COMPUTERS

COMPUTERS
THIRD EDITION

► **LARRY LONG**

► **NANCY LONG**

 PRENTICE HALL, ENGLEWOOD CLIFFS, NEW JERSEY 07632

Library of Congress Cataloging-in-Publication Data

LONG, LARRY E.
    Computers / Larry Long, Nancy Long.—3rd ed.

      p. cm.
    Includes index.
  ISBN 0–13–156241–X
    1. Computers. 2. Electronic data processing. I. Long, Nancy.
II. Title.
QA76.5.L654 1993   92–30998
004—dc20   CIP

Acquisition Editor: P.J. McCue
Editor-in-Chief: Joe Heider
Development Editor: Ray Mullaney
Production Editor: Nancy DeWolfe
Marketing Manager: Patti Arneson

Copy Editor: Nancy Savio-Marcello
Cover and Interior Design: Jerry Votta
Prepress Buyer: Trudy Pisciotti
Manufacturing Buyer: Patrice Fraccio
Page Layout: Diane Koromhas

Cover: This computerized interpretation of the classic Japanese woodcut "The Great Wave" is reprinted with permission from "The Wave of the Future" poster, designed by Grafik Communications, illustrated in part by B. Pomeroy, published by Nokes Berry Graphics as a poster.

All trademarks and registered trademarks are copyrighted and protected by their respective manufacturers.

Printed in the United States of America
10 9 8 7 6 5 4 3 2 1

ISBN 0-13-156241-X   01

Prentice-Hall International (UK) Limited, *London*
Prentice-Hall of Australia Pty. Limited, *Sydney*
Prentice-Hall Canada Inc., *Toronto*
Prentice-Hall Hispanoamericana. S.A., *Mexico*
Prentice-Hall of India Private Limited, *New Delhi*
Prentice-Hall of Japan, Inc., *Tokyo*
Simon & Schuster Asia Pte. Ltd., *Singapore*
Editora a Prentice-Hall do Brasil, Ltda., *Rio de Janeiro*

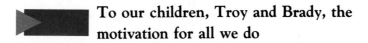 To our children, Troy and Brady, the
motivation for all we do

OVERVIEW

CONTENTS

PREFACE TO THE STUDENT

We are in the midst of a technological revolution that is changing our way of life. The cornerstone of this revolution, the computer, is transforming the way we learn, communicate, and do business. This text provides an overview of computers—what they are, what they are doing, and what they can do. Once you have read and understood its content, you will be poised to play an active role in this revolution.

Getting the Most from This Text

The layout and organization of the text and its content are designed to present concepts in a logical, interesting, and informative manner and to reinforce classroom lectures. A good way to approach each chapter is to:

1. Look over the Student Learning Objectives on the chapter opener.
2. Turn to the end of the chapter and read the Important Terms and Summary Outline.
3. Read over the major headings and subheadings and think about how they are related.
4. Read the chapter and note the important terms that are in **boldface** type and in *italic* type.
5. Relate photos and photo captions to the text. ("A picture is worth a thousand words.") *Note:* The chapter openers throughout the book provide a gallery for a new form of art created with computers.
6. Go over the Important Terms and Summary Outline again, paying particular attention to the boldface terms.
7. Take the Self-Test. Reread those sections you do not fully understand.
8. Answer the *concepts* and *discussion* questions in the Review Exercises.
9. Complete the *problem solving* Review Exercises as directed by your instructor.

Computers is supported by a comprehensive learning assistance package. The package is detailed in the "Preface to the Instructor." Ask your instructor about the availability of these learning supplements.

You, Computers, and the Future

Whether you are pursuing a career as an actuary, a social worker, an attorney, a dancer, an accountant, a computer specialist, a sales manager, or virtually any other job from shop supervisor to politician, the knowledge you gain from this course will prove beneficial. For most of you, this knowledge will be a fundamental prerequisite to performing your job. The chapter material addresses a broad range of computer concepts that occur frequently in other classes, at work, and even at home. Keep your course notes and this book, because they will be a valuable reference in these courses and in your career.

Computers are all around us, yet the application of computers is in its infancy. By taking this course, you are getting in "on the ground floor." Each class you attend and each page you turn will present a learning experience that will advance you one step further in your understanding of how computers are making the world a better place in which to live and work.

PREFACE TO THE INSTRUCTOR

This is the year of the computer. So was last year. And so it will be next year. Indeed, every year seems to be the year of the computer. A never-ending string of innovative applications of computer and information technology continues to affect virtually everything we do. We wrote this third edition of *Computers* to reflect the excitement associated with on-going technological change. To achieve this, we included discussions of hundreds of stimulating computer-based applications throughout the book. We feel that both the learning and teaching experiences are enriched when concepts are related to practice.

Intended Audience

The target course for the third edition of *Computers* and its teaching/learning system:

- Provides comprehensive coverage of a broad range of introductory computer and information processing concepts, applications, issues, concerns, and trends.
- Consists of students who have a variety of skill levels, interests, and career orientations.
- May or may not include a laboratory component. (The teaching/learning system includes an extensive array of optional hands-on laboratory materials that can be packaged with the text to meet the needs of most lab environments.)

The student completing this course will use his or her newly acquired knowledge to become an effective end user of computers or as a stepping-stone to a computer-related career.

The Third Edition

What's Retained in the Third Edition?   The third edition of *Computers* retains the basic pedagogical philosophy that prompted thousands of your colleagues in the United States and around the world to adopt its earlier editions. The third edition continues to cover all the angles: *what, why, when, where, how,* and *who.*

- *What?* All terms and concepts are discussed in the depth and in a manner in which they can be understood and applied to personal and business computing needs.
- *Why?* We explain why hundreds of times throughout the book—why use this DBMS, why use this printer, why use this programming language, or why use computers.
- *When?* As needed, we describe when or under what circumstances a concept or tool is applied or implemented (prototyping or proprietary software, for example).
- *Where?* We feel that students should know where concepts are applied (for example, in which industry or at which level in a company).
- *How?* We address the "How?" aspect of pedagogy many times in every chapter—how a compiler works; how an information system is developed; or how data are stored on a magnetic disk. (The supplements package includes "how to" books on micro applications software and BASIC programming.)
- *Who? Computers* identifies who is responsible for accomplishing particular tasks (functional specifications, maintenance of operating systems) or who employs a particular aspect of automation (CASE tools or decision support systems).

Traditional *Computers* features remain intact.

- *Applications-oriented.* Throughout the book, intangible concepts spring to life through dynamic, real-world applications.
- *Presentation style. Computers* is written in a style that conveys the energy and excitement of computers to the student.
- *Readability.* All elements (boxed features, photos, figures, Memory Bits, and so on) are integrated with the text to create a reading and study rhythm that complements and reinforces learning.
- *Currency-plus.* The material is more than current, it's "current-plus"—anticipating the emergence and implementation of computer technology such as virtual reality and wearable PCs.
- *Flexibility.* The text and its teaching/learning system are organized to permit maximum flexibility in course design and in the selection, assignment, and presentation of material.

What's New in the Third Edition?   The following summary of revisions may help you to better evaluate *Computers* in relation to your college's educational needs.

- *Exciting new boxed features.* Emerging Technology boxes address virtual reality, multimedia, smart houses, and other innovative applications of technology. PCs and You boxes explore telecommuting, shareware, add-ins, notebooks, EISA versus MCA, and many more areas of interest to PC users. Brief margin notes, called *Sidelights*, feature the human side of automation (for example, computer campaigning and personalized greeting cards).

- *Colorful Image Banks.* The Image Banks combine dynamic photos with in-depth discussions of topics that are of interest to students: computer graphics, how chips are made, how to buy a PC, the history of computers, and computers at the movies.

- *Emphasis on information systems.* Information systems move to the front and center: Coverage of systems development is expanded; management information systems, decision support systems, and expert systems are discussed and illustrated in detail; many application examples are added; and a comprehensive MIS case study is included as an appendix.

- *Continuous coverage of personal computing.* The growing importance of personal computing is underscored throughout the book.

- *More on communications and networking.* Communications topics now encompass two chapters: "Connectivity and Data Communications" (hardware) and "Networks and Networking" (software and applications).

- *Improved chapter pedagogy.* The basic elements of the familiar Long chapter format remain intact (*Student Learning Objectives, Memory Bits* summaries of key points, *numbered section heads, Summary Outline, Review Exercises* [Concepts and Discussion], and *Self-Test*). Three new elements help students learn: a *Chapter Outline,* an alphabetical list of *Important Terms,* and *Problem-Solving* exercises to encourage critical thinking.

- *Reorganized for better flow.* The chapters and appendices have been reorganized for better flow and to reflect changes in the technology, in student awareness, and in curriculums. Every page of the third edition has been revised but the following changes are major: an introduction to all computer systems in a single chapter; a new chapter on networking; consolidation of all software categories, including PC applications software, in "Part III: Software"; integration of programming concepts from an appendix into the body of the text; reduced coverage of design techniques; and the addition of an MIS case study as an appendix.

The *Computers* Teaching/Learning System

The third edition of *Computers* is the cornerstone of a comprehensive teaching/learning system. The other components of the system are described here.

***Computers* Annotated Instructor's Edition**   We introduced the first Annotated Instructor's Edition (AIE) for introductory computer education with the second edition of *Computers.* The well-received AIE is continued with the third edition. It is a four-color instructor's version of *Computers* that includes lecture notes, teaching tips, interesting supplemental material, in-class discussion questions and exercises, supplemental examples, warnings, quotes, cross-references to other components of the teaching/learning system, and much more—all in the margin of the text! When you open your book, you not only see what the student sees, you see what you need to deliver an interesting and informative lecture on the accompanying material.

CAPS (Computer-Assisted Presentation System)—Electronic Transparencies *CAPS*, a breakthrough in teaching technology, provides instructors with an integrated set of dynamic graphics, sometimes called *electronic transparencies*. Graphic displays are used in conjunction with a personal computer and a screen-image projector to enhance and facilitate classroom lectures. These computer-based "transparencies" enable the *dynamic* presentation of graphics, text, and animation. The transparencies contain key lecture points and appropriate graphics; they can be recalled from a menu and displayed as needed.

The Instructor's Resource Manual (IRM) The *IRM* contains detailed teaching hints, chapter outlines with key terms and concepts, solutions to exercises, and instruction on the use of all of the teaching and learning materials, and the hard copy of the *Test Item File*. Other sections contain information to help you prepare, develop, and teach the course.

The New York Times Dodger *The New York Times* and Prentice Hall are sponsoring A CONTEMPORARY VIEW: a program designed to enhance student access to current information of relevance in the classroom.

Through this program, the core subject matter provided in the text is supplemented by a collection of time-sensitive articles from one of the world's most distinguished newspapers, *The New York Times*. These articles demonstrate the vital, ongoing connection between what is learned in the classroom and what is happening in the world around us.

To enjoy the wealth of information of *The New York Times* daily, a reduced subscription rate is available. For information, call toll-free: 1-800-631-1222.

Prentice Hall and *The New York Times* are proud to cosponsor A CONTEMPORARY VIEW. We hope it will make the reading of both textbooks and newspapers a more dynamic, involving process.

ABC News/Prentice Hall Video Library Prentice Hall and *ABC News* have joined forces to provide you with a video library that offers a variety of documentary and feature-style stories on computers and applications of computer technology.

Study Guide The *Study Guide* is a supplementary book designed to support the student learning objectives in the text. It contains self-tests and hand-in exercises.

Test Item File The *Test Item File* contains over 3000 multiple-choice, true/false, essay, and matching questions. The questions are listed by numbered section head in the *IRM*. The *Test Item File* diskettes are distributed for use with *ParSystem Testing*, Prentice Hall's test preparation and classroom management software.

ParSystem Testing *ParSystem Testing* is a comprehensive, user-friendly testing package. *ParSystem* software allows you to interact with the *Computers Test Item File* to construct and print exams. Use this system to create your own customized exam, or request that the exams be generated randomly. You can also edit *Test Item File* questions and add questions of your own. You can even include graphic images in the printed exams, and a test can be generated and printed in multiple versions. When printed, the exam is ready for duplication. Student answer sheets and the answer key are also produced. *ParSystem* software interfaces with SCANTRON optical readers. *ParSystem* generates a wide variety of test reports and rosters including test item analysis, roster printout, score distribution, grade distributions, error logs, and many more.

ParSystem Testing gives you the option to test students on-line. The system also provides student feedback reports with correct answers and textbook references.

Computerized Testing Service   The Computerized Testing Service is available free of charge to all instructors who adopt *Computers*. This service eliminates the tasks associated with test preparation by providing a customized exam based on the questions in the *Test Item File*. To take advantage of this service, simply call in your test order to Prentice Hall.

Color Transparency Acetates   Over 70 color transparency acetates, which support material in the text and the *Computers* Annotated Instructor's Edition, are provided to facilitate in-class explanation.

Source 1: The Prentice Hall Custom Lab Program   Skills modules are available for MS-DOS, Windows, and a variety of popular word processing, spreadsheet, and database packages. Each skills module includes an *application description, step-by-step keystroke tutorials*, and *hands-on exercises*. You select the ones you need. Through custom publishing, Prentice Hall binds the applications software skills modules you selected. (Your Prentice Hall representative can provide details on publication deadlines.)

Laboratory Software and Support Materials   Prentice Hall is the largest and most prolific publisher of computer textbooks in the world. In many instances, full-function and educational versions of commercial software are distributed with these books (Microsoft Works, Quattro 1.01, and dBASE III PLUS, for example). Prentice Hall also publishes a variety of programming texts.

SuperSoftware   The dual-purpose *SuperSoftware* is equally effective as a stand-alone educational software package or as a vehicle for in-class demonstration of a myriad of computer-related concepts. When used as a hands-on educational package, *SuperSoftware* actively involves students through interactive communication with the computer. *SuperSoftware*, which contains 60 hands-on lab activities, is designed to instruct, intrigue, and motivate.

Author Hotline   If you have questions about the text, its package, or course planning, call us on the hotline. The telephone number appears in the *IRM*.

Acknowledgments

Computers imply change—lots of it. In that regard, the *Computers* text mirrors its namesake. As authors, we feel obligated to write a textbook that reflects changes in computer technology and in the evolution of curriculums and teaching methods. However, to do so effectively we needed help—and we got lots of it. We would like to extend our deep appreciation to our colleagues in academe for their help and insight.

- Ray Fanselau, American River College
- Fred Homeyer, Angelo State University
- Robert Keim, Arizona State University
- Carl Clavadetscher, California Polytechnic State University, Pomona
- Barry Floyd, California Polytechnic State University, San Luis Obispo
- Dr. Diane Visor, University of Central Oklahoma
- Dr. Diane Fischer, Dowling College
- Dr. Adolph Katz, Fairfield University
- Constance Knapp, Pace University
- Dr. John Sanford, Philadelphia College of Textiles and Science
- Peter Irwin, Richland College
- Al Schroeder, Richland College
- Amir Afzal, Strayer College
- James Johnson, Valencia Community College

In addition, we would like to thank the many professors who provided valuable feedback via the author hotline.

More than 100 organizations have made contributions to this book and its teaching/learning system. A grateful academic community appreciates their pledge to quality education.

The publication of *Computers*, third edition, marks the fifteenth anniversary of our association with Prentice Hall. We are proud of this association and of the dedicated professionals at PH with whom we work. We are honored to acknowledge their contributions. P. J. McCue brought vision and focus, Nancy DeWolfe added structure and achievement, and Ray Mullaney furnished wisdom and harmony. Managers Garret White, Joe Heider, Valerie Ashton, Joyce Turner, Patti Arneson, and Janet Schmid provided encouragement, timely support, and a commitment to excellence. A focus group of field sales representatives Beth Casey, Bill Hendee, Bruce Collin, Charlotte Morrissey, Clarissa Seager, Elizabeth Wood, Kate Moore, and Pamela Lancaster used their collective experiences to tell us what professors want in a text and a support package. Lisamarie Brassini, Delores Kenny, Nancy Savio-Marcello, Teri Stratford, Linda Muterspaugh, Virginia Feury-Gagnon, and Jerry Votta left a little of themselves in the project. We thank them all, for *Computers* is their book too. Finally, we would like to thank you, our customer, for your confidence and encouragement.

NANCY LONG, Ph.D.   LARRY LONG, Ph.D.

Dr. Larry Long is a lecturer, author, consultant, and educator in the computer and information services fields. He has written over 25 books on a broad spectrum of computer/MIS-related topics from introductory computing, to programming, to MIS strategic planning. Dr. Long has addressed a breadth of management, computer, and MIS issues in his executive seminars.

Dr. Long has served as a consultant to all levels of management in virtually every major type of industry. He has over 25 years of classroom experience at IBM, the University of Oklahoma, Lehigh University, and the University of Arkansas, where he continues to be an active lecturer. He received his Ph.D., M.S., and B.S. degrees in Industrial Engineering at the University of Oklahoma and holds certification as a C.D.P. and a Professional Engineer.

Dr. Nancy Long has coauthored a number of books with her husband. She has a decade of teaching and administrative experience at all levels of education: elementary, secondary, college, and continuing education. Dr. Long received a Ph.D in Reading Education and Educational Psychology, an M.S. in Personnel Services, and a B.S. in Elementary Education at the University of Oklahoma. Her wealth of knowledge in the areas of pedagogy and reading education is evident throughout the text and the supplements.

COMPUTERS

The World of Computers

STUDENT LEARNING OBJECTIVES

▶ To comprehend the significance of the computer revolution.

▶ To grasp the scope of computer understanding needed by someone living in an information society.

▶ To distinguish between data and information.

▶ To describe the fundamental components and the operational capabilities of a computer system.

▶ To identify and describe uses of the computer.

▶ To describe the general function of these microcomputer productivity software tools: word processing, desktop publishing, spreadsheet, database, and graphics.

CHAPTER OUTLINE

 Computers: The Revolution Is On

Rev·o·lu·tion (rev′ ə lü′ shən), *n.* a sudden, radical, or complete change.

Revolution: The Up Side

We are in the midst of a technological revolution that is changing our way of life. The cornerstone of this revolution, the *computer*, is transforming the way we communicate, do business, and learn. This text is about computers—what they are, what they are doing, and what they can do. Once you have read and understood its content, you will be poised to play an active role in this revolution.

The computer revolution is having a profound impact on the business community. Retailers are making it possible for us to do more shopping from the comfort of our own homes. Automobile manufacturers are integrating as many as a dozen computers in automobiles to enhance functionality, creature comforts, and safety. Computers in one company routinely communicate information to computers in another. Some factories have no windows or lights: The computer-controlled robots inside don't need to see!

In our private lives, computers speed the checkout at supermarkets, enable 24-hour banking, provide up-to-the-minute weather information, and, of course, entertain us with video games. If that is not enough, computers are the culprits behind our "conversations" with elevators, automobiles, and vending machines.

The computer revolution is changing every aspect of society, including the way we meet and interact with one another. These people are meeting to design a test for Space Station Freedom's *power system.*

In our professional lives, the computer is an integral tool in the performance of many jobs. Managers use word processing systems to compose memos and to check spelling, grammar, and style. Geologists rely on an "expert" computer system for guidance in the quest for minerals. Bankers examine up-to-the-minute securities information from their computers. Set directors in the theater and cinema create and view sets on the computer before constructing them. Retailers query their computer systems to determine which products are selling and which are not. Sociologists use the computer to analyze demographic patterns. Financial analysts examine up-to-the-minute securities information on their computers. Computer artists have millions (yes, millions!) of colors from which to choose.

Revolution: The Down Side

The computer revolution has raised serious social issues. Personal information is more accessible and therefore more vulnerable to abuse. The "take" in an average "electronic heist" is a hundred times that of the more traditional bank robbery. One computer-controlled robot can replace four or more workers. These and other automation issues are discussed in Chapter 18, "Computers in Society: Today and Tomorrow," and throughout the book.

Architects rely on computers for everything from design to cost analysis. An architect prepared the elevations (different views) for this beach house using computer graphics. The computer has dramatically changed the way architects do their jobs. The same is true for hundreds of other professions.

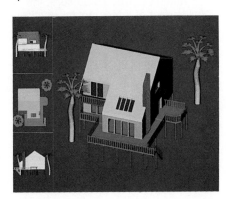

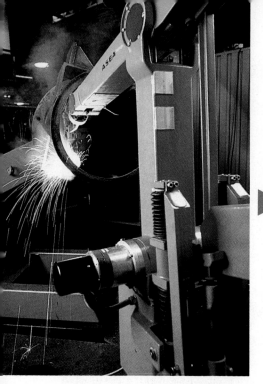

The precise, untiring movement of computer-controlled industrial robots helps assure quality in the assembly of everything from electrical components to automobiles. Here a robot applies spot welds.

Computer Revolution Still to Come? Few would argue that the business community is committed to the computer revolution. Surprisingly, however, only 15% of American homes have joined the revolution. Perhaps many of us are waiting for the unveiling of a computer that can communicate with us on human terms. To be sure, the full impact of the computer revolution is yet to come on the domestic front. This relatively low percentage hasn't dampened the spirits of computer industries who continue to slave away to be the first to invent the unimaginable. A machine that reads scrawled handwriting and pocket communicators that can communicate messages, documents, voices, and pictures around the neighborhood (or the world) are just a few of the many new devices that will soon be on the market.

Computers and technology in general have potential for both good and bad. Numerous surveys have attempted to evaluate public opinion on computers and automation. The findings show that the overwhelming majority believe that computers enhance the quality of life. People have become committed to a better way of life through computers, and it is unlikely that the momentum toward this goal will change. It is our responsibility to ensure that this inevitable evolution of computer technology is directed toward the benefit of society.

1-2 Learning About Computers

Computer Competency: Certificate for Success

Companies promote *it* for their employees. Parents demand *it* for their children. Those who have *it* believe they possess a competitive advantage. Those who don't have *it* seek *it* out. "*It*" is **computer competency**. The computer-competent person will

1. Feel comfortable using and operating a computer system.
2. Be able to make the computer work for him or herself through judicious development *or* use of **software**. (*Software* refers collectively to a set of machine-readable instructions, called **programs**, that cause the computer to perform desired functions.)
3. Be able to interact with the computer—that is, generate input to the computer and interpret output from it.
4. Understand the impact of computers on society, now and in the future.
5. Be an intelligent consumer of **hardware**, computers and computer equipment.
6. Be an intelligent consumer of computer-related products and services.

By the time you complete this course, you will have achieved a level of computer competency enabling you to be an active and effective participant in the emerging information society.

Fifteen years ago people who pursued a career in almost any facet of business, education, or government were content to leave computers to computer professionals. Well, things have changed. Computer competency is emerging as a prerequisite for employment in a growing number of career fields. As a result, the study of computers and computer-related topics are now an integral part of the learning experience.

Why Study Computers?

To thrive in today's highly competitive business world, you need to be computer-competent. *Network*, *data base*, *micro*, *macro*, *output*, and hundreds of other computer-related terms are used in everyday conversation by those who aspire to be successful in business—accountants, secretaries, salespeople, hospital administrators, lawyers, engineers, newspaper reporters, financial analysts, and people in most professions. The same can be said about people in education and government.

Up until twenty years ago, computers were found only in environmentally controlled rooms behind locked doors. Only computer professionals and duly authorized personnel were permitted entry to these secured premises. In contrast, computers today are found in millions of homes and just about every office. In fact, most office workers have a computer or **video display terminal** at or near their desks. The video display terminal, or **VDT**, is a device with a televisionlike screen and a keyboard that permits communication with a remote computer. Everywhere we look we see someone in front of a computer or VDT: ticket agents at airports, tellers at banks, professors at your college, and people at many other places.

Computers serve a growing army of workers who seldom see a desk. Police, overnight mail couriers, and others on the go are beginning to rely more and more on the power and versatility of portable computers. Computers and VDTs have become commonplace on the shop floor and in the warehouse. Eventually, all of us will have at least one computer and use it every day in our work and leisure. That day is not too far away.

Computers help foster a sense of adventure in any job. Here, meteorologists at the FAA's Air Traffic Control System Command Center in Washington, D.C., rely on computer systems to receive and process weather information critical to flight planning.

Cyberphobia

Computers are synonymous with change, and any type of change is usually met with some resistance. Much of this resistance to computers comes from a lack of knowledge about them and, perhaps, to a fear of the unknown. People seem to perceive computers as something mystical. And it is human nature to fear what we don't understand. Less than 5% of the population is comfortable enough with computers to deem themselves computer-competent. Computers will continue to be associated with the radical change implied by a revolution until the majority of workers are computer-competent. That may not happen until the turn of the century.

The fear of the computers brought on by rapid change is so widespread that psychologists have created a name for it: **cyberphobia**. Cyberphobia is the irrational fear of, and aversion to, computers. Keep in mind that computers are merely machines and don't merit such fear. If you are a cyberphobic, you will soon see that your fears are unfounded.

Today we are rapidly becoming an information society where "knowledge workers" depend on computer-generated information to accomplish their jobs. A portable personal computer is a constant companion of this investment banker.

A few years ago, Nan Davis stunned the world. A paraplegic since an automobile accident on the night of her high school graduation, she walked to the podium to receive her college diploma—with the help of a rehabilitative tool called FES, or functional electrical stimulation.

FES uses low-level electrical stimulation to restore or supplement the minute electrical currents the nervous system generates to control different parts of the body. In many cases, this electrical stimulation is controlled by a microprocessor—a computer—that uses feedback from the body to adjust the electrical stimulation's length and intensity.

In Nan's case, FES took the form of electrodes, to stimulate her leg muscles; a sensory feedback system; and a small, portable computer. The sensory feedback system tells the computer the position and movement of the legs so that it knows which muscles it must electrically stimulate next to produce a coordinated gait.

FES AS AN ACCEPTABLE MEDICAL PRACTICE

FES to restore the ability to stand, walk, and use the arms and hands is still in the experimental stage. Many other FES applications are accepted medical practice, though. The best-known application is probably the cardiac pacemaker, in which electrodes are attached directly to a faulty heart. FES can also be used to control chronic pain, correct spinal deformities, and pace the rise and fall of the diaphragm during breathing.

One of the most amazing applications of FES is an auditory prosthesis—a miniature computer system that

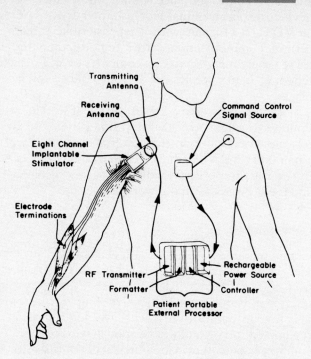

This illustration shows the components of a neural-muscular stimulation system for restoration of upper extremity function.

helps people with defects in their inner ear or auditory nerve. Some of the system's components are implanted surgically. These include a receiver/stimulator that is implanted beneath the skin behind the ear and an array

Computerese

A by-product of the computer revolution is **computerese**. A by-product of the computer learning experience is learning to speak computerese. Computerese is a mixture of English and computer jargon, which could just as well be ancient hieroglyphics to the computer novice. With the expanded use and acceptance of computers both at home and at work, it is becoming more and more important to be fluent in computerese. You may be surprised to know that you are already well along your way to this fluency. You are probably familiar with most of its vocabulary. For example, you know:

of electrodes that extends from the receiver/stimulator into the inner ear. An external directional microphone, which looks like a behind-the-ear hearing aid, is connected to a speech processor and transmitter by two cords. Sounds picked up by the microphone are transmitted to the speech processor, which amplifies, filters, and digitizes them into coded signals. The transmitter then sends these signals to the appropriate electrodes in the inner ear. The electrodes then stimulate the auditory nerve, which sends the signals to the brain. Many of the people who have received the auditory implants can recognize 60% to 70% of the speech they hear—a major achievement, especially for children who were born deaf.

FES AS A THERAPEUTIC TOOL

FES can also be used as a therapeutic tool to strengthen muscles idled by paralysis. Without exercise, muscles atrophy, circulation becomes sluggish, cardiovascular fitness declines, and pressure sores develop. These FES devices, which look like high-tech exercise bicycles, use a microprocessor to coordinate a system of electrodes and feedback sensors, allowing the user to push the pedals and turn a hand crank. Like anyone who engages in a regular exercise program, users of the FES devices report noticeable improvements in muscle tone, mass, and cardiovascular fitness. These devices cannot restore function, of course. But they can help the paralyzed to maintain their bodies while researchers continue to seek ways to help them walk again. In the meantime, many are thrilled just to see their bodies move again.

Paraplegic Nan Davis is demonstrating an experimental outdoor tricycle that uses functional electrical stimulation (FES) to stimulate paralyzed muscles to pedal the tricycle. Eventually researchers hope that paraplegics will be able to do much more than take a few crude steps or pedal tricycles. If research goes as planned, a pocket-sized computer will control sensors implanted in the skin that will give paraplegics the ability to walk forward and backward, sit, stand, and even climb stairs.

window	block	write	record
read	bug	job	flag
run	page	word	trace
bit	host	memory	loop
menu	gateway	field	load

Your familiarity with these terms is the good news. Now for the bad news: They mean something different in computerese. In computerese, you don't "walk through a *gateway*," "apply for a *job*," "wave a *flag*," or "*load* a truck." But, as you will learn, a parallel often exists between the computerese usage and the common definition of familiar words. Think about this parallel as you progress toward computer competency and fluency in computerese. Of course, you will learn many new vocabulary words, such as *byte*, *opcode*, and *ROM*.

The Computer Adventure

You will achieve computer competency through study, practice, and interest in the topic. There is no "quick fix" that will result in your becoming a computer-competent person. A magazine article, a few television shows, or a computer demonstration may serve to heighten your interest, but these are side trips on the way to computer competency. You are about to embark on an emotional and intellectual *journey* that will stimulate your imagination, challenge your every resource from physical dexterity to intellect, and, perhaps, alter your sense of perspective. Learning about computers is more than just education. It's an adventure!

 1–3 The Emerging Information Society

From Dirt to Data

Two centuries ago, 90 of every 100 people worked to produce food. As people became more efficient in food production, an *agrarian society* gave way to the growth of an *industrial society*. Our transition to an industrial society was slow and marked with social strife. Each new technological innovation had a profound impact. For example, the steam shovel did the work of 100 men.

We know now that the Industrial Revolution shortened the work week, provided greater opportunities for employment, and generally improved the quality of life for all. But at the time no argument could convince any of the 100 men who had lost their jobs to a steam shovel that the Industrial Revolution eventually would improve everyone's standard of living.

Today 2 people produce enough food for the remaining 98, and we are in the middle of a transition from an *industrial society* to an *information society*. The trend in today's offices and factories is paralleling that of the farm 200 years earlier. If history repeats itself—and most experts believe it will—automation will continue to reduce the number of workers needed to accomplish unskilled and semiskilled tasks. Automation also will provide workers with valuable information that will help them to better do their jobs.

In the information society, **knowledge workers** will focus their energies on providing a myriad of information services. The knowledge worker's job function revolves around the use, manipulation, and dissemination of information. Today it is a bit difficult to imagine a society that may become desperately dependent on certain information services. But let's put this concern in its proper perspective. Can you imagine our nineteenth-century ancestors becoming as desperately dependent on the speed of air travel or hair dryers as we are? Who among us would give up our hair dryer!

Just a few years ago, paperwork, dated reports, manually completed forms, and telephone tag were the norm in the business world. Today we are making a transition to an information society. Computer-based information systems enable knowledge workers at this management consulting firm to have ready access to the information they need to accomplish their jobs.

Our acceptance and dependence on a myriad of information services may be inevitable. For example, in a few years you will be able to do grocery shopping from the comfort of your own kitchen. This information-based service will accept a detailed shopping list. The items will be picked and boxed automatically for your pickup or delivery. If you wish, the information service will prepare a shopping list for you based on a profile of your family and its eating habits. Life will become more and more convenient as our emerging information society matures. As another example, consider this scenario: You are traveling to a meeting on a rainy election day and do not have time to stop off and mark your ballot. In the information society of the not-too-distant future, you will be able to register you votes from any telephone, including a mobile cellular system!

Data: Foundation for the Information Society

Up to now we have talked about *information*, but little about its origin—*data*. **Data** (the plural of *datum*) are the raw material from which information is derived. **Information** is data that have been collected and processed into a meaningful form. Computers are very good at producing information from data.

We routinely deal with the concepts of data and information in our everyday experiences. We use data to produce information that will help us make decisions. For example, when we wake up in the morning, we collect two pieces of data. We look at the clock, then recall from our memory the time our first class begins or when we are due at work. Then we subtract the current time from the starting time of class or work. This mental computation provides information on how much time we have

Data are collected in many ways. Here inventory data are being entered with a portable bar-code reader similar to those used in retail stores. Data are transmitted via radio waves directly to the company's main computer system.

to get ready and go. Based on this information, we make a decision to hurry up or to relax and take it easy. We produce information from data to help us make decisions for thousands of situations each day. In many ways, the content of this book is just an extension of concepts with which you are already familiar.

Data are all around us. We, as members of the information society, are continuously generating data. When you call a mail-order merchandiser, the data you give the sales representative (name, address, product number) is entered directly to computer. When you make a long-distance telephone call, your number, the number you call, and the length of the conversation is entered to a computer system. When you return the preprinted stub with your check for last month's electric bill, you are providing data for a computer system. When you press on the accelerator of a modern automobile, you are entering data to a computerized fuel-control system. When you travel down a busy avenue, chances are that you are feeding data to an automated traffic-control system. When you run short of cash and stop at an automatic teller machine, all data you enter, including that on the magnetic strip on your bank card, are processed immediately by the bank's computer system. All of these data are eventually manipulated by a computer system to produce information.

1–4 Computers Are For Everyone

Computer Systems in "the Old Days"

In "the old days" (that is, during the 1950s, 1960s, and even into the 1970s) business computer systems were designed so that a computer professional served as an intermediary between the **user** and the computer system. Users, who are sometimes called end users, are blue-and-white-collar workers who use the computer to help them do their jobs better. In the past, plant supervisors, financial directors, and marketing managers would relate their information needs to computer professionals, such as *programmers* or *systems analysts*, who would then work with the computer system to generate the necessary information. In "the old days," elapsed time between the submission of a request for information and the distribution of the results could be several days or as much as a month. The resulting time-sensitive information was often of little value by the time it reached the manager.

Computer Systems Today

The *timeliness of information* is critical in today's fast-paced business world. Managers cannot wait for the information they need. They want it now, not next week or next month. In response to managers' requests for more timely information, computer systems are now designed to be *interactive*. **Interactive computer systems** eliminate the need to go through an intermediary (the computer professional) and permit users to extract information directly from the computer system. This interactive mode of operation gives managers the flexibility to analyze the results of one inquiry, then make subsequent inquiries based on more information.

Today, computers and software are being designed to be **user-friendly**. This means that someone with a fundamental knowledge of and exposure to computers can make effective use of the computer and its software. Ten years ago this was not the case. If you didn't have a computer science degree and the mental agility of a wizard, you were out of luck.

Romancing the Computer

For almost a century, men and women have had ongoing love affairs with their automobiles. During the last decade, people in all walks of life are experiencing similar love affairs with their **personal computers**. Personal computers, or **PCs**, are designed primarily for use by *one person at a time*. For literally millions of people, their relationship with PCs is far stronger than a mere work interest. They also use their PCs as a source of recreation. These computer enthusiasts spend much of their time learning about the latest personal computers and software innovations. Many can write their own programs and are comfortable with a variety of sophisticated software and hardware.

PC users all over the country have formed clubs and associations to share interesting computer discoveries. They are old and young, manager and laborer, ecologist and geologist, all sharing a common bond: to explore the seemingly infinite capabilities of their computers.

1–5 Uncovering the "Mystery" of Computers

The Computer System

Technically speaking, the computer is any counting device. But in the context of modern technology, we will define the **computer** as *an electronic device capable of interpreting and executing programmed commands for input, output, computation, and logic operations*.

Computers may be technically complex, but they are conceptually simple. The computer, also called a **processor**, is the "intelligence" of a **computer system**. A computer system has only four fundamental components: *input, processing, output,* and *storage*. Note that a computer system (not a computer) is made up of the four components. The actual computer is the processing component; when combined with the other three components, it forms a *computer system* (see Figures 1–1 and 1–2).

The relationship of data to a computer system is best explained by showing an analogy to gasoline and an automobile. Data are to a computer system as gas is to a car. Data provide the fuel for a computer system. A computer system without data is like a car with an empty gas tank: No gas, no go; no data, no information.

How a Computer System Works

A computer system also can be likened to the biological system of the human body (see Figure 1–3). Your brain is the processing component. Your eyes and ears are input components that send signals to the brain. If you see someone approaching, your brain matches the visual image of

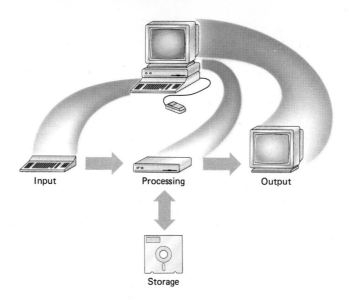

**FIGURE 1–1　The Four Fundamental Components
of a Microcomputer System**

*In a microcomputer system, the storage and processing components are often
contained in the same physical unit. In the illustration, the diskette storage
medium is inserted into the unit that contains the processor.*

this person with others in your memory (storage component). If the visual
image matches that of a friend, your brain sends signals to your vocal
chords and right arm (output components) to greet your friend with a
hello and a handshake. The brain interacts with the input, output, and
storage components of the body through the central nervous system. The
processing component of a computer system interacts with the system's
other components in a similar way.

The payroll system in Figure 1–4 illustrates how data are entered
into a microcomputer system and how the four system components interact
to produce information (a year-to-date overtime report) and payroll
checks. The following steps are illustrated in Figure 1–4.

FIGURE 1–2　The Four Fundamental Components of a Computer System

*In larger computer systems, each of the four components is contained in a
separate physical unit.*

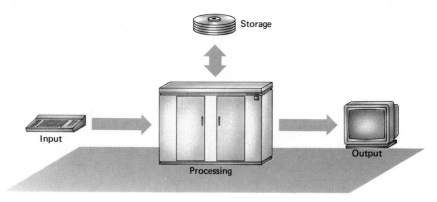

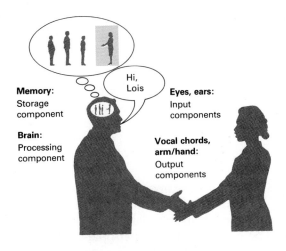

Memory:
Storage
component

Brain:
Processing
component

Eyes, ears:
Input
components

**Vocal chords,
arm/hand:**
Output
components

**FIGURE 1–3 The Biological
System: Input, Processing,
Output, and Storage**

1. At the end of each work week, the supervisor manually records the number of hours worked for each employee on the Payroll Work Sheet, a **source document**. The source document is the original document from which data are entered.
2. The hours-worked data are keyed in, or *input*, to the system by the supervisor or a data entry operator.
3. The data are *stored* on the personnel **master file**. The master file is made up of **records**, each of which contains data about a particular employee (for example: name, hours worked). Files, records, and other data management concepts are discussed in detail in Chapter 6, "Data Storage and Organization."

FIGURE 1–4 Microcomputer-Based Payroll System
This microcomputer-based payroll system illustrates input, storage, processing, and output. The six steps are discussed in the section How a Computer System Works.

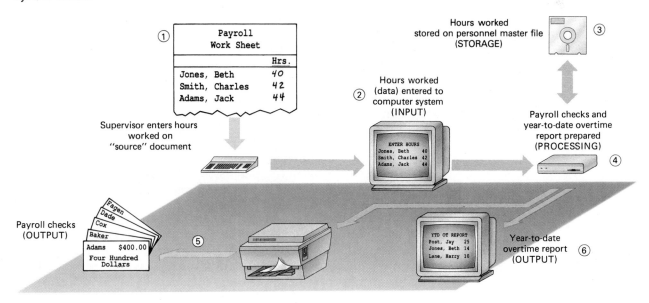

4. The payroll checks are produced when the *processing* component, or the computer, executes a program. In this example, the employee records are recalled from storage, and the pay amounts are calculated.

5. The *output* is the printed payroll checks.

6. Other programs extract data from the personnel master file to produce a year-to-date overtime report and any other *output* that might help in the management decision-making process.

The Hardware

The principles illustrated and discussed here apply equally to personal computers (Figures 1–1 and 1–4) and **mainframe computers** (Figure 1–2). Each has the four components and each uses data to produce information in a similar manner. The difference is that personal computers, also called **microcomputers**, are more limited in their capabilities and are designed primarily for use by *one person at a time*. Mainframe computers can service *many users*, perhaps every manager in the company, all at once. We discuss microcomputers and mainframe computers in more detail in Chapter 2, "Micros, Minis, Mainframes, and Supercomputers."

In the payroll example of Figure 1–4, data are entered (input) and processed on a microcomputer. The PC has a typewriterlike **keyboard** for input and a televisionlike (video) screen, called a **monitor**, for output such as the year-to-date overtime report. The output on a monitor is temporary and is often referred to as **soft copy**. The payroll checks are output on a device called a **printer**. Printers produce **hard copy**, or printed output. Data are stored for later recall on **magnetic disk**. There are a wide variety of **input/output (I/O)** and storage devices. The variety of hardware devices that make up a computer system are discussed in detail in Part II, "Hardware."

There are more similarities than differences between a mainframe-based payroll system and a PC-based system. The main differences are that many people can use the mainframe system at the same time and their primary input/output device is the video display terminal. A video display terminal (VDT), or simply **terminal**, has a keyboard for input and a monitor for output. The VDTs are located in the user areas throughout the company and linked to the mainframe via communications lines (see Figure 1–5).

What Can a Computer Do?

Remember from our previous discussion that the *input/output* and *data storage* hardware components are *configured* with the *processing* component (the computer) to make a computer system (Figures 1–1 and 1–2). Let's discuss the operational capabilities of a computer system just a bit further.

Input/Output Operations   The computer *reads* from input and storage devices. The computer *writes* to output and storage devices. Before data can be processed, they must be "read" from an input device or data storage device. Input data are entered directly by end users and by professional data entry operators. Typically, data are enter on a VDT's or PC's keyboard

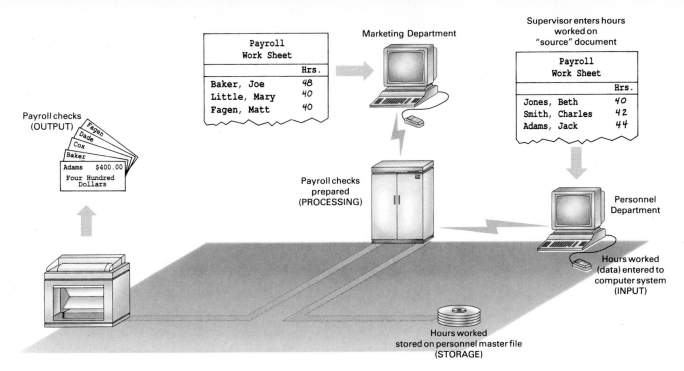

FIGURE 1–5 Mainframe-Based Payroll System
This mainframe-based payroll system illustrates input, storage, processing, and output.

or they are retrieved from a data storage, such as a magnetic disk. Once data have been processed, they are "written" to an output device, such as a printer, or to a magnetic disk.

Input/output (I/O) operations are illustrated in the payroll system example in Figure 1–4. Hours-worked data are entered, or "read," into the computer system. These data are "written" to magnetic disk storage for recall at a later date.

Processing Operations   The computer is totally objective. Any two computers instructed to perform the same operation will arrive at the same result. This is because the computer can perform only *computation* and *logic operations*.

■ *Computation operations.* The computational capabilities of the computer include adding (+), subtracting (−), multiplying (*), dividing (/), and exponentiation (∧). The commonly accepted symbols for these computation operations are shown in parentheses. In the payroll-system example of Figure 1–4, the computer calculates the gross pay in a computation operation. For example, it performs the calculations needed to determine the appropriate pay for someone who worked 40 hours and makes $15/hour.

$$\text{Pay} = 40 \text{ hours} * \$15/\text{hour} = \$600$$

■ *Logic operations.* The computer's logic capability enables comparisons between numbers and between words then, based on the result of the com-

Memory Bits

COMPUTER OPERATIONS
- Input/output
  Read
  Write
- Processing
  Computation
  Logic

parison, the computer performs appropriate functions. In the example of Figure 1–4, Charles Smith and Jack Adams had overtime hours since they worked in excess of 40 hours (the normal work week). The computer must use its logic capability to determine whether or not an employee is due overtime pay. To do this, hours-worked is compared to 40.

$$\text{Are hours-worked} > \text{(greater than) 40?}$$

For Charles Smith, who worked 42 hours, the comparison is true (42 is greater than 40). A comparison that is true causes the difference (2 hours) to be credited as overtime and paid at time and a half.

Computer System Capabilities

In a nutshell, computers are fast, accurate, and reliable; they don't forget anything; and they don't complain. Now for the details.

Speed The smallest unit of time in the human experience is, realistically, the second. Computer operations (for example, the execution of an instruction, such as multiplying the hours-worked times the rate of pay) are measured in **milliseconds**, **microseconds**, **nanoseconds**, and **picoseconds** (one thousandth, one millionth, one billionth, and one trillionth of a second, respectively). A beam of light travels down the length of this page in about one nanosecond. A millisecond can be sliced into a thousand microseconds and a microsecond can be sliced into a thousand nanoseconds. It takes about 18 milliseconds, 18,000 microseconds, or 18,000,000 nanoseconds for light to travel from New York to San Francisco.

On the Merrill Lynch & Company trading floor, literally billions of dollars' worth of securities are routinely bought and sold with nary a penny lost, a testament to the accuracy of computers.

Accuracy Errors do occur in computer-based information systems, but precious few can be directly attributed to the computer system itself. The vast majority can be traced to a program logic error, a procedural error, or erroneous data. These are *human errors*.

Reliability Computer systems are particularly adept at repetitive tasks. They don't take sick days and coffee breaks, and they seldom complain. Anything below 99.9% **uptime**, the time when the computer system is in operation, is usually unacceptable. For some companies, any **downtime** is unacceptable. These companies provide **backup** computers that take over automatically if the main computers fail.

Memory Capability Computer systems have total and instant recall of data and an almost unlimited capacity to store these data. A typical mainframe computer system will have many billions of characters stored and available for instant recall. High-end PCs have access to about a billion characters of data. To give you a benchmark for comparison, this book contains approximately a million characters. A 15-page report contains about 50,000 characters.

1–6 How Do We Use Computers?

For the purpose of this discussion, we will classify the uses of computers into seven general categories.

- Information systems/data processing
- Personal computing
- Science and research
- Process/device control
- Education
- Computer-aided design
- Artificial intelligence

Figure 1–6 shows how the sum total of existing computer capacity is apportioned to each of these general categories. Each category of computer usage is growing rapidly with the increase in the number of computers and their capabilities. However, in the years ahead, look for personal computing, education, and artificial intelligence to become larger shares of the computer "pie."

Information Systems/Data Processing

The bulk of existing computer power is dedicated to *information systems* and *data processing*. This category includes all uses of computers that support the administrative aspects of an organization. Example applications include payroll systems, airline reservation systems, student registration systems, hospital-patient billing systems, and countless others.

We combine *hardware*, *software*, *people*, *procedures*, and *data* to create an **information system**. A computer-based information system provides

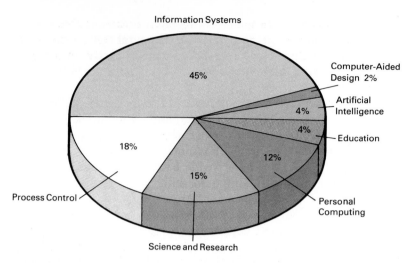

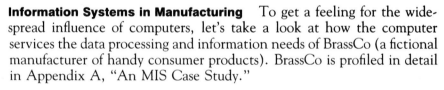

FIGURE 1–6   The Way We Use Computers
This pie chart is an estimate of how existing computer capacity is distributed among the general categories of computer usage.

Efficient inventory management is a goal of every manufacturing company. Improved shipping performance was a by-product of TRW's computer-based inventory-control system.

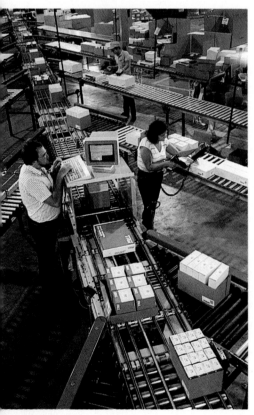

an organization with *data processing* capabilities and the knowledge workers in the organization with the *information* they need to make better, more informed decisions.

Information Systems in Manufacturing   To get a feeling for the widespread influence of computers, let's take a look at how the computer services the data processing and information needs of BrassCo (a fictional manufacturer of handy consumer products). BrassCo is profiled in detail in Appendix A, "An MIS Case Study."

- In the *accounting* division, all financial/accounting systems are computerized.
- BrassCo's *production* division uses information systems for such applications as inventory control and production scheduling.
- As competition becomes keener, the *marketing* division has turned to the information systems for assistance in fine-tuning the marketing effort.
- The *human resources development* division has automated the basic personnel functions of employment history, career planning, and benefits administration.
- The *purchasing* division has replaced cumbersome manual systems with computer-based systems that extend its buying power through selective, time-phased purchasing.
- The *research and development* division relies on the information systems to support a variety of technical programs that include simulation and computer-aided design.
- BrassCo's *headquarters staff* and top management routinely make "what if" inquiries to the decision support system. For example, "What if the advertising budget were increased by 20%? How might sales be affected?"

Information Systems in the Airline Industry   An airline reservation system is a classic example of an information system that reflects an up-to-the-minute status. Airline reservation agents communicate with a centralized computer via remote terminals to update the data base the moment a seat on any flight is filled or becomes available.

An airline reservation system does much more than keep track of flight reservations. Departure and arrival times are closely monitored so that ground crew activities can be coordinated. The system offers many kinds of management information needs: the number of passenger miles flown, profit per passenger on a particular flight, percent of arrivals on time, average number of empty seats on each flight for each day of the week, and so on.

The first airline reservation system, American Airlines' Sabre System, was implemented in 1976. The Apollo System of United Airlines was installed five months later. By being first, American Airlines and United Airlines grabbed the lion's share, over 60%, of the reservations market. Three other airline reservation systems share the other 40%. To give you an idea of the size and scope of these systems, the Sabre System involves more than 100,000 terminals and printers and can process 1,450 transactions per second!

You may be interested to know that airlines routinely overbook flights; that is, they book seats they do not have. The number of extra seats sold is based on historical "no-show" statistics compiled from the reservation system data base. Although these statistics provide good guidelines, occasionally everyone does show up!

Information Systems in Other Organizations   The influence of computer information systems is just as pervasive in hospitals (patient accounting systems), government agencies (revenue administration systems), insurance (claims-processing systems), and colleges (student registration systems). A wide variety of information systems in business, education, and government are described and discussed throughout the remainder of the book. Part IV, "Management Information Systems," provides a detailed discussion of information systems.

Personal Computing

Individuals and companies are purchasing small, inexpensive microcomputers for a variety of business and domestic applications. A microcomputer system, or **micro** for short, easily sits on, under, or to the side of a desk and can be controlled by one person. The growth of this general area, called **personal computing**, has surpassed even the most adventurous forecasts of a decade ago. Some high-tech companies actually have more personal computers than telephones. Personal computers far outnumber mainframe computers. But, of course, a single mainframe computer may have the processing capacity of 1000 personal computers.

Domestic Applications for Personal Computing   A variety of domestic and business applications form the foundation of personal computing. Domestic applications include some of the following: maintaining an up-

Bedside terminals enable doctors and nurses to enter patient data at the source. Doctors order blood tests, schedule operating rooms, and review medical records while interacting with the hospital's computer system.

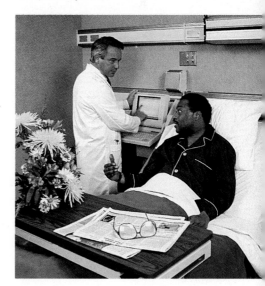

Like the Sunday newspaper, personal computers have something for everybody.

to-date inventory of household items; storing names and addresses for a personal mailing list; maintaining records for, preparing, and sending income tax returns; creating and monitoring a household budget; keeping an appointment and social calendar; handling household finances (for example, checkbook balancing, paying bills, coupon refunding); writing letters; education; and, of course, entertainment. You can purchase software for all these applications, and you can probably obtain software for your special interest, whether it be astrology, charting biorhythms, genealogy, religion, composing music, cooking, or dieting.

Business Applications for Personal Computing Inexpensive microcomputers have made automation financially feasible for virtually any business environment. As a result, microcomputer software is available to support thousands of common and not-so-common business applications. There is, of course, an established need for applications such as payroll, accounting, sales analysis, project management, and inventory control. There are also hundreds of industry-specific software packages for thoroughbred breeding, for medical laboratories, for professional football teams, for pre-owned car dealers, and for just about any other area of business.

The Microcomputer Family of Productivity Software Microcomputer-based *productivity software* is a series of commercially available programs that can help knowledge workers in the business community save time and get information they need to make more informed decisions. The family of productivity software is the foundation of personal computing in the business world and in the home. The most popular productivity tools include the following:

- *Word processing.* **Word processing software** enables users to enter text, to store it on magnetic storage media, to manipulate it in preparation for output, and to produce a hard copy (printed output).
- *Desktop publishing.* **Desktop publishing software** allows users to produce near-typeset-quality copy for newsletters, advertisements, and many other printing needs, all from the confines of a desktop.
- *Spreadsheet.* **Spreadsheet software** permits users to work with the rows and columns of a matrix (or spreadsheet) of data.
- *Database.* **Database software** permits users to create and maintain a data base and to extract information from the data base.
- *Graphics.* **Graphics software** facilitates the creation and management of computer-based images such as pie graphs, line drawings, company logos, maps, clip art, blueprints, and just about anything else that can be drawn in the traditional manner.

These software packages are general-purpose in that they provide the framework for a great number of business and personal applications. For example, desktop publishing software can be used to create an advertisement for a newspaper or an announcement for the annual office Christmas party. Graphics software can be used to create a bar graph of sales over the past quarter or to illustrate the landscaping plan for a new house.

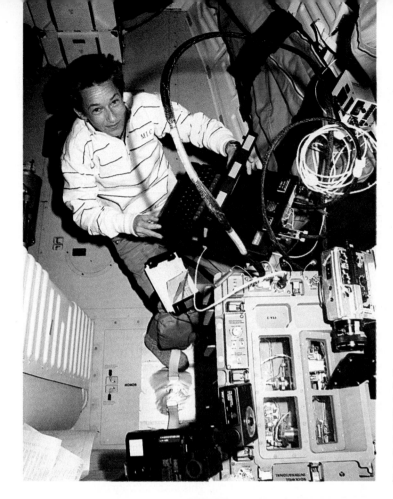

Microcomputers and productivity software have become fixtures in every business, educational, and government environment. On board the space shuttle, astronaut Mary Cleave relies on her laptop computer to help her analyze and document the results of a microgravity experiment.

The function and concepts of these productivity tools are described in Part III, "Software."

Information Network Services Although personal computers are normally used as stand-alone computer systems, they can also double as remote terminals. This *dual-function* capability provides you with the flexibility to work with the PC as a stand-alone system or to link it with a larger computer and take advantage of its increased capacity. With a PC, you have a world of information at your fingertips. The personal computer can be used in conjunction with the telephone system to transmit data to and receive data from an **information network**.

A growing trend among personal computer enthusiasts is to subscribe to the services of an information network. These information networks have one or several large computer systems that offer a variety of information services. These services include hotel reservations, home banking, shopping at home, daily horoscopes, financial information, games, up-to-the-minute news, and much more. Information networks are discussed in more detail in Chapter 8, "Networks and Networking."

The services provided by information networks, coupled with a vast array of applications software and the capabilities of microcomputer productivity software, eventually should make personal computers a "must-have" item in every home and business.

Apple Computer Corporation deserves a generous measure of credit for popularizing PCs. The company didn't actually invent the first personal computer, but soon after Stephen Wozniak and Steven Jobs got together in their California garage to build the first Apple computer in 1977, the little machines took the public by storm. Apple II computers (Apple I was a kit, but Apple II came preassembled) made their way into homes, schools, and offices across the nation. In those days, Apple wasn't "the other PC" but the main PC—the only kid of any significance on the block.

Four years later, in 1981, the venerable builder of mainframe computers, IBM, brought out its own PC, in tacit recognition of Apple's success. IBM's entry into the PC world announced to the business community what many individual executives had already found out: that PCs could boost productivity in the work place, particularly with electronic spreadsheet programs. Just as it had risen to stardom overnight, Apple Computer Corporation rapidly dropped into second place behind IBM.

TWO VERY DIFFERENT MACHINES

From the beginning, Apples were graphically oriented machines. The user moved around a mouse on the desk to choose a picture (icon) on the screen representing something to do. Then with a click of the mouse, the

THE MACINTOSH POWERBOOK   The Macintosh laptop PC offers capabilities similar to its desktop cousin with the added advantage of portability.

computer performed the function it was told to do. This was a very different way to interact with computers than that used by mainframe computers of the time (or indeed, of today).

With the IBM PC, the user typed in commands in written, rather than graphical, exchanges with an operating system (DOS). This was not very different from the way that programmers were used to communicating with mainframes.

The feel of using an Apple seemed as countercultural as Apple's inventors themselves, when compared to IBM's more button-down, establishment-oriented way of getting things done. The term *user-friendly* entered our vocabulary about the same time that Apples entered the computer world.

These two opposed approaches—Apple's graphics and IBM's keyboard—assured lack of compatibility between the two companies and helped divide the PC world into two opposing camps. This, too, however, would change.

THE MACINTOSH

In 1984, Apple brought out its most powerful PC, the Macintosh. From the start, the Macintosh was aimed directly at IBM's home turf—the business community. The Macintosh brought Apple's user-friendly graphical interface to offices. The Macintosh could also do things that an IBM PC could not, such as multitasking, or running more than one program at once—even transferring

THE MAC FAC   At the Apple "Mac Fac" (Macintosh factory), Macintosh computers are "burned in" for several days before shipment to lower the probability that a system will fail on delivery.

data back and forth between the programs. The IBM PC's DOS operating system, in contrast, ran one program at a time, without a graphical approach.

As IBM introduced new models of its PCs, Apple expanded its Macintosh line with machines fully as powerful as IBM's in terms of calculation speed and their ability to store and manipulate data, and with a continuing lead in graphical and multitasking ability.

Apple's fresh approach helped to find the Macintosh a comfortable niche in the business world: desktop publishing. A fundamental principle of desktop publishing is that pages made up of text and graphics are assembled on the display screen. When you are satisfied with a layout, you print it out. For a while, the Macintosh was the only system that combined the graphical interface needed to make up pages on screen with a printer—the Apple LaserWriter—that could produce near-typeset-quality. In fact, many of the leading desktop publishing software packages were first created for the Macintosh.

THE MACINTOSH HELPS SHAPE COMPUTING

Many computer designers, as well as users, conceded some time ago that the Macintosh's user-friendly graphical approach was superior to typing in keyboard commands. IBM and other personal computer makers have adapted their own operating systems to more closely resemble that of the Macintosh. For example, Microsoft Windows is a type of "shell" program designed to fit over the DOS operating system used by IBM PCs. This

MACINTOSH PERIPHERALS Apple manufactures a full line of peripherals for its Macintosh computers. Shown here are an elongated monitor, an image scanner, a laser printer, a keyboard, and a mouse.

THE EDUCATION COMPUTER COMPANY The Macintosh took off where the Apple II left off as a leader in education applications.

best-selling software product lets the DOS machine do multitasking, like the Macintosh, and uses a graphical interface—again, like the Macintosh.

At the same time, the Macintosh has grown more hospitable to its competing IBM PC. Recognizing that the bulk of today's business applications are designed for the IBM PC and other computers that use the DOS and OS/2 operating systems, Apple has gone to great lengths to make it possible to run these on the Macintosh.

THE BEST OF FRIENDS

With other PCs looking evermore like the Mac—and the Macintosh soliciting data and programs from other PCs—maybe it should come as no surprise that Apple and IBM have decided that they're not enemies after all. The two computer builders have recently signed agreements to increase further the compatibility between IBM systems and the Macintosh, develop jointly a powerful new microchip, and work together on PowerOpen, a UNIX-based operating system that both types of machines will be able to use. The two rivals have even agreed to found jointly two new research-intensive companies to develop video, animation, and sound processing techniques and to create yet more clever—and, of course, user-friendly—operating systems for the PCs of tomorrow.

Science and Research

Engineers and scientists routinely use the computer as a tool in experimentation and design. Aerospace engineers use computers to simulate the effects of a wind tunnel to analyze the aerodynamics of an airplane prototype. Political scientists collect and analyze demographic data, such as median income and housing starts, to predict voting trends. Chemists use computer graphics to create three-dimensional views of an experimental molecule. Researchers in the field of agriculture use computers to determine the fertilization programs that optimize yields for various crops. Metallurgists rely on computers to analyze stress and shear data as they work to create stronger alloys. There are at least as many science and research applications for the computer as there are scientists and engineers.

Process/Device Control

The number of applications for computer-based **process/device control** is growing rapidly. For example, computers control every step in the oil-refining process and they control thousands of devices from dishwashers to drawbridges. Computers that control processes accept data in a continuous **feedback loop**. In a feedback loop, the process itself generates data that become input to the computer. As the data are received and interpreted by the computer, the computer initiates action to control the ongoing process. An automated traffic-control system is a good example of the continuous feedback loop in a computerized process-control system. Have you ever driven an automobile through a city with an automated traffic-control system? If so, you would soon notice how the traffic signals are coordinated to minimize delays and optimize traffic flow. Traffic sensors are strategically placed throughout the city to feed data continuously to a central computer on the volume and direction of traffic flow (see Figure 1–7). The computer-based control system that activates the traffic signals is programmed to plan ahead. That is, if the sensors locate a group of cars traveling together, traffic signals are then timed accordingly.

Mainframe-sized process-control computers monitor and control the environment (temperature, humidity, lighting, security) inside skyscrapers. These computer-controlled skyscrapers are often referred to as "smart" buildings. At the other end of the process-control spectrum, tiny "computers on a chip" are being embedded in artificial hearts and other organs. Once the organs are implanted in the body, the computer monitors critical inputs, such as blood pressure and flow, then takes corrective action to ensure stability of operation in a continuous feedback loop.

All around us, computers are controlling devices of every shape and size, most of which can be programmed. Many domestic appliances are equipped with small computers. Your VCR has a small programmable computer. You are programming its computer when you set it to record several of your favorite TV shows during the coming week. The same is true of modern microwave ovens. You can program them to prepare a piping hot meal that will be ready for you when you return home from work. On a larger scale, computers control robots that perform the ma-

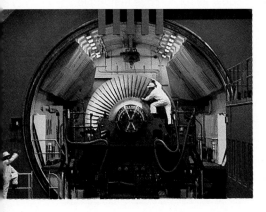

At the manufacturing operations division plant of Westinghouse Electric Corporation in Charlotte, North Carolina, technicians ready a turbine for balancing operations. The entire process is under computer control.

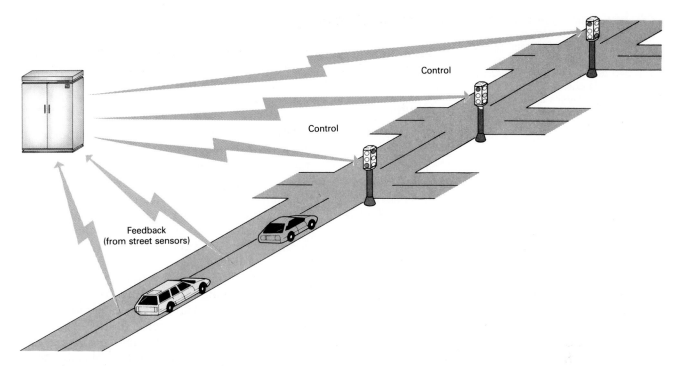

FIGURE 1–7 An Automated Traffic-Control System
In a continuous feedback loop, street sensors provide input to a process-control computer system about the direction and volume of traffic flow. Based on their feedback, the system controls the traffic lights to optimize the flow of traffic.

terials handling duties in five-acre warehouses. These robots, which navigate about the warehouse on a rail system, pick and place inventory items in bins under computer control.

Education

Computers can interact with students to enhance the learning process. Relatively inexpensive hardware capable of multidimensional communication (sound, print, graphics, and color) has resulted in the phenomenal growth of the computer as an educational tool in the home, in the classroom, and in business. Computer-based education will not replace teachers and books, but educators are in agreement that *computer-based training* (CBT) is having a profound impact on traditional modes of education.

Computers have been used for drill and practice for over a decade. Only recently has sophisticated CBT been economically feasible. Now powerful personal computers have added a dimension that is not possible with books and the traditional classroom lectures. The student controls the pace of learning and can interact directly with the computer system. Through interactive computer graphics, a CBT system can demonstrate certain concepts more effectively than can books or even teachers. The teacher-book-CBT approach has spawned a new era in education.

Crashware Have you ever wondered what would happen if your car hit a brick wall traveling at high speed? With DYNA 3D software you can actually see a simulation crash of this collision on your computer. The software is useful in many applications, particularly automobile crash testing. The computer simulation is less expensive and less time-consuming than using real automobiles. DYNA 3D is also helpful in designing products. Coors used it to design a tougher beer can. It also is used to predict injuries to passengers involved in train crashes. As you might imagine, DYNA 3D software is very complex. The simulation of a passenger going through a windshield involves more than a trillion arithmetic operations.

CBT programs are available that can help you learn keyboarding skills, increase your vocabulary, study algebra, learn about the makeup of the atom, and practice your Russian. These are just the tip of the CBT iceberg.

Computer-Aided Design

Computer-aided design (CAD), which is using the computer in the design process, is available on high-performance PCs or mainframe computers. CAD systems enable the creation and manipulation of an on-screen graphic image. CAD systems provide a sophisticated array of tools enabling designers to create three-dimensional objects that can be flipped, rotated, resized, viewed in detail, examined internally or externally, and much more. At a minimum, a CAD hardware configuration will include a high-performance computer, a large high-resolution monitor, and a variety of point/draw input devices.

CAD has all but eliminated the drawing table in many occupations. Engineers use CAD to design everything from toasters to locomotives. Architects use CAD to draw elevations and floor plans. Integrated circuit (chip) designers keep track of thousands of interconnected transistors with CAD. Software engineers use CAD to create graphic depictions of information systems. Chemists use CAD to examine the molecular structure of compounds. Photographs in this chapter and throughout the book illustrate a variety of CAD applications.

Computer-aided design (CAD) has revolutionized the way in which engineers and scientists design, draft, and document a product. With CAD, most of the "bugs" can be worked out of a design before a prototype is built.

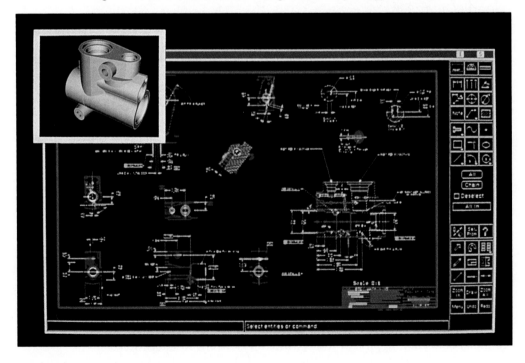

Artificial Intelligence

Human Beings Are Born, Not Manufactured   Today's computers can simulate many human capabilities such as reaching, grasping, calculating, speaking, remembering, comparing numbers, and drawing. Researchers are working to expand these capabilities and, therefore, the power of computers by developing hardware and software that can imitate intelligent human behavior. For example, researchers are working on systems that have the ability to reason, to learn or accumulate knowledge, to strive for self-improvement, and to simulate human sensory and mechanical capabilities. This general area of research is known as **artificial intelligence (AI)**.

Artificial intelligence? To some, the mere mention of artificial intelligence creates visions of electromechanical automatons replacing human beings. But as anyone involved in the area of artificial intelligence will tell you, there is a distinct difference between human beings and machines. Computers will never be capable of simulating the distinctly human qualities of creativity, humor, and emotions! However, computers can drive machines that mimic human movements (such as picking up objects and placing them at a prescribed location) and provide the "brains" for systems that simulate the human thought process within the domain of a particular area of expertise (tax preparation, medical diagnosis, and so on).

Categories of Artificial Intelligence   Research in the field of artificial intelligence can be divided into four categories (see Figure 1–8): knowledge-based and expert systems, natural languages, simulation of human sensory capabilities, and robotics.

FIGURE 1–8   Categories of Artificial Intelligence

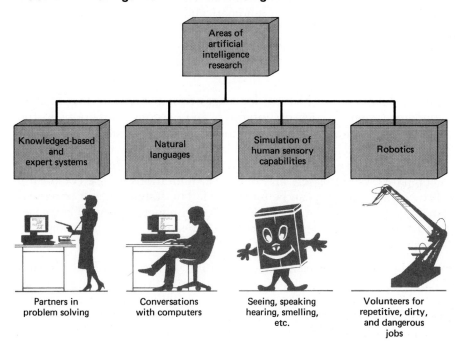

Knowledge-based and expert systems. A **knowledge-based system** relies on a **knowledge base** that is filled with "rules of thumb" (intuition, judgment, and inferences) about a specific application area, such as computer repair. Humans can use the knowledge-based system and the IF-THEN rules in the knowledge base to help them solve a particular problem. **Expert systems** are the most sophisticated implementation of a knowledge-based system. Once the knowledge of one or more human experts has been entered to an expert system's knowledge base, users can tap this knowledge by interacting with the system in much the same way they would interact with a human expert in that field. Both the user and the computer-based expert system ask and respond to each other's questions until a problem is resolved. Expert systems are beginning to make a major impact on the way people in the business community make decisions. In recent years, expert systems have been developed to support decision makers in a broad range of disciplines, including medical diagnosis, oil exploration, financial planning, chemical analysis, surgery, locomotive repair, weather prediction, computer repair, trouble-shooting satellites, computer systems configuration, operation of nuclear power plants, newspaper layout, interpreting government regulations, tax preparation, and many others.

Around tax time most of us are looking for someone to help us prepare our increasingly complex tax forms. Some of us are doing it ourselves with the help of an expert system. Several commercially available PC-based expert systems are designed to assist people in the preparation of their annual tax returns. Taxpayers and tax preparers can have a question-and-answer session with a computerized version of a tax expert. The expert system asks the user questions and, based on the answers provided, asks more detailed questions. The tax preparation expert system contains on-line facsimiles of the official IRS tax forms onto which users enter their data. The system automatically performs all needed calculations based on the data entered. Official IRS tax schedules can be printed directly by the system for submission to the Internal Revenue Service. Of course, tax expert systems are updated each year to reflect revisions in the tax laws.

Natural languages. **Natural languages** refer to software that enables computer systems to accept, interpret, and execute instructions in the native, or "natural," language of the end user, typically English. For example, the end user uses a natural language when he or she enters brief English commands such as "Show me a pie chart for regional sales" to a computer system. There are, of course, limitations on the complexity of the commands that can be interpreted. The state of the art of natural languages is still somewhat primitive. Most commercial natural languages are designed to provide end users with a means of communicating with a corporate data base or an expert system.

Simulation of human sensory capabilities. One area of AI research involves computer simulation of human capabilities. This area focuses on equipping computer systems with the capabilities of seeing, hearing, speaking, and feeling (touching). These artificial intelligence capabilities

By drawing on artificial-intelligence techniques, a General Electric research team has taught a computer the rudiments of how to read and digest a variety of printed material. In a demonstration, the system was fed a day's worth of stories from a financial news service (500 in all). At the user's request, it selected stories on mergers and acquisition and was then able to answer basic questions about them. The questions and the computer's answers are phrased in plain English, not in a specialized computer language. In the future, much of our interaction with the computer will be via a natural language; that is, we will communicate with computers in much the same way that we talk with one another.

are possible with current technology, to varying degrees. For example, some automobiles employ synthesized voice messages to warn the driver and passengers of problems: Have you ever heard, "A door is open"? Several of these capabilities are discussed in Chapter 5, "Input/Output Devices."

Robotics. **Robotics** is the integration of computers and **robots**. Industrial robots, which are usually equipped with an arm and a hand, can be "taught" to perform almost any repetitive manipulative task, such as painting a car, screwing on a bolt, moving material, and even such complex tasks as inspecting a manufactured part for defects. The topic of robotics is addressed in more detail in Chapter 14, "Applications of Information Technology."

Computers and Opportunity

Computers provide many opportunities for us to improve the quality of both our private and professional lives. The challenge is to take advantage of these opportunities. People like you who are willing to put forth the effort and accept the challenge will be the ones who benefit the most.

For some, this course will be a steppingstone to more advanced topics and, perhaps, a career in information systems or computer science. For others, this course will provide a solid foundation that will prove helpful in the pursuit of virtually any career. In either case, you will be prepared to play an active role in the computer revolution.

 Important Terms and Summary Outline

artificial intelligence (AI)
backup
computer
computer competency
computer system
computer-aided design (CAD)
computerese
cyberphobia
data
database software
desktop publishing software
downtime
expert system
feedback loop
graphics software
hard copy
hardware
information
information network

information system
input/output (I/O)
interactive computer system
keyboard
knowledge base
knowledge worker
knowledge-based system
magnetic disk
mainframe computer
master file
micro
microcomputer
microsecond
millisecond
monitor
nanosecond
natural language
personal computer (PC)

personal computing
picosecond
printer
process/device control
processor
program
record
robot
robotics
soft copy
software
source document
spreadsheet software
terminal
uptime
user
user-friendly
video display terminal (VDT)
word processing software

1–1 COMPUTERS: THE REVOLUTION IS ON. The computer revolution is transforming the way we communicate, do business, and learn. This technological revolution is having a profound impact on the business community and on our private and professional lives. The computer revolution, however, has raised serious social issues including the vulnerability of personal information and job security.

1–2 LEARNING ABOUT COMPUTERS. Computer competency is emerging as a universal goal in business and at home. Computer-competent people know how to purchase, use, and operate a computer system, and how to make it work for them. The computer-competent person is also aware of the computer's impact on society.

Cyberphobia, the irrational fear of, and aversion to, computers, is a result of people's fear of the unknown. They overcome cyberphobia by learning about computers and **computerese. Software** refers collectively to a set of machine-readable instructions, called **programs,** that cause the computer to perform desired functions.

We are entering an era where most office workers have a computer or **video display terminal (VDT)** at or near their desks.

1–3 THE EMERGING INFORMATION SOCIETY. After existing for millennia in an agrarian society, many countries progressed to industrial societies. Today we are being transformed into an information society. In the information society, **knowledge workers** will focus their energies on providing a myriad of information services. The knowledge worker's job function revolves around the use, manipulation, and dissemination of information.

Data are the raw material from which information is derived. **Information** consists of data that have been collected and processed into a meaningful form.

1–4 COMPUTERS ARE FOR EVERYONE. During the 1950s, 1960s, and 1970s, end users, or simply **users,** would relate their information needs to computer professionals, such as programmers or systems analysts, who would then work with the computer system to generate the necessary information. In "the old days," information was often obsolete by the time it reached the manager. In response to managers' requests for more timely information, **interactive computer systems** were created to permit users to communicate directly with the computer system via **user-friendly** software.

Personal computers, or **PCs,** are designed primarily for use by one person at a time. Many people have relationships with PCs that rival the romance that others have with automobiles.

1–5 UNCOVERING THE "MYSTERY" OF COMPUTERS. The **computer,** or **processor,** is an electronic device capable of interpreting and executing programmed commands for input, output, computation, and logic operations.

The data are stored on the **master file,** which is made up of **records.** The **source document** is the original document from which data are entered.

Computer system capabilities are defined as either input/output or processing. Processing capabilities are subdivided into computation and logic operations. A **computer system** is not as complex as we are sometimes led to believe. **Microcomputers** and **mainframe computers** are all computer systems, and each has only four fundamental components: **input** (for example, via the **keyboard** of a VDT, or **terminal**), processing (executing a program), **output** (via a **monitor** or a **printer**), and storage (for example, **magnetic disk**.) There are a wide variety of **input/output (I/O)** and storage devices. A monitor's output is **soft copy** and a printer's output is **hard copy**.

The computer is fast, accurate, reliable, and has an enormous memory capacity. Computer operations are measured in **milliseconds, microseconds, nanoseconds,** and **picoseconds.** For some companies, any **downtime** (versus **uptime**) is unacceptable. These companies provide **backup** computers that take over automatically if the main computers fail.

1–6 HOW DO WE USE COMPUTERS? The uses of computers can be classified into seven general categories:

■ *Information systems/data processing.* The computer is used to process data and produce business information. Hardware, software, people, procedures, and data are combined to create an **information system.**

■ *Personal computing.* The single-user **micro** is used by individuals for a variety of business and domestic applications, including such productivity tools as **word processing software, desktop publishing software, spreadsheet software, database software,** and **graphics software.** This area of computing is often referred to as **personal computing.** The dual-function personal computers, or **PC**s, can be used in conjunction with the telephone system to transmit data to and receive data from an **information network.**

■ *Science and research.* The computer is used as a tool in experimentation and design.

■ *Process/device control.* Applications that involve computer-based **process/device control** accept data in a continuous **feedback loop.**

■ *Education.* The computer interacts with a student to enhance the learning process.

■ *Computer-aided design.* **Computer-aided design (CAD)** is using the computer in the design process. CAD systems enable the creation and manipulation of an on-screen graphic image.

■ *Artificial intelligence.* **Artificial intelligence (AI)** is the area of research that involves creating computer systems with the ability to reason, to learn or accumulate knowledge, to strive for self-improvement, and to simulate human sensory and mechanical capabilities. There are four categories of AI research: **knowledge-based systems,** which rely on a **knowledge base,** and **expert systems; natural languages;** simulation of human sensory capabilities; and **robotics** (the integration of computers and **robots**).

A knowledge of computers opens the door to opportunity in many professions.

Review Exercises

Concepts

1. What are the four fundamental components of a computer system?

2. Which component of a computer system executes the program?

3. Name the four categories of artificial intelligence research.

4. Associate the following with the appropriate category of computer usage: continuous feedback loop, experimentation, home use, CBT, synthesized speech, architectural design, and business systems.

5. Compare the information processing capabilities of human beings to those of computers with respect to speed, accuracy, reliability, and memory capability.

6. What term is used to describe the integration of computers and robots?

7. Describe the relationship between data and information.

8. In computerese, what is meant by *read* and *write*?

9. Name the five microcomputer tools that are collectively referred to as productivity software.

10. Which microcomputer productivity tool would be most helpful in writing a term paper? Explain.

11. List at least six information network services.

12. The operational capabilities of a computer system include what two types of processing operations?

Discussion

13. The computer has had far-reaching effects on our lives. How has the computer affected your life?

14. What is your concept of computer competency? In what ways do you think achieving computer competency will affect your domestic life? Your business life?

15. At what age should computer competency education begin?

16. Discuss how the complexion of jobs will change as we evolve from an industrial society into an information society. Give several examples.

17. The use of computers tends to stifle creativity. Argue for or against this statement.

18. Comment on how computers are changing our traditional patterns of personal communication.

19. Comment on how computers are changing our traditional patterns of recreation.

Problem Solving

20. Describe the computation and logic operations that would take place within a computer while computing student grades for CIS 101. The results of two 100-point hourly exams and a 200-point final exam are added together to determine a student's raw score. Grades are awarded as follows: 90%

or above is an A; 80% up to 90% is a B; 70% up to 80% is a C; 60% up to 70% is a D; and below 60% is an F.

21. Describe at least three ways in which artificial intelligence applications can help disabled persons cope with the routine of everyday living.

22. Light travels at 186,000 miles per second. How many milliseconds does it take for a beam of light to travel across the United States, a distance of about 3000 miles?

 Self-Test (by section)

1–1 The "take" in an average "electronic heist" is less than that of the more traditional bank robbery. (T/*F*)

1–2 **a.** To be computer-competent, you must be able to write computer programs. (T/*F*)

b. The irrational fear of, or aversion to, computers is called _Cyberphobia_.

1–3 **a.** A person whose job revolves around the use, manipulation, and dissemination of information is called: (a) a computerphobe, (*b*) a knowledge worker, or (c) a data expert? ✳

b. _DATA_ are the raw material from which _Information_ is derived.

1–4 **a.** For the most part, a microcomputer is used by one person at a time. (*T*/F)

b. What type of system permits users to communicate directly with the computer: (a) a controlled-use system, (*b*) an interactive system, or (c) a loop system?

1–5 **a.** A printer is an example of which of the four computer system components? _Output_

b. The two types of processing operations performed by computers are ✳ _computation_ and _logic_.

c. A microsecond is 1000 times longer than a nanosecond. (*T*/F) ✳

1–6 **a.** Desktop publishing refers to the capability of producing _Near typeset_ ✳ _Quality_ copy from the confines of a desktop.

b. What type of computer-based system relies on a knowledge base to provide users with expert advice: (*a*) an expert system, (b) a master system, or (c) an intelligent system?

c. The greatest amount of available computing capacity is dedicated to the information systems/data processing category of computer usage. (*T*/F)

d. The microcomputer productivity tool that manipulates data organized in a tabular structure of rows and columns is called a _spreadsheet_.

e. Artificial intelligence refers to an area of research that uses computers to simulate human capabilities. (*T*/F)

Self-test answers. **1–1** F. **1–2 (a)** F; **(b)** cyberphobia. **1–3 (a)** b; **(b)** data, information. **1–4 (a)** T; **(b)** b. **1–5 (a)** output; **(b)** computation, logic; **(c)** T. **1–6 (a)** near-typeset-quality; **(b)** a; **(c)** T; **(d)** spreadsheet; **(e)** T.

THE IMAGE BANK
An Abbreviated History
of the Computer

Historians divide the history of the modern computer into generations, beginning with the introduction of the UNIVAC I, the first commercially viable computer, in 1951. But the quest for a mechanical servant—one that could free people from the more boring aspects of thinking—is centuries old.

Why did it take so long to develop the computer? Some of the "credit" goes to human foibles. Too often, brilliant insights were not recognized or given adequate support during an inventor's lifetime. Instead, these insights would lay dormant for as long as 100 years until someone else rediscovered—or reinvented—them. Some of the "credit" has to go to workers, too, who sabotaged labor-saving devices that threatened to put them out of work. The rest of the "credit" goes to technology; some insights were simply ahead of their time's technology. Here then is an abbreviated history of the stops and starts that have given us this marvel of the modern age, the computer.

THE ABACUS Probably the original mechanical counting device (it has been traced back 5000 years), the abacus is still used in education, to demonstrate the principles of counting and arithmetic, and in business, for speedy calculations.

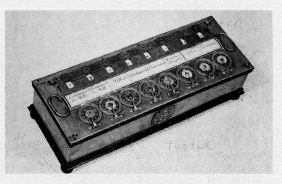

THE PASCALINE The Pascaline used a counting-wheel design: Numbers for each digit were arranged on wheels so that a single revolution of one wheel would engage gears that turned the wheel one tenth of a revolution to its immediate left. Although the Pascaline was abandoned as impractical, its counting-wheel design was used by all mechanical calculators until the mid-1960s, when they were made obsolete by electronic calculators.

BLAISE PASCAL Although inventor, painter, and sculptor Leonardo da Vinci (1425–1519) sketched ideas for a mechanical adding machine, it was another 150 years before French mathematician and philosopher Blaise Pascal (1623–62) finally invented and built the "Pascaline" in 1642 to help his father, a tax collector. Although Pascal was praised throughout Europe, his invention was a financial failure. The hand-built machines were expensive and delicate; moreover, Pascal was the only person who could repair them. Because human labor was actually cheaper, the Pascaline was abandoned as impractical.

JACQUARD'S LOOM A practicing weaver, Frenchman Joseph-Marie Jacquard (1753–1871) spent what little spare time he had trying to improve the lot of his fellow weavers. (They worked 16–hour days, with no days off!) His solution, the Jacquard loom, was created in 1801. Holes strategically punched in a card directed the movement of needles, thread, and fabric, creating the elaborate patterns still known as Jacquard weaves. Jacquard's loom was an immediate success with mill owners because they could hire cheaper and less skilled workers. But weavers, fearing unemployment, rioted and called Jacquard a traitor.

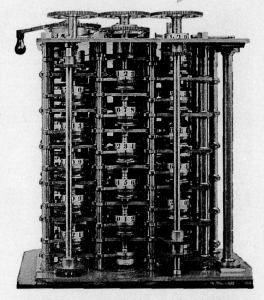

BABBAGE'S DIFFERENCE ENGINE AND THE ANALYTICAL ENGINE Convinced his machine would benefit England, Babbage applied for—and received—one of the first government grants to build the difference engine. Hampered by nineteenth-century machine technology, cost over-runs, and the possibility his chief engineer was padding the bills, Babbage completed only a portion of the difference engine (shown here) before the government withdrew its support in 1842, deeming the project "worthless to science." Meanwhile, Babbage had conceived the idea of a more advanced "analytical engine." In essence, this was a general-purpose computer that could add, subtract, multiply, and divide in automatic sequence at a rate of 60 additions per second. His 1833 design, which called for thousands of gears and drives, would cover the area of a football field and be powered by a locomotive engine. Babbage worked on this project until his death. In 1991 London's Science Museum spent $600,000 to build a working model of the difference engine (shown here), using Babbage's original plans. The result stands 6 feet high, 10 feet long, contains 4000 parts, and weighs 3 tons.

CHARLES BABBAGE Everyone from bankers to navigators depended on mathematical tables during the Industrial Revolution. However, these hand-calculated tables were usually full of errors. After discovering that his own tables were riddled with mistakes, Charles Babbage (1793–1871) envisioned a steam-powered "differential engine" and then an "analytical engine" that would perform tedious calculations accurately. Although Babbage never perfected his devices, they introduced many of the concepts used in today's general-purpose computer.

LADY ADA AUGUSTA LOVELACE The daughter of poet Lord Byron, Lady Ada Augusta Lovelace (1816–52) became a mentor to Babbage and translated his works, adding her own extensive footnotes. Her suggestion that punched cards could be prepared to instruct Babbage's engine to repeat certain operations has led some people to call her the first programmer.

HERMAN HOLLERITH With the help of a professor, Herman Hollerith (1860–1929) got a job as a special agent helping the U.S. Bureau of the Census tabulate the head count for the 1880 census—a process that took almost eight years. To speed up the 1890 census, Hollerith devised a punched-card tabulating machine. When his machine outperformed two other systems, Hollerith won a contract to tabulate the 1890 census. Hollerith earned a handsome income leasing his machinery to the governments of the United States, Canada, Austria, Russia, and others; he charged 65 cents for every 1000 people counted. (During the 1890 U.S. census alone, he earned over $40,000—a fortune in those days.) Hollerith may have earned even more selling the single-use punched cards. But the price was worth it. The bureau completed the census in just 2½ years and saved more than $5 million.

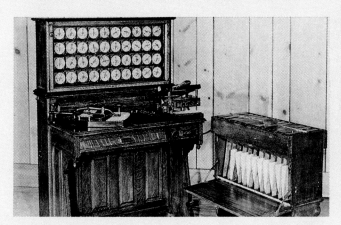

HOLLERITH'S TABULATING MACHINE
Hollerith's *punched-card tabulating machine* had three parts. Clerks at the U.S. Bureau of the Census used a hand punch to enter data into cards a little larger than a dollar bill. Cards were then read and sorted by a 24-bin sorter box (right) and summarized on numbered tabulating dials (left), which were connected electrically to the sorter box. Ironically, Hollerith's idea for the punched card came not from Jacquard or Babbage, but from "punch photography." Railroads of the day issued tickets indicating a passenger's hair and eye color. Conductors punched holes in the ticket to show that a passenger's hair and eye color matched those of the rightful owner. From this, Hollerith got the idea of making a punched "photograph" of every person to be tabulated.

IBM'S FIRST HEADQUARTERS BUILDING

In 1896 Herman Hollerith founded the Tabulating Machine Company which, in 1911, merged with several other companies to form the Computing-Tabulating-Recording Company. In 1924 the company's general manager, Thomas J. Watson, changed its name to International Business Machines Corporation and moved into this building.

THE EAM ERA From the 1920s throughout the mid–1950s, punched-card technology improved with the addition of more punched-card devices and more sophisticated capabilities. The *electromechanical accounting machine (EAM)* family of punched-card devices include the card punch, verifier, reproducer, summary punch, interpreter, sorter, collator, and accounting machine. Most of the devices in the 1940s machine room were "programmed" to perform a particular operation by the insertion of a pre-wired control panel. A machine-room operator in a punched-card installation had the physically challenging job of moving heavy boxes of punched cards and printed output from one device to the next on hand trucks.

THE ABC In 1939 Dr. John V. Atanasoff, a professor at Iowa State University, and graduate student Clifford E. Berry assembled a prototype of the *ABC* (for Atanasoff Berry Computer) to cut the time physics students spent making complicated calculations. A working model was finished in 1942. His decisions—to use an electronic medium with vacuum tubes, the base-2 numbering system, and memory and logic circuits—set the direction for the modern computer. Ironically, Iowa State failed to patent the device and IBM, when contacted about the ABC, airily responded, "IBM will never be interested in an electronic computing machine." A 1973 federal court ruling officially credited Atanasoff with the invention of the automatic electronic digital computer.

An Abbreviated History of the Computer

THE MARK I The first electromechanical computer, the *Mark I* was completed by Harvard University professor Howard Aiken in 1944 under the sponsorship of IBM. A monstrous 51 feet long and 8 feet high, the MARK I was essentially a serial collection of electromechanical calculators and had many similarities to Babbage's analytical machine. (Aiken was unaware of Babbage's work, though.) The Mark I was a significant improvement, but IBM's management still felt electromechanical computers would never replace punched-card equipment.

THE ENIAC Dr. John W. Mauchly (middle) collaborated with J. Presper Eckert, Jr., (foreground) at the University of Pennsylvania to develop a machine that would compute trajectory tables for the U.S. Army. (This was sorely needed; during World War II, only 20% of all bombs came within *1000 feet* of their targets.) The end product, the first fully operational electronic computer, was completed in 1946 and named the *ENIAC* (Electronic Numerical Integrator and Computer). A thousand times faster than its electromechanical predecessors, it occupied 15,000 square feet of floor space and weighed 30 tons. Its use of vacuum tubes signaled a major breakthrough. (Legend has it that the ENIAC's 18,000 vacuum tubes dimmed the lights of Philadelphia whenever it was activated.) Even before the ENIAC was finished, it was used in the secret research that went into building the first atomic bomb at Los Alamos.

THE UNIVAC I AND THE FIRST GENERATION OF COMPUTERS The first generation of computers (1951–1959), characterized by the use of vacuum tubes, is generally thought to have begun with the introduction of the first commercially viable electronic digital computer. The Universal Automatic Computer (*UNIVAC I* for short), developed by Mauchly and Eckert for the Remington-Rand Corporation, was installed in the U.S. Bureau of the Census in 1951. Later that year, CBS news gave the UNIVAC I national exposure when it correctly predicted Dwight Eisenhower's victory over Adlai Stevenson in the presidential election with only 5% of the votes counted. Mr. Eckert is shown here instructing news anchor Walter Cronkite in the use of the UNIVAC I.

THE IBM 650 Not until the success of the UNI-VAC I did IBM make a commitment to develop and market computers. IBM's first entry into the commercial computer market was the *IBM 701* in 1953. However, the *IBM 650* (shown here), introduced in 1954, is probably the reason IBM enjoys such a healthy share of today's computer market. Unlike some of its competitors, the IBM 650 was designed as a logical upgrade to existing punched-card machines. IBM management went out on a limb and estimated sales of 50—a figure greater than the number of installed computers in the entire nation at that time. IBM actually installed 1000. The rest is history.

THE HONEYWELL 400 AND THE SECOND GENERATION OF COMPUTERS The invention of the transistor signaled the start of the second generation of computers (1959–1964). Transistorized computers were more powerful, more reliable, less expensive, and cooler to operate than their vacuum-tubed predecessors. Honeywell (its *Honeywell 400* is shown here) established itself as a major player in the second generation of computers. Burroughs, Univac, NCR, CDC, and Honeywell—IBM's biggest competitors during the 1960s and early 1970s—became known as the BUNCH (the first initial of each name).

THE PDP-8 During the 1950s and early 1960s, only the largest companies could afford the six- and seven-digit price tags of *mainframe* computers. In 1963 Digital Equipment Corporation introduced the *PDP-8* (shown here). It is generally considered the first successful *minicomputer* (a nod, some claim, to the playful spirit behind the 1960s miniskirt). At a mere $18,000, the transistor-based PDP-8 was an instant hit. It confirmed the tremendous demand for small computers for business and scientific applications. By 1971 over 25 firms were manufacturing minicomputers, although Digital and Data General Corporation took an early lead in their sale and manufacture.

An Abbreviated History of the Computer

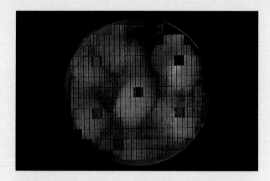

INTEGRATED CIRCUITS AND THE FOURTH GENERATION OF COMPUTERS Although most computer vendors would classify their computers as fourth generation, most people pinpoint 1971 as the generation's beginning. That was the year large-scale integration of circuitry (more circuits per unit space) was introduced. The base technology, though, is still the integrated circuit. This is not to say that two decades have passed without significant innovations. In truth, the computer industry has experienced a mind-boggling succession of advances in the further miniaturization of circuitry, data communications, and the design of computer hardware and software.

THE IBM SYSTEM 360 AND THE THIRD GENERATION OF COMPUTERS The third generation was characterized by computers built around integrated circuits. Of these, some historians consider IBM's *System 360* line of computers, introduced in 1964, the single most important innovation in the history of computers. System 360 was conceived as a family of computers with *upward compatibility*; when a company outgrew one model it could move up to the next model without worrying about converting its data. System 360 and other lines built around integrated circuits made all previous computers obsolete, but the advantages were so great that most users wrote the costs of conversion off as the price of progress.

THE IBM PC The enthusiastic reception of the *Altair 8800* in 1975 and the rags-to-riches success of Apple Computer and its *Apple II* finally convinced IBM there was a market for microcomputers. IBM responded with its 1981 announcement of the IBM Personal Computer, or PC. By the end of 1982, 835,000 had been sold. When software vendors began to orient their products to the IBM PC, many companies began offering *IBM-PC compatibles* or *clones*. Today, the IBM PC and its clones have become a powerful standard for the microcomputer industry.

Micros, Minis, Mainframes, and Supercomputers

2

STUDENT LEARNING OBJECTIVES

▶ To distinguish between microcomputers, minicomputers, mainframes, and supercomputers.

▶ To illustrate typical hardware configurations for microcomputers, minicomputers, and mainframes.

▶ To describe different types of microcomputers.

▶ To demonstrate awareness of the relative size, scope, characteristics, and variety of available computer systems.

▶ To describe the functions and relationships of the various processors in a mainframe computer system.

▶ To discuss the concept of distributed processing.

CHAPTER OUTLINE

2–1 Computer Systems Come in All Shapes and Sizes

Categories of Computer Systems

Most computers are boxlike, but they can be found in a variety of shapes, from U-shaped to cylindrical. However, the most distinguishing characteristic of any computer system is its *size*—not its physical size, but its *computing capacity*. Loosely speaking, size, or computer capacity, is the amount of processing that can be accomplished by a computer system per unit of time. **Minicomputers** have greater computing capacities than *microcomputers*. *Mainframe computers* have greater computing capacities than minicomputers. And **supercomputers**, the biggest of all, have greater computing capacities than mainframe computers. Some vendors are not content with pigeonholing their products into one of the four major categories, so they have created new niches, such as *supermicros* and *superminis*. In this chapter, we will focus on the four major categories.

Now and even in the past, these computer classifications have defied definition. Although it is doubtful that any two computer specialists would describe a minicomputer or a supercomputer in the same way, these terms are still frequently used. Rapid advances in computer technology have blurred what used to be distinguishing characteristics (physical size, cost, memory capacity, and so on).

All computers, no matter how small or large, have the same fundamental capabilities—processing, storage, input, and output. Just as "a rose, is a rose, is a rose . . ." (Gertrude Stein), "a computer, is a computer, is a computer. . . ." Keep this in mind as we discuss the four basic categories of computer systems. They are listed in ascending order of their processing capabilities:

- Microcomputer system
- Minicomputer system

- Mainframe computer system
- Supercomputer system

It should be emphasized that these are relative categories, and what people call a minicomputer system today may be called a microcomputer system at some time in the future.

The differences in computers is very much a matter of scale. A good analogy can be made between airplanes and computers. Try thinking of a wide-body jet as a supercomputer and a commuter plane as a micro. Both types of airplanes have the same fundamental capability: to carry passengers from one location to another. Wide-bodies, which fly at close to the speed of sound, can carry hundreds of passengers. In contrast, the commuter planes travel much slower and carry only 20 passengers. Wide-bodies travel between large international airports, across countries, and between continents. Commuter planes travel short distances between regional airports. The commuter plane, with its small crew, can land, unload, load, and be on its way to another destination in 15 or 20 minutes. The wide-body may take 30 minutes just to unload. A micro is much like the commuter plane in that one person can get it up and running in just a few minutes. All aspects of the micro are controlled by one person. The mainframe is like the wide-body in that a number of specialists

The clean lines of this mainframe computer system hide the thousands of integrated circuits, miles of wire, and even gold that make up the inner workings of a computer system. This data center provides information processing support for hundreds of end users.

are needed to keep it operational. No matter what their size, airplanes carry passengers and computers process data.

In keeping with conversational computerese, we will drop the word *system* when discussing the categories of computer systems. Keep in mind, however, that a reference to any of these categories (for example, supercomputer) implies a reference to the entire computer system.

Micros versus Minis, Mainframes, and Supercomputers

Minicomputers, mainframes, and supercomputers are computer systems. Micros also are computer systems. Each offers many input and output alternatives, that is, ways to enter data to the system and to present information generated by the system. In addition, each is supported by a wide variety of packaged software. There are, of course, obvious differences in size and capabilities. Everything associated with minicomputers, mainframes, and supercomputers is larger in scope than that associated with microcomputers: Execution of programs is faster; disk storage has more capacity; printer speeds are faster. Computers in these three categories can service many terminals and, of course, they cost more. (Interestingly, the execution of a million instructions costs more on a mainframe computer than on a microcomputer! So the economies of scale do not apply to computers.)

Besides size and capability, the single most distinguishing characteristic of minicomputers, mainframe computers, and supercomputers is the manner in which each type is used. The three larger computers, with their expanded processing capabilities, provide a computing resource that can be shared by many people. For example, finance, personnel, and accounting departments within a company share the resources of a mainframe, possibly all at the same time. In contrast, most microcomputers are used by one user at a time.

Another important difference between micros and the other categories of computers is that you, in all probability, will spend much of your working life within arm's reach of a micro. You will be the person who turns on the system, selects the software to be run, enters the data, and requests the information. In contrast, your association with larger computers will probably be via a VDT that is linked to a computer in a different building or even a different state. Since the micro will likely be the center of your computing experience, it is discussed in more detail in this chapter and throughout the book.

2–2 Microcomputers: Small but Powerful

Microprocessors

Here is a tough one. What is smaller than a dime and found in wristwatches, sewing machines, and jukeboxes? The answer: a **microprocessor**. Microprocessors play a very important role in our lives. You probably have a dozen or more of them at home and may not know it. They are used in telephones, ovens, televisions, thermostats, greeting cards, automobiles, and, of course, personal computers.

Memory Bits

CATEGORIES OF COMPUTER SYSTEMS
- Microcomputer system
- Minicomputer system
- Mainframe computer system
- Supercomputer system

What looks like a PC but isn't? It's a workstation and it's fast blurring some of the traditional distinctions between mainframes, minis, and microcomputers. What sets a workstation apart from a PC?

Clue One   One tip-off is the workstation's input/output devices. A typical engineering workstation will sport a large-screen, high-resolution color monitor for displaying graphics, with a smaller monochrome monitor for displaying data. For pointing and drawing, the engineer can call on such specialized input devices as a light pen, a digitizing tablet, or cross-hairs, which combines the precision of a gunsight with the convenience of a mouse. Add-on keypads may expand the number of specialized function keys. A plotter will produce plans and blueprints.

Clue Two   Another tip-off might be the operating system. Most PCs use MS-DOS or PC-DOS. Workstations tend to use UNIX, an operating system created by AT&T, which allows for multitasking and easy networking.

Clue Three   The most important difference between a workstation and a PC is speed and power. In fact, some people talk of workstations as "souped-up" PCs. To give you an idea of what they mean, consider one standard rating device, MIPS, which stands for millions of instructions per second. The first IBM PC, introduced in 1981, clocked in at $\frac{1}{10}$ to $\frac{1}{6}$ MIPS. The PC was fine for word processing, spreadsheets, and games, but for real "power users"—engineers doing computer-aided design, scientists, and other "number crunchers"—it was laughable. Power users needed the speed of a mini or mainframe at a fraction of the cost.

The workstation, introduced in the early 1980s, filled this gap. Today, many of the leading manufacturers offer entry-level workstations with 20 to 35 MIPS for about $5000. (In comparison, a typical 386 PC running at 33 megahertz, rated at 8 MIPS, sells for around $3000 and a mainframe serving 2000 terminals might be rated at 40 MIPS.) A fully equipped engineering workstation, rated as high as 75 MIPS, costs between $10,000 and $20,000—still a bargain compared to a mini or a mainframe. Most workstations get their speed from reduced-instruction-set computer (RISC) chips, which are generally seen as being faster than the complex-instruction-set computer (CISC) chips used in most PCs.

A RED HERRING

Until recently, another difference between a PC and a workstation might have been the person using it. Workstations were geared toward the power users—engineers, programmers, scientists, and the like.

The distinctions between technical and nontechnical user are blurring, though. Today anyone who uses graphics or a graphical user interface can quickly become a power user. Desktop publishing, for example, needs lots of power and speed, as do the special effects created for television and the movies. (Many of the special effects for *Terminator II: Judgment Day* were created on workstations.)

THE FUTURE FOR WORKSTATIONS

Many PC makers, IBM among them, are moving to incorporate RISC technology into PCs, a move that will further blur the PC–workstation distinction. Some experts predict a 2000 MIPS machine by the year 2000. This power, they speculate, will be used to improve graphical user interfaces, speech recognition, and handwriting recognition—all of which will make it easier and more natural to work with computers.

AN OVERWEIGHT TOWER PC?   No, it's a powerful graphics workstation with a variety of input/output devices to facilitate the creation of sophisticated graphic images.

The microprocessor is a product of the microminiaturization of electronic circuitry; it is literally a "computer on a chip." **Chip** refers to any self-contained integrated circuit. (See the feature entitled "Computer on a Chip" in this chapter.) The size of chips, which are about 30 thousandths of an inch thick, vary in area from fingernail size (about ¼-inch square) to postage-stamp size (about 1-inch square). The first fully operational microprocessor was demonstrated in March 1971. Since that time, these relatively inexpensive microprocessors have been integrated into thousands of mechanical and electronic devices—even elevators, band saws, and ski-boot bindings. In a few years virtually everything mechanical or electronic will incorporate microprocessor technology into its design.

Microcomputers

The microprocessor is sometimes confused with its famous offspring, the microcomputer. A keyboard, video monitor, and memory were attached to the microprocessor; power was added and the microcomputer was born! Suddenly owning a computer became an economic reality for individuals and small businesses. In all probability, your career will involve frequent interaction with a micro.

There is no commonly accepted definition of a microcomputer or, for that matter, of a minicomputer or a supercomputer. A microcomputer is just a small computer. However, it is a safe bet that any computer you can pick up and carry is probably a micro. But don't be misled by the *micro* prefix. You can pick up and carry some very powerful computers!

The System Board   In a microcomputer, the microprocessor, the electronic circuitry for handling input/output signals from the **peripheral devices** (keyboard, printer, and so on), and the memory chips are mounted on a single circuit board called a **system board**, or **motherboard**. Before being attached to the system board, the microprocessor and other chips are mounted onto a **carrier**. Carriers have standard-sized pin connectors that allow the chips to be attached to the system board. (See the feature entitled "Computer on a Chip.")

The system board, the "guts" of a microcomputer, is what distinguishes one microcomputer from another. The central component of the system board, the microprocessor, is not made by the manufacturers of micros but by companies, such as Motorola and Intel, that specialize in the development and manufacture of microprocessors. All of Apple's Macintosh-series micros use Motorola chips: the Motorola 68000 in earlier models, the Motorola 68020 in the Macintosh II, and the Motorola 68030 in recent models.

The system board for the original IBM PC, the IBM PC/XT, and most of the IBM-PC compatibles manufactured through 1984, used the Intel 8088 microprocessor chip. The Intel 8088 chip is a slower version of the Intel 8086, which was developed in 1979. At the time of the introduction of the IBM PC (1981), the Intel 8086 was thought to be too advanced for the emerging PC market. Ironically, the more powerful Intel 8086 chip was not used in micros until the introduction of the low-end models of the IBM PS/2 series in 1987. The 8086 is considered the

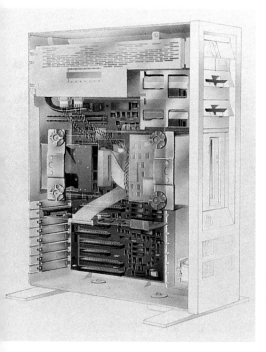

The system board on this tower PC is based on the high performance Intel 486 microprocessor. The chip packs 1.2 million transistors in a 0.414-inch by 0.619-inch die.

base technology for all microprocessors used in IBM-PC–compatible and PS/2 series computers.

The IBM PC/AT (Advanced Technology), which was introduced in 1984, employed an Intel 80286 microprocessor. As much as six times faster than the 8088, the 80286 provided a substantial increase in PC performance. High-end IBM-PC–compatible micros and PS/2s use the more advanced Intel 80386 and 80486 chips. When someone talks about a "286," "386," or "486" machine, he or she is referring to a micro that uses an Intel 80286, 80386, or 80486 chip.

The *SX* versions of Intel chips, such as the 386SX and 486SX, are less expensive and less powerful than the processors upon which they are based. Intel plans to introduce the 80586 and the 80686 soon. The performance of the 586 chip is expected to be double that of the 486. The 686 chip is being designed to accommodate multimedia applications that involve sound and motion video.

After the microprocessor and other chips have been mounted on the system board, it is simply inserted in the slot designed for the system board. The processing components of most micros are sold with several empty **expansion slots** so you can purchase and plug in optional capabilities in the form of **add-on boards**. Add-on boards are discussed in detail later in this chapter.

Pocket, Laptop, Desktop, and Tower PCs Personal computers come in four different physical sizes: **pocket PCs**, **laptop PCs**, **desktop PCs**, and **tower PCs**. The pocket and laptop PCs are light (a few ounces to about 15 pounds), compact, and can operate without an external power source, so they earn the "portable" label as well. The smallest laptops, which weigh from 6 to 8 pounds, are called **notebook** computers. Notebooks are so named because they are about the size of a three-ring notebook. There are also some "transportable" desktop PCs on the market, but they are more cumbersome. They fold up to about the size of a small suitcase, weigh about 25 pounds, and require an external power source. Desktop PCs and tower PCs are not designed for frequent movement and, therefore, are not considered portable. Typically, the monitor is positioned on top of the processing component of a desktop PC. The processing component of the tower PC is designed to rest on the floor, usually beside or under a desk. The tower PC resembles the processing component of a desktop PC that has been placed on end.

The power of a PC is not necessarily directly related to its size. A few laptop PCs can run circles around some of the desktop PCs. Some user conveniences, however, must be sacrificed to achieve portability. For instance, the miniature keyboards on pocket PCs, sometimes called **palmtop PCs**, make data entry and interaction with the computer difficult and slow. The only display screen available on most laptop PCs is monochrome (as opposed to color). Portable computers take up less space and, therefore, have a smaller capacity for permanent storage of data and programs.

Multiuser Micros In the early 1960s mainframe computer systems could service only one user at a time. By the mid-1960s technological im-

---

Memory Bits

TYPES OF PERSONAL COMPUTERS
- Pocket PC or palmtop PC
- Laptop PC
- Desktop PC (transportable)
- Desktop PC (stationary)
- Tower PC

(Top left) This high-performance palmtop computer can run the same applications as its desktop cousin. (Top right) When searching for a personal computer, this executive identified portability as her primary criterion. (Bottom left) Desktop Macintosh micros are made available to library patrons. (Bottom right) Some of the more powerful desktop microcomputers actually sit under or beside a desk, thus providing more space for the keyboard, monitor, printer, and other peripheral devices.

provements had made it possible for computers to service several users simultaneously. Now, a quarter century later, some mainframes service thousands of users at the same time!

We can draw a parallel between what happened to the mainframe in the 1960s and what is happening to microcomputers today. Until recently micros were "personal" computers—for individual use only. But technological improvements have been so rapid that it has become difficult for a single user to tap the full potential of state-of-the-art micros. To tap this unused potential, hardware and software vendors are marketing products that permit several people to use the system at once.

These **multiuser micros** are configured with as many as a dozen VDTs. These terminals, often located in the same office, share the microcomputer's resources and its peripheral devices. With a multiuser micro, a secretary can transcribe dictation at one terminal while a manager

Visitors to the Compaq Computer Corporation's Remote Terminal Emulation lab receive a vivid demonstration of the power of a micro in a multiuser environment. The lab consists of 144 terminals driven by a single PC system. Each terminal simulates the activity of a person engaged in intensive word processing, order entry, spreadsheet preparation, or other day-to-day activity.

does financial analysis at another terminal and a clerk enters data to a data base at yet another. All this can take place at the same time on the same multiuser micro. Multiuser microcomputer systems are installed in thousands of small businesses, from hardware stores to veterinarians' offices.

Configuring a Microcomputer System

Normally, computer professionals are called upon to select, configure, and install the hardware associated with minicomputers and mainframe computers. But for micros, the user typically selects, configures, and installs his or her own system; therefore, it is important that you know what makes up a microcomputer system and how it fits together.

A Typical Microcomputer Configuration   The computer and its peripheral devices are called the computer system **configuration**. The configuration of a microcomputer can vary. The most typical micro configuration consists of the following:

1. A microcomputer
2. A 101-key keyboard and a mouse for input
3. A color monitor for *soft-copy* (temporary) output
4. A printer for *hard-copy* (printed) output
5. Two disk drives for permanent storage of data and programs (one for a permanently installed disk and one to accommodate interchangeable disks)

Notebooks Reach New Heights
A group of mountain climbers from the United States used a solar-charged notebook PC to set a new record for Americans. The notebook came with a 1.8-pound solar panel for recharging its batteries. The climbers used the solar-powered notebook to record their use of supplies on a 30-day climb up the world's sixth highest peak, Cho Oyu, located in a remote part of China, stands 29,906 feet tall.

Imagine that your job is to monitor the operation of a vast telecommunications network. Cables snake underground and underwater. Data flows between communications satellites and earth and across wiring inside building walls. Now imagine that a graphic image of this vast grid and its data flows could be laid out below you, as you float above, an "infonaut" looking for the kink that is blocking service to millions of customers. Far below you see a pulsing light. There's the problem. With a gestured command, you fix it—without leaving your office. That's the promise of virtual reality, and it's fast moving from computer fantasy to computer fact. In fact, US West and a number of other telecommunications firms are already experimenting with such systems.

Virtual reality (VR) combines computer graphics with special hardware to immerse users in *cyberspace,* an artificial, three-dimensional world. Instead of passively viewing data or graphics on a screen, users can move about, handle "virtual" representations of data and objects, and get visual, aural, and tactile feedback. In the world of computers, the term *virtual* refers to an environment that is *simulated by hardware and software* (for example, virtual memory, virtual machine).

DRESSING FOR CYBERSPACE

To enter cyberspace, users must don special hardware.

- *Headpiece.* The goggles-like headpiece blocks out visual sensations from the real world and substitutes images presented on *two small video screens*—one for each eye, creating a three-dimensional effect.

The headpiece also contains *motion* or *balance sensors*; move your head and the computer will shift the view presented on the video screens.

- *Headphones.* Headphones block out room noise and substitute three-dimensional *holophononic* sounds.
- *Data glove.* The ensemble is completed by a data glove outlined with *fiber-optic sensors* and cables. The glove can be used, like a floating mouse, to "gesture" a command or to grasp and move virtual objects about.

Each piece of hardware is tethered to a power pack and to one or more powerful computers via two-way data transfer cables that record the user's movements and provide real-time feedback.

THE QUEST FOR COMMERCIAL APPLICATIONS

Virtual reality was born in the late 1960s, when the U.S. Air Force began experimenting with flight simulators. From there, the technology was picked up by NASA. Today, NASA and a number of universities and corporations are either developing or using virtual reality systems for the following applications:

- *Architecture and computer-aided design.* Architects already have access to a number of commercial VR systems that let them conduct electronic "walkthroughs" of proposed buildings.
- *Visualization of data.* NASA has created a virtual wind tunnel that lets a user climb inside an airstream.

In most microcomputer systems these components are purchased as separate physical units and then linked together. Micros that give users the flexibility to configure the system with a variety of peripheral devices (input/output and storage) are said to have an **open architecture**. We use the term *architecture* to refer to a computer system's design. A component stereo system provides a good analogy with which to illustrate the concept of open architecture. In a stereo system, the tuner is the central component to which equalizers, tape decks, compact disk players, speakers, and so on can be attached. An open-architecture microcomputer system is configured by linking any of a wide variety of peripheral devices to the processor component. As a rule of thumb, if there is a need for a special type of input/output or storage device, then someone markets

By gesturing with a data glove, the user can change the airflow and then walk around to view it from different angles.

- *Exploration of hostile environments.* NASA is using raw data to create a VR version of an Antarctic lake bottom that will let researchers study life forms beneath the frigid waters without risk.

- *Sales.* In the spring of 1991, a Japanese department store opened a "virtual kitchen" for planning custom-designed remodeling projects. After store personnel input a kitchen's existing layout and measurements, customers don the VR gear and play around with different appliances and arrangements—usually a half-hour process. Two weeks later, the store delivers the custom-designed kitchen. All hardware and software used in this high-tech application are made in the United States.

- *Education and training.* In addition to the flight and tank simulators used by the military, researchers are looking into VR systems that could be used to train firefighters and rookie police officers.

- *Entertainment.* Virtual reality arcades featuring space travel games are now appearing in the United States and Europe. In addition, a joint venture has been formed to build a series of test theaters that would use VR to let users "walk among" the on-screen actors.

WILL THE PROMISE BE KEPT?

At this point, virtual reality is still in its infancy. Although some VR applications can be run on powerful PCs, the

IT'S ALMOST REAL Virtual reality lets you walk into an imaginary home and meet people who do not exist in real life.

most realistic experiences are created with sophisticated systems that cost from $50,000 to $250,000 and up. Headsets alone can cost between $6000 to $50,000; a data glove will run between $6000 and $15,000. Moreover, the equipment is cumbersome and the graphics are often fairly crude. Still, many experts predict that hardware costs will continue to drop and software will become more refined. If so, another prediction—that virtual reality will emerge as the user interface of the future—will probably become a computer fact for you, perhaps by the year 2000.

it. The IBM family of computers, their compatibles, and most modern micros have open-architecture systems. In a **closed architecture**, the system is fully configured when it is sold.

Linking Micro Components   An open architecture, also called a **bus architecture**, is possible because all micro components are linked via a common electrical **bus**. In Chapter 1 we compared the processing component of a microcomputer to the human brain. Just as the brain sends and receives signals through the central nervous system, the processor sends and receives electrical signals through the bus. The bus is the path through which the processor sends data and commands to it **RAM** and all peripheral devices. (RAM, or **random-access memory**, provides temporary storage of data and programs during processing.) The micro sends the data and commands in the form of electronic signals. In short, the bus is the vehicle by which the processor communicates with its peripherals and vice versa. The processor, RAM, and disk-storage devices usually are connected directly to the bus—that is, without cables.

In an open architecture, external input/output devices (that is, devices external to the processor cabinet) and some storage devices are plugged into the bus in much the same way that you plug a lamp into an electrical outlet. The receptacle, called a **port**, provides a direct link to the micro's common electrical bus.

External peripheral devices are linked to, or *interfaced* with, the processor via cables through either a **serial port** or a **parallel port**.

- *Serial ports.* Serial ports facilitate the *serial transmission* of data, *one bit at a time*. The bit, which is discussed in detail in Chapter 4, "Inside the Computer," is the basic unit of data for computers. Serial ports provide an interface for low-speed printers and modems. The de facto standard for micro serial ports is the 9-pin or 25-pin (male or female) **RS-232C connector**.
- *Parallel ports.* Parallel ports facilitate the *parallel transmission* of data, that is, several bits are transmitted simultaneously. Parallel ports use the same 25-pin RS-232C connector or the 36-pin **centronics connector**. Parallel ports provide the interface for such devices as high-speed printers, magnetic tape backup units, and other computers.

Expansion Slots and Add-on Boards   Also connected to the common electrical bus are *expansion slots*, which usually are housed in the processor cabinet. These slots enable a micro owner to enhance the functionality of a basic micro configuration with a wide variety of special-function *add-on boards*, also called **add-on cards**. These "add-ons" contain the electronic circuitry for a wide variety of computer-related functions. The number of available expansion slots varies from computer to computer. Some of the more popular add-on boards are listed below.

- *RAM.* Expands memory, usually in increments of 256 KB or 1 MB. (A KB, or kilobyte, is roughly 1000 characters. A MB, or megabyte, is roughly 1,000,000 characters. The terms KB and MB are discussed in Chapter 4, "Inside the Computer.")
- *Color and graphics adapter.* Permits interfacing with video monitors that have graphics and/or color capabilities. The EGA (enhanced graphic adapter) and the VGA (video graphics array) boards enable the interfacing of high-resolution monitors with the processor. (The VGA monitor has emerged as the standard for contemporary micros.) These add-on boards usually come with at least 256 KB of *dedicated RAM*, RAM that is not available to the user. Monitors are discussed more in Chapter 5, "Input/Output Devices."
- *Modem.* A modem permits communication with remote computers via a telephone-line link. Modems are discussed more in Chapter 7, "Connectivity and Data Communications," and Chapter 8, "Networks and Networking."

Personal computers are everywhere and, as such, are particularly vulnerable to unauthorized use or malicious tampering. As an added layer of security, many companies are opting to use a magnetic card reader as part of the user sign-on procedure. The card reader comes with an add-on board that is inserted in one of the micro's expansion slots. The reader reads commonly carried credit cards, door-opener cards, telephone cards, and so on. When used in conjunction with authorization codes, a PC can have the same level of security as an automatic teller machine.

- *Internal battery-powered clock/calendar.* This board provides continuous and/or on-demand display of or access to the current date and time (e.g., Friday, March 12, 1994, 9:35 A.M.). The system board on all late-model micros includes this capability.
- *Serial port.* Installation of this board provides access to the bus via another serial port. Most micros are sold with at least one serial and one parallel port.
- *Parallel port.* Installation of this board provides access to the bus via another parallel port.
- *Printer spooler.* This add-on board enables data to be printed while the user continues with other processing activities. Data are transferred (spooled) at a high speed from RAM to a *print buffer* (an intermediate storage area) and then routed to the printer from the buffer.
- *Hard disk.* Hard disks with capacities of as much as 40 MB can be installed in expansion slots.
- *Coprocessor.* These "extra" processors, which are under the control of the main processor, help relieve the main processor of certain tasks, such as arithmetic functions. This sharing of duties helps increase system **throughput**, the rate at which work can be performed by the microcomputer system.
- *Accelerator.* The accelerator board gives the user the flexibility to upgrade a micro's processor. In effect, the higher speed processor on the accelerator board replaces the existing processor.
- *Network interface.* The network interface card (NIC) facilitates and controls the exchange of data between the micros in a PC *network* (several micros linked together). Each PC in a network must be equipped with an NIC. The cables that link the PCs are physically connected to the NICs.
- *Motion video.* This card enables full-motion color video with audio to be integrated with other output on the monitor's screen. Because the card accepts multiple inputs, videos can be shown full-screen (one video input) or in windows (multiple video inputs).
- *VCR backup.* This board enables an ordinary VHS or Beta videocassette recorder to be used as a tape backup device. One ordinary videocassette tape can hold up to 80 MB.

Most of the add-on boards are *multifunction:* They include two or more of these capabilities. For example, one popular **multifunction add-on board** comes with a serial port, a modem, and an internal battery-powered clock/calendar.

Expansion slots are at a premium. To make the most efficient use of these slots, circuit-board manufacturers have created **half-size expansion boards** that fit in a "short slot" (half an expansion slot). These half-size boards effectively double the number of expansion slots available for a given microcomputer.

The Dual-Purpose Micro: Two for the Price of One

A video display terminal (VDT) is the hardware that allows you to interact with a computer system, be it a mainframe or a multiuser micro. A microcomputer can also function as a VDT. With the installation of an

Upgrading PC Microprocessors If you want more speed and features than your PC has to offer, you might not have to buy an entirely new system. Installing a new motherboard (also called a system board) might give you the extras you are looking to find. Tearing into your PC sounds terrifying, but the installation of a motherboard is not all that difficult. Anyone who can install an internal Winchester disk drive probably can handle the job. When you upgrade your motherboard, you eliminate the compatibility worries that accompany conversion to a new PC. Motherboards are also relatively inexpensive, with prices ranging from about $500 to $1000.

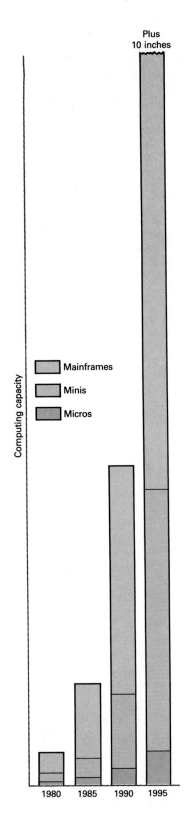

FIGURE 2–1 Micro, Mini, and Mainframe Computing Capacities
The computing capacity of a micro, mini, and mainframe increases with advancing technology. As a rule of thumb, the computing capacity of supercomputers is 10 times that of a mainframe computer.

optional data communications adapter, a micro has the flexibility to serve as a *stand-alone* computer system or as an "intelligent" terminal of a multiuser micro, a mini, a mainframe, or a supercomputer.

The term *intelligent* is applied to terminals that also can operate as stand-alone computer systems, independent of any other computer system. For example, you can dial up any one of a number of commercial information services on travel, securities, and consumer goods, link your micro to the telephone line and remote computer, then use your micro as a terminal to receive information. Or you can establish a communications link between your micro and your company's mainframe computer. Both the micro and the VDT can transmit and receive data from a remote computer, but only the micro in terminal mode can process and store the data independently.

2–3 Minis and Mainframes: Corporate Workhorses

Because minis and mainframes are functionally similar, they are discussed in the same section. Minis and mainframes are the workhorses that handle the bulk of the data and information processing duties in the business world.

What Is a Mini and How Is It Used?

Until the late 1960s all computers were mainframe computers, and they were expensive—too expensive for all but the larger companies. About that time vendors introduced smaller, slightly "watered down" computers that were more affordable for smaller companies. The industry dubbed these small computers *minicomputers*, or simply **minis**. The name has stuck, even though some of today's so-called minis are many times as powerful as the largest mainframes of the late 1960s (see Figure 2–1).

Early minicomputers were designed for and used primarily for research, engineering, and education. By 1970, the relatively inexpensive minis also were accomplishing processing tasks that traditionally have been associated with mainframes. Today's minicomputers address virtually all applications. They bridge the gap between micros and mainframes, but the way they are used makes them more like mainframes than micros. To distinguish between powerful multiuser micros, which look and function very much like small minis, we describe the minicomputer simply as the smallest computer *designed specifically* for the multiuser environment.

Minicomputers usually serve as stand-alone computer systems (see Figure 2–2) for small businesses (10 to 400 employees) and as remote **departmental computer systems**. In the latter case, these departmental systems are used both as stand-alone systems in support of a particular department and as part of a network of departmental minis, all linked

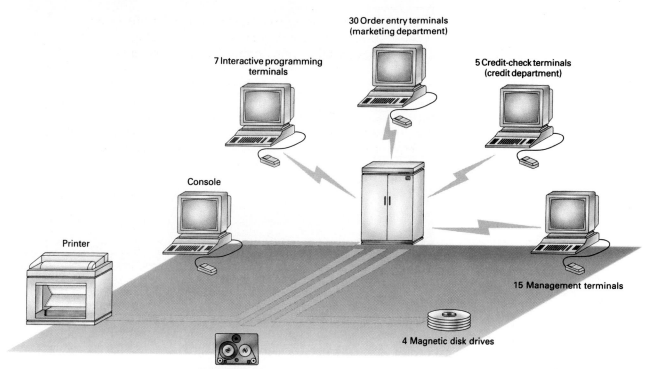

30 Order entry terminals
(marketing department)

7 Interactive programming
terminals

5 Credit-check terminals
(credit department)

Console

Printer

15 Management terminals

4 Magnetic disk drives

2 Magnetic tape drives

FIGURE 2–2 A Minicomputer System
This system supports a mail–order sporting goods retailer with $40 million in
sales and is representative of a midsized minicomputer.

to a large centralized mainframe computer. Minis are also common in
research groups, engineering firms, and colleges.

Configuring a Minicomputer System

Minis have most of the operational capabilities of mainframe computers
that may be 10 to 1000 times faster. They just perform their tasks more
slowly. Minicomputer input, output, and storage devices are similar in
appearance and function to those used on much larger systems. However,
the printers are not quite as fast, the storage capacity is smaller, and fewer
terminals can be serviced. Figure 2–2 illustrates a midsized minicomputer
system configuration that provides information systems support for a mail-
order sporting-goods retailer with $40 million in sales. The minicomputer
components illustrated in Figure 2–2 are described within the context of
the retailer.

■ *Processing.* The processor in the minicomputer system of Figure 2–2 has
  about 10 times the processing capability of a state-of-the-art single-user
  micro. The mini's processor works constantly throughout the day: processing orders, responding to management's requests for information (for
  example, the number of tennis racquet orders by manufacturer during June),
  checking credit, and much more.

This marketing consultant routinely uses his PC in terminal mode to obtain public domain demographic data directly from federal government mainframe computers. He analyzes the data in stand-alone mode.

- *Storage.* The minicomputer system in Figure 2–2 has four high-density magnetic *disk drives* and two magnetic *tape drives*. Up-to-date records on all customers and suppliers are maintained on magnetic disk. The disk files are periodically copied to magnetic tape for backup. Magnetic storage is discussed in Chapter 6, "Data Storage and Organization."
- *Input.* The primary means of data input to the system are the 35 VDTs (see Figure 2–2) installed in the marketing and credit departments. People in the marketing department enter the data to process orders received via phone, mail, and facsimile (fax). The credit department enters credit data for business accounts. The **operator console** in the machine room is also used to communicate instructions to the system. Seven terminals are used by programmers to write and test their programs.
- *Output.* A 1200-line-per-minute (lpm) printer provides hard-copy output (for example, shipping orders, invoices, catalog mailing labels, and microcomputer reports). The VDTs in the marketing, credit, and programming departments and the console in the machine room provide soft-copy output (for example, order entry display, credit history reports, and program listings). Fifteen VDTs are available to management so managers can make inquiries to the system (for example, total sales in California during 1993).

It is unlikely that you would find two minicomputers configured in exactly the same way. For example, another company may have a substantial volume of printed output and require a 2000-line-per-minute printer and a high-speed page printer that prints two pages of output each second. Figure 2–2 is an example of just one possible configuration.

The term *supermini* is often applied to a high-end minicomputer. Superminis typically have the capability of servicing one hundred or more users simultaneously. Such systems can be difficult to distinguish from mainframe computers.

Configuring a Mainframe Computer System

Aside from the obvious difference in the speeds at which they process data, the major difference between minicomputers and mainframe computers is in the number of remote terminals they can service. This rule of thumb may help you distinguish between minis and mainframes: Any computer that services more than 200 remote terminals is out of the minicomputer and into the mainframe range. Some very large mainframe computers provide service to over 10,000 remote terminals.

The speed at which medium-sized and large mainframe computers can perform operations allows more input, output, and storage devices with greater capabilities to be configured in the computer system. Let's take a closer look at a medium-sized mainframe computer system (Figure 2–3) used by the municipal government of a city of about one million people. This example should give you an appreciation of the relative size and potential of a medium-sized mainframe computer system. The hardware devices illustrated will be explained in detail in subsequent chapters. The components are described briefly below.

- *Processing.* Mainframe computer systems, including some minis, will normally be configured with the mainframe, or **host processor**, and several

FIGURE 2–3   A Mainframe Computer System
This midsized mainframe computer system supports the administrative processing needs for the municipal government of a city with a population of about one million.

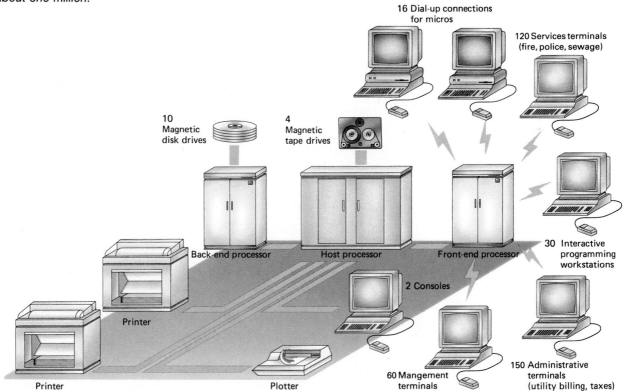

other *subordinate processors*. The host processor has direct control over all the other processors, storage devices, and input/output devices. The other processors relieve the host of certain routine processing requirements. For example, the **back-end processor** performs the task of locating a particular record on a data storage device. The **front-end processor** relieves the host processor of communications-related processing duties—that is, the transmission of data to and from remote terminals and other computers. In this way, the host can concentrate on overall system control and the execution of applications software.

A typical configuration would have a host processor, a *front-end processor*, and perhaps a *back-end processor*. The host is the main computer and is substantially larger and more powerful than the other subordinate processors. The front-end and back-end processors control the data flow in and out of the host processor. Although the host could handle the entire system, these subordinate processors provide a boost to overall system efficiency.

A large municipal government places a wide variety of processing demands on its mainframe. For example, each morning, the system prepares a maintenance schedule for the streets department. Court cases also are generated on the mainframe. Invoices for water and sewer usage are computed and printed every day.

■ *Storage.* All mainframe computer systems use similar direct and sequential storage media. The larger ones simply have more of them, and they usually

Minicomputers are being designed to operate in a normal office environment. Most minicomputers, such as the one in this real estate office (on the desk), do not require special accommodations for temperature and humidity control. More than a dozen terminals are connected to this mini.

work faster. Figure 2–3 shows 4 magnetic tape drives and 10 magnetic disk drives. The magnetic disks store data on land parcel usage, parking meter fines, taxes, and much more.

- *Input.* The primary means of entering data to the system is the same, no matter what the size of the computer system. The only difference between a large and a small system is in the number and location of the terminals. In the example of Figure 2–3, 270 terminals are dedicated to service and administrative functions, 30 are used for programming, 60 are used by management, and 16 *ports* are available for those who might wish to use their PCs to establish a link with the mainframe computer. A port on a mainframe is like the micro port discussed earlier in that it provides an access point in a computer system.

- *Output.* Like the minicomputer system in Figure 2–2, the hard copy is produced on high-speed printers and the soft copy on terminals. The Figure 2–3 example shows two printers: a line printer with a speed of 2000 lines per minute and a page printer that uses laser-printing technology to achieve speeds of over 40,000 lines per minute. A large municipal government generates a tremendous amount of external output (output which is directed to persons not affiliated with city government, such as utility bills and tax notices), thus the need for a high-speed printer. The plotter, also pictured in the configuration, is used by city engineers to produce large, high-precision hard copies of graphs, charts, blueprints, and drawings.

The dimensional integrity of a 1992 Crown Victoria body is verified to 1/1000th inch by computer-operated mechanical prods. Data from the verification process are transmitted directly to one of Ford's mainframe computers as part of its quality-control program.

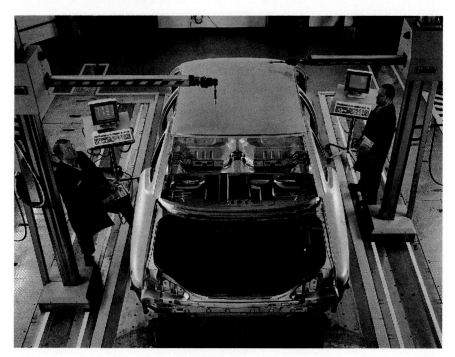

The Evolution of Supercomputers

During the early 1970s administrative data processing dominated computer applications. Bankers, college administrators, and advertising executives were amazed by the blinding speed at which million-dollar mainframes processed data. Engineers and scientists were grateful for this tremendous technological achievement, but they were far from satisfied. When business executives talked about unlimited capability, engineers and scientists knew they would have to wait for future enhancements before they could use computers to address complex problems. But, automotive engineers were still not able to build three-dimensional prototypes of automobiles inside a computer. Physicists could not explore the activities of an atom during a nuclear explosion. The engineering and scientific communities had a desperate need for more powerful computers. In response to that need, computer designers began work on what are now known as supercomputers.

Supercomputers primarily address applications that are **processor-bound**. Processor-bound applications, which are helpful to engineers and scientists, require relatively little in the way of input or output. In processor-bound applications, the amount of work that can be performed by the computer system is limited primarily by the speed of the computer. A typical scientific job involves the manipulation of a complex mathematical model, often requiring trillions of operations to resolve. During the early 1970s some of the complex processor-bound scientific jobs would tie up large mainframe computers at major universities for days at a time. This, of course, was unacceptable. In contrast, mainframe computers are oriented to **input/output-bound** applications; that is, the amount of work that can be performed by the computer system is limited primarily by the speeds of the I/O devices. Administrative data processing jobs, such as generating monthly statements for checking accounts at a bank, require relatively little calculation and a great deal of input and output. In I/O-bound applications, the computer is often waiting for data to be entered or for an output device to complete its current task.

Making Computers Faster

During the past two decades, computer designers have employed three basic strategies for increasing the speed of computers.

1. *Use faster components.* Essentially this means employing electronic circuitry that enables the fastest possible switching between the two electronic states, on and off.
2. *Reduce the distance that an electronic signal must travel.* This means increasing the density of the electronic circuitry.
3. *Improve the computer system architecture.* The architecture of a computer refers to the manner in which it handles data and performs logic operations and calculations. The architecture of supercomputers is substantially different from those of the other three categories of computers.

This double image depicts a typical application for supercomputing technology. A Cray YM-P supercomputer generates data for aerodynamics research using computational fluid dynamics, which are then fed to individual workstations.

To implement these strategies, designers of supercomputers must address a major obstacle—heat buildup. Densely packed integrated circuits produce a tremendous amount of heat. For example, imagine burning 3000 sixty-watt light bulbs in a space the size of an average clothes closet. Without some type of cooling mechanism, densely packed integrated circuits would literally melt. The air-cooling systems traditionally used in mainframe computers proved inadequate, so designers have tried a variety of *supercooling* methods, from freon-based refrigeration to bathing the circuit elements in a liquid coolant. Computer designers are continually trying to increase the density of the integrated circuits while allowing for adequate cooling. At this point in the evolution of supercomputers, innovation in supercooling is just as important as innovation in electronic circuitry.

Super Applications for Supercomputers

Supercomputers are known as much for their applications as they are for their speed or computing capacity, which may be 10 times that of a large mainframe computer. These are representative supercomputer applications:

- Supercomputers sort through and analyze mountains of seismic data gathered during oil-seeking explorations.

The graphics that introduce television newscasts, sports events, and movies are by-products of supercomputer technology. The processing power of supercomputers is needed to manipulate billions of picture elements into imaginative dynamic images.

- Supercomputers enable the simulation of airflow around an airplane at different speeds and altitudes.
- Auto manufacturers use supercomputers to simulate auto accidents on video screens. (It is less expensive, more revealing, and safer than crashing the real thing.)
- Physicists use supercomputers to study the results of explosions of nuclear weapons.
- Meteorologists employ supercomputers to study the formation of tornadoes.
- Hollywood production studios use advanced graphics to create special effects for movies and TV commercials.

All these applications are impractical, if not impossible, on mainframes.

Supercomputers are seldom called upon to do I/O-bound administrative processing, such as payroll processing or accounting. To do so would waste an expensive and relatively rare resource. (Only a few hundred supercomputers are currently installed in the world, and a supercomputer could not process the payroll any faster than a mainframe.) Because of their applications, supercomputers are more likely to be configured with sophisticated graphics workstations and plotters than with rows of high-speed printers.

 2–5 Integrated Computer Networks: Computers Working Together

Centralization versus Decentralization

Through the mid-1970s, executives sought to take advantage of the economy of scale by *centralizing* the information processing function at a single site within an organization. At the time, an organization could get more computing capacity for its dollar by purchasing larger and larger computer systems. This is no longer true.

Some centralized computer centers grew so big and complex that they were no longer responsive to the organization's information needs. This lack of responsiveness was a major factor in reversing the trend from centralization to *decentralization* through **distributed processing**. The introduction of inexpensive microcomputers and reasonably priced minis into the business community in the early 1980s offered the means by which to decentralize.

The trend toward distributed processing has prompted an explosion in **departmental computing**. Departmental computing has become a generic reference to any type of computing done at the departmental level. The concept of departmental computing has emerged because users are becoming sophisticated enough to assume responsibility for their own computer(s) and information systems. Departmental computing could be as basic as using a micro-based spreadsheet to do "what if" analysis or, at the other end of the spectrum, a superminicomputer which services 50 VDTs and several information systems. In more and more implementations of departmental computing, the department's computer is part of a network.

Distributed Processing: Moving Computers Closer to the People Who Use Them

Distributed processing is both a technological and an organizational concept. Its premise is that information processing can be more effective if computer *hardware* (usually micros and minis), *data*, *software*, and, in some cases, *personnel* are moved physically closer to the people who use these resources. For example, if the public relations people need access to a computer and information, these resources are made available to them in their work area. They don't need to go to the centralized mainframe-based information services department for every request. With distributed processing, users have greater control over their computing environment.

In distributed processing, computer systems are arranged in a **computer network**, with each system connected to one or more other systems. (Computer networks are discussed further in Chapter 7, "Connectivity and Data Communications," and Chapter 8, "Networks and Networking.") A distributed processing network of computer systems is usually designed around a combination of geographical and functional considerations. Figure 2–4, for example, illustrates a distributed processing net-

FIGURE 2–4   A Distributed Processing Network
This distributed processing network demonstrates both geographical and functional distribution of processing.

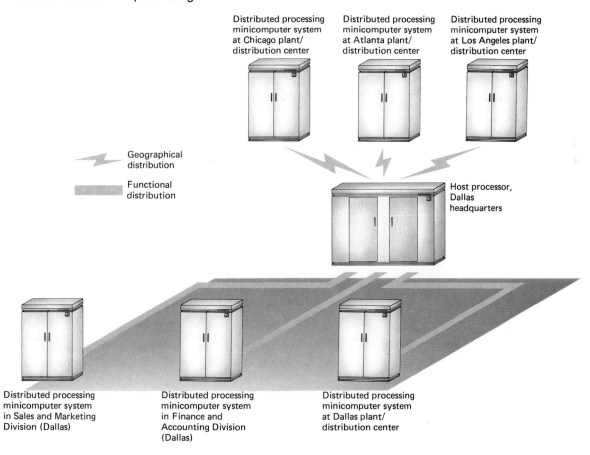

Distributed processing minicomputer system at Chicago plant/ distribution center

Distributed processing minicomputer system at Atlanta plant/ distribution center

Distributed processing minicomputer system at Los Angeles plant/ distribution center

Geographical distribution

Functional distribution

Host processor, Dallas headquarters

Distributed processing minicomputer system in Sales and Marketing Division (Dallas)

Distributed processing minicomputer system in Finance and Accounting Division (Dallas)

Distributed processing minicomputer system at Dallas plant/ distribution center

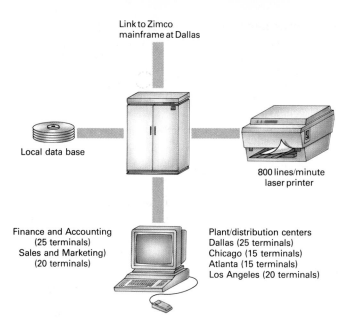

Link to Zimco
mainframe at Dallas

Local data base

800 lines/minute
laser printer

Finance and Accounting
(25 terminals)
Sales and Marketing)
(20 terminals)

Plant/distribution centers
Dallas (25 terminals)
Chicago (15 terminals)
Atlanta (15 terminals)
Los Angeles (20 terminals)

FIGURE 2–5   Configuration of a Minicomputer System in a Distributed Processing Network.

The distributed minis at the Zimco plants and at the home office (see Figure 2–4) have similar configurations. Each has a disk for a local data base, a laser printer, and from 15 to 25 terminals.

work for Zimco Enterprises. At the headquarters location in Dallas, Zimco has *functionally* distributed processing systems in the sales and marketing division, the finance and accounting division, and the home office plant/ distribution center. *Geographically* distributed processing systems are located at each of three plant/distribution centers in Chicago, Atlanta, and Los Angeles. At Zimco, all the distributed systems are minicomputers.

The host mainframe computer system at Dallas maintains the corporate data base and services those divisions without their own computer system. Although the distributed minis are part of the computer network, they are entirely self-contained and can operate as stand-alone systems. In this example, all the distributed systems are similarly configured minicomputers. The basic configuration for the functionally and geographically distributed minis is shown in Figure 2–5.

◤ **Important Terms and Summary Outline**

add-on board	closed architecture	distributed processing
add-on card	computer network	expansion slot
back-end processor	configuration	front-end processor
bus	departmental computer	half-size expansion
bus architecture	system	board
carrier	departmental	host processor
centronics connector	computing	input/output-bound
chip	desktop PC	laptop PC

microprocessor	open architecture	random-access
mini	operator console	memory (RAM)
minicomputer	palmtop PC	RS-232C connector
motherboard	parallel port	serial port
multifunction add-on	peripheral device	supercomputer
board	pocket PC	system board
multiuser micro	port	throughput
notebook	processor-bound	tower PC

2–1 COMPUTER SYSTEMS COME IN ALL SHAPES AND SIZES.   Each of the computers in the four main categories (micros, **minicomputers**, mainframes, and **supercomputers**) is a computer system, but they differ greatly in computing capacity and in how they are used. The three largest share functional similarities, including their ability to service many users. The microcomputer is designed primarily for the single-user environment.

2–2 MICROCOMPUTERS: SMALL BUT POWERFUL.   The **microprocessor**, a product of the microminiaturization of electronic circuitry, is literally a "computer on a chip." **Chip** refers to any self-contained integrated circuit. In a microcomputer, the microprocessor, the electronic circuitry for handling input/output signals from the **peripheral devices** (keyboard, printer, and so on), and the memory chips are mounted on a single circuit board called a **system board**, or **motherboard**. Before being attached to the system board, the microprocessor and other chips are mounted onto a **carrier**. The processing components of most micros are sold with several empty **expansion slots** so you can purchase and plug in optional capabilities in the form of **add-on boards**.

Personal computers come in four different physical sizes: **pocket PCs (palmtop)**, **laptop PCs** (small ones are **notebook** computers), **desktop PCs**, and **tower PCs**. Pocket and laptop PCs are considered portable. **Multiuser micros**, which are configured with as many as a dozen VDTs, permit several people to use the system at once.

The computer and its peripheral devices are called the computer system **configuration**. A typical micro configuration would be a computer, a keyboard, a monitor, a printer, and two disk drives. Micros that give users the flexibility to configure the system with a variety of peripheral devices are said to have an **open architecture**, or **bus architecture**. In a **closed architecture**, the system is fully configured when it is sold.

The electrical **bus** is the path through which the processor sends and receives data and commands to **RAM (random-access memory)** and all peripheral devices. A **port** provides a direct link to the micro's bus. External peripheral devices are interfaced with the processor through either a **serial port** or a **parallel port**. The de facto standard for micro serial ports is the **RS-232C connector**. The RS-232C and **centronics connectors** are used with parallel ports.

Expansion slots enable the addition of special-function **add-on cards**. Popular add-on boards include RAM, color and graphics adapter, modem, internal battery-powered clock/calendar, serial port, parallel port, printer spooler, hard disk, coprocessor (increases **throughput**), accelerator, network interface, motion video, and VCR backup. Most are **multifunction add-on boards**. **Half-size expansion boards** fit in a "short slot."

Micros can be used as stand-alone computer systems, or they can serve as "intelligent" terminals to mainframe computers.

2–3 MINIS AND MAINFRAMES: CORPORATE WORKHORSES. The term *mini-computer*, or **mini**, emerged in the late 1960s as a name for small computers. The name has stuck, even though some of today's minis are more powerful than any computer of the 1960s. Minis now accomplish processing tasks that traditionally have been associated with mainframe computers. Minicomputers usually serve as stand-alone computer systems for small businesses and as remote **departmental computer systems**.

Mainframe computers are the computer category between minicomputers and supercomputers. Aside from the obvious differences in processing speed, the major difference between minicomputers and mainframes is the number of remote terminals that can be serviced. A computer servicing more than 200 terminals is no longer considered a minicomputer.

The **operator console** in the machine room is used to communicate instructions to mini and mainframe computer systems.

A typical mainframe configuration might have a **host processor**, a **front-end processor**, and perhaps a **back-end processor**. The special-function processors help improve overall system efficiency.

2–4 SUPERCOMPUTERS: PROCESSING GIANTS. Mainframe computers are **input/output-bound**. In contrast, supercomputers handle the types of computer applications that are helpful to engineers and scientists. These applications are typically **processor-bound** and require relatively little in the way of input or output. Supercomputers are more likely to be configured with sophisticated graphics workstations and plotters than with high-speed printers.

2–5 INTEGRATED COMPUTER NETWORKS: COMPUTERS WORKING TO-GETHER. The trend through the 1970s was toward large centralized information services departments. The current trend is toward decentralizing people, hardware, and information systems through **distributed processing**. The trend toward distributed processing has prompted an explosion in **departmental computing**.

Distributed processing is the implementation of a **computer network** of geographically and functionally distributed processors. Distributed processing can result in more effective information processing because hardware, data, software, and personnel are closer to the people who use them.

 Review Exercises

Concepts

1. Describe the capabilities of a multiuser micro.
2. What is the relationship between a microprocessor, a motherboard, and a microcomputer?
3. In terms of physical size, how are PCs categorized?
4. What is the purpose of a mainframe computer's operator console?

5. Contrast the processing environment for mainframe computers with that of microcomputers.

6. Departmental computer systems are generally associated with which category of computer system?

7. Name three subordinate processors that might be configured with a mainframe computer system.

8. List five functional enhancements that can be added to a microcomputer by inserting one or more optional add-on boards into expansion slots.

9. Why are some microcomputers sold with empty expansion slots?

10. Describe an intelligent terminal.

11. Briefly describe one strategy for increasing the speed of supercomputers.

12. What term is used to describe the basic unit of work for a processor?

Discussion

13. Is the use of terms such as *microcomputer, minicomputer, supercomputer,* and so on a help or a hindrance in distinguishing between the processing capabilities of computer systems? Explain.

14. List at least 10 products that are smaller than a breadbox and use microprocessors. Select one and describe the function of its microprocessor.

15. What options would you like to have on your own personal micro that are not included in a minimum configuration? Why?

16. Ask two people who know and have worked with computers for at least three years to describe a minicomputer. What can you conclude from their responses?

17. Discuss centralization and decentralization as they are applied to computers and information processing.

18. Discuss how special-function processors can enhance the throughput of a mainframe computer system.

19. Explain the rationale for distributed processing.

Problem Solving

20. Departmental computer systems are often installed in accounting departments. How might this change the organizational structure of the department? Who should be responsible for the ongoing operation of the accounting department's computer system?

21. When three pediatricians decided to set up a clinic, they made a computer-based system a priority. They needed a computer system that would handle patient billing, insurance processing, inventory management, and enable word processing by the staff. One of the doctors expressed an interest in being able to tap into an information network. The staff consists of two nurses and four administrative personnel, each of whom is expected to have frequent interaction with the computer system. The three doctors expect minimal interaction with the system.
Select a type of computer system and configure it to meet the clinic's processing needs.

2–1 **a.** The most distinguishing characteristic of any computer system is physical size. (T/F)

b. At least _one_ (one, two, or three) person(s) are needed to control the operation of a PC.

2–2 **a.** The processing component of a motherboard is a _Microprocessor_

b. The four size categories of personal computers are miniature, portable, notebook, and business. (T/F)

c. The computer and its peripheral devices are called the computer system _configuration_

＊ **d.** The RS-232C connector provides the interface to a port. (T/F)

e. In an open architecture, all PC components are linked via a common electrical _bus_ .

2–3 **a.** A minicomputer is often referred to as a personal computer. (T/F)

＊ **b.** Micros can be linked to a mainframe computer through a: (a) base, (b) port, or (c) plug.

c. In a mainframe computer system, the processor in control of its subordinate processors is the: (a) front-end, (b) host, or (c) back-end?

2–4 **a.** Supercomputers are oriented to _processor_ -bound applications.

＊ **b.** One of the strategies employed by computer designers to increase the speed of computers involves reducing the distance that an electronic signal must travel. (T/F)

2–5 **a.** The trend in organizations is to centralize all information processing activities. (T/F)

＊ **b.** A distributed processing network of computer systems is usually designed around a combination of _functional_ and _geographic_ considerations.

Self-test answers. 2–1 (a) F; (b) one. 2–2 (a) microprocessor; (b) F; (c) configuration; (d) T; (e) bus. 2–3 (a) F; (b) port; (c) host. 2–4 (a) processor; (b) T. 2–5 (a) F; (b) functional, geographic.

3

Interacting with Personal Computers

STUDENT LEARNING OBJECTIVES

▶ To put the technological development of personal computers into historical perspective.

▶ To understand the scope of knowledge needed to interact effectively with a personal computer.

▶ To describe various keyboard, mouse, and data entry conventions.

▶ To grasp concepts related to the effective use of micros and micro software.

▶ To describe the proper care and maintenance of personal computers and disk storage media.

▶ To demonstrate file backup procedures.

CHAPTER OUTLINE

 Personal Computers in Perspective

The Personal Computer Boom

The personal computer is the foundation for personal computing. The attention given by the media to these desktop miracles of technology was intense during their infant years—the late 1970s and early 1980s. Fear of falling behind the competition motivated businesses to purchase personal computers by the truckload. Parents hurried to buy a personal computer so little Johnny or Mary could march to the head of the class.

Unfortunately, businesses, parents, and others bought PCs with very little knowledge of what they do or what to do with them. In fact, the first personal computer boom was actually a bust! A great many PCs were sold, but relatively few made significant contributions to businesses, homes, or educational institutions. Because they were misunderstood and did not live up to their fanfare, the buying public cooled toward PCs.

A decade later, these miniature marvels have vastly expanded capabilities, they are easier to use, and we have more realistic and informed expectations of them. Now people are educating themselves about the use and application of micros, and they are buying them with purpose and direction. The result is millions of micro enthusiasts.

Personal computers are everywhere, from kindergartens to corporate boardrooms. You can see them at work, at school, and possibly in your own home. The most recent boom has made it possible for people in every walk of life to see firsthand the usefulness of personal computers. Each passing month brings more power at less expense and an expansion of the seemingly endless array of microcomputer software.

Why Are Personal Computers So Popular?

The relatively low cost and almost unlimited applications for the microcomputer have made it the darling of the business community. Fifteen years ago very few people had heard of a microcomputer. Now the number of microcomputers sold in one month exceeds the total number of computers in existence in the United States 15 years ago.

When you use a micro or personal computer, the capabilities of a complete computer system are at your fingertips. Some are more powerful than computers that once handled the data processing requirements of large banks. Modern PCs and their support software are designed to be easy to use and understand. The wide variety of software available for microcomputers offers something for almost everyone, from video games to word processing, to education, to home finances, to inventory control.

A personal computer can be an electronic version of a scratch pad, a file cabinet, a drawing board, a teacher, a typewriter, a musical instrument, and even a friend. It can help you think logically, improve your spelling, select the right word, expand your memory, organize data, add numbers, and much more.

These reasons for the micro's popularity pale when we talk of the *real* reason for its unparalleled success—it can be plain fun to use, whether for personal, business, or scientific computing.

▶ 3–2 Interacting with the System

The thesaurus lists these synonyms for the word *interact*: *blend, associate, hobnob, mingle, combine, mix, stir,* and *socialize*. To some extent, we do all of these, even socialize, when we *interact* with personal computers. To interact effectively with a personal computer you need to be knowledgeable in four areas.

Computers are interactive—that is, in their own special way they can communicate with human beings. This capability makes them excellent educational tools. These children are learning about the concept of association. Computers also help adults learn about everything from auto mechanics to zoology.

Beginning in the mid-1970s, a visionary band of programmers, engineers, and hobbyists came together to launch a revolution that would change the way we perceive computers forever.

THE ALTAIR UNLEASHES A PENT-UP DEMAND

Today, we take the sight of sophisticated computers for granted. But in the early 1970s, few people saw, much less got a chance to use, a state-of-the art computer. These large, expensive, and delicate machines were locked away in sterile, air-conditioned rooms and guarded by hovering technicians.

The Altair 8800 computer, introduced in 1975, unleashed this demand. The Altair was built around one of the earliest computer "chips"—a product of the microminiaturization of electronic circuitry. First offered as a $395 kit, the Altair was sold through mail order by tiny Micro Instrumentation and Telemetry Systems (MITS). After *Popular Electronics* featured the Altair on its cover, MITS received thousands of orders.

Within two years, 30 other computer companies would be manufacturing personal computers. A host of special computer stores soon sprang into existence, followed by the first of many specialized computer magazines.

APPLICATIONS SOFTWARE INCREASES THE MARKET FOR PERSONAL COMPUTERS

In 1976, the Electric Pencil, a word processing package, became the first program to let nontechnical users perform practical tasks. Within three years, it was joined by WordStar, the first full-function word processing package; VisiCalc, the first electronic spreadsheet; and dBase II, a database software package. VisiCalc was especially important because it made the microcomputer a viable business tool.

At first, VisiCalc was available only for the Apple II, and this fact sold thousands of machines for Apple. This most famous of the start-up computer companies began in 1976, when two young computer enthusiasts, Steven Jobs and Steve Wozniak, collaborated to create and build the Apple I and then the Apple II. Raising $1300 by selling Jobs' Volkswagen and Wozniak's programmable calculator, they opened a makeshift production line in Jobs' garage. Seven years later, their company earned a spot on the Fortune 500, a list of the nation's largest corporations.

THE BIRTH OF A VIABLE BUSINESS TOOL
With the Apple II and VisiCalc, even small business owners could use a computer to keep their books.

IBM SETS THE STANDARD FOR BUSINESS USERS

Even before Apple made the Fortune 500, its success had challenged industry giant International Business Machines (IBM). In 1981, IBM responded by announcing the IBM PC. By the end of 1982, IBM had sold 835,000 IBM PCs, and its machine was fast becoming the standard for the microcomputer industry. IBM's success also helped Microsoft Corporation, which won the contract to create the IBM PC's operating system. Today, Microsoft's MS-DOS (called PC-DOS by IBM) is an industry standard for non-Apple microcomputers used by individuals. In 1985, AT&T introduced a powerful multiuser desktop PC based on the UNIX operating system. (Ironically, UNIX was created in 1969 for the single-user environment. The prefix *un* means one.) Now UNIX or versions of UNIX are the mainstay of IBM-PC–compatible computers that operate in a multiuser environment.

Microcomputer manufacturers jumped on the IBM bandwagon, creating compatible, but less expensive, machines called IBM-PC clones. In 1982, Compaq Computer Corporation bundled the equivalent of an IBM PC into a transportable case and named it the Compaq Portable. This began the era of portable computing. Although IBM tried to stem the growth of the clones in 1987 by introducing the IBM Personal System/2 (IBM

**PERSONAL COMPUTING GAINS STATUS IN THE BUSI-
NESS WORLD** The IBM reputation, coupled with powerful
software like Lotus 1-2-3, helped to sell thousands of IBM
PCs and clones to business people and professionals. Personal computer users no longer needed computer experts
to perform what-if calculations, prepare charts and graphs,
and manage data.

PS/2) line, the standards set by the original PC line and
its clones continue to be a major force in the business
world.

The success of the IBM PC and its clones quickly
eclipsed the Apple II and related models, which had
become associated with games and education, but not
business. Apple fought back in 1984 with the introduction of the Macintosh. Unlike the IBM PC and its clones,
the Macintosh used a "friendly" graphical interface—
proof that even powerful computers can be both easy
and fun to learn and use.

WINDOWS BRINGS MACINTOSH FEATURES TO THE IBM COMPATIBLES

An IBM-compatible package called Sidekick introduced
the concept of a memory-resident program during the
early 1980s. A memory-resident program remains operational while other applications programs are running.
Thus, SideKick users could call up its handy notepad,
calculator, or calendar without first closing their spreadsheet or word processing document. Sidekick and other
memory-resident programs whetted the IBM-PC user's
appetite for multitasking. And many IBM users secretly
coveted the Mac's easy-to-use graphical interface.

Microsoft tried to satisfy both these appetites in 1986
by introducing Windows, a graphical user interface for
the IBM PC and its clones. As with the Macintosh, Windows users can issue commands by using a mouse to
"click" on graphical icons. In addition, different applications can be running in separate "windows" or boxes
on the screen. Moving between applications is as simple
as clicking on a different window. Windows is significant
because software vendors and users are now embrac-
ing it as a foundation for single-user software for IBM
compatibles.

THE SHAPE OF THE FUTURE

By the early 1990s, a $3000 microcomputer offered as
much raw computing power as a mainframe computer
that once cost millions. Software developers have been
quick to take advantage of this power by devising new
and more sophisticated applications for graphics, such
as desktop publishing and computer-aided design.
Graphical user interfaces, like Windows, also require
more computing power, as does computer software that
can read handwriting, understand the human voice, and
synchronize the digitized images and sounds used in
the emerging field of multimedia. Today, the software
industry continues to grow at a fever pitch, putting ever
more computing power into the hands of the people.

THE LOOK OF THE FUTURE The combination of an
easy-to-use graphical user interface and multitasking offered by the Macintosh and, for the PC compatibles, Microsoft's Windows, is fast becoming the personal computing
standard.

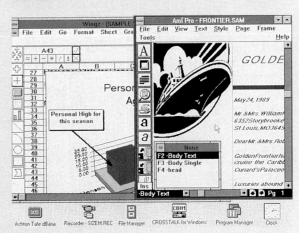

1. General software concepts (for example, windows, menus, uploading, and so on).

2. The operation and use of microcomputer hardware (such as magnetic disk, printers).

3. The function and use of **DOS**, the disk operating system, and/or a **graphical user interface**, both of which provide a link between the you, the microcomputer system, and the various applications programs (for example, the Lotus 1-2-3 spreadsheet program, the WordPerfect word processing program).

4. The specific applications programs you are using.

The first three areas are prerequisites to the fourth; that is, you will need a working knowledge of micro software concepts, hardware, and DOS and/or a **GUI** (graphical user interface) before you can make effective use of applications programs like Quicken (accounting), Harvard Graphics (presentation graphics), Paradox (database), or any of the thousands of micro software packages on the market today. We discuss the first two topics in this book. Also, we discuss concepts associated with DOS, GUIs, and common applications programs. Tutorials and exercises in supplemental material to this book teach you how to use DOS, GUIs, and applications programs, such as WordPerfect (word processing) and Paradox (database).

3-3 The Disk Operating System (DOS)

The nucleus of a microcomputer system is its *operating system*. The operating system monitors and controls all input/output and processing activities within a computer system. All hardware and software, including micro productivity software, are under the control of the operating system. Micro users need a working knowledge of their micro's operating system so they can interface, or link, their applications programs with microcomputer hardware.

PC Operating Systems

The four most popular micro operating systems based on number of installations are

- *MS-DOS (Microsoft Corporation).* **MS-DOS** is the operating system used with IBM-PC–compatible computers. The version of MS-DOS used with the IBM PC is called **PC-DOS.** The support material for this book includes tutorials and exercises for learning the use and application of this popular operating system.

- *Macintosh System (Apple Computer, Inc.).* **Macintosh System** is the operating system for the Macintosh line of computers.

- *Operating System/2 or OS/2 (Microsoft/IBM).* **OS/2** is the successor to MS-DOS. It is more sophisticated and offers greater capabilities, but it also requires more sophisticated and expensive hardware. Millions of users of IBM and IBM-compatible computers know and feel comfortable with MS-

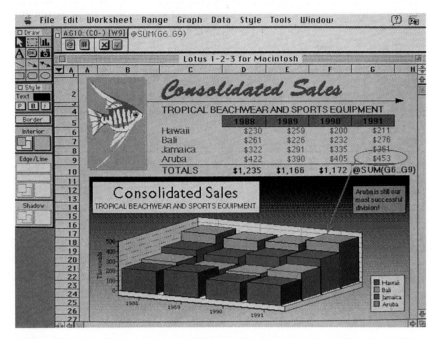

Lotus 1-2-3, a spreadsheet and graphics program, is one of many applications you can run once you have become familiar with software concepts, PC operation, and the PC's operating system and/or GUI.

DOS. Most of them are reluctant to upgrade their hardware to accommodate OS/2 and learn another operating system. In addition, relatively little software is available to run under OS/2. As a result, MS-DOS remains the preferred operating system for both end users and developers of micro software, at least for the present.

- *UNIX (AT&T).* Originally a mainframe operating system, **UNIX** and its spinoffs, such as **XENIX**, are used frequently with multiuser microcomputers.

The logic, structure, and nomenclature of the different operating systems vary considerably. Our emphasis will be on PC-DOS, the operating system used with the IBM-PC series of computers and the IBM Personal System/2 series of computers, and on MS-DOS, the operating system used with IBM-PC–compatible computers. In practice, these operating systems, which are essentially the same, are referred to simply as DOS (rhymes with *boss*), an acronym for *disk operating system.* DOS is a "disk" operating system because the operating system is stored on disk.

DOS Is the Boss

Just as the processor is the center of all hardware activity, DOS is the center of all software activity. The operating system is a family of **systems software** programs that must be installed on a microcomputer system before it can be used. Systems software is independent of any applications software. Because all hardware, software, and input/output are controlled by DOS, you might even call DOS "the boss."

One of the DOS family of programs is always *resident* in RAM during processing. This program, called COMMAND.COM, loads other operating system and applications programs into RAM as they are needed or as directed by you, the user. COMMAND.COM is usually referred to as COMMAND "dot" COM (rhymes with *mom*).

Besides controlling the ongoing operation of microcomputer systems, DOS has two other important functions.

- *Input/output control.* DOS facilitates the movement of data between peripheral devices, the processor, programs, and RAM. (Random-access memory provides temporary storage of data and programs during processing.)
- *File and disk management.* DOS and its file and disk management utility programs enable users to perform such tasks as making backup copies of work disks, erasing disk files that are no longer needed, making inquiries about the number and type of files on a particular disk, and preparing new disks for use. DOS also handles many file- and disk-oriented tasks that are *transparent* to the end user. For example, DOS keeps track of the physical location of disk files so that we, as users, need only refer to them by name (for example, *myfile*) when loading them from disk to RAM.

3–4 Microcomputer Operation

Installing Hardware and Software

When you purchase a microcomputer system, typically you will receive several boxes containing the various components of the system. Unless it is a portable PC, your system will come in several pieces: a keyboard, a monitor, a printer, and a processor unit that houses the disk drives. Normally you can complete the installation of the hardware simply by linking the pieces of the system with the various types of cables. A computer, however, does nothing without software.

Now you must install the software—first DOS, then any other software that you intend to run. Software installation is a three-step process for DOS and all applications software packages.

1. *Make a backup copy.* Seasoned users make duplicates of their vendor-supplied master disks prior to the initial installation of the software. This minimizes the risk of accidental loss of data or programs on their master disks. If a problem occurs, they can repeat the procedure with their backup disks. Be sure to store the master and backup disks in a safe place.

2. *Copy files.* Copy the program and data files from the master disks to the permanently installed hard disk. The first step usually is accomplished by entering "install" or "setup" at the DOS prompt for the disk drive containing the applications disk (for example, A:\> *install*).

3. *Set system information.* An applications software package is designed to accommodate a variety of microcomputer systems, so you must describe

Operating a notebook PC requires some understanding of power management. When operating his PC under battery power, this aerospace engineer will normally elect to conserve power by reducing the contrast on the monitor and choosing an option that spins the hard disk only when it is needed. He uses his notebook PC to manage a variety of aviation projects.

your system to the package. The software assumes you have a "typical" PC. If your system deviates from what is defined as "typical" in the software package, you will need to revise these **defaults** (standard settings) to fit the specifications of your system (for example, type of computer, monitor, keyboard layout, printer, and so on).

Power Up/Power Down

Booting the System   Micros are similar to copy machines, toasters, and other electrical devices—you must turn them on by applying electrical power. The power-on procedure on a micro is straightforward—flip the on/off switch on the processor unit to *on*. On some micros, the monitor may have a separate on/off switch. Turn on the printer as well if you anticipate using it.

When you **power up**, or add electrical power to a micro system, you also **boot** the system. The booting procedure is so named because the computer "pulls itself up by its own bootstraps" (without the assistance of humans). When you boot the system, several significant events take place (see Figure 3–1).

1. A program that is permanently stored in **read-only memory**, or **ROM** (rhymes with *mom*), is executed. ROM is discussed in Chapter 4, "Inside the Computer." The program verifies that the electronic components are

FIGURE 3–1   The Boot Procedure

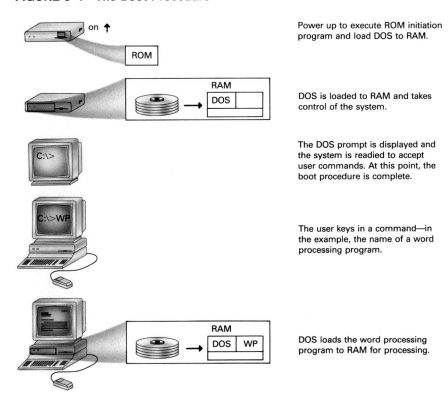

Power up to execute ROM initiation program and load DOS to RAM.

DOS is loaded to RAM and takes control of the system.

The DOS prompt is displayed and the system is readied to accept user commands. At this point, the boot procedure is complete.

The user keys in a command—in the example, the name of a word processing program.

DOS loads the word processing program to RAM for processing.

The Automated Court Clerk The county of Los Angeles has introduced Autoclerk, a system that uses personal computers equipped with a recorded human face to process traffic- and parking-ticket transactions. The new system is contained in an 800-pound, 7-foot kiosk outside the Long Beach Municipal Courthouse. Autoclerk contains a PC linked to minicomputer inside the courthouse. Victor, the actor that portrays a desk clerk, was videotaped responding to every imaginable inquiry by an offender. His image is stored on laser disk, also contained in the kiosk. Autoclerk is linked to a credit-card network; it includes a depository for accepting cash transactions and a printer for documentation of transactions. Autoclerk will aid the accused in the process of pleading guilty, paying fines, and scheduling future court dates. The system makes it easier for offenders to settle their claims without having to wait for the system of due process to fit them into its schedule.

operational and readies the computer for processing. After a short period, a beep signals the end of the **system check** and the program searches for the disk containing DOS, the operating system.

2. Upon finding DOS, the ROM program loads DOS from disk storage to RAM (internal memory) then passes control of the system to DOS.

3. DOS executes predefined user instructions, then usually—but not always—presents the user with a **system prompt** (C:\>, or A> when DOS is loaded from an interchangeable disk) and awaits a user command.

On micros with a permanently installed hard disk, the booting procedure takes place automatically when you flip the power on. On other micros, you must insert the interchangeable disk containing the operating system into the disk drive, close the disk-drive door, and flip the switch to *on*. All new micros sold after 1988 are configured with a hard disk and at least one interchangeable disk drive.

The Graceful Exit   Unlike electrical appliances, you do not simply flip the switch to *off*; you must **power down** in an orderly manner. This involves a **graceful exit** from all active applications programs prior to shutting off the power. All applications programs have an exit routine that, when activated, returns you to DOS or a higher-level applications program. For example, if you are running a grammar checker program within a word processing program, you must exit the grammar checker program, store your documents, and initiate the word processing exit routine. When all applications are *closed* (no longer active) and the DOS prompt is visible, it is safe to shut off the power.

It is not "graceful" to power down when an application is still active (for example, a spreadsheet is still being displayed). Exit routines perform some administrative processing that, if bypassed, can result in loss of user data and problems during subsequent sessions.

▶ 3–5 Entering Commands and Data

Micros Can Be Very Picky

A personal computer does *exactly* what you tell it to do—no more, no less. If you do something wrong, it tells you and then gives you another chance.

Whether entering a DOS command or an applications program command, you must be explicit. For example, if you wish to copy a word processing document file from one disk to another, you cannot just enter "copy" or even "copy MYFILE." You must enter the command that tells the micro to copy MYFILE from Disk A to Disk C (for example in MS-DOS, "copy a:myfile c:"). If you omit necessary information in a command or the format of the command is incorrect, an error message is displayed and/or an on-screen prompt will request that you reenter the command correctly. DOS, in particular, demands strict adherence to command **syntax**, the rules for entering commands, such as word spacing, punctuation, and so on.

Micros are not always so picky. You can enter DOS commands and filenames as either uppercase or lowercase characters. For example, the system interprets the command "copy a:myfile c:" and "COPY A:MYFILE C:" the same way. Some software packages do not distinguish between uppercase and lowercase commands; however, all software packages do make the distinction between uppercase and lowercase entries for *keyed-in data* (for example, an employee's last name in a document you are producing).

The Keyboard and Mouse: Input and Control Devices

The Keyboard A microcomputer's *keyboard* is normally its primary input and control device. You enter data and issue commands via the keyboard. Besides the standard typewriter keyboard, most micro keyboards have **function keys**, also called **soft keys** (see Figure 3–2). When tapped, these function keys trigger the execution of software, thus the name "soft key." For example, tapping one function key might call up a displayed list of user options commonly referred to as a **menu**. Another function key might cause a word processing document to be printed. Function keys are numbered and assigned different functions in different software packages. The software packages are usually distributed with **keyboard templates** that designate which commands are assigned to which function keys. For example, HELP (context-sensitive user assistance) is often assigned to F1, or Function Key 1. The templates usually are designed to fit over the keyboard or to be attached with an adhesive.

Most keyboards are equipped with a **key pad** and **cursor-control keys** (see Figure 3–2). The key pad permits rapid numeric data entry. It is normally positioned to the right of the standard alphanumeric keyboard.

FIGURE 3–2 Microcomputer Keyboard
This is representative of the microcomputer keyboard being configured with the latest IBM–compatible micros. In the figure, the alphanumeric characters follow the commonly used QWERTY layout. The positioning of the function keys, the cursor-control keys, and the keypad may vary substantially from keyboard to keyboard. On earlier versions of IBM-PC–compatible keyboards, the 10 function keys were aligned in two columns on the left end.

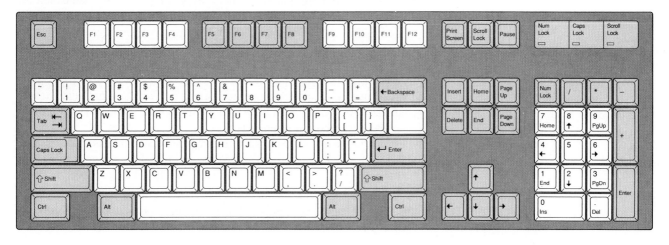

The keys on notebook PCs are the same size as those on desktop PCs; however, there are fewer of them. Notebooks have a standard QWERTY keyboard layout and all of the special-function keys discussed in this section, but they do not have a key pad.

The cursor-control keys, or "arrow" keys, allow you to move the text cursor *up* (↑) and *down* (↓), usually a line at a time, and *left* (←) and *right* (→), usually a character at a time. The **text cursor** always indicates the location of the next keyed-in character on the screen. The text cursor can appear as several shapes depending on the application, but frequently, you will encounter an underscore (__), a vertical line (|), or a rectangle (■). To move the text cursor rapidly about the screen, simply hold down the appropriate arrow key.

For many software packages, you can use the arrow keys to view parts of a document or worksheet that extend past the bottom, top, or sides of the screen. This is known as **scrolling**. Use the up and down arrow keys (↑ ↓) to *scroll vertically* and the left and right keys (← →) to *scroll horizontally*. For example, if you wish to scroll vertically through a word processing document, move the up or down arrow key to the edge of the current screen and continue to press the key to view more of the document, one line at a time. Figure 3–3 illustrates vertical and horizontal scrolling.

In summary, the keyboard provides three basic ways to enter commands:

- *Key in* the command using the alphanumeric portion of the keyboard.
- Tap a *function key*.
- Use the *arrow keys* to select a *menu option* from the displayed menu. (Menus are discussed in detail in the next section.)

Other important keys common to most keyboards are the *ENTER, HOME, END, PAGE UP* and *PAGE DOWN* (abbreviated as PGUP and PGDN), *DELETE* (DEL), *BACKSPACE* (BKSP), *Insert-typeover toggle* (INS), *ESCAPE* (ESC), *SPACEBAR, Shift Control* (CTRL), *Alternate* (ALT), TAB, SCROLL LOCK, CAPS LOCK, NUM LOCK, and PRINT SCREEN keys (see Figure 3–2).

ENTER   Traditionally the ENTER key is used to send keyed-in data or a selected command to RAM for processing. For example, when you want to enter data into an electronic spreadsheet, the characters you enter are displayed in an edit area until you tap ENTER, also called the *carriage return*. When you tap ENTER, the data are displayed in the appropriate area in the spreadsheet. Like most of the special keys, ENTER has other meanings, depending on the type of software package you are using. In word processing, for example, you would designate the end of a paragraph by tapping the ENTER key.

When you highlight a menu option in a software package with an arrow key, you tap ENTER to select that option. More often than not, ENTER can be interpreted as "Do."

In graphical user interfaces, the trend is away from using the ENTER key after each entry. In place of the ENTER key, the user clicks the mouse or taps TAB or a function key. Often ENTER is reserved to signal the system that all user options are set and processing can continue.

HOME   Tapping the HOME key results in different actions for different packages, but often the cursor is moved to the beginning of a work area

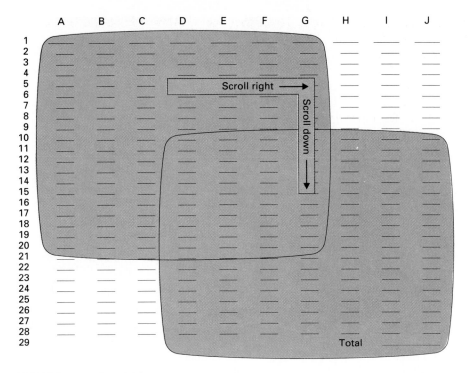

FIGURE 3–3 Scrolling
When an electronic spreadsheet does not fit on a single screen, you can scroll horizontally (to the right as shown in the figure) and vertically (down in the figure) to view other portions of the electronic spreadsheet.

(the beginning of the line, screen, or document in word processing; the upper left-hand corner of the spreadsheet; or the first record in a data base).

END   With most software packages, tap END to move the cursor to the end of the work area (the end of the line, screen, or document in word processing; the lower right corner of the spreadsheet, or the last record in a data base).

PAGE UP, PAGE DOWN   Tap PAGE UP (PGUP) and PAGE DOWN (PGDN) to vertically scroll *a page (or screen) at a time* to see parts of the document or spreadsheet that extend past the top or bottom of the screen, respectively. PGUP and PGDN are also used to position the cursor at the previous and next record when using database software.

DELETE   Tap DELETE (DEL) to delete the character at the cursor position.

BACKSPACE   Tap the BACKSPACE (BKSP) key to move the cursor one position to the left and delete the character in that position.

INSERT   Tap INS to **toggle** (switch) between the two modes of entering data and text—*insert* and *typeover*. Both modes are described and illustrated in the word processing discussion in Chapter 11, "Text and Image Processing Software." The term *toggle* is used to describe the action of tapping a single key to alternate between two or more modes of operation (insert and replace), functions (underline *on* and underline *off*), or

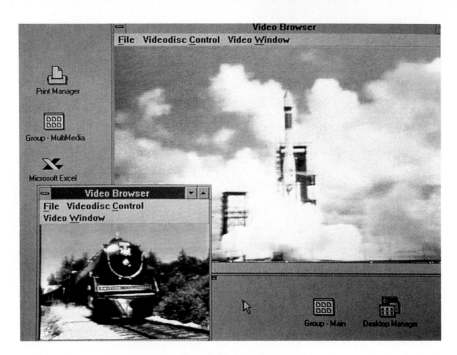

PCs have introduced two new dimensions in user interaction—sound and full-motion video. This multimedia capability enables the creation of more effective and stimulating presentations, training programs, and demonstrations. Multimedia presentations can combine full-motion video, slides, photographs, illustrations, text, graphics, animations, and narration.

operational specifications (for type of database field: character, numeric, date, memo).

ESCAPE The ESCAPE (ESC) key may have many functions, depending on the software package, but in most situations you can tap the ESC key to negate the current command or menu and return to the work screen.

SPACEBAR Tap the SPACEBAR at the bottom of the keyboard to key in a space at the cursor position. *Note:* On a computer, a space is recorded internally like any other character, even though it is not displayed or printed.

SHIFT, **CTRL**, **ALT** The SHIFT, CTRL (*control*), and ALT (*alternate*) keys are used in conjunction with another key to expand the functionality of the keyboard. Just as you depress the SHIFT key to enter a capital letter or one of the special characters above the numbers, you hold down a CTRL or ALT key to give a key new meaning. For example, on some word processing systems you tap HOME to move the cursor to the beginning of the current line. When you tap CTRL and HOME together, the cursor is positioned at the beginning of the document. When used in conjunction with the SHIFT, CTRL, and ALT keys, each function key can be assigned four meanings (for example, F1, SHIFT + F1, CTRL + F1, and ALT + F1).

TAB In word processing, the TAB key advances the text cursor to the next user-defined tab stop. In most other programs, it advances the text cursor to the next logical area into which data can be entered. For example, a program might position the cursor at the first of three data entry areas. After entering the required data in the first area, sometimes called a **field**, the user taps the TAB key to advance to the next. Tapping the TAB key with the text cursor in the last field positions the cursor at the first field again. The SHIFT + TAB combination (hold down SHIFT and tap TAB) moves the cursor to the previous field. Typically, you would tap the ENTER key to enter the data in all fields simultaneously.

SCROLL LOCK   Tap the SCROLL LOCK key to toggle the scroll lock feature on and off. When you tap the SCROLL LOCK key to activate the scroll lock feature, the cursor remains fixed and whatever is on the screen scrolls under the cursor. The scroll lock feature is only applicable to certain programs. For example, most spreadsheet programs enable the scroll lock feature to be used.

CAPS LOCK   Tap the CAPS LOCK key to toggle the capital letter lock feature on and off. When you tap the CAPS LOCK key to activate the caps lock feature, all letters entered from the keyboard are entered to the system as capital letters.

NUM LOCK   Tap the NUM LOCK key to toggle the number lock feature on and off. When you tap the NUM LOCK key to activate the num lock feature, numbers are entered when you tap the numbered keys on the keypad to the right of the alphanumeric keyboard.

PRINT SCREEN   Tap PRINT SCREEN (PRTSC) or SHIFT + PRINT SCREEN (press and hold the SHIFT key, then tap PRTSC) to print what is currently being displayed on the screen.

Each keystroke you enter is sent first to an intermediate keystroke buffer that can save from 15 to hundreds of keystrokes. Under normal processing conditions, the keystroke is sent immediately from the buffer to the processor. In many instances, however, you may have to wait for processing to finish (such as during a disk read operation). When this happens, you can key ahead. For example, if you know that the next prompt to be displayed is "Enter filename:" you can enter the desired filename in anticipation of the prompt. When the prompt appears, the filename you entered is loaded from the keystroke buffer and displayed after the prompt. Judicious use of the keystroke buffer can make your interaction with micro software packages much more efficient.

The Mouse   Another device used for input and control is the **mouse**. The hand-held mouse, sometimes called the "pet peripheral," is rapidly becoming a must-have item on micros. Attached to the computer by a cable (the mouse's "tail"), the mouse is a small device that, when moved across a desktop, moves the **graphics cursor** accordingly. The graphics cursor, which can be positioned anywhere on the screen, is displayed as a bracket ([), an arrow (↗), a crosshair (+), or a variety of other symbols (for example, ☞). Depending on the application, the text and graphics cursors may be displayed on the screen at the same time. The graphics cursor is used to *point* and *draw*.

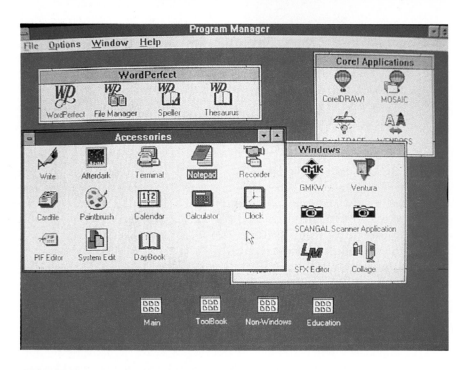

FIGURE 3–4 Symbolic Icons
Each of the icons in this Microsoft Windows display represents an available program. To run a program, simply use the mouse to point to and click on the desired icon.

Micro users frequently have one hand on the keyboard and one on the mouse. The mouse is rolled across the desktop to move the graphics cursor quickly about the screen.

All movements of the mouse are reproduced by the graphics cursor on the screen. For example, when a mouse positioned to the right of the keyboard is moved up and away from its user, the graphics cursor moves toward the top right corner of the screen. Use the mouse for quick positioning of the graphics cursor over the desired menu item or a graphic image, called an **icon** (a graphic rendering of a file cabinet or a disk, for example). When positioned at a menu item or an icon, the graphics cursor is said to "point" to that item or icon. Figure 3–4 shows a screen with a variety of symbolic icons.

Most mice have two buttons—left and right (Figure 3–5). Typically, you would tap, or **click**, the left button to select a menu item or execute the program represented by an icon. The function of the right button varies between software packages, but often it is used to call up a menu of options. A *double-click*, which is tapping a button twice in rapid succession, gives each button a different meaning. Some software packages permit a *simultaneous click*, or tapping both buttons simultaneously, to give the mouse added functionality.

Press and hold a button to **drag** the graphics cursor across the screen. When using a graphics software program, you drag the graphics cursor across the screen to create the image. When using a word processing program, you highlight a block of text to be deleted by dragging the graphics cursor from the beginning to the end of a block. Click and drag operations are demonstrated in Figure 3–5.

Levels of Command Interaction

You can interact with software packages, such as spreadsheet and database, at three different levels of sophistication: the *menu level*, the *macro level*, and the *programming level*. These three levels of command interaction are discussed in the following sections.

Menus When using micro applications software, you issue commands and initiate operations by selecting activities to be performed from a *hierarchy of menus*.

Menu trees. Menu hierarchies are sometimes called **menu trees** (see Figure 3–6). When you select an item from the **main menu**, you are often presented with another menu of activities, and so on. Depending on the items you select, you may progress through as few as one to as many as eight levels of menus before processing is started for the desired activity.

Let's use presentation graphics software to illustrate how you might use a hierarchy of menus. One of the options on the main menu of a graphics software package might be "Create Chart."

CREATE CHART	EDIT CHART	GET/SAVE	PRINT CHART	EXIT

If you select this option, you are presented with another menu and an opportunity to choose one of five types of charts.

FIGURE 3–6   A Hierarchy of Menus
This figure illustrates how a user of Lotus 1-2-3, a popular electronic spreadsheet program, progresses through a hierarchy of menus to format all numeric entries in a currency format with two decimal places. (For example, the entry 1234.56 would be displayed as $1,234.56.) Selecting the Worksheet option causes a display of the second-level menu. The Global option indicates that further menu options apply to all relevant spreadsheet entries. At the third and fourth levels, the user selects the Format and Currency options. Upon selecting the Currency option, the user is prompted to enter the desired number of decimal places.

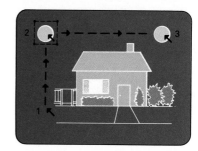

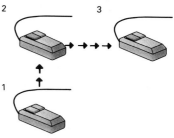

FIGURE 3–5   The Mouse and the Graphics Cursor
In the example, the user moved the sun image from the left to the right side of the screen. The graphics cursor, or pointer, was initially at Position 1 on the display screen. The user moved the mouse up (toward monitor) to position the pointer over the image to be moved (Position 2). The image, which includes the sun, is temporarily enclosed within a rectangular box. To reposition the sun to the right of the display (Position 3), the image within the box was dragged (by pressing and holding the left button) to the desired location. The drag operation was complete when the mouse button was released.

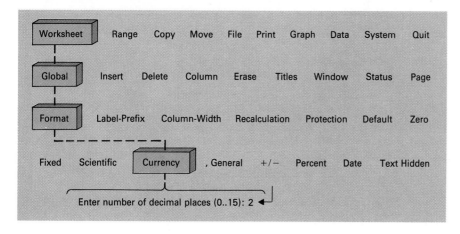

TEXT	BAR	PIE	LINE	ORGANIZATION

If you select the *text* option, another menu asks you to choose from three available types of text charts.

TITLE CHART	SIMPLE LIST	**BULLET LIST**

If you select the *bullet list* option, you are presented with the bullet list work screen.

Types of menus. The main menu is frequently presented as a **menu bar** in the **user interface** portion of the display. The user interface is from one line to about an inch of display at the bottom and/or top of the screen. The menu bar provides a *horizontal list* of menu options. The result of a menu selection from a menu bar at the top of the screen may be a subordinate menu bar (see Figure 3–6) or a **pull-down menu** (see Figure 3–7). The subordinate pull-down menu is "pulled down" from the selected menu bar option and displayed as a *vertical list* of menu options. The entire pull-down menu is shown in a box directly under the selected menu bar option and over whatever is currently on the screen (see Figure 3–7).

Like the pull-down menu, the pop-up menu is superimposed on the current screen in a window. The **pop-out menu** is displayed next to the menu option selected in a higher level pop-up or pull-down menu. The pop-out menu becomes the active menu, but the higher level menu continues to be displayed (see Figure 3–7).

FIGURE 3–7 Menus
The WordPerfect for Windows (WPwin) (a word processing program) main menu is presented in a menu bar above the user work area. In the example, the Layout *option in the bar menu is selected and the pull-down menu is presented. Selecting the* Justification *option results in a pop-out menu of justification options.*

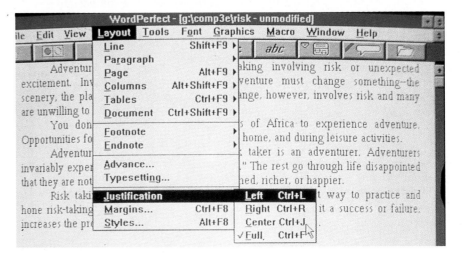

Menu item selection.   Micro software packages provide users with three ways to select an item from a menu.

1. Use the left/right or up/down arrow keys to highlight the desired menu option and tap ENTER.
2. Enter the **mnemonic** (pronounced *neh MON ik*) of the desired item. A letter or number within the text of the menu item is noted as its mnemonic, which means memory aid. The mnemonic is usually the first letter in the first word unless there is another option with the same first letter. For example, to work through the hierarchy of spreadsheet menus shown in Figure 3–6, the user would enter W, G, F, and C, for Worksheet, Global, Format, and Currency.
3. Use the mouse to position the graphics cursor at the desired option and click the left button.

Defaults, parameters, and dialog boxes.   As you progress through a series of menus, eventually you are asked to enter the specifications for data to be graphed (graphics software), the size of the output paper (word processing software), and so on. As a convenience to the user, many of the specification options are already filled in for common situations. For example, word processing packages set output document size at $8\frac{1}{2}$ by 11 inches. If the user is satisfied with these **default options**, no further specifications are required. The user can easily revise the default options to accommodate less common situations. So, to print a document on legal-sized paper, the default paper length of 11 inches would be revised to 14 inches.

Default options are normally revised in a dialog box. The text in a pop-up **dialog box** asks the user to change default options or enter further information. Often the dialog box appears when the user must choose among more options before the chosen menu option can be executed.

Those menu specifications which are not predefined by default values are called **parameters**. Parameters are user-defined variables that must be entered to execute the current command. For example, the parameters in the WPwin (WordPerfect for Windows) *Search and Replace* dialog box in Figure 3–8 are the search string (value) and the replace string (parameter). The default in the Search and Replace dialog box is to search *Forward* in the document.

Menu summary.   During any given point in a work session, the options available to the user of a micro productivity tool normally are displayed somewhere on the screen. For example, in spreadsheets, the active menu is displayed in the user interface. If you are ever confused about what to do next, the options usually are displayed on the current screen.

Macros and Programming   At the menu level of command interaction, you are initiating individual commands. At the macro and programming levels of interaction, you can string together commands and even introduce logic operations.

A handy feature available with most micro software packages is the macro. A **macro** is a sequence of frequently used operations or keystrokes that can be recalled as you need it. You create a macro by recording a

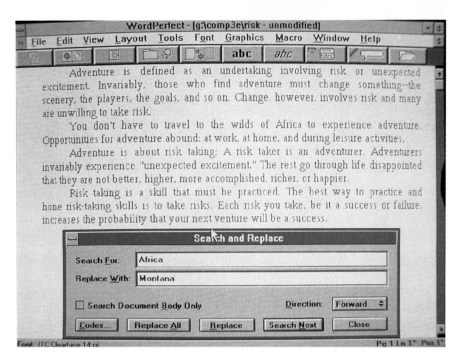

FIGURE 3–8 Dialog Box
The WordPerfect for Windows (WPwin) Search and Replace dialog box prompts the user to enter search and replacement strings.

sequence of operations or keystrokes and storing them on disk for later recall. To **invoke,** or execute, the macro, you either refer to it by name or enter a keystroke combination that identifies it (for example, ALT + D, CTRL + F4). Three common user-supplied macros in word processing could be the commands necessary to format the first-, second-, and third-level headings in a report. For example, you might want the first-level heading to be centered, boldface, in a large typeface, and followed by two line spaces. A single macro could be invoked to perform these operations on the first-level head. In electronic spreadsheets, macros are commonly used to produce graphs automatically from spreadsheet data.

Some software packages allow users the flexibility to do their own **programming**—that is, create logical sequences of instructions. For example, a database software program can be written that will retrieve records from a particular data base, depending on preset criteria; process the data according to programmed instructions; and print a report. The programming capability enables users to create microcomputer-based information systems for an endless number of applications, from payroll processing to tennis league scheduling.

3–6 User-Friendly Software

Software is said to be **user-friendly** when someone with limited computer experience has little difficulty using the system. User-friendly software communicates easily understood words, phrases, and icons to the end user, thus simplifying his or her interaction with the computer system. A user-friendly environment facilitates **navigation** between the elements of the software package. Navigation refers to movement within and between an application's work areas. A central focus of the design of any modern micro software package is user-friendliness.

Windows

The **window** has become symbolic of the user-friendly environment. A window is a rectangular display temporarily superimposed over whatever is currently on the screen. For example, the dialog box in Figure 3–8 is presented in a window. You can "look through" several windows on a single display screen; however, you can manipulate text, data, or graphics in only one window at a time. This is called the **current window**. Generally, each window contains a separate application. Figure 3–9 shows a variety of applications displayed in windows.

Windows can overlap one another on the display screen. For example, in Figure 3–9, you can view several software packages at once. With windows, you can work the way you think and think the way you work. Several projects are at your finger tips, and you can switch between them with relative ease.

You can perform work in one of several windows on a display screen, or you can **zoom** in on a particular window—that is, the window you

FIGURE 3–9 Viewing Multiple Applications in Windows
Five popular productivity software tools are shown in windows on the same screen: spreadsheet (Lotus 1-2-3), database (Paradox), word processing (WordPerfect for Windows), graphics (Harvard Graphics), and desktop publishing (Ventura Publisher).

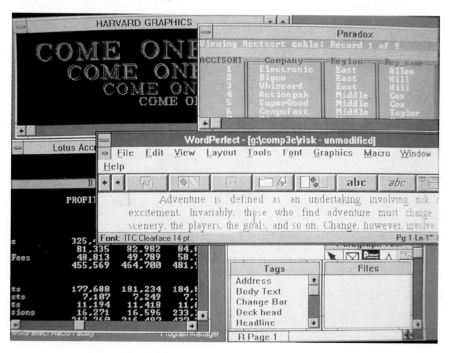

select expands to fill the entire screen. Tapping a program-specific key combination normally will return the screen to a multiwindow display. A multiwindow display permits you to see how a change in one window affects another window. For example, as you change the data in a spreadsheet, you can see how an accompanying pie graph is revised to reflect the new data.

You can even create **window panes**! As you might expect, a window is divided into panes so you can view several parts of the same window subarea at a time. For example, if you are writing a long report in a word processing window, you might wish to write the conclusions of the report in one window pane while viewing other portions of the report in another window pane.

Help Commands

A handy feature available on most software packages is the **help command**. When you find yourself in a corner, so to speak, tap the HELP key, often assigned to Function Key 1 (F1), to get a more detailed explanation or instructions on how to proceed. In most micro software packages, the help commands are **context-sensitive**—the explanation relates to what you were doing when you issued the help command. (For example, if you were entering data into a data base, the explanation would address how to enter data.) When you are finished reading the help information, the system returns you to your work at the same point you left it. Figure 3–10 shows a pop-up help window for a calendar application.

FIGURE 3–10   Help
A Help *window is displayed when* Help *is requested within Asymmetric's DayBook calendar program. Help information is available on a variety of topics through the* Help Index.

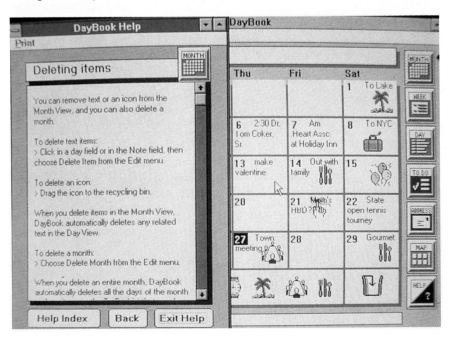

Graphical User Interfaces

The DOS Shell   Through the 1980s, DOS was strictly text-based, command-driven software. That is, we issued commands to DOS by entering them on the keyboard, one character at a time. For example, to copy a word processing document from one disk to another, we might enter "copy c:myfile a:" via the keyboard at the DOS prompt, "C:\>."

>   C:\> **copy c:myfile a:**

As we mentioned earlier, DOS commands are syntax-sensitive, so we must follow the rules for constructing the command, otherwise an error message is displayed. The trend, however, is away from command-driven interfaces to a user-friendly, graphics-oriented environment called a *graphical user interface*, or *GUI*.

GUIs provide an alternative to often cryptic text commands. With a GUI, you can interact with DOS and other software packages by selecting options from menus that are temporarily superimposed over whatever is currently on the screen or by using a mouse to position the graphics cursor over the appropriate icon.

Graphical user interfaces have effectively eliminated the need for users to memorize and enter cumbersome commands. In Windows, a GUI marketed by Microsoft Corporation, a file is copied from one disk to another disk by dragging the files icon from one window to another.

Virtually all new programs written for PCs are designed around a graphical user interface (GUI). ESYview, shown here, is a software program that provides solutions for the next generation of air traffic control and military systems.

The universal acceptance of GUIs has prompted software entre-preneurs to create GUI alternatives for DOS and several popular command-driven software packages. The software that provides a GUI alternative to a command-driven interface is called a **shell**. In effect, a shell is another layer of software between the user and a command-driven interface. Many people prefer using a DOS shell to entering text-based DOS commands.

Microsoft's Windows: Platform for the Foreseeable Future

Windows has emerged as the dominant graphical user interface (GUI) for the MS-DOS environment. The name *Windows* describes basically how the software functions. It runs one or more applications in "windows"—rectangular areas displayed on the screen.

The Windows platform. Windows, itself a commercial software package, is more than just another DOS application for micros. It also defines a new **platform,** or standard, for which other applications software packages are written. Moreover, it offers some very inviting solutions to the limitations of MS-DOS.

1. *Windows is user-friendly.* Windows employs a graphical user interface (GUI). In contrast, MS-DOS users must enter cryptic commands to the micro-computer system via the keyboard.
2. *Windows enables multiple programs to be run simultaneously.* A user can print out a WordPerfect report while engaged in a Lotus 1-2-3 session. The same user, running under the MS-DOS platform, would need to exit Lotus 1-2-3 and load WordPerfect to print out the report.
3. *Windows enables users to work with large files.* Data bases, spreadsheet files, and word processing documents can be as big as available memory will permit. Without Windows, a file containing one or two chapters of this book might not fit into available RAM.
4. *Windows permits information to be passed between applications.* With Windows, text in a word processing document can be transferred in seconds to a data base record. These types of information transfers, though not impossible, are cumbersome and time-consuming with MS-DOS.

Although Windows establishes a new platform, virtually all of the thousands of application software packages created for MS-DOS can run under Windows.

CUA Compliance. All software applications developed to run under Windows must adhere to Microsoft's **Common User Access,** or **CUA,** standard. By following the CUA standard, software developers give all Windows applications a similar look and feel. These CUA conventions describe the following.

- Type and style of window
- Arrangement and style of menus
- Use of the keyboard and mouse
- Format for screen-image display

Microsoft Mania In April 1992 Microsoft shipped 1.25 million copies of Windows 3.1. Microsoft said that 8 million disks were produced for the first month's shipment; the software was leased in 7 different languages; and workers at 9 Microsoft manufacturing factories worked 3 shifts each day to make the software. Microsoft launched its biggest advertising campaign ever on this new product, including its first television promotions. Windows 3.0 sold 10 million copies in about two years.

Care and Maintenance of a Micro

Micros, peripheral devices, and storage media are very reliable. Apply the dictates of common sense to their care and maintenance, and they will give you years of maintenance-free operation. A few helpful hints are listed here.

- Avoid excessive dust and extremes in temperature and humidity.
- Avoid frequent movement of desktop and tower micros.
- Install a *surge protector* between the power source and the micro. Micros as well as other electronic devices can be seriously damaged by a sudden surge of power caused by such things as a bolt of lightning striking a power line.

A blank interchangeable disk, costing only a dollar or so, has a very modest value. But once you begin to use the disk, its value, at least to you, increases greatly. Its value includes the many hours you have spent entering data, preparing spreadsheets, or writing programs. Such a valuable piece of property should be handled with care. The following are a few guidelines for handling interchangeable disks.

Computers in general and specifically portable PCs are designed to be used, even abused. PC manufacturers must assume that their portables will be dropped on occasion. Here, a Compaq LTE 386S/20 undergoes a mechanical shock test that simulates dropping it off a desk. Other tests involve subjecting PCs to severe vibrations, high humidity and altitudes, and extremes of heat and cold.

Do

- *Do* label each disk and use a felt-tipped pen on the label.
- *Do* cover the *write-protect notch* on all important 5¼-inch disks intended for read-only use, such as the program disks for micro software packages. On the 3½-inch microdisks, slide the *write-protect tab* to its open position.
- *Do* store 5¼-inch disks in their jackets so the exposed surface is covered.
- *Do* store 5¼-inch disks vertically or, if stored flat, place no more than 10 in a stack.
- *Do* store disks at temperatures between 50 to 125 degrees Fahrenheit.
- *Do* keep a backup of disks containing important data and programs.
- *Do* remove disks from disk drives before you turn off the computer.

Don't

- *Don't* fold, spindle, or mutilate disks.
- *Don't* force a disk into the disk drive. It should slip in with little or no resistance.
- *Don't* touch the disk surface.
- *Don't* place disks near a magnetic field, such as magnetic paper-clip holders, tape demagnetizers, or electric motors.
- *Don't* expose disks to direct sunlight for a prolonged period.
- *Don't* insert or remove a disk from a disk drive if the "drive active" light is on.

Personal computers can be replaced, but your data and programs can be lost forever if the disk malfunctions or you (or someone else) erases them. The best way to minimize this risk is to adopt a rigorous backup policy. Here, a user backs up files to a 3½-inch disk.

▶ 3–8 Backup: Better Safe Than Sorry

Safeguarding software and your data may be more important than safeguarding micro hardware. The first commandment in personal computing is

𝕭𝖆𝖈𝖐 𝖀𝖕 𝖄𝖔𝖚𝖗 𝕱𝖎𝖑𝖊𝖘

If data and program files are destroyed, it may be impossible for them to be re-created within a reasonable period of time. If, on the other hand, the hardware is destroyed, it can be replaced fairly quickly. The impact of losing critical software or files makes **backup** a major concern.

When you create a document, a spreadsheet, or a graph and you wish to recall it at a later time, you *store* the file on disk. You can, of course, store many files on a single disk. If the disk is in some way destroyed (scratched, demagnetized, and so on) or lost, you have lost your files unless you have a backup disk. To minimize the possibility of losing valuable files, you should periodically back up (make a copy of) your work disks.

The frequency with which a work disk is backed up depends on its *volatility*, or how often you use the files on the disk. If you spend time every day working with files on a work disk, you should back it up each day. Others are backed up no more often than they are used. Because some updating will occur between backup runs, the re-creation of lost files means that subsequent updates and changes must be redone from the point of the last backup.

Figure 3–11 illustrates the backup procedure for a work disk that is used daily. Two *generations* of backup are maintained on backup disks A and B. After each day's processing, the contents of the work disk are copied (or dumped) alternately to Disk A or B. In this manner, one backup is always current within a day's processing. If the work disk and the most recent backup are accidentally destroyed, a third backup is current within two days' processing. Disks A and B are alternated as the most current backup.

At one time or another, just about every computer specialist has experienced the trauma of losing work for which there was no backup. It is no fun seeing several days (or weeks) of work disappear, but it does emphasize the point that it is well worth the effort to make backup copies of your work.

FIGURE 3–11   Backup Procedure for Diskette-Based User Files
The diskette containing user files is backed up alternately to Diskette A or B at the end of each day so that one backup file is always current within one day's processing.

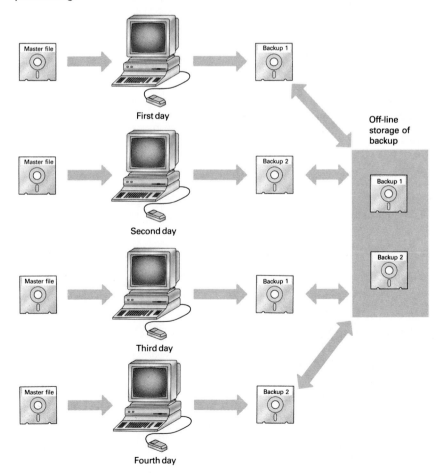

Computers can get sick just like people. A variety of highly contagious "diseases" can spread from computer to computer, much the way biological viruses do among human beings. A *computer virus* is a program that literally "infects" other programs and data bases upon contact. It can also hide duplicates of itself within legitimate programs, such as an operating system or word processing program.

There are many types of viruses. Some act quickly by erasing user programs and data bases. Others grow like a cancer, destroying small parts of a data base each day. Some act like a time bomb. They lay dormant for days or months, but eventually are activated and wreak havoc on any software on the system. Many companies warn their micro users to back up all software prior to every Friday the thirteenth, a favorite date of those who write virus programs. Some viruses attack the hardware and have been known to throw the mechanical components of a computer system, such as disk-access arms, into costly spasms.

In the microcomputer environment, there are three primary sources of computer viruses (see figure).

- *Electronic bulletin-board systems.* The most common source of viral infection is the public electronic bulletin board on which users exchange software. Typically, a user logs on to the bulletin board and downloads what he or she thinks is a game, a utility program, or some other enticing piece of freeware, but gets a virus instead.

- *Diskettes.* Viruses are also spread from one system to another via common diskettes. For example, a student with an infected applications disk might infect several other laboratory computers with a virus which, in turn, infects the applications software of other students. Software companies have unknowingly distributed viruses with their proprietary software products.

- *Computer networks.* In the minicomputer and mainframe environment, viruses generally are spread from one computer network to another.

Since they first appeared in the mid-1980s, viruses have erased bank records, damaged hospital records, destroyed the programs in thousands of microcomputers, and even infected part of the systems at NORAD (strategic defense) and NASA. Disgruntled employees have inserted viruses in disks that were distributed to customers.

How serious a problem are viruses? They have the potential of affecting an individual's career and even destroying companies. (A company that loses its accounts receivables records could be a candidate for bankruptcy.) Antiviral programs, also called *vaccines*, exist, but they can be circumvented by a persistent (and malicious) programmer. The best way to cope with viruses is to recognize their existence and to take precautionary measures.

More computer users are becoming aware of the threat of viruses, thanks to a recent spate of publicity about Michelangelo. This virus was set to wipe out hard disks on March 6, the anniversary of the artist's birth. Although few users were actually harmed by the Michelangelo virus, experts were heartened to see millions of PC users taking precautionary measures.

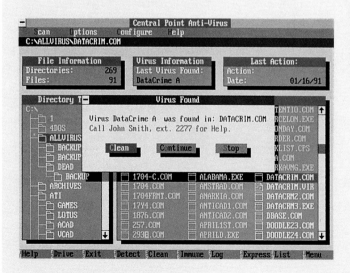

NO CATASTROPHE THIS TIME   The Central Point Anti-Virus program detects over 600 different viruses and can destroy most of them. With about 50 new viruses popping up every month, anti-virus programs have become a necessary tool for safe personal computing.

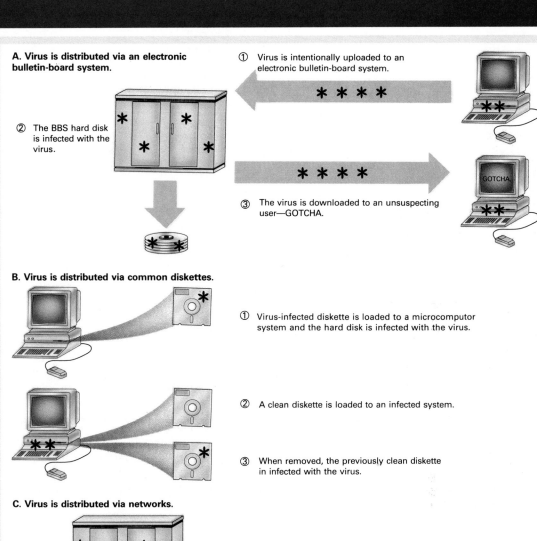

A. Virus is distributed via an electronic bulletin-board system.

① Virus is intentionally uploaded to an electronic bulletin-board system.

② The BBS hard disk is infected with the virus.

③ The virus is downloaded to an unsuspecting user—GOTCHA.

B. Virus is distributed via common diskettes.

① Virus-infected diskette is loaded to a microcomputor system and the hard disk is infected with the virus.

② A clean diskette is loaded to an infected system.

③ When removed, the previously clean diskette in infected with the virus.

C. Virus is distributed via networks.

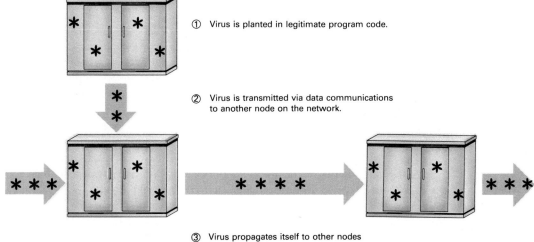

① Virus is planted in legitimate program code.

② Virus is transmitted via data communications to another node on the network.

③ Virus propagates itself to other nodes on the network.

THE WAYS IN WHICH VIRUSES ARE SPREAD

Important Terms and Summary Outline

Apple II
boot
click
clones
Common User Access
    (CUA)
context-sensitive
current window
cursor-control key
default
default option
dialog box
DOS
drag
field
function key
graceful exit
graphical user interface
    (GUI)
graphics cursor
help command
icon

invoke
key pad
keyboard template
Macintosh DOS
macro
main menu
menu
menu bar
menu tree
mnemonic
mouse
MS-DOS
navigation
operating system
OS/2
parameter
PC-DOS
platform
pop-out menu
power down
power up
programming

pull-down menu
read-only memory
    (ROM)
scrolling
shell
soft key
syntax
system check
system prompt
systems software
text cursor
toggle
UNIX
user interface
user-friendly
window
window pane
Windows
XENIX
zoom

3–1 PERSONAL COMPUTERS IN PERSPECTIVE. The first PC boom was a bust because people were not prepared to cope with them. Today a better educated and more deliberate buying public has spawned a second, very successful PC boom.

3–2 INTERACTING WITH THE SYSTEM. The effective micro user will understand general micro software concepts, how to operate and use the hardware, **DOS** and/or a **graphical user interface (GUI)**, and one or more applications programs.

3–3 THE DISK OPERATING SYSTEM (DOS). The operating system monitors and controls all input/output and processing activities within a computer system. The four most popular micro operating systems based on number of installations are: **MS-DOS** (or **PC-DOS**), **Macintosh System, OS/2**, and **UNIX** (and spinoffs, such as **XENIX**).

DOS, the center of all software activity, is a family of **systems software** programs that must be installed on a microcomputer system before it can be used. Systems software is independent of any applications software. The DOS COMMAND.COM program loads other operating system and applications programs into RAM as needed.

DOS has two primary functions. The DOS input/output control function facilitates the movement of data between peripheral devices, the processor, programs, and RAM. The DOS file- and disk-management function permits users to perform a variety of file maintenance tasks, such as copying files.

3–4 MICROCOMPUTER OPERATION. When you purchase a microcomputer system, you must install the software in a three-step process: make a backup copy; copy files to the permanently installed hard disk; and set system information, revising **defaults** (standard settings) as needed.

When you **power up** a micro, you **boot** the system. First, a program in **read-only memory**, or **ROM**, initializes the system and runs a **system check**. Next, DOS is loaded to RAM, takes control of the system, and presents the user with a **system prompt**.

To **power down** in an orderly manner, **gracefully exit** from all active applications programs prior to shutting off the power.

3–5 ENTERING COMMANDS AND DATA.   Whether entering a DOS command or an application program command, you must be explicit. DOS, in particular, demands strict adherence to command **syntax**.

A microcomputer's keyboard is normally its primary input and control device. In addition to the standard typewriter keyboard, most micro keyboards have **function keys**, also called **soft keys**. Tapping a function key might present the user with a **menu**, which is a displayed list of user options. The software packages are usually distributed with **keyboard templates** that designate which commands are assigned to which function keys. Most keyboards are equipped with a **key pad** and **cursor-control keys**. Use the cursor-control keys to position the **text cursor** and for **scrolling**.

Other important keys common to most keyboards are the *ENTER*, *HOME*, *END*, *PAGE UP* and *PAGE DOWN* (abbreviated as PGUP and PGDN), *DELETE* (DEL), *BACKSPACE* (BKSP), *insert-typeover* **toggle** (INS), *ESCAPE* (ESC), *SPACEBAR*, *SHIFT*, *Control* (CTRL), *Alternate* (ALT), *TAB*, *SCROLL LOCK*, *CAPS LOCK*, *NUM LOCK*, and *PRINT SCREEN* keys. In addition to its traditional function, the TAB key facilitates movement between data entry areas, sometimes called **fields**. Each keystroke you enter is sent first to an intermediate keystroke buffer.

The hand-held **mouse**, when moved across a desktop, moves the **graphics cursor** accordingly. The graphics cursor is used to *point* and *draw*. Use the mouse for quick positioning of the graphics cursor over the desired menu item or an **icon**. Typically, you would **click** the mouse's left button to select a menu item. You would press and hold a button to **drag** the graphics cursor across the screen.

You can interact with software packages, such as spreadsheet and database, at three different levels of sophistication: the *menu level*, the *macro level*, and the *programming level*. At the menu level you are initiating individual commands. At the macro and programming levels of interaction you can string together commands and even introduce logic operations.

Menu hierarchies are sometimes called **menu trees**. When you select an item from the **main menu**, you are often presented with another menu of activities, and so on. A menu can appear as a **menu bar** in the **user interface** portion of the display, a **pull-down menu**, or a **pop-out menu**.

Micro software packages provide users with three ways to select an item from a menu: Use the left/right or up/down arrow keys; enter the **mnemonic**; or use the mouse to position the graphics cursor at the desired option. Most menus present users with **default options** in a pop-up **dialog box**. Those menu specifications which are not predefined by default values are called **parameters**.

A **macro** is a sequence of frequently used operations or keystrokes that can be recalled as you need it. To **invoke** the macro, you either refer to it by name or enter the series of keystrokes that identify it. Micro software users can do their own **programming**.

3–6 USER-FRIENDLY SOFTWARE. **User-friendly** software communicates easily understood words, phrases, and icons to the end user, thus simplifying his or her interaction with the computer system. A user-friendly environment facilitates **navigation** between the elements of the software package.

Windows are rectangular displays temporarily superimposed over whatever is currently on the screen. You can manipulate text or data in only one window at a time, the **current window**. **Zoom** in on a particular window to fill the entire screen. **Window panes** enable users to view several parts of the same window subarea at a time.

The on-line **help command** provides **context-sensitive** explanations or instructions on how to proceed.

The trend is away from command-driven interfaces, like DOS, to a user-friendly, graphics-oriented environment called a *graphical user interface*, or *GUI*. The software that provides a GUI alternative to a command-driven interface is called a **shell**.

Windows software defines a new **platform** for which other applications software packages are written. All software applications developed to run under Windows must adhere to Microsoft's **Common User Access**, or **CUA**, standard.

3–7 CARE AND MAINTENANCE OF A MICRO. Apply the dictates of common sense to the care and maintenance of micros, peripheral devices, and storage media. For example, avoid excessive dust, extremes in temperature and humidity, and don't fold, spindle, or mutilate the disks.

3–8 BACKUP: BETTER SAFE THAN SORRY. Safeguarding software and your data may be more important than safeguarding micro hardware. The impact of losing critical software or files makes **backup** a major concern. The frequency with which a work disk is backed up depends on its volatility. It is common practice to maintain two generations of backup.

 Review Exercises

Concepts

1. What is the purpose of soft keys? Of cursor-control keys?
2. Describe the attributes of user-friendly software.
3. Contrast a menu bar with a pull-down menu.
4. Briefly describe two ways you can use a keyboard to enter commands to a microcomputer software package.
5. During a micro software session, which key would you commonly press to move to the beginning of the work area? To negate the current command?
6. Name three microcomputer operating systems.
7. How is a pop-out menu displayed?
8. What does "booting the system" mean?
9. What must be accomplished to power down in an orderly manner?
10. Which key is tapped to toggle between insert and typeover modes?
11. The help command is often assigned to which function key?

12. What is software called that provides a graphical user interface alternative to a software package's command-driven interface?

13. When multiple windows are open, the user manipulates text, data, or graphics in which window?

14. Which two cursor-control keys are used to scroll horizontally?

Discussion

15. Why would you use the mouse to drag the graphics cursor over text in a word processing document?

16. Most word processing packages have a default document size. What other defaults would a word processing package have?

17. What is a macro and how can using macros save time?

18. When would you use the zoom feature of a microcomputer software package?

Problem Solving

19. When you asked your boss to buy a mouse for your PC, your boss asked you to justify the expenditure in a brief memo. What would you say?

20. Most word processing packages have a default document size. What other defaults would a word processing package have?

21. **a.** You have just flipped your PC's power switch to on and nothing happened. What do you do?
b. During a word processing session, the system locks up and does not respond to any key or the mouse. What do you do? What are the consequences of your action(s)?
c. You insert an interchangeable disk in a disk drive. When you attempt to store data on it this message is displayed: "Write protected disk in disk drive." What do you do?

22. Suppose that life could be organized in a hierarchy of menus. Propose a menu bar and include *leisure* as one of the menu options. Propose options for the pull-down *leisure* menu. Select one of these options and propose a pop-out menu.

 Self-Test (by section)

3–1 PCs can be fun to use. (T̸F)

3–2 Both DOS and/or a ___G.U.I___ provide a link between the user, the ✱ microcomputer system, and the applications programs.

3–3 **a.** DOS is an acronym for disk operating system. (T̸F)
b. The name of the DOS program that is always resident in RAM during ✱ microcomputer operations is ___COMMAND___.COM.

3–4 **a.** A micro user must "kick the system" to load DOS to RAM prior to processing. (T/F̸)
b. DOS displays a system ___prompt___ to signal the user that it is ready to accept a user ___command___.

3–5 **a.** Use the _Keypad_ for rapid numeric data entry.

b. When interacting with a microcomputer via a keyboard, you must wait until the execution of one command is finished before issuing another. (T/Ⓕ)

c. Press and hold a mouse button to _drag_ the graphics cursor across the screen.

d. A sequence of frequently used operations or keystrokes that can be activated by the user is called a: (a) menu, Ⓑ macro, or (c) program?

e. A mouse can be used to point to a graphic image called an _icon_.

3–6 **a.** When software makes it easy for someone with limited computer experience to use it, the software is said to be: Ⓐ user-friendly, (b) a programming pal, or (c) simple software?

b. _Zoom_ in on a particular window to fill the entire screen.

3–7 Always label diskettes with a ballpoint pen. (T/Ⓕ)

✱**3–8** The frequency with which a work disk is backed up depends on its volatility. (Ⓣ/F)   (ChaNGAbility)

Self-test answers. 3-1 T. 3–2 graphical user interface (GUI). 3–3 (a) T; (b) COMMAND.COM. 3–4 (a) F; (b) prompt, command. 3-5 (a) keypad; (b) F; (c) drag; (d) b; (e) icon. 3–6 (a) a; (b) Zoom. 3–7 F. 3–8 T.

4

Inside the Computer

STUDENT LEARNING OBJECTIVES

▶ To describe how data are stored in a computer system.

▶ To demonstrate the relationships between bits, bytes, characters, and encoding systems.

▶ To understand the translation of alphanumeric data into a format for internal computer representation.

▶ To explain and illustrate the principles of computer operations.

▶ To identify and describe the relationships between the internal components of a computer.

▶ To distinguish processors by their word length, speed, and memory capacity.

CHAPTER OUTLINE

4–1 Data Storage: Data in the Computer

In Chapter 1 we learned that *data*, not *information*, are stored in a computer system. *Data are the raw material from which information is derived*, and *information is data that have been collected and manipulated into a meaningful form*. To manipulate data, we must have a way to store and retrieve this raw material.

It is easy to understand data storage in a manual system. For example, when a customer's address changes, we pull the folder, erase the old address, and write in the new one. We can see and easily interpret data that are kept manually. We cannot see or easily interpret data stored in a computer. Data are represented and stored in a computer system to take advantage of the physical characteristics of electronics and computer hardware, not human beings.

Data are stored *temporarily* during processing in a section of the computer system called **primary storage**. Primary storage is also called random-access memory (RAM). As you recall, RAM was introduced and discussed briefly in Chapter 2, "Micros, Minis, Mainframes, and Super-computers." Data are stored *permanently* on **secondary storage** devices such as magnetic tape and disk drives. We discuss primary storage (RAM) in detail later in this chapter. Secondary storage is covered in Chapter 6, "Data Storage and Organization." In this chapter we focus on the details of how data are represented electronically in a computer system and on the internal workings of a computer.

4–2 A Bit about the Bit

The computer's seemingly endless potential is, in fact, based on only two electronic states—*on* and *off*. The physical characteristics of the computer make it possible to combine these two electronic states to represent letters,

Programs and data are stored temporarily in these solid-state RAM chips (primary storage) during processing. Permanent storage can be on magnetic disk or optical laser disk (secondary storage). This optical laser disk contains the operating system and graphical user interface software for Sun Microsystems' workstations.

numbers, and colors. An "on" or "off" electronic state is represented by a **bit**. (*Bit* is short for *binary digit*.) The presence or absence of a bit is referred to as *on-bit* and *off-bit*, respectively. In the **binary** numbering system (base 2) and in written text, the on-bit is a 1 and the off-bit is a 0.

The vacuum tubes, transistors, and integrated circuits that characterize the generations of computers all enable them to distinguish between on and off and, therefore, to use binary logic.

Physically, these states are achieved in a variety of ways. In primary storage the two electronic states are represented by the direction of current flow. Another approach is to turn the circuit itself on or off. In secondary storage the two states are made possible by the magnetic arrangement of the surface coating on magnetic tapes and disks (see Chapter 6, "Data Storage and Organization").

Bits may be fine for computers, but human beings are more comfortable with letters, decimal numbers (the base-10 numerals 0 through 9), and colors. (Bits and colors are discussed in Chapter 11, "Text and Image Processing Software.") Therefore, the letters, decimal numbers, and colors that we input to a computer system must be translated into 1s and 0s for processing and storage. The computer translates the bits back into letters, decimal numbers, and colors on output. This translation is performed so we can recognize and understand the output. It is made possible by encoding systems.

Purity in Production In the manufacturing of computer chips, air purity is everything. The tiniest dirt particle could destroy the chip that is in production. One particle, half of a micron (a millionth of a meter) wide, is allowed per cubic foot of air in clean rooms where chips are assembled. A human sitting at rest sheds about 15,000 particles per second; therefore, employees must wear suits that cover their entire body.

In the first generation of computers (1951–1959), each bit was represented by a vacuum tube. Today computers use fingernail-sized chips, like this one, that can store over one million bits.

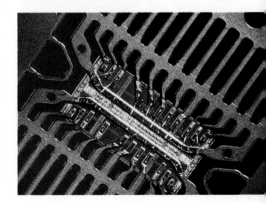

Encoding Systems: Combining Bits to Form Bytes

EBCDIC and ASCII

Computers do not speak to one another in English, Spanish, or French. They have their own languages, which are better suited to electronic communication. In these languages, bits are combined according to an **encoding system** to represent letters (**alpha** characters), numbers (**numeric** characters), and special characters (such as *, $, +, and &). For example, in the eight-bit **EBCDIC** encoding system (*Extended Binary-Coded Decimal Interchange Code*—pronounced *IB see dik*), used primarily in mainframe computers, 11000010 represents the letter *B*, and 11110011 represents a decimal number 3. In the seven-bit **ASCII** encoding system (*American Standard Code for Information Interchange*—pronounced *AS key*), which is used primarily in micros and data communications, a *B* and a 3 are represented by 1000010 and 0110011, respectively. There is also an eight-bit version of ASCII called **ASCII-8**.

An eight-bit encoding system, with its 256 unique bit configurations, is more than adequate to represent all of the alphanumeric characters used in the English language. The Japanese, however, need a 16-bit encoding system and a special keyboard to represent their 50,000 Kanji characters.

Letters, numbers, and special characters are collectively referred to as **alphanumeric** characters. Alphanumeric characters are *encoded* into a bit configuration on input so that the computer can interpret them. When you press the letter *B* on a PC keyboard, the *B* is transmitted to the processor as a coded string of binary digits (for example, 1000010 in ASCII). The characters are *decoded* on output so we can interpret them. For example, a monitor's device controller will interpret an ASCII 0110011 as a 3 and display a 3 on the screen. This coding, based on a particular encoding system, equates a unique series of bits and no-bits with a specific character. Just as the words *mother* and *father* are arbitrary English-language character strings that refer to our parents, 11000010 is an arbitrary EBCDIC code that refers to the letter *B*. The combination of bits used to represent a character is called a **byte** (pronounced *bite*). Figure 4–1 shows the binary value (the actual bit configuration) and the decimal equivalent of commonly used characters in ASCII.

The seven-bit ASCII code can represent up to 128 characters (2^7). Although the English language has considerably fewer than 128 *printable* characters, the extra bit configurations are needed to represent a variety of common and not-so-common special characters (such as - [hyphen]; @ [at]; | [a broken vertical bar]; and ~ [tilde]) and to signal a variety of activities to the computer (such as ringing a bell or telling the computer to accept a piece of datum).

ASCII is a seven-bit code, but the microcomputer byte can store eight bits. There are 256 (2^8) possible bit configurations in an eight-bit byte. Hardware and software vendors use the extra 128 bit configurations to represent control characters or noncharacter images to complement their hardware or software product. For example, the IBM-PC version of extended ASCII contains the characters of many foreign languages (such as Ä [umlaut] and é [acute]) and a wide variety of graphic images that can be combined on a text screen to produce larger images (for example, the box around a window on a display screen).

Character	ASCII Code Binary Value	Decimal Value
A	100 0001	65
B	100 0010	66
C	100 0011	67
D	100 0100	68
E	100 0101	69
F	100 0110	70
G	100 0111	71
H	100 1000	72
I	100 1001	73
J	100 1010	74
K	100 1011	75
L	100 1100	76
M	100 1101	77
N	100 1110	78
O	100 1111	79
P	101 0000	80
Q	101 0001	81
R	101 0010	82
S	101 0011	83
T	101 0100	84
U	101 0101	85
V	101 0110	86
W	101 0111	87
X	101 1000	88
Y	101 1001	89
Z	101 1010	90
a	110 0001	97
b	110 0010	98
c	110 0011	99
d	110 0100	100
e	110 0101	101
f	110 0110	102
g	110 0111	103
h	110 1000	104
i	110 1001	105
j	110 1010	106
k	110 1011	107
l	110 1100	108
m	110 1101	109
n	110 1110	110
o	110 1111	111
p	111 0000	112
q	111 0001	113
r	111 0010	114
s	111 0011	115
t	111 0100	116
u	111 0101	117
v	111 0110	118
w	111 0111	119
x	111 1000	120
y	111 1001	121
z	111 1010	122

Character	ASCII Code Binary Value	Decimal Value
0	011 0000	48
1	011 0001	49
2	011 0010	50
3	011 0011	51
4	011 0100	52
5	011 0101	53
6	011 0110	54
7	011 0111	55
8	011 1000	56
9	011 1001	57
Space	010 0000	32
.	010 1110	46
<	011 1100	60
(	010 1000	40
+	010 1011	43
&	010 0110	38
!	010 0001	33
$	010 0100	36
*	010 1010	42
)	010 1001	41
;	011 1011	59
,	010 1100	44
%	010 0101	37
—	101 1111	95
>	011 1110	62
?	011 1111	63
:	011 1010	58
#	010 0011	35
@	100 0000	64
'	010 0111	39
=	011 1101	61
"	010 0010	34
½	1010 1011	171
¼	1010 1100	172
▒	1011 0010	178
■	1101 1011	219
▬	1101 1100	220
▮	1101 1101	221
◾	1101 1110	222
▪	1101 1111	223
√	1111 1011	251
n	1111 1100	252
2	1111 1101	253
■	1111 1110	254
(blank)	1111 1111	255

FIGURE 4–1 ASCII Codes
This figure contains the binary and decimal values for commonly used ASCII characters.

Parity Checking

Within a computer system, data in the form of coded characters are continuously transferred at high rates of speed between the computer, the input/output (I/O) and storage devices, and the remote workstations. Each device uses a built-in checking procedure to help ensure that the

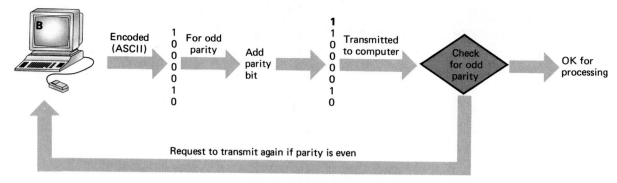

FIGURE 4–2 Parity Checking
The letter B *is entered and transmitted to the computer for processing. Because the ASCII* B *has an even number of bits, an on-bit must be added to maintain odd parity.*

transmission is complete and accurate. This procedure is called **parity checking**.

Logically, an ASCII character may have seven bits, but physically there are actually *eight* bits transmitted between hardware devices. Confused? Don't be. The extra **parity bit**, which is not part of the character code, is used in the parity-checking procedure to detect whether a bit has been accidentally changed, or "dropped," during transmission. A dropped bit results in a **parity error**.

To maintain *odd parity* (see Figure 4–2), the extra parity bit is turned *on* when the seven-bit ASCII byte has an *even* number of on-bits. When the ASCII byte has an *odd* number of on-bits, the parity bit is turned *off*. The receiving device checks for this condition. A parity error occurs when an even number of on-bits is encountered. Some computer systems are designed to maintain *even parity*, but odd and even parity work in a similar manner.

4–4 Numbering Systems and Computers

We humans use a **decimal**, or base-10, numbering system, presumably because people have 10 fingers. If we had three fingers and a thumb on each hand, as does the Extra-Terrestrial (E.T.) from the popular movie, then in all probability we would be using the **octal** numbering system, which has a base of 8.

Early computers were designed around the decimal numbering system. This approach made the creation of computer logic capabilities unnecessarily complex and did not make efficient use of resources. (For example, ten vacuum tubes were needed to represent one decimal digit.) In 1945, as computer pioneers were struggling to improve this cumbersome approach, John von Neumann suggested that the numbering system used by computers should take advantage of the physical characteristics of electronic circuitry. To deal with the basic electronic states of on and

```
38C070  29306294  4580623F  D20DD0AA  62A29640   8CECCC04  88F00010  80000004  88100010   41110003  5010D064  94FCD067  D703D06C
38C0A0  D06E0610  12114770  6202D203  D09F629D   4120D121  45B06236  5820D120  413062C4   477061A6  4810D06E  41110001  4010D06E
38C0D0  1A2C44E0  60701A1E  41818001  44F06076   9640D112  455062DA  94BFD112  4810D06C   02FF1302  FFC3C9D5  C5E240E2  C1D4C540
38C100  FF0098E0  D08012EE  47806310  D27CF000   48A0D06A  4BA0D06C  88A00002  45B0623E   D12094FC  D1235B00  D1201A10  5800D120
```

FIGURE 4–3 A Hexadecimal Dump

Each of the lines contains a hexadecimal representation of the contents of primary storage. The column of numbers farthest to the left consists of storage addresses. Each pair of hexadecimal digits represents the eight bits of an EBCDIC byte. The address of the first byte (29) in the memory dump is 0038C070 in hexadecimal (or 00000000001110001100000001110000 in binary). You can see how much space is saved by displaying dumps in "hex" rather than binary.

off, von Neumann suggested using the *binary* numbering system. His insight has vastly simplified the way computers handle data.

Computers *operate* in binary and *communicate* to us in decimal. A special program translates decimal into binary on input, and binary into decimal on output. Under normal circumstances, a programmer would see only decimal input and output. On occasion, though, he or she must deal with long and confusing strings of 1s and 0s in the form of a **memory dump**. A memory dump is like a snapshot of the contents of primary storage (on-bits and off-bits) at a given moment in time. To reduce at least part of the confusion of seeing only 1s and 0s on the output, the **hexadecimal** (base-16) numbering system is used as a shorthand to display the binary contents of both primary and secondary storage (see Figure 4–3).

The decimal equivalents for binary, decimal, and hexadecimal numbers are shown in Figure 4–4. We know that in decimal, any number greater than 9 is represented by a sequence of digits. When you count in decimal, you "carry" to the next position in groups of 10. As you examine Figure 4–4, notice that you carry in groups of 2 in binary and in groups of 16 in hexadecimal. Also note that any combination of *four* binary digits can be represented by one "hex" digit.

The hexadecimal numbering system is used only for the convenience of the programmer when reading and reviewing the binary output of a dump (see Figure 4–3) or the binary representation of an instruction or error message. Computers *do not operate or process in hex*. During the 1960s and early 1970s, programmers often had to examine the contents of primary storage to debug their programs (that is, to eliminate program errors). Today's programming languages display *error messages* in plain English. This increase in the sophistication of programming software has minimized the need for applications programmers to convert binary and hexadecimal numbers into their more familiar decimal equivalents. However, if you become familiar with these numbering systems, you should achieve a better overall understanding of computers.

Appendix B, "Working with Numbering Systems," presents the principles of numbering systems, discusses numbering-system arithmetic, and illustrates how to convert a value in one numbering system into its equivalent in another.

FIGURE 4–4 Numbering-System Equivalence Table

Binary (base 2)	Decimal (base 10)	Hexadecimal (base 16)
0	0	0
1	1	1
10	2	2
11	3	3
100	4	4
101	5	5
110	6	6
111	7	7
1000	8	8
1001	9	9
1010	10	A
1011	11	B
1100	12	C
1101	13	D
1110	14	E
1111	15	F
10000	16	10

At the peak of the evening rush hour on October 17, 1989, San Francisco and the surrounding area experienced a severe earthquake that registered 7.1 on the Richter scale. The rest of the country watched fires, fallen bridges, and evacuation efforts on television, and became deeply concerned about the people of northern California. Some were also concerned about the fate of the 1989 World Series. Those in San Francisco and the Silicon Valley were worried about their families, friends, property, and their computer systems—yes, their computer systems. PCs were jumping off desks. Mainframes and minis were rocking and literally rolling on the floor. Racks filled with communications hardware and data storage media tipped over. A data center director at a San Francisco hospital compared his machine room to the aftermath of a bomb explosion.

The Hewlett-Packard Company reacted to the earthquake as many other companies did. Executives gave all of Hewlett-Packard's 18,000 employees the day off—all except its information services staff. When a company's computer system goes down, the company's survival is at stake.

The earthquake forced many companies to test their disaster recovery plans. The first order of business was to get the computer system up and running as soon as possible. If the computer system is intact, the company's only concern is power. Power was cut off for hours and even days throughout northern California. As power went out in much of San Francisco, companies switched to their UPS (uninterruptible power supply) system, at least those that worked. Backup batteries, connections, and generators also had fallen to the earthquake.

Companies with damaged computers either transferred critical systems to a backup site, repaired damaged hardware, or ordered new hardware. Companies with undamaged hardware pitched in and provided limited backup support to less-fortunate companies. Computer manufacturers such as IBM and Digital Equipment Company made every resource available to their customers. Disaster recovery firms, which are set up to handle one disaster at a time, did everything possible to accommodate subscribers.

People cooperated and disaster plans worked. Computer centers in northern California experienced minimal damage, and operations at all but a few companies were restored by the next day, a truly amazing recovery from a major disaster.

4-5   Components of a Computer System: A Closer Look at the Processor and RAM

Let's review. We have learned that all computers have similar capabilities and perform essentially the same functions, although some might be faster than others. We have also learned that a computer system has input, output, storage, and processing components; that the *processor* is the "intelligence" of a computer system; and that a single computer system may have several processors. We have discussed how data are represented inside a computer system in electronic states called bits. We are now ready to expose the inner workings of the nucleus of the computer system—the processor.

Contrary to popular thinking, the internal operation of a computer is far more interesting than mysterious. The mystery is in the minds of those who listen to hearsay and believe science-fiction writers. The computer is a nonthinking electronic device that has to be plugged into an electrical power source, just like a toaster or a lamp.

Literally hundreds of different types of computers are marketed by scores of manufacturers. The complexity of each type may vary considerably, but in the end each processor, sometimes called the **central processing unit** or **CPU**, has only two fundamental sections: the *control unit* and the *arithmetic and logic unit*. *Primary storage* also plays an integral part in the internal operation of a processor. These three—primary storage, the control unit, and the arithmetic and logic unit—work together. Let's look at their functions and the relationships between them.

RAM: Random-Access Storage

The Technology   Unlike magnetic secondary storage devices, such as tape and disk, *RAM* (primary storage) has no moving parts. With no mechanical movement, data can be accessed from RAM at electronic speeds, or close to the speed of light. Most of today's computers use CMOS (Complementary Metal-Oxide Semiconductor) technology for RAM. A state-of-the-art CMOS memory chip about one-eighth the size of a postage stamp can store about 4 million bits, or over 400,000 characters of data!

But there is one major problem with semiconductor storage. When the electrical current is turned off or interrupted, the data are lost. Researchers are working to perfect a RAM technology that will retain its contents after an electrical interruption. Several "nonvolatile" technologies, such as **bubble memory**, have emerged, but none has exhibited the qualities necessary for widespread application. However, bubble memory is superior to CMOS for use in certain computers. It is highly reliable, it is not susceptible to environmental fluctuations, and it can operate on battery power for a considerable length of time. These qualities make bubble memory well-suited for use with industrial robots and in portable computers.

Function   RAM provides the processor with *temporary* storage for programs and data. *All programs and data must be transferred to RAM from an input device (such as a keyboard) or from secondary storage (such as a disk) before programs can be executed or data can be processed.* RAM space is always at a premium; therefore, after a program has been executed, the storage space it occupied is reallocated to another program awaiting execution.

Figure 4–5 illustrates how all input/output (I/O) is "read to" or "written from" RAM. In the figure, an inquiry (input) is made on a VDT. The inquiry, in the form of a message, is routed to RAM over a **channel** (such as a coaxial cable). The message is interpreted, and the processor initiates action to retrieve the appropriate program and data from secondary storage. The program and data are "loaded," or moved, to RAM from secondary storage. This is a *nondestructive read* process. That is, the program and data that are read reside in both RAM (temporarily) and secondary storage (permanently). The data are manipulated according to program instructions, and a report is written from RAM to a printer.

A program instruction or a piece of data is stored in a specific RAM location called an **address**. Addresses permit program instructions and data to be located, accessed, and processed. The content of each address is constantly changing as different programs are executed and new data are processed.

CMOS is magnified 5000 times so that we can see its physical structure.

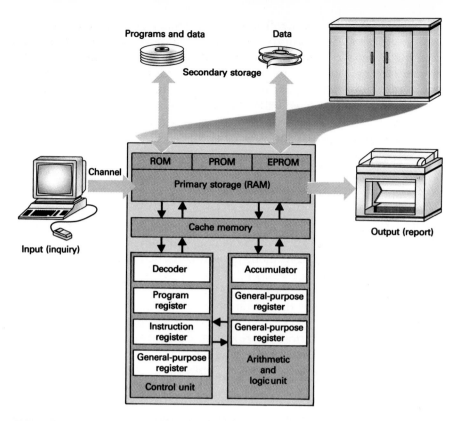

Programs and data

Data

Secondary storage

FIGURE 4–5   Interaction between Primary Storage and Computer System Components

All programs and data must be transferred from an input device or from secondary storage before programs can be executed and data can be processed. During processing, instructions and data are passed between the various types of internal memories, the control unit, and the arithmetic and logic unit. Output is transferred to the printer from primary storage.

RAM, ROM, PROM, and EPROM   A special type of RAM, called **read-only memory (ROM)**, cannot be altered by the programmer. The contents of ROM are "hard-wired" (designed into the logic of the memory chip) by the manufacturer and can be "read only." When you turn on a microcomputer system, a program in ROM automatically readies the computer system for use. Then the ROM program produces the initial display-screen prompt.

A variation of ROM is **programmable read-only memory (PROM)**. PROM (rhymes with *mom*) is ROM into which you, the user, can load "read-only" programs and data. Some microcomputer software packages, such as electronic spreadsheets, are available as PROM units as well as on diskette. Once a program is loaded to PROM, it is seldom, if ever, changed. However, if you need to be able to revise the contents of PROM, there is **EPROM** (pronounced *E prom*), erasable PROM.

Cache Memory   Programs and data are loaded to RAM from secondary storage because the time required to access a program instruction or piece of data from RAM is significantly less than from secondary storage. Thousands of instructions or pieces of data can be accessed from RAM in the time it would take to access a single piece of data from disk storage. RAM is essentially a high-speed holding area for data and programs. In fact, nothing really happens in a computer system until the program instructions and data are moved to the processor. This transfer of instructions and data to the processor can be time-consuming, even at microsecond speeds. To facilitate an even faster transfer of instructions and data to the processor, some computers are designed with **cache memory** (see Figure 4–5). Cache memory is employed by computer designers to increase the computer system **throughput** (the rate at which work is performed).

Like RAM, cache is a high-speed holding area for program instructions and data. However, cache memory uses a technology that is about 10 times faster than RAM and about 100 times more expensive. With only a fraction of the capacity of RAM, cache memory holds only those instructions and data that are likely to be needed next by the processor.

The Control Unit

Just as the processor is the nucleus of a computer system, the **control unit** is the nucleus of the processor. If you will recall from an earlier discussion, the control unit and the arithmetic and logic unit are the two fundamental sections of a processor. The control unit has three primary functions:

1. To read and interpret program instructions
2. To direct the operation of internal processor components
3. To control the flow of programs and data in and out of RAM

Modern technology has taken away some of the romance associated with the computer mystique. Today's computers don't have hundreds of multicolored blinking lights and swirling tapes. The processing component of this Amdahl mainframe computer system (behind people) has only one switch—on/off.

Memory Bits

INTERNAL STORAGE
- RAM (primary storage)
- ROM, PROM, and EPROM
- Cache
- Registers

DSP: Unlimited Applications
Digital signal processing (DSP), an up-and-coming technology, allows the transcription of analog signals into the digital language of computing. Once signals are converted into the 1s and 0s, they can be manipulated into combinations that were never possible using analog signals. DSP has many applications. For example, DSP allows compression of signals so that three telephone calls can be transmitted over the same radio band that used to carry one analog conversation. DSP also allows for hundreds of cable TV channels to be brought into a home. DSP chips are being installed in car, lawn mower, and leaf blower mufflers to reduce noise. To do this, the DSP chip generates a series of continuous antinoise signals that cancel out the bothersome sounds of the muffler.

A program must first be loaded to RAM before it can be executed. During execution, the first in a sequence of program instructions is moved from RAM to the control unit, where it is decoded and interpreted by the **decoder**. The control unit then directs other processor components to carry out the operations necessary to execute the instruction.

The control unit contains high-speed working storage areas called **registers** that can store no more than a few bytes (see Figure 4–5). Registers handle instructions and data at a speed about 10 times faster than that of cache memory and are used for a variety of processing functions. One register, called the **instruction register**, contains the instruction being executed. Other general-purpose registers store data needed for immediate processing. Registers also store status information. For example, the **program register** contains the RAM address of the next instruction to be executed. Registers facilitate the movement of data and instructions between RAM, the control unit, and the arithmetic and logic unit.

The Arithmetic and Logic Unit

The **arithmetic and logic unit** performs all computations (addition, subtraction, multiplication, and division) and all logic operations (comparisons).

Examples of *computations* include the payroll deduction for social security, the day-end inventory, and the balance on a bank statement. A *logic* operation compares two pieces of data. Then, based on the result of the comparison, the program "branches" to one of several alternative sets of program instructions. Let's use an inventory system to illustrate the logic operation. At the end of each day the inventory level of each item in stock is compared to a reorder point. For each comparison indicating an inventory level that falls below ($<$) the reorder point, a sequence of program instructions is executed that produces a purchase order. For each comparison indicating an inventory level at or above ($=$ or $>$) the reorder point, another sequence of instructions is executed.

The arithmetic and logic unit also does alphabetic comparisons. For example, when comparing Smyth and Smith, Smyth is evaluated as being greater alphabetically, so it is positioned after Smith.

The Machine Cycle

You have probably heard of computer programming languages such as COBOL, BASIC, and RPG. There are dozens of programming languages in common usage. However, in the end, COBOL, BASIC, RPG, and the other languages are translated into the only language that a computer understands—its machine language. Machine-language instructions are represented inside the computer as strings of binary digits, up to 64 digits in length. An overview of machine languages and of some of the more popular higher-level programming languages is provided in Chapter 10, "Programming Concepts and Program Languages."

Every machine language has a predefined format for each type of instruction. The relative position within the instruction designates whether a sequence of characters is an **operation code**, an **operand**, or irrelevant. The typical machine language will have from 50 to 200 separate

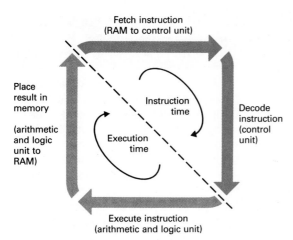

Fetch instruction
(RAM to control unit)

Place
result in
memory

(arithmetic
and logic
unit to
RAM)

Instruction
time

Decode
instruction
(control
unit)

Execution
time

Execute instruction
(arithmetic and logic unit)

FIGURE 4–6
The Machine Cycle

operation codes. The operation code, or **op-code**, is that portion of the fundamental computer instruction that designates the operation to be performed (add, compare, retrieve data from RAM, and so on). The operand is that portion of the instruction that designates data or refers to one or more addresses in RAM in which data can be found or placed. The op-code determines whether the operand contains data, addresses, or both.

Every computer has a **machine cycle**. The following actions take place during the machine cycle (see Figure 4–6):

- *Fetch instruction.* The next machine language instruction to be executed (op-code and operand) is retrieved, or "fetched," from RAM or cache memory and loaded to the instruction register in the control unit (see Figure 4–5).
- *Decode instruction.* The instruction is decoded and interpreted.
- *Execute instruction.* Using whatever processor resources are needed (primarily the arithmetic and logic unit), the instruction is executed.
- *Place result in memory.* The results are placed in the appropriate memory position (usually RAM or a register in the arithmetic and logic unit called the **accumulator**). (See Figure 4–5.)

The speed of a processor is sometimes measured by how long it takes to complete a machine cycle. The timed interval that comprises the machine cycle is the total of the **instruction time**, or **I-time**, and the **execution time**, or **E-time** (see Figure 4–6). The I-time is made up of the first two activities of the machine cycle—fetch and decode the instruction. The E-time comprises the last two activities of the machine cycle—execute the instruction and store the results.

Alternative Design Architectures

RISC: More Is Not Always Better   Most mainframe computers and personal computers use **CISC** (*complex instruction set computer*) architecture. In Chapter 2, "Micro, Minis, Mainframes, and Supercomputers,"

Since the emergence of microcomputers in the mid-1970s, four systems—the Apple II series, the Apple Macintosh series, the IBM-PC series (and its compatibles), and the IBM PS/2 series—have dominated the field. Dozens of manufacturers make clones of the IBM PC and the low-end PS/2 micros; however, the cloning may end with the next generation of microcomputers. The new micros permit concurrent processing; that is, more than one computer can compete for the resources linked to the common 32-bit electrical bus. In effect, this means that the user can assign one processor to one job (word processing) and another to a different job (printing invoices).

A group of prominent manufacturers of IBM-PC–compatible computers, known as the Gang of Nine (Compaq Computer Corporation, Hewlett Packard

Company, AST Research Inc., Zenith Data Systems, Tandy Corporation, and others), has decided to break away from IBM design architectures. The Gang of Nine, which has grown to a gang of many, is banking on their collective strength being great enough to offset the market dominance that IBM has enjoyed for decades. Now, we as users are being asked to make a choice that may affect our computing environment for years. For the overwhelming majority of micro users, the choice used to be between IBM and Apple. Now the Gang of Nine is proposing a third alternative.

The concurrent processing environment being pursued by IBM is called Micro Channel Architecture, or MCA for short. MCA is found on the high-end PS/2 line of computers. Apple's state-of-the-art architecture, called NuBus, is being installed on high-end Macintosh computers. The Gang of Nine created and adopted the Extended Industry Standard Architecture, or EISA (rhymes with *visa*). These maverick manufacturers are using EISA architecture as the basis for micros powered by the Intel 80386 and 80486 microprocessors.

The MCA and EISA architectures enable processors to take greater advantage of computing resources, especially random-access memory (RAM). The IBM-PC and compatible computers limit the applications software to 1 MB of RAM. This limits the size and, therefore, the potential of applications software developed for IBM-PC–compatible computers. The RAM limit for applications software on MCA- and EISA-based micros is 16 MB. Unlike the MCA, EISA is compatible with the millions of 8-bit and 16-bit add-on boards that users have been combining with IBM-PC and compatible computers.

IBM-PC COMPATIBLE WITH EISA ARCHITECTURE

we learned that the term *architecture*, when applied to a computer, refers to a computer system's design. A CISC computer's machine language offers programmers a wide variety of instructions from which to choose (add, multiply, compare, move data, and so on). CISC computers reflect the evolution of increasingly sophisticated machine languages. Computer designers, however, are rediscovering the beauty of simplicity. Computers designed around much smaller instruction sets can realize significantly increased throughput for certain applications, especially those that involve graphics (for example, computer-aided design). These computers use **RISC** (reduced instruction set computer) architecture.

Although RISC architecture is implemented in everything from PCs to supercomputers, RISC has experienced its greatest success in profes-

IBM PS/2 WITH MCA ARCHITECTURE

Many power users of IBM-PC–compatible micro-computers are ready to make the transition to the next generation of micros. Corporate decision makers also are aware that a transition to the next level is inevitable. The question remains: "Which architecture will emerge as the industry standard—MCA, EISA, or NuBus?" Most will agree that Apple has an established niche in the marketplace and enough loyal followers to maintain its position. The real question is whether IBM with MCA or the Gang of Nine (and others) with EISA will emerge as the architecture of choice for the next generation of micros.

The vast majority of the IBM-PC–compatible users has yet to exploit the potential of the Intel 8088, 8086,

80286, and 80386 microprocessors. These people will not be directly affected by the resolution of the MCA versus EISA debate until well into the 1990s. However, anyone needing the power of the Intel 80486 micro-processor (roughly equivalent to an average minicom-puter), may have to make a big decision.

Which system will the customer choose? So far no one knows. Computer customers have become skep-tical and confused. Each of the three groups claims its product is the standard for the field. So far the customers are sitting tight waiting for the confusion to be clarified. But an interesting development has occurred. One major computer magazine noted in 1992 that more vendors are supplying boards for EISA than for the IBM or the Apple standard.

APPLE MACINTOSH WITH NuBus ARCHITECTURE

sional workstations. (Professional workstations are discussed in Chapter 2.) The dominant application among workstations is graphics. Work-station manufacturers feel that the limitations of a reduced instruction set are easily offset by increased processing speed and the lower cost of RISC microprocessors.

Parallel Processing   Computer manufacturers have relied on the single processor design architecture since the late 1940s. In this environment, the processor addresses the programming problem sequentially, from be-ginning to end. Today designers are doing research on computers that will be able to break a programming problem into pieces. Work on each of these pieces will then be executed simultaneously in separate processors, all of which are part of the same computer. The concept of using multiple processors in the same computer is known as **parallel processing**.

In Chapter 2, "Micros, Minis, Mainframes, and Supercomputers," the point was made that a computer system may be made up of several special-function processors. For example, a single computer system may have a host, a front-end processor, and a back-end processor. By dividing the workload among several special-function processors, the system throughput is increased. Computer designers began asking themselves, "If three or four processors can enhance throughput, what could be accomplished with twenty, or even a thousand, processors?"

In parallel processing, one main processor (a mini or a host mainframe) examines the programming problem and determines what portions, if any, of the problem can be solved in pieces (see Figure 4–7). Those pieces that can be addressed separately are routed to other processors and solved. The individual pieces are then reassembled in the main processor for further computation, output, or storage. The net result of parallel processing is better throughput. Research and design in this area, which some say characterizes a fifth generation of computers, is still in the formative stages.

Neural Networks: Wave of the Future?   The best processor is the human brain. Scientists are studying the way the human brain and nervous system work in an attempt to build computers that mimic the incredible human mind. The base technology for these computers will be **neural networks**. Neural networks are made up of millions of interconnected artificial neurons (essentially integrated circuits). (The biological neuron is the functional unit of human nerve tissue.) The neural networked computer will be able to perform human-oriented tasks such as pattern recognition, reading handwriting, and learning.

The primary difference between traditional digital computer architectures and neural networks is that digital computers process data sequentially whereas neural networks process data simultaneously. Digital

FIGURE 4–7   Parallel Processing
In parallel processing, auxiliary processors solve pieces of a problem to enhance system throughput.

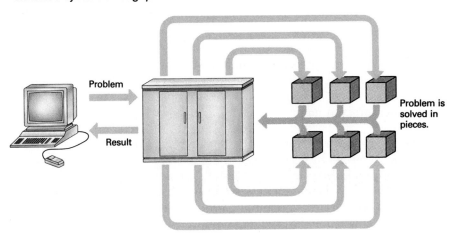

Problem

Result

Problem is solved in pieces.

computers will always be able to outperform neural networked computers and the human brain when it comes to fast, accurate numeric computation. However, if neural networks live up to their potential, they will be able to handle tasks that are currently very time-consuming or impossible for conventional computers, such as recognizing a face in the crowd.

4–6 Computer Operation: What Happens Inside

Some automobiles have the engine in the front, some have it in the rear, and a few have it in the middle. It's the same with computers. Computer architecture—the way in which they are designed—varies considerably. For example, one vendor's computers might have separate RAM areas for data and programs. In some microcomputers the *motherboard*, a circuit board, holds the electronic circuitry for the processor, memory, and the input/output interface with the peripheral devices. A knowledge of these idiosyncrasies is not required of the user; therefore, the following example focuses on the *essentials* of computer operation.

The BASIC program in Figure 4–8 computes and displays the sum of any two numbers. BASIC is a popular programming language. The instructions in the example BASIC program are intuitive; that is, a knowledge of BASIC is not required to understand what the program is doing. Figure 4–9 illustrates how a processor works by showing the interaction between RAM, the control unit, and the arithmetic and logic unit during the execution of the BASIC program in Figure 4–8. RAM in Figure 4–9 has only 10 RAM locations, and these are used only for data. In practice, both program and data would be stored in RAM, which usually has a minimum of 640,000 storage locations.

During execution of the BASIC program, one of the numbers (5 in the example) is loaded to the accumulator. The other number in RAM (2 in the example) is added to the 5 in the accumulator, and the value in the accumulator becomes 7. The following statement-by-statement discussion of the BASIC program of Figure 4–8 illustrates exactly what happens as each instruction is executed.

- *Statement 10* (INPUT "INPUT NO."; X) permits the terminal operator to enter any numeric value. The control unit arbitrarily assigns the value to RAM location *six*. In Figure 4–9, the value entered is 5. Future program references to X recall the content of the storage location whose address is *six*.

FIGURE 4–8   A BASIC Program
This program, written in the BASIC programming language, adds any two numbers and displays the sum. The execution of this program is illustrated in Figure 4–9.

```
10   INPUT "INPUT NO."; X
20   INPUT "INPUT NO."; Y
30   LET SUM=X+Y
40   PRINT "THE SUM IS"; SUM
50   END
```

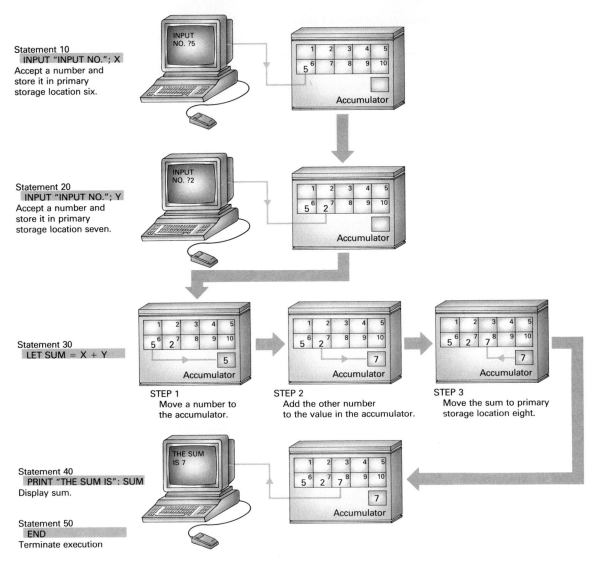

Statement 10
  INPUT "INPUT NO."; X
Accept a number and
store it in primary
storage location six.

Statement 20
  INPUT "INPUT NO."; Y
Accept a number and
store it in primary
storage location seven.

Statement 30
  LET SUM = X + Y

STEP 1
  Move a number to
  the accumulator.

STEP 2
  Add the other number
  to the value in the accumulator.

STEP 3
  Move the sum to primary
  storage location eight.

Statement 40
  PRINT "THE SUM IS": SUM
Display sum.

Statement 50
  END
Terminate execution

FIGURE 4–9 Internal Computer Operation
This figure, which is explained in the text, illustrates what happens inside the computer when the BASIC program of Figure 4–8 is executed. Primary storage is shown with 10 numbered storage locations.

■ *Statement 20* (INPUT "INPUT NO."; Y) permits the terminal operator to enter any numeric value. The control unit arbitrarily assigns the value to RAM location *seven*. In the figure, the value entered is 2.

■ *Statement 30* (LET SUM = X + Y) adds the content of location *six* to that of location *seven*. The sum is then stored in location *eight*. This addition is accomplished in three steps.

Step 1. The 5 in location *six* is copied to the *accumulator*. The 5 remains in location *six*, and the value of the *accumulator* becomes 5.

Step 2. The content of location *seven* (value = 2) is added to the content of the *accumulator* (value = 5). The addition changes the content of the *accumulator* to 7.

Step 3. The 7 cannot be output directly from the *accumulator*; therefore, the content of the *accumulator* (value = 7) is copied arbitrarily to location *eight*. The value of the *accumulator* is unchanged.

- *Statement 40* (PRINT "THE SUM IS"; SUM) displays, on the terminal screen, "THE SUM IS" and the result of the addition (content of location *eight*), or 7 in the figure.
- *Statement 50* (END) signals the end of the program.

More complex arithmetic and I/O tasks involve further repetitions of these fundamental operations. Logic operations are similar, with values being compared between RAM locations, the accumulator, and registers.

4–7 Describing the Processor: Distinguishing Characteristics

People are people, and computers are computers, but how do we distinguish one from another? We describe people in terms of height, build, age, and so on. We describe computers or processors in terms of *word length*, *speed*, and the *capacity* of their associated RAM. For example, a computer might be described as a 32-bit, 20-MHz, 4-MB micro. Let's see what this means.

Word Length

A **word** is the number of bits that are handled as a unit for a particular computer system. The word length of modern microcomputers is normally 32 bits; that is, the system's bus, which connects the processor, RAM, and the system's peripherals, can move 32 bits (four 8-bit bytes) at a time. Early micros had word lengths of 8 bits (one byte) and 16 bits (two bytes). Minis and mainframes typically have 32-bit or 36-bit word lengths. Supercomputers have 64-bit (eight bytes) words.

Processor Speed: Minis, Mainframes, and Supercomputers

Processor speed is often measured in **MIPS**, or millions of instructions per second. The processing speed of today's minis, mainframes, and supercomputers is in the range of 20 to 1000 MIPS.

The timed intervals of the machine cycle also provide a measure of processor speed (see Section 4–5). The shorter the machine cycle, the faster the processor. Machine cycles are measured in milliseconds, microseconds, and nanoseconds—or thousandths, millionths, and billionths of a second. As technology advances, machine cycles eventually will be measured in picoseconds—or trillionths of a second.

Processor Speed: Micros

A *crystal oscillator* paces the execution of instructions within the processor of a microcomputer. A micro's processor speed is rated by its frequency of oscillation, or the number of clock cycles per second. Most personal

This supercomputer helps an oil company process mountains of data into pictures of the underground. It has a machine cycle of 4.1 nanoseconds (4.1 billionths of a second), a word size of 64 bits, and 2048 megabytes of primary storage.

computers are rated between 5 and 50 **megahertz**, or **MHz** (millions of clock cycles). The elapsed time for one clock cycle is 1/frequency (1 divided by the frequency). For example, the time it takes to complete one cycle on a 25-MHz processor is 1/25,000,000, or 0.00000004 seconds, or 40 nanoseconds. Normally several clock cycles are required to retrieve, decode, and execute a single program instruction. The shorter the clock cycle, the faster the processor.

To properly evaluate the processing capability of a micro, you must consider both the processor speed and the word length. A 32-bit micro with a 25-MHz processor has more processing capability than a 16-bit micro with a 25-MHz processor.

We seldom think in time units of less than a second; consequently, it is almost impossible for us to think in terms of computer speeds. Imagine, today's microcomputers can execute more instructions in a minute than the number of times your heart has beat since the day you were born!

The microcomputer being used by these retail consultants is based on the Intel 80486 chip. It has a processor speed of 40 MHz, a RAM capacity of 16 MB, and a word length of 32 bits.

Capacity of RAM

The capacity of RAM is stated in terms of the number of bytes it can store. As we learned in this chapter, a byte, or eight bits, is roughly equivalent to a character (such as A, 1, &).

Memory capacity usually is stated in terms of **kilobytes (KB)**, a convenient designation for 1024 (2^{10}) bytes of storage, and in terms of **megabytes (MB)**, which is 1,048,576 (2^{20}) bytes. Notice that 1 KB is about 1000 and 1 MB is about 1,000,000, thus the origin of the prefixes *kilo* (thousand) and *mega* (million). Memory capacities of modern micros range from 640 KB to 16 MB. Occasionally you will see memory capacities of individual chips stated in terms of **kilobits (Kb)** and **megabits (Mb)**.

Now if anyone ever asks you what a 32-bit, 25-MHz, 4-MB micro is, you've got the answer! This describes the processor of what is emerging as the entry-level PC.

Differences in Processor Personality

Word length, speed, and RAM *capacity* are the primary descriptors of processors. However, computers, like people, have their own "personalities."

Memory Bits

PROCESSOR DESCRIPTION
Word length: Bits handled as a unit
Speed (mainframes): MIPS and machine cycle
Speed (micros): MHz (clock cycles)
RAM Capacity: KB, Kb, MB, or Mb

That is, two similarly described computers might possess attributes which give one more capability than the other. For example, one 32-bit, 25-MHz, 4-MB PC might permit the connection of three peripheral devices and another six peripheral devices. Or, one might be configured with an accelerator to speed up processing of numeric data. Just remember, when you buy a PC that the basic descriptors tell most of the story, but not the whole story.

 Important Terms and Summary Outline

accumulator	EBCDIC	operation code (op-code)
address	encoding system	parallel processing
alpha	EPROM	parity bit
alphanumeric	execution time (E-time)	parity checking
arithmetic and logic unit	hexadecimal	parity error
ASCII	instruction register	primary storage
ASCII-8	instruction time (I-time)	program register
binary	kilobits (Kb)	programmable read-only memory (PROM)
bit	kilobytes (KB)	
bubble memory	machine cycle	read-only memory (ROM)
byte	megabits (Mb)	register
cache memory	megabytes (MB)	RISC
central processing unit (CPU)	megahertz (MHz)	secondary storage
channel	memory dump	throughput
CISC	MIPS	word
control unit	neural network	
decimal	numeric	
decoder	octal	
	operand	

4–1 DATA STORAGE: DATA IN THE COMPUTER. Data, not information, are stored in a computer system. Data are stored temporarily during processing in **primary storage** (RAM), and permanently on **secondary storage** devices, such as magnetic tape and disk drives.

4–2 A BIT ABOUT THE BIT. The two electronic states of the computer—on and off—are represented by a **bit**, short for *binary digit*. These electronic states are compatible with the **binary** numbering system. Letters and decimal numbers are translated into bits for storage and processing on computer systems.

4–3 ENCODING SYSTEMS: COMBINING BITS TO FORM BYTES. **Alphanumeric** (**alpha** and **numeric**) characters are represented in computer storage by combining strings of bits to form unique bit configurations for each character. Characters are translated into these bit configurations, also called **bytes**, according to a particular coding scheme, called an **encoding system**. Popular encoding systems include **EBCDIC**, **ASCII**, and **ASCII-8**.

Parity-checking procedures ensure that data transmission between hardware devices is complete and accurate. A dropped **parity bit** results in a **parity error**.

4–4 NUMBERING SYSTEMS AND COMPUTERS. The two primary numbering systems used in conjunction with computers are binary and **decimal**. Decimal is translated into binary on input and binary is translated into decimal on output. The **hexadecimal** numbering system is used primarily as a programmer convenience in reading and reviewing binary output in the form of a **memory dump**. The **octal** numbering system has a base of 8.

4–5 COMPONENTS OF A COMPUTER SYSTEM: A CLOSER LOOK AT THE PROCESSOR AND RAM. The processor is the "intelligence" of a computer system. A processor, which is also called the **central processing unit** or **CPU**, has only two fundamental sections, the **control unit** and the **arithmetic and logic unit**, which work together with RAM to execute programs. The control unit interprets instructions and directs the arithmetic and logic unit to perform computation and logic operations.

RAM, or random-access memory, provides the processor with temporary storage for programs and data. Input/output (I/O) is "read to" or "written from" RAM over a **channel**. In RAM, datum is stored at a specific **address**. Most of today's computers use CMOS technology for RAM. However, with CMOS, the data are lost when the electrical current is turned off or interrupted. In contrast, **bubble memory** provides nonvolatile memory. All input/output, including programs, must enter and exit RAM. Other variations of internal storage are **ROM**, **PROM**, and **EPROM**.

Some computers employ **cache memory** to increase **throughput**. Like RAM, cache is a high-speed holding area for program instructions and data. However, cache memory holds only those instructions and data likely to be needed next by the processor. During execution, instructions and data are passed between very high-speed **registers** (for example, the **instruction register**, **program register**, and the **accumulator**) in the control unit and the arithmetic and logic unit.

Every machine language has a predefined format for each type of instruction. Each instruction has an **operation code (op-code)** and an **operand**. During one **machine cycle**, an instruction is "fetched" from RAM, decoded by the **decoder** in the control unit, executed, and the results are placed in memory. The machine cycle time is the total of the **instruction time (I-time)** and the **execution time (E-time)**.

Most mainframes and PCs use **CISC** (complex instruction set computer) architecture. Those using **RISC** (reduced instruction set computer) architecture realize increased throughput for certain applications.

In **parallel processing**, one main processor examines the programming problem and determines what portions, if any, of the problem can be solved in pieces. Those pieces that can be addressed separately are routed to other processors, solved, then recombined in the main processor to produce the result.

Neural network–designed computers mimic the human mind. When perfected, they are expected to excel at human-oriented tasks such as pattern recognition and reading handwriting.

4–6 COMPUTER OPERATION: WHAT HAPPENS INSIDE. Data are passed between RAM and the accumulator of the arithmetic and logic unit for both computation and logic operations.

4–7 DESCRIBING THE PROCESSOR: DISTINGUISHING CHARACTERIS-

TICS. A processor is described in terms of its word length, speed, and RAM capacity. The **word** (the number of bits handled as a unit) length of computers ranges from 16 bits for the smaller micros to 64 bits for supercomputers. Mini, mainframe, and supercomputer speed is measured in **MIPS** and by the timed intervals that make up the machine cycle. Microcomputer speed is measured in **megahertz (MHz)**. Memory capacity is measured in **kilobytes (KB)**, **megabytes (MB)**, **kilobits (Kb)**, and **megabits (Mb)**.

 Review Exercises

Concepts

1. Distinguish between RAM, ROM, PROM, and EPROM.
2. How many EBCDIC bytes can be stored in a 32-bit word?
3. Which two functions are performed by the arithmetic and logic unit?
4. List examples of alpha, numeric, and alphanumeric characters.
5. Write your first name as an ASCII bit configuration.
6. What are the functions of the control unit?
7. We describe computers in terms of what three characteristics?
8. What are the binary and hexadecimal equivalents of a decimal 12?
9. What is the basic difference between CMOS technology and nonvolatile technology, such as bubble memory?
10. For a given computer, which type of memory would have the greatest capacity to store data and programs: cache or RAM? RAM or registers? registers or cache?
11. Name three types of registers.
12. Which portion of the fundamental computer instruction designates the operation to be performed?
13. Which type of computer architecture has the smaller instruction set, RISC or CISC?
14. The *I* and the *E* in I-time and E-time stand for what?

Discussion

15. *KB* is used to represent 1024 bytes of storage. Would it not have been much easier to let *KB* represent 1000 bytes? Explain.
16. Millions of bytes of data are transferred routinely between computing hardware devices without any errors in transmission. Very seldom is a parity error detected. In your opinion, is it worth all the trouble to add and check parity bits every time a byte is transmitted from one device to another? Why?
17. If neural networks realize their potential, the distinction between what has traditionally been human-oriented task and machine-oriented task may begin to blur. Should society be doing anything that we are not already doing to prepare for this?

Problem Solving

18. Create a five-bit encoding system to be used for storing uppercase alpha characters, punctuation symbols, and the apostrophe. Discuss the advantages and disadvantages of your encoding system in relation to the ASCII encoding system.

19. Compute the time it takes to complete one cycle on a 50-MHz processor in both seconds and nanoseconds.

20. Convert 5 MB to KB, Mb, and Kb. Assume a byte contains eight bits.

21. Complete a numbering-system table that shows the binary, octal, and hexadecimal equivalents for the decimal numbers 1 through 20.

 ### Self-Test (by section)

4–1 Data are stored permanently on secondary storage devices, such as magnetic tape. (T̸/F)

4–2 **a.** *Bit* is the singular of *byte*. (T̸/F̸) �

 b. The base of the binary number system is: ⒜ 2, (b) 8, or (c) 16?

4–3 **a.** The combination of bits used to represent a character is called a ___byte___.

 b. The procedure that ensures complete and accurate transmission of data is called ASCII checking. (T/F̸)

4–4 **a.** A ___memory dump___ is a "snapshot" of the contents of RAM at a given ✖ moment in time.

 b. When you count in hexadecimal, you carry to the next position in ✖ groups of ___16___.

4–5 **a.** Data are loaded from secondary to RAM in a nondestructive read process. (T̸/F)

 b. The ___control unit___ is that part of the processor that reads and interprets ✖ program instructions.

 c. The arithmetic and logic unit controls the flow of programs and data in and out of main memory. (T/F̸)

 d. Put the following memories in order based on speed: cache, registers, ✖ and RAM. ___RAM, CACHE, REGISTERS.___

 e. The timed interval that comprises the machine cycle is the total of the ___instruction___ time and the ___execution___ time.

4–6 A single BASIC program instruction can cause several internal operations to take place. (T̸/F)

4–7 **a.** The word length of most microcomputers is 64 bits. (T/F̸) ✖

 b. MIPS is an acronym for "millions of instructions per second." (T̸/F)

 c. The time it takes to complete one cycle on a 10-MHz processor is ✖ ___100___ nanoseconds.

Self-test answers. **4–1** T. **4–2** (a) F; (b) a. **4–3** (a) byte; (b) F. **4–4** (a) memory dump; (b) 16. **4–5** (a) T; (b) control unit; (c) F; (d) from the slowest memory: RAM, cache, registers; (e) instruction, execution. **4–6** T. **4–7** (a) F; (b) T; (c) 100.

The invention of the light bulb in 1879 symbolized the beginning of electronics. Electronics then evolved into the use of vacuum tubes, then transistors, and now integrated circuits. Today's microminiaturization of electronic circuitry is continuing to have a profound effect on the way we live and work.

Current technology permits the placement of hundreds of thousands of transistors and electronic switches on a single chip. Chips already fit into wristwatches and credit cards, but electrical and computer engineers want them even smaller. In electronics, smaller is better. The ENIAC, the first full-scale digital electronic computer, weighed 50 tons and occupied an entire room. Today a complete computer is fabricated within a single piece of silicon the size of a child's fingernail.

Chip designers think in terms of nanoseconds (1/1,000,000,000 of a second) and microns (1/1,000,000 of a meter). They want to pack as many circuit elements as they can into the structure of a chip. High-density packing reduces the time required for an electrical signal to travel from one circuit element to the next—resulting in faster computers. Current research indicates that eventually chips containing millions of circuit elements will be produced!

The fabrication of integrated circuits involves a multistep process using various photochemical etching and metallurgical techniques. This complex and interesting process is illustrated here with photos, from silicon to the finished product.

Chips are designed and manufactured to perform a particular function. One chip might be a microprocessor for a personal computer. Another might be primary storage. Another might be the logic for a talking vending machine.

DESIGN

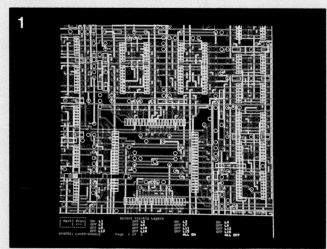

USING CAD FOR CHIP DESIGN Chip designers use computer-aided design (CAD) systems to create the logic for individual circuits. A chip contains from one to thirty layers of circuits. In this multilayer circuit design, each layer is color-coded so the designer can distinguish between the various layers.

CREATING A MASK An electron-beam exposure system etches the circuitry into a glass stencil called a *mask*. A mask such as this one is produced for each circuit layer. The number of layers depends on the complexity of the chip's logic.

FABRICATION

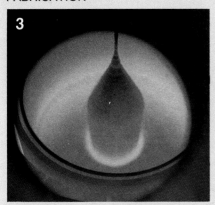

CREATING SILICON INGOTS Molten silicon is spun into cylindrical ingots. Because silicon, the second most abundant substance, is used in the fabrication of integrated circuits, chips are sometimes referred to as "intelligent grains of sand."

CUTTING THE SILICON WAFERS The ingot is shaped and prepared prior to being cut into silicon wafers. Once the wafers are cut, they are polished to a perfect finish.

COATING THE WAFERS Silicon wafers that eventually will contain several hundred chips are placed in an oxygen furnace at 1200 degrees Celsius. In the furnace each wafer is coated with other minerals to create the physical properties needed to produce transistors and electronic switches on the wafer's surface.

ETCHING THE WAFERS The mask is placed over the wafer and both are exposed to ultraviolet light. In this way the circuit pattern is transferred onto each wafer. Plasma (superhot gases) technology is used to etch the circuit pattern permanently into the wafer. This is one of several techniques used in the etching process. The wafer is returned to the furnace and given another coating on which to etch another circuit layer. The procedure is repeated for each circuit layer until the wafer is complete.

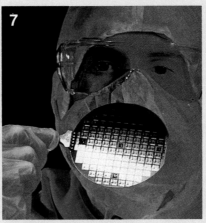

REMOVING THE ETCHED WAFERS The result of the coating/etching process are silicon wafers that contain from 100 to 400 integrated circuits each.

DRILLING THE WAFERS It takes only a second for this instrument to drill 1440 tiny holes in each wafer. The holes enable the interconnection of the layers of circuits. Each layer must be perfectly aligned (within a millionth of a meter) with the others.

The Computer on a Chip

TESTING

TESTING THE CHIPS   The chips are tested while they are still part of the wafer. Each integrated circuit on the wafer is powered up and given a series of tests. Fine needles make the connection for these computer-controlled tests. The precision demands are so great that as many as half the chips are found to be defective. A drop of ink is deposited on defective chips.

PACKAGING

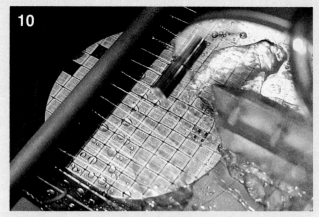

DICING THE WAFERS   A diamond saw separates the wafers into individual chips in a process called *dicing*.

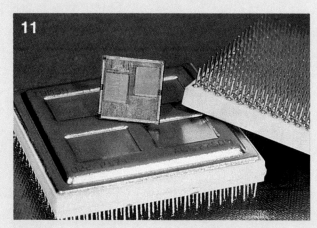

PACKAGING THE CHIPS   The chips are packaged in protective ceramic or metal carriers. The carriers have standard-sized electrical pin connectors that allow the chip to be plugged conveniently into circuit boards. Because the pins tend to corrode, the pin connectors are the most vulnerable part of a computer system. To avoid corrosion and a bad connection, the pins on some carriers are made of gold.

INSTALLING THE FINISHED CHIPS   The completed circuit boards are installed in computers and thousands of other computer-controlled devices.

Input/Output Devices

STUDENT LEARNING OBJECTIVES

▶ To explain alternative approaches to and devices for data entry.

▶ To describe the operation and application of common output devices.

▶ To describe the use and characteristics of the different types of terminals.

CHAPTER OUTLINE

 ## 5–1 I/O Devices: Our Interface with the Computer

Data are created in many places and in many ways. Before data can be processed and stored, they must be translated into a form the computer can interpret. For this, we need *input* devices. Once the data have been processed, they must be translated back into a form that *we* can understand. For this, we need *output* devices. These input/output (I/O) devices, or peripheral devices, enable communication between us and the computer.

Just about everyone routinely communicates directly or indirectly with a computer via I/O devices, even people who have never sat in front of a personal computer or video display terminal.

- Have you ever been hungry and short of cash? It's lunch time and you have only 47 cents in your pocket. No problem. Just stop at an automatic teller machine (ATM) and ask for some "lunch money." The ATM's keyboard (input) and monitor (output) enable you to hold an interactive conversation with the bank's computer. The ATM's printer (output) provides you with a hard copy of your transactions when you leave.
- Have you paid your latest electric bill? Sometimes we interact with the computer indirectly. Did you return a preprinted stub with your check when you paid last month's electric bill? If you did, you were providing input into a computer system. The information on the stub, which is computer-readable, is entered directly into the computer system.
- Have you ever called a mail-order merchandiser and been greeted by a message like this: "Thank you for calling Zimco Enterprises Customer Service. If you wish to place an order, press one. If you wish to inquire about the status of an order, press two. To speak to a particular person,

There are many ways to interact with a computer system. The people in this computerized control room help to operate the OxyMar vinyl chloride monomer complex near Corpus Christi, Texas. For output, each operator has a couple of monitors plus three large common displays.

enter that person's four-digit extension, or hold and an operator will process your call momentarily." The message is produced by an output device called a voice-response unit. Your telephone serves as an input device.

As you can see, input/output devices are quietly playing an increasingly significant role in our lives.

In this chapter we discuss input, output, and, finally, terminals with I/O capabilities.

5–2 Traditional Input Devices

The Keyboard

Alphanumeric Keyboards All PCs and VDTs have a keyboard, the mainstay device for user input to the computer system. The standard for the PC today is the 101-key keyboard with the *QWERTY* key layout, 12 function keys, a keypad, a variety of special-function keys, and dedicated cursor-control keys. We discuss this keyboard and its important keys in Chapter 3, "Interacting with Personal Computers," (see Figure 3–2). The original 83-key IBM-PC keyboard, which has only 10 function keys, is still in use on millions of PCs.

The QWERTY keyboard design, which derived its name from the first six letters on the top row of letters, was created in 1890 to slow down

The QWERTY keyboard design that you see on most typewriters and keyboards derived its name from the first six letters in the top row. Patented in the 1890s, it was designed to slow down fast typists who would otherwise entangle slow-moving type bars.

The Dvorak keyboard layout, named after its inventor, August Dvorak, places the most frequently used characters in the center. You can enter nearly 4000 different words from the "home row" on the Dvorak keyboard, as opposed to 100 with the traditional QWERTY layout.

Professor Dvorak invented this keyboard arrangement in 1932. Through ergonomic studies of typists, he noticed that the QWERTY layout forces the majority of the work to be done by the weakest fingers—the fourth and fifth fingers of the left hand. The stronger, quicker right hand and middle fingers are used only for the least frequently typed characters.

On Dvorak's keyboard, the most frequently used keys are on the home row (the vowels plus *d, h, t, n,* and *s*). The next most frequently used characters are placed up one row because it is easier to reach up than down. Because this layout distributes the typing workload among the fingers according to their strengths, awkward strokes are reduced by 90%. Word processing operators who have switched to Dvorak are experiencing as much as a 75% improvement in productivity.

PC users who want to try the Dvorak layout do not need to replace their QWERTY keyboard. The switch can be made electronically. Windows users can open the control panel's international dialog box and change the keyboard layout to US-Dvorak. DOS and DOS applications users will need to purchase a keyboard redefinition utility. One such utility is a shareware memory-resident program called Dvorak.KB, which lets users "hot key" between Dvorak and QWERTY. With the widespread availability of the Dvorak keyboard, look for it to grow in popularity in the coming years.

RAPID DATA ENTRY   Directory assistance operators and others whose jobs demand rapid data entry often opt for the Dvorak keyboard layout.

typists. This intentionally inefficient design kept fast typists from entangling the slow-moving type bars of nineteenth-century typewriters. The alternative is the *Dvorak* keyboard layout, which places the most frequently used characters on the home row (the vowels plus *d, h, t, n,* and *s*). You can enter nearly 4000 different words from the home row on the Dvorak keyboard, as opposed to 100 with the traditional QWERTY layout. Word processing operators who have switched to Dvorak are experiencing as much as a 75% improvement in productivity. The 101-key keyboard is available in both QWERTY and Dvorak layouts. VDT keyboards vary considerably, from a simple QWERTY keyboard with no function keys to something similar to the familiar 101-key PC keyboard.

Special-Function Keyboards Some keyboards are designed for specific applications. For example, the cash-register-like terminals at most fast-food restaurants have special-purpose keyboards. Rather than type in the name and price of an order of French fries, attendants need only press the key marked "French fries" to record the sale. These keyboards enable rapid interaction with computer systems for shop supervisors, airline ticket agents, retail sales clerks, and many others.

A game of cat and mouse? This cat finds this mouse more interesting than appetizing.

The Mouse

The keyboard is too cumbersome for some applications, especially those that rely on a graphical user interface (GUI) or require the user to point or draw. The effectiveness of GUIs depends on the user's ability to make a rapid selection from a screen full of graphic icons. In these instances the mouse can position the pointer (graphics cursor) over an icon quickly and efficiently. Computer artists use mice to create images. Engineers use them to "draw" lines that connect points on a graph. We discuss the operation of the mouse in Chapter 3, "Interacting with Personal Computers."

Other Point-and-Draw Devices

The mouse is one of several devices that move the graphics cursor to point and draw. The *joystick, track ball, digitizer tablet and pen,* and *light pen* are also input devices that move the graphics cursor to point or draw.

Video arcade wizards are no doubt familiar with the joystick and track ball. The **joystick** is a vertical stick that moves the graphics cursor in the direction the stick is pushed. The **track ball** is a ball inset in a small external box or adjacent to and in the same unit as the keyboard of some portable computers. The ball is "rolled" with the fingers to move the graphics cursor. Some people find it helpful to think of a track ball as an upside-down mouse with a bigger ball on the bottom.

The **digitizer tablet and pen** are a pen and a pressure-sensitive tablet with the same X–Y coordinates as the screen. Some digitizing tablets also use a *crosshair* device instead of a pen. The movement of the pen or crosshair is reproduced simultaneously on the display screen.

When it is moved close to the screen, the **light pen** detects light being emitted from the monitor's display. The graphics cursor automatically locks on to the position of the pen and tracks its movement over the screen. An engineer may create or modify images directly on the screen with a light pen. A city planner may select from a menu of possible computer functions by simply pointing the light pen to a display of the desired function.

The Macintosh Powerbook PC is configured with a built-in track ball. Users can use the track ball to position the graphics cursor without having to remove their fingers from the keyboard.

At Ford Motor Company designers use a dramatic new process to help bring new products to customers sooner. This designer uses a digitizer tablet and pen to work on a new car idea. The image can be instantly reshaped or repainted in any of 16 million color combinations.

 5–3 Source-Data Automation: Getting Closer to the Action

Trends in Data Entry

The trend in data entry has been toward decreasing the number of transcription steps. This is accomplished by entering the data as close to the source as possible. For example, in most sales departments, salespeople key in orders directly to the system. In many accounting departments, bookkeepers and accountants record and enter financial transactions into the system from their VDT keyboards. However, whenever possible, the need for key entry transcription of data can be eliminated altogether. This is known as **source-data automation**.

Until recently, data entry has been synonymous with *keystrokes*. The keystroke will continue to be the basic mode of data entry for the foreseeable future, but recent innovations have eliminated the need for key-driven data entry in many applications. For example, you have probably noticed the preprinted **bar codes** on grocery products. At some supermarket checkout counters these bar codes have eliminated the need for most key entry. Checkers need only pass the product over the *laser scanner*, the price is entered, and the shelf inventory is updated as well.

Data entry is an area in which enormous potential exists for increases in productivity. The technology of data entry devices is constantly changing. New and improved methods of transcribing raw data are being invented and put on the market each month. These data entry methods and associated devices are discussed next.

Optical Character Recognition

Optical character recognition (OCR) is a way to encode (write) certain data in machine-readable format on the original source document. For example, the International Standard Book Number (ISBN) on the back cover of this book is printed in machine-readable OCR. This eliminates the need for publishers and bookstore clerks to key these data manually. OCR equipment consists of a family of devices that encode and read OCR data.

OCR Scanners   OCR characters are identified by light-sensitive devices called **OCR scanners**. There are two types of scanners, *contact* and *laser*. Both bounce a beam of light off an image, then measure the reflected light to determine the value of the image. Hand-held contact scanners make contact as they are brushed over the printed matter to be read. Laser-based scanners are more versatile and can read data passed near the scanning area. Scanners of both technologies can recognize printed characters and various types of codes.

OCR devices can "learn" to read almost any typeface, including the one used for this book! The "learning" takes place when the structure of the character set is described to the OCR device. Special OCR devices can even read hand-printed letters if they are recorded on a standard form and written according to specific rules.

OCR scanners can be classified into the following six categories:

- *Hand-held label scanners.* These devices read data on price tags, shipping labels, inventory part numbers, book ISBNs, and the like. Hand-held label scanners, sometimes called **wand scanners**, use either contact or laser technology. You have probably seen both types used in various retail stores. Wand scanners also are used to read package labels in shipping and receiving and in inventory management. Passport inspection is even being automated with the use of wand scanners. Customs officials enter passport numbers via wand scanners to help speed the processing of international travelers.
- *Stationary label scanners.* These devices, which rely exclusively on laser technology, are used in the same types of applications as wand scanners. Stationary scanners are common in grocery stores.
- *Page scanners.* These devices scan and interpret the alphanumeric characters on regular printed pages. People use page scanners to translate printed hard copy to machine-readable format. For applications that demand this type of translation, page scanners can minimize or eliminate the need for key entry.
- *Document scanners.* Document scanners are capable of scanning documents of varying sizes (for example, utility-bill invoice stubs and sales slips from credit-card transactions).
- *Continuous-form scanners.* These devices read data printed on continuous forms, such as cash register tapes.
- *Optical mark scanners.* Optical mark scanners scan preprinted forms, such as multiple-choice test answer forms. The position of the "sense mark" indicates a particular response or character.

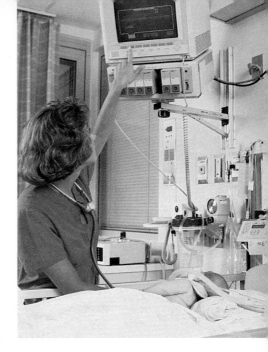

Life-threatening circumstances in hospitals demand greater use of source-data automation. Data collected in this critical-care unit for infants are continuously monitored and analyzed by a computer system. Appropriate persons are alerted automatically on their terminals of any changes in an infant's vital signs.

Supermarket checkout systems are now an established cost-saving technology. The automated systems use stationary laser scanners to read the bar codes that identify each item. Price and product descriptions are retrieved from a data base and recorded on the sales slip.

Bar Codes   Stationary scanners, such as those in supermarkets, use lasers to interpret the bar codes printed on products. Bar codes represent alphanumeric data by varying the width and combination of adjacent vertical lines. Just as there are a variety of internal bit encoding systems, there are a variety of bar-coding systems (see Figure 5–1). One of the most visible of these systems is the Universal Product Code (UPC). The UPC, originally used for supermarket items, is now being printed on other consumer goods. The advantage of bar codes over characters is that the position or orientation of the code being read is not as critical to the scanner. In a supermarket, for example, the data can be recorded even if a bottle of ketchup is rolled over the laser scanner.

Applications of Optical Scanners   Source-data automation has resulted in the use of optical scanners for a variety of applications. Below are a few examples of how optical scanners are applied in the work place.

Speeding the delivery of mail.   The U.S. Postal Service has special-purpose computer systems that employ OCR technology to process all metered mail (bank statements and utility bills, for example). Bulk mailers deliver the mail to post offices in trays; the mail is fed into multifont document scanners capable of reading many different type styles. The OCR scanner first locates the address on the envelope. It then reads the last line, containing the city, state, and ZIP code. To verify that the ZIP code in the address matches the city and state, it is compared to a ZIP code retrieved from a city/state master file. The OCR scanner then reads the next line up, usually the delivery address. The delivery address (for example, 1701 El Camino) is converted into a four-digit code (such as 5483) and combined with the five-digit ZIP (74604 for Ponca City, OK) to make up the nine-digit ZIP (74604-5483). An ink-jet printer inscribes the "ZIP + 4" code in the form of a POSTNET bar code in the lower

FIGURE 5–1   Various Codes That Can Be Interpreted by OCR Scanners

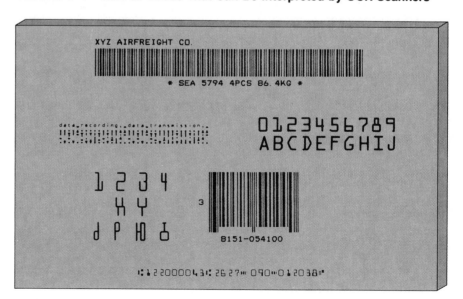

right corner of the envelope. Mail is processed by these special-purpose computer systems at the rate of 700 pieces per minute.

Data at the point-of-sale. As we mentioned earlier, the hand-held wand scanner and the stationary scanner are now common in point-of-sale (POS) systems in retail stores throughout the world. Clerks need only brush the wand over the price tag or move the item past the stationary scanner to record the sale. Because the POS terminal is linked with the store's host computer system, the inventory also is updated as each item is sold.

High-speed data gathering: automating toll booths. One of the more innovative uses of stationary scanners is along toll roads. Drivers who frequently use a particular toll road pay tolls in advance and receive labels for their cars. Stationary scanners along the toll road read the labels as cars pass at highway speeds. The electronic toll booths transmit the data directly to a central computer system. At the central site, the drivers' accounts are debited the amount of the toll.

The round-trip journey: OCR turnaround documents. OCR devices are custom-made for situations where data can be encoded by the computer system on a **turnaround document** when visual recognition is important. A turnaround document is *computer-produced output* that is ultimately returned as *machine-readable input* to a computer system. The billing system of Pocono Power and Light is a good example of this OCR application.

The utility billing system procedures illustrated in Figure 5–2 are described below.

1. The invoices (turnaround documents) are generated from PP&L's customer master file and the electricity usage file. Data on the invoice are printed in a format that can be read by an OCR document scanner. Therefore, no data entry is required unless the amount of the payment is less than the amount due.

2. The XYZ Corporation and other customers return the OCR-readable invoice stubs (turnaround documents) with the payment. Clerks cross-check the payment against the amount due. Partial payments are separated from full payments.

3. An OCR scanner reads the original turnaround document of full-payment customers to acknowledge receipt of payment.

4. The only data entry required is on partial payments. The amount of the payment is encoded on the partial-payment invoice stubs, and these are read by the OCR device.

5. The XYZ Corporation and other customer accounts are credited by the amount of their payment.

In an attempt to cut costs and speed tax-return processing, the Internal Revenue Service is already distributing the short form as a turnaround document. The long form will be next!

Credit-card purchases: original source-data collection. Optical character recognition is also used for original source-data collection. An example is data collection for credit-card purchases. When you make a

Clerks in retail stores use wand scanners to expedite the recording of sales. The possibility of entering erroneous data is significantly less with a wand scanner than with a keyboard.

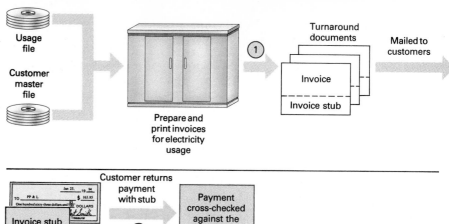

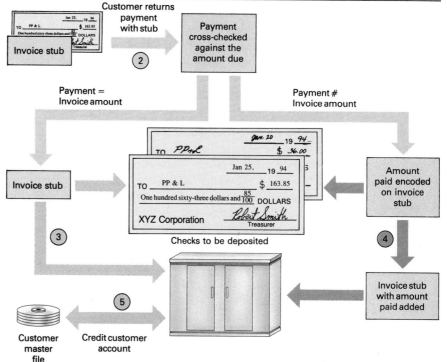

FIGURE 5–2   Electricity Utility Billing System

This system invoices customers with OCR turnaround documents, thereby minimizing the amount of key entry required. The five steps are discussed in the text.

credit-card purchase, your card, a multicopy form, and a portable imprint device are used to record the sales data in machine-readable OCR format. The data recorded on the form for most credit-card purchases include the *account number of the buyer* (imprinted from the customer's credit card), the *account number of the retailer* (imprinted from a permanently installed merchant card in the portable imprint device), and the *amount of the purchase* (entered by the salesperson or automatically by a cash register). The customer is given one copy of the form as a record of purchase, one copy is retained by the retailer, and the third copy, a stiffer card, is sent to the company, often a bank, that issued the credit card. With the data already in OCR format, no further data entry is required. During processing, the amount charged is recorded as a debit to the buyer's account and as a credit to the retailer's account.

The next time United Parcel Service visits your house, don't be surprised if the driver gives you a clipboard-shaped device, hands you an electronic stylus, and asks you to sign your name on a pressure-sensitive display screen. Congratulations. You've just entered the world of pen-based computing, a world where electronic pens replace the keyboards found on most portable PCs.

The first pen-based computers (notepad or slate computers) came from Grid Systems Corporation, whose GridPad computers offer a rugged but compact tool for managing the paperwork involved in delivering packages, taking inventory, recording sales orders, and making service calls. Users report the pen-based systems are easy to learn, reduce errors, and save time. In addition, the ability to capture signatures is important for legal reasons.

Now pen-based computers are poised to make an entry into the world of mobile professionals who can't or won't use keyboard-based portables. Many professionals can't type, and in meetings, colleagues find the click-clack of a portable's keyboard an annoying distraction. In other situations, typing on a laptop is simply impractical. State Farm Insurance, for example, recently began testing notepads with agents and claims adjusters who need to work at accident or disaster scenes.

The computers State Farm is testing pair IBM hardware with Pinpoint, an operating system from Go Corporation. Applications written for Pinpoint and the operating system for the GridPads are examples of *pen-based* or *pen-centric* software; they are designed around the pen and use it both as a mouse and as the primary input device. To enter text, you can either write or print on the screen. To create a sketch or diagram anywhere in a document, just use the pen to draw on the screen.

A second approach is offered by Microsoft Windows for Pen Computing, an extension of the popular Windows operating system. Although Pen Windows lets users make notes or draw on the screen, the pen is used mainly as a replacement for the mouse. Microsoft's hope here is that millions of Windows users will like the idea of using familiar Windows applications with their new pen-based computers. Microsoft is also offering flexibility; one scenario they paint shows a notepad computer being attached to a desktop PC, like a second monitor, so that users can quickly type in a sales presentation and then add handwritten notes. When they're done, all they have to do is detach the notepad and bustle off to a client's office, where they can make additional handwritten changes as needed.

PEN-BASED PC With the advent of user-friendly pen-based computers, insurance adjusters spend less time documenting the details of an accident.

Image Scanners

In recent years, source-data automation has expanded to allow the direct entry of graphic information, as well as text-based information via scanners. An **image scanner** employs laser technology to scan and **digitize** an image. That is, the hard-copy image is translated into an electronic format that can be interpreted by and stored on computers. The digitized image is then stored on magnetic disk. The image to be scanned can be handwritten notes, a photograph, a drawing, an insurance form—anything that can be digitized. Once an image has been digitized and entered to the computer system, it can be retrieved, displayed, altered, merged

Relatively inexpensive image scanners have given rise to image processing. In many applications, it is more efficient to capture the image in its original format. On the left a dental assistant is using a page scanner to scan hard-copy dental records into storage. On the right a reporter is using a hand scanner to read quotes from a newspaper into memory for inclusion in an article.

with text, stored, and sent via data communications to one or several remote locations. Image scanners are becoming a must-have peripheral for people doing desktop publishing (see Chapter 11, "Text and Image Processing Software").

Image scanners are of two types: *page* and *hand*. Either can be gray scale (the image is presented in shades of gray) or color. (Gray scale is discussed later in this chapter.) The *page image scanner* works like a desktop duplicating machine. That is, the image to be scanned is placed face down on the letter-sized scanning surface, covered, then scanned. The result is a high-resolution digitized image. The *hand image scanner* is rolled manually over the image to be scanned. Because it must be guided across the image by the human hand, the resolution of a hand image scanner is not as high. Hand image scanners, about five inches in width, are appropriate for capturing small images or portions of very large images.

If you purchase optional hardware and software, you can turn your image scanner into an OCR page scanner. That is, the image scanner can read and interpret the characters from most typewritten or typeset documents, such as a printed letter or a page from this book.

Magnetic-Ink Character Recognition

Magnetic-ink character recognition (MICR) is similar to optical character recognition and is used exclusively by the banking industry. MICR readers are used to read and sort checks and deposits. You probably have noticed the *account number* and *bank number* encoded on all your checks and personalized deposit slips. The *date* of the transaction is automatically recorded for all checks processed that day; therefore, only the *amount*

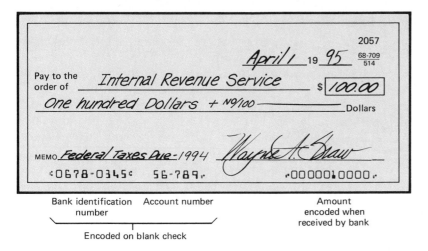

FIGURE 5–3 A Magnetic-Ink Character-Recognition (MICR) Encoded Check

Notice that the amount is entered on the check when it is received by the bank.

must be keyed in (see Figure 5–3) on an **MICR inscriber**. An **MICR reader-sorter** reads the data on the checks and sorts the checks for distribution to other banks and customers or for further processing.

Magnetic-ink character-recognition devices are faster and more accurate than OCR scanners. The special magnetic characters permit the speeds that banks need to sort and process more than 500 million checks each day.

Magnetic Stripes and Smart Cards

The magnetic stripes on the back of charge cards and badges offer another means of data entry at the source. The magnetic stripes are encoded with data appropriate for the application. For example, your account number and privacy code are encoded on a card for automatic teller machines.

Magnetic stripes contain much more data per unit of space than do printed characters or bar codes. Moreover, because they cannot be read visually, they are perfect for storing confidential data such as the privacy code. Employee cards and security badges often contain authorization data for access to physically secured areas, such as the computer center. To gain access, an employee inserts a card or badge into a **badge reader**. This device reads and checks the authorization code before permitting the individual to enter a secured area. When badge readers are linked to a central computer, a chronological log of people entering or leaving secured areas can be maintained.

The enhanced version of cards with a magnetic stripe is called the **smart card**. The smart card, similar in appearance to other cards, contains a microprocessor that retains certain security and personal data in its memory at all times. Because the smart card can hold more information, has some processing capability, and is almost impossible to duplicate, smart cards may soon replace cards with magnetic stripes.

This grocery store has an automated checkout system with the capability of operating without cash transfers. The customer slides her bank card (containing account number and authorization data) through a badge reader and enters a personal identification number on the keyboard, both of which are connected to a network of banking computers. The customer then enters the amount of the purchase. This amount is deducted from her bank account and credited to that of the store.

Voice Data Entry

Speech-recognition systems can be used to enter limited kinds and quantities of information. Despite its limitations, speech recognition has a number of applications. Salespeople in the field can enter an order simply by calling the computer and stating the customer number, item number, and quantity. Quality-control personnel who must use their hands call out defects as they are detected. Baggage handlers at airports simply state the three-letter destination identifier ("L-A-X" for Los Angeles International), and luggage is routed to the appropriate conveyer system. Physicians in the operating room can request certain information about a patient while operating. A computer-based *audio response unit* or a *speech synthesizer* makes the conversation two-way.

The four steps in Figure 5–4 illustrate how speech recognition works.

1. *Say the word.* When you speak into a microphone, each sound is broken down into its various frequencies.
2. *Digitize the word.* The sounds in each frequency are digitized so they can be manipulated by the computer.

FIGURE 5–4   Speech Recognition
The sound waves created by the spoken word Move *are digitized by the computer. The digitized template is matched against templates of other words in the electronic dictionary. When the computer finds a match, it displays a written version of the word.*

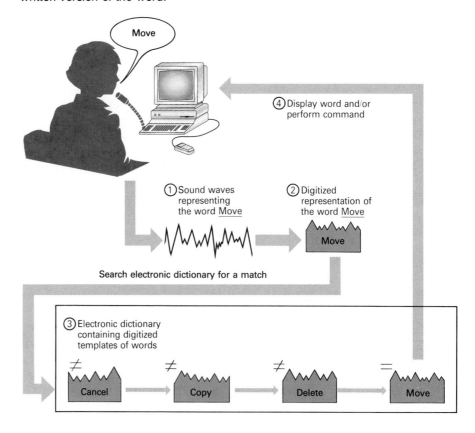

3. *Match the word.* The digitized version of the word is matched against similarly formed *templates* in the computer's electronic dictionary. The digitized template is a form that can be stored and interpreted by computers (in 1s and 0s).

4. *Display the word or perform the command.* When a match is found, the word (*Move* in Figure 5–4) is displayed on a VDT or the appropriate command is performed (for example, move the marked text). In some cases, the word is repeated by a speech synthesizer for confirmation. If no match is found, the speaker is asked to repeat the word.

In speech recognition, the creation of the data base is called *training.* Most speech-recognition systems are *speaker-dependent;* that is, they respond to the speech of a particular individual. Therefore, a data base of words must be created for each person using the system. To create this data base, each person using the system must repeat—as many as 20 times—each word to be interpreted by the system. This training is necessary because we seldom say a word the same way each time. Even if we say the word twice in succession, it will probably have a different inflection or nasal quality.

State-of-the-art *speaker-independent* systems have a limited vocabulary: perhaps *yes, no,* and the 10 numeric digits. Although the vocabulary is limited, speaker-independent systems do not require training and can be used by anyone. However, they do require a very large data base to accommodate anyone's voice pattern.

Computers are great talkers, but they are not very good listeners. Voice inflections, grammatical exceptions, and words that have several meanings make speech interpretation difficult, but not impossible. For example, "I'm OK!" differs from "I'm OK?" For human beings, distinguishing these subtle differences is second nature. However, these subtleties are difficult for computer systems. Even so, researchers are developing speaker-independent data bases of several thousand words that enable the transcription of complete spoken sentences with a high degree of accuracy. It is only a matter of time before programmers can enter their programs in spoken English rather than through time-consuming keystrokes and before managers can dictate their correspondence directly to the computer. Today we must see and touch our PCs and terminals to interact with a computer, but in a few years we will be talking with computers as we move about our offices and homes.

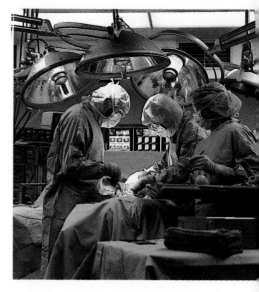

Surgeons in some operating rooms are able to obtain pertinent patient information through voice data entry. They work through a hierarchy of menus by speaking the number of the desired menu item. The resulting text information can be displayed on a monitor or output as spoken words on a speech synthesizer.

Vision-Input Systems

The simulation of human senses, especially vision, is extremely complex. A computer does not actually see and interpret an image the way a human being does. A camera is needed to give computers "eyesight." To create the data base, a vision system, via a camera, digitizes the images of all objects to be identified, then stores the digitized form of each image in the data base. When the system is placed in operation, the camera enters the image into a digitizer. The system then compares the digitized image to be interpreted to the prerecorded digitized images in the computer's data base. The computer identifies the image by matching the structure

This technician's "third eye" is a vision-input system that can detect tiny, but critical, flaws in circuit boards. The system performs inspections at a speed and precision unattainable with the human eye.

of the input image with those images in the data base. This process is illustrated by the digital vision-inspection system in Figure 5–5.

As you can imagine, **vision-input systems** are best suited to very specialized tasks in which only a few images will be encountered. These tasks are usually simple, monotonous ones, such as inspection. For example, in Figure 5–5 a digital vision-inspection system on an assembly line rejects those parts that do not meet certain quality-control specifications. The vision system performs rudimentary gauging inspections, and then signals the computer to take appropriate action.

FIGURE 5–5   Digital Vision-Inspection System
In this digital vision-inspection system, the system examines parts for defects. If the digitized image of the part does not match a standard digital image, the defective part is placed in a reject bin.

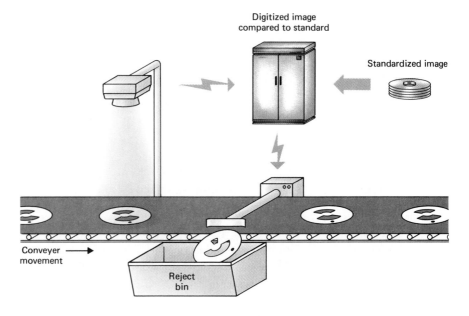

Hand-held Data Entry Devices

The typical *hand-held data entry device* would have a limited keyboard and some kind of storage capability for the data, usually random-access memory or magnetic cassette tape. After the data have been entered, the portable data entry device is linked with the host computer and data are *uploaded* (transmitted from the data entry device to host) for processing.

One hand-held data entry device combines a hand-held optical wand with a keyboard. Stock clerks in department stores routinely use such devices to collect and enter reorder data. As clerks visually check the inventory level, they identify the items that need to be restocked. First they scan the price tag with the wand, then enter the number to be ordered on the keyboard.

Another hand-held data entry device contains a pressure-sensitive writing pad that recognizes hand-printed alphanumeric characters.

This hand-held data entry device is designed for remote data collection in manufacturing environments. The shipping clerk is using a keyboard and a wand scanner to enter data to the device. At the end of the day, he transmits the data to the company's host computer via a telephone hookup.

5–4 Output Devices: Computers Communicate with Us

Output devices translate bits and bytes into a form we can understand. Terminals are both input and output devices. The monitors of terminals and workstations provide soft copy, or temporary output. The most common "output only" devices are discussed in this section. These include printers, plotters, desktop film recorders, screen-image projectors, voice-response units, and computer output microform.

Monitors

Alphanumeric and graphic output are displayed on the televisionlike monitor. The three primary attributes of monitors are the *size* of the display screen; the *resolution*, or detail, of the display; and whether the display is *monochrome* or in *color*. Display screens vary in size from 5 to 25 inches (diagonal dimension). Output on a monitor is *soft copy*; that is, it is temporary and is available to the end user only until another display is requested, as opposed to the permanent *hard-copy* output of printers.

Resolution   Monitors vary in their quality of output or **resolution.** Resolution refers to the number of addressable points on the screen—the number of points to which light can be directed under program control. These points are sometimes called **pixels**, short for *picture elements*. Each pixel can be assigned a shade of gray or a color. A low-resolution monitor has about 64,000 (320 by 200) addressable points. A monitor used primarily for computer graphics and computer-aided design may have more than 16 million addressable points. The high-resolution monitors project extremely clear images that almost look like photographs.

PC displays are in either **text mode** or **graphics mode**. Some word processing and spreadsheet programs operate in text mode, with 25 rows of up to 80 characters in length. All graphical user interfaces (GUIs) and

Memory Bits

INPUT DEVICES

- Keyboard (*alphanumeric keys*, *function keys*, *keypad*, *special-function keys*, and *cursor-control keys*)
- Point-and-draw devices (*mouse*, *joystick*, *track ball*, *digitizing tablet and pen or crosshair*, and *light pen*)
- OCR scanners (*hand-held label*, *stationary label*, *page*, *document*, *continuous-form*, and *optical mark*)
- Image scanners (*page* and *hand*)
- Magnetic-ink character recognition (MICR)
- Magnetic stripes and smart cards
- Speech-recognition systems (*speaker-dependent* and *speaker-independent*)
- Vision-input systems
- Hand-held data entry devices

Monitors are designed to accomplish a particular function. (Top left) An engineer at John Deere needs a large high-resolution monitor for computer-aided design (CAD) applications and a smaller monochrome monitor for the display of text and graphic information. (Top right) This full-page color monitor can be tilted 90 degrees to enable both long and wide presentations. (Bottom left) Some notebook PCs are equipped with flat-panel color monitors. (Bottom right) This shopper is interacting with a touch screen monitor by simply touching the desired menu item. The shopper can request a printed recipe, a display of nutritional content, and even an actual video of food preparation.

draw and design programs operate in graphics mode. The trend in software development is toward the exclusive use of the graphics mode, even in word processing and spreadsheet software.

Monochrome Monitors Monitors are either monochrome or color. Monochrome monitors display images in a single color, usually white, green, blue, red, or amber. A monochrome monitor can, however, display shades of its one color. The industry uses the term **gray scales** to refer to the number of shades of a color that can be shown on a monochrome monitor's screen.

Color Monitors Color monitors add another dimension to the display. Their use of colors can focus attention on different aspects of the output.

For example, an engineer designing pipelines for an oil refinery can use colors to highlight such things as the direction and type of fluid flow, the size of the pipes, and so on.

Most color monitors mix red, green, and blue to achieve a spectrum of colors, and are called **RGB monitors**. Several color video display standards have evolved since the introduction of the IBM PC in 1981. Each is implemented by installing an add-on board and connecting it to the appropriate monitor. The four most popular monitors are listed below.

- CGA. The initial color graphics adapter standard was low-resolution (320 by 200 pixels). CGA monitors do an adequate job of presenting graphics, but their text mode displays are hard on the eyes. During the era of CGA, higher-resolution monochrome monitors (720 by 350) were preferred for text mode displays.
- EGA. The enhanced graphics adapter provided higher resolution (640 by 350), greater variety in the selection of colors (from 4 to 16), and a substantially improved presentation of text. The EGA monitor started the era of the all-purpose color monitor.
- VGA. The video graphics array standard provides a slightly improved resolution to 640 by 480 and uses up to 256 colors. (The original standard called for 16 colors, but vendors have enhanced this specification to 256.)
- Super VGA. The Super VGA provides resolutions from 800 by 600 to 1280 by 1024.

All four—CGA, EGA, VGA, and Super VGA—are in widespread use today. Add-on graphics boards and monitors are available that enable very high resolution; however, these can be more expensive than the PC.

Flat-panel Monitors   Some space-saving monitors are flat. Most **flat-panel monitors** are used in conjunction with laptop PCs. Flat-panel monitors use three basic types of technology: *LCD* (liquid crystal display), the technology commonly used in digital wristwatches; *gas plasma*; and *EL* (electroluminescent). Each has its advantages. For example, LCD displays use relatively little power and EL displays provide a wider viewing angle. Up until the late 1980s all flat-panel monitors were monochrome. With the recent introduction of color LCD monitors, portable-PC buyers now have a choice.

Printers

Printers produce hard-copy output, such as management reports, memos, payroll checks, and program listings. Generally classified as **serial printers**, **line printers**, or **page printers,** printers are rated by their print speed. Print speeds are measured in *characters per second* (*cps*) for serial printers, in *lines per minute* (*lpm*) for line printers, and in *pages per minute* (*ppm*) for page printers. The print-speed ranges for the three types of printers are 40–450 cps, 1000–5000 lpm, and 4–800 ppm. The maximum speed for PC page printers is about 22 ppm.

Printers are further categorized as *impact* or *nonimpact*. An impact printer uses some type of hammer or hammers to hit the ribbon and the paper, much as a typewriter does. Nonimpact printers use chemicals, lasers, and heat to form the images on the paper. All page printers are nonimpact printers. Only nonimpact printers can achieve print speeds in excess of 5000 lpm.

Serial Printers Impact serial printers rely on *dot-matrix* and *daisy-wheel* technology. Nonimpact serial printers employ *ink-jet* and *thermal* technology. Regardless of the technology, the images are formed *one character at a time* as the print head moves across the paper. Virtually all serial printers are *bidirectional*; that is, they print whether the print head is moving left to right or right to left.

Most serial printers can accommodate both *single-sheet paper* and *continuous-form paper*, sometimes called fan-fold paper. If your output is mostly single sheet (for example, letters and envelopes), you may need to purchase an *automatic sheet feeder*. The *tractor-feed* that handles fan-fold paper is standard with most serial printers.

The impact dot-matrix printer. The **impact dot-matrix printer** arranges printed dots to form characters and all kinds of images in much the same way as lights display time and temperature on bank signs. One or several vertical columns of small print hammers, referred to as *pins*, are contained in a rectangular print head. The hammers are activated independently to form a dotted character image as the print head moves horizontally across the paper. The characters in Figure 5–6 are formed by a nine-pin

FIGURE 5–6 Dot-Matrix-Printer Character Formation
Each character is formed in a 7 x 5 matrix as the nine-pin print head moves across the paper. The two bottom pins are used for lowercase letters that extend below the line (for example, g and p).

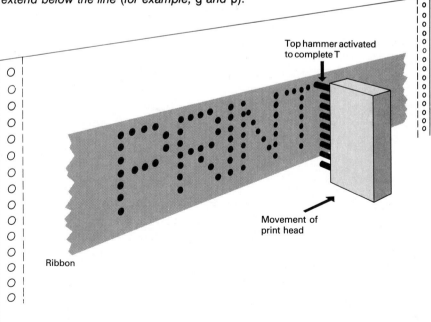

Top hammer activated
to complete T

Movement of
print head

Ribbon

print head within a matrix that is seven dots high and five dots wide (7 × 5). The number of dots within the matrix varies from one printer to the next.

The quality of the printed output is directly proportional to the density of the dots in the matrix. The 18-pin and 24-pin dot-matrix printers form characters that appear solid, and they can be used for business letters as well as for routine data processing output. Figure 5–7 illustrates how the dots can be overlapped with an 18-pin print head to create a *near-letter-quality* (NLQ) appearance. These printers are called *dual-mode* because of their dual-function capabilities (draft and NLQ).

Dot-matrix printers are further categorized as *monochrome* and *color*. The monochrome printer prints in the color of the ribbon, usually black. Color dot-matrix printers can select and print any of the colors on a multicolored ribbon (usually bands of black, yellow, red, and blue), or the printer can mix these colors via multiple passes and overstrikes to create the appearance of other colors in the rainbow. As you might imagine, you have to wait a little longer for a color graph than you would for a monochrome graph.

Dot-matrix printers are more flexible than serial printers of fully formed characters (printers that use an embossed rendering of a character to reproduce the image on paper). Depending on the model, dot-matrix printers can print a variety of sizes and types of characters (even old English and script characters), graphics, and bar codes.

Features common to most dot-matrix printers include boldface, underline, subscript and superscript, and compressed print (narrower letters). Optional features include proportional spacing (using more or less space, depending on the width of the character) and italics.

Small businesses need the flexibility of impact dot-matrix printers (foreground). This man can adjust the feed mechanism on the printer to accommodate a variety of print jobs, from mailing labels to 15-inch–wide spreadsheets.

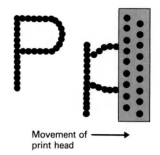

Movement of ——→
print head

FIGURE 5–7   Near-Letter-Quality Dot-Matrix Character Formation
The 18-pin print head permits dots to overlap to increase the density and, therefore, the quality of the image.

The daisy-wheel printer.   The **daisy-wheel printer** produces *letter-qual-ity (LQ)* output for word processing applications. An interchangeable daisy wheel containing a set of fully formed characters spins to the desired character. A print hammer strikes the character embossed on the print wheel to form the image on the paper. Although daisy-wheel printers have the highest quality text output of serial printers, they are the slowest and cannot produce graphic output. These disadvantages and the emergence of high-quality dot-matrix printers have driven the once-popular daisy-wheel printer from the market during the past few years. However, they are still found in the office.

The ink-jet printer.   Monochrome and color **ink-jet printers** employ several independently controlled injection chambers to squirt ink droplets on the paper. The droplets, which dry instantly as dots, form the images. The big advantage that nonimpact ink-jet printers have over impact dot-matrix printers is the quality of the output, especially color output. Sales of color ink-jet printers are expected to increase substantially as users, accustomed to color output on their video monitors, come to want hard-copy output in color.

The thermal printer.   The **thermal printer** is an alternative to the other serial printers. Heat elements produce dot-matrix images on heat-sensitive paper. The major disadvantage is the cost of the heat-sensitive paper. The advantages include compact size, limited noise, and low purchase price.

Line Printers   Line printers are impact printers that print *one line at a time*. Line printers are used primarily in the mini/mainframe processing environments. The most popular types of line printers are the band printer, chain printer, and matrix line printer.

Band and chain printers.   Both band and chain printers have a print hammer for each character position in the line of print (usually 132). On a band printer, several similar sets of fully formed characters are embossed on a horizontal band that is continuously moving in front of the print hammers. On a chain printer, the characters are embossed on each link of the print chain. With both types, the paper is momentarily stopped and, as the desired character passes over a given column, the hammer activates, pressing the ribbon against the paper to form the image.

Band and chain printers are capable of printing on continuous-feed paper as well as on cards and on documents of varying sizes (even mailing labels). Interchangeable bands and chains make it easy for operators to change the style of print (typeface).

The matrix line printer.   Matrix line printers print one line of *dots* at a time. Needlelike hammers are lined up across the width of the paper. Like serial matrix printers, the characters are formed in rectangular dot configurations as the paper passes the line of print hammers. Matrix printers are much more flexible than band printers, and they can perform the same types of print operations as serial matrix printers (see above), including graphic output and machine-readable bar codes.

This line printer (left) uses 132 print hammers in conjunction with an operator-changeable steel band to achieve print speeds of 1000 lines per minute. To load the continuous-feed paper, an acoustical enclosure is raised (right), and the "gate" containing the band and ribbon is swung open.

Page Printers   Page printers are of the nonimpact type and use a variety of technologies to achieve high-speed hard-copy output by printing *a page at a time*. Most page printers employ laser technology; however, other technologies are used: ink-jet, thermal-transfer, LED (light-emitting diode), and LCS (liquid crystal shutter). The majority of page printers print shades of gray; however, color page printers are becoming increasingly popular as their price continues to drop.

Page printers have the capability of printing graphs and charts and offer considerable flexibility in the size and style of print. They can also print in portrait or landscape format. **Portrait** and **landscape** refer to the orientation of the print on the page. Portrait format is like the page on this book—the lines run parallel to the shorter side of the page. In contrast, landscape output runs parallel to the longer side of the page. Landscape is frequently the orientation of choice for spreadsheet outputs with many columns.

Desktop page printers.   Until the mid-1980s, virtually all printers configured with microcomputers were serial printers. Now economically priced desktop page printers are becoming the standard for office microcomputer systems. These printers, capable of print speeds up to 22 pages per minute, have redefined the hard-copy output potential of micros. Automatic sheet feeders, which hold from 100 to 200 blank pages, are standard equipment on desktop page printers.

Desktop page printers are capable of producing *near-typeset-quality* (*NTQ*) text and graphics. The operation of a laser-based page printer is

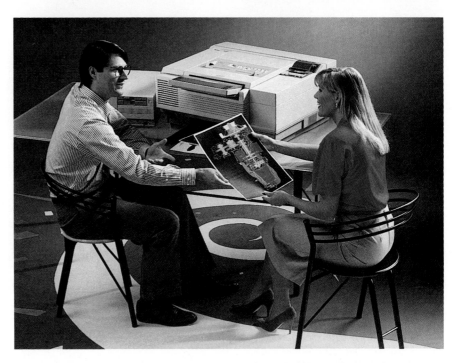

This 300-dpi color page printer employs ink-jet technology. Color printing is more time-consuming than monochrome printing. Printing a high-resolution graphic image on this printer takes about eight minutes per page.

illustrated in Figure 5–8. The resolution (quality of output) of the typical desktop page printer is *300 dpi* (dots per inch). High-end desktop page printers, which are sometimes called *desktop typesetters*, are capable of 1000 dpi. The dpi qualifier refers to the number of dots that can be printed per linear inch, horizontally or vertically. That is, a 300-dpi printer is capable of printing 90,000 (300 times 300) dots per square inch.

Commercial typesetting quality is a minimum of 1200 dpi and is usually in excess of 2000 dpi. Contrast the desktop page-printer output (300 dpi) in Figure 5–9 with the typeset print in this book. Desktop page printers are also quiet (an important consideration in an office setting), and they can combine type styles and sizes with graphics on the same page. The emergence of desktop page printers has fueled the explosion of *desktop publishing* (discussed in detail in Chapter 11, "Text and Image Processing Software").

Figure 5–9 contrasts the output of a dot-matrix printer, in both draft and near-letter-quality (NLQ) modes; a daisy-wheel printer (letter-quality); and a desktop page printer (near-typeset-quality).

Mainframe-based page printers. Operating at peak capacity during an 8-hour shift, the fastest page printer can produce almost a quarter of a million pages—that's 50 miles of output. This enormous output capability is normally directed to people outside an organization. For example, large banks use page printers to produce statements for checking and savings accounts; insurance companies print policies on page printers; and electric utility companies use them to bill their customers.

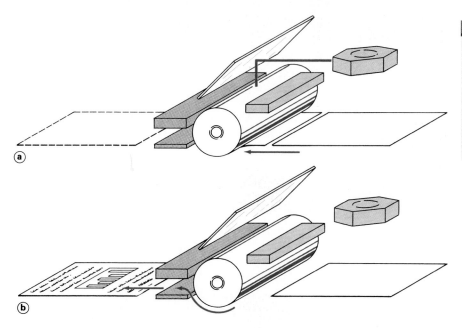

(a)

(b)

FIGURE 5–8   Desktop Page Printer Operation
The enclosure of a desktop page printer is removed to expose its inner workings. (a) Prior to printing, an electrostatic charge is applied to a drum. Then laser beam paths to the drum are altered by a spinning multisided mirror. The reflected beams selectively remove the electrostatic charge from the drum. (b) Toner is deposited on those portions of the drum that were affected by the laser beams. The drum is rotated and the toner is fused to the paper to create the image.

Very high-speed laser printers used in the mainframe environment have the capability of superimposing preprinted forms on continuous-feed stock paper. This eliminates a company's need to purchase expensive preprinted forms.

Printer summary.   Hundreds of printers are produced by dozens of manufacturers. There is a printer manufactured to meet the hard-copy output requirements of any individual or company, and almost any combination of features can be obtained. You can specify its size (some weigh less than a pound), speed, quality of output, color requirements, flexibility requirements, and even noise level. Micro printers sell for as little as a good pair of shoes or for as much as a small automobile.

FIGURE 5–9   Printer Output Comparison

```
This sentence was printed in draft mode on a 24-pin dot-matrix printer.

This sentence was printed in NLQ mode on a 24-pin dot-matrix printer.

This sentence was printed on a daisy-wheel printer.

This sentence was printed on a desktop page printer.
```

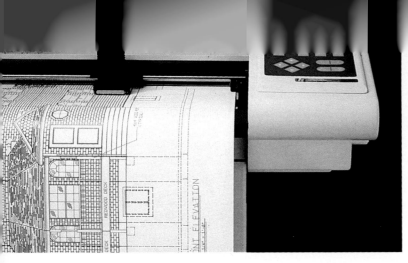

(Left) This drum pen plotter is capable of a mechanical resolution of 0.0005 inch; that is, the output is accurate to within five ten-thousandths of an inch. The plot is an architect's rendering of the front elevation for an office building. (Right) Flatbed pen plotters can draw the image on paper or directly on a blank acetate for presentations.

Plotters

Dot-matrix, ink-jet, thermal, and page printers are capable of producing page-size graphic output, but are limited in their ability to generate high-quality, perfectly proportioned graphic output. For example, on a blueprint the sides of a 12-foot-square room are exactly the same length. Architects, engineers, city planners, and others who routinely generate high-precision, hard-copy graphic output of widely varying sizes use the other hard-copy alternative—**pen plotters**.

The two basic types of pen plotters are the *drum plotter* and the *flatbed plotter*. Both have one or more pens that move over the paper under computer control to produce an image. Several pens are required to vary the width and color of the line, and the computer selects and manipulates them. On the drum plotter, the pens and the drum move concurrently in different axes to produce the image. Drum plotters are used to produce continuous output, such as plotting earthquake activity, or for long graphic output, such as the structural view of a skyscraper. On some flatbed plotters, the pen moves in both axes while the paper remains stationary. However, on most desktop plotters, both paper and pen move concurrently in much the same way as drum plotters.

Presentation Graphics: Desktop Film Recorders and Screen Image Projectors

Business people have found that sophisticated and colorful graphics add an aura of professionalism to any report or presentation. This demand for *presentation graphics* has created a need for corresponding output devices. Computer-generated graphic images can be re-created on paper and transparency acetates with printers and plotters. Graphic images also can be captured on 35-mm slides, or they can be displayed on a monitor or projected onto a large screen.

Screen image projectors can fill a room with information.

Desktop film recorders reproduce a high-resolution graphic image on 35-mm film in either black and white or color. Some models allow users to process and mount their own slides. Others require outside processing. **Screen image projectors** project the graphic image onto a large screen, similar to the way television programs are projected onto a large TV screen. Another type of screen image projector transfers the graphic image displayed on the monitor onto a large screen with the use of an ordinary overhead projector.

Voice-Response Units

If you have ever called directory assistance, you probably have heard something like: "The number is five-seven-five-six-one-three-one." You may have driven a car that advised you to "fasten your seat belt." These are examples of talking machines, output from voice-response units. There are two types of **voice-response units**: One uses a *reproduction* of a human voice and other sounds, and the other uses a **speech synthesizer**. Like monitors, voice-response units provide a temporary, soft-copy output.

The first type of voice-response unit selects output from user-recorded words, phrases, music, alarms, or anything you might record on audiotape, just as a printer would select characters. In these recorded voice-response units, the actual analog recordings of sounds are converted into digital data, then permanently stored on a memory chip. When output, a particular sound is converted back into analog before being routed to a speaker. These chips are mass-produced for specific applications, such as output for automatic teller machines, microwave ovens, smoke detectors, elevators, alarm clocks, automobile warning systems, video games, and vending machines, to mention only a few.

Speech synthesizers, which convert raw data into electronically produced speech, are more popular in the microcomputer environment.

To produce speech, these devices combine sounds resembling the *phonemes* (basic sound units) that make up speech. A speech synthesizer is capable of producing at least 64 unique sounds. The existing technology produces synthesized speech with only limited vocal inflections and phrasing, however.

Even with its limitations, the number of speech synthesizer applications is growing. For example, a person who is visually impaired can use the speech synthesizer to translate printed words into spoken words. In another application, speech synthesizers are used by people unable to communicate through speech. The person types the information and the speech synthesizer translates it into spoken words. Speech synthesizers have opened a new world to speech-impaired children who were once placed in institutions because they could not communicate verbally. Speech synthesizers are also used in domestic alarm systems and computer-based training. As the quality of the output improves, speech synthesizers will enjoy a broader base of applications. They are relatively inexpensive and are becoming increasingly popular with many personal computer owners.

Computer Output Microform

Computer output microform (COM) devices prepare microfiche that can be read on microform viewers. Microfiche is hard-copy output that becomes a permanent record able to be referenced over and over. Each COM device contains an image-to-film recorder and a duplicator for making multiple copies of a microfiche.

In the COM process (see Figure 5–10), the images (output) to be miniaturized are prepared, as if to be printed, on a computer system. This output is then sent to the COM device. Here the images are miniaturized for microform viewers.

In the miniaturization process, images are displayed on a small high-resolution video display. A camera exposes a segment of the microfilm for each display, thereby creating a grid pattern of images, or frames. The microfilm is then developed and cut into 4- by 6-inch sheets of microfiche, each containing up to 270 frames. The duplicator section makes multiple copies of the microfiche. Each sheet of microfiche is titled and indexed so the appropriate frame, or "page," can be retrieved quickly on a viewer.

This PC-based system can read novels, newspapers, or any printed matter to visually impaired people. An image scanner's output is automatically converted to computer signals which in turn are converted to full-word English speech using a speech synthesizer.

FIGURE 5–10 The Computer Output Microform (COM) Process
In the on-line COM process, data are routed directly from the computer to the COM system.

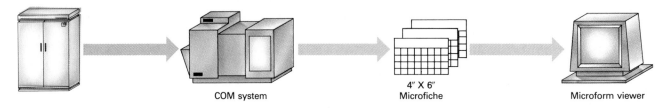

COM system

4″ X 6″
Microfiche

Microform viewer

COM is an alternative to an on-line computer-based system when up-to-the-minute information is not critical. COM is also used extensively instead of hard copy for archival storage (old income tax records, for example).

COM equipment can produce in minutes what may take hours to produce on a printer. But the real advantage of COM is the elimination of cumbersome volumes of printed output. Nevertheless, these advantages are overshadowed by the potential of systems that are integrated through computer network. As terminals and networks become commonplace, a trend will be to replace COM with integrated systems. Computer networks offer the added advantages of direct access to and immediate update of the data base.

5–5 Terminals: Input and Output

The Tube and the Telephone

General-purpose terminals enable interaction with a remote computer system in a wide variety of applications. The two most popular general-purpose terminals are the *video display terminal* (*VDT*) and the *telephone*. VDTs, or *terminals*, were first introduced in Chapter 1. The VDT is affectionately known as "the tube," short for **cathode-ray tube**. A VDT's primary input mechanism is usually a *keyboard*, and the output is usually displayed on a *monitor*. Terminals come in all shapes and sizes and have a variety of input/output capabilities.

The telephone's widespread availability is causing greater use of it as a terminal. You can enter alphanumeric data on the touch-tone keypad of a telephone (keyboard) or by speaking into the receiver (voice input). You would then receive computer-generated voice output. Salespeople use telephones as terminals for entering orders and inquiries about the availability of certain products into their company's mainframe computer.

Although the telephone, with its touch-tone keypad and computer-generated voice output, is the terminal with which we are most familiar, the VDT and the microcomputer remain the most commonly used general-purpose terminals. From our past discussions (Chapter 2, "Micros, Minis, Mainframes, and Supercomputers"), we know that a microcomputer can serve as a stand-alone computer or as a terminal linked to a mainframe.

Special-Function Terminals

The number and variety of special-function terminals is growing rapidly. Special-function terminals are designed for a specific application, such as convenience banking. You probably are familiar with the *automatic teller machine* (*ATM*) and its input/output capabilities (see Figure 5–11). A badge reader (magnetic stripe) and keypad enable input to the system. A monitor and printer (for printing transaction receipts) provide output. Some ATMs use voice response as a backup to the monitor to alert people when to perform certain actions (for example, take their receipts).

Another ubiquitous special-function terminal is the *point-of-sale* (*POS*) terminal. At a minimum, POS terminals in retail establishments

Memory Bits

OUTPUT DEVICES
- Monitors
  Described by size and resolution
  Display is:
  Text or graphics mode
  Monochrome or color
- Printers
  Serial (40–450 cps)
  • Impact
    Dot-matrix (color option)
    Daisy-wheel
  • Nonimpact
    Ink-jet (color option)
    Thermal
  Line (1000–5000 lpm)
  • Band and chain
  • Matrix
  Page (4–800 ppm)
  • Desktop (color option)
  • Mainframe-based
- Plotters
  Drum
  Flatbed
- Presentation graphics
  Desktop film recorder
  Screen image projector
- Voice-response units
  Recorded voice
  Speech synthesizer
- Computer output microform (COM)

Memory Bits

TERMINALS
- General-purpose
  Video display terminal (VDT)
  also, cathode-ray tube or the tube
  Telephone
- Special-function
  Automatic teller machine (ATM)
  Point-of-sale (POS) terminal

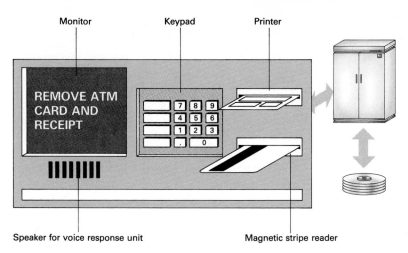

Monitor　　　　Keypad　　　　Printer

REMOVE ATM
CARD AND
RECEIPT

Speaker for voice response unit　　　　Magnetic stripe reader

**FIGURE 5–11　Terminals for Banking Customers:
Automatic Teller Machines**

*The widely used automatic teller machine (ATM) supports a variety of input/
output methods. The magnetic stripe on the ATM card contains identification
and security information that, when read, is sent to the bank's computer
system. The ATM responds with instructions via its monitor. The customer
enters an identification number and data via a keypad. In the figure, the
computer processes the customer's request, then provides instructions for the
customer via the monitor and verbally with a voice-response unit.*

have a keypad for input and at least one small monitor. Some have other
input devices, such as a badge reader for credit cards and a wand scanner
to read price and inventory data. Many grocery stores have POS terminals
with voice-response units that verbally confirm the price on each item.

*Terminals are being created to meet a variety of needs. Cashiers at fast-food
restaurants are coming out from behind the counter to greet customers. This
portable special-function terminal transmits orders directly to the kitchen via
the restaurant's computer system. An order for an entire baseball team can be
entered from the parking lot or the playground.*

Important Terms and Summary Outline

badge reader
bar code
cathode-ray tube
computer output
  microform (COM)
daisy-wheel printer
desktop film recorder
digitize
digitizer tablet and pen
flat-panel monitor
graphics mode
gray scales
image scanner
impact dot-matrix
  printer
ink-jet printer

joystick
landscape
light pen
line printer
magnetic-ink character
  recognition (MICR)
MICR inscriber
MICR reader-sorter
OCR scanner
optical character
  recognition (OCR)
page printer
pen plotter
pixel
portrait
resolution

RGB monitor
screen image projector
serial printer
smart card
source-data automation
speech-recognition
  system
speech synthesizer
text mode
thermal printer
track ball
turnaround document
vision-input system
voice-response unit
wand scanner

5–1 I/O DEVICES: OUR INTERFACE WITH THE COMPUTER. A variety of input/output peripheral devices provide the interface between us and the computer system.

5–2 TRADITIONAL INPUT DEVICES. All PCs and VDTs are configured with a keyboard. The QWERTY 101-key version is popular with PCs. Some keyboards are designed for specific applications. The mouse, which is now standard on most PCs, is one of several devices that move the graphics cursor to point and draw. The **joystick**, **track ball**, **digitizer tablet and pen**, and **light pen** are also input devices that move the graphics cursor.

5–3 SOURCE-DATA AUTOMATION: GETTING CLOSER TO THE ACTION. The trend in data entry has been toward **source-data automation**, where the need for the key entry transcription of data is eliminated altogether.

Optical character recognition (OCR) reduces the need for manual data entry by encoding certain data in machine-readable format. **OCR scanners** (hand-held label or **wand**, stationary label, page, document, continuous-form, and optical mark) recognize printed characters and certain coded symbols, such as **bar codes**. OCR scanners are used for original source-data collection and with **turnaround documents**.

An **image scanner** enables **digitized** images of photos, drawings, and other images to be stored on magnetic disk. **Magnetic-ink character recognition (MICR)** devices, which are used almost exclusively in banking, are similar to OCR scanners in function but are faster and more accurate.

Magnetic stripes and **smart cards** provide input to **badge readers**. **Speech-recognition systems** can be used to enter limited kinds and quantities of data. They do this by comparing digitized representations of words to similarly formed templates in the computer's electronic dictionary. **Vision-input systems** are best suited for tasks that involve only a few images. Hand-held data entry devices may or may not be linked to the central computer during data collection activities.

5–4 OUTPUT DEVICES: COMPUTERS COMMUNICATE WITH US. Output devices translate data stored in binary into a form that can be interpreted by the end user. A soft copy of alphanumeric and graphic output is displayed on a monitor. The three attributes of monitors are size (diagonal dimension 5 to 25 inches), color (monochrome or color), and **resolution**. A monochrome monitor can display shades of one color, called **gray scales**. A monitor's resolution is determined by the number of **pixels** it has. Space-saving monochrome and color **flat-panel monitors** use LCD, gas plasma, and EL technologies.

Several **RGB monitor** standards have evolved since the introduction of the IBM PC in 1981: CGA, EGA, VGA, and super VGA. PC displays are in either **text mode** or **graphics mode**.

Printers prepare hard-copy output at speeds of 40 characters per second to 800 pages per minute. **Serial printers** are both impact (**impact dot-matrix** and **daisy-wheel**) and nonimpact (**ink-jet** and **thermal**). **Line printers** are impact only, and **page printers** are nonimpact only. The emergence of desktop page printers has fueled the explosion of desktop publishing. Page printers can print in **portrait** and **landscape**.

Pen plotters (drum and flatbed) convert stored data into high-precision hard-copy graphs, charts, and line drawings. **Desktop film recorders** reproduce a high-resolution graphic image on 35-mm film in either black and white or color. **Screen image projectors** project the graphic image onto a large screen. **Voice-response units** provide recorded or synthesized voice output (via **speech synthesizers**).

Computer output microform (COM) devices prepare microfiche as a space- and time-saving alternative to printed output.

5–5 TERMINALS: INPUT AND OUTPUT. General-purpose terminals, such as the VDT and telephone, enable interaction with a remote computer system. The VDT is often called "the tube," short for **cathode-ray tube**. Terminals come in all shapes and sizes and have a variety of input/output capabilities.

A variety of special-function terminals, such as automatic teller machines and point-of-sale terminals, are designed for a specific application.

 Review Exercises

Concepts

1. Which output device generates graphs with the greatest precision, a pen plotter or a dot-matrix printer?
2. What is meant when someone says that speech-recognition devices are "speaker-dependent"?
3. List devices, other than key-driven, that are used to input data into a computer system.
4. Name an impact printer that prints fully formed characters.
5. What is the relationship between a joystick and a graphics cursor?
6. What output device reproduces high-resolution graphic images on 35-mm film?
7. Name a device other than a monitor that produces soft-copy output.

8. Which kind of printer can produce near-typeset-quality output?

9. Which type of OCR scanner is designed to read documents of varying sizes?

10. What are the two modes of IBM-PC display?

11. List the following in order of increasing resolution: VGA, CGA, and EGA.

12. What is a turnaround document? Give two examples.

13. Identify all input and output methods used by an automatic teller machine.

14. What is a smart card?

15. Give two applications for bar codes.

16. Why do banks use MICR rather than OCR for data entry?

Discussion

17. Describe the input/output characteristics of a terminal that would be used by engineers for computer-aided design.

18. Some department stores use hand-held label scanners and others use stationary label scanners to interpret the bar codes printed on the price tags of merchandise. What advantages does one scanner have over the other?

19. What input/output capabilities are available at your college?

20. Compare today's vision-input systems with those portrayed in such films as *2001* and *2010*. Do you believe we will have a comparable vision technology by the year 2001?

Problem Solving

21. The four PCs at a police precinct are networked and currently share a 100-cps impact dot-matrix printer. The captain has budgeted enough money to purchase one desktop page printer (8 ppm) or two more 100-cps dot-matrix printers. Which option would you suggest the precinct choose and why?

22. Twenty-five secretaries at a large law firm spend 50% of each day working with PCs, doing primarily word processing. All the secretaries know and use the conventional QWERTY keyboard; however, the office manager is considering a switch to the Dvorak keyboard. How long will it take to break even if:

- The secretaries make an average of $25,000 a year?
- Each secretary must spend four hours each working day for two months to learn the use of the new keyboard. The cost of administering the two-month keyboarding course is $20,000?
- The QWERTY keyboards must be replaced with Dvorak keyboards at a cost of $150 each?
- Use of the Dvorak keyboard is expected to increase productivity by 75% once the secretaries complete the course?

23. In the next generation of credit cards, the familiar magnetic stripe probably will be replaced by embedded microprocessors. Each will have limited processing capability. Suggest applications for this capability.

5–1 **a.** Input devices translate data into a form that can be interpreted by a computer. (T̂/F)

b. The primary function of I/O peripherals is to facilitate computer-to-computer data transmission. (T/F̂)

5–2 **a.** Only VDT keyboards have function keys. (T/F̂)

b. Which of the following is not a point-and-draw device: (a) joystick, (b̂) document scanner, or (c) light pen?

5–3 **a.** Optical character recognition is a means of source-data automation. (T̂/F)

b. In speech recognition, words are ‾digitized‾ and matched against
✗ similarly formed ‾templates‾ in the computer's electronic dictionary.

✗ **c.** Vision-input systems are best suited to generalized tasks in which a wide variety of images will be encountered. (T/F̂)

5–4 **a.** The quality of output on a monitor is determined by its ‾resolution‾.

b. Most flat-panel monitors are used in conjunction with desktop PCs. (T/F̂)

c. The Universal Product Code (UPC) was originally used by which industry: (â) supermarket, (b) hardware, or (c) mail-order merchandising?

d. Ink-jet printers are classified as nonimpact printers. (T̂/F)

e. Dot-matrix printing technology is available in serial and line printers. (T̂/F)

f. What type of printers are becoming the standard for office microcomputer systems: (â) desktop page printers, (b) daisy-wheel printers, or (c) thermal printers?

✗ **g.** ‾Synthesizers‾ (speech) convert raw data into electronically produced speech.

✗ **5–5** The terminal that is familiar to most people is the: (a) VDT, (b̂) telephone, or (c) graphics workstation?

Self-test answers. **5–1 (a)** T; **(b)** F. **5–2 (a)** F; **(b)** b. **5–3 (a)** T; **(b)** digitized, templates; **(c)** F. **5–4 (a)** resolution; **(b)** F; **(c)** a; **(d)** T; **(e)** T; **(f)** a; **(g)** Speech synthesizers. **5–5** b.

6 ▶

Data Storage and Organization

STUDENT LEARNING OBJECTIVES

▶ To distinguish between primary and secondary storage.

▶ To describe and illustrate the relationships between the levels of the hierarchy of data organization.

▶ To describe how data are stored, retrieved, and manipulated in computer systems.

▶ To demonstrate an understanding of the principles and use of sequential processing and random processing.

▶ To distinguish between secondary storage devices and secondary storage media.

▶ To describe the principles of operation, methods of data storage, and use of magnetic tape and disk drives.

▶ To discuss the applications and use of optical laser disk storage.

CHAPTER OUTLINE

6–1 Secondary Storage: Permanent Data Storage

The most common secondary storage devices are the magnetic disk drive and magnetic tape drive. However, for certain applications, optical laser disk storage technology (shown here) is emerging as a viable alternative to disk and tape storage.

Within a computer system, programs and data are stored in *primary storage* and in *secondary storage* (see Figure 6–1). Programs and data are stored *permanently* for periodic retrieval in **secondary storage**. Programs and data are retrieved from secondary storage and stored *temporarily* in high-speed primary storage, also called random-access memory, or RAM, for processing. RAM is discussed in detail in Chapter 4, "Inside the Computer."

"Why two types of storage?" you might ask. Remember from Chapter 4 that most primary storage is semiconductor memory, and the data are lost when the electricity is interrupted. Primary storage is also expensive and has a limited capacity. The RAM capacity of a large mainframe computer would not come close to meeting the data and program storage needs of even a small company. Secondary storage, however, is relatively inexpensive and has an enormous capacity.

Over the years, manufacturers have developed a variety of devices and media for the permanent storage of data and programs. *Paper tape*, *punched cards*, the *data cell*, and a variety of others have become obsolete. Today the various types of **magnetic disk drives** and their respective storage media are the state of the art for permanent storage of programs and data. **Magnetic tape drives** complement magnetic disk storage by providing inexpensive *backup* capability and *archival* storage. We will discuss these as well as the potential and applications of **optical laser disk**

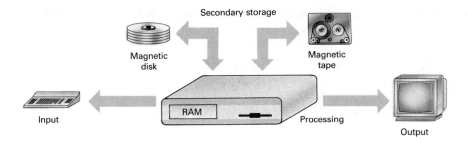

FIGURE 6–1   Primary and Secondary Storage
Programs and data are stored permanently in secondary storage and temporarily in primary storage.

technology, a rapidly emerging alternative to magnetic disk and magnetic tape storage. The terminology, principles, operation, and trade-offs of these secondary storage devices are covered in the context of data organization.

6–2 The Hierarchy of Data Organization: Bits to Data Bases

The six levels of the *hierarchy of data organization* are illustrated in Figure 6–2. They are *bit, character, field, record, file,* and *data base.* You are already familiar with several levels of the hierarchy. Bits and characters are discussed in some detail in Chapter 4, "Inside the Computer." Records and files are introduced in Chapter 1, "The World of Computers."

Each information system has a hierarchy of data organization, and each succeeding level in the hierarchy is the result of combining the elements of the preceding level (see Figure 6–2). Data are logically combined in this fashion until a data base is achieved. Bits—the first level—

FIGURE 6–2   The Hierarchy of Data Organization

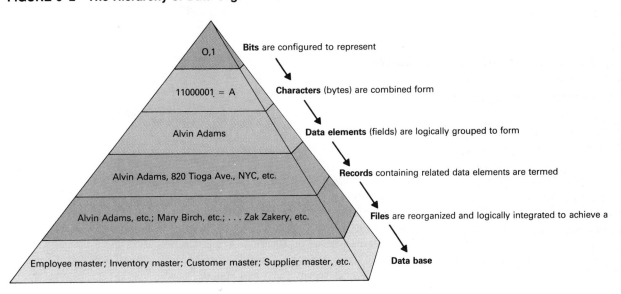

are handled automatically, without action on the part of either the programmer or the end user. The other five levels are important design considerations for any information processing activity. The following paragraphs explain each level of the hierarchy and how it relates to the succeeding level.

Bits and Characters

A *character* is represented by a group of *bits* that are configured according to an encoding system, such as ASCII or EBCDIC. Whereas the bit is the basic unit of primary and secondary storage, the character is the basic unit for human perception. When we enter a program instruction on a terminal, each character is automatically encoded into a bit configuration. The bit configurations are decoded on output so we can read and understand the output. In terms of data storage, a character is usually the same as a *byte*. (See Chapter 4 for more on bits, bytes, and encoding systems.)

Fields

The **field** is the lowest level *logical* unit in the data hierarchy. For example, a single character (such as A) has little meaning out of context. But when characters are combined to form a name (for example, *Alicia* or *Alvin*), they form a logical unit. A field is best described by example: social security number, first name, street address, marital status. These are all fields.

The Associates' commercial-paper trading room in Dallas, Texas, is a source of thousands of pieces of data. An information system continually updates a data base so that brokers in offices all over the country have access to up-to-the-minute quotations.

An address is not one, but four fields: street address, city, state, and ZIP code. If we treated the entire address as one field, it would be cumbersome to print because the street address is normally placed on a separate line from the city, state, and ZIP code. Because name-and-address files are often sorted by ZIP code, it is also a good idea to store the ZIP code as a separate field.

When it is stored in secondary storage, a field is allocated a certain number of character positions. The number of these positions is called the *field length*. The field length of a telephone area code is 3. The field length of a telephone number is 7.

Whereas the field is the general (or generic) reference, the specific content of a field is called the **data item**. For example, a social security number is a field, but the actual number, *445487279*, is a data item. A street address is a field, but *1701 El Camino* and *134 East Himes Street* are data items.

Records

A *record* is a description of an event (a sale, a hotel reservation) or an item (for example, a customer, a part). Related fields describing an event or item are logically grouped to form a record. For example, Figure 6–3 contains a partial list of fields for a typical employee record. It also shows the data items for an *occurrence* of a particular employee record (Alvin E. Smith): "Department," "Sex," and "Marital status" are *coded* for ease of data entry and to save storage space.

In general, the record is the lowest level logical unit that can be accessed from a file. For instance, if the personnel manager needs to know only the marital status of Alvin E. Smith, he will have to retrieve Smith's entire record from secondary storage and transmit it to primary storage for processing.

Files

A **file** is a collection of related records. The employee file contains a record for each employee. An inventory file contains a record for each inventory item. The accounts receivable file contains a record for each customer. The term *file* is also used to refer to a named area on a secondary storage device that contains a *program*, *textual material* (such as a letter), or even an *image*.

Data Bases

The **data base** is the data resource for every computer-based information system. In essence, a data base is a collection of files that are in some way logically related to one another. In a data base, the data are integrated and related so that data redundancy is minimized. For example, if records are kept in a traditional file environment and an employee moves, his or her address must be changed in all files that maintain address data. In a data base, employee address data are stored only once and are made available to all departments. Therefore, only one update is needed.

Database management system software, which is discussed in Chapter 9, "System Software and Platforms," has enabled many organizations to move from traditional file organization to data base organization, thereby enjoying the benefits of a higher level of data management sophistication.

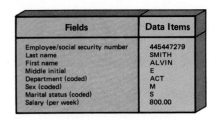

FIGURE 6–3 A Portion of an Employee Record
The fields listed are commonly found in employee records. Data items appear next to each field.

 6–3 Traditional Approaches to Data Manipulation and Retrieval

The Flat File

Data management encompasses the storage, retrieval, and manipulation of data. In the remainder of this chapter we will discuss the concepts, methods, and storage devices involved in traditional file-oriented computer-based data management. The data base approach to data management, which uses disk storage, is covered in Chapter 9.

Your present or future employer will probably use both the traditional file-oriented and the data base approaches to data management. Many existing information systems were designed using traditional approaches to data management, but the trend now is to use the data base approach to develop new information systems.

In traditional, or **flat file**, processing, files are sorted, merged, and processed by a **key field**. For example, in a payroll file the key might be "social security number," and in an inventory file the key might be "part number."

Memory Bits

HIERARCHY OF DATA ORGANIZATION

- Bit
- Character (byte)
- Field
- Record
- File
- Data base

For Shearson Lehman Hutton Inc., it was a sobering realization. They were paying more than $1 million to use their PCs to access on-line financial information services that charge $20 to $400 an hour. Clearly, they needed the data. An investment banker's recommendations are only as good as the data backing up those recommendations. But wasn't there a cheaper way to gather it? For Shearson Lehman and an increasing number of companies, research centers, universities, and libraries, CD-ROM publishing was the answer.

CD-ROM publishing refers to the collection and distribution of large financial, scientific, technical, legal, medical, and bibliographic data bases, as well as reference works, catalogs, and manuals, on CD-ROM disks. Shearson Lehman's solution was to order a $30,000 subscription to One Source, a CD-ROM–based financial, business, and reference data base from Lotus Development Corporation, which is updated weekly.

INFORMATION SERVICE OFFERINGS

One Source is just one of the more than 4000 data bases offered on CD-ROM disks, often by the same information services that operate the on-line data bases. Dialog Information Services, Inc., for example, offers many of its 400 data bases both on-line and on CD-ROM. Other offerings include regularly updated data bases on engineering developments, cancer research, and environmental issues surrounding pollution and hazardous wastes. Some of the data bases contain

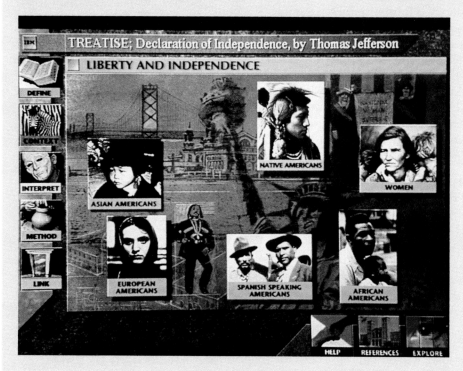

THE NEXT DIMENSION IN PUBLISHING Traditional publishing (books) is sequential—one page after another. Publishing via CD-ROM lets the reader choose what comes next. In the example, the viewer can explore the Declaration of Independence's impact on any of six minority groups.

Sequential and Direct Access: New Terms for Old Concepts

An important consideration in both the design of an information system and the purchase of a computer system is the way that data are accessed. Magnetic tape can be used for *sequential access* only. Magnetic disks have *random-*, or *direct-access*, capabilities as well as sequential-access capa-

bibliographic citations only; others contain the full text of articles, sometimes including all illustrations.

And at many public libraries, the dog-eared *Reader's Guide to Periodical Literature* has been replaced by workstations that sport a CD-ROM drive, an ink-jet printer, and InfoTrac, a service from Information Access Company. InfoTrac is a collection of CD-ROM–based indexes for more than 1100 popular magazines and journals; about 800 business, management, and trade journals; and such leading newspapers as *The New York Times* and *The Wall Street Journal*. Other InfoTrac CD-ROM disks let users retrieve financial and investment data.

CD-ROM–based data bases are also available for specific industries. One example is Sabrevision, a national data base for travel agencies that is updated quarterly.

GOVERNMENT DATA ON CD-ROM

CD-ROM publishing is proving invaluable to the U.S. government, which collects, maintains, and distributes the world's largest storehouse of information. Consider just one example from the U.S. Geological Survey's Geological Division, which maintains vast data bases of satellite images of the earth for use by its scientists and by the public. The division once stored the data base on 125 MB tapes; the price to the public was $2000 each. The CD equivalent offers 680 MB of data for only $32 per disk.

Other government data available on CD-ROM disks include complete demographic data (from the U.S. Bureau of the Census); high-resolution displays of sonar-scanned oceanographic data (the product of a cooperative project between the U.S. Geological Survey, NOAA, and NASA); as well as CD-ROM disks on aquaculture, the Agent Orange defoliant, and acid rain (from the National Agricultural Library). And, over at the Library of Congress, the American Memory project is developing CD-ROM disks of sound recordings, book ex-

cerpts, manuscripts, photographs, and other primary source material that is organized about specific themes.

MANUALS, CATALOGS, AND SOFTWARE

The federal government is also turning to CD-ROM publishing as a cost-effective way to publish the thousands of manuals, specifications, and guidelines the government issues for its own use. An 800-page manual from the Army Corps of Engineers, for example, costs more than $6 to print on paper, weighs 4 pounds, and costs $6 to mail. The same information can be put on one CD-ROM disk for a fraction of the cost. As a bonus, the disk can be searched more quickly than a paper document.

Shop manuals and parts catalogs also lend themselves to CD-ROM publishing. The catalog from Intel Corporation, the major semiconductor manufacturer, delivers some 25,000 pages of technical data, wiring diagrams, schematics, and photographs to 300,000 design engineers worldwide. The massive amount of data can be stored on just two CD-ROM disks. Automobile and truck manufacturers are also providing parts catalogs to dealers on CD-ROM; the dealers find it faster and easier than going on-line to access a central mainframe.

REFERENCE WORKS

A representative title here is the *New Grolier Electronic Encyclopedia,* which packs all 21 volumes of *Grolier's Academic American Encyclopedia* onto a single CD-ROM disk. Like other CD-ROM titles, the encyclopedia includes audio excerpts, such as excerpts from famous speeches, musical passages, and the sounds of animals and birds. Many of these titles qualify as *multimedia*—computer applications that combine text, computer graphics, animation, and sound with full-motion video. In fact, many experts feel multimedia will be one of the decade's most exciting applications for CD-ROM technology.

---

bilities. You are quite familiar with these concepts, but you may not realize it. Operationally, the magnetic tape is the same as the one in home and automobile tape decks. The magnetic disk can be compared to a phonograph record.

Suppose you have the Beatles' classic record album *Sgt. Pepper's Lonely Hearts Club Band.* The first four songs on this album are: (1) "Sgt.

Pepper's Lonely Hearts Club Band," (2) "With a Little Help from My Friends," (3) "Lucy in the Sky with Diamonds," and (4) "Getting Better." Now suppose you also have this Beatles album on a tape cassette. To play the third song on the cassette, "Lucy in the Sky with Diamonds," you would have to wind the tape forward and search for it sequentially. To play "Lucy in the Sky with Diamonds" on the phonograph record, all you would have to do is move the needle directly to the track containing the third song. This simple analogy demonstrates the two fundamental methods of storing and accessing data—*sequential* and *random*.

Magnetic disk drives are secondary storage devices that provide a computer system with **random-** *and* **sequential-processing** capabilities. In random processing, the desired programs and data are accessed *directly* from the storage medium. In sequential processing, the computer system must search the storage medium to find the desired programs or data. Magnetic tapes have only sequential-processing capabilities. Both methods and their storage media are discussed in detail in the pages that follow. First, sequential processing is addressed with magnetic tape storage. Then random processing is covered with magnetic-disk storage. In each case, the presentation of the data management technique is prefaced by a discussion of applicable storage technology (magnetic tape for sequential processing and magnetic disk for random processing).

6–4 Magnetic Tape: Ribbons of Data

During the 1950s and 1960s, the foundation of many information systems was *sequential processing*. Today, however, magnetic tape storage is used primarily as a backup medium for magnetic disk storage. Relatively few applications involve sequential processing. A magnetic tape medium, such as the **magnetic tape reel** or the **magnetic tape cartridge**, can be loaded conveniently to a tape drive (the hardware device) for processing. Once loaded to a tape drive, the magnetic tape is said to be **on-line**; that is, the data and programs on the tape are accessible to the computer system. When processing is complete, the tape is removed for **off-line** storage (that is, not accessible to the computer system) until it is needed again for processing.

Hardware and Storage Media

The mechanical operation of a magnetic tape drive is similar to that of a reel-to-reel or audiocassette tape deck. The tape, a thin polyester ribbon coated with a magnetic material on one side, passes under a **read/write head**, and the data are either (1) read and transmitted to primary storage or (2) transmitted from primary storage and written to the tape. The $\frac{1}{2}$-inch tape reel has been around since the mid-1950s. This form of "mag" tape was the main type of secondary storage medium until the advent of economically priced and reliable magnetic disk storage (the mid-1960s). Thousands of reel-to-reel mag tape drives are still in service today, primarily because they remain the standard for the physical distribution of mainframe software and data. For example, in the mainframe environment, vendors distribute their software via mag tape reels, just as micro vendors distribute theirs via diskettes. For this reason, most mainframe installations will have one or two mag tape reel drives. For routine processing and backup, tape reels are being replaced by the more convenient, less costly, and space-saving tape cartridges.

Two types of tape cartridges are in common use, the $\frac{1}{4}$-*inch* and the $\frac{1}{2}$-*inch* versions. Both are self-contained and are inserted into and removed from the tape drive in much the same way you would load or remove a videotape from a VCR. Like the videotape, the supply and the take-up reels for the $\frac{1}{4}$-inch cartridges are encased in a plastic shell. However, the shell for the $\frac{1}{2}$-inch tape cartridge contains only the supply reel. The take-up reel is permanently installed in the tape drive unit.

The mag tape reel and the $\frac{1}{2}$-inch tape cartridge are used exclusively in the mini, mainframe, and supercomputer environments. The $\frac{1}{4}$-inch cartridges, popular with micros and minis, are being used more frequently in the mainframe environment.

A tape drive is rated by the density at which the data can be stored on a magnetic tape as well as by the speed of the tape as it passes under the read/write head. Combined, these determine the **transfer rate**, or the number of characters per second that can be transmitted to primary storage. **Tape density** is measured in **bytes per inch (bpi)**, or the number of bytes (characters) that can be stored per linear inch of tape. Tape density varies from 800 to 77,000 bpi. A 77,000 bpi tape traveling under the read/write head at 80 inches per second is capable of a transfer rate of 6,160,000 bytes per second (77,000 bpi times 80 inches per second equals 6.16 MB/sec). Some tape drives move the tape under the read/write head at speeds in excess of 50 miles per hour!

The most common lengths of magnetic tape reels are 600, 1200, and 2400 feet. The capacity of a tape is equal to the tape density (bpi) times the length of the tape in inches. A 6250-bpi, 2400-foot (28,800-inch) tape has a capacity of approximately 180 MB (million bytes). Significant advances have been made in tape cartridge technology. Magnetic tape cartridges are available in a variety of sizes and are capable of storing up to 2.4 gigabytes on a single cartridge. Each **gigabyte (GB)** consists of a billion bytes.

Two gigabytes sounds like ample storage for just about anything, but this is not the case. For example, 10 high-capacity tape cartridges would be required to store just the names and addresses of all the people living in the United States.

Principles of Operation: $\frac{1}{2}$-Inch Magnetic Tape

The $\frac{1}{2}$-Inch Tape Reel   Because of the physical nature of magnetic tape, files must be processed sequentially from beginning to end for each computer run. On any given run, a *single* tape is either input or output, not both. Sequential processing with magnetic tape is discussed in detail in Section 6–5.

The principles of data storage for $\frac{1}{2}$-inch mag tape are illustrated in Figure 6–4. The film coating on the tape is electronically magnetized by the read/write head to form bit configurations. In EBCDIC, eight bits (the EBCDIC code) plus the *parity bit* are needed to represent a character.

Up to sixteen $\frac{1}{2}$-inch tape cartridges can be mounted to this magnetic tape subsystem for processing. Up to six cartridges can be mounted in a stacker for each of the sixteen tape drives. Stacked tapes are automatically loaded and unloaded in the order in which they are stacked.

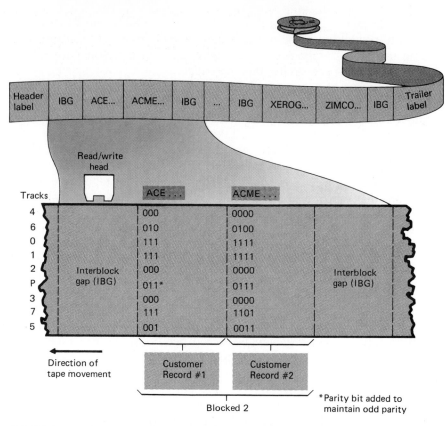

FIGURE 6–4 Cross-Section of a Magnetic Tape: Parallel Representation
The ¹/₂-inch magnetic tape has evolved from 9 to 18 to 36 tracks over the past four decades. The 9-track tape, which is still in common use, is used for illustrative purposes. Parallel representation is used to store the customer master file on this 9-track magnetic tape. This cross-section of mag tape contains two records from a customer master file. Those tracks in which an "on" bit appears most often (0, 1, 2, P, 3) are clustered in the center of the tape. Those tracks that are least likely to be magnetized to an "on" bit (4, 6, 7, 5) are placed toward the outside so the data on a tape with damaged edges are less likely to be affected. The tape travels past the write head, then the read head. This enables the computer to read and check the data immediately after they are written to the tape.

The parity bit is used to ensure the accuracy of the data transmission to and from the tape drive. Each of the nine bits is stored in one of nine *tracks* that run the length of the tape. In the *nine-track mag tape reel of* Figure 6–4, characters are represented by parallel EBCDIC bit configurations. This method of storing data in adjacent bit configurations is known as **parallel representation**. In parallel representation, data are read or written a byte at a time.

Figure 6–4 portrays a cross-section of a magnetic tape that contains a *customer master file.* The data relating to each customer are grouped and stored in a *customer record.* The records are stored *alphabetically by customer name* (from ACE, ACME... to ZEROG, ZIMCO).

Records are usually grouped in blocks of two or more, separated by an **interblock gap (IBG)**. The IBGs not only signal a stop in the reading process but also provide some margin for error in the rapid *start/stop* operation of the tape drive.

Blocking permits additional records to be transmitted with each "read" or "write." Each time the computer is instructed to read from a magnetic tape, all data between adjacent interblock gaps are transmitted to primary storage for processing. The next "read" transmits the next **block** of records to primary storage. When the computer is instructed to write to a tape, the data are transmitted from primary storage to the tape drive. Then a block of data and an IBG are written to the tape.

In Figure 6–4, the records have a blocking factor of two and are said to be "blocked two." Figure 6–5 shows how the same file would appear blocked three and unblocked. Notice how the tape blocked three contains more records than the unblocked tape.

To signal the beginning and end of a particular tape file, the computer adds a *header label* and a *trailer label*, respectively (see Figure 6–4). The header label contains the name of the file and the date it was created. The trailer label is written at the end of the data file and shows the number of records in the file.

The ½-Inch Tape Cartridge   The operation of the ½-inch tape cartridge is similar to that of the ½-inch mag tape reel. Aside from the obvious differences in mechanical operation, there are two main differences. The mag tape reel reads in one direction, then must be rewound. The mag tape cartridge reads the top half of the tape in one direction and the bottom half in the other. The ½-inch tape cartridge has 36 tracks, as opposed to 9 for most mag tape reels. Like the 9-track mag tape reel, the *36-track tape cartridge* stores data using parallel representation; however, it stacks four bytes of data across the width of the tape such that 18 tracks are read in each direction. This enables more bytes of data to be stored on the same length of tape. Both ½-inch tapes block records for processing.

FIGURE 6–5   Customer Records Blocked Three (top) and Unblocked (bottom)

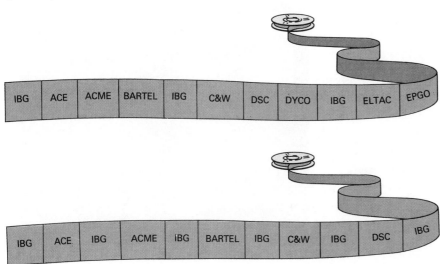

Multimedia. Probably no other "buzzword" is causing as much excitement today. To understand the excitement, just consider the "show biz" appeal of these few examples.

- *Microsoft Bookshelf for Windows*, a single CD-ROM disk, contains seven reference works, including a "talking" dictionary that demonstrates correct pronunciations, a book of quotations that includes digitized recordings of such luminaries as John F. Kennedy, an atlas that plays every country's national anthem, and a concise encyclopedia illustrated with high-resolution graphics and narrated animations showing how certain processes work. And, like any computer file, the CD-ROM can be searched by key word or phrase, taking a lot of the tedium out of research. *Bookshelf* is just one of a growing list of multimedia software titles that merge entertainment and education.

- A computerized information kiosk at the Montreux Jazz Festival allowed users to call up biographies, photos, and performance videos of all performers.

- Thousands of workers are now learning WordPerfect, Lotus 1-2-3, and other popular applications via interactive multimedia tutorials that are enlivened with music, graphics, and motion. A 1990 Department of Defense study concluded that such tutorials take about a third less time, cost about a third less, and are more effective than traditional training methods.

The lure and range of such applications have sparked predictions that a multimedia revolution is just over the horizon. The revolution is still in the making, though, in part because multimedia generates almost as much confusion as excitement.

MULTIMEDIA: A DEFINITION

One source of confusion is the misuse of the term *multimedia* itself. You may see it used to describe everything from an animated, talking, and singing children's book on CD-ROM to a high-resolution monitor. Although there's no official definition, most computer experts agree that *multimedia* refers to a computer system that lets users access and interact with computerized text,

high-resolution still graphics, motion visuals, and sound. Three elements in particular distinguish multimedia: sound, motion, and the opportunity for interaction.

TECHNICAL CHALLENGES: TEACHING THE PC TO SING AND DANCE

Given the sophistication of today's computer graphics, animation, and sound, creating a multimedia system may seem like a simple task. In reality, it poses at least three technical challenges.

The first challenge is simply assembling the additional hardware and software needed to convert the digitized signals of light and sound into the analog signals humans can understand or vice versa.

The second challenge lies in augmenting the PC's processor, memory, and storage. Managing and manipulating the user-friendly interface of multimedia at acceptable speeds takes a lot of computer power, memory, and storage.

A third challenge is devising software to make all the pieces work together. At one level, this is similar to the challenge that faced early movie makers: synchronizing sound and motion. But the computer adds its own wrinkle. Most computer processors work on a contention system, in which peripherals take turns accessing the processor. Given the speed of most processors, users are never aware of this. But for multimedia, several

THE MULTIMEDIA ADVENTURE   Explore the coral reefs of the U.S. Virgin Islands without getting wet! In the illustration, a diver takes the user on a full-motion and sound tour of the coral reefs off St. Thomas.

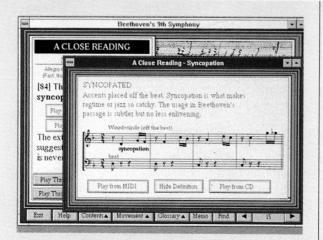

BEETHOVEN'S NINTH SYMPHONY We can still learn a thing or two from the old masters. This multimedia presentation demonstrates how Ludwig van Beethoven used syncopation in his Ninth Symphony. Selected passages are displayed, then played at the user's request.

peripherals have to access the processor at the same time. This will ultimately require more sophisticated operating systems.

THE CONSUMER'S CHALLENGE: FOOTING THE BILL

How much will it cost to put the thrill of multimedia into your computing life? The answer depends, to a great extent, on what you want to do with multimedia. You might even approach it in stages.

Do you merely want to experience multimedia? If you own any of the current Macintosh models, you already have the main hardware needed to play back multimedia. Just attach a *CD-ROM drive* (available at discount for about $400 to $1000) and you're ready to go. If you already own a reasonably powerful IBM-PC compatible, look for an upgrade kit. These kits contain a CD-ROM drive, an audio board (and sometimes *external speakers* or *headphones*), and Microsoft Windows with Multimedia Extensions, which provides a software-based method of playing back motion. Such kits average about $1000. Or, if you need to upgrade your computer anyway, consider paying 10% to 30% more for one of the emerging multimedia computers, which comes with multimedia hardware already built in. At this point, you will probably still be *playing* multimedia titles, which cost from $70 to $600 each.

The next stage comes when you decide to *develop* multimedia applications—either your own multimedia title, a computer-based tutorial, or a business presentation. At this point, you may need to invest in additional hardware, such as a *microphone*, *tape cassette player*, *CD-audio player*, or *music synthesizer* (for inputting sound); a *color scanner*, *video camera*, *videocassette recorder*, and *video board* (for inputting and manipulating still and motion graphics, including input to and output from a television set); plus software for creating graphics and animation, as well as an authoring system. An *authoring system* is software that lets nonprogrammers use English-like commands to create interactive computer programs. One popular authoring system is HyperCard; it is bundled with all Macintosh computers.

THE WILD CARD OF KALEIDA

In 1991, IBM and Apple shocked the computer world by announcing they would collaborate on a long-range five-point plan. One of the most significant points, at least for multimedia, is the creation of Kaleida, a company that will merge Apple and IBM research into animation, video, and multimedia, and create tiny multimedia machines that can run both Apple and IBM software. The move has both intrigued and unnerved computer pundits. Because the first products won't be released for a few years, many are afraid that consumers will become even more hesitant to invest in multimedia. Others take the long view and applaud the effort. After all, if the Number 1 and Number 2 forces in the computer world can't spark a multimedia revolution, who can?

INFORMATIVE KIOSKS Many retail establishments are installing multimedia-based kiosks to better assist their customers. This kiosk is designed to introduce customers to the latest fashion trends.

Principles of Operation: ¼-Inch Magnetic Tape

In the past the simplicity and lower cost of magnetic tape processing often made it preferable to magnetic disk processing. This is no longer true, and today magnetic tape is used primarily for backup. During backup or recovery runs, backup tapes are processed continuously from beginning to end. Because there is seldom a need for selective access of records from magnetic tape, there is no reason to start and stop the tapes.

Most ¼-inch tape cartridges record data in a continuous stream, thereby eliminating the need for the start/stop operation of traditional tape drives. Drives for ¼-inch tape cartridges, often called **streamer tape drives**, store data in a **serpentine** manner (Figure 6–6). Data are recorded using **serial representation**; that is, the bits are aligned in a row, one after another, in tracks. A tape cartridge can have from four to fifteen tracks, depending on the tape drive. The read/write head reads or writes data to one, two, or four tracks at a time. Figure 6–6 illustrates how data are written two tracks at a time. In the figure, data are written serially on the top two tracks for the entire length of the tape or until the data are exhausted. The tape is reversed, the read/write head is positioned over the next two tracks, and writing continues in a similar manner. If more backup capacity is needed, the computer operator is informed. He or she inserts a clean tape and writing continues.

Having no start/stop mechanisms, streamer tape drives can store data much more efficiently than the traditional tape drives that stop, then start the tape's movement over the read/write head at each IBG. Streamer tape drives use 97% of the tape for data storage, whereas traditional start/stop tapes use only 35% to 70%, depending on the blocking factors.

FIGURE 6–6 Cross-Section of a Magnetic Tape: Serial Representation
Data are recorded serially on this eight-track tape in a serpentine manner, two tracks at a time.

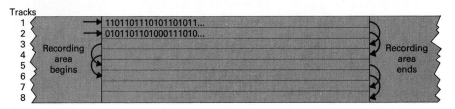

Magnetic Tape Summary

Both mag tape technology and the way we use magnetic tape are changing rapidly. In this section, we address the fundamental technologies that are in use today, though there are many variations on these technologies. As for the way we use magnetic tape, the trend toward on-line system is a trend away from magnetic tape for routine information processing. In contrast, high-density magnetic tape will continue to be a cost-effective medium for backup of critical data and software and for archival storage.

6-5 Sequential Processing: One after Another

Sequential files, used for *sequential processing,* contain records ordered according to a key field. The key field in an employee record might be social security number or employee name. If the key is social security number, the employee records are ordered and processed *numerically* by social security number. If the key is employee name, the records are ordered and processed *alphabetically* by last name. *A sequential file is processed from start to finish. The entire file must be processed, even if only one record is to be updated.*

The principal storage medium for sequential files is magnetic tape. Magnetic disks also can be used for sequential processing.

Principles of Sequential Processing

Sequential-processing procedures for updating an inventory file are illustrated in Figures 6–7, 6–8, and 6–9. Figure 6–7 lists the contents of an inventory *master file,* which is the permanent source of inventory data, and a *transaction file,* which reflects the daily inventory activity.

In most data centers, magnetic tapes are manually mounted. The alternative is an automated tape library. Under computer control, the automated tape library retrieves the appropriate tape from the library and mounts it on a tape drive for processing. The tape is automatically returned to the library at the end of the job.

FIGURE 6–7   Inventory Master and Transaction Files
Both files are sorted by part number. The numbers in brackets [ ] reflect the inventory master file after the update. Figures 6–9 and 6–12 illustrate the update process for sequential and random processing.

Inventory master file (sorted by part number)

	Part no.	Price	No. used to date	No. in stock
One record →	2	25	40	200
	4	1.40	100 [106] *	100 [94]
	8	.80	500	450
	•	•	•	•
	•	•	•	•
	•	•	•	•
	20	4.60	60 [72]	14 [2]
	21	2.20	50	18

*[ ] reflects updated values

Transaction file (sorted by part number)

Part no.	No. used today
4	6
20	12

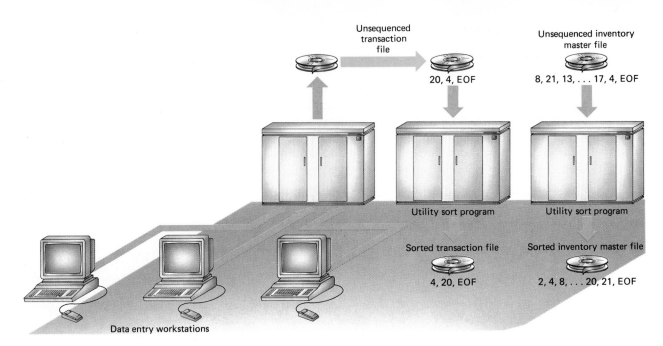

FIGURE 6–8　Sorting
Unsequenced inventory master and transaction files are sorted prior to sequential processing. Normally, the master file would have been sorted as a result of prior processing.

Prior to processing, the records on both files are sorted and arranged in ascending sequence by part number (the key). A utility sort program takes a file of unsequenced records and creates a new file with the records sorted according to the values of the key. The sort process is illustrated in Figure 6–8.

Figure 6–9 shows both the inventory master and transaction files as input and the *new inventory master file* as output. Because the technology does not permit records to be "rewritten" on the magnetic tape master file, a new master file tape is created to reflect the updates to the master file. *A new master file is always created for master file updates in tape sequential processing.* The processing steps are illustrated in Figure 6–9 and explained as follows:

- *Prior to processing.* If the two input tapes are *not sorted* by part number, they must be sorted as shown in Figure 6–8. The sorted tapes are then mounted on the tape drives. A blank tape, mounted on a third tape drive, will ultimately contain the updated master file. The arrows under the part numbers in Figure 6–9 indicate which records are positioned at the read/write heads on the respective tape drives. These records are the *next* to be read. Each file has an **end-of-file marker (EOF)** that signals the end of the file.

- *Step 1.* The first record (4) on the transaction file (T) is read and loaded to primary storage. Then the first record (2) on the master file (M) is loaded to primary storage. A comparison is made of the two keys. Because there is not a match (4 ≠ [is not equal to] 2), the first record on the master file is written to the new master file tape without being changed.

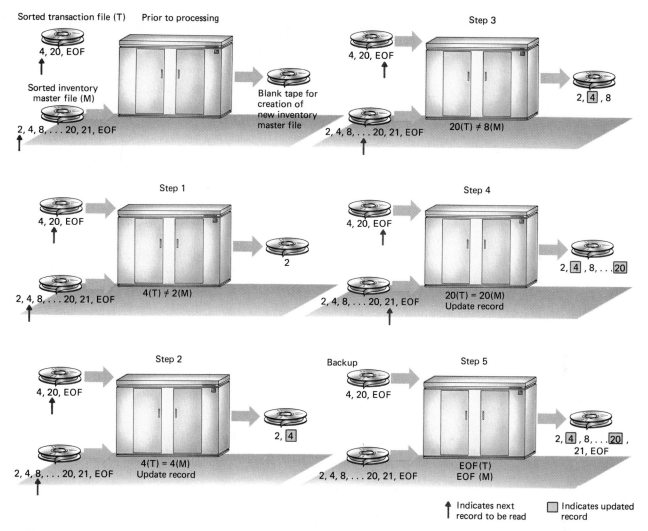

FIGURE 6–9 Sequential Processing

An inventory master file is updated using sequential processing and magnetic tapes. Processing steps are discussed in the text. Notice in Step 5 that the backup is a by-product of sequential processing.

- *Step 2.* The next record (4) on the master file is read and loaded to primary storage. After a positive comparison (4 = 4), the record of Part Number 4 is updated (see Figure 6–7) to reflect the use of six items and then written to the new master file tape. In Figure 6–7 note that the Number in Stock data item is reduced from 100 to 94 and the Number Used to Date is increased from 100 to 106. Updated records in Figure 6–9 are enclosed in boxes.

- *Step 3.* The next record from the transaction file (20) and the next record from the master file (8) are read and loaded to primary storage. A comparison is made. Because the comparison is negative (20 ≠ 8), the record for Part Number 8 is written to the new master file tape without being changed.

- *Step 4.* Records from the master file are individually read and loaded, and the part number is compared to that of the transaction record (20). With each negative comparison (for example, 20 ≠ 17), the record from the old master file is written, without change, to the new master file tape. The read-and-compare process continues until a match is made (20 = 20). Record 20 is then updated and written to the new master file tape.

- *Step 5.* A "read" is issued to the transaction file and an end-of-file marker is found. All records on the master file tape following the record for Part Number 20 are written to the new master file tape, and the end-of-file marker is recorded on the new master file tape. All tapes are then automatically rewound and removed from the tape drives for off-line storage and processing at a later time.

Backup

The transaction file and old master file are retained as *backup* to the new master file. Fortunately, *backup is a by-product of sequential processing.* After the new master file is created, the old master file and the transaction file become the backup. If the new master is destroyed, the transaction file can simply be run against the old master file to re-create the new master file.

Backup files are handled and maintained by *generation*, the up-to-date master file being the current generation. This tape cycling procedure is called the **grandfather-father-son method** of file backup. The "son" file is the up-to-date master file. The "father" generation is noted in Step 5 of Figure 6–9. Most computer centers maintain a grandfather file (from the last update run) as a backup to the backup.

 6–6 **Magnetic Disks: Rotating Storage Media**

Hardware and Storage Media

Because of its random- and sequential-processing capabilities, magnetic disk storage is the overwhelming choice of computer users, whether on micros or on supercomputers. A variety of magnetic disk drives (the hardware device) and magnetic disks (the media) are manufactured for different business requirements. There are two fundamental types of magnetic disks: interchangeable and fixed.

- **Interchangeable magnetic disks** can be stored off-line and loaded to the magnetic disk drives as they are needed.
- **Fixed magnetic disks**, also called *hard disks*, are permanently installed, or fixed. The trend in magnetic storage media is to fixed disks. All fixed disks are rigid and are usually made of aluminum with a surface coating of easily magnetized elements, such as iron, cobalt, chromium, and nickel.

In the past, interchangeable disks containing certain files and programs were taken from the shelf and loaded to the disk drives as needed. This is still true today but to a much lesser extent. Today's integrated software and data bases require all data and programs to be on-line at all times.

The different types of interchangeable magnetic disks and fixed disks are shown in the accompanying photographs. As you can see, magnetic

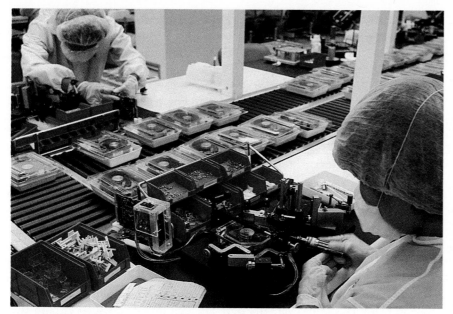

The trend in disk storage is toward permanently installed storage media. Fixed disks are manufactured in rooms that are 1000 times cleaner than hospital operating rooms.

disk drives are available in a wide variety of shapes and storage capacities. The type used would depend on the volume of data you have and the frequency with which those data are accessed. Disk drives are sometimes called **direct access storage devices**, or **DASD** (*DAZ dee*).

Magnetic Disks: The Microcomputer Environment

Microcomputer Disk Media   Virtually all micros sold today are configured with at least one hard disk drive and one interchangeable disk drive. The interchangeable disk drive provides a vehicle for the distribution of data and software, a means for backup and archival storage, and, of course, on-line storage. The high-capacity hard-disk storage has made it possible for today's micro user to enjoy the convenience of having all data and software readily accessible at all times.

The diskette.   PC disk drives use two sizes of interchangeable magnetic disks. Both are called **diskettes**.

- *5¼-inch diskette.* The 5¼-inch diskette is a thin, flexible disk that is permanently enclosed in a soft, 5¼-inch-square jacket. Because the magnetic-coated mylar diskette and its jacket are flexible like a page in this book, the diskette is also called a **floppy disk**.

   Early 5¼-inch diskettes recorded data on only one side of the disk. These were *single-sided* (SS) diskettes. Today all common-usage diskettes are *double-sided* and are labeled "DS" or simply "2." Similarly, the technological evolution of the early diskettes are classified as *double-density*

(DD), as opposed to *single-density*. **Disk density** refers to the number of bits that can be stored per unit of area on the disk-face surface.

The *360-KB DS/DD* (double-sided, double-density) 5¼-inch diskette dominated during the 1980s and is still the only diskette that can be used on many PCs. However, the new 5¼-inch disk drives support both the popular 360-KB diskette and the *1.2-MB DS/HD* (double-sided, high-density) diskette. The 1.2-MB diskette can store more programs and data than three 360-KB diskettes.

■ *3½-inch diskette.* The 3½-inch diskette is enclosed in a rigid plastic jacket. Like its 5¼-inch cousin, the 3½-inch diskette comes in two capacities, the 720-KB DS/DD and the 1.44-MB DS/HD diskettes. The diskette is slowly displacing the 5¼-inch diskette because of its durability, convenient size, and higher capacity.

Winchester disk. The microcomputer hard disk is called the **Winchester disk**. The Winchester disk got its nickname from the 30-30 Winchester rifle. Early disk drives had two 30-MB disks—thus the nickname "Winchester." Most of the newer personal computers are configured with at least one diskette drive and one fixed Winchester disk. Having two disks increases system throughput. The storage capacity of these 3½- and 5¼-inch hard disks ranges from about 40 MB to 760 MB. The 760-MB hard disk has over 2000 times the capacity of a 360-KB diskette.

A Winchester hard disk contains several disk platters stacked on a single rotating spindle. Data are stored on all *recording surfaces*. For a disk with four platters, there are eight recording surfaces on which data can be stored (see Figure 6–10). The disks spin continuously at a high speed (usually 3600 revolutions per minute) within a sealed enclosure. The enclosure keeps the disk-face surfaces free from contaminants such as dust and cigarette smoke. This contaminant-free environment allows Winchester disks to have greater density of data storage than the interchangeable diskettes. In contrast to the Winchester disk, the diskettes are set in motion only when a command is issued to read from or write to the disk. An indicator light near the disk drive is illuminated only when the diskette is spinning.

The rotational movement of a magnetic disk passes all data under or over a *read/write head*, thereby making all data available for access on

As PCs downsize, so must disk drives. This multiplatter 2½-inch Winchester disk, which has a capacity of 42.8 MB, is designed for use in notebook PCs.

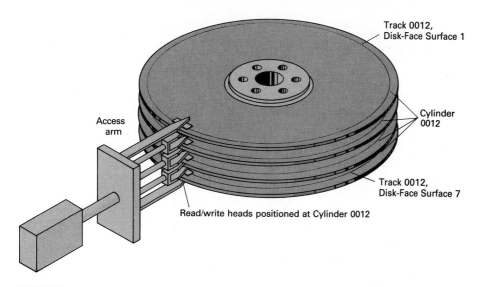

FIGURE 6–10   Fixed Hard Disk with Four Platters and Eight Recording Surfaces
A cylinder refers to similarly numbered concentric tracks on the disk-face surfaces. In the illustration, the read/write heads are positioned over Cylinder 0012. At this position, the data on any one of the eight tracks numbered 0012 are accessible to the computer on each revolution of the disk. The read/write heads must be moved to access data on other cylinders.

each revolution of the disk (see Figure 6–10). A fixed disk will have at least one read/write head for each recording surface. The heads are mounted on **access arms** that move together and literally float on a cushion of air over (or under) the spinning recording surfaces. The tolerance is so close that a particle of smoke from a cigarette will not fit between these "flying" heads and the recording surface!

Winchester disks normally are permanently installed in the same physical unit as the processor and diskette drives. There are, however, interchangeable hard disks on the market. These interchangeable Winchester modules are inserted and removed in a manner that is similar to the way you insert and remove tapes on a VCR. Only a small percentage of PCs are configured to accept interchangeable Winchester disks.

The capacity of Winchester disks is increasing steadily. Already, very high-density fixed disks can store over 62 million characters on one square inch of recording surface. That's the text of this and 50 other books in a space the size of a postage stamp!

Micro Disk Organization   The way in which data and programs are stored and accessed is similar for both hard and interchangeable disks. The disk-storage medium has a thin film coating of one of the easily magnetized elements (cobalt, for example). The thin film coating on the disk can be magnetized electronically by the read/write head to represent the absence or presence of a bit (0 or 1).

Data are stored in concentric circles called **tracks** by magnetizing the surface to represent bit configurations (see Figure 6–11). Bits are recorded using *serial representation*. The number of tracks varies greatly

This highly magnified area of a magnetic disk-face surface shows elongated information bits recorded serially along 8 of the disk's 1774 concentric tracks. One square inch of this disk's surface can hold 22 million bits of information.

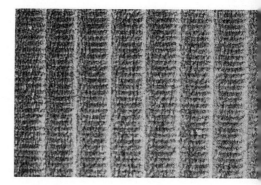

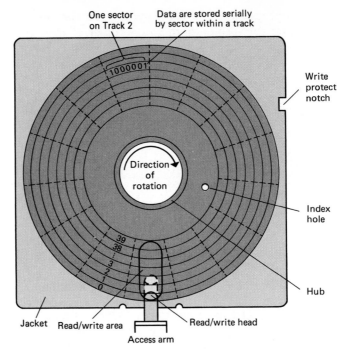

FIGURE 6–11 Cutaway of a 5¼-Inch Diskette
Photoelectric cells sense light as it passes through the index hole. This feedback enables the computer to monitor which sector is under or over the read/write head at any given time. Data are read or written serially in tracks within a given sector.

between disks, from as few as 40 on some 5¼-inch diskettes to several thousand on high-capacity Winchester disks. The spacing of tracks is measured in **tracks per inch**, or **TPI**. The 5¼-inch diskettes are rated at 48 and 96 TPI and the 3½-inch diskettes are rated at 135 TPI. The TPI for Winchester disks can be in the thousands.

The *track density* (TPI) tells only part of the story. The *recording density* tells the rest. Recording density, which is measured in *bits per inch*, refers to the number of bits (1s and 0s) that can be stored per inch of track. Note that magnetic disk density is measured in *bits* per linear inch of track, not *bytes* per inch (as is the case with mag tape). Both the 720-KB and 1.44-MB diskettes have a track density of 135 TPI, but the recording density of the high-density disk is twice that of the double-density disk.

Microcomputer disks use **sector organization** to store and retrieve data. In sector organization, the recording surface is divided into from 9 to 33 pie-shaped **sectors**. The surface of the diskette in Figure 6–11 is logically divided into 15 sectors. Typically, the storage capacity of each sector on a particular track is 512 bytes, regardless of the number of sectors per track. Each sector is assigned a unique number; therefore, the *sector number* and *track number* are all that are needed for a **disk address** on a particular disk-face surface. The disk address represents the physical location of a particular set of data or a program. To read from or write to a disk, an access arm containing the read/write head is moved, under program control, to the appropriate *track* (see Figures 6–10 and 6–11). When the sector containing the desired data passes under or over the read/write head, the data are read or written.

Each of the high-density disk-face surfaces of a Winchester disk may have several thousand tracks, numbered consecutively from outside to inside. A particular **cylinder** refers to every track with the same number on all recording surfaces (see Figure 6–10). When reading from or writing to a Winchester disk, all access arms are moved to the appropriate *cylinder*. For example, each recording surface has a track numbered 0012, so the disk has a cylinder numbered 0012. If the data to be accessed are on Recording Surface 01, Track 0012, then the access arms and the read/write heads for all eight recording surfaces are moved to Cylinder 0012.

In Figure 6–10 the access arm is positioned over Cylinder 0012. In this position, data on any of the sectors on the tracks in Cylinder 0012 can be accessed without further movement of the access arm. If data on Surface 5, Track 0145, are to be read, the access arm must be positioned over Cylinder 0145 until the desired record passes under the read/write head.

Fortunately, software automatically monitors the location, or address, of our files and programs. We need only enter someone's name to retrieve his or her personnel record. The computer system locates the record and loads it to primary storage for processing. Although the addressing schemes vary considerably between disks, the address normally will include the *cylinder (or track)*, the *recording surface*, and the *sector number*.

Disk Access Time   **Access time** is the interval between the instant a computer makes a request for transfer of data from a disk-storage device to RAM and the instant this operation is completed. The access of data from RAM is performed at electronic speeds—approximately the speed of light. But the access of data from disk storage depends on mechanical apparatus. Any mechanical movement significantly increases the access time. The access time for hard disks is significantly less than for floppy disks because the hard disk is in continuous motion.

The *seek time*, the largest portion of the total access time, consists of how long it takes the mechanical access arm to move the read/write head to the desired track or cylinder. Some Winchester disk drives have two sets of access arms, one for reading and writing on the inside tracks and another for the outside tracks. Two independent sets of access arms

---

Memory Bits

CHARACTERISTICS OF MAGNETIC DISK

Media	Fixed (hard) and interchangeable disks
Type access	Direct (random) or sequential
Data representation	Serial
Storage scheme	Sector

significantly reduce the average seek time because they have a shorter distance to move and one can move while the other is reading or writing.

The *rotational delay time* is the time it takes for the appropriate data to be positioned under the read/write head. On the average, it would be half the time it takes for one revolution of the disk, or about 8 milliseconds for a hard disk spinning at 3600 rpm. The rotational delay time for a diskette spinning at 400 rpm is 75 milliseconds, almost 10 times that of a hard disk. The *transmission time*, or the time it takes to transmit the data to primary storage, is negligible. The average access time for most hard-disk drives is less than 20 milliseconds—still very slow when compared with the microsecond-to-nanosecond processing speeds of computers.

Disk Caching   Even though the data transfer rate from magnetic disk to RAM may be millions of bytes per second, the rate of transfer between one part of RAM to another is much faster. **Disk caching** (pronounced *cashing*) enhances system performance by placing programs and data that are likely to be called into RAM for processing from a disk into an area of RAM that simulates disk storage. When an applications program issues a call for the data or programs in the disk cache area, called the **RAM disk**, the request is serviced directly from RAM rather than magnetic disk. Data or programs in the RAM disk eventually must be transferred to a disk for permanent storage.

All state-of-the-art PCs come with software that takes full advantage of the potential of RAM disks.

Magnetic Disks: The Mainframe Environment

Sitting atop rows of disk drives are interchangeable magnetic disk packs that provide billions of characters of direct-access storage for this superminicomputer system.

Mainframe Disk Media   Direct access storage devices (DASD) are prerequisites for all information systems where the data must be on-line and accessed directly. An airline reservation system provides a good mainframe-oriented example of this need. Direct-access capability is required to retrieve the record for any flight at any time from any reservations office. The data must be current, or flights may be overbooked or underbooked. Because of the random nature of the reservations data, sequential-only magnetic tape cannot be used as a storage medium for this or any other system that requires random processing. File and data base organization for random processing, also called **direct-access processing**, is covered in Section 6–7.

The demand for on-line systems during the past decade has caused the virtual disappearance of interchangeable disk-storage media in the mainframe environment. The once popular **disk cartridge** and the **disk pack** (see accompanying photos) have been replaced with permanently installed high-density fixed disks. The current technology enables a single disk drive, which might include four platters (see Figure 6–10) to store over 20 gigabytes of data.

Minis, mainframes, and supercomputers use a wide variety of fixed-disk media. The differences are primarily the size of the platter (2 inches to 14 inches in diameter), the number of platters per disk drive, and the density at which data are recorded.

Mainframe Disk Organization The way data are organized on mainframe disk systems is similar to that on microcomputer disk systems. That is, the read/write heads are positioned over/under the track containing the desired data or software (see Figure 6–10). The data are read from or written to the appropriate sector as it passes over/under the read/write head.

6–7 Random, or Direct-Access, Processing: Pick and Choose

A **direct-access file**, or a **random file**, is a collection of records that can be processed randomly (in any order). Only the value of the record's key field is needed in order to retrieve or update a record in random processing. More often than not magnetic disks are the storage medium for random processing.

You can access records on a direct-access file by more than one key. For example, a salesperson inquiring about the availability of a particular product could inquire by *product number* and, if the product number is not known, by *product name*. The file, however, must be created with the intent of having multiple keys.

Random-Access Methods

The procedures and mechanics of the way a particular record is accessed directly are, for the most part, transparent (not a concern) to users and even to programmers. However, some familiarity will help you understand the capabilities and limitations of direct-access methods. **Indexed-sequential organization** is a popular method that permits both sequential and random processing.

Federal Express couriers and handlers use the SuperTracker (left), a hand-held OCR data collection device, to track the progress of packages from source to destination. Package status information, such as pickup or delivery times, is transmitted directly to the company's centralized data base through the DADS (Digitally Assisted Dispatch System) units in the courier vans and sorting facilities. These customer service agents (right) access the up-to-the-minute data base for package status information when responding to customer inquiries.

In indexed-sequential organization there are actually two files: The *data file* contains the records (for each student, for each inventory item, and so on); the smaller *index file* contains the key and disk address of each record on the data file. A request for a particular record is first directed to the smaller, more accessible index file which, in turn, "points" to the physical location of the desired record on magnetic disk.

Principles of Random Processing

In Figure 6–12, the inventory master file of Figure 6–7 is updated from an *on-line* terminal to illustrate the principles of random processing. The following activities take place during the update:

- *Step 1.* The first transaction (for Part Number 20) is entered into primary storage from an on-line terminal. The computer issues a read for the record of Part Number 20 on the inventory master file. The record is retrieved and transmitted to primary storage for processing. The record is updated and written back to the *same* location on the master file. The updated record is simply written over the old record.
- *Step 2.* A second transaction (for Part Number 4) is entered into primary storage. The computer issues a read for the record of Part Number 4 on the inventory master file. The record is retrieved and transmitted to primary storage for processing. The record is then updated.

Because only two updates are to be made to the inventory master file, processing is complete. However, unlike sequential processing where the backup is built in, random processing requires a special run to provide backup to the inventory master file. In the backup activity illustrated in Figure 6–13, the master file is "dumped" from disk to tape at frequent intervals, usually daily. If the inventory master file is destroyed, it can

FIGURE 6–12   Random Processing
An inventory master file is updated using random processing and magnetic disks. Processing steps are discussed in the text.

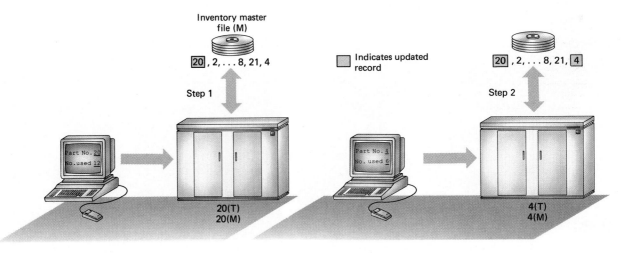

Inventory master file

Backup

Inventory master file

FIGURE 6–13   Backup Procedure for Random Processing
Unlike sequential processing, a separate run is required to create the backup for random processing.

be re-created by dumping the backup file (on tape) to disk (the reverse of Figure 6–13).

As you can see, random processing is more straightforward than sequential processing, and it has those advantages associated with on-line, interactive processing. Figure 6–14 summarizes the differences between sequential and random processing.

6–8   Optical Laser Disks: High-Density Storage

Some industry analysts have predicted that *optical laser disk* technology, now in its infant stage of use and development, eventually may make magnetic disk and tape storage obsolete. With this technology, the read/write head used in magnetic storage is replaced by two lasers. One laser beam writes to the recording surface by scoring microscopic pits in the disk, and another laser reads the data from the light-sensitive recording surface. A light beam is easily deflected to the desired place on the optical disk, so a mechanical access arm is not needed.

Optical laser disks are becoming a very inviting option for users. They are less sensitive to environmental fluctuations, and they provide

FIGURE 6–14   Differences between Sequential and Random Processing

	Sequential Processing	Random Processing
Primary storage medium		
Preprocessing	Files must be sorted	None required
File updating	Requires complete processing of file and creation of new master file	Only active records are processed, then rewritten to the same storage area
Data currency	Batch (at best, data are a day old)	On-line (up-to-the-minute)
Backup	Built-in (old master file and transaction file)	Requires special provisions

more direct-access storage at a cost that is much less per megabyte of storage than the magnetic disk alternative. Optical laser disk technology is still emerging and has yet to stabilize; however, at present there are three main categories of optical laser disks. They are *CD-ROM*, *WORM disks*, and *magneto-optical disks*.

CD-ROM

Introduced in 1980 for stereo buffs, the extraordinarily successful CD, or compact disk, is an optical laser disk designed to enhance the reproduction of recorded music. To make a CD recording, the analog sounds of music are translated into their digital equivalents and stored on a 4.72-inch optical laser disk. Seventy-four minutes of music can be recorded on each disk in digital format by 2 billion digital bits. (A bit is represented by the presence or absence of a pit on the disk.) With its tremendous storage capacity per square inch, computer industry entrepreneurs immediately recognized the potential of optical laser disk technology. In effect, anything that can be digitized can be stored on optical laser disk: data, text, voice, still pictures, music, graphics, and video.

CD-ROM, a spinoff of audio CD technology, stands for *compact disk–read only memory*. The name implies its application. CD-ROM disks are created at a mastering facility, just as audio CDs are created at a recording studio. The master copy is duplicated or "pressed" at the factory and the copies are distributed with their prerecorded contents (for example, the complete works of Shakespeare or the first 30 minutes of *Gone with the Wind*). Once inserted into the CD-ROM disk drive, the text,

A single CD-ROM disk can hold the equivalent of 13,000 images, 250,000 pages of text, or 1500 floppy disks. This tremendous storage capacity has opened the door to a variety of multimedia applications. Multimedia can provide needed flexibility during a presentation. Unlike a videotape, CD-ROM gives the presenter instant random access to any sequence of images on the disk.

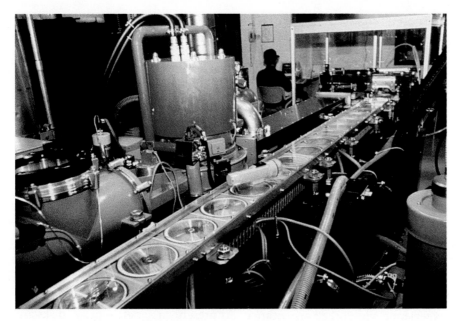

Most commercial CD-ROM disks contain reference material. This mastering facility creates the actual disks from the source material supplied by CD-ROM publishers.

video images, and so on can be read into primary storage for processing or display; however, the data on the disk are fixed—they cannot be altered. This is in contrast, of course, to the read/write capability of magnetic disks.

The capacity of a single CD-ROM is over 550 MB—about that of 400 DS/HD 3½-inch diskettes. To put the density of CD-ROM into perspective, the words in every book ever written could be stored on a hypothetical CD-ROM that is seven feet in diameter.

The tremendous amount of low-cost direct-access storage made possible by optical laser disks has opened the door to many new applications. Currently, most of the commercially produced CD-ROM disks contain reference material. A sampling of these disks follows: *The Groliers Electronic Encyclopedia*; *The Oxford English Dictionary*; the 1990 U.S. Census (county level); maps at the national, state, regional, and metropolitan levels; a world history tutorial; the text of 450 titles (including *Moby Dick*, the *King James version of the Bible*, *Beowolf*, *The Odyssey*, and many more); multilingual dictionaries (one disk contains translation dictionaries for 12 languages); scientific writings for the Apple Macintosh; and *The Daily Oklahoman* (1981–1986). The cost of commercially produced CD-ROMs varies considerably from as little as $50 to several thousand dollars.

WORM Disks

Write once, read many optical laser disks, or **WORM disks**, are used by end user companies to store their own, proprietary information. Once the data have been written to the medium, they only can be read, not

The IBM PS/2 Rewritable Optical Drive uses 3½-inch interchangeable optical cartridges that store up to 127 MB each. The optical cartridge stores the equivalent of eighty-eight 1.44-MB diskettes. Optical cartridge applications include distribution of data bases to branch offices, multimedia presentations, distribution of PC software, hard disk backup, and archival storage.

updated or changed. The PC version of a WORM disk cartridge, which looks like a 5¼-inch version of the 3½-inch diskette, has a capacity of 200 MB.

The WORM disks cartridge is a feasible alternative to magnetic tape for archival storage. For example, a company might wish to keep a permanent record of all financial transactions during the last year. Another popular application of WORM disks is in information systems that require the merging of text and images that do not change for a period of time. A good example is an "electronic catalog." A customer can peruse a retailer's electronic catalog on a VDT, or perhaps a PC, and see the item while he or she reads about it. And, with a few keystrokes the customer can order the item as well. The Library of Congress is using WORM technology to alleviate a serious shelf-space problem.

Magneto-Optical Disks

Magneto-optical disks integrate optical and magnetic disk technology to enable read-*and*-write storage. The 5¼-inch disks can store up to 1000 Mb. However, the technology must be improved before the disks can experience widespread acceptance. At present, magneto-optical disks are too expensive and do not offer anywhere near the kind of reliability that users have come to expect of magnetic media. In addition, the access times are relatively slow, about the same as a low-end Winchester disk.

As optical laser disk technology matures to offer reliable, cost-effective, read/write operation, it eventually may dominate secondary storage in the future as magnetic disks and tape do today.

 ## Important Terms and Summary Outline

access arm	field	parallel representation
access time	file	RAM disk
block	fixed magnetic disk	random file
blocking	flat file	random processing
bytes per inch (bpi)	floppy disk	read/write head
CD-ROM	gigabyte (GB)	secondary storage
cylinder	grandfather-father-son	sector
data base	method	sector organization
data item	indexed-sequential	sequential files
direct access storage	organization	sequential processing
devices (DASD)	interblock gap (IBG)	serial representation
direct-access file	interchangeable	serpentine
direct-access	magnetic disk	streamer tape drive
processing	key field	tape density
disk address	magnetic disk drive	track
disk caching	magnetic tape cartridge	tracks per inch (TPI)
disk cartridge	magnetic tape drive	transfer rate
disk density	magnetic tape reel	Winchester disk
disk pack	magneto-optical disk	WORM disk
diskette	off-line	
end-of-file marker	on-line	
(EOF)	optical laser disk	

6–1 SECONDARY STORAGE: PERMANENT DATA STORAGE. Data and programs are stored on **secondary storage** for permanent storage. **Magnetic disk drives** and **magnetic tape drives** are the primary devices for secondary storage. **Optical laser disk** technology is emerging as an alternative to magnetic disks and magnetic tapes.

6–2 THE HIERARCHY OF DATA ORGANIZATION: BITS TO DATA bASES. The six levels of the hierarchy of data organization are bit, character (or byte), **field**, record, **file**, and **data base**. The first level is transparent to the programmer and end user, but the other five are integral to the design of any information processing activity. A string of bits is combined to form a character. Characters are combined to represent the content of fields— **data items**. Related fields are combined to form records. Records with the same data elements combine to form a file. The data base is the company's data resource for all information systems.

6–3 TRADITIONAL APPROACHES TO DATA MANIPULATION AND RE- TRIEVAL. In traditional **flat file** processing, files are sorted, merged, and processed by a **key field**. Data are retrieved and manipulated either sequentially or randomly. Magnetic disk drives enable **random-** and **sequential-processing** capabilities. Magnetic tapes have only sequential-processing capabilities.

6–4 MAGNETIC TAPE: RIBBONS OF DATA. Once loaded, a **magnetic tape reel** or **magnetic tape cartridge** is said to be **on-line** (accessible to the computer system). When processing is complete, the tape is removed for **off-line** storage.

A magnetic tape is loaded onto a tape drive, where data are read or written as the tape is passed under a **read/write head**. The physical nature of the magnetic tape results in data being stored and accessed sequentially. On ½-inch magnetic tape, data are stored using **parallel representation**, and **blocking** in blocks between **interblock gaps (IBGs)** minimizes the start/ stop movement of the tape. The standard 9-track, 2400-foot tape reel stores data at a **tape density** of 6250 **bytes per inch (bpi)**. Magnetic tape density and its speed over the read/write head combine to determine the **transfer rate**. The density of the 36-track, ½-inch tape cartridge is much greater than its tape reel predecessor which can store up to 2.4 **gigabytes (GB)**.

Most ¼-inch tape cartridges record data using **serial representation** in a continuous stream, eliminating the need for the start/stop operation of traditional tape drives. These cartridges use **streamer tape drives**, which store data in a **serpentine** manner.

6–5 SEQUENTIAL PROCESSING: ONE AFTER ANOTHER. **Sequential files**, used for sequential processing, contain records ordered according to a key field. A sequential file is processed from start to finish, and a particular record cannot be updated without processing the entire file. The **end-of- file marker (EOF)** signals the end of the file.

In tape sequential processing, the records on both the transaction and the master file must be sorted prior to processing. A new master file is created for each computer run in which records are added or changed. The **grand- father-father-son method** is a file backup procedure.

6–6 MAGNETIC DISKS: ROTATING STORAGE MEDIA. **Direct access storage devices (DASD)**, such as magnetic disk, permit random processing of records.

In the microcomputer environment, the two most popular types of **interchangeable magnetic disks** are the 5¼-inch and 3½-inch **diskettes** (or **floppy disks**). The microcomputer **fixed magnetic disk** is called the **Winchester disk.**

In **sector organization**, the recording surface is divided into pie-shaped **sectors**, and each sector is assigned a number. Data are stored via serial representation within **tracks** on each recording surface. The spacing of tracks is measured in **tracks per inch**, or **TPI.** A particular **cylinder** refers to every track with the same number on all recording surfaces. **Disk density** refers to the number of bits that can be stored per unit of area on the disk-face surface. A particular set of data stored on a disk is assigned a **disk address** that designates its physical location (disk-face surface, track, sector). An **access arm** is moved to the appropriate track to retrieve the data.

The **access time** for a magnetic disk is the sum of the seek time, the rotational delay time, and the transmission time.

The data transfer rate from magnetic disk to RAM is measured in bytes per second. **Disk caching** enhances system performance by placing programs and data that are likely to be called into RAM for processing from a disk into an area of RAM that simulates disk storage, called the **RAM disk.**

In the mainframe environment, DASD are the prerequisite for virtually all information systems which demand **direct-access processing**. The once popular **disk cartridge** and the **disk pack** have been replaced with permanently installed high-density fixed disks. Mainframe disks are organized like PC disks.

6–7 RANDOM, OR DIRECT-ACCESS, PROCESSING: PICK AND CHOOSE. A **direct-access file**, or a **random file**, is a collection of records that can be processed in any order. **Indexed-sequential organization** is one of several access methods that permit a programmer random access to any record on a file. In indexed-sequential organization, access to any given record begins with a search through an index file. This search results in the disk address of the record in question.

In random processing, the unsorted transaction file is run against a random master file. Only the records needed to complete the transaction are retrieved from secondary storage.

6–8 OPTICAL LASER DISKS: HIGH-DENSITY STORAGE. Optical laser disk storage is capable of storing vast amounts of data. The three main categories of optical laser disks are **CD-ROM, WORM disk,** and **magneto-optical disk**. Most of the commercially produced read-only CD-ROM disks contain reference material. The *write once, read many* (WORM) optical laser disks are used by end user companies to store their own, proprietary information. The new magneto-optical disk offers the promise that optical laser disks will become commercially viable as a read-and-write storage technology.

 Review Exercises

Concepts

1. What are other names for diskette and direct processing?
2. CD-ROM is a spinoff of what technology?

3. What is the purpose of the interblock gap?

4. What information is contained on a magnetic tape header label?

5. A program issues a "read" command for data to be retrieved from a magnetic tape. Describe the resulting movement of the data.

6. Use the initials of your name and the ASCII encoding system to graphically contrast parallel and serial data representation.

7. What are the three main categories of optical laser disks?

8. What is the nickname of the hard disk used with microcomputers?

9. What are the six levels of the hierarchy of data organization?

10. What is the lowest level logical unit in the hierarchy of data organization?

11. Name two possible key fields for a personnel file. Name two for an inventory file.

12. In the grandfather-father-son method of file backup, which of the three files is the most current?

13. What is the purpose of an end-of-file marker?

14. Under what circumstances is a new master file created in sequential processing?

Discussion

15. If increasing the blocking factor for a magnetic tape file improves tape utilization, why not eliminate all IBGs and put all the records in one big block? Explain.

16. A floppy disk does not move until a read or write command is issued. Once it is issued, the floppy begins to spin. It stops spinning after the command is executed. Why is a disk pack not set in motion in the same manner? Why is a floppy not made to spin continuously?

17. Every Friday night a company makes backup copies of all master files and programs. Why is this necessary? The company has both tape and disk drives. What storage medium would you suggest for the backup? Why?

18. Describe the potential impact of optical laser disk technology on public and university libraries. On home libraries.

19. Contrast the advantages and disadvantages of sequential and random processing. Do you feel there will be a place for sequential processing in 1995? If so, where?

Problem Solving

20. How many megabytes are there in a gigabyte?

21. A company's employee master file contains 120,000 employee records. Each record is 1800 bytes in length. How many 2400-foot, 6250-bpi magnetic tapes (interblock gap = 0.6 inch) will be required to store the file? Assume records are blocked five. Next, assume records are unblocked, and perform the same calculations.

22. A 20-sectored disk contains 8 recording surfaces and 1000 cylinders. Each sector of a disk-face surface can store 512 bytes of data. What is the storage capacity of 8 such disks?

23. Use the technique of Figure 6–9 to illustrate graphically the sequential-processing steps required to update the inventory master file of Figure 6–7. The transaction file contains activity for Part Numbers 8 and 21. Assume that the transaction file is unsequenced.

24. Use the technique of Figure 6–12 to illustrate graphically the random-processing steps required to update the inventory master file of Figure 6–7. The transaction file contains activity for Part Numbers 8 and 21. Provide for backup.

Self-Test (by section)

6–1 Data are retrieved from temporary auxiliary storage and stored permanently in RAM. (T/F)

✱ **6–2** The specific value of a field is called the _data item_.

6–3 Flat files are sorted, merged, and processed by what kind of field: (a) solution field, (b) key field, or (c) central field?

6–4 **a.** Tape density is based on the linear distance between IBGs. (T/F)

b. The data on a ½-inch mag tape cartridge are stored in the same manner as the data on a ¼-inch tape cartridge. (T/F)

c. Streamer tape drives store data in a _serpentine_ manner.

✱ **6–5** **a.** A key field is needed for sequential processing. (T/F)

b. The entire magnetic tape master file must be processed even if only one record is to be updated. (T/F)

6–6 **a.** Magnetic disks have both _random_- and _sequential_-access capabilities.

b. In a disk drive, the read/write heads are mounted on an access arm. (T/F)

c. Fixed disks can be removed and stored off-line. (T/F)

d. The two diskette sizes are __5¼__ inch and __3½__ inch.

e. What percentage of the data on a magnetic disk is available to the system with each complete revolution of the disk: (a) 10%, (b) 50%, or (c) 100%?

✗ **f.** The _disk address_ denotes the physical location of a particular set of data or a program on a magnetic disk.

✱**6–7** In indexed-sequential organization, the data file contains the key and disk address. (T/F)

6–8 **a.** _Optical Laser Disk_ technology permits on-line direct access of both still pictures and video.

b. CD-ROM is read-only. (T/F)

Self-test answers. **6–1** F. **6–2** data item. **6–3** b. **6–4** (a) F; (b) F; (c) serpentine. **6–5** (a) T; (b) T. **6–6** (a) random, sequential; (b) T; (c) F; (d) 5¼, 3½; (e) c; (f) disk address. **6–7** F. **6–8** (a) Optical laser disk; (b) T.

7

Connectivity and Data Communications

STUDENT LEARNING OBJECTIVES

▶ To describe the concept of connectivity and the challenge associated with its implementation.

▶ To demonstrate an understanding of data communications terminology and applications.

▶ To detail the function and operation of data communications hardware.

▶ To describe alternatives and sources of data transmission services.

CHAPTER OUTLINE

 ## 7–1 Data Communications: From One Room to the World

In the 1960s computers numbered in the tens of thousands. Today computers number in the tens of millions. Information is everywhere. The challenge of the next decade is to make this information more accessible to a greater number of people. To do this, the business and computer communities are seeking ways to interface, or connect, a diverse set of hardware, software, and data bases. **Connectivity**, as it is called, is necessary to facilitate the electronic communication between companies, end user computing, and the free flow of information within an enterprise.

Today, workers at all levels are knowledge workers. Their scope of responsibility continues to expand as does their need for ready access to information. In today's competitive environment, relying solely on verbal communication for information transfer can be inefficient, untimely, and very expensive. Of course, knowledge workers continue to interact with co-workers, but they need a more efficient way of retrieving information. To achieve an efficient and effective interface between knowledge workers, links need to be established between their terminals and data bases. This chapter focuses on connectivity concepts and the base technology of connectivity—data communications.

Data communications is, very simply, the collection and distribution of the electronic representation of information from and to remote facilities. The information can appear in a variety of formats: data, text, voice, still pictures, graphics, and video. Prior to transmission, the raw information must be digitized. (For example, data and text might be translated into their corresponding ASCII codes.) Ultimately all forms of information are sent over the transmission media as a series of binary bits (1s and 0s). Information is transmitted from computers to terminals

This is the nerve center of EDSNET, Electronic Data Systems Corporation's global communications system. EDSNET facilitates data, voice, and video communication between a quarter of a million sites on five continents. Here in Plano, Texas, (near Dallas) more than 100 operators manage the system. Operators view 12-by-16-foot screens to keep abreast of system activity. Fourteen smaller screens provide detailed information for trouble-shooting situations, and 13 clocks display times from around the world.

and other computers over land via fiber optic cable, through the air by satellites, and under the sea through coaxial cable. The technical aspects of data communications are discussed later in this chapter.

Two other terms describe the general area of data communications. **Telecommunications** encompasses not only data communications but any type of remote communication, such as transmitting a television signal. The *computer network*, first introduced in Chapter 2, "Micros, Minis, Mainframes, and Supercomputers," is the integration of computer systems, terminals, and communication links. Computer networks and networking are discussed in detail in Chapter 8, "Networks and Networking."

Through the mid-1960s, a company's computing hardware was located in a single room called the machine room. Only the people working in the machine room had direct access to the computer. Since that time, microcomputers, terminals, and data communications have made it possible to move hardware and information systems "closer to the source"— to the people who use them. Before long, terminals will be as much a part of our work environment as desks and telephones are now.

What do these people have in common?

- The CEO of a multinational corporation who routinely visits foreign offices, reviewing and generating documents from the back seat of a limousine, on a plane, or in a hotel room
- A sales representative who creates and presents a polished proposal to clients and then taps into the home office's data base to confirm product availability and delivery dates
- A journalist who travels around the world covering fast-breaking stories for major publications
- A student who needs to take accurate notes in class, compile detailed research in the library, and still meet deadlines, even when lured outside by a sunny day

They're all part of a new generation of "computing nomads" who are building their work lives around laptop, notebook, and palmtop computers that offer desktop power in a portable package.

GEARING UP FOR COMPUTING ON THE ROAD

Because they spend so much time traveling and working at different locations, computing nomads need light-weight but powerful computers they can carry with them.

The earliest portables weighed about 45 pounds, as much as a portable sewing machine. Small wonder, then, that users turned with gratitude to the laptop, which has shrunk to about the size of a hard-side briefcase and weighs from 6 to 15 pounds. Most models can run on AC power or on rechargeable batteries; all use flat-panel monitors, which further reduce size and power consumption. A down-sized modem or fax/modem combination allows users to send and receive files over a telephone line; small (three to four pound) printers can produce hard copy on site. In addition, most laptop and notebook computers offer as much RAM and power as a desktop, a hard drive, an internal 3.5-inch high-density disk drive, and some sort of pointing device, such as a mouse or a trackball. This means a laptop computer can run the same productivity software as a desktop model. Many computing nomads supplement their portable PCs with cellular telephones, giving them the flexibility to link up with mainframes and information services from just about anywhere.

Computing nomads are also intrigued by the subnotebook computer, a slightly thinner, lighter (five pounds or less) version of the notebook computer that offers much the same computing power and peripherals. Some of these subnotebooks have lost weight

---

 The Beginning of an Era: Cooperative Computing

Intracompany Networking

This is the era of **cooperative computing**. Information is the password to success in today's business environment. To get meaningful, accurate, and timely information, businesses must cooperate internally and externally to take full advantage of what is available. To promote internal cooperation, businesses are setting up *intracompany networking* (see Figure 7–1). For example, information maintained in the personnel department is readily accessible to people throughout the company on a *need-to-know* basis. The same is true of information maintained by purchasing, engineering, or any other department. At the individual level, managers or knowledge workers create microcomputer-based systems and data bases to help them do their jobs. These personalized systems and data bases can be made a part of the company's larger computer network when other managers need these information resources.

by omitting an internal disk drive. In its place, a few provide a slot for an I/O or memory card. These cards, which look like thick credit cards, use integrated circuits to store data, ranging from computer files to programs. Although more expensive than disk-based storage, memory cards are durable, an important consideration for computing on the go.

WEIGHING THE TRADE-OFFS

Nomadic computing is not without its drawbacks, of course. Anyone who has experienced computing on the road has a horror story of trying to work around a dead battery or finding a phone that could be attached to a computer's modem. Other aggravations include the hard-to-see LCD screens and the limited expansion options; most of the smaller notebook PCs simply don't have room to expand. The portables, especially the notebook computers, are easily stolen, and some don't react well to being dropped or subjected to extreme cold, heat, vibration, or spills. And then there is the matter of price. Although prices continue to drop, a portable PC may cost twice that of a similarly configured desktop PC.

Still, for most computing nomads, time is money; if they can't work while on the go, they can't make money. This simple equation makes it easy to justify the portable's cost—or any other trade-off.

THE PC AS A SALES TOOL   To help market Nike shoes, the company has equipped its sales force with Compaq notebook computers. The PCs can display images and specifications of the company's current product line. The computers are also set up for order entry, inventory status, and electronic mail.

FIGURE 7–1   Intracompany and Intercompany Networking

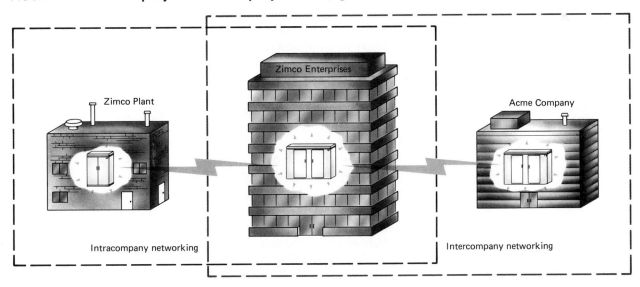

This office is one of eight regional customer support centers, each of which is part of a computer network. The terminals and PCs at this office are linked to a local minicomputer that is connected via a high-speed communications line to the company's headquarters in Omaha, Nebraska. The regional minis also are used for local processing.

Intercompany Networking

Companies have recognized that they must cooperate with one another to compete effectively in a world market. They cooperate via *intercompany networking* (Figure 7–1) or, more specifically, **electronic data interchange (EDI)**. EDI uses computers and data communications to transmit data electronically between companies. Invoices, orders, and many other intercompany transactions, including the exchange of information, can be transmitted from the computer of one company to the computer of another. For example, at General Foods, over 50% of all shipments result from computer-to-computer order processing—customers submitting their orders to General Foods via EDI. Figure 7–2 contrasts the traditional interaction between a customer and supplier company with interactions via EDI. EDI is a *strategic advantage* that some companies have over their competitors. We list some of the reasons below.

- EDI reduces paper-processing costs and delays.
- EDI reduces errors and correction costs.
- EDI minimizes receivables and inventory disputes.
- EDI improves relations between trading partners.

Executives no longer debate whether to implement EDI; they are more concerned about the speed at which it can be put to work in their companies. Essentially, they have two choices. They can elect to create the hardware- and software-based EDI system in-house, or they can use

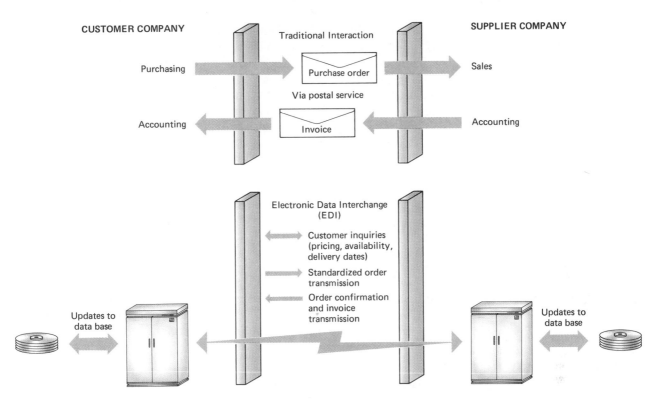

FIGURE 7–2 Interactions between Customer and Supplier
In the figure, the traditional interaction between a customer company and a supplier company is contrasted with similar interactions via electronic data interchange.

a **third-party provider** of EDI services. A third-party provider is an intermediary who helps facilitate EDI between trading partners with incompatible hardware and software. By far the fastest way to take advantage of EDI is to contract for the services of a third-party provider. Although developing EDI capabilities within a company may be less costly, it will take longer to implement.

External Computing Support: Service via Computer

The phenomenal growth of the use of micros in the home is causing companies to expand their information system capabilities to permit linkages with home and portable PCs. This form of cooperative computing increases system efficiency while lowering costs. For example, in over 100 banks, services have been extended to home micro owners in the form of home banking systems. Subscribers to a home banking service use their personal computers as terminals linked to the bank's mainframe computer system to pay bills, transfer funds, and inquire about account status.

Also, the Internal Revenue Service (IRS) now permits tax returns to be filed by professional preparers from their PCs. This service saves both the taxpayer and the IRS time and money. For the taxpayer and

Ford Motor Company's CREDITNET system is a good example of intercompany networking. CREDITNET lets a salesman at Tate's Auto Center in Holbrook, Arizona, process a customer's credit application right from the showroom floor.

the preparer, the on-line system performs all the necessary table searches and computations, and it even cross-checks the accuracy and consistency of the input data. For the IRS, no further data entry or personal assistance is required. A third example of cooperative computing are the brokerage firms now permitting customers to access up-to-the-minute stock market quotations and to issue buy/sell orders directly through their personal computers. Several supermarkets are experimenting with electronic shopping. In the 1990s virtually every type of industry will provide the facility for external links to its mainframe computer systems.

7-3 ## Connectivity: Linking Hardware, Software, and Data Bases

The scope of computer and information system technology is doubling every two years. Accompanying this rapid growth is an equal increase in the number of catch phrases, buzz words, and new terms. If computer specialists were asked to vote on which of these phrases, words, or terms would represent the driving force of computers in the 1990s, they would probably say *connectivity*.

Theory and Practice

Connectivity refers to the degree to which hardware devices can be functionally linked to one another. Some people expand the scope of connectivity to include other aspects of computers and information processing, such as software and data bases. Connectivity has become such an important consideration that virtually all future decisions involving hardware, software, and data base management must be evaluated with respect to connectivity. Corporate management has made connectivity a high-priority strategy. Management realizes that connectivity is the key to unlocking the full potential of the information resource.

To get the most out of the information resource, it must be shared. To do this, the company must strive toward full connectivity.

- Connectivity means that a marketing manager can use a microcomputer to access information in a data base on the finance department's minicomputer.
- Connectivity means that a network of microcomputers can route output to the same laser printer.
- Connectivity means that a manufacturing company's mainframe computer can communicate with the mainframe computers of suppliers.

In these examples there must be an electronic connection between these hardware devices—thus the derivation of the term *connectivity*.

In practice, people interpret the meaning of connectivity within the context of their own perspectives. A personal computer enthusiast sees it as the capability to transfer files between personal computers. Computer professionals, in particular, data communications specialists,

Many insurance companies say that they are quick to process claims, but some are more effective than others. This insurance claims adjuster brings a cellular laptop, which is capable of transmitting voice, data, and images, plus a video camera to the site of an accident or a natural disaster. While writing up the claim, he transmits videos, frame by frame, to the company's home office. Normally, electronic approval for issuing a check is sent to him via his laptop. He then issues a check on the spot to the policyholder.

see it as the passing of data between hardware devices of any kind. Vendors of user-oriented query languages see it as the degree of connection between software products that use query languages. In its broadest sense, connectivity is more than the physical connection of hardware devices; it is the functional connection of an organization's information resources.

The Technological Challenge

Technologically, it is relatively easy to make an electronic connection between two computer systems, but realizing any meaningful transfer of information from the connection is another matter. Most computer systems and database software packages were not designed to permit the efficient sharing of resources with different types of computer systems and data bases. *Incompatible* computer systems differ, often dramatically, in architecture (basic design) and the manner in which they store data. In essence, they do not speak the same language. This incompatibility is best explained by an analogy. You can pick up a telephone and dial anywhere in the world, even China. However, if you do not speak Chinese or the person on the other end does not speak English, information transfer is impossible without the assistance of a translator.

The technological challenge confronting connectivity in an incompatible environment is formidable. To achieve connectivity, a hardware and/or software interface must be designed and implemented that enables the efficient modification of the output of one system such that it can be intercepted and interpreted by another system. Efficiency is the key word. Connectivity is possible in almost every situation, but in some situations, the *system overhead* is prohibitively high. That is, the expense of the extra processing required to modify the output may make connectivity infeasible.

A Hardware Vendor's Perspective

Until recently, vendors and business were not very concerned about data communications compatibility. Traditionally, companies had all their computer needs handled by a centralized information services division. This centralized division made certain that their hardware and software purchases were all compatible. Now the situation has changed. The widespread use of micros and the emergence of departmental computing has diluted centralized control. Users purchase and install micros, minis, and a wide variety of applications software. Now these users want to connect their incompatible hardware and software to the company's mainframe resources and the resources of other users. This connectivity challenge is shared by small mom-and-pop organizations and by billion-dollar multinationals.

The information services divisions in today's organizations must accommodate user requests for greater connectivity. They must also make the most effective use of all computing and information resources. This requires handling a wide variety of hardware, software, and data bases. A particular connectivity issue has arisen as companies push to implement electronic funds transfer and electronic data interchange applications.

Computers Solve the Disappearing Act In 1960, Robert Switzer's first wife vanished with his two children. After 29 years of looking for his sons, Switzer took a chance and entered a message on an CompuServe electronic bulletin board that would be read by PC enthusiasts across the country. The message read, "If your name is Robert Switzer, please call me." Switzer received a phone call three weeks after he had sent the message. The phone call was from a comptroller at CompuServe relaying that Switzer had an important message. He turned on his computer and read the message: "I am the son you're looking for. My brother and I have been looking for you for many years." As this story portrays, the computer is no longer just for cranking out numbers—it is a wonderful new way to communicate.

Automatic teller machines (ATMs) provide the link between us and our money via EFT. The banking industry would prefer that its customers use ATMs for banking transactions rather than tellers. The average ATM transaction takes less time, but more importantly, it costs less than half that of a teller transaction. We can expect the cost of banking services to drop as more and more people use ATMs.

Electronic funds transfer, or **EFT**, involves the transfer of funds from one organization to another via data communications. Connectivity concerns have actually changed the buying habits of companies. Executives are much more deliberate in their decision making. They do not want to buy into a technology that may be obsolete in a few years because of changing connectivity standards. This need for internal and external connectivity has prompted top management personnel in companies throughout the world to demand that vendors focus their efforts on providing better connectivity.

Vendors, usually reluctant to cooperate with each other, are beginning to respond to the growing need for connectivity. For example, IBM, Digital, and others are committed to providing the facility to link all hardware devices and software products within their respective product lines.

A User's Perspective

To the user, the ideal implementation of connectivity would be to make all corporate computer and information resources accessible from his or her PC or terminal. This ideal is referred to as **total connectivity**. Realistically, industry analysts are predicting that total connectivity is still a decade or more away. Nevertheless, users are expecting, even demanding, that the information services divisions at least strive for total connectivity.

Total connectivity, or the networking of all hardware, software, and data bases, is a goal of many companies. Total connectivity will permit user access to

- Mainframe computers
- Computer networks of all kinds
- Outside information services
- Departmental computers
- Other companies' computers via EDI
- All other hardware/software environments in the company

In total connectivity, a message can be sent from any user to any other point in the network, be it a workstation, a micro, a printer, or a mainframe.

One of the fundamental assumptions of connectivity is that the linking of hardware, software, and data bases be *transparent* to the user. That is, the user would simply request the information he or she needs without being concerned about the technical complexities of connectivity.

A Technological Perspective

To the computer/communications specialists charged with establishing the link between the various elements of a system, the implementation of connectivity can be incredibly complex. To achieve almost any level of connectivity (connectivity is implemented in degrees), these technical specialists must juggle communication protocols (rules), official and de facto standards, different approaches to data base design, different computer system architectures, and user information requirements. Each of these considerations poses formidable technological hurdles. To overcome these hurdles while shielding users from the complexity of connectivity is a herculean task. Nevertheless, organizations are making the commitment to strive for a higher level of connectivity.

Connectivity Summary

Technologically, total connectivity is possible; however, it is not likely in the near future. If vendors were to cooperate and set standards for connectivity, it would still take them years to redesign their product lines to accommodate the standards. Also, companies have enormous investments in their existing hardware and software environments. It is not likely that a company would scrap its current environment and replace it with a compatible environment, even if such an environment were available on the open market. One industry analyst described the prospects for improved connectivity as a "muddy mess." For example, if vendors change their product lines to accommodate connectivity better, they run the risk of being shunned by existing customers for leaving them with obsolete equipment and software.

For the time being, companies are using jury-rigged solutions to implement connectivity. For example, to permit communication between a network of microcomputers in the marketing department and a departmental minicomputer in the plant may require substantial interim processing. In the ideal implementation of connectivity, the connection is direct with no interim processing needed. Approaches to linking incompatible environments are discussed later in this chapter.

Even a "muddy mess" has some clear water. The greatest strides have been in the area of intercompany networking. The ANSI **X.12** communications protocol has been adopted for the exchange of invoices, orders, corporate electronic payments (via participating banks), and other electronic data interchange transactions. International standards-making bodies are developing standards, such as the *Open Systems Interconnection* (*OSI*) and *Integrated Services Digital Network* (*ISDN*). Others are gaining de facto standard status, such as IBM's *Systems Network Architecture* (*SNA*).

7–4 Data Communications Hardware

Data communications hardware is used to transmit data between terminals (including PCs that emulate terminals) and computers and between computers in a computer network. These primary hardware components include the modem, down-line processor, front-end processor, and PBX. The integration of these devices (except the PBX) with terminals and computer systems is illustrated in Figure 7–3 and discussed in the paragraphs that follow.

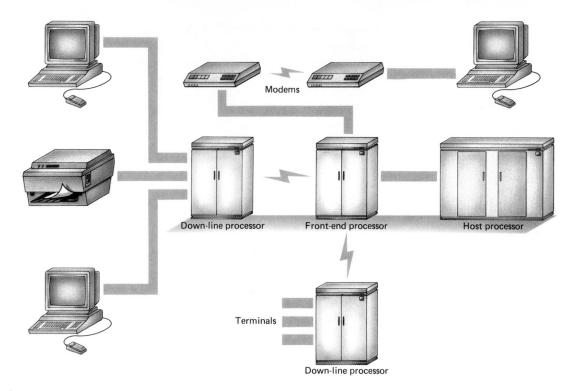

FIGURE 7–3 Hardware Components in Data Communications
Devices that handle the movement of data in a computer network are the modem, down-line processor, front-end processor, and host processor.

The Modem

If you have a micro, you have the capability of establishing a communications link between your microcomputer and any remote computer system in the world. However, to do this you must have ready access to a telephone line and your micro must be equipped with a *modem*. Currently, a little over 50% of all PCs are equipped with modems.

Telephone lines were designed for voice communication, not data communication. The **modem** (*modulator-demodulator*) converts micro-to-computer and terminal-to-computer electrical *digital* signals into *analog* signals so that the data can be transmitted over telephone lines (see Figure 7–4). The digital electrical signals are modulated to make sounds similar to those you hear on a touch-tone telephone. Upon reaching their destination, these analog signals are demodulated by another modem into computer-compatible electrical signals for processing. The procedure is reversed for computer-to-terminal or computer-to-micro communication. A modem is always required when you dial up the computer on a telephone line. The modulation-demodulation process is not needed when a micro or terminal is linked directly to a network by a transmission medium such as a coaxial cable.

Internal and External Modems   There are two types of modems for micros and terminals: *internal* and *external*. Most micros and terminals have

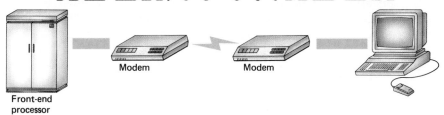

FIGURE 7–4   The Modulation-Demodulation Process
Electrical digital signals are modulated into analog signals for transmission over telephone lines and then demodulated for processing at the destination.

internal modems; that is, the modem is on an optional add-on circuit board that is simply plugged into an empty expansion slot in the micro's processor unit or the terminal's housing. The external modem is a separate component, as illustrated in Figure 7–4, and is connected via a serial interface port (see Chapter 2, "Micros, Minis, Mainframes, and Super-computers"). To make the connection with a telephone line and either type of modem, you simply plug the telephone line into the modem just as you would when connecting the line to a telephone.

Smart Modems   Modems have varying degrees of "intelligence" produced by embedded microprocessors. For instance, some modems can

This advertising executive's notebook PC is configured with an internal modem. She has only to establish a communications link via a telephone line to keep in touch with office activities and retrieve critical information wherever she travels.

automatically dial up the computer (*auto-dial*), establish a link (*log on*), and even answer incoming calls from other computers (*auto-answer*). **Smart modems** also have made it possible to increase the rate at which data can be transmitted and received.

Fax Modems   The **fax modem** performs the same function as a regular modem plus it has an added capability—it enables a PC to simulate a **facsimile** or **fax** machine. Fax machines transfer images of hard-copy documents via telephone lines to another location. The process is similar to using a copying machine except that the original is inserted in a fax machine at one location and a hard copy is produced on a fax machine at another location. PCs configured with a fax modem (usually an add-on board) can fax text files and images (send an electronic version) directly from an electronic file to a remote facsimile machine or another similarly equipped micro. The uses of fax modems are discussed in more detail in Chapter 8, "Networks and Networking."

Acoustical Couplers   If you need a telephone hookup for voice conversations on the same telephone line used for data communication and do not want to disconnect the phone each time, you can purchase a modem with an **acoustical coupler**. To make the connection, you mount the telephone handset directly on the acoustical coupler. Acoustical couplers are essential items for travelers who routinely make micro/mainframe connections from public telephones.

A "Host" of Computers

Twenty-five years ago, most processors were simply called central processing units, or CPUs for short; today, however, not all processors are "central." In this era of cooperative computing, special-function processors, such as the front-end processor and the down-line processor, are strategically located throughout a computer system to increase efficiency and throughput.

The Need for Special-Function Processors   A processor executes only one instruction at a time, even though it appears to be handling many tasks simultaneously. A **task** is the basic unit of work for a processor. At any given time, several tasks will compete for processor time. For example, one task might involve calculating finance charges and another, the analysis of data from a research project.

Since a single processor is capable of executing only one instruction at a time, one task will be given priority; the others will have to wait. The processor rotates between competing tasks so quickly, however, that it appears as if all are being executed at once. Even so, this rotation eventually takes its toll on processor efficiency. To improve the overall efficiency of a computer system, the *processing load* is *distributed* among several other special-function processors.

In Figure 7–3, the *host*, or *mainframe*, processor is responsible for overall control of the computer system and for the execution of applications programs, such as payroll or accounting. The two communications-related processors in the computer system, the down-line processor and the front-end processor, are under the control of and subordinate to the host.

The down-line processor. The **down-line processor**, also called a **multiplexer**, is an extension of the front-end processor. Its name is derived from its physical location relative to the host processor. It is located "down-line"—at or near a remote site. The down-line processor collects data from a number of low-speed devices, such as terminals and serial printers, then "concentrates" the data—sending the data over a single communications channel (see Figure 7–5) to the front-end processor. The down-line processor also receives and distributes host output to the appropriate remote terminals.

The down-line processor is an economic necessity when several low-speed terminals are located at one remote site. One high-speed line connecting the down-line processor to the host is considerably less expensive than several low-speed lines connecting each terminal to the host. An airline reservations counter might have 10 terminals. Each terminal is connected to a common down-line processor, which in turn is connected to a central host computer. An airline might have one or several down-line processors at a given airport, depending on the volume of passenger traffic.

A microcomputer can be made to emulate the function of a down-line processor. This often occurs when a network of micros is linked to a mainframe computer.

Terminals at this branch bank are connected to a down-line processor. The down-line processor facilitates communications with the bank's mainframe computer.

FIGURE 7–5 "Concentrating" Data for Remote Transmission
The down-line processor "concentrates" the data from several low-speed devices for transmission over a single high-speed line. At the host site, the front-end processor separates the data for processing. Data received from a front-end processor are interpreted by the down-line processor and routed to the appropriate device.

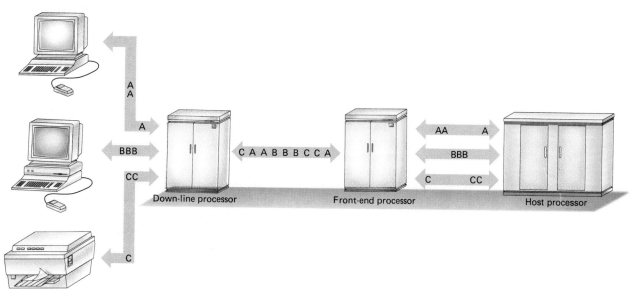

Although most of us like the idea of cash, it does have its drawbacks, it's bulky and heavy, it gets dirty, and it attracts pickpockets and thieves. For all these reasons, futurists have long predicted the evolution of a cashless society. If you'd like a preview, visit Parris Island, the Marine Corps' training base in South Carolina. Recruits are paid, make purchases, and even use pay phones—without touching a check, paper money, or coins. They use smart cards instead.

WHAT MAKES A SMART CARD SMART

Some smart cards look like a traditional credit card, down to the raised lettering on the front and the magnetic strip on the back. The only visible difference might be a few flat metal contacts on one end. Inside, though, the smart card hides 1 to 8 KB of memory and sometimes a microprocessor, which allows it to store, manipulate, and communicate information to another computer—something no credit card or "greenback" can do.

The simplest and most widely used type of smart card acts as an "electronic purse." Instead of carrying change for a pay phone, you could buy a smart card that is good for a certain dollar value of phone calls. In use, the smart card is inserted into a special reader, which deducts the call's cost from the card's dollar value. When the card's dollar value is used up, you buy a new card. The only drawback is that the cards are specialized; the "money" they contain has, in effect, been spent on phone calls. To pay a parking meter, you need a different smart card. Several European resorts and at least one American race track use this type of smart card to let guests prepay for such expenses as food or bets.

More sophisticated smart cards can carry detailed, personalized records of transactions, as well as such security measures as a personal identification number (PIN). Of course, smart cards can carry more than just financial information. A smart card under consideration by several major insurance companies would contain a patient's complete medical records. When passed through a card reader in a hospital, doctor's office, or pharmacy, the medical records on the card could be read and then updated. Medical records and transaction information captured by the reader could be transmitted to a central computer on-line or at the end of the day, so that insurance claims could be filed electronically.

Smart cards are widely used in Europe, especially France, where they were invented in the late 1970s, and in Japan, where they have largely replaced the pocket change needed for parking meters and pay phones. In Japan, every Nissan automobile comes with a smart card, which is used to store both maintenance and loan payment records. In Europe, some hotels allow guests to charge meals and other expenses to a smart card; at the end of their stay, they plug the smart card into a special terminal, which prints out an itemized bill.

Smart cards have been slow to catch on in the United States, however. One reason is that smart cards and their readers seem expensive, especially when compared to credit cards and their readers. This perception may change, though, thanks to a number of pilot programs that show how smart cards can actually cut costs.

Some of the most ambitious and successful programs are being conducted by the U.S. government. Based on the success of experimental programs, the U.S. Department of Agriculture recently announced guidelines for replacing $17.3 billion in traditional food stamps with smart cards. Besides reducing theft and fraud, the smart cards will cut the massive expense of processing 2.5 billion paper coupons. The Social Security Administration, the U.S. Department of Veterans Affairs, and other agencies are also looking into using smart cards as a way of distributing government benefits.

AT&T is investing heavily in smart card research, too, and its smart cards are already being used to collect tolls in Italy and on selected toll roads in this country. IBM, meanwhile, is just one company that is developing smart cards that can be used as ID cards or to "unlock" computer systems or offices. Because smart cards offer superior security and instant verification of credit lines, the major credit-card companies are also experimenting with them.

As the technology develops, experts predict, even more applications will become apparent. One proposal, for example, would replace military dog tags with smart cards that supplement name, rank, and serial number with medical information that would be invaluable to battlefield medics.

The front-end processor. The terminal or computer sending a **message** is the *source*. The terminal or computer receiving the message is the *destination*. The *front-end processor* establishes the link between the source and destination in a process called **handshaking**.

If you think of messages as mail to be delivered to various points in a computer network, the front-end processor is the post office. Each computer system and terminal is assigned a **network address**. The front-end processor uses these addresses to route messages to their destinations. The content of a message could be a prompt to the user, a user inquiry, a program instruction, an "electronic memo," or any type of information that can be transmitted electronically—even the image of a handwritten report. Figure 7–6 illustrates how a memo would be sent from the president of a company to two vice presidents and the plant manager. It is not uncommon for a front-end processor to control communications between a dozen down-line processors and 100 or more terminals.

FIGURE 7–6 Message Routing
In the illustration, the president sends a message to two vice presidents and the plant manager. The front-end processor accepts the president's message for processing and routes it to the appropriate addresses.

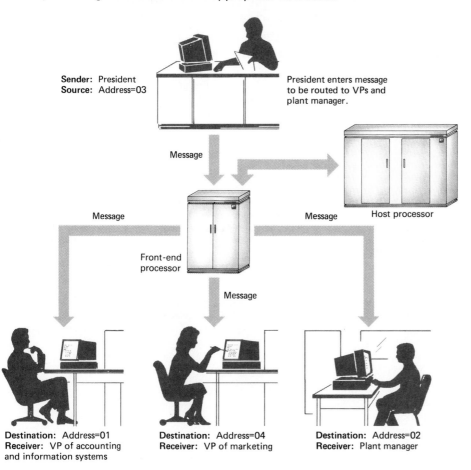

Sender: President
Source: Address=03

President enters message to be routed to VPs and plant manager.

Message

Host processor

Message

Message

Front-end processor

Message

Destination: Address=01
Receiver: VP of accounting and information systems

Destination: Address=04
Receiver: VP of marketing

Destination: Address=02
Receiver: Plant manager

The front-end processor relieves the host processor of communications-related tasks, such as message routing, parity checking, code translation, editing, and cryptography (the encryption/decryption of data for security purposes). All data transmitted *to* the host processor *from* remote locations or *from* the host processor *to* remote locations are handled by the front-end processor. This processor specialization permits the host to operate more efficiently and to devote more of its resources to processing applications programs.

Another Host and Other Subordinate Processors   Figure 7–3 demonstrates how a computer system can have three processors: a host, a front-end, and a down-line processor. Figure 7–7 illustrates an even greater variety of subordinate processors, each one performing a different function. A computer system can be configured with the host plus none or all of the subordinate processors shown in Figure 7–7. Circumstances dictate which, if any, of these subordinate processors should be included.

The parallel host processor.   Figure 7–7 includes a **parallel host**. A parallel host is necessary where downtime (host not operational) is unacceptable. This is the case in many on-line information systems. For example, in an airline reservation system, thousands of reservations are made and canceled each hour, 24 hours a day, 7 days a week. If the host

FIGURE 7–7   Host and Subordinate Processors

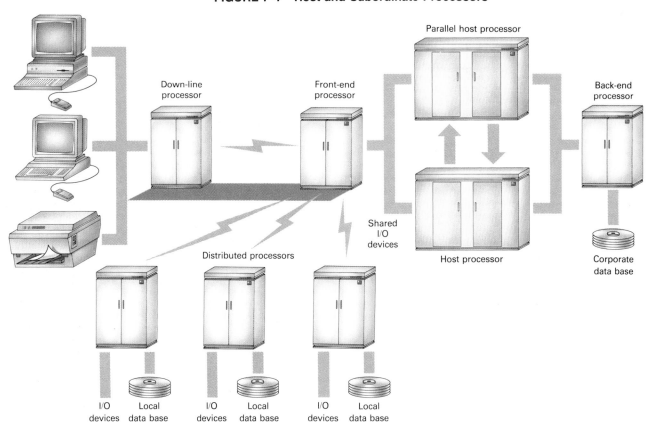

fails, the parallel host takes over and provides backup to keep the system in continuous operation.

The back-end processor. The *back-end processor* handles tasks associated with the retrieval and manipulation of data from secondary storage devices, such as magnetic disk. For example, suppose a program that is executing in the host requires Sally Smith's record from the personnel master file. The host processor issues a request to the back-end processor to retrieve the record of Sally Smith. It is then the responsibility of the back-end processor to issue the commands necessary to retrieve the record from magnetic disk storage and transmit it to the host for processing. By handling the logic and the mechanics of tasks involving the data base, the back-end processor substantially reduces the processing load of the host, thereby speeding the execution of applications programs.

The distributed processor. The **distributed processor** is an extension of the host. In effect, it is a *host* processor system that is *distributed*, or physically located, in a functional area department (such as accounting, marketing, or manufacturing). These microcomputer and minicomputer systems, also known as *departmental computer systems*, have their own input/output (I/O), terminals, and storage capabilities and can operate as a stand-alone system (independent of the host) or as a distributed system (an extension of the host). Distributed processing is introduced in Chapter 2, "Micros, Minis, Mainframes, and Supercomputers."

The PBX

The old-time telephone **PBX** (private branch exchange) switchboard has evolved into a sophisticated device capable of switching not only voice but also digital electronic signals. The PBX is actually a computer that electronically connects computers and terminals much as telephone operators manually connected telephone lines on the old PBX switchboards. Approximately 70% of the traffic handled by a modern PBX is voice; the remainder consists of digital electronic signals.

As we discussed earlier, we are moving toward making information systems more responsive to end users by "distributing" processing capabilities closer to the people who use them. Because of this trend, a single organization is likely to have at least one mainframe computer, several minis, and many micros and terminals. The PBX, serving as the hub of data activity, permits these computers and terminals to "talk" to one another. Figure 7–8 illustrates how several computer systems can be linked via a PBX.

Memory Bits

HARDWARE FOR DATA COMMUNICATIONS

- Modem
- Down-line processor
- Front-end processor
- PBX

Computer Campaigning Politics and computers? It was only a matter of time. On-line information services such as Prodigy and Compuserve offer their users insights on politics. Both have set up bulletin boards so their users can view information about political candidates and issues. When someone finds out something interesting, possibly incriminating, about a candidate, he or she posts it to the bulletin board. Candidates can go on-line to defend themselves and answer questions. One candidate held an on-line meeting. Once the meeting was in progress, people submitted questions and the candidate answered them by dictating to a fast keyboarder.

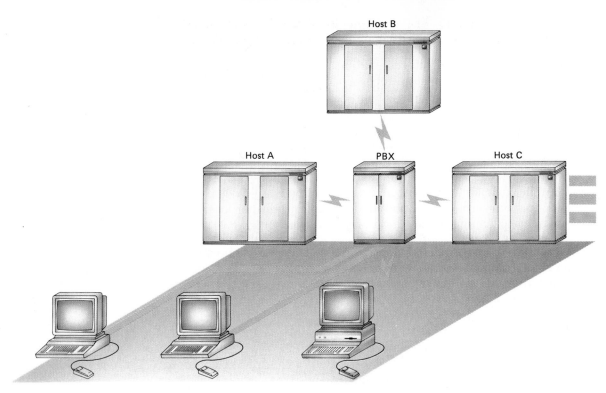

FIGURE 7–8 Computers and Terminals Linked by a PBX
Any two of the host computers or terminals can be linked together for data transmission by the PBX.

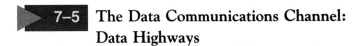

7–5 The Data Communications Channel: Data Highways

Transmission Media

A **communications channel** is the facility through which electronic signals are transmitted between locations in a computer network. Data, text, and digitized images are transmitted as combinations of bits (0s and 1s). A *channel's capacity* is rated by the number of bits it can transmit per second. A regular telephone line can transmit up to 9600 **bits per second (bps)**, or 9.6 K bps (thousands of bits per second). Under normal circumstances, a 9.6 K-bps line would fill the screen of a typical video monitor with text in one or two seconds.

In practice, the word **baud** is often used interchangeably with bits per second. But in reality, they are quite different. Baud is a measure of the maximum number of electronic signals that can be transmitted via a communications channel. It is true that a 300-bps modem operates at 300 baud, but both 1200-bps and 2400-bps modems operate at 600 baud. A technical differentiation between baud and bits per second is beyond the scope of this book. Suffice it to say that when someone says *baud* when talking about computer-based communications, that person probably means bits per second. The erroneous use of *baud* is so common that some software packages that facilitate data communication ask you to specify baud when they actually want bits per second.

Data rates of 1540 K bps are available through common carriers such as American Telephone & Telegraph (AT&T). The channel may comprise one or a combination of the transmission media discussed next.

Telephone Lines   The same transmission facilities we use for voice communication via telephones can also be used to transmit data. This capability is provided by communications companies throughout the country and the world.

Coaxial Cable   **Coaxial cable** contains electrical wire and is constructed to permit high-speed data transmission with a minimum of signal distortion. If you have ever hooked up a television, you probably are familiar with coaxial cable. Coaxial cable is laid along the ocean floor for intercontinental voice and data transmission. It is also used to connect terminals and computers in a "local" area (from a few feet to a few miles).

Fiber Optic Cable   Very thin transparent fibers have been developed that will eventually replace the twisted-pair copper wire traditionally used in the telephone system. These hairlike **fiber optic cables** carry data faster and are lighter and less expensive than their copper-wire counterparts. Twisted-pair wire and coaxial cable carry data as electrical signals. Fiber optic cable carries data as laser-generated light beams.

The differences between the data transmission rates of copper wire and fiber optic cable are tremendous. In the time it takes to transmit a single page of *Webster's Unabridged Dictionary* over twisted-pair copper wire (about 6 seconds), the entire dictionary could be transmitted over a single fiber optic cable.

Another of the many advantages of fiber optic cable is its contribution to data security. It is much more difficult for a computer criminal to intercept a signal sent over fiber optic cable (via a beam of light) than it is over copper wire (an electrical signal).

Fiber optic technology has opened the door for some very interesting domestic applications. The high-capacity cable will service our telephone, our TV, and our PC. Fiber optic cable will enable us to see the party on the other end of a telephone conversation. As for TV viewing, we will be able to choose from hundreds of movies, including current releases, and we will be able to choose when we watch them. In the PC world, tapping into an information network will be an increasingly visual experience, with plenty of high-resolution color graphics. For example, instead of reading a buying service's product description, we'll be able to view a photo-quality display of it. However, we may need to wait a few years to enjoy these services. The expense of fiber optic cable may delay its widespread implementation in the home until the turn of the century.

Microwave   Communications channels do not have to be wires or fibers. Data can also be transmitted via **microwave radio signals**. Transmission of these signals is *line-of-sight*; that is, the radio signal travels in a direct

Copper wire in the telephone network is being replaced by the more versatile fiber optic cable. Laser-generated light pulses are transmitted through these ultra-thin glass fibers. A pair of optic fibers can simultaneously carry 1344 voice conversations and interactive data communications sessions.

Microwave repeater stations, such as this one amidst the icy drifts atop Echo Summit in California, relay signals to transceivers or other repeater stations. This microwave station opens a telecommunications link between Sacramento, California, and Salt Lake City, Utah.

Computers and data communications have turned our world into a "global village." This satellite, which has served as a data communications link between North America and Europe, is being loaded in the bay of a space shuttle craft and brought back to earth for repair.

line from one repeater station to the next until it reaches its destination. Because of the curvature of the earth, microwave repeater stations are placed on the tops of mountains and towers, usually about 30 miles apart.

Satellites have made it possible to minimize the line-of-sight limitation. Satellites routinely are launched into orbit for the sole purpose of relaying data communications signals to and from earth stations. A satellite, which is essentially a repeater station, is launched and set in a **geosynchronous orbit** 22,300 miles above the earth. A geosynchronous orbit permits the communications satellite to maintain a fixed position relative to the surface of the earth. Each satellite can receive and retransmit signals to slightly less than half of the earth's surface; therefore, three satellites are required to cover the earth effectively (see Figure 7–9). The big advantage of satellites is that data can be transmitted from one location to any number of other locations anywhere on (or near) our planet.

Wireless Transceivers   Perhaps the greatest challenge and one of the biggest expenses in a computer network is the installation of the physical links between its components. The *wireless transceiver* provides an alternative when the expense of running a permanent physical line (twisted-pair wire, coaxial cable, and fiber optic cable) is prohibitive. Two wireless transceivers, each smaller than this book, replace a physical line between source and destination (micro and mainframe, terminal and down-line

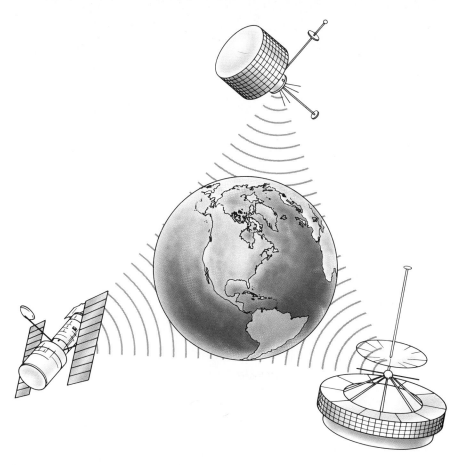

FIGURE 7–9 Satellite Data Transmission
Three satellites in geosynchronous orbit provide worldwide data transmission service.

In satellite communications, data are transmitted first to an earth station where giant antennae route signals to another earth station via a communications satellite. The signals are then transmitted to their destination over another type of communications channel.

processor, and so on). The source transmits digital signals via a physical link to a nearby transceiver, which in turn retransmits the signals over radio waves to another transceiver. Transceivers provide users with tremendous flexibility in the location of PCs and terminals in a network; however, the flexibility advantage is offset by the transceivers' limited channel capacity. Also, the number of terminals/PCs that can linked via transceivers is limited by the frequencies allotted for this purpose.

Data Transmission in Practice

A communications channel from Computer A in Seattle, Washington, to Computer B in Orlando, Florida (see Figure 7–10), usually would consist of several different transmission media. The connection between Computer A and a terminal in the same building is probably coaxial cable. The Seattle company might use a communications company such as AT&T to transmit the data. AT&T would then send the data through a combination of transmission facilities that might include copper wire, fiber optic cable, and microwave radio signals.

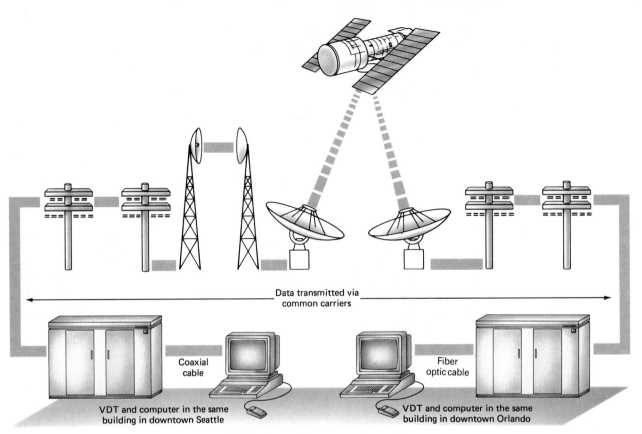

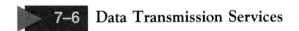

Data transmitted via
common carriers

Coaxial
cable

Fiber
optic cable

VDT and computer in the same
building in downtown Seattle

VDT and computer in the same
building in downtown Orlando

FIGURE 7–10   Data Transmission Path
*It's more the rule than the exception that data are carried over several
transmission media between source and destination.*

7–6   Data Transmission Services

Common Carriers

It is impractical, not to mention illegal, for companies to string their
own coaxial cables between two locations, such as Philadelphia and New
York City. It is also impractical for them to set their own satellites in
orbit. Therefore, companies turn to **common carriers** for data communications, such as AT&T, MCI, Western Union, and GTE, to provide
communications channels. Communications common carriers, which are
regulated by the Federal Communications Commission (FCC), offer two
basic types of service: private lines and switched lines.

A **private line** (or **leased line**) provides a dedicated data communications channel between any two points in a computer network. The
charge for a private line is based on channel capacity (bps) and distance
(air miles).

A **switched line** (or **dial-up line**) is available strictly on a time-and-
distance charge, similar to a long-distance telephone call. You make a

connection by "dialing up" the computer, then a modem sends and receives data. Switched lines offer greater flexibility than private lines in that a link can be made with any computer near a telephone.

Low-speed modem-assisted transmission over conventional telephone lines will suffice for many applications, but some applications demand a higher channel capacity. Some common carriers offer a source-to-destination digital alternative using the **Integrated Services Digital Network (ISDN)** telecommunications standard. High-speed electronic data interchange (EDI) between computers is all digital. There is no need for modems in ISDN communication. ISDN services include two channel options, a 144 K-bps channel or a 1540 K-bps channel.

Specialized Common Carriers

A **specialized common carrier**, such as a **value-added network (VAN)**, may or may not use the transmission facilities of a common carrier, but in each case it "adds value" to the transmission service. The value added over and above the standard services of the common carriers may include electronic mail, data encryption/decryption, access to commercial data bases, and code conversion for communication between incompatible computers. Not only do VANs such as Tymshares's Tymnet and GTE's Telenet offer expanded services but the basic communications service provided by the VAN also may be less expensive than the same service from a common carrier.

To illustrate how a VAN can offer the same or better service at a reduced rate, consider the following. The Ace Corporation wishes to lease a 9.6 K-bps private line between New York and Philadelphia from a common carrier. Ace is likely to use only 15% of the capacity of the line. A VAN could lease the same line from the same common carrier (or use its own) and use the line to capacity by combining the New York/Philadelphia data transmission requirements of Ace Corporation with those of several other companies (see Figure 7–11). The VAN uses computers on each end of the line to collect the data and redistribute them to appropriate destinations. In effect, several corporations share the same line and its cost with little or no loss in performance.

One of the services offered by common carriers is the facilitation of conferencing via telecommunications, or teleconferencing. These people in Charleston, South Carolina, saved the cost and time of a cross-country flight by teleconferencing with their colleagues in Portland, Oregon. The participants can see and talk with one another and pass information back and forth via computer and facsimile machines.

FIGURE 7–11 Part of a Value-Added Network (VAN)
A VAN uses transmission media more efficiently and, therefore, is able to offer transmission service at a reduced rate.

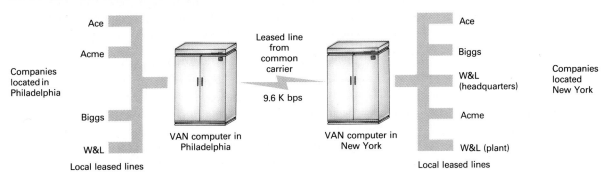

Important Terms and Summary Outline

acoustical coupler	electronic funds	network address
baud	transfer (EFT)	parallel host
bits per second (bps)	facsimile (fax)	PBX
coaxial cable	fax modem	private line
common carrier	fiber optic cable	smart modem
communications	geosynchronous orbit	specialized common
channel	handshaking	carrier
connectivity	Integrated Services	switched line
cooperative computing	Digital Network	task
data communications	(ISDN)	telecommunications
dial-up line	leased line	third-party provider
distributed processor	message	total connectivity
down-line processor	microwave radio signal	value-added network
electronic data	modem	(VAN)
interchange (EDI)	multiplexer	X.12

7–1 DATA COMMUNICATIONS: FROM ONE ROOM TO THE WORLD. **Connectivity** facilitates the electronic communication between companies, end user computing, and the free flow of information within an enterprise. Modern businesses use **data communications** to transmit data and information at high speeds from one location to the next. Data communications makes an information system more accessible to the people who use it. **Telecommunications** encompasses not only data communications but any type of remote communication. The integration of computer systems via data communications is referred to as a computer network.

7–2 THE BEGINNING OF AN ERA: COOPERATIVE COMPUTING. This is the era of **cooperative computing**. To obtain meaningful, accurate, and timely information, businesses have decided that they must cooperate internally and externally to take full advantage of available information. To promote internal cooperation, they are promoting intracompany networking. To compete in a world market, they are encouraging intercompany networking or **electronic data interchange (EDI)**. A **third-party provider** is an intermediary who helps facilitate EDI between trading partners.

7–3 CONNECTIVITY: LINKING HARDWARE, SOFTWARE, AND DATA BASES. *Connectivity* refers to the degree to which hardware devices can be functionally linked to one another. Some people expand the scope of connectivity to include other aspects of computers and information processing, such as software and data bases. Connectivity is viewed differently, depending on the perspective of the observer (user, vendor, computer specialist). The ideal implementation of connectivity is referred to as **total connectivity**.

Electronic funds transfer, or **EFT**, involves the transfer of funds from one organization to another via data communications.

The ANSI **X.12** communications protocol has been adopted for the exchange of invoices, orders, corporate electronic payments, and other EDI transactions.

7–4 DATA COMMUNICATIONS HARDWARE. The data communications hardware used to facilitate the transmission of data from one remote location to another includes **modems**, **down-line processors** (also called **multiplexers**), front-end processors, and **PBXs**. Modems modulate and demodulate signals so that data can be transmitted over telephone lines. The **fax modem** acts as a modem and enables a PC to simulate a **facsimile** or **fax** machine. **Acoustical couplers** are helpful when a single line serves both data and voice communication.

A processor rotates between competing **tasks**. To improve the overall efficiency of a computer system, the processing load is distributed among several other special-function processors. The down-line processor collects data from a number of devices then "concentrates" the data—sending the data over a single communications channel to the front-end processor. The front-end processor establishes the link between the source and destination in a process called **handshaking**, then sends a **message** to a **network address**. The front-end processor relieves the host processor of communications-related tasks.

A **parallel host** is necessary where downtime is unacceptable. The back-end processor handles tasks associated with the retrieval and manipulation of data from secondary storage devices. The **distributed processor** is, in effect, a host processor system that is physically located in a functional area department.

The PBX makes needed connections between computers and terminals.

7–5 THE DATA COMMUNICATIONS CHANNEL: DATA HIGHWAYS. A **communications channel** is the facility through which electronic signals are transmitted between locations in a computer network. A channel's capacity is rated by the number of bits it can transmit per second (**bits per second** or **bps**). In practice, the word **baud** is often used interchangeably with bits per second; in reality, they are quite different.

A channel may be composed of one or more of the following transmission media: telephone lines, **coaxial cable**, **fiber optic cable**, **microwave radio signal**, and wireless transceivers. Satellites are essentially microwave repeater stations that maintain a **geosynchronous orbit** around the earth.

7–6 DATA TRANSMISSION SERVICES. **Common carriers** provide communications channels to the public, and lines can be arranged to suit the application. A **private**, or **leased**, **line** provides a dedicated communications channel. A **switched**, or **dial-up**, **line** is available on a time-and-distance charge basis. Some common carriers offer a source-to-destination digital alternative using the **Integrated Services Digital Network (ISDN)** telecommunications standard. **Specialized common carriers**, such as **value-added networks (VANs)**, offer expanded transmission services.

 Review Exercises

Concepts

1. Would EDI be more closely associated with intercompany networking or intracompany networking?

2. What is meant by *geosynchronous orbit*, and how does it relate to data transmission via satellite?

3. What is the unit of measure for the capacity of a data communications channel?

4. Expand the following acronyms: EFT, bps, VAN, and EFT.

5. What is the purpose of a multiplexer?

6. What is the relationship between a communications channel and a computer network?

7. At what channel capacity is the bits per second equal to the baud?

8. What computerese term refers to the degree to which hardware devices can be functionally linked to one another?

9. What device converts digital signals into analog signals for transmission over telephone lines? Why is it necessary?

10. Why is it not advisable to increase the distance between microwave relay stations to 200 miles?

11. What is the ideal implementation of connectivity called?

12. Briefly describe the function of a PBX.

13. What is the purpose of the X.12 communications protocol?

14. Describe circumstances in which a leased line would be preferred to a dial-up line.

15. What is the name of the machine that transfers images of hard-copy documents via telephone lines to another location?

16. Name three subordinate processors that might be configured with a host processor to improve the overall efficiency of the computer system.

Discussion

17. What is the relationship between EDI, electronic funds transfer (EFT), and connectivity?

18. Discuss connectivity from the perspective of any non-IBM hardware vendor. From the perspective of IBM.

19. Describe how information can be made readily accessible, but only on a need-to-know basis.

20. List and discuss those characteristics that would typify a knowledge worker.

Problem Solving

21. Consider this situation: A remote line printer is capable of printing 800 lines per minute (70 characters per line average). Line capacity options are 2.4 K, 4.8 K, or 9.6 K bps. Data are transmitted according to the ASCII encoding system (7 bits per character). What capacity would you recommend for a communications channel to permit the printer to operate at capacity?

22. Suppose that you are a systems analyst for a municipal government. You have been asked to justify the conversion from the current system to an on-line incident-reporting system to the city council. In the current system, transactions are batched for processing at the end of each day. What points would you make?

23. Que Realty Software has developed an expert system that matches clients with houses. The company plans to market the system, called Que-List, to regional realtor associations who want an on-line multiple listing system. Such systems permit any member realtor access to information on any real estate listing in the region. A realtor association would purchase the hardware and software as a turnkey system (installed and ready to use) from Que Realty Software and then operate the system for its members. Que-List will have the following functions:

- Entering a new listing from a seller
- Printing the listing book of all current listings
- Entering a sale
- Making inquiries by criteria

The Que-List system can be accessed from any terminal or PC equipped with dial-up communication capabilities.

a. Specify the data communications hardware that will be needed at the realtor association's data center. Justify your recommendations.

b. Specify the data communications hardware at these user locations: a real estate office with eight PCs, a real estate office with a single PC, and an agent's laptop PC. Justify your recommendations.

c. List the alternatives for data transmission services. Discuss the economics of the various alternatives, including speed versus cost trade-offs as well as other considerations.

Self-Test (by section)

7–1 **a.** The general area of data communications encompasses telecommunications. (T/F̶)

b. The integration of computer systems, terminals, and communication links is referred to as a _computer networking_.

7–2 Using computers and data communications to transmit data electronically between companies is called: (a) EDI, (b) DIE, or (c) DEI?

7–3 A company either has total connectivity or it has no connectivity. (T/F̶)

7–4 **a.** The modem converts computer-to-terminal electrical _____ (digital or analog) signals to _____ (digital or analog) signals so that the data can be transmitted over telephone lines.

b. The terminal sending a message is the source and the computer receiving the message is the destination. (T̶/F)

c. Another name for a front-end processor is a multiplexer. (T/F̶)

d. Which of the following provides backup to the host processor: (a) back-end processor, (b) duplicate processor, or (c) parallel host?

7–5 **a.** It is more difficult for a computer criminal to tap into an fiber optic cable than a copper telephone line. (T̶/F)

b. A 9600-bits-per-second channel is the same as a: (a) 9.6-kps line, (b) 9.6 K-bps line, or (c) dual 4800X2 K-bps line.

c. The wireless transceiver replaces the physical link between the source and destination in a network. (T/F)

7–6 a. The two basic types of service offered by common carriers are a private line and a leased line. (T/F)

b. The ISDN telecommunications standard promotes source-to-destination analog data transmission. (T/F)

c. A value-added network is not required by law to use the transmission facilities of a common carrier. (T/F)

Self-test answers.   7–1 **(a)** F; **(b)** computer network. 7–2 a. 7–3 F. **7–4 (a)** digital, analog; **(b)** T; **(c)** F; **(d)** c. 7–5 **(a)** T; **(b)** b; **(c)** T. **7–6 (a)** F; **(b)** F; **(c)** T.

8

Networks and Networking

STUDENT LEARNING OBJECTIVES

▶ To illustrate the various kinds of network topologies.

▶ To describe a local area network and its associated hardware and software.

▶ To demonstrate an understanding of network design considerations.

▶ To describe the purpose, use, and applications of micro-based communications software.

CHAPTER OUTLINE

Each time you use the telephone, you use the world's largest computer network—the telephone system. A telephone is an end point, or a **node**, connected to a network of computers that route your voice signals to any one of the 500 million telephones (other nodes) in the world. In a computer network the node can be a terminal or a computer. Computer networks are configured to meet the specific requirements of an organization. Some have 5 nodes; others have 10,000 nodes. This chapter addresses the various approaches used to link nodes within an organization into a computer network.

Network Topologies

The basic computer **network topologies**—star, ring, and bus—are illustrated in Figure 8–1. A network topology is a description of the possible physical connections within a network. The topology is the configuration of the hardware and indicates which pairs of nodes are able to communicate.

Star Topology The **star topology** involves a centralized host computer connected to a number of smaller computer systems. The smaller computer systems communicate with one another through the host and usually share the host computer's data base. Both the central computer and the distributed computer systems are connected to terminals (micros or VDTs). Any terminal can communicate with any other terminal in the network. Banks usually have a large home-office computer system with a star network of minicomputer systems in the branch banks.

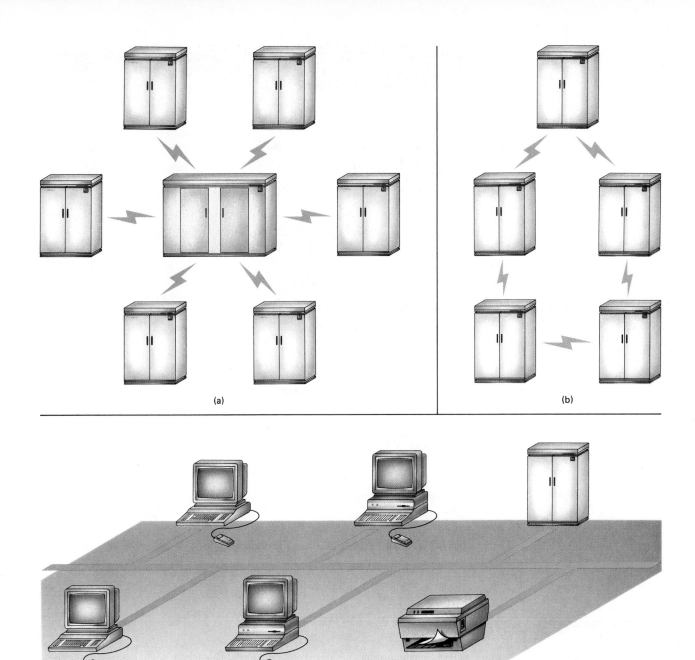

FIGURE 8–1   Network Topologies
(a) star (b) ring (c) bus

Ring Topology   The **ring topology** involves computer systems that are approximately the same size, with no one computer system as the focal point of the network. When one system routes a message to another system, it is passed around the ring until it reaches its destination address.

Crude-oil traders keep close watch on oil prices for future trading operations. They do this through a complex system of computer-based networks. Trading allows a company both to "hedge" or protect against future price changes and to gain insights about oil-market trends.

Bus Topology   The **bus topology** permits the connection of terminals, peripheral devices, and microcomputers along a central cable called a **transmission medium**. It is easy to add devices or delete them from the network. Bus topologies are most appropriate when the linked devices are physically close to one another. (See the discussion of local area networks that follows.)

Topology Summary   A pure form of any of these three basic topologies is seldom found in practice. Most computer networks are *hybrids*—combinations of these topologies.

Three-Tier and Two-Tier Networks

The different types of networks are sometimes classified as **three-tier** or **two-tier networks**, referring to the number of layers of computers in the network. A three-tier network contains three layers of computers. At the top is the host mainframe that is linked to multiple minicomputers. Each mini is linked to multiple micros. The three-tier concept was the norm until the capabilities of micros began to approach those of the multiuser minis of the mid-1980s. The increased power of the microcomputer made three-tier networks redundant at the bottom level, thus prompting the concept of the two-tier network. A two-tier network has only two layers of computers, usually a mainframe computer that is linked directly to multiple minicomputers and/or microcomputers. The tier concept is most often associated with the star topology or a hybrid based on the star topology.

This office is part of a two-tier network that links distributed minis (foreground) in seven locations with a host mainframe computer.

The Micro/Mainframe Link

Micros, initially designed for use by a single individual, have even greater potential when they can be linked with mainframe computers. To give micros this dual-function capability, vendors have developed the necessary hardware and software to enable some **micro/mainframe links**. There are three types of micro/mainframe links:

1. The microcomputer serves as a "dumb" terminal (that is, I/O only with no processing) linked to the mainframe. Micros can be set up via software to emulate (act like) any popular terminal.
2. Microcomputer users request that data be **downloaded** (mainframe-to-micro transmission of data) from the mainframe to their micros for processing. Upon completion of processing, user data may be **uploaded** from their microcomputers to the mainframe.
3. Both microcomputer and mainframe work together to process data and produce information.

Micro/mainframe links of the first two types are well within the state of the art, but achieving the third is more involved. The tremendous differences in the way computers and software are designed make complete integration of micro/mainframe processing difficult and, for some combinations of micros and mainframes, impossible. Nevertheless, the integrated processing is the ultimate goal of hardware/software vendors and users.

If PC-based local area networks are at one end of the network scale, then global networks are at the other end. A global network is to a PC-based LAN what a multinational corporation is to a mom-and-pop grocery store.

Global networks, also known as *wide-area networks* (WANs) or *enterprise networks,* span North America, reach out across oceans, and unite computer users throughout the world. Giant corporations such as IBM maintain their own global networks. Others are shared by different firms and organizations.

The goal of a global network is to allow users to send electronic messages, data, graphics, programs, documents, and even video and audio information rapidly and economically. Global networks make judicious use of data-communications common carriers throughout the world and/or private microwave links to connect its computers. The network's computers accept transmissions, route them to their destinations via the other computers, and alert addressees to waiting messages and other transmissions.

IS BIGGER BETTER?

The short answer is yes. If you're in Paris and want to get up-to-the-minute inventory information from Boise, Idaho, you can. This also could be done with a modem and a conventional telephone connection, but at considerable expense. Networks provide immediate access at a lower cost than the telephone system, and they're less expensive and faster than the postal system. The bigger the network, the greater the number of people and locations it can serve.

INTERNET

The original global network (founded in 1969 by the Department of Defense) and still the largest is Internet. The National Science Foundation manages Internet, which is used mainly by research-oriented users in colleges, government agencies, and other organizations coast to coast and in 33 other countries. Internet links over a thousand government and academic networks. Many pioneering ideas in telecommunications, such as electronic mail, originated on Internet.

OTHER NETWORKS

SmithKline Beecham, a pharmaceutical company, has a network linking 160 international sites and carrying data files, voice messages, faxed documents, and other information. General Electric maintains a private global network for the exclusive use of its employees throughout the world. The GE network uses its own microwave links, thereby eliminating the need for common carriers. Electronic Data Systems Corporation's EDSNET links 250,000 sites on five continents. Among others, EDSNET supports General Motors and its suppliers.

Major telecommunications carriers like AT&T offer both the hardware and the expertise to help corporations use shared global networks or develop their own. British Telecommunications, AT&T, and other companies are currently scrambling to unite the European Economic Community with a global network. In the United States, the National Science Foundation plans to replace the venerable Internet with a new network that is quicker

8–2   Line Control: Rules for Data Transmission

Polling and Contention

When a terminal or a microcomputer is connected to a computer over a single communications channel, this is a **point-to-point connection**. When more than one terminal or micro is connected via a single communications channel, the channel is called a **multidrop line**. Terminals on a multidrop line must share the data communications channel. Because all terminals cannot use the same channel at once, line-control procedures are needed. The most common line-control procedures are *polling* and *contention*.

and more user-friendly. The new version will be known as the National Research and Education Network (NREN).

SECURITY RISKS

Being connected to a network does expose your data as well as your software and computer equipment to possible unauthorized use by others. In one notorious case in 1988, graduate computer student Robert Morris, Jr., found a way to spread a "worm" program through Internet, forcing thousands of research computers to grind to a halt. Morris was sentenced to three years' probation (which many feel was too light a sentence).

Morris's exploit and others like it make some global network users nervous. Most, however, share the view of Clifford Stoll, whose best-seller *The Cuckoo's Nest* describes his success in nabbing a computer hacker: "Security risks are no reason to abandon computer networks. After all, a computer that can't communicate with other computers is like a hermit. It can't contribute very much to society."

LINKING THE WORLD NASA's Mission Control Center is the epicenter of one of the world's most sophisticated global networks. Computer-based tracking stations around the world gather data directly from the computers on-board the space shuttle. These data are transmitted via satellite to the Mission Control Center where a host mainframe computer provides position reports and makes trajectory predictions.

In **polling,** the front-end processor "polls" each terminal in rotation to determine whether a message is ready to be sent (see Figure 8–2). If a particular terminal has a message ready to be sent and the line is available, the front-end processor accepts the message and polls the next terminal.

Programmers can adjust the polling procedure so that some terminals are polled more often than others. For example, tellers in a bank are continuously interacting with the system. A loan officer, however, may average only two inquiries in an hour. In this case, the teller terminals might be polled four times for each poll of a loan officer's terminal.

In the **contention** line-control procedure, a terminal with a message to be sent automatically requests service from the host processor. The request might result in a "line busy" signal, in which case the terminal waits a fraction of a second and tries again, and again, until the line is

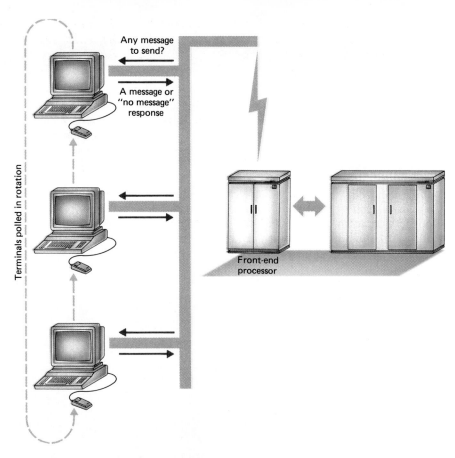

Terminals polled in rotation

Any message to send?

A message or "no message" response

Front-end processor

FIGURE 8–2 The Polling Process

Each terminal is polled in rotation to determine if a message is ready to be sent.

free. Upon assuming control of the line, the terminal sends the message and then relinquishes control of the line to another terminal.

Polling is commonly used in star-based networks where the host computer polls each node in rotation for messages. The contention procedure is popular in bus-based networks.

Communications Protocols

Communications protocols are rules established to govern the way data are transmitted in a computer network. Communications protocols are defined in *layers*, the first of which is the physical layer or the manner in which nodes in a network are connected to one another. The RS-232C connector, introduced in Chapter 2, "Micros, Minis, Mainframes, and Supercomputers," is the standard for some communications protocols. Subsequent layers, the number of which vary between protocols, describe how messages are packaged for transmission, how messages are routed through the network, security procedures, and the manner in which messages are displayed.

A number of different protocols are in common use. For example, X.12 is the standard for electronic data interchange (EDI); X.25 is used for packet switching (a procedure in which messages are routed as packets then reassembled at the source); X.75 is used for interconnections between networks of different countries; XON/XOFF is the de facto standard for microcomputer data communications; and XMODEM is used for uploading and downloading files.

IBM created an overall communications strategy **Systems Network Architecture (SNA)** that encompasses hardware, software, and communications protocols (Synchronous Data Link Control or SDLC and token ring). The SNA strategy is widely used throughout the world.

Asynchronous and Synchronous Transmission

Protocols fall into two general classifications, *asynchronous* and *synchronous* (see Figure 8–3). In **asynchronous transmission**, data are transmitted at irregular intervals on an as-needed basis. A modem is usually involved in asynchronous transmission. *Start/stop bits* are appended to the beginning and end of each message. The start/stop bits signal the receiving terminal/computer at the beginning and end of the message. In microcomputer data communications, the message is a single byte or character. Asynchronous transmission, sometimes called *start/stop transmission*, is best suited for data communication involving low-speed I/O devices, such as serial printers and micros functioning as remote terminals.

Network software enables those who control the network to display network status. The display in the photo indicates data transmissions between Dallas, New York City, and Atlanta.

In **synchronous transmission**, the source and destination operate in timed synchronization to enable high-speed data transfer. Start/stop bits are not required in synchronous transmission. Data transmission between computers and between down-line processors and front-end processors is normally synchronous.

FIGURE 8–3 Asynchronous and Synchronous Transmission of Data
Asynchronous data transmission takes place at irregular intervals. In asynchronous transmission, the message is typically a single character.
Synchronous data transmission requires timed synchronization between sending and receiving devices. The message is typically a block of characters.

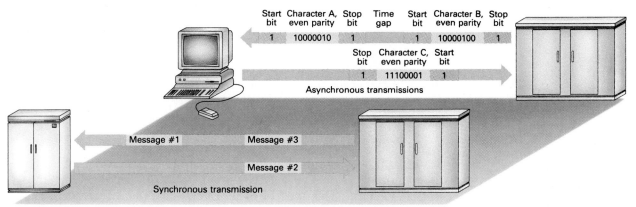

LAN Defined

A **local area network** (**LAN**), or **local net**, is a system of hardware, software, and communications channels that connects devices in close proximity, such as in a suite of offices. A local net permits the movement of data (including text, voice, and graphic images) between mainframe computers, personal computers, terminals, and I/O devices. For example, your micro can be connected to another micro, to mainframes, and to shared resources such as printers and disk storage. The distance separating devices in the local net may vary from a few feet to a few miles. As few as two and as many as several hundred micros can be linked on a single local area network.

The unique feature of a local net is that a common carrier is not necessary for transmitting data between computers, terminals, and shared resources. Because of the proximity of devices in local nets, a company can install its own communications channels (such as coaxial cable, fiber optic cable, or wireless transceivers).

The ability to share valuable resources is the fundamental reason that the trend is to incorporate more and more PCs into local area networks. Currently about 20% of all PCs are part of a LAN. Industry forecasters are predicting that the percentage will grow rapidly during the decade of the 1990s, perhaps to 70% or 80%. In a LAN, data, applications software, links to mainframes, communications capabilities (for example, modems), CD-ROM data bases (for example, an on-line national telephone directory), add-on boards (for example, fax boards), and other resources can be shared among users of the system. LANs make good business sense because available resources can be shared. For example, the cost of a LAN-based spreadsheet is far less than the cost of a spreadsheet for each PC in the LAN. Also, in a normal office setting, a single page printer can service the printing needs of up to 10 micro users.

LANs have opened the door to applications that are not possible in the one-person, one-computer environment. For example, users linked together via a local area network can send electronic mail to one another. Also, scheduling meetings with other users on the LAN is a snap. Scheduling software automatically checks appropriate users' electronic calendars for possible meeting times, schedules the meeting, and informs the participants via electronic mail.

Like computers, automobiles, and just about everything else, local nets can be built at various levels of sophistication. At the most basic level, they permit the interconnection of PCs in a department so that users can send messages to one another and share files and printers. The more sophisticated local nets permit the interconnection of mainframes, micros, and the gamut of peripheral devices throughout a large but geographically constrained area, such as a cluster of buildings.

In the near future you will be able to plug a terminal into a communications channel just as you would plug a telephone line into a telephone jack. This type of data communications capability is being

A network within a network? Yes, the Home Shopping Network operators rely on a local area network to enter orders.

installed in the new "smart" office buildings and even in some hotel rooms.

Local nets are often integrated into "long-haul" networks. For example, a bank will link home-office teller terminals to the central computer via a local net. But for long-haul data communication, the bank's branch offices must rely on common carriers.

LAN Hardware

As we mentioned before, most LANs link micros in the local area. The three basic hardware components in a PC-based LAN are the network interface cards, or NICs; the cables that connect the nodes in the network; and the servers.

Network Interface Cards   The NIC, which we described briefly in Chapter 2, is an PC add-on card that facilitates and controls the exchange of data between the micros in a LAN. Each PC in a LAN must be equipped with an NIC. As an add-on card, the NIC is connected directly to the PC's bus. The cables that link the PCs are physically connected to the NICs.

The transfer of data and programs between nodes is controlled by the access method embedded in the network interface card's ROM. The two most popular access methods are *token-ring* and *Ethernet*.

Token-ring access method.   In a token-ring network, an electronic *token* travels around a ring of nodes in the form of a *header* (see Figure 8–4). The header contains control signals, including one specifying whether the token is "free" or carrying a message. A sender node captures a free token as it travels from node to node, changes it to "busy," and adds the message. The resulting *message frame* travels around the ring to the ad-

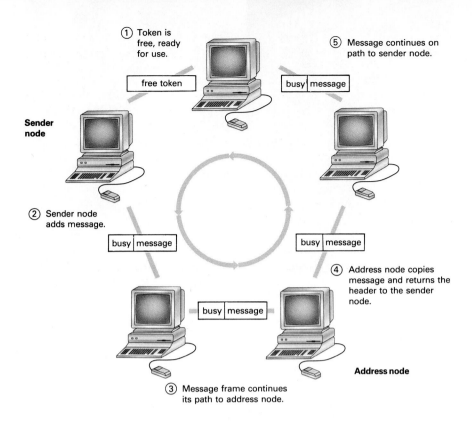

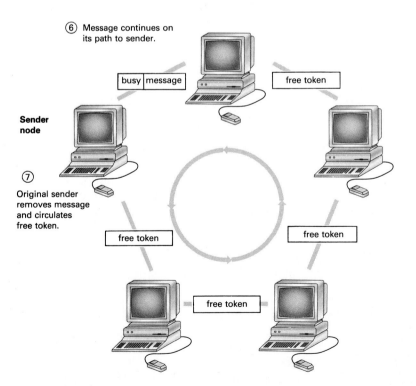

FIGURE 8–4 The Token-Ring Local Area Network

dressee's NIC, which copies the message and returns the message frame to the sender. The sender's NIC removes the message frame from the ring and circulates a new free token.

Ethernet access method. Ethernet, which employs the *CSMA/CD* (Carrier Sense Multiple Access/Collision Detection) access method, is based on the bus network topology. CSMA/CD uses the contention line-control procedure discussed in Section 8–2. To gain access to the network, a node with a message to be sent automatically requests network service from the network software. The request might result in a "line busy" signal, in which case the node waits a fraction of a second and tries again, and again, until the line is free. Upon assuming control of the line, the node sends the message and then relinquishes control of the line to another node.

Cables Three kinds of cables are connected to the network interface cards: twisted-pair cable (the same four-wire cables used to connect telephones in a home), coaxial cable, and fiber optic cable.

Servers A **server** is a LAN component that can be shared by users on the LAN. The three most popular servers are the **file server**, **print server**, and **communications server**. These server functions may reside in a single micro or can be distributed among the micros that make up the LAN. When the server functions are consolidated, the server micro usually is *dedicated* to servicing the LAN and, therefore, is not used for applications.

Until recently, you would purchase a traditional single-user micro and make it a dedicated server. This continues to be a viable option with

France Gets the Gold for Networking The 1992 Winter Olympics was highly automated with Info92, an impressive network that consisted of 10 token-ring networks and 1800 IBM PS/2s dispersed at 15 venues over 700 square miles of France, including the French Alps. Authorized users could access everything from up-to-the-minute scores to weather reports. The PCs were linked by OS/2 LAN Server, then linked to an IBM 3090 mainframe. An IBM AS/400 was also connected with the mainframe for various business and financial affairs.

The knowledge workers in the public relations office of a large company are linked with one another by a LAN. The tower PC on the floor under the table is a dedicated file server for the 25 micros on the LAN.

small to medium-sized LANs, but not in large LANs with 100 or more users. Now, micro vendors manufacture powerful micros designed specifically as network servers. These micros can comfortably handle hundreds of micros on a single LAN.

The file server normally is a dedicated micro with a high-capacity disk for storing the data and programs shared by the network users. For example, the master client file, word processing software, spreadsheet software, and so on would be stored on the server disk. When a user wants to begin a spreadsheet session, the spreadsheet software is downloaded from the file server to the user's RAM.

The print server typically is housed in the same dedicated micro as the file server. The print server handles user print jobs and controls at least one printer. If needed, the server *spools* print jobs; that is, it saves print jobs to disk until the requested printer is available, then routes the print file to the printer.

The communications server provides communications links external to the LAN—that is, micro/mainframe links and links to other networks. To accomplish this service, the communications server controls one or more modems.

LAN Software

Network Operating Systems   The **LAN operating system**, the nucleus of a local area network, is actually several pieces of software. Each processing component in the LAN has a piece of the LAN operating system resident in its RAM. The controlling software resides in the file server's RAM. The pieces interact with one another to enable the nodes to share resources and communication. Two of the most popular LAN operating systems are Novell's *NetWare* and Microsoft's *LAN Manager*.

The individual user in a LAN might appear to be interacting with an operating system, such as MS-DOS or OS/2. However, the RAM-resident LAN software *redirects* certain requests to the appropriate LAN component. For example, a print request would be redirected to the print server.

Shared Applications Software and Groupware   LANs enable the sharing of applications software, such as WordPerfect and Excel, and the use of groupware. **Groupware** is software whose application is designed to benefit a group of people. Electronic mail, electronic bulletin-board, on-line appointment calendar, and project/resource scheduling software are examples of groupware.

The PCs on the LAN interact with a central file server to use groupware or load applications programs. When a LAN-based PC is booted, software that enables the use of the network interface card, communication with the file server, and interaction with DOS is loaded from the PC's hard disk to RAM. Depending on how the LAN system administrator configured the LAN you may see a menu of available groupware and applications software on the file server, or you may see a prompt from the operating system.

Project managers in a midwestern construction firm use LAN-based groupware to coordinate a variety of projects. All project managers schedule activities and the company's resources through a common project management system.

Network Design Considerations

The design of any network, even a small 10-node LAN, can be complex. The design of a large national or international network redefines the word *complex*. Beyond the technical details of linking incompatible systems via data communications in the most efficient manner, network designers must consider the workload at each node, response time, system reliability, and data security.

Workload Analysis at Each Node

The first task in designing a computer network is to analyze the workload at each location such that the transmission of messages can be distributed evenly among the communications channels. To do this, the analysis must determine:

- Average daily and hourly message volume
- Peak daily and hourly message volume
- Type of message sent (long, short, requires response, and so on)
- From where and to where sent

Designers use interview techniques to gather information from users relative to message volume, type, and routing. Based on the data, they propose several combinations of network topologies, communications channels, and hardware. The network design alternatives are tested using computer simulate. Ultimately, network designers want to make connections between all nodes, minimize channel expense, and avoid line overloads. The network design alternative that meets these design objectives is chosen.

Response Time

Response time is the elapsed time between when a message is sent and a response is received. A message could be the update of a name and address file, and a response could be a visual display of the updated record. The response time will vary considerably depending upon the complexity of the inquiry, the number of terminals contending for processing time, the speed of the host, and the channel capacity.

Response time is an important consideration when designing a network. It has a direct impact on worker efficiency and on system cost. The lower the response time, the higher the cost. Network designers must determine what is an acceptable response time. Typically anything over two seconds is unacceptable for a simple inquiry.

System Reliability

Any complex system is subject to failure. However, for many organizations, network failure is simply unacceptable. For example, if the network supporting the Hilton Hotel reservation system went down for couple of

At Compaq's Network Control Center in Houston, specialists monitor all major elements of a vast internal PC network. These specialists ensure that data flows smoothly through the system that links offices, manufacturing plants, and service facilities in more than 20 countries.

hours, thousands of reservations would be lost and, perhaps, millions of dollars. When network downtime is unacceptable, the network must be made **fault-tolerant**; that is, the network must be designed to permit continuous operation, even if important components of the network fail. To accomplish this, parts of the system must be duplicated. For example, the system might have a parallel host. Fault-tolerant networks are designed to enable alternate routing of messages.

No network can be made totally fault-tolerant. The degree to which a network is made fault-tolerant depends on the amount of money an organization is willing to spend on its system.

Data Security

The mere existence of data communications capabilities poses a threat to security. A knowledgeable criminal can tap into the system from a remote location and use it for personal gain. In a well-designed system, this is not an easy task. But it can be and has been done! When one criminal broke a company's security code and tapped into the network of computers, he was able to order certain products without being billed. He filled a warehouse before he eventually was caught. Another tapped into an international banking exchange system to reroute funds to an account of his own in a Swiss bank. In another case, an oil company consistently was able to outbid a competitor by "listening in" on the latter's data transmissions. On several occasions, overzealous hackers have tapped into sensitive defense computer systems; fortunately, no harm was done.

How do companies protect themselves from these criminal activities? Some companies use **cryptography** to scramble messages sent over data communications channels. Someone who unlawfully intercepts such a message would find meaningless strings of characters. Cryptography is analogous to the code book used by intelligence people during the "cloak-and-dagger" days. Instead of a code book, however, a key is used in conjunction with **encryption/decryption** hardware to unscramble the message. Both sender and receiver must have the key, which is actually an algorithm that rearranges the bit structure of a message. Companies that routinely transmit sensitive data over communications channels are moving to data encryption as a means by which to limit access to their information systems and their data bases.

8–5   Using Micro-Based Communications Software

Now that you have studied the concepts associated with data communications and networks, you are ready to unlock the door to a new world of information. That key is micro-based communications software.

The Function of Communications Software

Communications software expands the capability of a microcomputer. With communications software, a micro becomes more than a small stand-alone computer: It becomes capable of interacting with a remote computer, in the next room or in Japan.

In a nutshell, communications software performs two basic functions.

1. *Terminal emulation.* Communications software transforms a micro into a video display terminal (VDT) that can be linked to another computer.
2. *File transfer.* Communications software enables the transfer of files between a micro and another computer.

Before accomplishing either of these functions, an electronic link must be established between the micro and the other computer. To establish this link the micro user initiates the **log-on procedure**. Typically, the log-on procedure involves the following:

1. A remote computer (another micro or a mainframe) is dialed up via the telephone system. The remote computer answers with a high-pitched tone.
2. A preassigned **password** and **personal identification number**, or **PIN**, is entered. The use of passwords and PINs helps protect a computer system against unauthorized access and use.

Once the remote computer validates the password, PIN, or both, the link is established. At this time, the remote computer normally will prompt the end user to enter a command or it will present the user with a menu of options.

This engineer is using communications software to enable his PC to emulate a VT–100 terminal. By doing this he can establish an on-line link to his company's mainframe computer.

Terminal Emulation　Supercomputers, mainframes, minis, and multiuser micros are host processors that can provide service to remote terminals. Supercomputers and mainframes can serve thousands of end users at remote terminals. Multiuser micros can serve about a dozen end users. When an end user at a terminal logs on to (establishes a link with) a host computer, the host immediately responds by asking the end user to enter the type of terminal he or she is using. Of course, a micro is not a terminal, but with the aid of communications software, a micro can emulate, or act like, one of the terminals that can be interfaced with the host. Communications software can transform a micro into any of a variety of popular terminals.

The two most distinguishing characteristics of terminals are the keyboard layout and the manner in which they send and receive data. When a micro is in **terminal emulation mode**, the keyboard, monitor, and data interface function like that of the terminal being emulated. From the host computer's perspective, the workstation being serviced is a terminal (for example, the DEC VT-100 terminal), not a micro.

Most terminals are *dumb terminals*; that is, they do not have stand-alone processing or storage capabilities. Communications software transforms a micro into an *intelligent terminal* that can provide capabilities above and beyond that of the terminal being emulated: For example, it can store an interactive session on a disk file.

File Transfers　Once the link between the micro and host has been established, data, program, or text files can be downloaded from disk storage on the host computer to disk storage on the micro. Files also can be uploaded. The file transfer capability afforded by communications software can be invaluable when you need to transfer files between computers.

Preparing for an Interactive Session with a Remote Computer

When you use a PC, modem, and data communications software to establish a link with another computer, the communications software will prompt you to specify the *telephone number* to be called and certain data communications **parameters**. A parameter is a descriptor that can take on different values. These parameters may include

- *Terminal emulation.* Specify the type of terminal to be emulated. The options might include the generic TTY, the DEC VT-100, DEC VT-52, IBM 3101, and others.
- *Communications protocol.* Select protocol (for example, XON/XOFF, XMODEM).
- *Data flow.* Select half- or full-duplex. Communication channels that transmit data in both directions, but not at the same time, are called **half-duplex**. A channel that transmits data in both directions at the same time is called **full-duplex**. A full-duplex line is simply two half-duplex lines dedicated to the same link. Half-duplex channels do not permit the echoing of user keystrokes on the display screen.
- *Data bits.* Specify the number of bits in the message (the bits within the start/stop bits). Typically, the character is transmitted with *seven* or *eight* bits.
- *Parity checking.* In data communications, as in a computer system, data in the form of coded characters are continuously transferred at high rates of speed. In the case of data communications, data are transferred between the micro and the remote computer. Like computer systems, data communications uses the parity checking procedure to insure the accuracy of the transmission. Parity checking is discussed in Chapter 4, "Inside the Computer."
- *Bits per second* (sometimes labeled as *baud*). Select the appropriate transmission rate: 300, 1200, 2400, 4800, or 9600 bps.
- *Stop bits.* Stop is actually a misnomer in that it is actually a timing unit. Usually you would select *1* for micro-based data communications. Other options might be *1.5* or *2*.
- *Echo.* Typically, the host computer will **echo**, or return, the characters that are received from a micro; that is, the characters entered at the micro appear on the micro's monitor in the context of those originated by the host computer. In effect, the entire interactive session is displayed when the echo is on. When the host does not echo characters, the user will have to specify *local echo* to display characters entered via the keyboard.

Depending on the protocol and communications package, you may need to specify other parameters as well.

Communications software offers a variety of handy, time-saving features. For example, you can store the settings (parameters) for a particular bulletin board, information service, or mainframe computer in a *communications profile*. To establish a link with another computer, simply recall and activate the appropriate communications profile. From there, the communications software takes over and automatically dials and logs on to the remote computer. It will even redial if it gets a busy signal. A micro with a modem and communications software can be on the receiving end as well: It can automatically answer "calls" from other computers.

Most communications software packages provide the feature that enables the micro to *capture* all input/output during an interactive session in an ASCII file on disk. At a later time the user can recall the session from disk storage with word processing software and browse through it at a more leisurely pace. Of course, all or part of the information gathered during an interactive session can be integrated into word processing documents, such as memos, letters, and reports.

Microcomputer Communications Software in Practice

Personal computers that can double as remote terminals can take advantage of a wide variety of communications-based applications.

Electronic Bulletin Boards   Most cities with a population of 25,000 or more have at least one electronic **bulletin-board system (BBS)**, often sponsored by a local computer club. Members "post" messages, announcements, for-sale notices, and so on, "on" the computer bulletin board by transmitting them to a central computer—usually another micro. To scan the bulletin board, members again use communications software to link to the central computer. The person or group sponsoring the BBS is referred to as the **system operator**, or **sysop**.

There are hundreds of regional and national special-interest bulletin boards that focus on anything from matchmaking to UFOs. The Clean Air BBS deals with health and smoking topics. The U.S. Census Bureau sponsors several BBSs. People looking for jobs might scan the listings on the Employ-Net BBS. Catch up on which fish are biting and which are not by tapping into the Fly-Fishers Forum BBS. The do-it-yourselfer might want to log on to the Popular Mechanics Online BBS. Enter your own movie review on the Take 3 BBS. Lawyers talk with one another on the Ye Olde Bailey BBS. A Denver BBS is devoted to parapsychology. Some senators and members of Congress sponsor BBSs to facilitate communication with their constituents. A number of BBSs are devoted to religious topics.

Information Services   More and more PC users are subscribing to a commercial **information service** (also called an *information network*), such as CompuServe, Prodigy, GEnie, The Source, Dow Jones News/Retrieval Service, Western Union, and NewsNet. The largest information services, CompuServe and Prodigy, have over a million subscribers each. These information services have one or several large computer systems that offer a variety of information services, from hotel reservations to daily horoscopes. Some, like Dow Jones News/Retrieval (financial news and information), offer specialized services.

Minding Your Manners on a BBS
Taking part in one of the many forums offered on a bulletin board system (BBS) is a great way to make new friends across the nation. Becoming aware of BBS etiquette will make your on-line visits even more enjoyable. Courtesy is the rule of the day; most bulletin boards discourage sarcasm and personal attacks. And, because everyone is paying for access time, the well-mannered BBSer will learn to keep messages short and to the point. Abbreviations, such as BION ("believe it or not"), save both time and keystrokes. And to express feelings concisely, there are *emotions* built from common keyboard symbols. Can you guess what this means?
:-)
If not, turn this book 90 degrees clockwise and look again.

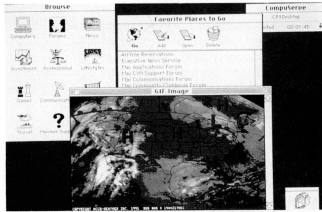
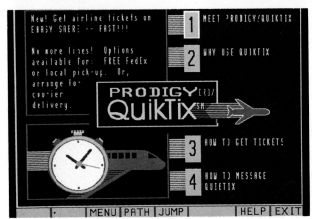

An information network includes such services as home shopping (top left), weather (top right), airline reservations (bottom left), and electronic mail (bottom right).

In addition to a micro, all you need to take advantage of these information services is a modem (the interface between the telephone line and a micro), a telephone line, and a few dollars. You normally pay a one-time fee. For the fee, you get a password and personal identification number (PIN) that permit you to establish a communications link with the service. You also receive a booklet that lists the telephone numbers you dial to establish a link with the information service. If you live in a medium-to-large city, the telephone number you would dial is usually local. Your bill is based on how much you use the information service.

The following list summarizes the types of services available commercially.

- *News, weather, sports.* Get the latest releases directly from the wire services. You can request general news or news about a specific topic. For example, you can request news about Australia, French politics, the plastics industry, or whatever interests you. You can request a short- or long-term weather forecast for any region in the world. You can obtain up-to-the-minute scores for college and professional sporting events, or, if you wish, only that of your favorite teams.

- *Entertainment.* Read reviews of the most recently released movies, videos, and records. Chart your biorhythms or ask the advice of an astrologer.
- *Games.* Hundreds of single-player games, such as digital football, and multiplayer games, such as MegaWars, are available. You can even play a game of chess with a friend in another state! Or you might prefer to match wits with another trivia buff.
- *Home banking.* Check your account balances, transfer money, and pay bills in the comfort of your home or office.
- *Financial information.* Get up-to-the-minute quotes on stocks, securities, bonds, options, and commodities. You also can use this service to help you manage a securities portfolio and to keep tax records.
- *Brokerage services.* Purchase and sell securities 24 hours a day from your microcomputer.
- *Bulletin boards.* Use special-interest electronic bulletin boards as a forum for the exchange of ideas and information. Information services have hundreds of bulletin-board systems to choose from on topics ranging from gardening, to astrology, to IBM personal computers, to wine, to human sexuality, to computer art, to aviation, to graphics showing the FBI's most wanted fugitives.
- *Electronic mail.* Send **electronic mail** to and receive it from other users of the information service. Each subscriber is assigned an ID and an electronic mailbox. **E-mail**, another name for electronic mail, sent to a particular subscriber can be "opened" and read only by that subscriber.
- *Shop at home.* Select what you want from a list of thousands of items offered at discount prices. Unless you plan on ordering an automobile or a truck (which you can do), your order is delivered to your doorstep. Payment may be made via electronic funds transfer (EFT); that is, money is exchanged electronically between your account and that of the shopping service.
- *Reference.* Look up items of interest in an electronic encyclopedia. Scan through various government publications. Recall articles on a particular subject from dozens of newspapers, trade periodicals, and newsletters. Students seeking a college might want to query the service for information about certain schools.
- *Education.* Choose from a variety of educational packages, from learning arithmetic to preparing for the Scholastic Aptitude Test (SAT). You can even determine your IQ!
- *Real estate.* Moving? Check out available real estate by scanning the listings for the city to which you are moving.
- *Cooking.* Use your micro to access thousands of culinary delights. For example, if you're hungry for a particular type of cuisine, enter appropriate descriptors to obtain a recipe (for example: entree, Spanish, rice, crab).
- *Health.* Address medical questions to a team of top physicians. Diagnose your own illness while interacting with an on-line expert system. Plan and monitor your next diet.
- *Travel.* Plan your own vacation or business trip. You can check airline, train, and cruise schedules and make your own reservations. You can even charter a yacht in the Caribbean, locate the nearest bed-and-breakfast inn, or rent a lodge in the Rockies.

Traditionally, people get up in the morning, get dressed, and fight through rush hour to go to the office because that is where the work is. However, for many knowledge workers, work is really at a micro or terminal, whether at the office or at home. More and more employees are beginning to question the wisdom of going to the office in the traditional sense. Many would prefer to telecommute and work in the more comfortable surroundings of home. Telecommuting is "commuting" to work via a data communications link between home and office.

In theory, millions of people could telecommute to work at least a few days a week. People whose jobs involve considerable interaction with a computer system are perfect candidates (such as those who process insurance claims and programmers). Managers who need a few hours, or perhaps a few days, of uninterrupted time to accomplish tasks that do not require direct personal interaction are beginning to consider the merits of telecommuting.

At present, telecommuting is seldom an employee option. Most companies that permit telecommuting are restricting it to management and computer professionals. However, it is only a matter of time before self-motivated individuals at all levels and in a variety of disciplines are given the option of telecommuting at least part of the time. Most workers would view telecommuting and the accompanying flexible work hours as "perks" of employment. The company that does not offer them may be at a disadvantage in recruiting quality workers.

The trend is definitely to an increased level of telecommuting, especially with the proliferation of facsimile (fax) machines and sophisticated telephone systems that include voice mail and call forwarding. In effect, a knowledge worker's home office could function much like his or her "at work" office. In some cases, the at work office could be eliminated.

Everyone has a different reason for wanting to telecommute. A programmer with two school-age children says, "I want to say good-bye when the kids leave for school and greet them when they return." A writer goes into the office once a week, the day before the magazine goes to press. He says, "I write all my stories from the comfort of my home. An office that puts out a weekly magazine is not conducive to creative thinking." A financial analyst telecommutes to prepare quarterly financial statements. He says, "All the information I need is at my finger tips and I finish in one day at home what used to take me a week at the office." The president of the same company stated emphatically, "I got sick and tired of spending nights up in my office. By telecommuting, I'm at least within earshot of my wife and kids. Also, I like to get into more comfortable clothes." The director of an MIS department describes one of many telecommuting applications: "Every Monday evening I write out the agenda for my Tuesday morning staff meeting. I then send a summary of the agenda via electronic mail to my managers so they will see it first thing Tuesday morning when they log in."

Of course, there are differing opinions. One sales manager says, "I'm more productive working at the office, where household and family distractions fade into the distance."

Telecommuting may never catch on as a general alternative to working in the office, but for some applications it has proved to be a boon to productivity. As a personnel director observed: "With the elimination of travel time, coffee breaks, idle conversations, and numerous office distractions, we have found that conscientious, self-motivated employees can be more productive at home when working on certain projects." However, management at this company encourages workers to select their telecommuting activities carefully. Telecommuting is fine for interaction with the computer and the data base, but for interaction with other people, it has its limitations. Telecommuting does not permit "pressing of the flesh" and the transmittal of the nonverbal cues that are essential to personal interaction.

WORKING AT HOME   The familiar surroundings of home inspire some people to do their best work. Others, however, are more comfortable working in a traditional office setting.

These and many other time-saving applications eventually should make personal computers more of a necessity than a luxury item in every home and office.

Telecommuting and the Cottage Industry   In the coming years, we will probably see business people carrying less work to and from the office. Why? With communications software and an ever-growing number of home computers, people won't need to lug their paperwork between home and office every day. A great many white-collar workers do much of their work on computers. Working at home is simply a matter of establishing a link between home and office computers. This is sometimes referred to as **telecommuting**. In the years to come, many white-collar workers will elect to telecommute at least one day a week.

The combination of microcomputers and communications software has also fueled the growth of *cottage industries*. The world has been made a little more compact with the computer revolution. Stockbrokers, financial planners, writers, programmers, and people from a wide variety of professions may not need to "go to the office," so they can live wherever they choose. Micros make it possible for these people to access needed information, communicate with their clients, and even deliver their work (programs, stories, reports, or recommendations) in electronic or hard-copy format.

Telecommuters use facsimile machines or fax modems (see Chapter 7, "Connectivity and Data Communications") in conjunction with communications software to fax hard-copy material back and forth between the office. When using a PC to simulate a fax machine, the electronic image received via data communications can be viewed on the display, or if a hard copy is desired, it must be printed. An image in any electronic format is sent easily via fax modem. However, in order to send the image of a hard-copy document, the image must be scanned with a scanner to obtain an electronic image before it can be faxed.

Summary   Microcomputers have placed the power of computers at our fingertips. Communications software expands that capability by enabling micro users to become a part of any number of computer networks. Once part of the network, a user can take advantage of the awesome power of mainframe computers, the information in their data bases, and the opportunity to communicate electronically with others on the network.

▶ 8-6   **Approaches to Connectivity: Gateways and Bridges**

Now that you are familiar with the technologies associated with data communications and have an appreciation of the technological challenges of connectivity, it is time to discuss approaches to achieving degrees of hardware connectivity. Perhaps the most effective way to overcome compatibility problems and achieve hardware connectivity within the confines of an organization is to stay with one vendor. Even then, purchases must be limited to those hardware devices that are compatible. Very small companies and start-up companies can follow this approach. But for larger companies with established multiple vendor environments, this straight-

By providing more and better information at a centralized location, networks improve security at prison complexes, such as Rikers Island, New York.

forward solution is not an option. These companies already use many different vendors, and the expense of a total conversion is prohibitive.

Companies with established operating environments use gateway and bridge technologies to achieve connectivity. **Gateways** help alleviate the problems of linking incompatible micros, minis, and mainframes. A gateway is a combination of hardware and software that permits networks using different communications protocols (rules) to "talk" to one another. The use of a gateway normally implies a requirement for a protocol conversion.

Most commercially available gateways connect microcomputer-based local area networks to mainframes. In the micro/mainframe link, discussed earlier in this chapter, the micro is linked to a down-line processor that in turn is connected to a front-end processor, which is linked to the mainframe. A LAN-to-mainframe gateway makes it possible for one of the micros in a LAN to emulate the function of a down-line processor. Although efficiency may suffer slightly, the company can actually save money because down-line processors are considerably more expensive than microcomputers.

Some companies have many small, departmental local area networks. Instead of integrating these microcomputer-based LANs into a large network, they use **bridges** to enable these LANs to continue operation in their present format with the added advantage of being able to "talk" to each other. Bridges, which are protocol-independent hardware devices, permit communication between devices in separate local area networks. Bridges provide a relatively straightforward solution to enable LANs to communicate with one another.

For the foreseeable future, many connectivity questions can be answered with planning, restrictive policies, gateways, and bridges. However, with total connectivity the goal of most progressive companies, the computer community will continue to focus its sights on overcoming the barriers to it.

 Important Terms and Summary Outline

asynchronous transmission	gateway	polling
bridge	groupware	print server
bulletin-board system (BBS)	half-duplex	response time
bus topology	information service	ring topology
communications protocol	LAN operating system	server
communications server	local area network (LAN)	star topology
contention	local net	synchronous transmission
cryptography	log-on procedure	system operator (sysop)
downloaded	micro/mainframe link	Systems Network Architecture (SNA)
echo	multidrop line	telecommuting
electronic mail (E-mail)	network topology	terminal emulation mode
encryption/decryption	node	three-tier network
fault-tolerant	parameters	transmission medium
file server	password	two-tier network
full-duplex	personal identification number (PIN)	uploaded
	point-to-point connection	

8–1 NETWORKS: LINKING COMPUTERS AND PEOPLE.   Computer systems are linked together to form a computer network. In a computer network the **node** can be a terminal or a computer. The basic patterns for configuring computer systems within a computer network are **star topology, ring topology,** and **bus topology.** The bus topology permits the connection of nodes along a **transmission medium.** In practice, most networks are actually hybrids of these **network topologies.** Networks are sometimes classified as **three-tier** or **two-tier networks.**

The connection of microcomputers to a mainframe computer is called a **micro/mainframe link.** With this link, microcomputer users **download/ upload** data from/to the mainframe as needed.

8–2 LINE CONTROL: RULES FOR DATA TRANSMISSION.   A communications channel servicing a single workstation is a **point-to-point connection.** A communications channel servicing more than one workstation is called a **multidrop line.** The most common line-control procedures are called **polling** and **contention.**

Communications protocols are rules for transmitting data. Communications protocols are defined in layers.

The **Systems Network Architecture (SNA)** communications strategy is widely used throughout the world.

Asynchronous transmission begins and ends each message with start/ stop bits and is used primarily for low-speed data transmission. **Synchronous transmission** permits the source and destination to communicate in timed synchronization for high-speed data transmission.

8–3 LOCAL AREA NETWORKS.   A **local area network (LAN),** or **local net,** is a system of hardware, software, and communications channels that connects devices in close proximity and does not involve a common carrier. A local net permits the movement of data between mainframe computers, personal computers, terminals, and I/O devices. The ability to share valuable resources is the fundamental reason that the trend is to incorporate more and more PCs into local area networks.

The three basic hardware components in a PC-based LAN are the network interface cards, or NICs; the cables that connect the nodes in the network; and the servers. The physical transfer of data and programs between LAN nodes is controlled by the access method embedded in the network interface card's ROM, usually the *token-ring* or *Ethernet* access method.

A **server** is a LAN component that can be shared by users on the LAN. The three most popular servers are the **file server, print server,** and **communications server.**

The **LAN operating system** is actually several pieces of software, a part of which resides in each LAN component's RAM. LANs enable the sharing of applications software, such as WordPerfect and Excel, and the use of **groupware.** The PCs on the LAN interact with a central file server to use groupware or load applications programs.

8–4 NETWORK DESIGN CONSIDERATIONS.   Workload analysis at each node, response time, system reliability, and data security are important network design considerations. The first task in designing a computer network is to analyze the workload at each location. **Response time** is the elapsed time between when a message is sent and a response is received.

When network downtime is unacceptable, the network must be made **fault-tolerant**.

Cryptography is the scrambling of messages sent over data communications channels. Messages are scrambled and unscrambled with **encryption/decryption** hardware.

8–5 USING MICRO-BASED COMMUNICATIONS SOFTWARE. Communications software performs two basic functions: *terminal emulation* and *file transfer*. Typically, the **log-on procedure** involves dialing the remote computer and entering a **password** and **personal identification number**, or **PIN**.

When a micro is in **terminal emulation mode**, the keyboard, monitor, and data interface are like that of the terminal being emulated. Communications software transforms a micro into an *intelligent terminal* that can provide capabilities above and beyond that of the terminal being emulated.

When using communications software, specify the following **parameters**: type of terminal to be emulated, communications protocol, data flow (**half-duplex** or **full-duplex**), data bits, parity checking activated, type of parity checking, bits per second (sometimes labeled as *baud*), stop bits, and **echo**.

A variety of information services are available to microcomputer owners with communications capabilities. **Bulletin-board systems (BBSs)** are popular throughout the country. The person or group sponsoring the BBS is referred to as the **system operator**, or **sysop**.

PC users can subscribe to a commercial **information service**. Some of the services are news, weather, sports, entertainment, games, home banking, financial information, brokerage services, bulletin boards, electronic mail, shop at home, reference, education, real estate, cooking, health, and travel. Communications software also opens the door to sending and receiving **electronic mail (E-mail)**.

In the years to come, many white-collar workers will elect to **telecommute** at least one day a week. The combination of microcomputers and communications software has fueled the growth of cottage industries.

8–6 APPROACHES TO CONNECTIVITY: GATEWAYS AND BRIDGES. Companies with established operating environments use **gateway** and **bridge** technologies to achieve connectivity. Gateways help alleviate the problems associated with incompatible hardware. A gateway permits networks using different communications protocols to "talk" to one another. Bridges enable LANs to continue operation in their present format with the added advantage of being able to "talk" to other LANs.

 Review Exercises

Concepts

1. Name the three basic computer network topologies.
2. In a three-tier network, would a mainframe computer be at the bottom or the top of the tier? How about a micro?
3. What communications protocols are associated with Systems Network Architecture?

4. Expand the following acronyms: sysop, NIC, PIN, and LAN.

5. What are the two basic functions performed by micro-based communications software?

6. Name two popular LAN access methods. Which one passes a token from node to node?

7. Name three types of LAN servers.

8. Give two examples of groupware.

9. What term is used to describe the elapsed time between when a message is sent and a response is received?

10. Describe what is involved in a typical log-on procedure.

11. What is the advantage of a communications profile?

12. What technologies do companies with established operating environments use to achieve connectivity?

13. What is the purpose of a key in cryptography?

14. List at least six services that might be provided by a commercial information service.

Discussion

15. For the most part, *Fortune* 500 companies are relying primarily on gateways and bridges to achieve connectivity. What is the alternative?

16. The five PCs in the purchasing department of a large consumer goods manufacturer are used primarily for word processing and database applications. What would be the benefits and burdens associated with connecting the PCs in a local area network?

17. The mere fact that a system uses data communications poses a threat to security. Why?

Problem Solving

18. Corporate management at a large publishing company is planning to allow salaried employees to telecommute one day each week—that is, to work at home with a direct link to the company via a PC. Suggest key points that you feel should be included in the company's formal telecommuting policy.

19. The Dean of the School of Business at Peterson College has asked you to develop a plan for the support of academic computing. Current computing facilities at the main campus consist of an eight-year-old minicomputer with 16 terminals and a line printer and a microcomputer laboratory containing 10 IBM PCs, 12 IBM-PC compatibles, 7 Apple IIe computers, 7 dot-matrix printers, 1 desktop page printer, and 1 plotter. Each of the printers are shared by 3 or 4 microcomputers that use "share switches." The satellite location has a laboratory containing 4 IBM-PC compatibles, 3 Apple IIe's, and 2 dot-matrix printers. The minicomputer is used primarily to support instruction in BASIC and COBOL. The stand-alone PCs are used for instruction in word processing, database, spreadsheet, desktop publishing, and graphics software. All professors and administrators have their own PC.

Suggest a data communications alternative that would provide greater flexibility, save money, and position the college's academic computing for the future. Be specific in your recommendations. Justify each recommendation.

 Self-Test (by section)

★**8–1** **a.** An endpoint in a network of computers is called a __ₙₒdₑ__.

★ **b.** The central cable called a transmission medium is most closely associated with which network topology: (a) ring, (b) star, or ⓒ bus?

8–2 **a.** In asynchronous data transmission, start/stop bits are appended to the beginning and end of each message. (Ⓣ/F)

★ **b.** The __X.12__ communications protocol is the standard for electronic data interchange.

★ **c.** Which line-control procedure demands that a terminal request service from the host: (a) polling, Ⓑ contention, or (c) request-driven?

8–3 **a.** A LAN is designed for "long-haul" data communications. (T/Ⓕ)

b. Which of the following is not a popular LAN access method: (a) token-ring, (b) Ethernet, or ⓒ parity checking?

c. The LAN operating system resides entirely in the server processor's RAM. (T/Ⓕ)

8–4 **a.** One of the tasks in designing a computer network is to analyze the workload at each location. (Ⓣ/F)

✓ **b.** A _ᶠᵃᵘˡᵗ ₜₒₗₑᵣₐₙₜ_ network is designed to permit continuous operation, even if important components of the network fail.

8–5 **a.** Parity checking is not needed or used in data communications. (T/Ⓕ)

b. A micro with a modem and communications software can make calls to other computers but it cannot receive calls. (T/Ⓕ)

★ **c.** When acting like a terminal, the micro is said to be in _ₑₘᵤₗₐₜᵢₒₙ_ mode. ᵗᵉʳᵐⁱⁿᵃˡ

✓ **d.** A channel that transmits data in both directions at the same time is called _ᶠᵘˡˡ ᵈᵘᵖˡᵉˣ_.

8–6 The use of a gateway normally implies a requirement for a protocol conversion. (Ⓣ/F)

Self-test answers. **8–1 (a)** node; **(b)** c. **8–2 (a)** T; **(b)** X.12; **(c)** b. **8–3 (a)** F; **(b)** c; **(c)** F. **8–4 (a)** T; **(b)** fault-tolerant. **8–5 (a)** F; **(b)** F; **(c)** terminal emulation; **(d)** full-duplex. **8–6** T.

System Software and Platforms

STUDENT LEARNING OBJECTIVES

▶ To distinguish between the three categories of software: general-purpose, applications, and system software.

▶ To demonstrate an understanding of common system software concepts.

▶ To detail the purpose and objectives of an operating system.

▶ To describe the function of program language compilers and interpreters.

▶ To demonstrate an understanding of the principles and use of database management systems.

▶ To discuss the differences between file-oriented and data base organization.

▶ To describe what constitutes a platform.

▶ To distinguish between common platforms available to microcomputer users.

9-1 Categories of Software

We use the term *software* to refer to programs that direct the activities of the computer system. Software falls into three major categories: general-purpose software, applications software, and system software (see Figure 9–1).

General-Purpose Software

General-purpose software provides the framework for a great number of business, scientific, and personal applications. Spreadsheet, computer-aided design (CAD), and word processing software fall into this category. Most general-purpose software is sold as a package—that is, with software and user-oriented documentation (reference manuals, keyboard templates, and so on). It is then up to the user of the software to create the application. For example, a professor can use spreadsheet software to create a template for computing grades or one for maintaining an inventory of laboratory equipment. An aeronautical engineer can use CAD software

FIGURE 9–1 Categories of Software

SOFTWARE		
General-Purpose	**Applications**	**System**
Word Processing	Payroll Processing	Operating System
Spreadsheet	Inventory Mgt.	Programming Language
Expert System Shell	Class Scheduling	Compiler/interpreter
Paint and Draw	Human Resorce Mgt.	Database Mgt. System (DBMS)
Desktop Publishing	Insurance Claims Proc.	Utility
Presentation Graphics	Utility Billing	Performance Monitoring
Computer-Aided Design	General Ledger	Communications
Database		

to design an airplane or an airport. A personnel manager can use word processing software to create a letter or the camera copy for a newsletter. A number of PC-based general-purpose software packages are discussed in Chapter 11, "Text and Image Processing Software," and Chapter 12, "Data Management Software."

Applications Software

Applications software is designed and written to perform specific personal, business, or scientific processing tasks, such as payroll processing, order entry, or financial analysis. Notice that all of these applications process data (orders) and generate information (payroll register) for the user. The development procedure that results in the creation of applications software is covered in Chapter 15, "Analysis and Design of Business Information Systems," and Chapter 16, "System Implementation: Programming, System Conversion, and Controls." Examples of applications supported by applications software are presented in Chapter 14, "Applications of Information Technology."

System Software

System software is independent of any general-purpose software package or any specific application area. Software in this category controls or in some way supports software in the other two. The operating system, introduced in Chapter 3, "Interacting with Personal Computers," is classified as system software.

System software can be divided into six subcategories (see Figure 9–1): *operating systems*, *programming language compilers/interpreters*, *database management systems (DBMSs)*, *utility programs*, *performance monitoring software*, and *communications software*.

Operating Systems Every computer has an operating system that controls all hardware and software activities within a computer system. Section 9–2 is devoted to a discussion of operating systems.

Programming Language Compilers/Interpreters *Compilers* and *interpreters* translate programming languages, such as COBOL and BASIC, into a form that can be interpreted and executed by a computer system. Section 9–3 discusses compilers and interpreters.

Database Management System Software **Database management system (DBMS) software** provides the interface between application programs and the data base. For example, if you wrote a program to update employee records, the only instructions you would need to retrieve a record are those required to accept the employee's name at a VDT. Once the employee's name is entered, the database management system software does the rest. The employee record is retrieved from magnetic disk storage and moved to RAM for processing. Control is then returned to your application program to complete the update. Section 9–4 covers DBMS concepts.

A quality-control system at Ford's Explorer production facility is representative of applications software. Workers use a touch screen to enter any production variations from established standards into the system's computer.

Utility Programs   Utility programs are service routines that make life easier for us. They eliminate the need to write a program every time we need to perform certain computer operations. For example, in the mainframe environment, a utility program dumps (copies) an employee master file from magnetic disk to magnetic tape for backup. Another utility program sorts the employee master file by social security number. In the microcomputer environment, utility programs help us reorganize our hard disk to conserve storage space, manage and use available RAM more efficiently, find a file lost in the maze of a hundred directories, and reduce the file size for more efficient transmission over a data communications link, to mention a few types.

Performance Monitoring Software   Performance monitoring software is used to monitor, analyze, and report on the performance of the overall computer system and the computer system components. This software provides such information as the percentage of processor utilization and the number of disk accesses during any given period of time. This type of information enables the scheduler to make the most efficient use of hardware resources, and it helps management plan for future hardware upgrades.

Communications Software   In the mainframe environment, communications software is executed on the front-end processor, the down-line processor, and the host processor. This software controls the flow of traffic (data) to and from remote locations. Functions performed by communications software include preparing data for transmission (inserting start/

This user-friendly communications software package has the capability to display a graphic overview of the overall network. Two host computers in New York (headquarters) are linked with distributed minis and token-ring-based LANs in regional offices in Dallas and Atlanta.

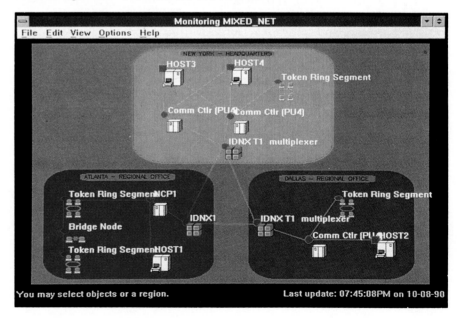

stop bits in messages), polling remote terminals for input, establishing the connection between two terminals, encoding and decoding data, and parity checking.

Micro-based communications software performs two basic functions: terminal emulation and file transfer. The function and use of micro communications software is discussed in detail in Chapter 8, "Networks and Networking."

9-2 The Operating System: The Boss

Just as the processor is the nucleus of the computer system, the *operating system* is the nucleus of all software activity. All hardware and software are controlled by the operating system. You might even call the operating system "the boss." The operating system is a family of *system software* programs that are usually, although not always, supplied by the computer system vendor.

The operating system is the first program to be loaded to RAM on any general-purpose computer system. Most dedicated computers, such as those that control appliances and electronic games, are controlled by a single program and do not need an operating system.

Microcomputer Operating Systems: A Review

The four most popular micro operating systems are: MS-DOS, Macintosh System, Operating System/2 (OS/2), and UNIX (a multiuser operating system).

A PC's operating system:

- Controls the ongoing operation of the microcomputer systems
- Facilitates the movement of data between peripheral devices, the processor, RAM, and programs
- Enables file and disk management

PC operating systems are discussed in Chapter 3, "Interacting with Personal Computers."

Mainframe Operating Systems

Because minicomputer, mainframe, and supercomputer operating systems are similar, all are discussed under this heading.

The Mainframe versus the Micro Operating System   The mainframe and micro operating systems are similar; however, they differ markedly in complexity and orientation. The mainframe operating system may coordinate a number of special-function processors, perform the concurrent execution of dozens of programs, and monitor interaction with hundreds of nodes in a network. Most micro operating systems are designed to support a single user on a single micro. In the mainframe environment, specially trained computer professionals interact with the operating system

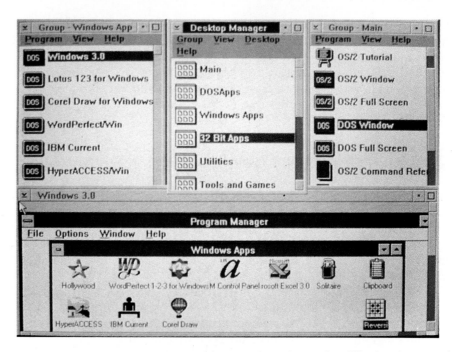

For occasional users, operating system commands can be difficult to learn and use. Designers of the OS/2 operating system for PCs address this concern by providing OS/2 users with a graphical user interface between the operating system, applications software, and user files. The photo shows how the user can view several applications at the same time.

so that end users can focus on their applications. In contrast, all micro users need a working knowledge of their micro's operating system because they must use it to interface their applications programs with the microcomputer hardware.

Design Objectives Some of the more popular mainframe operating systems include IBM's *MVS* and *VM*, DEC's *VMS*, and AT&T's *UNIX*. The logic, structure, and nomenclature of these (each of which has different versions) and other operating systems vary considerably. However, each is designed with the same five objectives in mind:

1. To minimize **turnaround time** (elapsed time between submittal of a job—for example, print payroll checks—and receipt of output)
2. To maximize *throughput* (amount of processing per unit of time)
3. To optimize the use of the computer system resources (processor, RAM, and peripheral devices)
4. To facilitate communication between the computer system and the people who run it
5. To provide an envelope of security about the computer system

Several operating system alternatives are available for minis, mainframes, and supercomputers. The choice of an operating system depends on the processing orientation of the company. Some operating systems are better for *timesharing* (servicing multiple end users), others for *processor-intensive jobs* (for example, jobs that involve complex mathematical operations), and still others for *distributed processing* (linking a central computer system with several smaller computer systems).

Interacting with the Operating System   Generally, interaction with a mainframe operating system is limited to computer professionals, usually operators and programmers.

Operator interaction.   The operating system interacts continuously with computer operators. The incredible speed of a mainframe computer system dictates that resource-allocation decisions be made at computer speeds. Most are decided automatically by the operating system. For decisions requiring human input, the operating system interrogates the operators through the operator consoles (VDTs in the machine room). The operating system also sends messages to the operator. A common message is: "Printer No. 1 is out of paper."

Operators enter commands to direct the operating system to perform specific tasks. For example, operators request the execution of certain programs, reallocate computing resources, and perform system shutdowns.

Programmer interaction.   Programmers can interact with the operating system within the context of their individual programs, or they can use **job-control language (JCL)**. Programmers often use JCL to specify the **job stream**, the sequence in which their programs are to be executed. They also use JCL to tell the operating system what programming language they are using and where to find the data (for example, which disk drive).

The Supervisor   One of the operating system programs is always *resident* in RAM (see Figure 9–2). This program, called the **supervisor**, loads other operating system and applications programs to RAM as they are needed. For example, when you request that a COBOL program be executed, the supervisor loads the necessary software (a COBOL compiler) to RAM and links your COBOL program to the compiler to translate it to an executable program. In preparing for execution, another program—the **linkage editor**—assigns a RAM address to each byte of the program you are executing.

Allocating Computer Resources   All computers, including micros, have **multitasking** capabilities. Multitasking is the *concurrent* execution of more than one program at a time. Actually, a computer can execute only one program at a time. But its internal processing speed is so fast that several programs can be allocated "slices" of computer time in rotation; this makes it appear that several programs are being executed at once.

The great difference in processor speed and the speeds of the peripheral devices makes multitasking possible. A 50-page-per-minute printer cannot even challenge the speed of a high-performance mainframe. The processor is continually waiting for the peripheral devices to complete such tasks as retrieving a record from disk storage or printing a report. During these waiting periods, the processor just continues processing other

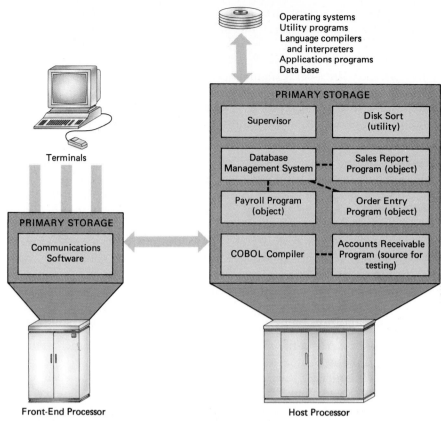

Operating systems
Utility programs
Language compilers
and interpreters
Applications programs
Data base

PRIMARY STORAGE

Supervisor	Disk Sort (utility)
Database Management System	Sales Report Program (object)
Payroll Program (object)	Order Entry Program (object)
COBOL Compiler	Accounts Receivable Program (source for testing)

Terminals

PRIMARY STORAGE

Communications Software

Front-End Processor

Host Processor

FIGURE 9–2 Software, Storage, and Execution

The supervisor program is always resident in RAM and calls other programs, as needed, from secondary storage. For example, applications programs rely on database management system software to assist in the retrieval of data from secondary storage. Software in the front-end processor handles data communications–related tasks.

programs. The operating system ensures that resources are allocated to competing tasks in the most efficient manner.

In a multitasking environment, programs running concurrently are controlled and assigned priorities by the operating system. The typical mainframe computer system will be processing several applications at the same time. For example, the BrassCo mainframe supports at least one on-line application (for example, order entry and E-mail) and one batch application (for example, printing invoices and sales analysis) at any given time. Its on-line order entry application, which runs during working hours, and other on-line applications are given the highest priority and run in the **foreground**. The foreground is that part of RAM that contains the highest priority programs. Other lower priority programs, such as the batch payroll job, are run in the **background** part of RAM. The operating system rotates allocation of the processor resource between foreground and background programs, with the foreground program receiving the lion's share of time.

The operating system also resolves conflicts over peripheral devices. For example, BrassCo's computer system has only two printers. Sometimes

The operating system of this Unisys mainframe computer system is the nerve center of a network of distributed computer systems. The system services hundreds of on-line users.

three or more applications are sending output to the printer at the same time. Obviously, some applications must wait. When this happens, printer output is temporarily loaded to magnetic disk. As the printer becomes available, the output is called from magnetic disk and printed. This process is called **spooling**.

The operating system continuously resolves these and other types of conflicts to optimize the allocation of computer resources.

The Virtual Machine: Imaginary Computer   An information system is designed and coded for a specific *computer* and *operating system*. This is true for both micros and mainframes. Therefore, programs that work well under one operating system may not be compatible with a different operating system. To minimize compatibility problems, some mainframe operating systems create a **virtual machine (VM)** environment. A VM-type operating system enables a single mainframe computer to emulate (imitate) other computers and their operating systems while executing programs in its own computing environment. That is, the specifications of a program may designate that it is to be run on Computer A using Operating System X. Upon interpreting the specifications, a VM computer loads the program to that portion of main memory that contains the emulation software for Computer A and Operating System X. Another portion of memory might contain the emulation software for Computer B and Operating System Y.

Virtual machine operating systems are especially valuable when a company is in transition from one computing environment to another. Typically, the new VM computer emulates the old computing environment while applications programs are being modified to run in the new environment. Virtual machine operating systems provide the best of both worlds by using working programs from the past and by taking advantage of the improved performance of new technology.

Virtual Memory: Imaginary RAM　We learned in Chapter 4, "Inside the Computer," that all data and programs must be resident in RAM in order to be processed. Therefore, RAM is a critical factor in determining the throughput—how much work can be done by a computer system per unit of time. Once RAM is full, no more programs can be executed until a portion of RAM is made available.

Virtual memory is a system software addition to the operating system that effectively expands the capacity of RAM through the use of software and secondary storage. This allows more data and programs to be resident in RAM at any given time.

The principle behind virtual memory is quite simple. Remember, a program is executed sequentially—one instruction after another. Programs are segmented into **pages**, so only that portion of the program being executed (one or more pages) is resident in RAM. The rest of the program is on disk storage. Appropriate pages are *rolled* (moved) into RAM from disk storage as they are needed to continue execution of the program. The paging process and use of virtual memory are illustrated in Figure 9–3.

The advantage of virtual memory is that RAM is effectively enlarged, giving programmers greater flexibility in what they can do. For example, some applications require several large programs to reside in RAM at the same time (see the order-processing and credit-checking programs illustrated in Figure 9–3). If the size of these programs exceeds the capacity of RAM, then virtual memory can be used as a supplement to complete the processing.

The disadvantage of virtual memory is the cost in efficiency during program execution. If the logic of a program causes frequent branching between pages, the program will execute more slowly because of the time

FIGURE 9–3　Virtual Memory
Pages of the order-processing and credit-checking programs are rolled from virtual memory on magnetic disk into "real" memory (RAM) as they are needed.

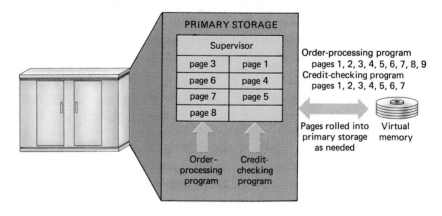

required to roll pages from secondary storage to RAM. Excessive page movement results in too much of the computer's time devoted to page handling and not enough to processing. This excessive data movement is appropriately named *thrashing* and actually can be counterproductive.

9–3 Compilers and Interpreters: Programs for Programs

All programs are ultimately executed in the computer's **machine language**. As this is a cumbersome process, we write programs in high-level language that must be translated into machine language before they can be executed. This conversion of high-level instructions to machine-level instructions is done by system software programs called *compilers* and *interpreters*.

Compilers

The **compiler** program translates the instructions of a high-level language, such as COBOL, to machine-language instructions that the computer can interpret and execute. A separate compiler (or an interpreter, discussed in the next section) is required for each programming language intended for use on a particular computer system. That is, to execute both COBOL and Pascal programs, you must have a COBOL compiler and a Pascal compiler.

High-level programming languages are simply a programmer convenience; they cannot be executed in their source, or original, form. The actual high-level programming-language instructions, called the **source program**, are translated, or **compiled**, into machine-language instructions by a compiler.

Suppose you want to write a COBOL program to process sales receipts. The circled numbers in Figure 9–4 cross-reference the numbered discussion of the compilation process presented below.

1. On a mainframe computer system you would enter the COBOL instructions into the computer system through an on-line terminal. (On a PC, you would enter the program as you would anything else.) Having done so, you identify the language (COBOL) in which you wrote the program and request that the program be compiled.

2. The COBOL compiler program is called from magnetic disk and loaded to RAM along with the COBOL source program. (*Note:* Step 3 will be attempted but not completed if the source program contains errors or **bugs** [see Step 4].)

3. The COBOL compiler translates the source program into a machine-language program called an **object program**. The object program is the output of the compilation process. At this point, the object program resides in RAM and can be executed upon your command.

   The compilation process can be time-consuming, especially for large programs. Therefore, if you intend to execute the program at another time, perhaps during another session, you should store the object program on

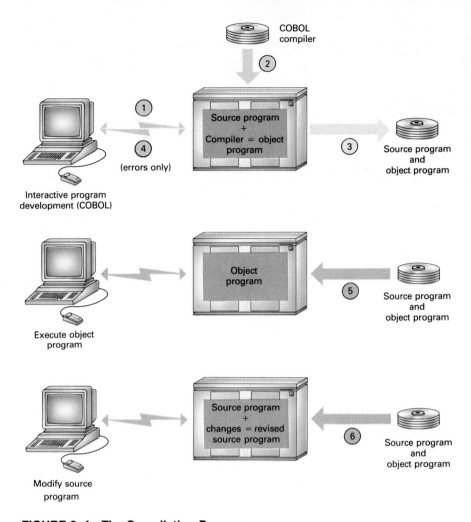

FIGURE 9–4 The Compilation Process

A source program is translated into an object program for execution. The steps of the compilation process are discussed in the text.

magnetic disk for later recall. On most mainframe computer systems this is done automatically.

4. If the source program contains a **syntax error** (for example, an invalid instruction format), the compiler will display an error message on the terminal screen, then terminate the compilation process. An error message identifies the program statement or statements in error and the cause of the error. Syntax errors usually involve invalid instructions. Consider the following COBOL statement: DISPLAY "WHOOPS". The statement is invalid because DISPLAY is misspelled.

   As a programmer, you will make the necessary corrections and attempt the compilation over and over and over again, until the program compiles and executes. Don't be discouraged. Very few programs compile on the first, second, or even third attempt. When your program finally compiles and executes, don't be surprised if the output is not what you expected. A "clean," or error-free, compilation is likely to surface un-

When Grace Murray Hopper died on New Year's Day in 1992 at the age of 85, the computer world lost its "Grand Old Lady of Software." Dubbed "Amazing Grace" by her many admirers, Dr. Hopper was widely respected as the driving force behind COBOL, the most popular programming language, and a champion of standardized programming languages that are hardware-independent.

Dr. Hopper was a professor of mathematics when she joined the Navy in 1943 and began her distinguished career in computers. She was assigned to the Bureau of Ordinance Computation Project at Harvard University, helping program the first large-scale digital computer, the Mark I. After World War II she continued her work on the Mark II and Mark III. (An outspoken and feisty computer advocate, Dr. Hopper liked to introduce herself at speaking engagements by saying that she was the third programmer on the first large-scale digital computer in the United States, and she'd been coping with it ever since.)

In 1949 she moved to the Eckert-Mauchly Computer Corporation in Philadelphia where she helped build UNIVAC I, the first commercial large-scale electronic digital computer. In 1959 Dr. Hopper led an effort that laid the foundation for the development of COBOL. She also created a compiler that enabled COBOL to run on many types of computers. Her reason: "Why start from scratch with every program you write when a computer could be developed to do a lot of the basic work for you over and over again?"

Although she retired from the Navy Reserve in 1966 at age 59, Dr. Hopper was recalled to active duty within a year to help the Navy standardize its programming languages. When she retired in 1986 at the age of 79, she was the oldest active-duty military officer and held the rank of Rear Admiral.

To Dr. Hopper's long list of honors, awards, and accomplishments, add the fact that she found the first "bug" in a computer—a real one. She repaired the Mark II by removing a moth that was caught in Relay Number II. From that day on, every programmer has *debugged* software by ferreting out its *bugs,* or errors, in programming syntax or logic.

GRACE MURRAY HOPPER, 1906–1992

detected **logic errors**. For example, your program logic might result in an attempted division by zero; this is mathematically and logically impossible and will result in a program error. In most cases, you will need to remove a few such bugs in the program logic and in the I/O formats before the program is finished.

5. Suppose you come back the next day and wish to execute your COBOL program again. Instead of repeating the compilation process of Step 2, you simply call the object program from magnetic disk and load it to RAM for execution. Since the object program is already in machine language, no compilation is necessary.

6. If you want to make any changes in the original source programs, you simply: Recall the original source program from magnetic disk, make the changes, recompile the program, and create an updated object program (repeat Steps 1 through 4).

Programs that are run frequently are stored and executed as object programs. Recompilation is necessary only when the program is modified.

Interpreters

An **interpreter** is a system software program that ultimately performs the same function as a compiler—but in a different manner. Instead of translating the entire source program in a single pass, an interpreter translates *and* executes each source program instruction before translating and executing the next.

The obvious advantage of interpreters over compilers is that an error in instruction syntax is brought to the attention of the programmer immediately, thereby prompting the programmer to make corrections during interactive program development. This is a tremendous help.

But, as we know, advantages are usually accompanied by disadvantages. The disadvantage of interpreters is that they do not use computing resources as efficiently as a program that has been compiled. Since the interpreter does not produce an object program, it must perform the translation process each time a program is executed.

Programmers can take advantage of the strengths of both interpreters and compilers for programs that are run often. First they develop and debug their programs using an interpreter. Then they compile the finished program to create a more efficient object program that can be used for routine processing.

 9–4 The DBMS: Solving the Data Puzzle

Data Integration

The traditional sequential and random files, discussed in Chapter 6, "Data Storage and Organization," typically are designed to meet the specific information and data processing requirements of a particular department such as accounting, sales, or purchasing. Different files are created to support these functions, but many of the fields on each of these files are the same. For example, each of these functional areas needs to maintain customer data, such as customer name, customer address, and the contact person at the customer location. When the name of the contact person changes in a traditional file environment, each file must be updated separately.

Through the early 1980s, most installed information systems were implemented in a crisis environment with a single functional objective in mind. The integration of information systems was not a priority. As a result, many companies are now saddled with massive system, procedural, and data redundancies. These redundancies promote inefficiencies and result in unnecessary expenses. Today companies are using *database man-*

The emergence of high-density optical laser disk technology has made it economically feasible to store images as well as text in a data base. AT&T has many applications that call for optical storage and retrieval of documents.

agement system (*DBMS*) software as a tool to integrate data management and information flow within an organization. DBMS software falls under system software since it is independent of any specific application.

Costly data redundancy can be minimized by designing an *integrated data base* to serve the organization as a whole, not just one specific department. The integrated data base is made possible by database management system software. Notice that *database* is one word when it refers to the software that manages the data base. *Data base* is two words when it refers to the most comprehensive level of the hierarchy of data organization (see Figure 6–2).

Benefits of an Integrated Data Base Environment

A company would begin with or convert to an integrated data base environment for a variety of reasons. Some of these are discussed below.

Greater Access to Information   Most organizations have accumulated a wealth of data, but translating these data into meaningful information has, at times, proved difficult, especially in a traditional file environment. The structure of an integrated data base provides enormous flexibility in the types of reports that can be generated and the types of on-line inquiries that can be made.

Better Control   A database management system allows data to be centralized for improved security. Also, by centralizing data, advanced *data structures* can be used to control data redundancy. The term *data structures* refers to the manner in which the fields and records are related to one another.

More Efficient Software Development   The programming task is simplified with a database management system because data are more readily

225 Files = 1 Data Base Ingersoll Milling Machine Company, a $550-million manufacturer of metal cutting and machinery systems, developed a customized, integrated data base to help cut costs. The data base took the place of 1300 programs and systems running from 225 different master files. The data base cut work-in-process by 48%, purchasing costs by 43%, and quality-control costs by 34%.

available. In addition, data in a data base are *independent* of the applications programs. That is, fields can be added, changed, and deleted from the data base without affecting existing programs. Adding a field to a record of a traditional *flat file* may require the modification and testing of dozens and sometimes hundreds of programs.

Approaches to Data Base Management

Database management system software has overcome the processing constraints of traditional files. To do this, such systems rely on sophisticated data structures. The data structures vary considerably from one commercially available DBMS software package to another. However, there are three fundamental approaches to the design of DBMS software:

- The **hierarchical DBMS**
- The **network DBMS**
- The **relational DBMS**

The examples presented in the following sections should help you better understand the principles and advantages of the three types of database management systems, all of which are in common use.

Hierarchical DBMS

Background. Although network and relational DBMS technologies are considered superior to hierarchical DBMS technology, the hierarchical approach remains widely used. This is more a result of momentum than choice. In 1968 IBM announced its *Information Management Systems* (*IMS*), a hierarchical DBMS product. At the time it was the only database management system available and became enormously popular. Although *IMS* has been upgraded many times, it is still a hierarchical system and does not have the scope of features of the more sophisticated network and relational DBMSs. It, however, has two decades of momentum, and *IMS* users are reluctant to scrap their sizable investments and start over with a network or relational DBMS. Nevertheless, virtually all new development in the area of database management systems uses network and/or relational technologies.

A hierarchical DBMS example. Hierarchical DBMSs are based on the tree data structure, actually an uprooted tree turned upside down. Hierarchies are easy to understand and conceptualize. A company's organizational chart is a good example of the tree structure. At the top of the chart is the president, with the vice presidents in the second level, subordinate to the president. Those people reporting to the vice presidents occupy the third level.

Hierarchical structures are equally appropriate for data management. Consider the employee data base for Winning Ways, Inc., a large investment company, in Figure 9–5. Winning Ways' commitment to employee education has prompted management to create an information center. The information center provides a variety of computer-related services, including education, for all Winning Ways employees. In the

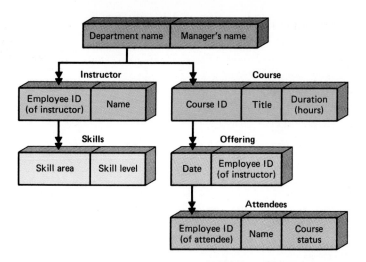

FIGURE 9–5 A Structure for a Hierarchical Data Base

The data base records for instructor, [instructor] skills, course, [course] offering, and [course] attendees are linked to the root in a hierarchical manner to form the structure of a hierarchical data base.

example, the information center has several full-time in-house instructors, each of whom gives courses on a variety of subjects. The data base includes the skill areas and associated skill levels for each instructor. For example, an instructor might have skills in word processing and local area networks at Skill Levels 4 and 3, respectively. A particular course (word processing) may be given several times a year, possibly by different instructors. Each offering of a course is attended by at least one employee who either completes (C) the course or withdraws (W), thereby prompting a C or W to be entered in the course status field (see Figures 9–5 and 9–6).

Figure 9–6 shows a partial *occurrence* of the information center's hierarchical data base structure. The hierarchical structure of the data base and the occurrence are analogous to the field and the data item (for example, employee name, Jack Beck). One is the definition—the category, or abstract—and the other is the actual value, or contents.

In hierarchical DBMSs, a group of fields is called a **segment**. The segment is similar to the record of a traditional file in that it is a collection of related fields and is read from, or written to, the data base as a unit. The relationship between a segment at a higher level to one connected by a line at a lower level is that of a *parent* and *child* or *children*. In Figure 9–5, the instructor segment is the parent of the skills segment. The possibility of "children" (for example, instructors with multiple skills) is denoted by a double arrow on the connector line. In a hierarchical data base, no segment has more than one parent. The **root**, or highest level, does not have a parent.

The Winning Ways information center tree illustrated in Figure 9–5 could be linked with other trees, perhaps the company's employee tree, to create informative reports. For example, the employee ID data items in the attendees' segments could be used to "point" to more detailed information about a particular attendee (department affiliation, extension number, and so on).

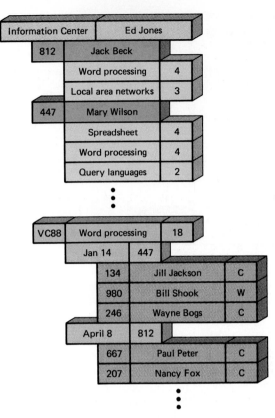

FIGURE 9–6 A Partial Occurrence of the Hierarchical Data Base Structure of Figure 9–5

Mary Wilson (employee ID 447) taught the January 14 offering of the word processing course.

If this application were designed using traditional approaches to data management, there would probably be two files, the course file and the instructor file. The record layout for these two files might appear as shown in Figure 9–7. Notice the redundancy that would result from the these flat files (for example, attendee information would be duplicated for each course taken).

Network DBMS The network approach to data management carries the hierarchical approach to the next level of sophistication by permitting "children" to have more than one "parent."

A network DBMS example. Consider the following situation. The Ozark Regional Library currently maintains a file that contains the following fields on each record:

- Title
- Author(s)
- Publisher
- Publisher's address
- ISBN
- Publication year

The head librarian wants more flexibility in obtaining decision-making information. Many of the librarian's requests would be impractical

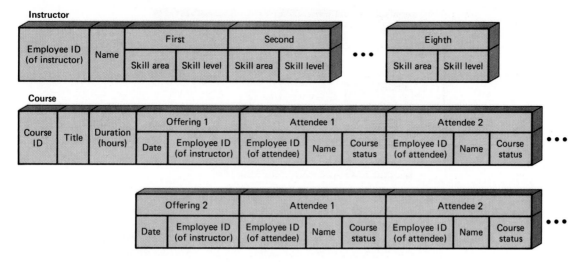

FIGURE 9–7 Record Layouts

These record layouts for a course file and an instructor file are traditional file alternatives to the hierarchical data base structure of Figure 9–5.

with the existing traditional file (see Figure 9–8). A data base administrator recommends restructuring the file as a network database management system. The data base administrator is a computer specialist who designs and maintains the data base.

Not surprisingly, the data base administrator finds certain data redundancies in the existing file. Because each book or title has a separate record, the *name* of an author who has written several books is repeated for each book written. A given publisher may have hundreds, even thousands, of books in the Ozark Regional Library—but in the present file, the *publisher* and *publisher's address* are repeated for each title. To eliminate these data redundancies, the data base administrator suggests the records, or segments, shown in Figure 9–9.

Next, the data base administrator establishes the relationships between the records. There is a *one-to-many* relationship between the publisher and title records. That is, one publisher may publish any number of titles. Notice that the publisher–title relationship is represented in Figure 9–9 by a connecting line between the two records. A double arrow toward the title record represents the possibility of more than one title per publisher. The publisher–title combination is called a **set**. Other sets defined by the data base administrator are title–author and author–title (*many-to-many*). Figure 9–9 is a graphic representation of the logical structure of the data base, called a **schema** (pronounced *SKEE muh*).

FIGURE 9–8 Record Layout

This record layout is for a traditional book inventory file in a library.

Title	ISBN	Publication year	Publisher	Publisher's address	Author 1	Author 2	Author 3	Author 4

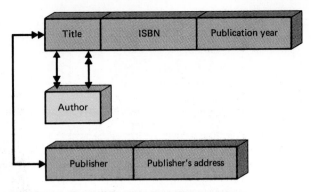

FIGURE 9–9 A Network Data Base Schema
The record layout of the traditional book inventory file in Figure 9–8 is reorganized into segments and integrated into a data base schema to minimize redundancy. Relationships are established between the segments so that authors, titles, and publishers can be linked as appropriate.

In the data base schema of Figure 9–9, a particular author's name appears only once. It is then linked to the title records of those books he or she has written. The publisher record is linked to all the titles it publishes. When accessing a record in a program, you simply request the record of a particular title, author, or publisher. Once you have the author's record, you can use the links between records to retrieve the titles of the books written by that author. Similarly, if you request the record of a particular publisher, you can obtain a list of all titles it has published.

Figure 9–9 is a representation of the schema and Figure 9–10 shows an occurrence of the data base structure.

FIGURE 9–10 An Occurrence of the Network Data Base Structure of Figure 9–9
Notice that publishers can be linked to authors via the title record, and vice versa.

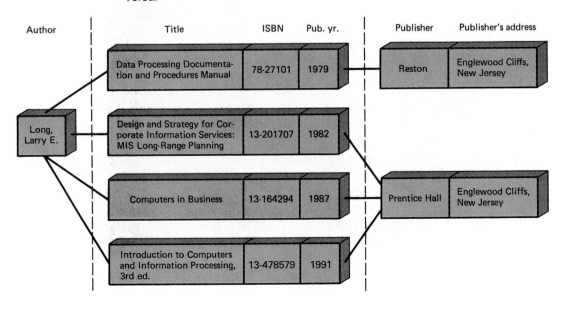

Queries to the data base. This data base design eliminates, or at least minimizes, data redundancy and permits the head librarian at Ozark Regional Library to make a wide range of inquiries. For example:

- What titles were written by Mark Twain?
- List those titles published by Prentice Hall in 1986 (alphabetically by title).

Responses to these and similar inquiries are relatively easy to obtain with a database management system. Similar inquiries of the library's existing traditional file (Figure 9–8) would require not only the complete processing of the file but perhaps several data preparation computer runs for sorting and merging.

If the head librarian decides after a year to add, for example, the Library of Congress number to the title record, the data base administrator can make the revision without affecting existing programs.

Relational DBMS

Relational versus network DBMSs. The relational approach to database management systems has been gaining momentum through the 1980s. In contrast to the network DBMSs, data are accessed by *content* rather than by *address*. That is, the relational approach uses the computer to search the data base for the desired data rather than accessing data through a series of indices and physical addresses, as with both the hierarchical and network DBMSs. In relational DBMSs, the data structures, or relationships between data, are defined in *logical* rather than *physical* terms. That is, the relational data base has no predetermined relationship between the data, such as the one-to-many sets in the network schemas (see Figure 9–9). In this way, data can be accessed at the *field* level. In network structures, the entire segment must be retrieved into RAM for processing in order to examine a single field.

Until recently, relational DBMSs have not been as effective in the real world, especially in transaction-oriented environments. Even with the increased speed of computers and innovations in relational technology, network database management systems outperform relational DBMSs for transaction processing. However, for applications in which the transaction volume is low and the need for flexible decision support systems (query and "what if") is high, relational DBMSs outperform network DBMSs. Because relational structures provide greater flexibility in accessing information, relational DBMSs provide companies with greater opportunities to increase productivity.

A relational DBMS example. Let's stay with library applications at Ozark Regional Library for our relational DBMS example, but let's shift emphasis from book inventory to book circulation. The objective of a circulation system is to keep track of who borrows which books, then monitor their timely return. In the traditional flat-file environment, the record layout might appear as shown in Figure 9–11. In the record shown, a library patron can borrow from one to four books. Precious magnetic disk storage space is wasted for patrons who borrow infrequently, and the four-book limit may force prolific readers to make more trips to the Ozark Regional Library.

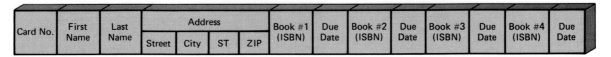

Card No.	First Name	Last Name	Address				Book #1 (ISBN)	Due Date	Book #2 (ISBN)	Due Date	Book #3 (ISBN)	Due Date	Book #4 (ISBN)	Due Date
			Street	City	ST	ZIP								

FIGURE 9–11 Record Layout

This record layout is for a traditional book circulation file in a library.

The data base administrator recommended the relational DBMS organization shown in Figure 9–12. The data base contains two *tables*, each containing rows and columns of data. A *row*, or **tuple**, in a table is roughly equivalent to an occurrence of a segment in a hierarchical or network data base. The column headings, called **attributes**, are analogous to fields of the hierarchical and network data bases.

The first table contains patron data, and the second table contains data relating to books on loan. Each new patron at Ozark Regional Library is assigned a number and issued a library card with a number that can be read with an optical wand scanner. The patron's card number, name, and address are added to the data base. When the patron borrows a book, the librarian at the circulation desk uses a wand scanner to enter the card number and the book's ISBN (International Standard Book Number). These data and the due date, which are entered on a keyboard, become a row in the books-on-loan data table. Notice that by using a relational DBMS, there is no limit to the number of borrowed books the system can handle for a particular patron.

Queries to the data base.   Suppose Ozark Regional's circulation librarian wanted a report of overdue books as of April 8 (4/8). The query would be: "List all books overdue" (query date is 4/8). The search criterion of "due date < [before] 4/8" is applied to the due date column in the books-on-loan data table (see Figure 9–13). The search surfaces two overdue books, then the system uses the card numbers to cross-reference delinquent patrons in the patron data table to obtain their names and addresses. The report at the bottom of Figure 9–13 is produced in response to the librarian's query. Data on each book, including publisher, author, and ISBN, might be maintained in another table in the relational data base.

FIGURE 9–12 A Relational Data Base Organization

The record layout of the traditional book circulation file of Figure 9–11 is reorganized and integrated into a relational data base with a "patron data" table and a "books-on-loan data" table.

Patron Data

Card No.	First Name	Last Name	Address			
			Street	City	ST	ZIP
1243	Jason	Jones	18 W. Oak	Ponca City	OK	74601
1618	Kay	Smith	108 10th St.	Newkirk	OK	74647
2380	Heather	Hall	2215 Pine Dr.	Ponca City	OK	74604
2644	Brett	Brown	1700 Sunset	Ponca City	OK	74604
3012	Melody	Beck	145 N. Brook	Ark. City	KS	67005
3376	Butch	Danner	RD#7	Tonkawa	OK	74653
3859	Abe	Michaels	333 Paul Ave.	Kaw City	OK	74641

Books-on-Loan Data

Card No.	Book No. (ISBN)	Due Date
1618	89303-530	4/7
1243	12-201702	4/20
3859	13-48049	4/9
2644	18-23614	4/14
2644	71606-214	4/14
2644	22-68111	4/3
1618	27-21675	4/12

Card No.	Book No. (ISBN)	Due Date	Overdue? (Due Date < 4/8)
1618	89303-530-0	4/7	→ Yes
1243	13-201702-5	4/20	→ No
3859	13-48049-8	4/9	→ No
2644	18-23614-1	4/14	→ No
2644	71606-214-0	4/14	→ No
2644	22-68111-7	4/3	→ Yes
1618	27-21675-2	4/12	→ No

Overdue Books (4/8)			
Card No.	Name	Due Date	ISBN
1618	Kay Smith	4/7	89303-530-0
2644	Brett Brown	4/3	22-68111-7

FIGURE 9–13 Queries to a Relational Data Base

The figure illustrates the resolution and output of an April 8 query to the data base: "List all books overdue."

Commercial Database Management Systems

Over 200 commercially available DBMS software packages are offered for sale. Each year unprofitable packages are removed from the market, but the gap is soon filled with innovative new products. Some microcomputer DBMSs sell for under $50 and some mainframe versions sell for over $250,000. Industry giant IBM dominates the minicomputer and mainframe DBMS market with the two-decade-old *IMS*, a hierarchical DBMS, and the recently introduced *DB2*, a relational DBMS. With *IMS* and *DB2*, IBM has 50 percent of the DBMS market. *DB2*, introduced in 1985, is far from the market leader, but all indicators show that it will be within a few years.

We cannot always pigeonhole a commercial DBMS as hierarchical, network, or relational. In practice, there are as many approaches to developing database management system software as there are DBMS products. To achieve the flexibility of relational technology and the transaction processing capabilities of network technology, a vendor might create a DBMS software package that embodies the best of both.

This workstation combines a relational database management system, a structured query language (SQL), and a digital world map to simplify data analysis for a government agency.

At some time or another, just about everybody is faced with resolving critical questions about college. Do I attend college? If so, where? College graduates must answer similar questions. Do I go on to graduate school? If so, where? To some prospective students, the answers are clear: continue the family tradition at State U., or perhaps attend the local college. Others are faced with the awesome task of evaluating several thousand options. Certainly a well-informed decision maker is more likely to make the right decision than one who is ill-informed.

In the past, prospective students have sought information from a variety of sources, including "how to" books, books that summarize information about colleges, and thousands of college catalogs. Scanning through this information can be cumbersome, time-consuming, and expensive. Today's computer-based data bases offer an easier, faster, and less expensive way to choose a college. There are two ways of accessing these data bases. You can use your microcomputer to tap into a commercial information service that supports a college data base, or you can purchase the database software on a diskette.

Peterson's College Selection Service Data Base is one of a hundred data bases made available to subscribers of CompuServe, the on-line information service with the most subscribers. Subscribers search its data base by identifying the features they desire in a college. The features include level of study, location, size, campus setting, housing, costs, majors, ethnic/geographic mix, admissions requirements, entrance difficulty, type of student body, and 10 other categories. Options are selected for each feature. For example, for level of study, the user could choose

1. Two-year college
2. Four-year college with no graduate work
3. University or four-year college with graduate work
4. Upper-level institution (starts at the junior year)

The data base is searched and only those colleges that meet the selection criteria are listed. The user can then request a display of an in-depth profile of any of the colleges on the list.

College Explorer is a database software product available for IBM-PC compatibles and for the Apple II series. The interface with this program is similar to the on-line Peterson's College Selection Service Data Base in that the prospective student must establish his or her search criteria. A search of the College Explorer data base results in two lists—one of colleges that meet all required and preferred conditions and the other consisting of colleges that meet all required conditions but not all the preferred conditions.

A criteria search of an on-line or diskette-based college data base can be completed in seconds. The advantages of computer-based data bases become vividly apparent when you consider that a similar but less rigorous search through printed college literature might take weeks, even months!

Besides the way they are designed, the application development tools that accompany commercial DBMS packages help differentiate them. A DBMS package can be purchased with none or all of the following development tools: user-oriented query language, code generator for programs, data dictionary, report generator, screen generator, prototyping tool, and others. These tools are discussed in later chapters.

Standards for Database Management Systems

For the most part, the 200-plus DBMS products on the market differ markedly in approach and the manner in which they store and retrieve data. Moreover, vendors have created their own proprietary data base query languages for data definition, retrieval, manipulation, and control. Typically, to respond to the query "List all books overdue" in the relational

DBMS example we discussed earlier, a query-language program would have to be written (or generated automatically). The existence of so many query languages has made it difficult, although not impossible, for data in one data base to be combined logically with that of another. However, this hurdle will be less of a concern in the coming years.

IBM's **SQL (Structured Query Language)**, pronounced *sequel*, has been the de facto standard data access query language for relational data bases for several years. Recently, *SQL* was made the official standard by both ANSI (American National Standards Institute) and ISO (International Standards Organization). As a result, vendors of future relational DBMS software will design their packages so that they can interpret *SQL* commands. It also means that *SQL* can be used to permit the sharing of data by dissimilar software packages and DBMSs. This should spur the growth of both intercompany and intracompany networking.

Most industry observers, even skeptics, are predicting that IBM's *DB2* will be the de facto industry standard and may someday garner as much as two thirds of the DBMS market. In fact, *DB2* is already a market itself: Software vendors are developing productivity tools designed specifically for the *DB2* environment.

With *SQL* and *DB2* becoming industry standards, human skills (programming, data base administration) and software will have greater portability. That is, both humans and software can move easily from one computing environment to the next. Humans will need little or no supplemental training and the software will need little or no modification. The overwhelming majority of people who have *SQL* programming skills and/or *DB2* design skills are MIS specialists.

DBMS Summary

The days of the centralized data base may be numbered. Emerging DBMS standards may enable computer specialists to overcome the hurdle of data base connectivity. The ideal data storage scheme would optimize the use of available resources. Such a scheme would store data in the most convenient places within a computer network, depending on data entry requirements, storage capacity availability, processing load requirements, and so on. To implement this ideal data storage scheme, computer specialists must use a **distributed DBMS**. A distributed DBMS permits the interfacing of data bases located in various places throughout a computer network (departmental minicomputers, micro-based local nets, the corporate mainframe, and so on). The distributed DBMS functions as if it were centralized. The fact that it is distributed is transparent (invisible) to the end user. That is, a user making a request would not be concerned about the source of the data or how they are retrieved. Unfortunately, the software for distributed DBMSs is still on the drawing board and will not be available for several years.

We all keep data, both at our place of business and at home. DBMS software and the availability of computing hardware make it easier for us to extract meaningful information from these data. In time, working with data bases will be as familiar to us as reaching in a desk drawer file for a manila folder.

Memory Bits

APPROACHES TO DBMS SOFTWARE
- Hierarchical DBMS
  Root plus parent/child(ren) relationships
- Network DBMS
  Schema
  One-to-many and many-to-many sets
- Relational DBMS
  Tables with tuples (rows) and attributes (columns)

Software is written to run under a specific platform. A *platform* defines the standards followed by those who create software. Specifically, the platform is defined by the *processor's design architecture* and the *operating system* being used. Generally, software that works on one platform is not compatible with any other platform. Platforms were introduced briefly in Chapter 3, "Interacting with Personal Computers." The term **operating environment** is used interchangeably with *platform*.

The typical computer system, large or small, runs under a single platform. However, some can be configured to run several platforms. A virtual machine-based mainframe computer (see Section 9–2) runs its native platform and emulates other platforms. In the PC environment, the UNIX and Macintosh System operating systems have software that emulates the popular MS-DOS operating system. Although emulation adds flexibility, programs running in emulation mode run more slowly than if run on the real thing.

The selection of a platform is important because it establishes boundaries for what you can and cannot do with your computer system. For example, for the same mainframe environment, one operating system option might support a distributed processing system and another might not. In the micro environment, one operating system option permits only a single user where another supports multiple users. Perhaps the single most important criteria in the selection of a platform is the availability of appropriate commercial applications and general-purpose software. Of course, this criteria is less important for companies and individuals who plan to create their own custom software.

Mainframe Platforms

Major mainframe vendors, such as IBM, Digital Equipment, Amdahl, and UNISYS, market a variety of mainframe computers, each of which has at least one operating system option. Each computer and each operating system defines a platform. The selection of a platform for corporate computing can be very complex, even for seasoned computer professionals. Most organizations have made at least one mainframe platform decision already and have made sizable investments in their platforms (software, hardware, personnel training, and so on). Eventually, advancing technology forces these organizations to choose between continuing with their existing platform or upgrading to another, which may or may not be compatible with the existing one.

A listing of actual mainframe platforms, of which there are many, is beyond the scope of this book. Suffice it to say that its selection defines the direction for computing within an organization for the foreseeable future.

PC Platforms

In the mainframe environment, platforms are the purview of computer specialists. In the PC environment, you, the individual user, select the platform. The following discussion will provide some insight into that decision process. You must first decide whether to go with a single-user or multiuser platform.

Single-User Platforms The three most popular single-user platforms combine any IBM-PC–compatible micro with MS-DOS or OS/2 and the Macintosh with its operating system (Macintosh System).

IBM-PC compatibles with MS-DOS and Windows. Through 1990 the platform of choice for the vast majority of PC users was defined by micros that are functionally compatible with the 1984 IBM PC-AT architecture (the Intel family of microprocessors) and run under MS-DOS. This platform dominated because

1. Most users operated in the single-user environment, one application at a time.
2. Thousands of software packages have been created for this platform.
3. Millions of people are familiar with this platform and are reluctant to change.
4. Users have a tremendous financial investment in software and hardware that run under this platform.

However, by itself, this platform permits relatively little multitasking capability (see Section 9–2), and modern users want multitasking capabilities.

Responding to this need, Microsoft Corporation introduced software that expanded this platform to include multitasking. Microsoft's Windows, by virtue of its warm acceptance in the marketplace, defines a new

Vendor-supplied software manuals must strike a balance between too little and too much information. Too little information precludes effective use of the software. Too much information tends to obscure fundamental instructions. As a result, vendor manuals often fall short of telling the whole story. To fill in the information gap, vendors provide call-in support for customers. At IBM's customer support center, technical experts help customers diagnose and solve problems over the telephone.

platform. Windows runs under MS-DOS, but programs written to take full advantage of its potential must conform to Windows CUA (Common User Interface) standards (see Chapter 3).

Most popular micro programs that gained their popularity as MS-DOS programs have been converted or they are being converted to run under the Windows platform. Moreover, most software packages that run under MS-DOS and do not conform to Windows standards can be run within Windows. These programs, called non-Windows programs, are no less effective when run within Windows, but they cannot take full advantage of the Windows capabilities.

IBM-PC compatibles with OS/2.   OS/2 is the next generation of MS-DOS. It is a single-user multitasking operating system that requires an Intel 286 or better microprocessor. In addition to multitasking, the great advantage of the OS/2 platform is that it enables up to 16 MB of RAM to be addressed directly (as opposed to 1 MB for MS-DOS). On the down side, OS/2 is a very sophisticated environment that requires up to 4 MB of dedicated RAM. OS/2 users interact with the system via a graphical user interface called *Presentation Manager*.

Even though OS/2 breaks the MS-DOS 1-MB barrier, it has been slow to catch on. Software vendors are reluctant to devote resources to creating OS/2-based software for a market dominated by MS-DOS. As you might expect, users are reluctant to switch to OS/2 because of the lack of software that runs under the OS/2 platform.

The Macintosh platform.   The Apple Macintosh family of PCs and its operating system (Macintosh System) define another major platform. Macintosh PCs, which are based on the Motorola family of microprocessors, use the NuBus 32-bit architecture. The Macintosh platform includes many sophisticated capabilities including multitasking, a GUI, virtual memory, and the ability to emulate the MS-DOS platform. Macintosh PCs also have the built-in ability to communicate with and share files with other Macintosh PCs on a network.

Multiuser Platforms   Each of the multiuser operating systems defines a different platform for which software is created, the most popular being UNIX and its spinoffs. Many of the popular PC software packages have been retrofitted to run under UNIX. For example, WordPerfect, a word processing package, has a product that runs under the UNIX platform. Much of the software written for this platform addresses office or department information systems. For example, a doctor's clinic might have three terminals for administration and three for inquiry.

With microcomputers being equipped with power beyond the need of most individual users, companies are looking to multiuser platforms to take advantage of emerging PC technology.

    Important Terms and Summary Outline

applications software	background	compile
attribute	bug	compiler

database management	machine language	source program
system (DBMS)	multitasking	spooling
distributed DBMS	network DBMS	Structured Query
foreground	object program	Language (SQL)
general-purpose	operating environment	supervisor
software	page	syntax error
hierarchical DBMS	performance monitoring	system software
interpreter	software	tuple
job stream	relational DBMS	turnaround time
job-control language	root	utility program
(JCL)	schema	virtual machine (VM)
linkage editor	segment	virtual memory
logic errors	set	

9–1 CATEGORIES OF SOFTWARE.   Software directs the activities of the computer system. Software falls into three major categories: general-purpose, applications, and system. **General-purpose software** provides the framework for a great number of business, scientific, and personal applications. **Applications software** is designed and written to perform specific personal, business, or scientific processing tasks. **System software** is usually independent of any general-purpose software package or any specific application area. System software is in these subcategories: operating systems, programming language compilers/interpreters, **database management systems (DBMSs)**, utility programs, performance monitoring software, and communications software.

9–2 THE OPERATING SYSTEM: THE BOSS.   The four most popular micro operating systems are MS-DOS, Macintosh System, Operating System/2 (OS/2), and UNIX.

The design objectives of an operating system, the nucleus of all software activity, are to minimize **turnaround time**, maximize throughput, optimize the use of computer resources, facilitate communication with people, and provide for security. Operating systems are oriented to a particular type of processing environment, such as timesharing, processor-intensive jobs, or distributed processing.

Programmers can interact with the operating system within the context of their individual programs or they can use the **job control language (JCL)**. Programmers often use JCL to specify the **job stream**.

The memory-resident **supervisor** program loads other operating system and applications programs to RAM as they are needed. The **linkage editor** assigns a RAM address to each byte of the object program.

Multitasking is the concurrent execution of more than one program at a time. The great difference in processor speed and the speeds of the peripheral devices makes multitasking possible. High-priority programs run in the **foreground** part of RAM. Lower-priority programs are run in the **background**. Routing printer output via magnetic disk is called **spooling**.

A **virtual machine (VM)** operating system enables a single computer to emulate other computers and their operating systems while executing programs in its own computing environment.

Virtual memory effectively expands the capacity of RAM through the use of software, **pages**, and secondary storage.

9–3 COMPILERS AND INTERPRETERS: PROGRAMS FOR PROGRAMS. High-level languages must be translated into **machine language** in order to be executed. They are a programmer convenience and facilitate the programmer/computer interaction. A **compiler** is needed to translate, or **compile**, a **source program** in a high-level language into an **object program** in machine language for execution. An **interpreter** performs a function similar to a compiler, but it translates one instruction at a time. To run properly a program must be free of **bugs**, including **syntax errors** and **logic errors**.

9–4 THE DBMS: SOLVING THE DATA PUZZLE. A traditional file is usually designed to meet the specific requirements of a particular functional area department. This approach to file design results in the same data being stored and maintained in several separate files. Data redundancy is costly and can be minimized by designing an integrated data base to serve the organization as a whole, not any specific department. The integrated data base is made possible by *database management system*, or *DBMS*, software.

Database management systems permit greater access to information, enable greater control of data, minimize data redundancy, and allow programmers more flexibility in the design and maintenance of information systems.

Database management systems rely on sophisticated data structures to overcome the processing constraints of traditional files. Three common types of DBMSs are the **hierarchical DBMS**, the **network DBMS**, and the **relational DBMS**.

Because of the tremendous momentum of IBM's *IMS* DBMS, the hierarchical approach to data base management remains the most commonly used. Hierarchical DBMSs are based on the tree data structure. In hierarchical DBMSs the **segment** is similar to the record of a traditional file in that it is a collection of related fields and is read from, or written to, the data base as a unit. The relationship between segments is that of a parent to a child or children. In a hierarchical data base, no segment has more than one parent. The **root**, or highest level, does not have a parent.

In network DBMSs, data links are established between segments. One-to-one and one-to-many relationships between segments are combined to form **sets**. The data base **schema** is a graphic representation of the logical structure of these sets.

In relational DBMSs, data are accessed by content rather than by address. There is no predetermined relationship between the data; therefore, the data can be accessed at the field (**attribute**) level. The data are organized in tables in which each row, or **tuple**, is roughly equivalent to an occurrence of a segment in a hierarchical or network DBMS.

IBM dominates a large minicomputer and mainframe DBMS market with *IMS* and *DB2*. IBM's **SQL (Structured Query Language)** was recently made the official standard data access query language for relational data bases. *DB2* may soon emerge as the de facto industry standard DBMS.

The **distributed DBMS** will permit the interfacing of data bases located in various places throughout a computer network.

9–5 PLATFORMS: HOMES FOR SOFTWARE. Software is written to run under a specific platform (or **operating environment**), which is defined by the processor's design architecture and the operating system being used. Computers can emulate other than their native platforms, but programs running in emulation mode run much slower.

The selection of a mainframe platform for corporate computing is done primarily by computer specialists whereas micro platform decisions are made by users.

Through 1990, the IBM PC-AT architecture and MS-DOS dominated. Responding to a need for multitasking, Microsoft Corporation introduced a GUI-based multitasking platform called Windows. OS/2 is a single-user, multitasking operating system that enables up to 16 MB of RAM to be addressed. OS/2's GUI is called *Presentation Manager*. The Apple Macintosh family of PCs and its operating system (Macintosh System) define a platform.

Each of the multiuser operating systems defines a different platform, the most popular being UNIX and its spinoffs.

 Review Exercises

Concepts

1. Why is it necessary to spool printed output in a multitasking environment?
2. Name the system software category associated with: (a) a company's data base, (b) file backup, and (c) overall software and hardware control.
3. What is meant when someone says that data are program-independent?
4. The attribute of a relational DBMS is analogous to which level of the hierarchy of data organization?
5. What are the programs called that translate source programs into machine language? Which one does the translation on a single pass? Which one translates one statement at a time?
6. Give two examples each of applications and system software.
7. Describe what defines a platform.
8. Which approach to data base management is based on the tree data structure?
9. What is the official ANSI and ISO standard for data access query languages for relational data bases?
10. Which level in a hierarchical data base does not have a parent?
11. Does the current program run in RAM's foreground or background?
12. What do programmers use to specify the job stream?

Discussion

13. What do you feel is the most significant advantage of using a database management system? Why?
14. Even though network and relational DBMS technologies are considered superior to hierarchical DBMS technology, the use of the latter remains strong because of the momentum of IBM's *IMS*. Why are *IMS* users reluctant to convert their data bases to more technologically advanced DBMSs?

15. Prior to the implementation of an integrated data base in 1981, a midwestern company maintained 113 separate computer-based files. Most of these files supported autonomous departmental information systems and contained many instances of redundant data. Discuss the impact that redundant data have on the integrity and accuracy of data.

16. *SQL* and *DB2* are well on their way to becoming industry standards. How will this impact the software industry in general and consumers of computer hardware and software in particular?

17. Identify some of the major hurdles that must be overcome before distributed DBMSs can become a reality.

Problem Solving

18. Assume that the registrar, housing office, and placement service at your college all have computer-based information systems that rely on traditional file organization. Identify possibly redundant fields.

19. Identify the fields that would provide the links between these four categories of data in an integrated data base: manufacturing/inventory, customer/sales, personnel, and general accounting. (For example, the customer account number field is common to all data categories except personnel.)

20. Peterson College is a small, private liberal arts school with an enrollment of 825 students. Approximately 70% of these students live on campus in four dormitories, in one remodeled house, and in rooms rented from a hospital within easy walking distance. A room may house 1, 2, or 3 students. Students are not permitted to bring household appliances into their rooms, but they can rent a minirefrigerator from the school for a monthly fee. A deposit, returnable at the end of the semester, is also required. The school does not require a general damage deposit, but it does assess room damages against the residents of the room and distributes general damages among all students on a floor.

Regina Dacey, the director of housing, feels that she could provide better service for resident students if she had ready access to timely, accurate information regarding the status of rooms, furnishings, and students. Specifically, she wants a data base that can respond to the following types of requests:

- Given a student's name, what is the dormitory and room number, and who are the roommates?
- Given a dormitory and room number, who are the residents?
- Given a dormitory and room number, what are the contents of the room as inventoried at the beginning of the current semester?
- Given a refrigerator number, to whom is it rented, and where?
- Given a dormitory and floor, who are the students who live on that floor?
- Given a dormitory and floor, who is resident advisor (R.A.) in charge?
- Given a student's name, what is the student's disciplinary history?

For Regina Dacey's requests as described,

a. Prepare a data organization design using traditional files. For each file, specify the following: the file name, the processing mode (sequential or random), the record layout, and the key field(s).

b. Prepare a data organization design using a network DBMS. Graphically illustrate the schema, including a name for each record, the fields in each record, the key field(s) for each record, and the sets connecting records (name each set and show the arrows entering all records).

c. Prepare a data organization design using a relational DBMS. For each tuple, specify the tuple name, the attributes in each tuple, and the key field(s) for each tuple.

Self-Test (by section)

9–1 a. A spreadsheet package is in the _general purpose_ category of software.

b. What type of system software provides information on processor utilization: (a) utility programs, (b) performance monitoring software, or (c) communications software?

9–2 a. The operating system program that is always resident in main memory is called the supervisor. (T/F)

b. Programmers often use JCL to specify the _job stream_, or the sequence in which their programs are to be executed.

c. All programs are segmented into pages. (T/F)

d. Virtual memory effectively expands the capacity of RAM through the use of software and secondary storage. (T/F)

9–3 a. An object program is always free of logic errors. (T/F)

b. What system software program ultimately performs the same function as a compiler: (a) utility program, (b) DBMS, or (c) interpreter?

9–4 a. Integrated data bases are made possible by DBMS software. (T/F)

b. One of the disadvantages of DBMS software is that applications programs must be modified when the data base design is changed. (T/F)

c. The logical structure of a network data base is called a _schema_.

d. Which of the following is not one of the fundamental approaches to the design of DBMS software: (a) hierarchical, (b) circle, or (c) relational?

e. IBM's *IMS* is a _hierarchical_ DBMS product.

f. In a relational DBMS, data are accessed by _content_ rather than by address.

g. The standard for data access query languages is: (a) *SQL*, (b), 4GL, or (c) ISO?

9–5 a. The most commonly used multiuser PC platform involves which of the following operating systems: (a) XIX, (b) UNIX, or (c) XINU?

b. The Macintosh family of PCs is unique in that they do not need an operating system. (T/F)

Self-test answers. **9–1 (a)** general-purpose; **(b)** b. **9–2 (a)** T; **(b)** job stream; **(c)** F; **(d)** T. **9–3 (a)** F; **(b)** c. **9–4 (a)** T; **(b)** F; **(c)** schema; **(d)** b; **(e)** hierarchical; **(f)** content; **(g)** a. **9–5 (a)** b; **(b)** F.

THE IMAGE BANK
Computer Graphics:
The Wave of the Future

Experts estimate that about one in fifteen workers uses a computer today. By the year 2000 that number is expected to double and perhaps triple. Luckily, computers promise to become increasingly easy to use, thanks to the growing use of computer graphics.

On the simplest level, *graphics* refers to any type of drawing, diagram, chart, graph, or icon. But graphics also refers to the way graphics—and even letter shapes—are stored inside the computer. One method is to store a "bit map" that represents the outline of a specific shape of a certain size. A second, more sophisticated method stores each graphic as a series of mathematical equations that represent every line and curve. Issue the appropriate command and the computer plots the equations, creating the graphic's outline on the computer screen. Issue another command and voilà—the graphic is bigger, smaller, rotated, squeezed, stretched, or even "painted" with different colors and textures. Couple this with the fact that graphics can also be scanned or digitized into computer-readable form and you have the makings of a powerful new way of envisioning data as information.

Why is the use of graphics so powerful? For one thing, it makes it easier to interact with computers. An increasing number of computers feature a graphical user interface, or GUI. A GUI protects users from having to memorize cryptic computer commands. Instead, a series of pull-down menus list the available options, while icons, or graphic symbols, make it easier to find certain functions. Want to add color to a graphic? Just look for the icon shaped like an artist's palette.

Computer graphics is also appealing because it automates laborious plotting and drawing tasks precisely. Relieved of the tedium, users are free to be creative and explore options that would be simply too time-consuming or difficult without the use of powerful computer graphics. Today computer graphics are being used to transform almost every aspect of our work lives.

And, finally, computer graphics help fulfill a primary goal of using computers: to convert data into useable information. Business, medicine, and all fields of research generate overwhelming amounts of raw data. By letting the computer plot this data and show it in graphic format, users can begin to see the underlying patterns and make reasoned decisions. In fact, both system designers and users are beginning to speak of these new and powerful graphics-based systems as tools for the visualization of heretofore unseen realities.

THE · WAVE · OF · THE · FUTURE

BEHIND THE SCENES WITH COMPUTER GRAPHICS This computer interpretation of the classic Japanese woodcut "The Great Wave of Kanagawa" shows how even the most complex shapes can be broken down to a "wire frame" of line segments and curves that can be "painted" to suggest three-dimensional shapes.

COMPUTER GRAPHICS SPEED TRAINING

In an age when managers in all fields are looking for ways to increase productivity, computer graphics can reduce or even eliminate the need for full-scale training. Instead of issuing a terse command—"Insert disk in Drive A"—a graphics-based computer system can run an animated sequence that shows exactly where the disk should go.

Computer graphics can help employees learn non-computer tasks, too. Instead of pulling employees off the job for classroom training, companies are turning to "just-in-time training." Just-in-time training uses an interactive computer system to deliver job-related information as needed. For instance, one large hotel and resort chain is developing a just-in-time training system for its telemarketing clerks. At the push of the button,

a clerk can call up a full-color graphic image of a room's ocean-front view and its furnishings, along with a description of its other features, its price, and its availability. This combination of graphics and words helps the clerks make more sales.

COMPUTER GRAPHICS STIMULATE ARTISTIC EXPRESSION

Artists have been quick to add computer graphics to their traditional toolbox. Rather than being put off by the technology, most artists find that graphics software frees them of the tedium of drawing and painting and makes it easier to create sophisticated works quickly.

COMPUTER GRAPHICS AND EDUCATION Computer graphics plays an important role in multimedia applications, especially those associated with learning. Graphic images, such as a simulated color palette, are recalled as needed to facilitate understanding.

THE ART OF REPRESENTING LIGHT This surreal scene is all the more remarkable for the way the computer artist has used graphics software to model light, shadow, and reflections, mimicking a photograph's realism.

Computer Graphics:
The Wave of the Future

COMPUTER GRAPHICS AND COMMERCIAL ART
Sports artist Joni Carter became the first to design a series
of stamps completely on the computer. Carter's PC-based
multimedia system let her program videos and photos from
past Olympics into the computer and then "freeze" frames
to create models for her initial computer-generated
sketches. The system also let her edit the designs to meet
the goals of using bright colors, representing a racial and
male–female balance, and being sure the athletes could not
be identified with a particular personality or nationality.

COMPUTER GRAPHICS AND BROADCASTING
Because they need dramatic images that quickly catch the
viewer's eye, television and advertising executives have
been an impetus behind some of the most artistic
innovations in computer graphics.

DESKTOP PUBLISHING FREES COMMUNICATION

Computer graphics has given new meaning to the
phrase "freedom of the press." Instead of being tied to
the typesetter and the print shop, millions of users now
create newsletters, brochures, ads, flyers, and other
publications without leaving their desk. Today advanced
desktop publishing techniques are standard operating
procedures at most major publications and advertising
agencies. Mail-order houses routinely use desktop publishing to combine a data base of product descriptions
with full-color photographs, creating eye-appealing catalogs in a fraction of the time required by traditional
methods.

THE SUBTLE MAGIC OF DESKTOP PUBLISHING   The
typical document produced by desktop publishing involves
the integration of text and computer graphics. Desktop
publishing lets professional designers use special effects
that once were time-consuming and extremely expensive.

COMPUTER GRAPHICS ENLIVEN BUSINESS PRESENTATIONS

Once upon a time, business people had two choices: They could supplement their business presentations with boring black-and-white handouts and flip-charts of statistics, or they could give their raw material to a professional designer, who would in time return a professional presentation—and a big bill. And woe to the hapless business person who found a mistake or needed to make a last-minute change.

Today, the increasing sophistication of presentation graphics software helps executives or their in-house staff quickly create colorful, compelling, and customized presentations that combine professional-looking type, charts, graphs, and artwork. According to one recent poll, 74% of all respondents use presentation graphics

software to prepare their own presentations. Among the advantages they cite: more control, lower costs, and the freedom to quickly produce last-minute but polished presentations—sometimes en route to a business meeting—that leave the competition in the dust.

COMPUTER GRAPHICS SERVE JUSTICE

Some of the nation's most important presentations take place in its courtrooms. How can a lawyer best present evidence to help a judge and jury understand the case? This is a special challenge in personal injury suits, where technical experts often present conflicting testimony. An increasing number of lawyers are illustrating expert testimony with animated computer graphics. In recreating a plane crash, for example, data from the plane's data recorder can be used to prepare an animated graphic showing the exact flight path, while the cockpit voice recorder plays in the background.

Motor Vehicle Production in Europe

Production

10,000	— 300,000
300,000	— 1,000,000
1,000,000	— 3,000,000
3,000,000	— 6,000,000

THE POWER OF PRESENTATION GRAPHICS
Presentation graphics software makes it easy to prepare charts, graphs, and bulleted lists that summarize the presentation's goals, persuasive points, and conclusions. To let presenters focus on their message, rather than on the technology, many presentation graphics packages include professionally designed templates, such as maps, clip art (the automobile in the photo), predefined color combinations, drawing tools, and special effects, such as user-defined shading.

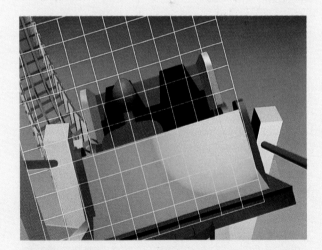

SEEING IS BELIEVING   How do you convince a skeptical jury that a ride on a seemingly harmless roller coaster caused a teenager to have a stroke? Commission a 15-minute computer animation. Arrows show the G-forces that caused the cerebral hemorrhage.

293

Computer Graphics: The Wave of the Future

Computer graphics are also a valuable aid in detective work. One growing application is fingerprint matching. Advanced computer systems can store millions of fingerprints as a data base of graphic images. The systems match up fingerprints by measuring the distance and angles between randomly chosen sets of points and then computing the difference. In as little as 30 minutes, the system can determine whether a fingerprint lifted from a crime scene matches any fingerprint already on file. Before, the same process might take months for hundreds of human fingerprint experts.

Another application is the computerized aging of missing children. These systems work by combining a child's snapshot with a data base of measurements showing how human facial dimensions change in a fairly predictable way over time. When done by hand, it might take as much as 20 hours to prepare an "aged" likeness of one child; the computer systems can do it in minutes. Such systems have helped find hundreds of children since the mid-1980s.

COMPUTER GRAPHICS HELP AUTOMATE PRODUCT DESIGN AND MANUFACTURE

Product designers, engineers, and architects have been among the most avid converts to computer graphics. And no wonder. Even in the best of circumstances, their work is a trial-and-error process that zig-zags between initial sketches and blueprints, the building and testing of models and prototypes, and trips "back to the drawing board" to fix the inevitable mistakes. And on complex projects, such as an airplane or a shopping mall, the work may be divided between teams of workers, who must then coordinate their efforts. Every zig and every zag means wasted time, money, and effort.

Today computer graphics can speed and simplify every step of a product's design and manufacture, every detail of designing and constructing a new building. In industry, the process begins with CAD, short for *computer-aided design*. CAD lets a designer or engineer draw a *wire-frame model* that can be rotated to show different views and filled in to create a *three-dimensional solid model*. Users can zoom in to see details or create exploded views that show how parts work together. These computerized models can then be tested through computerized simulations of real-world conditions. Errors caught with CAD can be fixed for as little as $1; the same error might cost $100,000 to fix once production starts.

In one of the newest developments, these computer-generated designs can also be employed to program machines that build a physical prototype or a mold that can be used in manufacturing. This innovation, known as desktop manufacturing, extends the frontiers of CIM, or computer-integrated manufacturing, which uses the output of CAD to plan and control the entire manufacturing process.

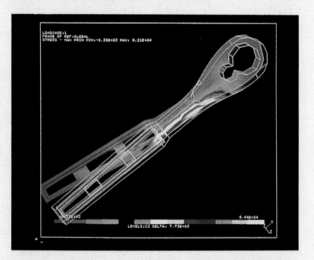

THE COMPUTER-AIDED DESIGN PROCESS Using a combination of computer-generated "primitives"—circles, ellipses, lines, and polygons—and free-hand drawing tools such as light pens and digitizing pads, engineers create a wire-frame model that can be rotated and sized as needed. Wire-frame models can then be computer-painted to simulate the color and texture of a finished product. In this illustration, a solid model of a part is torqued to the position of the wire-frame model to highlight stress points.

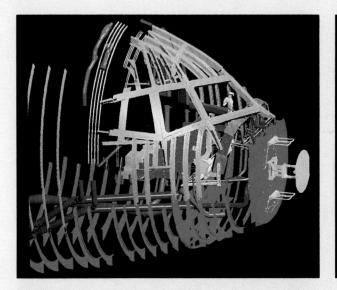

CATIA
THE BOEING CO.

CAD LETS BOEING SKIP TRADITIONAL PHYSICAL PROTOTYPES Boeing is using a three-dimensional computerized modeling system to design its 777 transport, the largest product ever designed entirely by computer. The project uses 8 mainframe computers and 2800 workstations to link the work of over 7000 specialists. Although the project cost billions of dollars, the company expects that reduced reworking and time savings will cut costs by 20 percent. Computer simulations of solid three-dimensional models let designers check for interferences between parts and, with the help of computer-generated human models, check the ergonomics, or the way the design and human users interact. Here the system is being used to make sure a maintenance worker would have easy access to a vertical stabilizer.

Rx FOR HEALTH CARE: COMPUTER GRAPHICS

Sophisticated computer graphics can now be found in almost every phase of medical training, diagnosis, and treatment. In fact, scholars of medical ethics predict that doctors who don't use these and other computer-based aids might eventually be sued for providing inadequate medical treatment.

Many of these tools, such as the graphic output of computerized diagnostic and monitoring devices, are already commonplace. One especially valuable diag-nostic technology is computed axial tomography, or the CAT scan, a rotating X-ray device that constructs a three-dimensional view of body structures.

What is new, though, is the way some of these tools are being combined. For example, medical schools are replacing traditional anatomy lessons and dissection labs with "electronic cadavers," data bases of three-dimensional images created by combining measurements taken from human cadavers with CAT scans, magnetic resonance imaging, and still and video photographic images. Real cadavers are hard to come by

Computer Graphics: The Wave of the Future

and an errant cut during dissection can't be undone. Not so with the computer. With an electronic cadaver, students can practice over and over again. Plus the computer can run interactive tutorials that both drill and then challenge students to apply their knowledge. Veterinary schools, too, are turning to similar systems, to improve training and to minimize the animal sacrifice decried by animal rights activists.

PRACTICING WITH A DIGITAL SCALPEL
Preparation and accuracy are especially important for any brain surgery. Today, neurosurgeons can minimize risk by performing practice surgery on three-dimensional images a computer generates from a patient's CAT scans and X-rays.

CREATING CUSTOMIZED SURGICAL IMPLANTS The same computer-aided design and manufacturing techniques used in industry are being used to create artificial hips and other replacement bones and joints. Special software translates CAT scans and other medical images of a patient's body into a precise drawing that doctors and medical engineers use to create a final design. The software then uses this design to control the manufacture of the finished implant. Similar techniques are being used to create other medical devices, such as replacement heart valves.

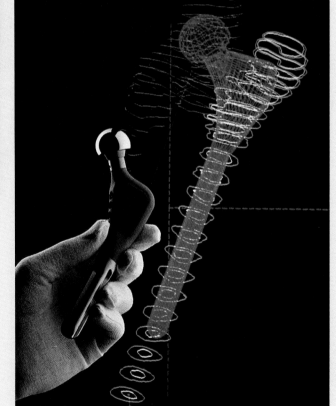

COMPUTER GRAPHICS HELP RESEARCHERS ANALYZE DATA

One of the computer world's basic maxims is "The goal of computing is insight, not numbers." The same could be said of scientific research, where a wealth of data is both a blessing and a curse. Computer graphics are now helping scientists of every type gain new insights. Consider just these few examples:

- **Paleontology.** Paleontologists, scientists who study the fossil remains of prehistoric plants and animals, have always been at a disadvantage, since their subjects are all extinct. This has been a special problem in the study of dinosaurs. Too often, the only way to study rare fossils was to destroy them, by cutting them open to study the inside of a skull, say, or how nerves branched out of a spinal cord. Comparing these findings to those of today's creatures gives researchers insight into a dinosaur's probable intelligence and the way it may have moved and lived.

Today, with the help of high-powered CAT scans, researchers can peer inside a fossil without destroying it. As a result, paleontologists are confirming their theories about which dinosaurs lumbered on four legs, which ran on two, and which were relatively intelligent. CAT scans are even helping researchers trace the evolutionary link between dinosaurs and today's birds.

- **Geophysics.** Computer-generated graphics are letting researchers go back 179 million years, when Pangea, the earth's land mass, began to drift apart to form the continents we know today. Understanding these ancient events can help us understand and predict today's earthquakes and volcanoes.

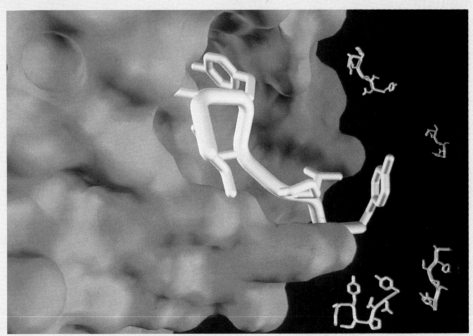

USING GRAPHICS TO DESIGN NEW MEDICINES This computer graphic shows what molecular biologists have long known: that certain chemical and biological structures fit together in a complementary fashion. In this case, an antigen, or toxic substance (shown in white), is locked to an antibody, the body's natural disease-fighting mechanism. When antibody and antigen lock together, the action of the antigen is blocked. Researchers today are combining biotech with computer modeling and chemical synthesis in an effort to create compounds that will put the lock on Alzheimer's disease, cancer, heart disease, multiple sclerosis, and AIDS.

Computer Graphics:
The Wave of the Future

■ **Archeology.** A blend of data base technology and three-dimensional computer mapping, modeling, and imaging have helped researchers reconstruct and preserve the ruins and artifacts of Pompeii. Like modern architects, archaeologists can now tour electronic models of ancient buildings and get a better idea of how the Pompeiians lived and died.

■ **Astrophysics.** With the help of extremely powerful computers, researchers have been able to create three-dimensional simulations of the sun's surface that will help them understand the boiling turbulence of the convection zone, where superheated material from the sun's core mixes with cooler material near the surface.

■ **Oceanography.** Computer-enhanced graphics can be used to plot raw data collected by satellite, creating three-dimensional color-coded maps that help oceanographers envision the interplay of water temperature and movement with the terrain of the ocean floor.

■ **Meteorology.** Color-coded graphics and simulations are helping meteorologists track cold fronts, predict flash floods, and detect wind sheers, sudden powerful wind shifts that can down commercial airliners and give rise to tornadoes.

These insights prove yet another truism of the computer world: "Computers really don't make difficult things easier; they make impossible things possible." This ability—to make the impossible possible—has made computer graphics one of the most exciting tools for computer users in all fields.

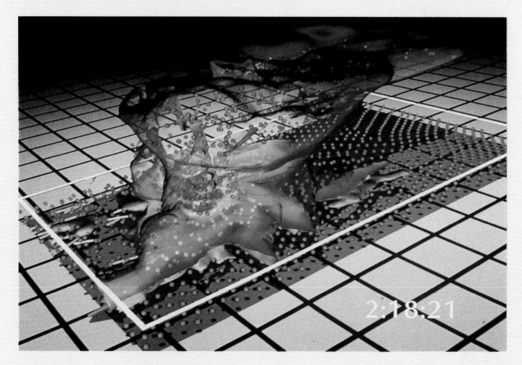

MODELING A THUNDERSTORM
Supercomputers analyze data on wind speed, water content, and air pressure and temperature to create this simulation of a thunderstorm, which will improve weather forecasting.

Programming Concepts and Languages

10

STUDENT LEARNING OBJECTIVES

▶ To discuss the terminology and concepts associated with programming languages and software.

▶ To identify approaches to solving a programming problem.

▶ To describe the concept of structured programming.

▶ To demonstrate an understanding of the principles and use of flowcharting and other program design techniques.

▶ To classify the various types of program instructions.

▶ To describe the steps and approaches to program development.

▶ To categorize programming languages by generation.

▶ To describe the function and purpose of application generators.

▶ To describe the capabilities and limitations of natural languages.

CHAPTER OUTLINE

10–1 Programming in Perspective

Programming is no longer limited to technical specialists. This architect has his own laptop PC and has learned to program. In the case of short programs, it may take less time for end users to write their own than to describe the problem to a professional programmer.

At this point on your journey toward computer competency you probably are feeling comfortable with computer hardware concepts and applications. *Hardware*, however, is useless without *software*, and software is useless without hardware. This chapter is about how we create software.

A computer system does nothing until directed to do so by a human. A computer is not capable of performing calculations or manipulating data without exact, step-by-step instructions. These instructions, which take the form of a computer *program*, are how we tell a computer to perform certain operations. Five, fifty, or even several hundred programs may be required for an information system. Spreadsheet software, for example, is made up of dozens of programs that work together so that you can perform spreadsheet tasks. The same is true of word processing software.

The instructions in programs are logically sequenced and assembled through the act of *programming*. **Programmers**, people who write programs, use a variety of **programming languages**, such as COBOL, BASIC, and dBASE IV Language, to communicate instructions to the computer. Twenty years ago, virtually all programmers were computer specialists. Today, office managers, management consultants, engineers, politicians, and people in all walks of life write programs to meet business and domestic needs. Some do it for fun.

Most of the programs you develop while you are a student will be independent of those developed by your classmates and, more often than not, independent of one another. In a business environment, however, programs often complement one another. For example, you might write one program to collect the data you need for a presentation and another to analyze it. Someone else might write one to print a report based on the analysis you provided.

A knowledge of programming will always be a plus, even if you don't plan to write programs at home or at work. The following are just a few of the many benefits of learning to program.

1. You will gain an appreciation for what the computer can and cannot do.
2. You will develop good logic skills.
3. You will be able to communicate more effectively with other programmers and systems analysts.
4. You will be able to write your own "custom" programs.

There is no such thing as an "easy" program. A programming task, whether in the classroom, in business, or at home, should challenge your intellect and logic capabilities. Just as you might want to succeed in business or lower your golf score, the programmer, professional or amateur, wants to write increasingly sophisticated programs. As soon as you develop competence at one level, your instructor will surely assign you a program that is more difficult than anything you have done in the past. Even when doing recreational programming on your personal computer, you won't be satisfied with an "easy" program. You will probably challenge yourself with increasingly complex programs.

10–2 Problem Solving and Programming Logic

Computer Programs: The Power of Logic

A single program addresses a particular problem: to compute and assign grades, to permit an update of a data base, to monitor a patient's heart rate, to analyze marketing data, and so on. In effect, when you write a program, you are solving a *problem*. To solve a problem you must use your powers of *logic* and develop an **algorithm**, or procedure, for solving a problem.

Creating a program is like constructing a building. Much of the brainwork involved in the construction goes into the blueprint. The location, appearance, and function of a building are determined long before the first brick is laid. With programming, the design of a program, or its *programming logic* (the blueprint), is completed before the program is written (the building is constructed). This section and the next discuss approaches to designing the logic for a programming task. Later in this chapter we discuss the program and the different types of program instructions.

Structured Program Design: Divide and Conquer

Figure 10–1 illustrates a common programming problem—the printing of weekly payroll checks for hourly and commission employees. In the

Changing the Way We Meet
A software product, called Groupware, helps increase productivity at meetings. Here's how it works. All participants sit at PCs, all of which are linked via a local area network. They key in their ideas and the software keeps track of each person's contribution. In the traditional meeting structure, 20% of the participants do 80% of the talking. Groupware gives each person an equal opportunity to present his or her ideas. One company used Groupware to cut the time needed to complete a series of team projects by 91%. Another stated that a job that would normally take about a year to complete took only 15 electronic meetings and 35 days.

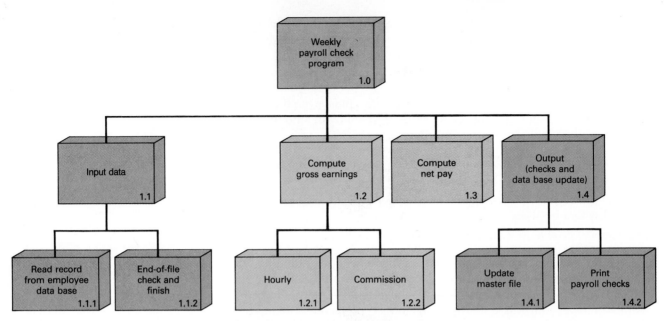

FIGURE 10–1 Program Structure Chart

The logic of a payroll program to print weekly payroll checks can be broken down into modules for ease of understanding, writing, and maintenance.

figure a **structure chart** is used to break the programming problem into a hierarchy of tasks. (Any task can be broken into subtasks if a finer level of detail is desired.) The most effective programs are designed to be written in **modules,** or independent tasks. It is much easier to address a complex programming problem in small, more manageable modules than as one big task. You use the principles of structured programming to accomplish this task.

In **structured programming,** the logic of the program is addressed hierarchically in logical modules (see Figure 10–1). In the end, the logic of each module is translated into a sequence of program instructions that can be executed independently. By dividing the program into modules, the structured approach to programming reduces the complexity of the programming task. Some programs are so complex that if taken as a single task, they would be almost impossible to conceptualize, design, and code. We must "divide and conquer."

A structure chart for a program to print monthly payroll checks for salaried employees would look similar to that of Figure 10–1, except that Task 1.2, Compute gross earnings, would not be required. The salary amount can be retrieved directly from the employee data base.

10–3 Program Design Techniques

A number of techniques are available to help programmers analyze a problem and design the program. Two popular techniques are *flowcharting* and *pseudocode.* These techniques also can be used as design tools for an information system.

These branch bank cashiers and tellers interact with the bank's mainframe-based information systems. Loan officers also work with micro-based information systems. The techniques used in designing the computer programs for these systems are the same for both mainframes and micros.

Flowcharting

In **flowcharting, flowcharts** are used to illustrate data, information, and work flow by the interconnection of *specialized symbols* with *flow lines*. The combination of symbols and flow lines portrays the logic of the program or system. The more commonly used flowchart symbols are shown in Figure 10–2.

Flowcharting Symbols   Each symbol indicates the type of operation to be performed, and the flowchart graphically illustrates the sequence in which the operations are to be performed. *Flow lines* depict the sequential flow of the program logic. A rectangle signifies some type of *computer process*. The process could be as specific as "Compute an individual's grade average" (in a program flowchart) or as general as "Prepare class schedules for the fall semester" (in an overview system flowchart). The *predefined process*, a special case of the process symbol, is represented by a rectangle with extra vertical lines. The predefined process refers to a group of operations that may be detailed in a separate flowchart. The parallelogram is a generalized *input/output* symbol that denotes any type of input to or output from the program or system. The diamond-shaped symbol marks the point at which a *decision* is to be made. In a program flowchart, a particular set of instructions is executed based on the outcome of a decision. For example, in a payroll program, gross pay is computed differently for hourly and commission employees; therefore, for each employee processed, a decision is made as to which set of instructions is to be executed.

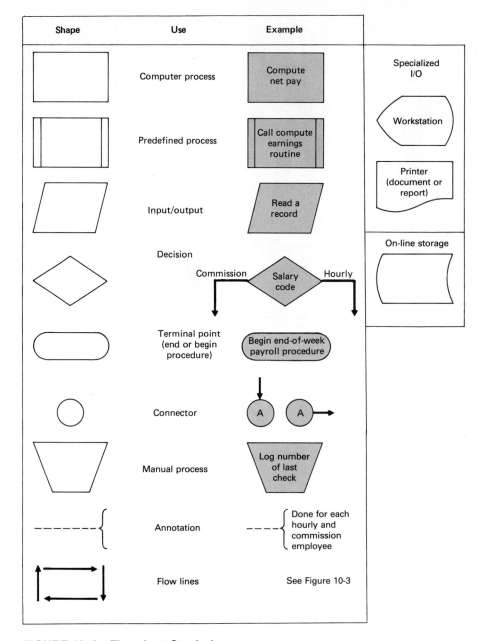

FIGURE 10–2 Flowchart Symbols

Each flowchart must begin and end with the oval *terminal point* symbol. A small circle is a *connector* and is used to break and then link flow lines. The connector symbol often is used to avoid having to cross lines. The trapezoid indicates that a *manual process* is to be performed. Contrast this with a computer process represented by a rectangle. The bracket permits descriptive notations to be added to flowcharts.

The *on-line storage symbol* represents a file or data base. The most common *specialized input/output* symbols are the *workstation* and the *printer* (hard copy) symbols.

"Macro magic" allows users to customize programs or automate frequent but tedious procedures. To put it simply, a macro is a series of recorded keystrokes. Any often-used sequence of keystrokes, whether they are keyboard characters, commands for a program, or a combination of both, could be a macro. You *play back* a sequence of keystrokes by tapping a key combination (for example, ALT + Y) or entering the name of a macro. Macros can be created for most popular software packages, from word processing to presentation graphics. Each package (Lotus 1-2-3, Word, Windows, and so on) has its own macro facility.

You can save a lot of time by spending a little time creating a macro. For example, if you write business letters as a matter of routine, a well-conceived macro can be invoked (played) that will enter the date, inside address, salutation, and closing—just about everything but the body of the letter.

A macro can be as straightforward as entering the name of your company or it can involve the use of logic and interactive communication with the user. The latter are very much like programs and generally require the skills of computer specialists. Of course, users need macros for both kinds of applications. This demand for sophisticated macros has spawned a new industry made up of companies that create and sell helpful macros. For example, one company sells advanced macros designed for assisting scriptwriters. Although scriptwriters routinely create personalized macros, few are willing to spend the time (possibly weeks) needed to create complex macros. Commercial scriptwriting macros offer advanced features, such as automatic scene numbering.

A macro is, by definition, intended to help you with repetitive procedures. If you do something over and over, chances are that others are faced with the same problem. Many of those who create macros to assist them in their work share their creations with colleagues by publishing them in trade periodicals, company newsletters, and the like. Some periodicals make user-submitted macros available on disks.

There is no limit to the variety of time-saving macros.

- A sales manager created a macro to prepare pie and bar graphs from sales data in a spreadsheet.
- A couple of teachers created word processing macros to format exams and to randomly shuffle questions and answers to generate multiple versions of an exam.
- An imaginative secretary created a macro to print documents in reverse order on her face-up printer so she would not have to restack the sheets.
- A writer created a macro to translate documents generated in an obsolete word processing package to Microsoft Word format.

Judicious use of macros can make your time at the PC more profitable and pleasurable.

These symbols are equally applicable to system and program flowcharting and can be used to develop and represent the logic for each. The program flowchart of Figure 10–3 portrays the logic for the structure chart of Figure 10–1. The instructions adjacent to the flowchart symbols will be discussed in the next section. The company in the example of Figure 10–1 processes hourly and commission employee checks each week. (Salary employee checks are processed monthly.) Gross earnings for hourly employees are computed by multiplying hours worked times the rate of pay. For salespeople on commission, gross earnings are computed as a percentage of sales.

The Driver Module   In structured programming, each program has a **driver module**, sometimes called the **main program**, that causes other program modules to be executed as they are needed. The driver module in the payroll program (see Figure 10–3) is a **loop** that "calls" each of

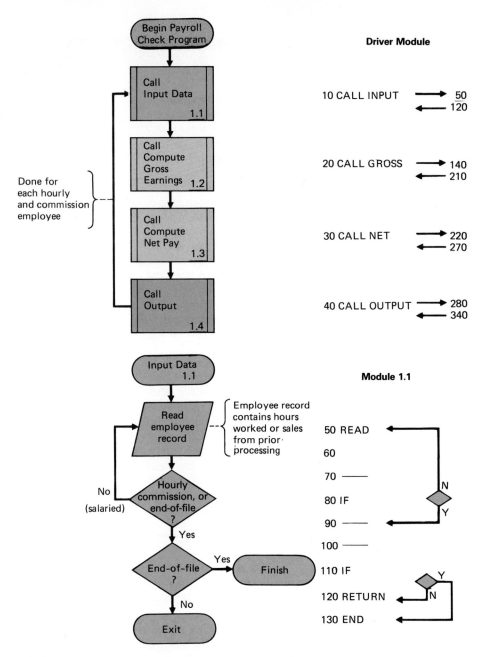

FIGURE 10–3   Program Flowchart with Language-Independent Instructions

The flowchart presents the logic of a payroll program to compute and print payroll checks for commission and hourly employees. (See the structure chart of Figure 10–1.) The logic is designed so that a driver module calls subroutines as they are needed to process each employee. The accompanying "program" has a few language-independent instructions to help illustrate the concepts and principles of programming. This figure is discussed in detail in the text.

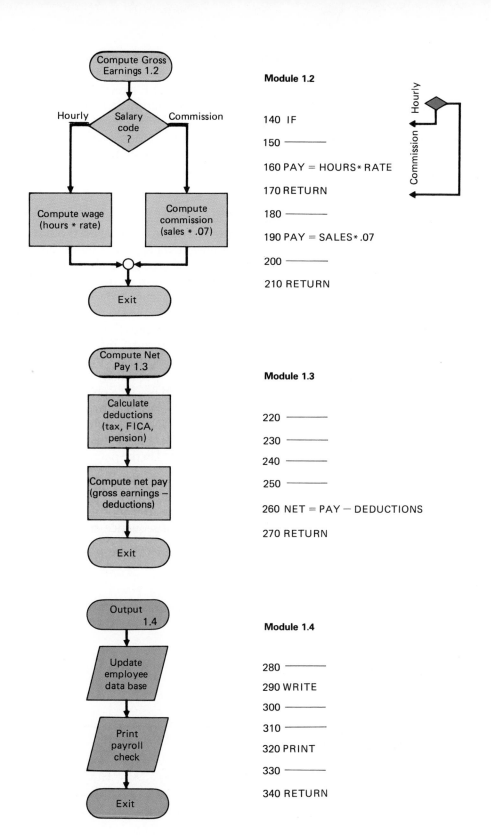

Module 1.2

140 IF

150 ———

160 PAY = HOURS * RATE

170 RETURN

180 ———

190 PAY = SALES * .07

200 ———

210 RETURN

Module 1.3

220 ———

230 ———

240 ———

250 ———

260 NET = PAY — DEDUCTIONS

270 RETURN

Module 1.4

280 ———

290 WRITE

300 ———

310 ———

320 PRINT

330 ———

340 RETURN

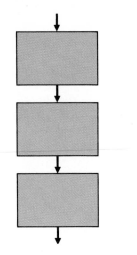

FIGURE 10–4   Sequence Control Structures

the subordinate modules, or **subroutines**, as needed for the processing of each employee. The program is designed so that when the payroll program is initiated, the "input data" module (1.1) is executed, or "performed," first. After execution, control is then returned to the driver module unless there are no more employees to be processed, in which case execution is terminated (the "Finish" terminal point). For each hourly or commission employee, Modules 1.2, 1.3, and 1.4 are performed, and at the completion of each subroutine, control is passed back to the driver module.

Programming Control Structures   Through the 1970s, many programmers unknowingly wrote what is now referred to as "spaghetti code." It was so named because their program flowcharts appeared more like a plate of spaghetti than like logical analyses of programming problems. The unnecessary branching (jumps from one portion of the program to another) of a spaghetti-style program resulted in confusing logic, even to the person who wrote it.

Computer scientists overcame this dead-end approach to developing program logic by identifying three basic *control structures* into which any program or subroutine can be segmented. By conceptualizing the logic of a program in these three structures—*sequence*, *selection*, and *loop*—programmers can avoid writing spaghetti code and produce programs easy to understand and maintain. The use of these three basic control structures has paved the way for a more rigorous and scientific approach to solving a programming problem. These control structures are illustrated in Figures 10–4, 10–5, and 10–6, and their use is demonstrated in the payroll example of Figure 10–3.

Sequence control structure.   In the sequence structure (Figure 10–4), the processing steps are performed in sequence, one after another. Modules 1.3 and 1.4 in Figure 10–3 are good examples of sequence structures.

Selection control structure. The selection structure (Figure 10–5) depicts

FIGURE 10–5   Selection Control Structures
Any number of options can result from a decision in a selection control structure.

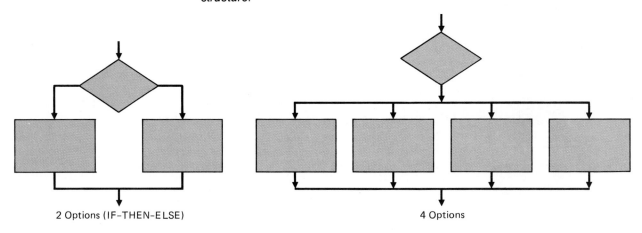

2 Options (IF–THEN–ELSE)   4 Options

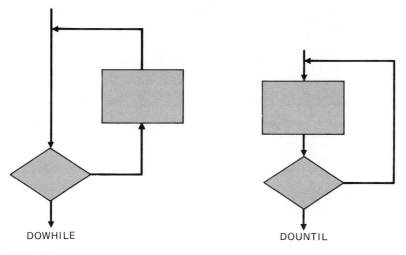

DOWHILE   DOUNTIL

FIGURE 10–6 Loop Control Structures
The two types of loop structures are DOWHILE and DOUNTIL.

the logic for selecting the appropriate sequence of statements. In Figure 10–3, our example payroll program, the selection structure is used to illustrate the logic for the computation of gross pay for hourly and commission employees (Module 1.2). In the selection structure, a decision is made as to which sequence of instructions is to be executed next.

The selection structure of Module 1.2 presents two options: hourly or commission. Other circumstances might call for three or more options.

Loop control structure.   The loop structure (Figure 10–6) is used to represent the program logic when a portion of the program is to be executed repeatedly until a particular condition is met. There are two variations of the loop structure (see Figure 10–6): (1) When the decision, or *test-on-condition*, is placed at the beginning of the statement sequence, it becomes a *DOWHILE loop*; (2) when placed at the end, it becomes a *DOUNTIL loop* (pronounced *doo while* and *doo until*). In the payroll flowchart of Figure 10–3, that portion of the input data module (1.1) that reads an employee record is illustrated in a DOUNTIL loop. That is, *do* the loop *until* the end of the file is reached.

Pseudocode

Another design technique used almost exclusively for program design is called **pseudocode**. While the other techniques graphically represent the logic of the program, pseudocode represents the logic in programlike statements written in plain English. Because pseudocode does not have any syntax guidelines (rules for formulating instructions), you can concentrate solely on developing the logic of your program. Once you feel that the logic is sound, the pseudocode is easily translated into a procedure-oriented language such as COBOL or BASIC that can be run on a computer. In Figure 10–7 the logic of a simple program is represented both in pseudocode and with a flowchart.

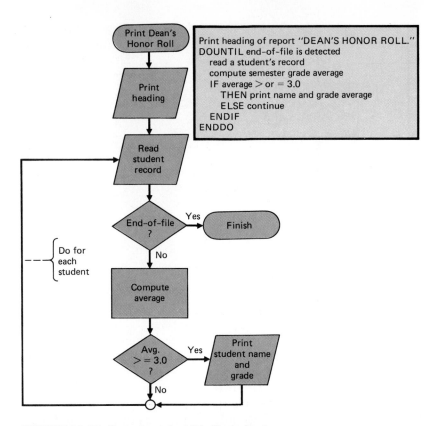

FIGURE 10–7 Pseudocode with Flowchart

This pseudocode program depicts the logic of a program to compile a list of students who have qualified for the dean's honor roll. The same logic is shown in a flowchart.

There is no substitute for good, sound logic in programming. If you follow the guidelines of structured programming and make judicious use of these and other program design techniques, your program will be easier to write, use, and maintain.

10–4 So What's a Program? Concepts and Principles of Programming

A computer program consists of a sequence of instructions that are executed one after another. These instructions, also called **statements**, are executed in sequence unless their order is altered by a "test-on-condition" instruction or a "branch" instruction.

The flowchart of our payroll program (Figure 10–3) is accompanied by a sequence of language-independent instructions. Except for the computation of gross earnings, the processing steps are similar for both types of employees. Two sequences of instructions are needed to compute gross earnings for *hourly* and *commission* employees. We can also see from the flowchart that the sequence in which the instructions are executed may be altered at three places (decision symbols), depending on the results of the test-on-condition. In Module 1.2, for example, the sequence of instructions to be executed depends on whether the test-on-condition detects an hourly or a commission employee.

To the right of the flowchart in Figure 10–3 is a representation of a sequence of language-independent instructions and the order in which they are executed. *Statement numbers* are included, as they are in most program listings. This program could be written in any common programming language. The purpose of the discussion that follows is to familiarize you with general types of programming instructions, not those of any particular programming language. Each language has an instruction set with at least one instruction in each of the following *instruction classifications:* input/output, computation, control, data transfer and assignment, and format.

Input/Output

Input/output instructions direct the computer to "read from" or "write to" a peripheral device (for example, printer or disk drive). *Statement 50* of Figure 10–3 requests that an employee record, including pay data, be read from the data base.

Computation

Computation instructions perform arithmetic operations (add, subtract, multiply, divide, and raise a number to a power). *Statement 160* (PAY = HOURS * RATE) computes gross earnings for hourly employees.

Control (Decision and/or Branch)

Control instructions can alter the sequence of the program's execution or terminate execution. In Figure 10–3, *Statements 10 through 40, 80, 110, 120, 130, 140, 170, 210, 270,* and *340* are control instructions. The two types of control instructions are *unconditional branch* and *conditional branch* instructions.

Statements 10 through 40 are unconditional branch instructions. An unconditional branch instruction disrupts the normal sequence of execution by causing an unconditional branch to another part of the program or to a subroutine. In *Statements 10 through 40,* the branch is from the driver module to a subroutine. The CALL statement works in conjunction with the RETURN statement to branch to another location, then RETURN control back to the statement following the CALL.

Statements 80 and 110 are conditional branch instructions and are generally referred to as IF statements: If certain conditions are met, then a branch is made to a certain part of the program. The conditional branch at *Statement 80* causes the program to "loop" until the employee record read is for either an hourly or a commission employee, or the end-of-file marker is reached. The sequence of instructions, *Statements 50 through 80,* comprise a DOUNTIL loop. The END (*Statement 130*) causes the program to terminate.

The National Weather Service uses a mix of manual procedures and computer-based technology to make its weather forecasts. This man created a program that maintains a 12-hour plot of weather variables.

If you ever feel intimidated by the idea of programming a computer, just remember how much easier it is today than in the computer's early days. Programming has come a long way in the last half century. Prior to the invention of the electronic digital computer, companies relied on electromechanical accounting machines (EAM) for automated data processing. The EAM family consisted of about a dozen punched-card devices (sorter, accounting machine, collator). The act of programming these devices was referred to as "wiring the program." Early programmers, called *operators* during this era, literally created the circuitry for the devices by inserting wires into interchangeable removable control panels. A different panel was wired for each type of operation to be performed (merge the employee and name/address files, print payroll checks). A typical company might have 50 of the two-foot-square prewired control panels for use with an accounting machine, the central device in punched-card processing. The company would have scores of other prewired control panels for other devices. Each control panel might involve hundreds of wires. For example, to read and add the numbers in Columns 4 through 6 and 12 through 14 of a punched card and to print the results using Print Hammers 56 through 60, the operator would have to insert wires to accept the data, to add them, and to print the result. Punched-card devices were used by thousands of companies well into the third generation of computers (1964–1971).

In 1946 Dr. John W. Mauchly and J. Presper Eckert, Jr., created the first large-scale fully operational electronic digital computer called the ENIAC (see the Image

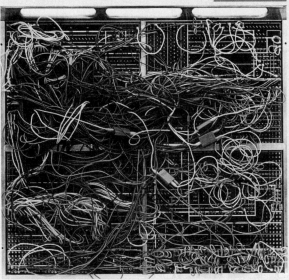

"PROGRAMMING" THE EAM   This hand-wired EAM control panel was inserted in an accounting machine to provide it with the logic to calculate and print a payroll register.

Bank, "An Abbreviated History of the Computer," following Chapter 1). However, the quantum leap in technology brought about by the ENIAC was offset by the cumbersome method of programming the machine. Switches had to be set and wires inserted into a series of panels resembling those used by telephone operators of the period. Each time a different program was to be run, the switches had to be reset and the wires repo-

Data Transfer and Assignment

Data can be transferred internally from one RAM location to another. In procedure-oriented languages, data are transferred, or "moved," by *assignment instructions*. These instructions permit a *string constant*, also called a *literal value*, such as "The net pay is," or a *numeric value*, such as 234, to be assigned to a named location in RAM.

In a program, a RAM location is represented by a **variable name** (for example, PAY, HOURS, NET). A variable name in a program statement refers to the *contents* of a particular RAM location. For example, a programmer may use the variable name HOURS in a computation

sitioned—a task often taking several hours. Not only did early programmers spend countless hours setting switches and wiring boards, but they hoped that the computer would run long enough to complete the program without breaking down!

Mauchly and Eckert realized that a better method of programming was necessary to make their computer truly a general-purpose machine. In 1949 they worked with a mathematician named John Von Neumann to develop a computer that would store a program the way it stored data. The introduction of the "stored-program" concept enabled computers to execute one program, then electronically load and ready another program for execution within a matter of minutes. All early programs were written in machine language that consisted entirely of 1s and 0s. Imagine the difficulty in keeping track of the sequence of program instructions made up entirely of 1s and 0s, not to mention the eyestrain!

Von Neumann reconceived one of Lady Ada Augusta Lovelace's concepts 90 years after her death. Lady Lovelace had suggested the use of a conditional transfer instruction long before the existence of electronic computers. This type of instruction would permit the sequence in which the instructions were executed to be altered, based on certain criterion. For example, in a payroll processing program, the criteria might be type of pay. One set of instructions is executed for salaried personnel and a different set for hourly personnel.

The conditional transfer instruction and the introduction of the stored-program concept made the general-purpose computer a reality. By the early 1950s the business and scientific communities had recognized the

"PROGRAMMING" AN EARLY ELECTRONIC DIGITAL COMPUTER Early programmers had to set hundreds of switches to enter a program into the computer.

utility of these "giant brains." However, programmers had little relief from the tedium of writing programs in low-level languages until the introduction of the first high-level one in 1955, a scientific language called FORTRAN. COBOL, still the most frequently used business-oriented language, was introduced in 1959. Today, software engineers are working to develop natural programming languages that will enable us to articulate our processing and information needs in plain English. Won't it be nice.

statement to refer to the numeric value of the *hours worked* by a particular employee.

Format

Format instructions are used in conjunction with input and output instructions; they describe how the data are to be entered to or outputted from RAM. On output, format instructions print headings on reports and present data in a readable format.

With these few types of instructions, you can model almost any business or scientific procedure, whether it be sales forecasting or guiding rockets to the moon.

Writing Programs

Each program is a project. You should follow these steps for each programming project.

Step 1. Describe the problem.
Step 2. Analyze the problem.
Step 3. Design the general logic of the program.
Step 4. Design the detailed logic of the program.
Step 5. Code the program.
Step 6. Test and debug the program.
Step 7. Document the program.

Step 1. Describe the Problem

Identify exactly what needs to be done. It often helps to describe the problem in words.

Step 2. Analyze the Problem

In this step you break the problem into its basic components for analysis. Remember to "divide and conquer." Although different programs have different components, a good starting place for most is to analyze the *output*, *input*, *processing*, and *file-interaction* components.

Steps 3 and 4. Design the General and Detailed Logic of the Program

Now you need to put the pieces together in the form of a logical program design. A program is designed in a hierarchical manner—that is, from general to specific.

The General Design (Step 3) The *general* design of the program is oriented primarily to the major processing activities and the relationships between these activities. The structure chart of Figure 10–1 and the flowchart of Figure 10–3, both discussed earlier in this chapter, illustrate the general design of a weekly payroll program to compute and print paychecks. By first completing a general program design, you make it easier to investigate alternative design approaches. Once you are confident of which approach is best, you may complete a more detailed design.

The Detailed Design (Step 4) In the *detailed* design you will produce a graphic representation of the program logic that includes *all* processing activities and their relationships, calculations, data manipulations, logic operations, and all input/output.

Step 5. Code the Program

Whether you "write" or "code" the program is a matter of personal preference. In this context, the terms are the same. In Step 5, the graphic

and narrative design of program development Steps 1 through 4 are translated into machine-readable instructions, or programs. If the logic is sound and the design documentation (flowcharts, pseudocode, and so on) is thorough, the coding process is relatively straightforward.

Step 6. Test and Debug the Program

Once the program has been entered into the system, it is likely that you will encounter at least one of those cantankerous **bugs**. A bug is either a *syntax error* (violation of one of the rules for writing instructions) or a *logic error*. Ridding a program of bugs is the process of **debugging**.

A good programmer lives by Murphy's Law, which assumes that if anything can go wrong, it will! Don't assume that whoever uses your program will not make certain errors in data entry.

Step 7. Document the Program

Procedures and information requirements change over the life of a system. For example, because the social security tax rate is revised each year, certain payroll programs must be modified. To keep up with these changes, programs must be updated periodically, or *maintained*. Program maintenance can be difficult if the program documentation is not complete and up-to-date.

The programs you write in college are not put into production and therefore are not maintained. You may ask, "Why document them?" The reason is simple. Good documentation now helps to develop good programming habits that you will need later. *Documentation* is part of the *programming process*. It's not something you do after the program is written.

All the example programs in the BASIC supplement to this text, *BASIC for Introductory Computing*, provide good examples of program documentation. Each program is documented with a *program description*, a *structure chart*, a *flowchart*, a *program listing* (with internal comments), and an *interactive session*.

10–6 Generations of Programming Languages

We "talk" to computers within the framework of a particular programming language. There are many different programming languages, most of which have highly structured sets of rules. The selection of a programming language depends on who is involved and the nature of the "conversation."

Low- and High-Level Languages

Programming languages fall into two fundamental categories—low- and high-level languages. **Low-level languages** are machine-dependent; that is, they are designed to be run on a particular computer. In contrast, **high-level languages** (for example, COBOL and BASIC) are machine independent and can be run on a variety of computers.

The hierarchy of programming languages in Figure 10–8 summarizes the relationships between the various types of programming languages, each of which we discuss in this chapter. Through the first four decades of computing, programming languages evolved in generations. The first two generations were low-level and the next two were high-level (see Figure 10–8) generations of programming languages. The higher-level languages do not necessarily provide us with greater programming capabilities, but they do provide a *more sophisticated programmer/computer interaction*. In short, *the higher the level of the language, the easier it is to understand and use.* For example, in a fourth-generation language you need only instruct the computer system *what to do,* not necessarily *how to do it.* When programming in one of the first three generations of languages, you have to tell the computer what to do *and* how to do it. What comprises a new generation is less clear; therefore, languages after the fourth generation are referred to as *very high-level languages.*

FIGURE 10–8 The Hierarchy of Programming Languages
As you progress up the ladder of the hierarchy of programming languages, fewer instructions are required to perform a particular programming task.

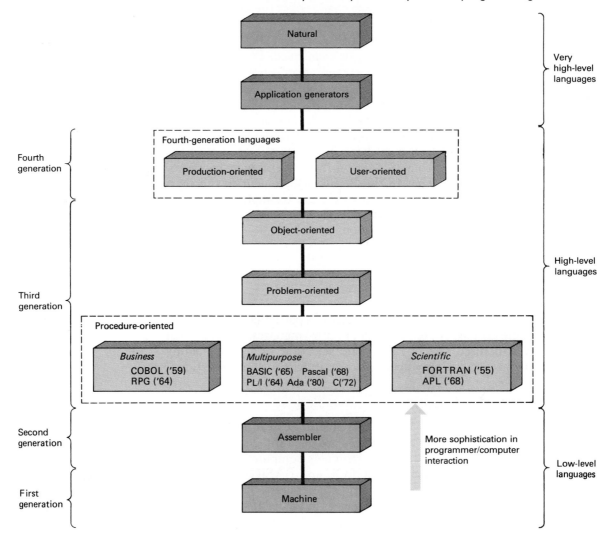

With each new level, fewer instructions are needed to tell the computer to perform a particular task. A program written in a second-generation language that computes the total sales for each sales representative, then lists those over quota may require 100 or more instructions; the same program in a fourth-generation language may have fewer than 10 instructions.

The ease with which the later generations can be used is certainly appealing, but the earlier languages also have their advantages. All generations of languages are in use today.

The First and Second Generations: "Low-Level"

Machine Language   In Chapter 9, "System Software and Platforms," we learned that each computer has only *one* programming language that can be executed—the *machine language*. We talk of programming in COBOL, Pascal, and BASIC, but all these languages must be translated into the computer's native language, or machine language, prior to execution. These and other high-level languages are simply a convenience for the programmer.

Machine-language programs, the *first generation*, are written at the most basic level of computer operation. In machine language, instructions are coded as a series of 1s and 0s. As you might expect, machine-language programs are cumbersome and difficult to write. Early programmers had no alternative. Fortunately, we do.

Assembler Language   A set of instructions for an **assembler language** essentially correspond on a one-to-one basis with those of a machine language. Like machine languages, assembler languages are unique to a particular computer. This computer dependency makes them low-level languages. The big difference between the two is the way the instructions are represented by the programmer. Rather than a cumbersome series of 1s and 0s, assembler languages use easily recognized symbols, called **mnemonics**, to represent instructions (see Figure 10–9). For example, most assembler languages use the mnemonic *MUL* to represent a "Multiply"

FIGURE 10–9   An Assembler Program Procedure
These assembler instructions compute PAY by multiplying the number of HOURS times the RATE.

```
COMP$PAY        PROC PUBLIC
;
;        COMP$PAY - procedure to compute gross pay (PAY = HOURS * RATE)
;
        MOV     AX,HOURS                ;multiplicand
        MUL     RATE+2                  ;  times second word of multiplier
        MOV     PAY+2,AX                ;store the product in PAY
;
        MOV     AX,HOURS                ;multiplicand
        MUL     RATE                    ;  times first word of multiplier
        ADD     PAY+2,AX                ;add the product to PAY
        ADC     PAY,DX                  ;add the carry, if any
        RET                             ;end procedure
COMP$PAY        ENDP
```

instruction. The assembler languages ushered in the *second generation* of programming languages.

The Third Generation: For Programmer Convenience

No matter which high-level language (third and later generations) a program is written in, it must be translated into machine language before it can be executed. System software programs called *compilers* and *interpreters* perform this task. Compilers and interpreters were covered in Chapter 9, "System Software and Platforms."

Third-generation programming languages fall into three categories: *procedure-oriented languages*, *problem-oriented languages*, and *object-oriented languages*.

Procedure-Oriented Languages   The introduction of the *third generation* of programming languages, most of which would be classified as **procedure-oriented languages**, resulted in a quantum leap in programmer convenience. The flexibility of procedure-oriented languages permits programmers to model almost any scientific or business procedure. Instructions are **coded**, or written, sequentially and processed according to program specifications.

Procedure-oriented languages are classified as *business*, *scientific*, or *multipurpose*.

Business languages.   Business programming languages are designed to be effective tools for developing business information systems. The strength of business-oriented languages lies in their ability to store, retrieve, and manipulate alphanumeric data.

A point-of-sale system installed in a department store chain enables consumer sales data to be gathered from more than a thousand POS terminals located in 50 stores. The system was developed in COBOL, a third-generation language.

COBOL, the first business programming language, was introduced in 1959. It remains the most popular. The original intent of the developers of COBOL (*Common Business Oriented Language*) was to make its instructions approximate the English language. Here is a typical COBOL *sentence*:

IF SALARY-CODE IS EQUAL TO 'H' MULTIPLY SALARY BY HOURLY-RATE GIVING GROSS-PAY ELSE PERFORM SALARIED-EMPLOYEE-ROUTINE.

Note that the sentence contains several instructions and even a period.

The American National Standards Institute (ANSI) has established standards for COBOL and other languages to make these programs *portable*. A program is said to be portable if it can be run on a variety of computers. Unfortunately, the ANSI standards are followed only casually; it is unlikely that a COBOL program written for a UNISYS computer, for example, can be executed on a Digital computer without some modification.

Figure 10–10 illustrates a COBOL program that computes gross pay for hourly wage earners. Notice that the program is divided into four divisions: identification, environment, data, and procedure.

For purposes of comparison, the COBOL program in Figure 10–10 and the other examples of third-generation programs (Figures 10–11

FIGURE 10–10 A COBOL Program
This COBOL program accepts the number of hours worked and the pay rate for an hourly wage earner, then computes and displays the gross pay amount. The interactive session shows the input prompt, the values entered by the user, and the result.

```
0100 IDENTIFICATION DIVISION.
0200 PROGRAM-ID.            PAYPROG.
0300 REMARKS.               PROGRAM TO COMPUTE GROSS PAY.
0400 ENVIRONMENT DIVISION.
0500 DATA DIVISION.
0600 WORKING-STORAGE SECTION.
0700 01 PAY-DATA.
0800         05 HOURS       PIC 99V99.
0900         05 RATE        PIC 99V99.
1000         05 PAY         PIC 9999V99.
1100 01 LINE-1.
1200         03 FILLER      PIC X(5)       VALUE SPACES.
1300         03 FILLER      PIC X(12)      VALUE "GROSS PAY IS  ".
1400         03 GROSS-PAY   PIC $$$$9.99.
1500 01 PRINT-LINE.         PIC X(27).
1600 PROCEDURE DIVISION.
1700 MAINLINE-PROCEDURE.
1800         PERFORM ENTER-PAY.
1900         PERFORM COMPUTE-PAY.
2000         PERFORM PRINT-PAY.
2100         STOP RUN.
2200 ENTER-PAY.
2300         DISPLAY "ENTER HOURS AND RATE OF PAY".
2400         ACCEPT HOURS, RATE.
2500 COMPUTE-PAY.
2600         MULTIPLY HOURS BY RATE GIVING PAY ROUNDED.
2700 PRINT-PAY.
2800         MOVE PAY TO GROSS-PAY.
2900         MOVE LINE-1 TO PRINT-LINE.
3000         DISPLAY PRINT-LINE.
```

```
Enter hours and rate of pay
43, 8.25
        Gross pay is $354.75
```

```
        program payprog
c
c       payprog        - Program to compute the pay for an employee,
c                        given hours worked and the employee's pay rate.
c
        real hours, rate, pay                    !define the variables
c
        write(6,1)                               !input prompt
1       format(1H,'Enter hours and rate of pay')
        read(5,*) hours, rate                    !accept hours & pay rate
        pay = hours * rate                       !compute pay
        write(6,2) pay                           !display gross pay
2       format(1H,5X,'Gross pay is $',F7.2)
        end
```

FIGURE 10–11   A FORTRAN Program
This FORTRAN program accepts the number of hours worked and the pay rate for an hourly wage earner, then computes and displays the gross pay amount. The resulting interactive session is the same as that of Figure 10–10.

through 10–13) are written to perform the same input, processing, and output activities: Compute gross pay for hourly wage earners. The interactive session (see Figure 10–10) is the same for all four programs.

Another popular business programming language is **RPG** (*Report Program Generator*). RPG, introduced in 1964, has always differed somewhat from other procedure-oriented languages in that the programmer specifies certain processing requirements by selecting the desired programming options.

Scientific languages.   These algebraic formula-type languages are specifically designed to meet typical scientific processing requirements, such as matrix manipulation, precision calculations, iterative processing, the expression and resolution of mathematical equations, and so on.

FORTRAN (*Formula Translator*), the first procedure-oriented language, was developed in 1955. It was and remains the most popular scientific language. The FORTRAN program in Figure 10–11 performs the same processing functions as the COBOL program in Figure 10–10.

APL (*A Programming Language*), introduced in 1968, is a symbolic interactive programming language that is popular with engineers, mathematicians, and scientists. A special keyboard with "shorthand" symbols helps speed the coding process.

FIGURE 10–12   A C-Language Program
This C program accepts the number of hours worked and the pay rate for an hourly wage earner, then computes and displays the gross pay amount. The resulting interactive session is the same as that of Figure 10–10.

```
/*      payprog.c      - Program to compute the pay for an employee,
                         given hours worked and the employee's pay rate. */

main()
{
        float hours, rate, pay;                  /* define the
                                                    variables used */
        printf("Enter hours and rate of pay\n"); /* input prompt */
        scanf("%f %f", &hours, &rate);           /* accept hours
                                                    and pay rate */
        pay = hours * rate;                      /* compute pay */
        printf("\tGross pay is $%.2f\n",pay);    /* print gross pay */
}
```

```
100 REM payprog          Program to compute the pay for an employee,
110 REM                  given hours worked and the employee's pay rate.
120 REM
130 PRINT "Enter hours and rate of pay"      'input prompt
140 INPUT HOURS, RATE                        'accept hours & pay rate
150 LET PAY = HOURS * RATE                    'compute pay
160 PRINT TAB(5);"Gross pay is $";PAY        'display gross pay
170 END
```

FIGURE 10–13   A BASIC Program
This BASIC program accepts the number of hours worked and the pay rate for an hourly wage earner, then computes and displays the gross pay amount. The resulting interactive session is the same as that of Figure 10–10.

Multipurpose languages.   Multipurpose languages are equally effective for both business and scientific applications. They are an outgrowth of the need to simplify the programming environment by providing programmers with one language capable of addressing all programming needs of a company.

C programmers, according to a recent employment survey, are in the greatest demand. Developers of proprietary packaged software are very interested in C because it is considered more transportable than other languages. That is, it is relatively machine-independent: A C program written for one type of computer (see Figure 10–12) can be run on another type with little or no modification.

BASIC, developed in 1965, is the primary language supported by millions of personal computers. BASIC is also used extensively on mainframe computer systems, primarily for one-time "quick-and-dirty" programs. It is arguably the easiest third-generation language to learn and use (see Figure 10–13). BASIC was originally developed to help teach programming. Now, it is commonly used in both scientific and business applications—and even in developing video games. The widespread use of BASIC attests to the versatility of its features. In fact, it is the only programming language supported on virtually every computer.

Pascal, named after the seventeenth-century French mathematician Blaise Pascal, has experienced tremendous growth during the last decade. Introduced in 1968, Pascal is considered the state of the art among widely used procedure-oriented languages (see Figure 10–14). Pascal's power,

FIGURE 10–14   A Pascal Program
This Pascal program accepts the number of hours worked and the pay rate for an hourly wage earner, then computes and displays the gross pay amount. The resulting interactive session is the same as that of Figure 10–10.

```
program payprog(input,output);
{        Program to compute the pay for an employee,
         given hours worked and the employee's pay rate. }

var      hours, rate, pay : real;                (define the variables)

begin
  writeln(output,'Enter hours and rate of pay');  (input prompt)
  readln(input,hours,rate);                        (accept hours & pay rate)
  pay := hours * rate;                             (compute pay)
  writeln(output,'     Gross pay is $',pay:0:2)    (display gross pay)
end.
```

flexibility, and self-documenting structure have made it the language of choice in many computer science curriculums and for many developers of system software. Although only a small percentage of the business-system programs are currently written in Pascal, it is enjoying a growing acceptance in the business community.

PL/I (*Programming Language/I*), introduced in 1964, was hailed as the answer to many of the problems of existing programming languages such as COBOL and FORTRAN. Even though it has not won the widespread acceptance originally anticipated, it is widely used.

Ada, introduced relatively recently (1980), is a very sophisticated procedure-oriented language. It is a multipurpose language developed for the U.S. Department of Defense. The language was named in honor of the nineteenth-century pioneer, Lady Augusta Ada Lovelace, considered by some to be the first programmer. Its developers are optimistic that as more people begin to study it, Ada will gain widespread acceptance not only in the military but also in the private sector.

Other procedure-oriented languages. The foregoing coverage of procedure-oriented languages is not intended to be exhaustive. The languages presented were selected to provide an overview of some you might encounter in practice. Many other programming languages are commonly used in business and taught in academic institutions. These include the following:

- *LISP* (*List Processing*, 1959). A list-processing language that is good at manipulating non-numeric data, such as symbols and strings of text (used in artificial intelligence and compiler development).

Pascal, a multipurpose programming language, is often used to develop software for scientific applications. Here, a Kerr-McGee explorationist maps seismic data at a three-dimensional workstation. The system provides computer support for preparation of detailed seismic analyses.

- LOGO (1967). Uses a "turtle" to teach children geometry, mathematics, and programming.
- FORTH (1971). Used for device control applications, arcade games, and robotics.
- Prolog (*Programming* in *Logic*, 1972). Can manipulate relationships between facts (used in the development of expert systems).
- Modula-2 (1981). Enables self-contained modules to be combined in a program.

Problem-Oriented Languages   A problem-oriented language is designed to address a particular application area or to solve a particular set of problems. Problem-oriented languages do not require the programming detail of procedure-oriented ones. The emphasis of problem-oriented languages is more on *input* and *the desired output* than on the *procedures* or *mathematics involved*.

Problem-oriented languages have been designed for scores of applications: simulation (for example, GPSS, SLAM); programming machine tools (APT); and analysis of stress points in buildings and bridges (COGO).

Object-Oriented Languages   In procedure-oriented languages, the emphasis is on *what* is done (the action). In **object-oriented languages**, the emphasis is on the *object* of the action, thus the object orientation. Programs are developed such that objects are linked together in a hierarchy. An object at one level inherits the characteristics of an object at a higher level. This facilitates programming in that the programmer need only address the differences in the objects rather than starting from scratch for each object.

Some programs for computer-based tools, such as this chip testing device, are written in problem-oriented languages.

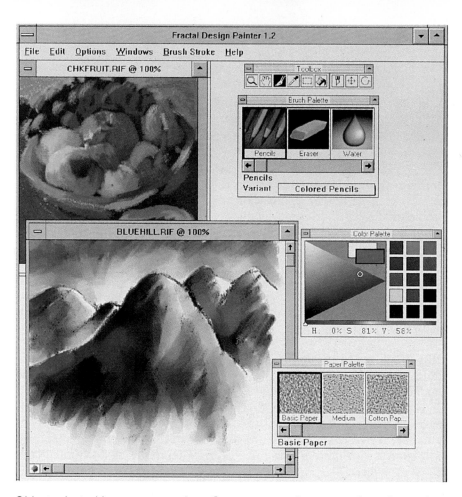

Object-oriented languages, such as C + +, are used to create the software for PC packages such as Fractal Design Painter (shown here), Lotus 1-2-3, and others.

Object-oriented languages provide programmers with the flexibility needed to address abstract programming problems, such as the creation of icon-based graphical user interfaces. When programming a GUI (graphical user interface), the icons are the objects.

Two examples of these languages are Smalltalk and C++. The first, and still popular, object-oriented language is **Smalltalk**. Smalltalk was used to create the first GUI. **C++** is popular because it embodies the features of object-oriented languages while permitting the programmer to use the features of C.

The Fourth Generation: 4GLs

Types of 4GLs   The trend in software development is toward using high-level user-friendly **fourth-generation languages (4GLs)**. There are two types of 4GLs.

- *Production-oriented 4GLs.* Production-oriented 4GLs are designed primarily for computer professionals. They use 4GLs such as ADR's Ideal, Software AG's Natural 2, and Cincom's Mantis to create information systems. Professional programmers who use 4GLs claim productivity improvements over third-generation procedure-oriented languages (COBOL, FORTRAN, BASIC, and so on) of 200% to 1000%.

- *User-oriented 4GLs.* This type of 4GL is designed primarily for end users. Users write 4GL programs to query (extract information from) a data base and to create personal or departmental information systems. User-oriented 4GLs include Mathematica Products Group's RAMIS II and Information Builders' FOCUS.

Over the years most companies have accumulated large quantities of computer-based data. Prior to fourth-generation languages (the mid-1970s), these data were not directly accessible to users. They had to describe their information needs to a professional programmer, who would then write a program in a procedure-oriented language like PL/I to produce the desired results. Fulfilling a typical user request would take at least a couple of days and as long as two weeks. By then the desired information might no longer be needed. With fourth-generation languages, these same ad hoc requests, or queries, can be completed in minutes. When 4GLs are available, many users elect to handle their own information needs without involving computer professionals at all!

With a day or so of training and practice, a computer-competent user can learn to write programs, make inquiries, and get reports in user-oriented 4GLs. Once they become familiar with user-oriented 4GLs, users often find it is easier and quicker to sit down and write a program themselves than to relate inquiry or report specifications to a professional programmer. With 4GLs, managers can attend to their own seemingly endless ad hoc requests for information and even write their own production information systems. If the data base is already in place, about 75% of a typical user's information needs can be met with 4GLs. 4GLs benefit everyone concerned: Users quickly get the needed information, and, because programmers have fewer ad hoc programming assignments, they can focus their efforts on the ever-increasing backlog of information systems projects.

Principles and Use Fourth-generation languages use high-level English-like instructions, the trademark of 4GLs, to retrieve and format data for inquiries and reporting. Most of the procedure portion of a 4GL program is generated automatically by the computer and the language software. That is, for the most part the programmer specifies what to do, *not* how to do it. In contrast, a Pascal or FORTRAN programmer writes instructions for what to do *and* how to do it.

The features of a 4GL include English-like instructions, limited mathematical manipulation of data, automatic report formatting, sequencing (sorting), and record selection by criteria.

Using 4GLs. The 4GL example presented here gives you a sense of the difference between a procedure-oriented language such as COBOL and a 4GL. About 20 4GLs are commercially available. The example that

Some City of Miami police officers learn fourth-generation query languages to make inquiries to the city's data bases without the assistance of a computer specialist.

follows shows how a 4GL program can be used to generate a management report. Suppose, for example, that Peggy Peoples, the personnel manager for Zimco Enterprises, wants to make the following request for information:

List the employee ID, sex, net pay, and gross pay for all employees in Departments 911 and 914.

To obtain the report, Ms. Peoples wrote the query-language program in Figure 10–15; the report generated by this program is shown in Figure 10–16.

- *Instruction 1* specifies that the payroll data are stored on a FILE called PAYROLL. The payroll file contains a record for each employee. Although the data of only one file are needed in this example, requests requiring data from several files are no more difficult.
- *Instruction 2* specifies the basic format of the report. Employee records are *sorted* and LISTed BY DEPARTMENT. It also specifies which data elements within the file (NAME and ID, for example) are to be included in the report of Figure 10–16. If the instruction had been LIST BY DEPARTMENT BY NAME, then the employee names would be listed in alphabetical order for each department.
- *Instruction 3* specifies the criterion by which records are SELECTed. The personnel manager is interested in only those employees from Departments 911 and 914. Other criteria could be included for further record selections. For example, the criterion "GROSS > 400" could be added to select only those people (from Departments 911 and 914) whose gross pay is greater than $400.
- *Instruction 4* causes SUBTOTALS to be computed and displayed BY DEPARTMENT.
- *Instructions 5 and 6* allow Peggy Peoples, the personnel manager, to improve the report's appearance and readability by including a title and labeling the columns. Instruction 5 produces the report title, and Instruction 6 specifies descriptive column headings.

The COBOL equivalent of this request would require over 150 lines of code (instructions)!

Fourth-generation languages are effective tools for generating responses to a variety of requests for information. Short programs, similar

FIGURE 10–15   A 4GL Program
This representative 4GL program generates the report shown in Figure 10–16. Each instruction is discussed in detail in the text.

```
1.  FILE IS PAYROLL
2.  LIST BY DEPARTMENT:   NAME ID SEX NET GROSS
3.  SELECT DEPARTMENT = 911, 914
4.  SUBTOTALS BY DEPARTMENT
5.  TITLE: "PAYROLL FOR DEPARTMENTS 911, 914"
6.  COLUMN HEADINGS:   "DEPARTMENT", "EMPLOYEE, NAME";
    "EMPLOYEE, NUMBER"; "SEX"; "NET, PAY"; "GROSS, PAY"
```

PAYROLL FOR DEPARTMENTS 911, 914

DEPARTMENT	EMPLOYEE NAME	EMPLOYEE NUMBER	SEX	NET PAY	GROSS PAY
911	ARNOLD	01963	1	356.87	445.50
911	LARSON	11357	2	215.47	283.92
911	POWELL	11710	1	167.96	243.20
911	POST	00445	1	206.60	292.00
911	KRUSE	03571	2	182.09	242.40
911	SMOTH	01730	1	202.43	315.20
911	GREEN	12829	1	238.04	365.60
911	ISAAC	12641	1	219.91	313.60
911	STRIDE	03890	1	272.53	386.40
911	REYNOLDS	05805	2	134.03	174.15
911	YOUNG	04589	1	229.69	313.60
911	HAFER	09764	2	96.64	121.95
DEPARTMENT TOTAL				2,522.26	3,497.52
914	MANHART	11602	1	250.89	344.80
914	VETTER	01895	1	189.06	279.36
914	GRECO	07231	1	685.23	1,004.00
914	CROCI	08262	1	215.95	376.00
914	RYAN	10961	1	291.70	399.20
DEPARTMENT TOTAL				1,632.83	2,403.36
FINAL TOTAL 17 RECORDS TOTALED				4,155.09	5,900.88

FIGURE 10–16   A Payroll Report
This payroll report is the result of the execution of the 4GL program shown in Figure 10–15.

to the one in Figure 10–15, are all that are needed to respond to the following typical management requests:

- Which employees have accumulated over 20 sick days since May 1?
- Which deluxe single hospital rooms, if any, will be vacated by the end of the day?
- What is a particular student's average in all English courses?
- List departments that have exceeded their budgets alphabetically by the department head's name.

Strengths and weaknesses. The problem with 4GLs is that they are less efficient than third-generation languages. That is, 4GLs require more computer capacity to perform a particular operation. Proponents of 4GLs claim that the added cost of the hardware is more than offset by the time saved in creating the programs. On the other hand, critics claim that 4GL capabilities are limited (when compared to third-generation languages) and that users end up fitting their problems to the capabilities of the software.

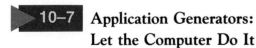
10–7 Application Generators: Let the Computer Do It

Application generators are designed primarily for use by computer professionals. The concept of an application generator is not well defined, nor will it ever be, because entrepreneurs are continually working to provide better ways of creating information systems. In general, application generators are designed to assist in the development of full-scale information systems.

When using application generators, also called **code generators**, to develop information systems, programmers specify what information processing tasks are to be performed by engaging in an interactive dialogue with the system. This is essentially a fill-in-the-blank process. The code generator asks a question, and the programmer responds by filling in the blank. For example, the code generator might ask the user to categorize the proposed program as data entry, inquiry, report generation, or file maintenance. If the programmer responds "Inquiry," then the code generator will ask the programmer to identify appropriate data bases. Code generators interpret the programmer-supplied information and actually generate the program code or instructions, usually in the form of COBOL or PL/I programs. These instructions become commands to the computer to make a data base inquiry, update a data base, and so on.

When using application generators to create an information system, systems analysts and programmers describe the data base, then specify screen layouts for file creation and maintenance, data entry, management reports, and menus. The application generator software consists of modules of **reusable code** that are pulled together and integrated automatically to complete the system.

Application generators are currently in the infant stage of development. Existing application generators do not have the flexibility of procedure-oriented languages; therefore, the generic reusable code of application generators must occasionally be supplemented with **custom code** to handle unique situations. Normally, about 10% to 15% of the code would be custom code. Application generators provide the framework in which to integrate custom code with generated code. When used properly, application generators can quadruple the output of programmers and systems analysts. With this kind of contribution to productivity, application generators are sure to play an ever-increasing role in information systems development.

 10–8 Natural Languages: The Ultimate Programming Language

Natural languages refer to software that enables computer systems to accept, interpret, and execute instructions in the native, or "natural," language of the end user—typically, English. The premise behind a natural language is that the programmer or user needs little or no training. The programmer simply writes, or perhaps verbalizes, processing specifications without regard for instruction syntax (the rules by which instructions are formulated). In theory, people using natural languages are not constrained by the instruction syntax inherent in traditional programming languages. In practice, however, there are limitations.

The State of the Art of Natural Languages

The state of the art of natural languages is still somewhat primitive. To date, there are no pure natural languages. However, natural languages

By drawing on artificial intelligence techniques, a GE research team has taught a computer the rudiments of how to read and digest a variety of printed material. In a demonstration, the system was fed a day's worth of stories from a financial news service (500 in all). At the user's request, it selected stories on mergers and acquisitions and was then able to answer basic questions about them. The questions and the computer's answers are phrased in plain English, not in a specialized computer language. In the future, much of our interaction with the computer will be via a natural language; that is, we will communicate with computers in much the same way that we talk with one another.

with certain syntax restrictions are available. Most commercial natural languages are designed to provide the *front end*, or the user interface, for a variety of domain-specific applications. These applications could involve an interface with the corporate data base, an expert system, or certain micro-based software products, such as electronic spreadsheets.

Researchers are currently working to develop pure natural languages that permit an unrestricted dialogue between us and a computer. Although the creation of such a language is difficult to comprehend, it is probably inevitable. In the interim, the complexities involved in translating one language into another are substantial. For example, a program designed to translate English into Russian and Russian into English was used to translate "The spirit is willing, but the flesh is weak" into Russian and than back into English. The result of the double translation was: "The vodka is good, but the meat is rotten." This example gives you an idea of the complexities involved in the creation of natural language programs. Similar subtleties must be considered when translating English into the language of computers, and vice versa.

What are the advantages of natural languages? Existing natural languages enable more people to take advantage of available information because even casual users can articulate their information needs in their native tongue. For limited information processing tasks, such as ad hoc inquiries and report generation for a specific application area (inventory management, purchasing, and so on), existing natural languages work quite well. Eventually, as natural languages mature, they will provide the front end for all categories of software, from word processing to operating systems.

Natural Language Concepts

Here is how a natural language works. Take, for example, the following request:

Let me see the average salaries by job category in the marketing department.

The natural language software analyzes the sentence in much the same way that we used to diagram sentences during our studies of grammar. This process, known as **parsing**, results in a **parse tree** (see Figure 10–17). The components of the requests are translated into applications commands through a semantic analysis. In the semantic analysis, the components are matched, typically beginning with the verb, against key words in the user-created application dictionary. The dictionary is essentially a list of command synonyms for English words that might be used in a request for a particular applications environment (marketing, medical diagnosis, and so on).

In the example inquiry, the verb *see* would be translated into the applications command *display*. For example, at its most fundamental level, the request is interpreted as "[Let me] see...salaries" or, simply, "Display salaries." The *salaries* part of the request indicates that access to the salary field, and, therefore, the employee record in the data base, is critical to the response. On closer examination, *average* specifies a function that is to be applied to the salary field. The phrase *by job category in the marketing department* identifies the user's selection criteria: Include in the response

FIGURE 10–17 Interpreting a Natural-Language User Request
Following the parsing process, a natural-language user request is translated into applications commands through a semantic analysis.

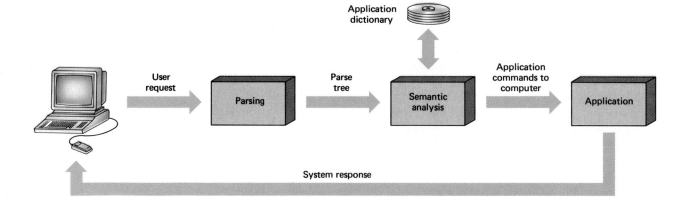

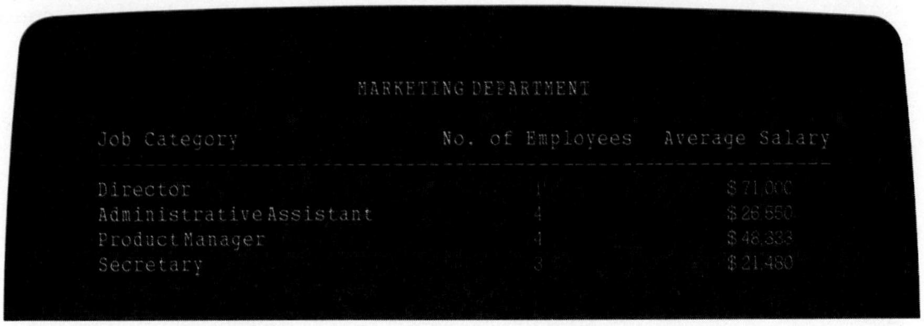

```
                    MARKETING DEPARTMENT

Job Category              No. of Employees   Average Salary
-----------------------------------------------------------
Director                         1               $ 71,000
Administrative Assistant         4               $ 26,650
Product Manager                  4               $ 48,333
Secretary                        3               $ 21,480
```

FIGURE 10–18   The Results of a Natural Language Inquiry
The inquiry: Let me see the average salaries by job category in the marketing department.

only those employees in the marketing department and compute the average salary for each job category. The response to the example inquiry is shown in Figure 10–18.

The user would get the same results if he or she had entered the following request:

> What is the average salary in the marketing department for each job classification?

If your query is unclear, the natural language software might ask you questions that will clarify any ambiguities. For example, in the preceding request the system might respond, "I do not understand 'What is'. Do you mean 'Let me see' or 'display'?"

A natural language interprets many common words, but the user must add other words peculiar to a specific application or company. All common and user-supplied words comprise the **lexicon,** or the dictionary of words that can be interpreted by the natural language. The sophistication of the types of queries that can be accepted depends on the comprehensiveness of the lexicon. In the example inquiry, the words *Let, me,* and *see;* their meaning; and the context in which they are used would have to be entered into the lexicon before the phrase *Let me see* could be interpreted by the natural language software. In addition, references to job *category* and *classification* must be defined in the lexicon to mean the same thing.

Usually state-of-the-art natural language software can interpret no more than a one-sentence query at a time. Even so, much can be accomplished with a brief command. For example, instead of writing the 4GL program in Figure 10–15, the user could have entered this request directly to the natural language interface:

> List the employee ID, sex, net pay, and gross pay for all employees in Departments 911 and 914.

The natural language interface analyzes the request and translates it into instructions that can be interpreted by the 4GL. Other typical natural language queries might be:

- Are there any managers between the ages of 30 and 40 with MBA degrees in the northwest region?
- Show me a pie graph that compares voter registrations for Alabama, Georgia, North Carolina, South Carolina, and Florida.
- What are the top 10 best-selling books of fiction in California?

 Important Terms and Summary Outline

Ada	flowcharting	Pascal
algorithm	FORTRAN	PL/I
APL	fourth-generation	procedure-oriented
application generator	language (4GL)	language
assembler language	high-level language	programmer
BASIC	lexicon	programming language
bug	loop	pseudocode
C	low-level language	reusable code
C++	main program	RPG
COBOL	mnemonic	Smalltalk
code	module	statement
code generator	natural language	structure chart
custom code	object-oriented	structured programming
debug	language	subroutine
driver module	parse tree	variable name
flowchart	parsing	

10–1 PROGRAMMING IN PERSPECTIVE. A program directs a computer to perform certain operations. The program is produced by a **programmer**, who uses any of a variety of **programming languages** to communicate with the computer. A knowledge of programming will always be a plus, even if you don't plan to write programs at home or at work.

10–2 PROBLEM SOLVING AND PROGRAMMING LOGIC. We direct computers to perform calculations and manipulate data by describing step-by-step instructions in the form of a program. Programs can provide solutions to particular problems. The creativity in programming is in the application of logic, or the creation of the **algorithm**, to problem solving.

The most effective programs are designed so that they can be written in **modules**. A **structure chart** is used to illustrate a program in modules. Addressing a programming problem in logical modules is known as **structured programming**.

10–3 PROGRAM DESIGN TECHNIQUES. Design techniques such as **flowcharting** and **pseudocode** are commonly used to represent systems and programming logic.

Flowcharts illustrate data, information, and work flow by the interconnection of specialized symbols with flow lines. In structured programming, each program is designed with a **driver module**, or **main program**, that calls **subroutines** as they are needed.

Program logic can be conceptualized in three basic control structures: sequence, selection, and **loop**. There are two variations on the loop structure: DOWHILE and DOUNTIL.

Pseudocode represents program logic in programlike statements that are written in plain English. There are no syntax guidelines for formulating pseudocode statements.

10–4 SO WHAT'S A PROGRAM? CONCEPTS AND PRINCIPLES OF PROGRAMMING. A computer program is made up of a sequence of instructions, or **statements**. There are five classifications of instructions.

- Input/output instructions direct the computer to read from or write to a peripheral device.
- Computation instructions perform arithmetic operations. A **variable name** in computation instruction refers to the contents of a particular RAM location.
- Control instructions can alter the sequence of a program's execution.
- Data transfer and assignment instructions permit data to be transferred internally.
- Format instructions describe how data are to be entered to or outputted from RAM.

10–5 WRITING PROGRAMS. Writing a program is a project in itself and follows these seven steps:

Step 1. Describe the problem.

Step 2. Analyze the problem. Examine the output, input, processing, and file-interaction components.

Step 3. Design the general logic of the program.

Step 4. Design the detailed logic of the program.

Step 5. Code the program.

Step 6. Test and debug the program. Programs are **debugged** to eliminate syntax and logic errors (**bugs**) and to clean up the input/output.

Step 7. Document the program.

10–6 GENERATIONS OF PROGRAMMING LANGUAGES. Through the first four decades of computing, programming languages evolved in generations. Each new generation permits a more sophisticated programmer/computer interaction.

The first two generations of programming languages are **low-level languages**; that is, the programmer must identify each fundamental operation the computer is to perform. The machine language is the only language that can be executed on a particular computer. **High-level languages** have surpassed machine language and **assembler language**, which uses **mnemonics**, in terms of human efficiency. They must be translated into the computer's native language. High-level languages are a programmer convenience and facilitate the programmer/computer interaction.

Third-generation programming languages fall into three categories: *procedure-oriented languages*, *problem-oriented languages*, and *object-oriented languages*.

Procedure-oriented languages are **coded** sequentially and processed according to program specifications. They are generally classified as business (**COBOL** and **RPG**), scientific (**FORTRAN** and **APL**), or multipurpose (**C, BASIC, Pascal, PL/I,** and **Ada**). Other third-generation languages include LISP, LOGO, FORTH, Prolog, and Modula-2.

Problem-oriented languages are designed to address a particular application area or to solve a particular set of problems.

Object-oriented languages, such as **Smalltalk** and **C++**, emphasize the *object* of the action.

In **fourth-generation languages**, the programmer need only specify *what* to do, not *how* to do it. The features of **4GLs** include English-like instructions, limited mathematical manipulation of data, automatic report formatting, sequencing (sorting), and record selection by criteria.

10–7 APPLICATION GENERATORS: LET THE COMPUTER DO IT. When using **application generators**, or **code generators**, to develop information systems, programmers specify what information processing tasks are to be performed by engaging in an interactive dialogue with the system. Code generators interpret the programmer-supplied information and actually generate the program code.

The generic **reusable code** of application generators occasionally must be supplemented with **custom code** to handle unique situations.

10–8 NATURAL LANGUAGES: THE ULTIMATE PROGRAMMING LANGUAGE. **Natural languages** are programs that permit a computer to accept instructions without regard to format or syntax in the native language of the end user. To date, there are no pure natural languages.

The natural language software **parses** a user inquiry into a **parse tree** that is translated into applications commands through a semantic analysis. All common and user-supplied words comprise the **lexicon**.

 Review Exercises

Concepts

1. Draw the flowcharting symbols for manual process, terminal point, workstation, and decision.
2. Where is the test-on-condition placed in a DOWHILE loop? In a DOUNTIL loop?
3. Assign meaningful variable names to at least six fields you might expect to find in a personnel record.
4. Write a pseudocode program that represents the logic of Module 1.1 (Input Data) in Figure 10–3.
5. Give an original example of a computation instruction.
6. Name and illustrate the three basic program control structures.
7. What is the purpose of a test-on-condition instruction?
8. What are the benefits of structured programming?
9. Associate each of the following with a particular generation of language: 4GLs, mnemonics, and Ada.
10. Name two types of program errors.
11. Name a procedure-oriented programming language in each of the three classifications—business, scientific, and multipurpose.
12. Name two object-oriented programming languages.
13. Contrast 4GLs with code generators.

Discussion

14. Discuss the rationale for the "divide and conquer" approach to programming.

15. What is the rationale for completing the general design of a program's logic before completing a detailed design?

16. Discuss the justification for the extra effort required to document a program fully.

17. Discuss the difference between a program and a programming language.

18. If each new generation of language enhances interaction between programmers and the computer, why not write programs using the most recent generation of languages?

19. Which generation of language would a public relations manager be most likely to use? Why?

20. If code generators can produce functional COBOL and PL/I programs, why would anyone ever write a COBOL or PL/I program?

Problem Solving

21. Complete a flowchart to illustrate the programming logic for a program that accepts three quiz grades from each of any number of students. The program should compute and display the average for each student. Include a driver module in your logic.

22. Write the pseudocode for the programming problem described in Review Exercise 22.

23. Explain in general terms what a natural language would do with the following command: "List all fixed inventory items in the purchasing department purchased prior to 1985." Give an example of what a response to the request might look like. Fixed inventory items would include items such as desks, chairs, lamps, and so on.

Self-Test (by section)

10–1 ✗Programmers use a variety of _~~programming~~ languages_ to communicate instructions to the computer.

10–2 **a.** The software for an electronic spreadsheet package is contained in a single program. (T/**F**)
b. Computer programs direct the computer to perform calculations and manipulate data. (**T**/F)
✗ **c.** Programs are written in _modules_, or independent tasks.
d. The effectiveness of structured programming is still a matter of debate. (T/**F**)

10–3 ✗Flowcharting is used primarily for program design, rarely for systems design. (T/**F**)

10–4 ✗In programming, "Subtotal Amount" is not a: **(a)** numeric value, (b) string constant, or (c) literal value?

10–5 ✗Once all the syntax errors have been removed from a program, no further testing is required. (T/**F**)

10–6   **a.** When programming in a procedure-oriented language, you tell the computer what to do and how to do it. (T/F)

b. C++ is: (a) a procedure-oriented language, (b) a problem-oriented language, or (c) an object-oriented language?

c. Assembler-level languages use mnemonics to represent instructions. (T/F)

d. A fourth-generation program normally will have fewer instructions than the same program written in a third-generation language. (T/F)

10-7   **a.** Application generators are used almost exclusively for ad hoc requests for information. (T/F)

b. The generic reusable code of application generators must occasionally be supplemented with ___custom code___ to handle unique situations.

10-8   **a.** An individual must undergo extensive training before he or she can write programs in a natural language. (T/F)

b. The dictionary of words that can be interpreted by the computer in a natural language is called the ___lexicon___.

Self-test answers.   10–1 programming languages. 10–2 **(a)** F; **(b)** T; **(c)** modules; **(d)** F. 10–3 F. 10–4 a. 10–5 F. 10–6 **(a)** T; **(b)** c; **(c)** T; **(d)** T. 10–7 **(a)** F; **(b)** custom code. 10–8 **(a)** F; **(b)** lexicon.

11

Text and Image Processing Software

STUDENT LEARNING OBJECTIVES

▶ To describe the function and applications of word processing software.

▶ To understand word processing concepts.

▶ To identify and describe add-on capabilities of word processing software packages.

▶ To describe the function and applications of desktop publishing software.

▶ To understand desktop publishing concepts.

▶ To describe the functions of different types of graphics software.

▶ To understand graphics software concepts.

CHAPTER OUTLINE

▶ 11–1 Word Processing

This chapter discusses microcomputer software tools that perform text and image processing. The primary tools for text processing (letters, reports, and so on) are word processing software and desktop publishing software. A variety of software tools address image processing, including paint software and presentation graphics. Word processing, which is installed on virtually every PC, is discussed first, then desktop publishing and image processing packages.

Function

Word processing is using the computer to enter, store, manipulate, and print text in letters, reports, books, and so on. Once you have used word processing software, you will probably wonder (like a million others before you) how in the world you ever survived without it!

Word processing has virtually eliminated the need for opaque correction fluid and the need to rekey revised letters and reports. Revising a hard copy is time-consuming and cumbersome, but revising the same text in electronic format is quick and easy. You simply make corrections and revisions on the computer before the document is displayed or printed in final form.

Concepts

Creating a Document

Formatting a document.   Before you begin keying in the text of a word processing document, you may need to *format* the document to meet your application needs. However, if you are satisfied with the software's preset format specifications, you can begin keying in text right away. Typically, the preset format, or *default settings*, fit most word processing applications. For example, the size of the output document is set at letter size ($8\frac{1}{2}$ by 11 inches); the left, right, top, and bottom margins are set at 1 inch; tabs are set every $\frac{1}{2}$ inch; and line spacing is set at 6 lines per inch.

At USA Today, *word processing skills are critical. Here several of the 425* USA Today *reporters, editors, and researchers are writing and editing copy at their computer terminals. Their late-breaking stories are entered directly into a central computer system. The system processes the copy and sends it to phototypesetters. Within minutes the stories are transmitted via satellite to 33 print sites across the United States. A couple of hours later, you can pick up a copy of* USA Today *and read the stories.*

Therefore, if you want to print your document on legal-size paper, you would need to reset the size of the output document to $8\frac{1}{2}$ by 14 inches.

Depending on the software package, some or all of these specifications are made in a *layout line*. You can have as many layout lines as you want in a single document. Text is printed according to specifications in the most recent layout line in the running text of the document.

Entering text. Text is entered in either **typeover mode** or **insert mode**. On most word processing systems you *toggle*, or switch, between typeover and insert modes by tapping the insert (or INS) key.

Let's use the draft copy of a memo written by Pat Kline (see Figure 11–1), the national sales manager for Zimco Enterprises (a manufacturer of high-tech products) to illustrate the two modes of data entry. When in typeover mode, the character you enter *types over* the character at the cursor position. For example, in the last sentence of the memo, Pat began with *The* and realized that *Our* is a better word. To make the correction in typeover mode, Pat positioned the cursor at the *T* and typed *O-u-r*, thereby replacing *The* with *Our*. When in insert mode, any text entered is *additional* text.

Pat forgot to enter the full name of the hotel (Bayside Hotel and Marina) in the last sentence. To complete the name, Pat selected the insert mode, placed the cursor at the *i* in the word *in* (after *Bayside Hotel*), and entered *and Marina* followed by a space (see Figure 11–2).

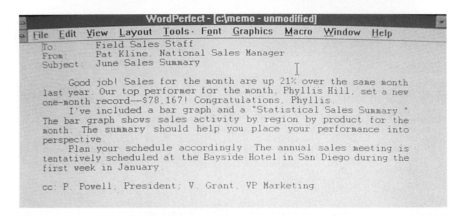

FIGURE 11–1   A Word Processing Memorandum

*This first-draft memo is revised for illustrative purposes in Figures 11–2, 11–4 through 11–7, and 11–10. The word processing software used in the examples is WP*win *(WordPerfect for Windows).*

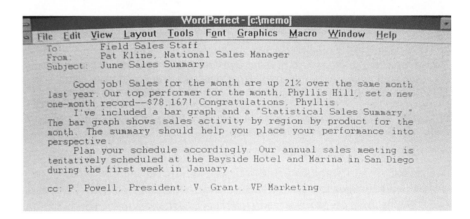

FIGURE 11–2   Typeover and Insert Mode

This memo is the result of two revisions of the first sentence of the last paragraph. The is replaced with Our in typeover mode. The phrase and Marina and a space are added in insert mode. Notice how the text wraps around to make room for the additional words.

On most word processing packages, text that extends past the defined margins is automatically *wrapped* to the next line. That is, the words that extend past the right margin are automatically moved down to the next line, and so on, to the end of the paragraph. Consider this modified version of the first two sentences of this book.

> We are in the midst of a revolution that is changing
> our way of life. The cornerstone of this revolution,
> the computer, is transforming the way we communicate,
> do business, and learn.

Notice that the remaining lines are wrapped when the word *technological* is inserted in the first line.

We are in the midst of a technological revolution that is changing our way of life. The cornerstone of this revolution, the computer, is transforming the way we communicate, do business, and learn.

When you enter text in insert mode, the computer manipulates the text so it wraps around. This type of text movement is called **word wrap**. In Figures 11–1 and 11–2, notice how the word *during* (in the last sentence) is wrapped to the next line when *and Marina* is inserted. When you enter text in typeover mode, the cursor automatically moves to the next line when you reach the right-hand margin.

Word processing permits **full-screen editing**. In other words, you can move the text cursor to any position in the document to insert or type over text. You can browse through a multiscreen document by *scrolling* a line at a time, a screen at a time, or a page (the text that corresponds to a printed page) at a time. You can edit (revise) any part of any screen.

When you enter text, *tap the ENTER key only when you wish to begin a new line of text*. In the memo of Figure 11–1, Pat tapped ENTER after each of the three information lines, after each paragraph in the body of the memo, and after the "copy to" (cc) line. Pat also tapped ENTER to insert each of the blank lines. The TAB key was tapped at the beginning of each paragraph to indent the first line of the paragraph.

What you see is what you get. Most modern word processing packages are considered **WYSIWYG** (pronounced *WIZ e wig*), short for "What you see is what you get." What you see on the screen is essentially what the document will look like when it is printed—font size, graphics, and all (see Figure 11–3). These word processing packages employ high resolution graphics. However, text-based WYSIWYG is slightly misleading in that what you see while editing a document is *not exactly* what you get. For example, the text you see on the screen may have a right-justified margin. However, most of the text-based word processing packages have a *preview* feature that permits you to see what the document will look like when it is printed—almost. The display screen fonts may be slightly different than the printer fonts. These differences have prompted the occasional use of a more accurate term **WYSIWYG–MOL**, short for

FIGURE 11–3   A WYSIWYG Word Processing Display: Text and Graphics

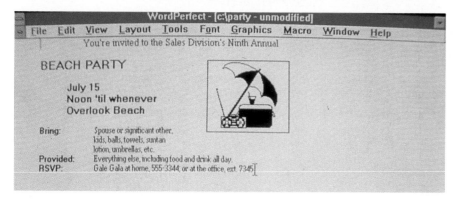

"What you see is what you get—more or less." Text-based and graphics-based displays are discussed in detail later in this chapter.

Block Operations   Features common to most word processing software packages are discussed briefly in this section. *Block* operations are among the handiest word processing features. They are the block-*move*, the block-*copy*, and the block-*delete* commands. These commands are the electronic equivalent of a "cut-and-paste job."

Let's discuss the move command first. With this feature you can select a block of text (for example, a word, a sentence, a paragraph, a section of a report, or as much contiguous text as you desire) and move it to another portion of the document. To do this, follow these steps:

1. Indicate the start and ending positions of the block of text to be moved (*mark* the text).
2. Issue the move command (a main-menu option or a function key).
3. Move the text cursor to the beginning of the destination location (where you wish the text to be moved).
4. Tap ENTER (or the appropriate function key) to complete the move operation.

At the end of the move procedure, the entire block of text you selected is moved to the designated location, and the text is adjusted accordingly (wrapped).

The following example demonstrates the procedure for marking and moving a block of text. After reading over the memo to the field staff (Figure 11–2), Pat decided to edit the memo to make it more readable. Pat moved the first sentence in the last paragraph to the end of the memo. To perform this operation, Pat marked the beginning (*P* in *Plan*) and end (the position following the period at the end of the next sentence) of the block. On most word processing systems, the portions of text marked

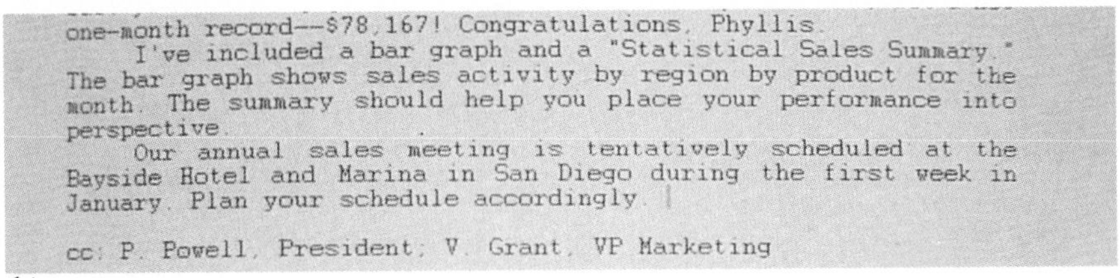

FIGURE 11–4   Marking and Moving Text
(a) The first sentence of the last paragraph of the memo is marked to be moved. (b) The marked sentence is moved to the end of the paragraph.

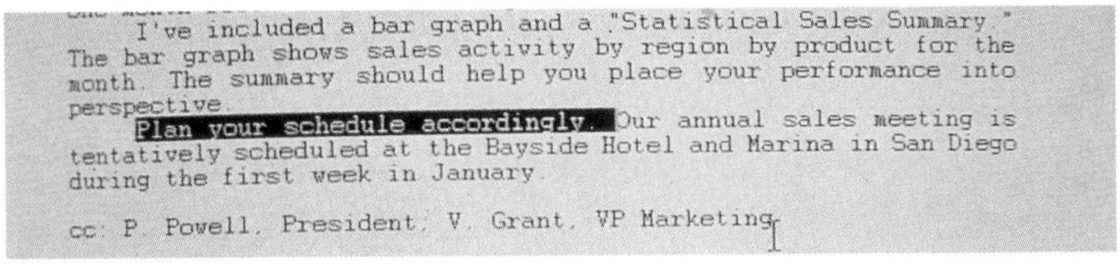

(a)

(b)

for a block operation are usually displayed in **reverse video** (see Figure 11–4a). To complete the operation (see Figure 11–4b), Pat selected the move option, positioned the cursor at the destination location (after a space following the end of the paragraph), and tapped the appropriate key. Notice that the text in the last paragraph is wrapped to accommodate the move operation.

The copy command works in a similar manner, except that the text block you select is copied to the location you designate. When the operation is completed, the text block in question appears twice in the document.

In keeping with the "cut-and-paste" terminology associated with page makeup, modern word processing programs are beginning to use cut-and-paste commands in lieu of the move command. To move a marked block, cut it (remove the block from the screen and store it in memory), then paste (insert) it at the cursor location. To copy a marked block, issue the copy command, then paste (insert) it at the cursor location.

To delete a block of text, mark the block in the same manner, then select the block-delete option. The meeting at the Bayside Hotel and Marina was confirmed while Pat was composing the memo in Figure 11–1. To reflect the confirmation, Pat used the block-delete command to drop the phrase *tentatively scheduled*, then inserted the word *set*. This operation is illustrated in sequence in Figure 11–5.

FIGURE 11–5 Marking and Deleting Text
(a) The phrase tentatively scheduled *in the first sentence of the last paragraph is marked to be deleted. (b) The phrase is deleted. (c) The word* set *is inserted at the cursor position.*

```
        Good job! Sales for the month are up 21% over the same month
last year  Our top performer for the month, Phyllis Hill, set a new
one-month record--$78,167! Congratulations, Phyllis.
        I've included a bar graph and a "Statistical Sales Summary."
The bar graph shows sales activity by region by product for the
month. The summary should help you place your performance into
perspective.
        Our annual sales meeting is tentatively scheduled at the
Bayside Hotel and Marina in San Diego during the first week in
January  Plan your schedule accordingly.
```
(a)

```
        Good job! Sales for the month are up 21% over the same month
last year  Our top performer for the month, Phyllis Hill, set a new
one-month record--$78,167! Congratulations, Phyllis.
        I've included a bar graph and a "Statistical Sales Summary."
The bar graph shows sales activity by region by product for the
month. The summary should help you place your performance into
perspective.
        Our annual sales meeting is at the Bayside Hotel and Marina in
San Diego during the first week in January. Plan your schedule
accordingly
```
(b)

```
        Good job! Sales for the month are up 21% over the same month
last year  Our top performer for the month, Phyllis Hill, set a new
one-month record--$78,167! Congratulations, Phyllis.
        I've included a bar graph and a "Statistical Sales Summary."
The bar graph shows sales activity by region by product for the
month. The summary should help you place your performance into
perspective.
        Our annual sales meeting is set at the Bayside Hotel and
Marina in San Diego during the first week in January. Plan your
schedule accordingly.
```
(c)

The Search Features   While looking over the memo, Pat Kline decided that it would read better if all generic references to *the month* were replaced by the name of the month, *June*. The necessary revisions in the memo can be made by using any of several word processing features. One option is to use the *search*, or *find*, feature. This feature allows Pat to search the entire document and identify all occurrences of a particular character string. For example, if Pat wanted to search for all occurrences of *the month* in the memo, the manager simply would initiate the search command and type in the desired *search string—the month*, in this example. Immediately, the cursor is positioned at the first occurrence of the character string *the month* so Pat can easily edit the text to reflect the new meeting day. From there, other occurrences of *the month* can be located by tapping the appropriate search key.

An alternative to changing each occurrence of *the month* to *June* involves using the *search-and-replace* feature. This feature enables *selective* replacement of *the month* with *June*. Issuing the *global search-and-replace* command causes *all* occurrences of *the month* to be replaced with *June*. Opting for the global search-and-replace command, Pat replaced all three occurrences of *the month* with *June* (see Figure 11–6).

FIGURE 11–6   Search and Replace
(a) The memo contains three occurrences of the string the month. *(b) The search-and-replace command is used to replace all occurrences of* the month *with* June.

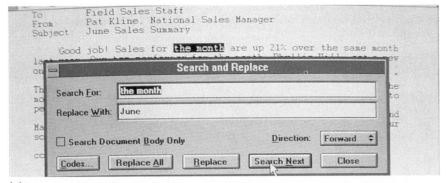

(a)

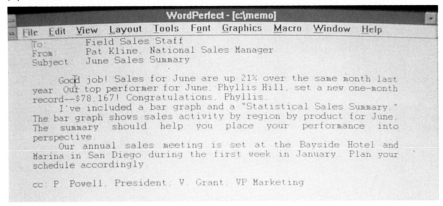

(b)

Features That Enhance Appearance and Readability   Pat used several other valuable word processing features to enhance the appearance and readability of the memo before distributing it to the field sales staff. First, the manager decided to enter the current date at the top of the memo and use the automatic *centering* feature to position it at the center of the page. On most word processing systems, centering a particular line is as easy as moving the text cursor to the desired line and tapping the *center* function key. The rest is automatic (see Figure 11–7).

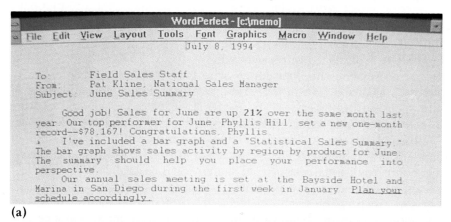

(a)

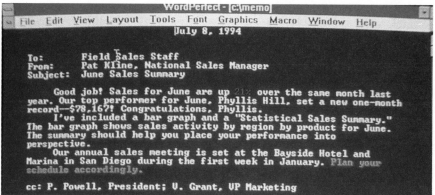

(b)

(c)

FIGURE 11–7   Center, Boldface, and Underline
The date is centered at the top of the memo. (a) In a WYSIWYG display, text is shown as boldface and underlined. (b) On a color monitor, text to be printed in boldface type or underlined is displayed in different colors. (c) The memo is printed on a desktop page printer.

Word processing provides the facility to *boldface* and/or *underline* parts of the text for emphasis. In the memo, Pat decided to highlight the remarkable 21% increase in sales by requesting that it be printed in boldface type (see Figure 11–7c). To do so, the manager marked *21%* and issued the boldface command. To make the point that sales representatives should plan now for the January meeting, Pat followed a similar procedure to make sure the last sentence is underlined on output (see Figure 11–7c).

Text-based WYSIWYG–MOL word processing packages highlight boldface and underline words by displaying them in different colors (Figure 11–7b). Sometimes text that is to be printed in boldface type or underlined on output is displayed in reverse video.

To enhance the appearance of a document, some people like to *justify* (align) text on the left or the right margin, or on both margins, like the print in newspapers and in this book. Word processing software is able to produce "clean" margins on both sides by adding small spaces between characters and words in a line as it is output. The right and left margins of the memo in Figure 11–7c are justified. However, Pat prefers the more traditional *ragged right* margin on personal letters. The first paragraph in Figure 11–8 is printed as ragged right.

In creating the memo of Figure 11–7, Pat used many but not all the word processing features available to enhance its appearance and readability. Figure 11–8 illustrates other such features. Users can *indent* a block of text, cause *header* and *footer labels* to be printed on each page, and request that pages be numbered (*pagination* feature). On long reports, Pat usually repeats the report title at the top of each page (header label) and numbers each page at the bottom (pagination).

The example in Figure 11–8 also illustrates hyphenation, footnotes, numbered list/outline, bulleted list, line draw, superscripts and subscripts, and the insertion of an image into the running text. The *hyphenation* feature automatically breaks and hyphenates words to create a smoother appearing right margin. One of the most tedious typing chores, *footnoting*, is done automatically. Footnote spacing is resolved electronically before anything is printed. The *numbered list* and *outline* features enable descriptive items to be presented in a numbered list or in outline format (shown in Figure 11–8). The numbers and/or letters are inserted automatically by the word processing program. The *bulleted list* is created in a similar manner. Users can create special effects with the *line-draw* feature. This feature permits the drawing of vertical and horizontal lines of varying widths. *Superscripts* and *subscripts* are common in technical writing. One of the most popular features of the more sophisticated word processing programs is the ability to *insert images* into the running text. In Figure 11–8, notice how the text wraps around the image. Not shown in Figure 11–8 is the feature that permits *multicolumn output*, one or more columns of text on a single page. The Multicolumn option is used frequently in newsletters.

Depending on the type of software and printer you have, you may even be able to mix the size and style of typefaces, called **fonts**, in a single document. In Figure 11–8, the heading, headers, footer, quotation, and figure caption are printed in a different size and style of type than

At many companies all office workers, including executives, are trained to use word processing. Workers save time and money by using word processing to create and edit their written work. While waiting to make a presentation, this executive reviews and refines his notes for the meeting.

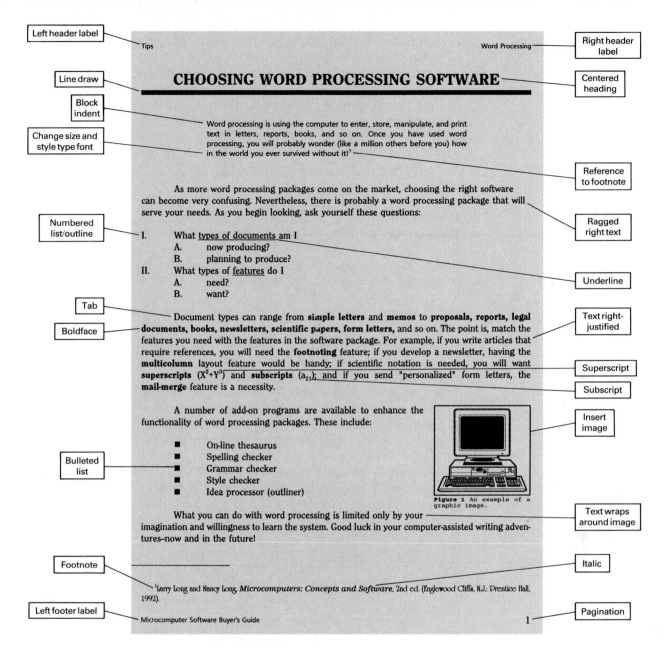

The figure illustrates the following labeled parts:

- Left header label — Tips
- Line draw
- Block indent
- Change size and style type font
- Numbered list/outline
- Tab
- Boldface
- Bulleted list
- Footnote
- Left footer label
- Right header label — Word Processing
- Centered heading
- Reference to footnote
- Ragged right text
- Underline
- Text right-justified
- Superscript
- Subscript
- Insert image
- Text wraps around image
- Italic
- Pagination

CHOOSING WORD PROCESSING SOFTWARE

Word processing is using the computer to enter, store, manipulate, and print text in letters, reports, books, and so on. Once you have used word processing, you will probably wonder (like a million others before you) how in the world you ever survived without it![1]

As more word processing packages come on the market, choosing the right software can become very confusing. Nevertheless, there is probably a word processing package that will serve your needs. As you begin looking, ask yourself these questions:

I.   What types of documents am I
     A.   now producing?
     B.   planning to produce?
II. What types of features do I
     A.   need?
     B.   want?

Document types can range from **simple letters** and **memos** to **proposals, reports, legal documents, books, newsletters, scientific papers, form letters,** and so on. The point is, match the features you need with the features in the software package. For example, if you write articles that require references, you will need the **footnoting** feature; if you develop a newsletter, having the **multicolumn** layout feature would be handy; if scientific notation is needed, you will want **superscripts** (X^2+Y^3) and **subscripts** (a_{21}); and if you send "personalized" form letters, the **mail-merge** feature is a necessity.

A number of add-on programs are available to enhance the functionality of word processing packages. These include:

- On-line thesaurus
- Spelling checker
- Grammar checker
- Style checker
- Idea processor (outliner)

Figure 1 An example of a graphic image.

What you can do with word processing is limited only by your imagination and willingness to learn the system. Good luck in your computer-assisted writing adventures–now and in the future!

[1]Larry Long and Nancy Long, *Microcomputers: Concepts and Software*, 2nd ed. (Englewood Cliffs, N.J.: Prentice Hall, 1992).

Microcomputer Software Buyer's Guide   1

FIGURE 11–8   Word Processing Features Overview
Many of the more common capabilities of word processing software are illustrated in this printout.

the rest of the document. The heading is a larger type font and the others are in a smaller type font. Fonts are discussed in more detail in the section on desktop publishing.

Some word processing software contains sophisticated features for writers and people who are charged with the preparation of long, involved documents (strategic plans, annual reports, procedures manuals, and so on). A simple command creates a *table of contents* with page references for chapters and up to five levels of headings. An alphabetical *index of key words* can be compiled that lists the page numbers for each occurrence of user-designated words.

Some word processing packages have a *table* feature that expedites the tabular presentation of data. The user sets up a table format with the appropriate number of lined boxes by entering the number of rows and columns desired. Once data have been entered into the table, simple arithmetic can be performed (for example, column totals).

The more sophisticated word processing packages provide users with the capability of doing *desktop publishing*. We discuss desktop publishing in detail later in this chapter.

Printing a Document   To print a document, ready the printer and select the print option on the main menu. Some word processing systems present you with other print options. For example, you can choose to print in draft (low resolution with no graphics) or graphics mode; you also could be given the option of printing specific pages or the whole document.

File Features   Certainly one of the most important features of a word processing package is the ability to store a document on disk for later recall. The stored version of a document is referred to as a *document file*. The *file* feature permits you to save, retrieve, and delete a document file. At a minimum, most word processing systems provide users with the save-, retrieve-, and delete-file options. No matter which option you choose, the system asks you to identify the file (document). You then enter an arbitrary name that in some way identifies the document (for example, MEMO). To retrieve or delete an existing file, you enter its file name.

Pat Kline "saved" the memo in Figure 11–7 (stored it on disk) under the file name MEMO. Because the memo is stored in electronic format on disk, Pat can retrieve and edit it to report the sales results for another month.

Add-on Capabilities   A number of programs are designed to enhance the function of word processing programs. These add-on capabilities are usually separate programs that can interface with a word processing package. Generally, they come with the word processing software package or, if not, they can be purchased separately.

On-line thesaurus.   Have you ever been in the middle of writing a letter or memo and been unable to put your finger on the right word? Some word processing packages have an **on-line thesaurus**! Suppose you have just written: *The Grand Canyon certainly is beautiful.* But *beautiful* is not quite the right word. Your electronic thesaurus is always ready with suggestions: *pretty, gorgeous, exquisite, angelic, stunning, ravishing, divine,* and so on.

Spelling checker.   If spelling is a problem, then word processing can be the answer. Once you have entered the text and formatted the document, you can call on the **spelling checker** capability. The spelling checker checks every word in the text against an **electronic dictionary** (usually from 75,000 to 150,000 words) and alerts you if a word is not

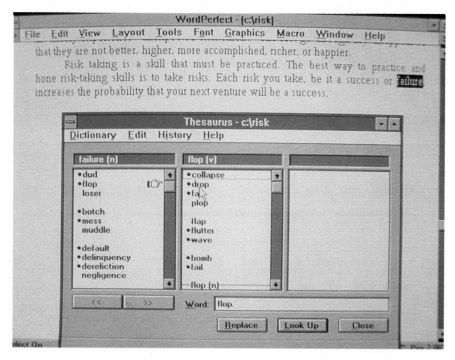

The WordPerfect for Windows thesaurus feature helps you find the right word. In the example, the user requested synonyms for the word failure. The user extended the search by requesting synonyms for the word flop.

in the dictionary. Upon finding an unidentified word, the spell function normally will give you several options:

1. You can correct the spelling.
2. You can ignore the word and continue scanning the text. Normally you do this when a word is spelled correctly but is not in the dictionary (for example, a company name such as Zimco).
3. You can ask for possible spellings. The spell function then gives you a list of words of similar spellings from which to choose. For example, assume that Pat left out the *o* in *month*. Upon finding the nonword *mnth*, the spelling checker might suggest the following alternatives: *math*, *month*, *moth*, *myth*, and *nth*.
4. You can add the word to the dictionary and continue scanning.

Grammar and style checkers. Grammar and style checkers are the electronic version of a copy editor. A **grammar checker** highlights grammatical concerns and deviations from conventions. For example, it highlights split infinitives, phrases with redundant words (*very highest*), misuse of capital letters (*JOhn* or *MarY*), subject and verb mismatches (*they was*), double words (*and and*), and punctuation errors. When applied to the memo in Figure 11–7, the grammar checker noted the incomplete sentence at the end of the first paragraph ("Congratulations, Phyllis"). A **style checker** alerts users to such writing concerns as sexist words or

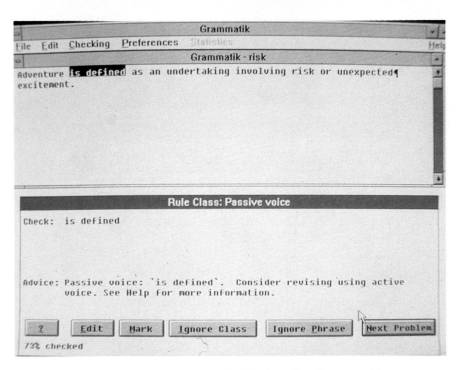

This screen illustrates how Grammatik for Windows handles a problem encountered while scanning a word processing document for grammar, style, usage, punctuation, and spelling errors. In the example, the program advises the user to consider using the active voice in the displayed sentence. The user has the option of taking no action and going on to the next problem; editing the problem; marking it for later examination; or ignoring similar problems for the rest of the scan.

phrases (*chairman*), long or complex sentence structures, clichés (for example, *the bottom line*), and sentences written in the passive (*The letter was written by Sherry*) rather than the active voice (*Sherry wrote the letter*).

Idea processor. Like word processing software, an **idea processor** permits the manipulation of text, but with a different twist. It deals with brief explanations of items—for example: ideas, points, notes, and so on. Idea processors, or **outliners**, can organize these brief items into an outline format. Referred to by some as an electronic version of the yellow notepad, the idea processor lets you focus your attention on the thought process by letting the computer help document your ideas.

Document-conversion programs. Although a handful of word processing packages dominate the marketplace, about 30 are commonly used. It is not unusual for people within a company to use half a dozen incompatible word processing packages and, of course, these people frequently need to share text in their word processing documents. There are two ways to do this.

1. *Create an ASCII file.* When you save a word processing document, you save all the text in the file *plus* the hidden control characters that end paragraphs, start and end boldface, cause page breaks, and so on. These control characters are unique to each word processing package; therefore,

one package cannot read a file produced by another. However, all word processing packages can read **ASCII files.** An ASCII file is a generic text file that is stripped of program-specific control characters. One way to pass text from one word processing package to another is to create a generic ASCII file with one and read it with another. Of course, when you do this, you lose everything (tabs, underlines, and so on) except the text in the transfer.

2. *Use a document-conversion program.* **Document-conversion programs** help solve the dilemma created when several word processing packages are used within one company. This add-on converts documents generated on one word processing package into a format consistent with another. For example, document-conversion programs enable a Microsoft Word user to convert files to WordPerfect files—control characters and all.

Use

Mail Merge   You can create just about any kind of text-based document with word processing: letters, reports, books, articles, forms, memos, tables, and so on. The features of some word processing packages go beyond the generation of text documents, however. For example, some word processing systems provide the capability of merging parts of a data base with the text of a document. Figure 11–9 illustrates an example of this **mail-merge** application. In the example, Zimco Enterprises announced the enhanced version of its Qwert, one of its hottest selling items. Each regional sales manager sent a "personal" letter to every one of the thousands of Zimco customers in his or her region. Using word processing, a secretary enters the text of the letter once, stores it on the disk, then simply merges the customer name-and-address file (also stored on the disk) with the letter. The letters then can be printed with the proper addresses and salutations. Figure 11–9 illustrates how the Qwert announcement letter is merged with the customer name-and-address file to produce a "personalized" letter.

Boilerplate   The mail-merge example is a good illustration of the use of **boilerplate.** Boilerplate is existing text that can be customized for a variety of word processing applications. One of the beauties of word processing is that you can accumulate text on disk storage that eventually will help you meet other word processing needs. You can even *buy* boilerplate.

The legal profession offers some of the best examples of the use of boilerplate. Simple wills, uncontested divorces, individual bankruptcies, real estate transfers, and other straightforward legal documents may be as much as 95% boilerplate. Even more-complex legal documents may be as much as 80% boilerplate. Once the appropriate boilerplate has been merged into a document, the lawyer edits the document to add transition sentences and the variables, such as the names of the litigants. Besides the obvious improvement in productivity, lawyers can be relatively confident that their documents are accurate and complete. The use of boilerplate is common in all areas of business, education, government, and personal endeavor.

Memory Bits

WORD PROCESSING
Entering text
- Typeover mode
- Insert mode

Block operations on marked text
- Move
- Copy
- Delete

Search or find
- Search only
- Selective search and replace
- Global search and replace

Add-ons
- On-line thesaurus
- Spelling checker
- Grammar and style checkers
- Idea processor
- Document-conversion program

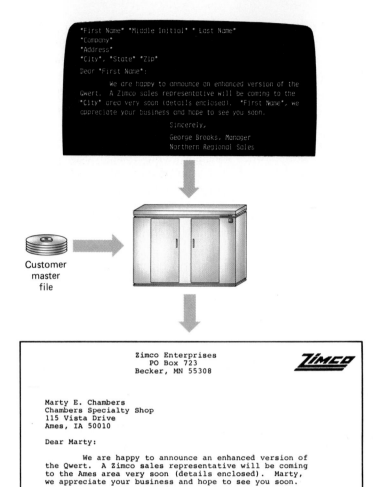

FIGURE 11–9 Merging Data with Word Processing
The names and addresses from a customer master file are retrieved from secondary storage and are merged with the text of a letter. In the actual letter, the appropriate data items are inserted for *First Name*, *Company*, *Address*, *City*, and so on. In this way, a "personalized" letter can be sent to each customer.

Integration of Text and Graphics   Most state-of-the-art word processing packages permit the integration of text and graphic images. For example, the text in Figure 11–10 refers to a "bar graph" and a "Statistical Sales Summary." Figure 11–10 shows how the memo, the bar graph (produced with electronic spreadsheet software), and the sales summary (from an electronic spreadsheet file) can be integrated into a single word processing document.

Summary   Word processing is the perfect example of how automation can be used to increase productivity and foster creativity. It minimizes

July 8, 1994

To: Field Sales Staff
From: Pat Kline, National Sales Manager
Subject: June Sales Summary

    Good job! Sales for June are up **21%** over the same month last
year. Our top performer for June, Phyllis Hill, set a new one-month
record--$78,167! Congratulations, Phyllis.
    I've included a bar graph and a "Statistical Sales Summary."
The bar graph shows sales activity by region by product for June.
The summary should help you place your performance into
perspective.
    Our annual sales meeting is set at the Bayside Hotel and
Marina in San Diego during the first week in January. Plan your
schedule accordingly.

cc: P. Powell, President; V. Grant, VP Marketing

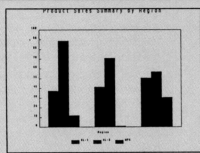

Figure 1   Region/Product Graph

***** STATISTICAL SALES SUMMARY *****			
SALES BY REP.	**XL-1**	**XL-2**	**MPX**	**TOTAL**
LOW	$15,570	$24,660	$0	$48,305
AVG.	$21,551	$36,069	$7,250	$64,869
HIGH	$28,067	$58,388	$25,440	$78,167
RANGE	$12,497	$33,728	$25,440	$29,862

Figure 2   Sales Stats

FIGURE 11–10   Integrating Text with Graphics
*The bar graph and the "Statistical Sales Summary" referred to in the memo of
Figure 11–7 are combined in the same word processing document and printed
on a desktop page printer. The bar graph and summary were produced using
electronic spreadsheet software.*

the effort you must devote to the routine aspects of writing so you can
focus your attention on its creative aspects. Most word processing users
will agree that their writing styles have improved. The finished product
is less verbose, better organized, devoid of spelling errors, and, of course,
more visually appealing.

Desktop Publishing

Function

The ultimate extension of word processing is *desktop publishing*, sometimes
abbreviated as **DTP**. Desktop publishing refers to the capability of producing *near-typeset-quality copy* from the confines of a desktop. This con-

Frustration! You imagine how much better your writing could be if your word processing program checked grammar, as well as spelling. Or, you imagine how much time you could save if your presentation graphics program stored files in a variety of graphics formats. Add-in programs promise to help when you can do almost everything you need to . . . but not quite!

Add-in software in some way enhances the functionality of a major PC software package, such as WordPerfect or Lotus 1-2-3, or it provides you with alternative ways to use the package. For example, the work area for WordPerfect 5.1 is limited to 25 rows and 80 columns. An add-in effectively extends the display so that you can view more lines in the work area. Add-ins may be supplied with the basic applications software or, as is normally the case, marketed by another company.

Add-ins evolve from need. Once a PC software package has been on the market for a while, the vendor or software entrepreneurs create ingenious solutions to problems users are having.

- Microsoft's *Windows* enables the viewing of multiple applications on a single screen; however, only parts of the applications are shown in each window. *WideAngle*, an add-in, compresses the individual application such that up to nine applications can be shown in their entirety on a single screen.

- Most presentation graphics packages are accompanied by a variety of clip art (prepackaged electronic images). Several companies offer supplemental extensive arrays of clip art that are electronically pre-indexed for fast identification and retrieval. For example, you could call up images that relate to a particular season, holiday, geographic location, business scenario, and so on.

- Several companies offer add-ins for word processing packages that expand the number of typefaces available to the user.

- *Perfect Exchange*, an add-in for WordPerfect, converts documents between WordPerfect and 55 word processor, spreadsheet, and database formats. This gives offices which use several packages the flexibility to exchange text without losing markings such as boldface and underline.

- *PC-Translator*, an add-in for word processors, helps international businesses translate technical manuals, business letters, purchase orders, invoices, and so on to English.

- *Grammatik*, a word processor add-in, analyzes a document to point out problems in grammar and style.

- Several companies market rhymer add-ins to help writers, educators, language teachers, songwriters, and others find just the right word.

cept is changing the way companies, government agencies, and individuals approach printing newsletters, brochures, business cards, user manuals, pamphlets, restaurant menus, periodicals, greeting cards, and thousands of other items.

Concepts

Traditionally, drafts of documents to be printed are delivered to commercial typographers to be typeset. The typeset text is physically pasted together with photos, artwork, ruled lines, and so on to achieve the final layout. Desktop publishing eliminates the typesetting and pasteup process for those documents that require only near-typeset-quality (for example, those documents produced by desktop page printers with resolutions [quality of output] of 300 to 1000 dots per inch [dpi]). In practice, near-typeset-quality copy is acceptable for most printed documents. Relatively few need to be prepared using the expensive commercial phototypesetting process (which uses 1200 dpi or greater). The output of the desktop

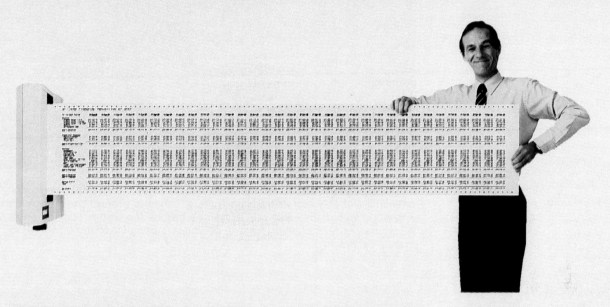

SPREADSHEETS TOO WIDE FOR THE PRINTER? A PC add-on solves this problem by printing the spreadsheet sideways.

- An add-in called *Compare and Contrast* helps you keep tabs on spreadsheets by comparing two spreadsheets cell by cell and informing you of any differences.
- *R & R Report Writer* turns your raw data into useful information by creating reports that relate, analyze, summarize, and handsomely present the data in spreadsheets and data bases.

If you and others have an add-in–type problem, there is a good chance that someone has a product on the market or, if not, is planning to create one in the near future.

publishing process is called *camera-ready copy*. The camera-ready copy is reproduced by a variety of means, from duplicating machines to commercial offset printing.

The Components of Desktop Publishing   The components required for desktop publishing include

- Document-composition software
- Microcomputer
- Desktop page printer
- Image scanner
- Typefaces and fonts
- Clip art

Document-composition software.   The document-composition software enables users to design and make up the page or pages of a document.

Desktop publishing software certainly has captured the business community's attention. Not only can users bypass the expense of professional typesetting and page layout, they also can drastically reduce the time needed to prepare a camera-ready document. Here, a designer is completing the layout for a trade newsweekly.

The image scanner is one of the six components required for desktop publishing. Relatively inexpensive hand image scanners have made it possible for the casual PC user to get into desktop publishing.

When people talk of desktop publishing software, they are actually talking about document-composition software. Two of the most popular packages are Xerox's *Ventura Publisher* and Aldus Corporation's *PageMaker*.

Microcomputer. Of all of the microcomputer productivity tools, DTP is the most technologically demanding. A high-end microcomputer is a prerequisite for effective desktop publishing. The typical micro used for DTP will be fast and will be configured with a high-resolution *monitor*, a *mouse*, plenty of RAM, and a high-capacity *hard disk*.

Desktop page printer. The overwhelming majority of desktop page printers configured with DTP systems are laser printers that print at 300 dpi. However, affordable desktop page printers with 1000 dpi resolution are available.

Image scanner. Image scanners (see Chapter 5, "Input/Output Devices"), found on high-end DTP systems, are used to digitize images, such as photographs. Image scanners re-create an electronic version of text or an image (photograph or line drawing) that can be manipulated and reproduced under computer control.

Typefaces and fonts. Most DTP-produced documents use a variety of **typefaces**. A typeface refers to a set of characters that are of the same type style (**Helvetica**, `Clarinda Typewriter`, *Park Avenue*, and so on). A *font* is described by its typeface, its height in points (8, 10, 14, 24, and so on; 72 points to the inch), and its presentation attribute (light, roman [or normal], medium, bold, italic, bold italic, extra bold, and so on). A variety of typefaces and point sizes are illustrated in Figure 11–11.

Typefaces fall into three categories:

Serif:	those that have short crosslines projecting from the ends of the strokes.
Sans Serif:	those without serifs.
Decorative:	*those used for headlines and special effects.*

The lowercase *x* sits on the baseline and defines the x-height. That portion of a character that is below the baseline is the descender (as in *g, p* and *y*) and that which is above the x-height is the ascender (as in *d, f,* and *H*).

A typeface's style is defined in terms of

Weight:	light, **medium, heavy** or **bold** (with *extra* and *ultra* prefixes).
Slant:	*italic (for serif typefaces);* oblique (for sans serif typefaces).
Proportion:	condensed, **regular,** or extended.

Typeface families (those typefaces with similar shapes) are usually named for their designers (Frederick Goudy, Oswald **Cooper**) or their function (Bookman). Examples of the Claude Garamond family are illustrated below.

Garamond Book	***Garamond Bold Italic***
Garamond Book Italic	Garamond Book Condensed
Garamond Bold	*Garamond Book Condensed* Italic

A font refers to a particular typeface size and style. All previous fonts in this illustration are 12 point (72 points to an inch). Other fonts follow.

Brody:	(4 point) and 8 point.
Chaucer (Old English):	24 point and
	36 point
Old Towne:	72 point

Bitmapped fonts, which are made up of pixels, require a separate character set file for each point size. Outline fonts of any size (and orientation) for a particular typeface are generated from a single typeface file.

FIGURE 11–11 Typeface Tutorial

Each font (such as 24-point Helvetica Bold) is stored on disk or in ROM (read-only memory). When needed to print a document, the **soft font** for a particular font is retrieved from disk storage and downloaded to the printer's memory. A **resident font** is accessed directly from the printer's built-in ROM. Some printers have removable ROM cartridges, each of which contains a variety of fonts. The cartridges must be inserted manually in the printer when the fonts are needed for a print job. People engaged in DTP typically will have a minimum of a dozen soft or resident fonts available for use. The more sophisticated user will have access to hundreds of fonts.

The latest round of high-speed micros have made it possible to generate fonts as they are needed. To do this, they use **scalable typefaces** that are stored in outline format. The outline is essentially a template, described in mathematical terms, from which fonts of any point size can be created. Scalable typefaces provide the user with tremendous flexibility in font selection. For example, you might elect to print your first-level headings in 20-point Goudy (bold) and your second-level headings in 16-point Goudy (bold). These two fonts are generated by the processor from the Goudy (bold) scalable typeface, then downloaded to the printer's memory.

Clip art. No DTP environment would be complete without a healthy supply of **clip art**. Clip art refers to prepackaged electronic images that are stored on disk to be used as needed. The clock in Figure 11–8 is clip art. Clip art items could be a computer, a rose, two people talking, a hamburger, or just about anything you can imagine.

Desktop Publishing Files Typically, a DTP-produced document such as a newsletter consists of several files. A long report or a book may be made up of hundreds of files. During the document-composition process, each file is assigned to a rectangular **frame**. A frame holds the text or an image of a particular file. Each page is a frame. There also can be frames within a frame (for example, figures and photos on a page).

A DTP document will involve one or more text files, perhaps one or more picture files, a style-sheet file, and a print file.

- *Text files.* The *text files* are created by a word processing program, such as WordPerfect. Although DTP software provides the facility to create and edit text, it is much easier to do these tasks with a word processing program.
- *Picture files. Picture files* are made up of clip art, line art, scanned-in graphics and photos, and renderings of screen displays (for example, the summary at the bottom of Figure 11–10).
- *Style-sheet file.* In the traditional approach to publishing, the designer of a print job (a book or a restaurant menu) creates a style sheet that provides the information needed by the typesetter (for example, typeface size and attributes for first-level headings). In DTP, the user creates a *style-sheet file* that tells the document-composition software what do with the text. To create the style-sheet file, the user must go into the document and *tag* each paragraph with the appropriate typographical attributes (such as typeface and size).
- *Print file.* The *print file* contains all the information needed to combine the text and picture files with the style sheet and print the document.

The Document-Composition Process The document-composition process involves integrating graphics, photos, text, and other elements into a visually appealing *document layout*. With DTP, you can produce finished, professional-looking documents in four steps (see Figure 11–12).

1. *Prepare text and graphics.* Use your word processing software to create and edit the text of your document. For illustrations you can use clip art, computer-created graphics (such as a pie graph), or scanned images (photos).

2. *Create the style sheet.* Define the document format (for example, margins and number of columns) and text attributes. Once a style-sheet file for a particular job is created, it can be applied to similar text files (for example, monthly newsletters).

3. *Combine text and picture files.* Create and position needed frames, then insert text and picture files to fit your needs. The DTP display is WYSIWYG—that is, "What you see is what you get" when the document is printed. If what you see is not what you want, then you can use the mouse to reposition frames containing text and graphics to the desired locations.

4. *Print the document.* Once the WYSIWYG display shows what you want, use a desktop page printer to produce the finished camera-ready copy.

Desktop Publishing and Word Processing Traditionally, users have combined the text manipulation capabilities of word processing software with the document-composition capabilities of DTP software to produce camera copy for reproduction. Word processing–generated text provides input to the document-composition process. This distinction may begin to blur in the near future. Already state-of-the-art word processing programs, such as Microsoft Word and WordPerfect, provide users with sophisticated DTP capabilities. Word processing users routinely produce camera-ready copy for everything from letterheads to books—all without the aid of DTP software.

By now you are probably thinking, "If word processing software does it all, why do we need DTP software?" At this time, word processing software doesn't do it all. DTP software offers a full range of sophisticated capabilities that are not available with word processing software. For example, suppose the last sentence of a paragraph was, "The binary digits are 0 and 1." and "1." ended up alone on the last line. With DTP software, you can force the "1." onto the previous line. You can't do that with word processing software. In general, DTP software provides users with tremendous flexibility in formatting documents. The document-composition capabilities of word processing software are typically more cumbersome and time-consuming than similar DTP capabilities.

It is inevitable that future generations of high-end word processing software will incorporate more and more document-composition capabilities. In time, word processing software will be all that is needed for most jobs that require camera-ready copy. On the other hand, vendors of desktop publishing software plan to incorporate advanced text-manipulation capabilities, thereby eliminating the need for word processing–generated text. Look for the differences between the two to diminish over the next few years.

Inclinations toward Imagesetting Many companies that routinely publish printed matter are shying away from conventional typesetting and warming up to imagesetting. An imagesetter allows every process in the development of publications to be done in-house without the aid of outside services. After a publication has been created on a PC or Macintosh, it is sent to a raster image processor (RIP). It is then sent to the imagesetter where lasers expose film or photosensitive paper with an image made of dots—a raster image. From here, the film is processed and a negative is produced. Even though imagesetters are a large initial investment (prices range from $14,000 to $50,000), the venture usually pays for itself in one or two years, depending on the publication's volume.

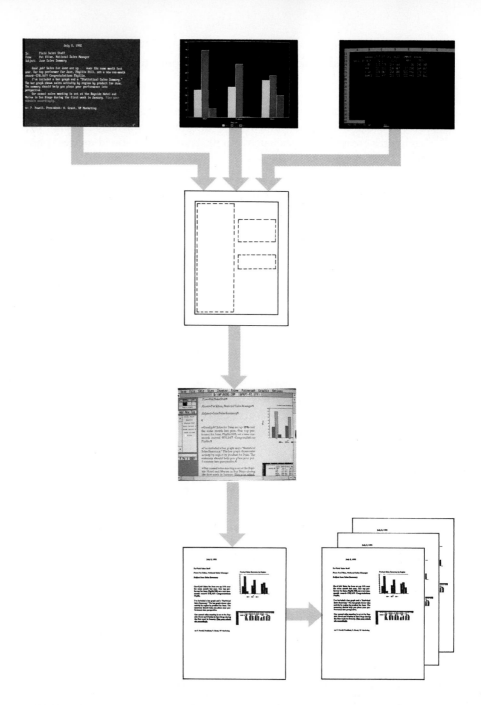

FIGURE 11–12 Preparing a Document with Desktop Publishing Software

Desktop publishing software combines text prepared using word processing software with images from a variety of sources and loads each into prepositioned frames. The graph and spreadsheet frames appear within the larger frame of the word processing text. The style sheet combines the elements, and the document is printed. The camera-ready document is reproduced in multiples.

Use

Desktop publishing software today can produce camera-ready copy for every conceivable type of printed matter, from graduation certificates to catalogs. However, many people who know DTP are not trained in the basics of creating aesthetically pleasing professional camera-ready documents. Recognizing this, businesses normally set standards for all who prepare company documents distributed to the public.

11–3 Graphics

A dollar may not buy what it used to, but a picture is still worth a thousand words. This time-honored maxim may be one of the many reasons for the explosion of **graphics software** as a productivity tool. Graphics software facilitates the creation and management of computer-based images. It can help you create pie graphs, line drawings, company logos, maps, clip art, blueprints, and just about anything else that can be drawn in the traditional manner.

The five dominant categories of graphics software are

- Paint
- Draw
- Presentation graphics
- Computer-aided design
- Screen capture and graphics conversion

Reasonably priced workstations, such as this one by Sun Microsystems, and user-friendly graphics software are major contributors to the rapid growth of computer art. Workstations have the power necessary to enable users to work efficiently with high-resolution graphic images.

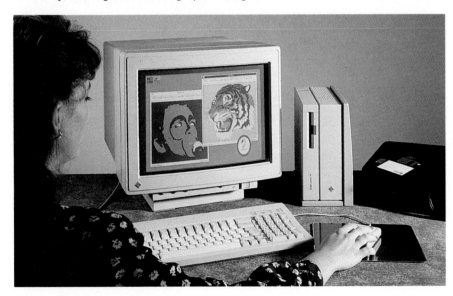

Ever since "thinking machines" first captured the public imagination, users have dreamed of conversing with a computer—a feat immortalized in science fiction tales from *2001: A Space Odyssey* to *Star Trek*. Today, advances in both *voice response* and *speech recognition* are helping to keep the dream alive.

VOICE RESPONSE: AN ACCOMPLISHED FACT

Voice response takes two forms: digitized recordings of a human voice and speech synthesis, which combines digitized phonemes to "speak" words and phrases. A *phoneme* is the smallest unit of recognizable speech; about 50 phonemes can be combined to pronounce every word in the English language.

The most prevalent application of voice response is probably directory assistance. Callers give their requests to human operators, who initiate a data base search and sometimes verify the entry desired, perhaps by confirming an address. From there, the system's audio unit takes over. A digitized recording—"The number is . . ."—is followed by a synthesized reading of the number, followed by a second recording, "If you need further assistance, . . ."

Microcomputer systems are also gaining a voice, thanks to speech-synthesizing utilities like Monologue for Windows, which will read aloud any words or numbers users highlight within Windows applications.

SPEECH RECOGNITION: A STILL EMERGING TECHNOLOGY

Building a talking computer is simple compared to the challenge of creating a computer that obeys spoken commands. First, the computer has to be equipped with artificial ears, in the form of a microphone or headset and a voice processor chip or sound board that converts the audio signals of the human voice into digital signals the computer can process. Second, the computer must be equipped with software that can decipher speech. This is an enormous programming challenge, given the vagaries of human speech.

- *Assembly-line work.* General Motors and a number of other major organizations are using speech recognition software to simplify quality control, safety reporting, and inventory recording.
- *Computer control for the disabled.* Thousands of disabled workers are using speech-recognition systems to perform such traditional applications as word processing, spreadsheets, and data base management. (One senior programmer at a major insurance company, a quadriplegic since a car accident, has resumed all professional duties, using a system he has taught about 5000 words.)
- *Telephone service.* By 1994, AT&T plans to have phased in a voice-recognition system that will au-

---

We describe the function, concepts, and use of each in this section. However, before you can fully understand the capabilities of the various categories of graphics software, first you need to know the fundamentals of how images are displayed.

Displaying and Printing Graphic Images

Depending on the software and hardware you are using, graphic images are maintained as **raster graphics** or **vector graphics**. In raster graphics, the image is composed of patterns of dots called **picture elements** or **pixels**. (The enlarged view shown in Figure 11–15 illustrates the pixel makeup of the original image.) In vector graphics, the image is composed of patterns of lines, points, and other geometric shapes (vectors). The naked eye cannot distinguish one method of graphics display from another; however, the differences are quite apparent when you try to manipulate them.

tomate the processing of most collect and third-party billing calls. The new system would combine digitized recordings ("This is a collect call from . . .") and sophisticated speech-recognition software that uses "word spotting" to filter out room noise and irrelevant words, "hearing" only the key words "yes," "no," or "operator." (The latter response would summon a human operator.)

- *Office work.* Securities traders are using speech-recognition systems to issue buy and sell orders. Another system under development would let law-enforcement officers dictate, rather than type, arrest reports. And at a major newspaper chain, copy editors are experimenting with a speech-recognition system that lets them work with spoken, not written, commands.

And what about the dream of conversing with the computer in continuous language without unnatural pauses or limited vocabulary? Two trends will be important here. One is the development of more advanced software. Sophisticated error-checking algorithms, for example, promise to improve the analysis of context and syntax needed to distinguish between similar phrases, such as "I need to check in" and "I need two chickens." The second trend is the development of more powerful, economically feasible computer systems that

can operate at 100 MIPS (millions of instructions per second)—a target that is clearly within sight. Given these two trends, experts predict, speech recognition may well replace the keyboard or the mouse by the twenty-first century.

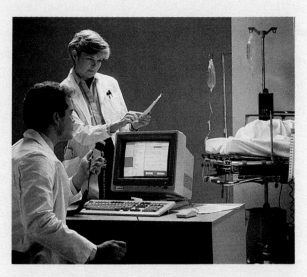

QUICK REPORTS Speech-recognition technology allows emergency-room physicians to prepare complete reports rapidly using spoken key words and phrases.

Raster Graphics Raster graphics, displayed as dot patterns, are created by digital cameras, scanners, graphics paint software, presentation graphics software, and screen capture software. Dots on the screen are arranged in rows and columns. The typical PC monitor has about 300,000 pixels in 480 rows and 640 columns. Very high-resolution monitors will have thousands of rows and columns and millions of pixels. Each dot or pixel on a monitor is assigned a number that denotes its position on the screen grid (120th row and 323rd column) and its color. On a monochrome (one-color) monitor, the pixel denotes the position and a shade of one color.

As with all internal numbers in a computer system, the numbers that describe the pixel attributes (position and color) are binary bits (1s and 0s). The number of bits needed to describe a pixel increases with the monitor's resolution and the number of colors that can be presented. Because the image is projected, or "mapped," onto the screen based on binary bits, the image is said to be **bit-mapped**. In conversation, the term *bit-mapped* may be used more frequently than the term *raster graphics.*

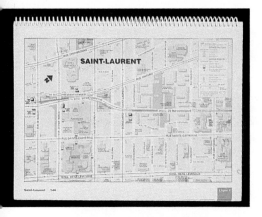

Cartographer Marie de Jocas used vector graphics–based Aldus FreeHand to develop 65 maps of the Montreal subway system. Shown here is one page of a subway booklet.

A bit-mapped image and the display of a word processing document share many similarities. Just as you can replace one word with another in word processing, you can replace one color with another in a bit-mapped image. Carrying the analogy one step further, you also can do block operations—move, copy, and delete on a user-defined area in a graphics display.

Like television, a bit-mapped image is continuously projected onto the screen, one line of dots at a time. Any changes in the display are reflected immediately. **Animation**, or movement, is accomplished by rapid repositioning (moving) of an area of the screen. For example, animation techniques give life to video-game characters.

Vector Graphics   Vectors, which are lines, points, and other geometric shapes, are configured to create the vector graphics image. The vector graphics display, in contrast to the raster graphics display, permits the user to work with objects, such as a drawing of a computer. Draw software and computer-aided design software employ vector graphics to meet the need to manipulate individual objects on the screen.

Vector graphics images take up less storage than bit-mapped images. Each pixel in the bit-mapped image must be fully described, even the background colors. Vector graphics are defined in geometric shapes, each of which can define the attributes of many pixels.

Printing/Plotting Graphics Images   In general, printers and plotters provide higher resolution output than screen displays. The resolution of a 300-dpi page printer is four times that of a VGA monitor, and lines that may appear uneven on a monitor will be more uniform when printed.

Paint Software

Paint software provides the user with a sophisticated electronic canvas. Although you can perform amazing feats with paint software, one important similarity remains between it and the traditional canvas. Whatever you draw on either one becomes part of the whole drawing. Because the canvas is a bit map, you must erase or draw over any part with which you are dissatisfied. For example, suppose you draw a green circle. You would not be able simply to replace the circle with a blue square. The paint software does not remember the circle or any other representation of an object on the screen. To replace the circle with the square, you would have to draw over (or erase) the pixels that make up the green circle, then draw in the blue square.

The user interfaces of paint programs are similar. Once you are familiar with the six items in the user interface on a typical paint screen, you are ready to use the program. Paintbrush is a paint program distributed with Microsoft's Windows. The Paintbrush user interface is illustrated in Figure 11–13 and discussed here.

- *Drawing area.* The image is created in this area.
- *Graphics cursor.* Typically, the mouse is used to move the graphics cursor to draw images and to select options. However, other pointing devices

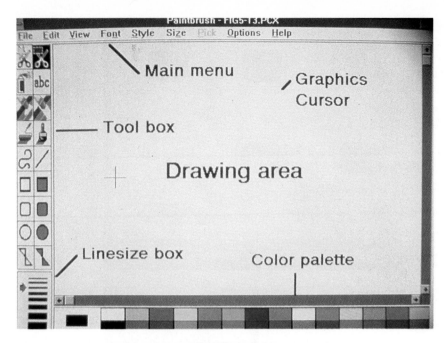

FIGURE 11–13 The Paint-Software User Interface
The user interface for Paintbrush, which is distributed with Windows, is representative of paint programs.

(discussed in Chapter 5, "Input/Output Devices") can be used to move the graphics cursor. When positioned in the drawing area, the graphics cursor takes on a variety of shapes, depending on the tool selected. Outside the drawing area, it is an arrow.

- *Main menu.* Pull-down menus appear when any of the items in the main bar menu (top of screen) are selected. Go to the main menu to load and save drawings, zoom in on a particular area for detailed editing, change the attributes of the screen fonts, copy parts of the screen, and so on.
- *Tool box.* One of the tools in the tool box is active at any given time. Use the tools to draw; to move, copy, or delete parts of the screen; to create geometric shapes; to fill defined areas with colors; to add text; and to erase.
- *Linesize box.* This box contains the width options for the drawing line.
- *Color palette.* This box contains colors and patterns that are used with the drawing tools.

The examples in Figures 11–14, 11–15, and 11–16 illustrate some of the features of paint software. The screen in Figure 11–14 illustrates the steps in creating a PC image. Each step is described here.

Step A. The *box* and *rounded box tools* (see tool box in Figure 11–13) are used to create the outlines for the monitor and the processor unit. Notice that Figure 11–14 uses the *text tool* to cross-reference the steps with letters.

Step B. The area containing the image created in Step A was *copied* to a position B, then the *paint roller tool* was used to fill in *background colors.*

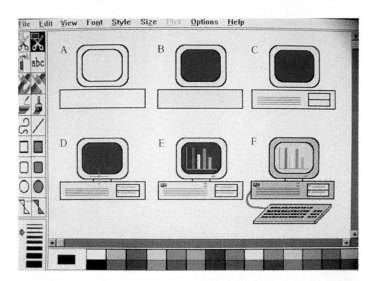

FIGURE 11–14 Creating an Image with Paint Software

This screen shows various stages in the development of a PC image.

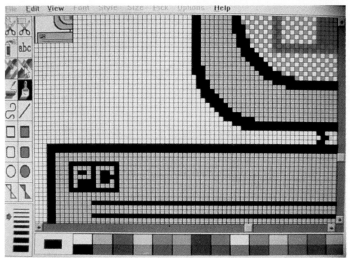

FIGURE 11–15 The Zoom Feature

In the illustration, the paint-software user has zoomed in on the upper-left corner of the processor box and the lower-right corner of the screen in the completed PC image in Figure 11–14 (Step F). Each square is a pixel. Any changes made in the enlarged version of the image are reflected in the window in the upper-left corner of the work area, which is the actual size, and in the actual image.

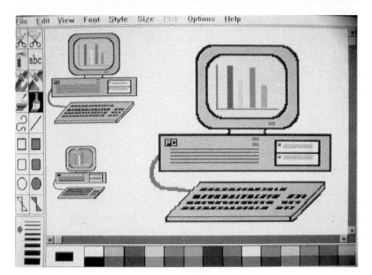

FIGURE 11–16 The Shrink–Grow Feature

The completed PC image in Figure 11–14 (Step F) is reduced and enlarged with the shrink–grow feature of paint software.

The image in each of the following steps was created from a copy of the image of the preceding step.

Step C. The *line tool* is used to draw the vents on the front of the processor unit. Drag the graphics cursor from one point to another and release the mouse button to draw the line. The two box areas for the microdisks were created with the box and line tools.

Step D. When the *brush tool* is active, the *foreground color* is drawn at the graphics cursor position. Use the brush tool for freehand drawing, such as the addition of the pedestal for the monitor. The microdisk slots and the disk-active lights are drawn with the line tool. Notice that the line width and the foreground color were changed to draw the disk slots and the lights.

Step E. A logo (upper-left corner of processor box) and a bar graph are added. The *PC* in the black logo box was drawn one pixel at a time. The *zoom-in* feature explodes a small segment of the draw area to enable the user to draw one pixel at a time (see Figure 11–15). The bar graph is drawn with the line tool. Notice that each line is drawn with a different color from the color palette.

Step F. In this final step, the beige color is *erased* to gray. Paint software permits the user to selectively switch one color for another within a user-defined area or in the entire drawing area. The keyboard was drawn with the box, line, and erase tools, then *tilted* for a three-dimensional look.

Several other important paint-software features are illustrated in Figure 11–16. The medium-sized micro in the upper-left corner of Figure 11–16 is an exact duplicate of the Step F bit-mapped image from Figure 11–14. The original image was selected with the *cutout tool*, then saved to disk. The stored image was then loaded from disk and displayed in a clear drawing area. The paint software *shrink-grow* feature was employed to shrink and enlarge the image. Notice that parts of the image may be distorted when the image is shrunk (for example, the microdisk slots) and that image resolution suffers when the image is enlarged.

Once stored as a paint graphics file, images can be manipulated in many ways. For example, scanned images can be modified or colored. Even a frame from a video recording can be integrated into a paint drawing.

Draw Software

Both paint and **draw software** enable users to create imaginative images. Perhaps the best way to explain draw software is to address the differences between it and paint software. Consider the same example we used in the paint software discussion—a drawing of a green circle, to be replaced with a blue square. As draw software permits you to isolate and manipulate representations of individual objects, you simply delete the entire green circle and copy a blue square to that position. This is not possible with paint software.

Draw software relies on vector graphics, so a specific object can be moved, copied, deleted, rotated, tilted, flipped horizontally or vertically, stretched, and squeezed. A screen image produced by draw software is actually a collage of one or more objects.

The zoom feature, available with paint and draw software, lets the user make adjustments to an enlarged view of a section of the drawing.

Presentation Graphics

Using Technology to Make the Point   Computer-generated business graphics is one of the more recent applications of computers. With few exceptions, most computer-generated graphic outputs of a decade ago were for engineers and researchers. Managers of business units who wanted a pie graph or a bar graph had it produced manually by the drafting department. This could take anywhere from a few days to weeks. Most managers, unwilling to wait, continued preparing reports and presentations in the traditional tabular manner—rows and columns of data.

Today managers of business units have powerful microcomputers and user-friendly **presentation graphics software** that allow them to create in seconds a wide variety of visually appealing and informative presentation graphics. To capture and reproduce these graphic images, they use printers and desktop plotters (for paper and transparency acetates), desktop film recorders (for 35-mm slides), and screen image projectors (to project an image onto a large screen).

During the past decade, the use of presentation graphics has become a business imperative. A progressive sales manager would never consider reporting a sales increase in tabular format. A successful year that otherwise would be obscured in rows and columns of sales figures will be vividly apparent in a colorful bar graph. Those in other areas of business also want to "put their best foot forward." To do so, they use computer-generated presentation graphics.

A number of studies confirm the power of presentation graphics. These studies uniformly support the following conclusions:

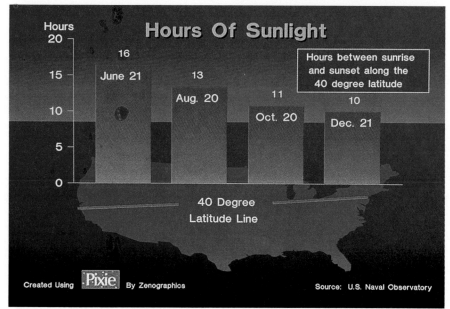

Computer graphics is a natural for the preparation of exciting presentation graphics. This bar chart vividly illustrates the variation in hours of daylight throughout the year at the fortieth parallel.

- People who use presentation graphics are perceived as being better prepared and more professional than those who do not.
- Presentation graphics can help persuade attendees or readers to adopt a particular point of view.
- Judicious use of presentation graphics tends to make meetings shorter. (Perhaps it's true that a picture is worth a thousand words!)

Whether you're preparing a report, a presentation, a newsletter, or any other form of business communication, it pays—immediately and over the long term—to take advantage of the capabilities of presentation graphics.

Output Options With presentation graphics software, you can create a variety of graphics from data in a spreadsheet or a data base, or you can enter the data within the presentation graphics program. Among the most popular presentation graphics are **pie graphs** and **bar graphs** (see Figures 11–17 and 11–18). It is also possible to produce other types of graphs, range bar charts, and scatter diagrams, annotated with *titles*, *labels*, and *legends*.

Most spreadsheet and database packages come with presentation graphics software. However, dedicated presentation graphics packages have a wider range of features that enable you to prepare more dynamic and visually appealing graphics (such as three-dimensional pie and bar graphs). Dedicated presentation graphics packages provide users with the tools they need to customize their graphs. For example, a transportation company can add another dimension to a sales-summary bar graph by

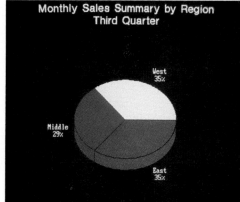

FIGURE 11–17 Pie Graph

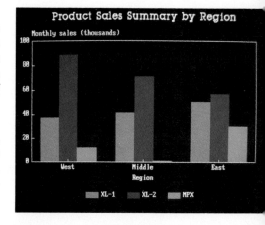

FIGURE 11–18 Bar Graph

GRAPHICS SOFTWARE
CATEGORIES

- Paint
- Draw
- Presentation graphics
- Computer-aided design
- Screen capture and conversion

FIGURE 11–19   Text Chart

topping the bars with clip art that represents the sales area (a bar of soap, an airplane, a refrigerator).

In addition to traditional business graphs, presentation graphics software provides the ability to prepare *text charts* (see lists of key points in Figure 11–19), *organization charts* (such as block charts showing the hierarchical structure of an organization, see Figure 11–20), and *maps*.

Besides offering the ability to prepare graphs and charts from user-supplied data, some presentation graphics packages let you create and store original drawings. This capability is functionally similar to that of paint and draw packages, but without their sophisticated features. Companies frequently use this capability to draw and store the image of their company logo to insert on memos, reports, and graphs.

Another recently introduced feature of presentation graphics software is the *dynamic show* capability. The dynamic show capability enables you to assemble presentation graphics in a synchronized demonstration. The show is usually presented to a small group on a single PC, or it is projected onto a large screen with a screen image projector. The dynamic show capability provides a visually interesting transition between the various graphics. For example, the current graph or image can be made to *fade out* (dissolve to a blank screen) while the next is fading in. Or the current image can be *wiped* away with the next.

The dynamic show can be further enhanced with rudimentary *animation*. Animating presentation graphics involves the rapid movement of an object, perhaps the image of an automobile, from one part of the screen to another. The animation is accomplished by moving the object in small increments of about $\frac{1}{4}$ inch in rapid succession, giving the illusion of movement. The judicious use of this capability can enliven any presentation.

FIGURE 11–20   Organization Chart

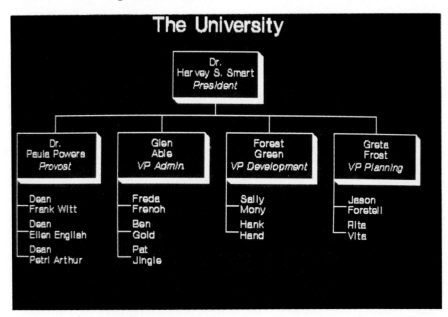

Preparing a Business Graph   Usually the data needed to produce a graph already exist in a spreadsheet or data base. The graphics software leads you through a series of prompts, the first of which asks you what type of graph is to be produced—a bar graph, a pie graph, a line graph, and so on. You then select the data to be plotted. You can also enter names for the labels. Once you have identified the source of the data (perhaps a spreadsheet or a data base), have entered the labels, and perhaps have added a title, you can plot, display, and print the graph. The preparation of bar, pie, and line graphs from spreadsheet data is illustrated in Chapter 12, "Data Management Software."

Presenting a Graph   The use of sophisticated and colorful graphics adds an aura of professionalism to any report or presentation. The actual physical presentation of a graph depends on the available hardware (for example, color page printer, plotter, and so on). Computer-generated graphic images can be re-created on paper, transparency acetates, 35-mm slides, or they can be displayed on a monitor or projected onto a large screen. These output devices are discussed in Chapter 5, "Input/Output Devices."

Computer-Aided Design

Until recently, sophisticated **computer-aided design (CAD)** was not possible in the PC environment. Now high-performance micros can be configured with very high-resolution large-screen monitors, a variety of pointing and drawing devices, plotters (of any size), and whatever else is needed to produce computer-aided graphics design. Traditionally, CAD applications have been associated with engineers and scientists; however, today PC-based CAD has opened the door to all who do design work.

Perhaps the best way to describe computer-aided design is visually, through its applications. Look at the adjacent photos to see how engineers design parts and assemblies, how artists design logos for television programs, how architects design buildings, and how others use CAD. Although generic CAD packages can accommodate almost any design application, in some application areas they can be cumbersome. In those areas where CAD has become critical to success, specialized packages have emerged. For example, specialized CAD packages are available to help industrial engineers in plant layout, to help programmers and systems analysts with the design of an information system, to help architects with the design of buildings, and to help electrical engineers with the design of integrated circuits.

Screen Capture and Graphics Conversion

Screen-capture programs are memory-resident TSRs (terminate-and-stay-resident programs) that enable users to transfer all or part of the current screen image to a disk file. For example, you can capture the summary portion of a Lotus 1-2-3 display and integrate it into a report (a word processing document). A screen is captured as a bit-mapped image (pixel format). Once on disk, it can be recalled and manipulated with a paint program.

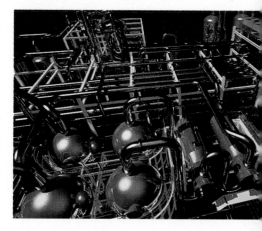

Computer-aided design (CAD) is one of the most sophisticated uses of computer graphics. This 3-D plant model was created by engineers on a CAD system at Mutoh Industries, Tokyo.

Unfortunately, there are no standards for the way graphic images are stored. Therefore, **graphics conversion** programs are needed so that graphics files can be passed between programs. Most of the popular programs that create graphic images (paint, draw, presentation graphics, spreadsheet graphics) do so in their own unique formats. Graphics conversion programs provide dozens of options. For example, you can convert an image created with a popular CAD program, AutoCAD (a vector graphics image), into Microsoft Windows Paintbrush (a bit-mapped image) for pixel-level editing. You also can convert a bit-mapped Harvard Graphics (presentation graphics program) file into a format that is compatible with a fax modem (an add-on board that can send and receive facsimile documents). If you do much work with graphics files, a good graphics conversion program is invaluable.

 Important Terms and Summary Outline

animation	full-screen editing	raster graphics
ASCII file	grammar checker	resident font
bar graph	graphics conversion	reverse video
bit-mapped	graphics software	scalable typeface
boilerplate	idea processor	screen capture
clip art	insert mode	soft font
computer-aided design	mail merge	spelling checker
(CAD)	on-line thesaurus	style checker
document-conversion	outliner	typeface
program	paint software	typeover mode
draw software	picture element	vector graphics
DTP	pie graph	word wrap
electronic dictionary	pixel	WYSIWYG
font	presentation graphics	WYSIWYG–MOL
frame	software	

11–1 WORD PROCESSING. Word processing is using the computer to enter, store, manipulate, and print text in letters, reports, books, and so on.

When you format a document, you are describing the size of the page to be printed and how you want the document to look when it is printed. To enter and edit text, you toggle between **typeover mode** and **insert mode**. **Word wrap** occurs when text that extends past the defined margins automatically wraps around to the next line. Word processing permits **full-screen editing**.

Most word processing packages are considered **WYSIWYG**, short for "What you see is what you get." Some are **WYSIWYG–MOL**.

The block-move, the block-copy, and the block-delete commands are known collectively as *block operations*, the electronic equivalent of "cut and paste." The search, or find, feature permits the user to search the entire word processing document and identify all occurrences of a particular search string.

Word processing has several features that enable users to enhance the appearance and readability of their documents. These include left and/or right justification, automatic centering, boldface, underlining, indentation, header and footer labels, pagination, hyphenation, footnotes, numbered-list/outline format, bulleted-list format, line draw, superscripts and subscripts, the insertion of an image into the running text, a variety of **fonts**, and multicolumn text.

Some word processing packages enable the automatic generation of a table of contents and an alphabetical index of key words; have a table feature that expedites the presentation of tabular data; and enable rudimentary desktop publishing.

All word processing packages allow users to save, retrieve, and delete files that contain word processing documents. The print function transforms your electronic document into a hard-copy document.

Several add-on programs are designed to enhance the functionality of word processing programs. An **on-line thesaurus** is always ready with synonyms for any word in a document. The **spelling checker** program checks every word in the text against an **electronic dictionary** and alerts the user when a word is not in the dictionary. A **grammar checker** highlights grammatical concerns and deviations from conventions. A **style checker** alerts users to such writing concerns as sexist words and hackneyed clichés. **Idea processors**, or **outliners**, can be used to organize single-line items into an outline format.

There are two ways to pass documents between different types of word processing programs—via **ASCII files** and the use of **document-conversion programs**.

Any kind of text-based document can be created with word processing software. **Boilerplate** is existing text that can in some way be customized so it can be used in a variety of word processing applications (for example, **mail merge**). Most state-of-the-art word processing packages enable the integration of text and graphic images.

11–2 DESKTOP PUBLISHING. Desktop publishing (**DTP**) refers to the capability of producing near-typeset-quality copy from the confines of a desktop. The components required for desktop publishing include document-composition software, a high-end microcomputer, a desktop page printer, an image scanner, **typefaces** and fonts, and **clip art**.

Most DTP-produced documents use a variety of typefaces, all of which fall in one of two categories—serif and sans-serif. **Soft fonts** are retrieved from disk storage and downloaded to the printer's memory as needed. A **resident font** is accessed directly from the printer's built-in ROM. **Scalable typefaces** give users the flexibility to scale them to any point size.

Typically, a DTP-produced document consists of several (often many) files. During the document-composition process, each file is assigned to a rectangular **frame**. A frame holds the text or an image of a particular file.

A DTP document will involve one or more text files, perhaps one or more picture files, a style-sheet file, and a print file. Text files are created by a word processing program. Picture files are made up of clip art and other images. The style-sheet file tells the document-composition software what to do with the text. The print file contains all the information needed to combine the text and picture files with the style sheet and print the document.

The document-composition process involves integrating graphics, photos, text, and other elements into a visually appealing layout. The steps are (1) prepare text and graphics; (2) create the style sheet; (3) combine text and picture files in frames; and (4) print the document.

11–3 GRAPHICS. **Graphics software** facilitates the creation and management of computer-based images. The five dominant categories of graphics software are paint, draw, presentation graphics, computer-aided design, and screen capture and graphics conversion.

Graphic images are presented as **raster graphics** or **vector graphics**. In raster, or **bit-mapped**, graphics, the image is composed of patterns of dots (**picture elements**, or **pixels**). In vector graphics, the image is composed of patterns of lines, points, and other geometric shapes (vectors). **Animation**, or movement, is accomplished by rapidly repositioning an area of the screen.

Paint software provides the user with a sophisticated electronic canvas. Whatever you draw on either the traditional or the electronic canvas becomes part of the whole drawing. The six items in a paint program's user interface are the drawing area, graphics cursor, main menu, tool box, linesize box, and color palette.

Draw software permits you to create a screen image, then isolate and manipulate representations of individual objects within the overall image. Draw software relies on vector graphics, so a specific object can be dealt with independently.

User-friendly **presentation graphics software** enables users to create a wide variety of visually appealing and informative presentation graphics. Among the most popular are **bar graphs** and **pie graphs**. Presentation graphics software also permits the preparation of text charts, organization charts, maps, and original drawings. These graphic images are captured and reproduced on printers, desktop plotters, desktop film recorders, and screen image projectors. Some sophisticated packages allow you to present dynamic shows.

High-performance microcomputers that support **computer-aided design (CAD)** are configured with very high-resolution large-screen monitors, a variety of pointing and drawing devices, plotters, and sometimes other design-oriented devices. CAD applications include everything from television graphics to engineering design.

Screen-capture programs are TSRs that enable users to transfer all or part of the current screen image to a disk file. **Graphics conversion** programs help users pass graphics files between programs.

 Review Exercises

Concepts

1. What is the function of word processing software?

2. What must be specified when formatting a document?

3. What is meant when a document is formatted to be justified on the right and on the left?

4. Text is entered in either of which two modes? Which mode would you select to change *the table* to *the long table*? Which mode would you select to change *pick the choose* to *pick and choose*?

5. What causes text to wrap around?

6. Give an example of when you might issue a global search-and-replace command.

7. When running the spelling checker, what options does the system present when it encounters an unidentified word?

8. What productivity software package has the capability of producing near-typeset-quality copy for printing jobs?

9. Name two software components and two hardware components of a desktop publishing system.

10. What is the shape of a desktop publishing frame?

11. What term is used to refer to prepackaged electronic images?

12. Which DTP file tells the document-composition software what do with the text?

13. What term is frequently used in place of *raster graphics*?

14. Which type of graphics software package provides a computer-based version of the painter's canvas?

15. What type of graphics software package enables the generation of a wide variety of presentation graphics?

16. What presentation graphics software capability enables users to assemble presentation graphics in a synchronized show?

17. What type of TSR program enables users to transfer all or part of the current screen image to a disk file?

Discussion

18. Customer-service representatives at Zimco Enterprises spend almost 70% of their day interacting directly with customers. Approximately one hour each day is spent preparing courtesy follow-up letters, primarily to enhance good will between Zimco and its customers. Do you think the "personalized" letters are a worthwhile effort? Why or why not?

19. Describe the relationship between word processing, electronic images, and desktop publishing software.

20. With the advent of desktop publishing, the number of printed items bearing the company logo has increased dramatically. Many companies require that all such documents be approved by a central DTP review board prior to distribution. What concerns prompted these managers to establish the review board?

Problem Solving

21. You work for a large department store chain and have been given the task of designing an internal monthly newsletter that will be distributed to all employees who sell men's and women's clothing. Suggest a name for the newsletter and an overall layout (for example, how many columns, size of title, location of page number, headers, footers, font sizes, scheme for numbering issues, and so on). Draw a rough sketch of the layout, noting dimensions where applicable.

22. A bar graph that was created with a presentation graphics package needs to be integrated into a report that is being created camera-ready with DTP software. The bar graph is in Lotus 1-2-3 PIC format, but the DTP package accepts only graphics files in PCX format. Describe two approaches that would enable you to integrate the bar graph into the report.

 Self-Test (by section)

11–1 a. Preset format specifications are referred to as <u>default</u>.

b. To add a word in the middle of an existing sentence in a word processing document, you would use the insert mode. (T̶/F)

c. Which word processing feature enables the automatic numbering of pages of a document: (a̶) pagination, (b) page breaking, or (c) footers?

d. The word processing feature that automatically breaks long words that fall at the end of a line is called <u>hyphenation</u>

e. An on-line thesaurus can be used to suggest synonyms for a word in a word processing document. (T̶/F)

11–2 a. The type of printer normally associated with desktop publishing is the daisy-wheel printer. (T/F̶)

✗ **b.** The output of the desktop publishing process is <u>ready</u> ^{CAMERA} copy.

✗ **c.** What device re-creates a black-and-white version of an image in an electronic format: (a̶) image scanner, (b) image-reduction aid, or (c) vision-entry device?

✗ **d.** The height of a 36-point typeface is: (a) ¼ inch, (b̶) ½ inch, or (c) 1 inch?

✗ **e.** Fontware is that component of the document-composition software that enables WYSIWYG display of DTP documents. (T/F̶)

11–3 a. Presentation graphics software allows users to create charts and line drawings. (T̶/F)

b. In raster graphics, the image is composed of patterns of: (a) vectors, (b) pictures, or (c̶) dots?

✗ **c.** Which of the following would be an unlikely entry in a paint program's tool box: (a) create rectangle, (b̶) select color palette, or (c) erase?

d. <u>Organization</u> charts show the hierarchical structure of an organization.

✗ **e.** Bit-mapped files cannot be converted to a format that is compatible with fax modems. (T/F̶)

Self-test answers.   11–1 **(a)** default settings; **(b)** T; **(c)** a; **(d)** hyphenation; **(e)** T. 11–2 **(a)** F; **(b)** camera-ready; **(c)** a; **(d)** b; **(e)** F. 11–3 **(a)** T; **(b)** c; **(c)** b; **(d)** Organization; **(e)** F.

Data Management Software

STUDENT LEARNING OBJECTIVES

▶ To describe the function, purpose, and applications of spreadsheet software.

▶ To discuss common spreadsheet concepts.

▶ To describe how presentation graphics can be created from spreadsheet data.

▶ To describe the function, purpose, and applications of database software.

▶ To discuss common database software concepts.

▶ To grasp the applications and potential of hypertext and hypermedia.

▶ To be familiar with a variety of applications-specific data management tools.

12–1 Spreadsheet: The Magic Matrix

Function

The name *spreadsheet* aptly describes this software's fundamental application. The spreadsheet has been a common business tool for centuries. Before computers, the ledger (a book of spreadsheets) was the accountant's primary tool for keeping a record of financial transactions. A professor's grade book is also set up in spreadsheet format.

The information contained in a spreadsheet full of numbers is seldom obvious and, consequently, may not be apparent to the reader. However, trends, extraordinary efforts, and problem areas become easy to perceive when the same data are summarized in graph form. Quattro Pro (shown here) and other spreadsheets have the capability to display numerical results in illustrative presentation graphics.

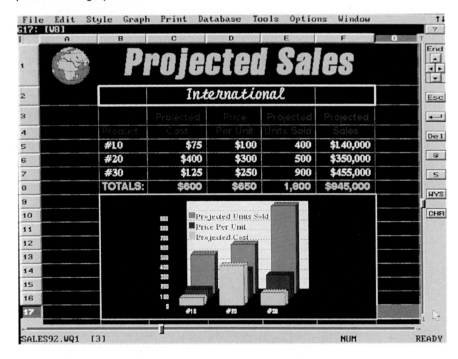

Spreadsheets are simply an electronic alternative to thousands of traditionally manual tasks. No longer are we confined to using pencils, erasers, and hand calculators to deal with rows and columns of data. Think of anything that has rows and columns of data and you have identified an application for spreadsheet software: income (profit-and-loss) statements, personnel profiles, demographic data, and budget summaries, just to mention a few. Because spreadsheets parallel so many of our manual tasks, they are enjoying widespread acceptance.

All commercially available spreadsheet packages enable you to manipulate rows and columns of data. However, the *user interface,* or the manner in which you enter data and commands, differs from one package to the next. The conceptual coverage that follows is generic: It applies to all spreadsheets.

Concepts

Pat Kline, the national sales manager for Zimco Enterprises, a manufacturer of high-tech products (the XL-1, the XL-2, and the MPX) uses spreadsheet software to compile a monthly sales summary. We will use Pat's June sales summary, shown in Figure 12–1, to demonstrate spreadsheet concepts. Pat uses a monthly sales **template** each month. The template, simply a spreadsheet model, contains the layout and formulas needed to produce the summary in Figure 12–1. Pat entered only the data for the current month (June in the example) and the spreadsheet template did all the needed calculations.

Viewing Data in a Spreadsheet   Scrolling through a spreadsheet is much like looking through a magnifying glass as you move it around a newspaper page. You scroll left and right (horizontal scrolling) and/or up and down (vertical scrolling) to see different portions of a large spreadsheet. In

FIGURE 12–1   A Monthly Sales Summary Spreadsheet Template
This spreadsheet template is the basis for the explanation and demonstration of spreadsheet concepts.

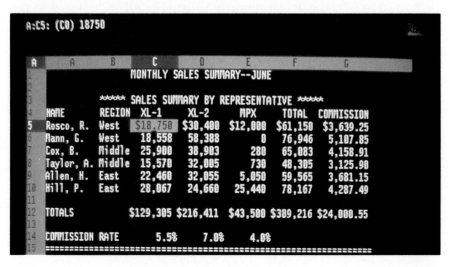

Figure 12–1, the entire sales summary can be displayed on a single screen. However, if 5 more products or 20 more salespeople were added, Pat would scroll horizontally and vertically to view the entire spreadsheet. Scrolling is discussed and illustrated in Chapter 3, "Interacting with Personal Computers."

Organization   Spreadsheets are organized in a *tabular structure* with *rows* and *columns*. The intersection of a particular row and column designates a **cell**. As you can see in Figure 12–1, the rows are *numbered* and the columns are *lettered*. Single letters identify the first 26 columns; double letters are used thereafter (A, B, . . . Z; AA, AB, . . . AZ; BA, BB, . . . BZ). The number of rows or columns available to you depends on the size of your micro's RAM (random-access memory). Most spreadsheets permit hundreds of columns and thousands of rows.

Data are entered and stored in a cell at the intersection of a column and a row. During operations, data are referred to by their **cell address**. A cell address identifies the location of a cell in the spreadsheet by its column and row, with the column designator first. For example, in the monthly sales summary of Figure 12–1, C4 is the address of the column heading for product XL-1, and D5 is the address of the total amount of XL-2 sales for R. Rosco ($30,400).

In the spreadsheet work area (the rows and columns), a movable highlighted area "points" to the *current cell*. This highlighted area, called the **pointer**, can be moved around the spreadsheet with the arrow keys (→ ← ↑ ↓) to any cell address. To add or edit (revise) an entry at a particular cell, the pointer must be moved to that cell. The address and content of the current cell (the location of the pointer) are displayed in the user-interface portion of the spreadsheet, the area above and/or below the spreadsheet work area (above in Figure 12–1). Specifically, the information for a particular cell (Cell C5 in Figure 12–1) is displayed in a *cell status line*. The content, or resulting value (for example, from a formula), of each cell is shown in the spreadsheet work area. The current cell is displayed in reverse video (black on white or, for color monitors, black on a color). Also notice in Figure 12–1 that when the pointer is positioned at C5, the actual numeric value (18750) is displayed as the cell contents in the user interface, and an optional *formatted* version ($18,750) is displayed in C5.

Cell Entries   To make an entry in the spreadsheet, simply move the pointer with the arrow keys to the appropriate cell, and key in the data. To *edit* (revise) or replace an existing entry, you also move the pointer to the appropriate cell. Key in the new or revised entry in the user-interface panel beside the cell address (see Figure 12–1). Once you have completed work on a particular entry, press the ENTER key or an arrow key to insert the entry in the actual spreadsheet.

Spreadsheet packages allow the user to vary the column width to improve readability. The width for Column A in Figure 12–1 is set at 11 positions; the width for Column B is set at 6 positions.

Ranges   Many spreadsheet operations ask you to designate a **range** of cells. The four types of ranges are highlighted in Figure 12–2:

11						
12	TOTALS		$129,305	$216,411	$43,500	$389,216	$24,000.55
13						
14	COMMISSION RATE		5.5%	7.0%	4.0%	

(a)

			***** SALES SUMMARY BY REPRESENTATIVE *****				
3							
4	NAME	REGION	XL-1	XL-2	MPX	TOTAL	COMMISSION
5	Rosco, R.	West	$18,750	$30,400	$12,000	$61,150	$3,639.25
6	Mann, G.	West	18,558	58,388	0	76,946	5,107.85
7	Cox, B.	Middle	25,900	38,903	280	65,083	4,158.91
8	Taylor, A.	Middle	15,570	32,005	730	48,305	3,125.90
9	Allen, H.	East	22,460	32,055	5,050	59,565	3,681.15
10	Hill, P.	East	28,067	24,660	25,440	78,167	4,287.49
11							

(b)

11						
12	TOTALS		$129,305	$216,411	$43,500	$389,216	$24,000.55
13						
14	COMMISSION RATE		5.5%	7.0%	4.0%	

(c)

			***** SALES SUMMARY BY REPRESENTATIVE *****				
3							
4	NAME	REGION	XL-1	XL-2	MPX	TOTAL	COMMISSION
5	Rosco, R.	West	$18,750	$30,400	$12,000	$61,150	$3,639.25
6	Mann, G.	West	18,558	58,388	0	76,946	5,107.85
7	Cox, B.	Middle	25,900	38,903	280	65,083	4,158.91
8	Taylor, A.	Middle	15,570	32,005	730	48,305	3,125.90
9	Allen, H.	East	22,460	32,055	5,050	59,565	3,681.15
10	Hill, P.	East	28,067	24,660	25,440	78,167	4,287.49
11							

(d)

FIGURE 12–2 Spreadsheet Ranges

The highlighted cells in these spreadsheet displays illustrate the four types of ranges: (a) cell (G12), (b) column (A5..A10), (c) row (C14..E14), and (d) block (C5..E10).

    a. A single cell (Example range is G12.)

    b. All or part of a column of adjacent cells (Example range is A5..A10.)

    c. All or part of a row of adjacent cells (Example range is C14..E14.)

    d. A rectangular block of cells (Example range is C5..E10.)

A particular range is indicated by the addresses of the endpoint cells separated by two periods. (Some packages use only one period or a colon, for example: C5.E10 or C5:E10.) Any cell can comprise a single-cell range. The range for the commission percentages in Figure 12–2 is C14..E14, and the range for the row labels (salespeople's names) is A5..A10. The range of sales amounts for the three products is indicated by any two opposite-corner cell addresses (for example, C5..E10 or E5..C10).

When you want to copy, move, or erase a portion of the spreadsheet, you must first define the range you wish to copy, move, or erase.

Types of Cell Entries   An entry to a cell is classified as either a *text* (also called *label*) entry, a *numeric* entry, or a *formula* entry.

Text entries. A text entry, or a label, is a word, a phrase, or any string of alphanumeric text (spaces included) that occupies a particular cell. In Figure 12–1, "NAME" in Cell A4 is a text entry, as is "COMMISSION" in G4 and "MONTHLY SALES SUMMARY—JUNE" in C1. Notice that the label in C1 extends across Columns C, D, and E. This is possible when the adjacent cells (D1 and E1) are blank. If an entry were made in D1, only the first nine positions (the width of Column C) of the entry in Cell C1 would be visible on the spreadsheet (that is, "MONTHLY S"). Unless otherwise specified, text entries are left-justified and numeric entries are right-justified (lined up on the right edge of the column). However, you can specify that any entry be left- or right-justified or centered in the column. In Figure 12–1 all column headings except "NAME" are centered.

Numeric and formula entries. In Figure 12–1, the dollar sales values in the range C5..E10 are numeric. The dollar sales values in the ranges F5..G10 and C12..G12 are results of formulas. Cell F5 contains a formula, but it is the numeric result (for example, $61,150 in Figure 12–3) that is displayed in the spreadsheet work area. With the pointer positioned at F5, the formula appears in the cell contents line in the user-interface panel, and the actual numeric value appears in the spreadsheet work area (see Figure 12–3). The formula value in F5 computes the total sales made by the salesperson in Row 5 for all three products (that is, total sales is +C5+D5+E5).

Spreadsheet formulas use standard notation for **arithmetic operators**: + (add), − (subtract), * (multiply), / (divide), ^ (raise to a power, or exponentiation). The formula in F5 (top of Figure 12–3) computes the total sales for R. Rosco. The range F6..F10 contains similar formulas that apply to their respective rows (+C6+D6+E6, +C7+D7+E7, and so on). For example, the formula in F6 computes the total sales for G. Mann. More examples of formulas from the MONTHLY SALES SUMMARY spreadsheet are shown in Figure 12–8.

Spreadsheet Formulas This section expands on the use and application of formulas—the essence of spreadsheet operations. A formula enables the spreadsheet software to perform numeric and/or string calculations

FIGURE 12–3 Spreadsheet Formulas
The actual content of F5 is the formula in the user-interface panel in the upper-left part of the screen. The result of the formula appears in the spreadsheet at F5.

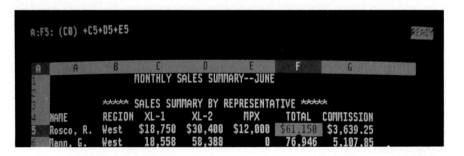

and/or logic operations that result in a numeric value (for example, 18750) or an alphanumeric character string (for example, *ABOVE QUOTA* or *BELOW QUOTA*).

Relative and absolute cell addressing. The formulas in the range G5..G10 (see Figures 12–4 and 12–8) compute the commission for the salespeople based on the commission rates listed in Row 14. The commission rates vary from month to month. The percentages in Row 14 reflect the rates for June. The commission for R. Rosco is computed by the following formula.

G5: +$C$14*C5+$D$14*D5+$E$14*E5

The distinction between the way the sales amounts and the commission-rate variables are represented in the formula highlights an important concept in spreadsheets, that of **relative cell addressing** and **absolute cell addressing**. The dollar signs ($), which preface both the column and row in an absolute cell address ($C$14), distinguish it from a relative cell address (C5). *The relative cell address is based on its position relative to the cell containing the formula.* If the contents of a cell containing a formula are copied to another cell, the relative cell addresses in the copied formula are revised to reflect its new position, but the absolute cell addresses are unchanged.

The two types of cell addressing are illustrated in the spreadsheet in Figure 12–5. Suppose the formula B3*$E$1 is in Cell A1. B3 is a relative cell address that is one column to the right of and two rows down from A1. If this formula is copied to C2, the formula in C2 is D4*$E$1.

FIGURE 12–4 Spreadsheet Formulas with Relative and Absolute Cell Addresses

Each of the commission computation formulas in the range G5..G10 has the same multipliers—the commission rates in the range C14..E14. Because the relative positions between the commission formulas in G5..G10 and the commission rates in C14..E14 vary from row to row, the commission rates are entered as absolute cell addresses.

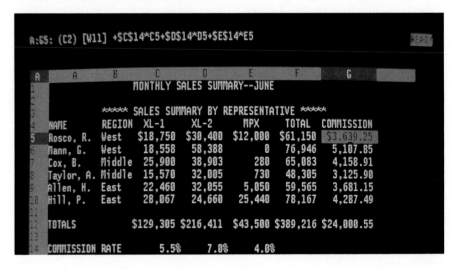

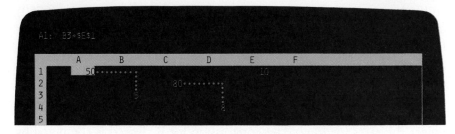

FIGURE 12–5 Relative and Absolute Cell Addressing
When the formula in A1 is copied to C2, the formula in C2 becomes D4*$E$1.

Notice that D4 has the same *relative position* to the formula in Cell C2 as B3 has to the formula in Cell A1: one column to the right and two rows down. The *absolute cell address* ($E$1) remains the same in both formulas.

Copying formulas. In creating the spreadsheet template for the monthly sales summary, Pat Kline entered only one formula to compute salesperson commission—in G5 (see Figure 12–4). Then spreadsheet commands were selected that *copied*, or *replicated*, the formula into each cell in the range G6..G10. Notice in the following copied formulas for G. Mann and B. Cox (rows 6 and 7) how the absolute addresses ($C$14, $D$14, and $E$14) remained the same in each formula and the relative addresses were revised to reflect the applicable row.

G6: +$C$14*C6+$D$14*D6+$E$14*E6

G7: +$C$14*C7+$D$14*D7+$E$14*E7

The formula in G6 (above) applies to the sales data in the cells adjacent to G. Mann, not R. Rosco (as in the formula in G5). The same is true of other formulas in the range G5..G10.

Creating spreadsheet formulas. A formula may include one or all of the following: *arithmetic operations, functions, string operations,* and *logic operations.* The first two are discussed here in more detail. String operations (for example, joining, or *concatenating,* character strings) and logic operations (formulas that involve relational operators, such as < and >, and logic operators, such as *AND* and *OR*) are beyond the scope of this presentation.

When you design the spreadsheet, keep in mind where you want to place the formulas and what you want them to accomplish. Because formulas are based on relative position, you will need a knowledge of the layout and organization of the data in the spreadsheet. When you define a formula, you must first determine what you wish to achieve (for example, to calculate total sales for the first salesperson). Then select a cell location for the formula (for example, F5), and create the formula by connecting relative cell addresses, absolute cell addresses, and/or numbers with operators, as appropriate. In many instances, you will copy the formula to other locations. For example, in Figure 12–4, F5 (total for a salesperson) was copied to each cell in F6..F10.

Memory Bits

SPREADSHEET ORGANIZATION

- Tabular structure
  Numbered rows
  Lettered columns
- Row/column intersect at cell
- Cell address locates cell
- Pointer highlights current cell
- Cell entry types
  Text (label)
  Numeric
  Formula
- Cell addressing
  Relative
  Absolute

Spreadsheet applications begin with a blank screen and an idea. The spreadsheet you create is a product of skill and imagination. What you get from a spreadsheet depends on how effectively you use formulas.

Arithmetic operations. Formulas containing arithmetic operators are resolved according to a hierarchy of operations. That is, when more than one operator is included in a single formula, the spreadsheet software uses a set of rules to determine which operation to do first, second, and so on. In the hierarchy of operations illustrated in Figure 12–6, exponentiation has the highest priority, followed by multiplication-division and addition-subtraction. In the case of a tie (for example, * and /, or + and −), the formula is evaluated *from left to right*. *Parentheses*, however, override the priority rules. Expressions placed in parentheses have priority and are evaluated innermost first and left to right.

The steps in the evaluation of the formula that results in the value in G5 ($3639.25) of Figure 12–4 is shown below:

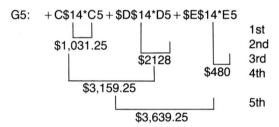

Following the hierarchy of operations, the three multiplications are performed first (leftmost first). The products are then added to arrive at the result in G5.

Pat Kline's monthly sales summary template also includes a "Sales Summary by Region" in Rows 16 through 20 (see Figure 12–7). All the formulas in the spreadsheet of Figure 12–7 are listed in Figure 12–8.

Functions. Spreadsheets offer users a wide variety of predefined operations called **functions**. These functions can be used to create formulas that perform mathematical, logical, statistical, financial, and character-string operations on spreadsheet data. To use a function, simply enter the desired function name (for example, SUM for "Compute the sum") and enter the **argument**. Some spreadsheet programs require the user to prefix the function with a symbol such as @. (The symbol may vary from

FIGURE 12–6   Hierarchy of Operations

The Hierarchy of Operations	
OPERATION	**OPERATOR**
Exponentiation	∧
Multiplication-Division	* /
Addition-Subtraction	+ −

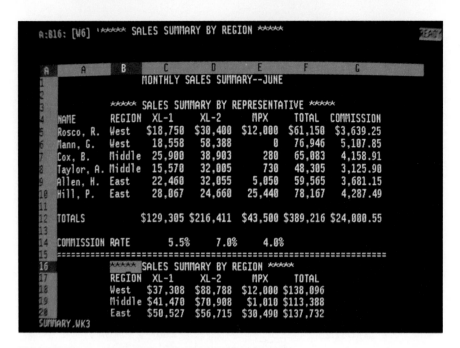

FIGURE 12–7 Expanding an Existing Template

The "Sales Summary by Region" portion of the template is extrapolated from the data in the "Sales Summary by Representative" portion.

one software package to the next.) The argument, which is placed in parentheses, identifies the data to be operated on. The argument can be one or several numbers, character strings, or ranges that represent data.

In the spreadsheet in Figure 12–7, the "TOTALS" for each column (C12..G12) are determined by adding the amounts in the respective

FIGURE 12–8 Actual Content of Formula Cells

This figure illustrates the actual content of the cells in Figure 12–7 that contain formulas. In an actual spreadsheet display, the formulas would be resolved when displayed (F5 would appear as $61,150).

	A	B	C	D	E	F	G	H	I
1			MONTHLY SALES SUMMARY--JUNE						
2									
3			***** SALES SUMMARY BY REPRESENTATIVE *****						
4	NAME	REGION	XL-1	XL-2	MPX	TOTAL		COMMISSION	
5	Rosco, R.	West	$18,750	$30,400	$12,000	+C5+D5+E5	+$C$14*C5+$D$14*D5+$E$14*E5		
6	Mann, G.	West	18,558	58,388	0	+C6+D6+E6	+$C$14*C6+$D$14*D6+$E$14*E6		
7	Cox, B.	Middle	25,900	38,903	280	+C7+D7+E7	+$C$14*C7+$D$14*D7+$E$14*E7		
8	Taylor, A.	Middle	15,570	32,005	730	+C8+D8+E8	+$C$14*C8+$D$14*D8+$E$14*E8		
9	Allen, H.	East	22,460	32,055	5,050	+C9+D9+E9	+$C$14*C9+$D$14*D9+$E$14*E9		
10	Hill, P.	East	28,067	24,660	25,440	+C10+D10+E10	+$C$14*C10+$D$14*D10+$E$14*E10		
11									
12	TOTALS		@SUM(C5..C10)	@SUM(D5..D10)	@SUM(E5..E10)	@SUM(F5..F10)	@SUM(G5..G10)		
13									
14	COMMISSION RATE		5.5%	7.0%	4.0%				
15		===							
16			***** SALES SUMMARY BY REGION *****						
17		REGION	XL-1	XL-2	MPX	TOTAL			
18		West	+C5+C6	+D5+D6	+E5+E6	+C18+D18+E18			
19		Middle	+C7+C8	+D7+D8	+E7+E8	+C19+D19+E19			
20		East	+C9+C10	+D9+D10	+E9+E10	+C20+D20+E20			

columns. For example, the total sales for the XL-1 is determined with the following formula.

C12: +C5+C6+C7+C8+C9+C10

Or the total sales for the XL-1 can be computed with a function and its argument:

C10: @SUM(C5..C10)

The use of predefined functions can save a lot of time. What if the range to be added were C5..C100? Other spreadsheet functions include trigonometric functions, square roots, comparisons of values, manipulations of strings of data, computation of net present value and internal rate of return, and a variety of techniques for statistical analysis.

Pat Kline has included a "Statistical Sales Summary" on the second screen of the spreadsheet template in Rows 21 through 27 (see Figure 12–9). The summary uses three common statistical functions: low or minimum (@MIN), average (@AVG), and high or maximum (@MAX). For example, @MIN(C5..C10), the statistical function in C24 of Figure 12–9, determines the minimum sales amount for the XL-1. The actual formulas in Rows 21 through 27 are shown in Figure 12–10. Vendors of spreadsheet software create slightly different names for their functions.

Formatting Data for Readability   The appearance of data in the spreadsheet of Figures 12–7 and 12–9 has been modified to enhance readability. For example, the value .055 was entered as the rate of commission for the XL-1 in C14 (Figure 12–7), but it appears in the spreadsheet display as a percent (5.5%). This is because the range C14..E14 was *formatted* so the values are automatically displayed as percentages with one decimal place rather than as decimals.

FIGURE 12–9   Spreadsheet Functions
The "Statistical Sales Summary" portion of the template is extrapolated from the data in the "Sales Summary by Representative" portion (see Figure 12–7). The statistical summary employs the minimum (@MIN), average (@AVG), and maximum (@MAX) functions (see Figure 12–10).

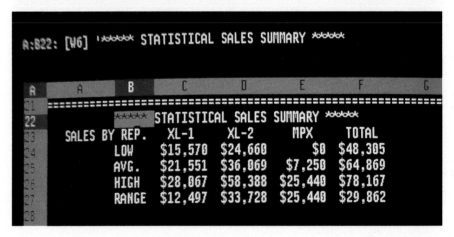

```
        A        B          C              D              E              F
21  ===============================================================================
22            ***** STATISTICAL SALES SUMMARY *****
23  SALES BY REP.   XL-1           XL-2           MPX            TOTAL
24            LOW   @MIN(C5..C10)  @MIN(D5..D10)  @MIN(E5..E10)  @MIN(F5..F10)
25            AVG.  @AVG(C5..C10)  @AVG(D5..D10)  @AVG(E5..E10)  @AVG(F5..F10)
26            HIGH  @MAX(C5..C10)  @MAX(D5..D10)  @MAX(E5..E10)  @MAX(F5..F10)
27            RANGE +C26-C24       +D26-D24       +E26-E24       +F26-F24
```

FIGURE 12–10 Actual Content of Formula Cells
This figure illustrates the actual content of the cells in Figure 12–9 that contain formulas.

All currency amounts entered in the spreadsheet template of Figure 12–7 were entered without commas or dollar signs. The currency amounts are formatted so that commas and a dollar sign (first row and totals) are inserted. For example, in Figure 12–7 the value for R. Rosco's XL-1 sales was entered as 18750 in C4, which is formatted for currency. Notice that it is displayed as $18,750.

Numeric data can be defined so they are displayed with a fixed number of places to the right of the decimal point. In Figure 12–7, the format of the sales data in the range C5..F10 is currency with the number

The monthly sales summary example in the text is presented on a two-dimensional worksheet in rows and columns. Some electronic spreadsheet packages permit three-dimensional spreadsheets. A 3-D spreadsheet has multiple worksheets. This 3-D example contains a monthly sales summary for the current month (June) and the previous two months (May and April). The cell references in 3-D spreadsheets are prefaced with the letter of the worksheet. In the photo, the pointer is on Cell C:C1, the title of the report. The titles of the other two reports are in Cells A:C1 and B:C1. A quarterly sales summary can be compiled in a fourth worksheet (D) by adding like cells in Worksheets A, B, and C. For example, the XL-1 sales by R. Rosco for the quarter would be computed in Cell D:C5 by the formula A:C5 + B:C5 + C:C5.

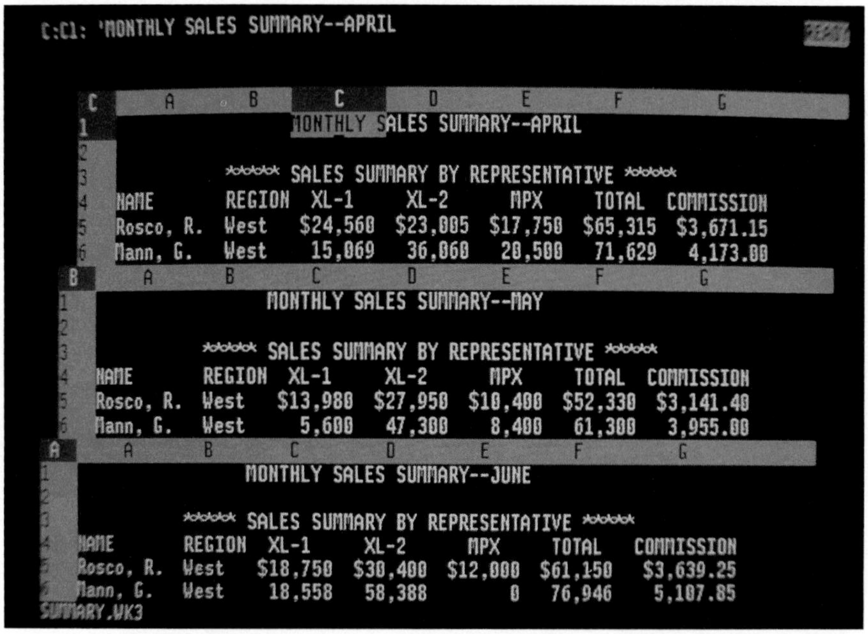

of decimal places fixed at zero. Numbers with more decimal digits than specified in the format are rounded when displayed. The amounts in the "COMMISSION" column of the spreadsheet of Figure 12–7 are formatted to be displayed as currency with two decimal places.

Use

The possibilities of what Pat Kline, you, and others can do with spreadsheet software and micros are endless. Find any set of numbers and you have identified a potential application for spreadsheet software.

Spreadsheet Templates　The spreadsheet in Figures 12–7 and 12–9 is a *template*, or a model, for Pat Kline's monthly sales summary. All Pat has to do is enter the sales data for the current month in the range C5.. E10. All other data are calculated with formulas.

Most spreadsheet applications eventually take the form of a spreadsheet template. Once created, the template becomes the basis for handling a certain type of data (for example, monthly sales data).

Spreadsheet templates are modified easily. For example, any of these modifications of Figures 12–7 and 12–9 would require only a few minutes: Add another column to accommodate a new product; delete a row to accommodate one less salesperson; compute the standard deviation for XL-1 sales data; and change the rate of commission for the XL-1 to 6.0%.

"What If" Analysis　The real beauty of a spreadsheet is that if you change the value of a cell, all other affected cells are revised accordingly. This capability makes spreadsheet software the perfect tool for "what if" analysis. For example, Pat Kline used the current data to assess how commissions might be affected if each of the rates of commission were increased by 0.5% (for example, from 5.5% to 6.0% for the XL-1). The resulting spreadsheet in Figure 12–11 indicates that the salesperson earning the highest commission (G. Mann) would have earned almost $400 more— $5,493 versus $5,108) under the proposed commission rates.

Spreadsheet Graphics　Most commercial spreadsheet packages are *integrated packages*, combining spreadsheet, presentation graphics, and database capabilities. The graphics component enables users to present spreadsheet data as business graphs (see Chapter 11, "Text and Image Processing Software"), the most popular of which are the *bar*, *pie*, and *line graphs* (as seen in Figures 12–13, 12–15, and 12–16, respectively). The user responds to a series of prompts to generate a graph. The first prompt asks the user to select the type of graph to be generated. The user then identifies the source of the data, enters labels and titles, and so on.

Pat Kline, the national sales manager who produced the monthly sales summary spreadsheet in the last section, is an avid user of spreadsheet and presentation graphics software. The spreadsheet segment in Figure 12–12 consists of Rows 15 through 20 of the monthly sales summary spreadsheet in Figure 12–7. The spreadsheet in Figure 12–12 is the basis for the preparation of bar, pie, and line graphs in the following sections.

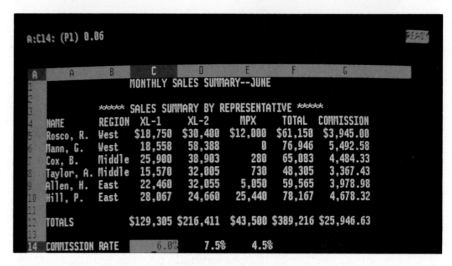

FIGURE 12–11   Spreadsheet "What If" Analysis
"What if" each of the commission rates were increased by 0.5%? This spreadsheet reflects the commissions that would have been earned had the increase been in effect.

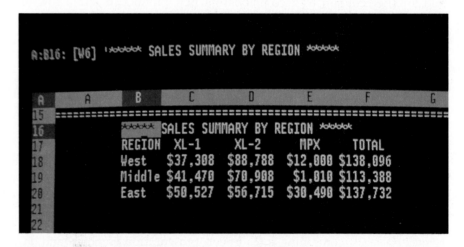

FIGURE 12–12   Spreadsheet Sales Data for Graphs
The bar, pie, and line graphs of Figures 12–13 through 12–16 are derived from these sales figures.

Bar graphs.   To prepare the bar graph in Figure 12–13, Pat had to specify appropriate ranges; that is, the values in the "TOTAL" column (Range F18..B20 of Figure 12–12) are to be plotted, and the region names (Range B18..B20 in Figure 12–12) are to be inserted as labels along the horizontal, or *x*, axis. Pat also added a title for the graph ("Monthly Sales Summary by Region"), and titles for the *x* axis ("Region"), and the vertical, or *y*, axis ("Monthly Sales").

The sales figures for each region in Figure 12–12 (Range C18..E20) can be plotted in a *stacked-bar graph*. The resulting graph, shown in Figure 12–14, permits Pat Kline to better understand the regional distribution

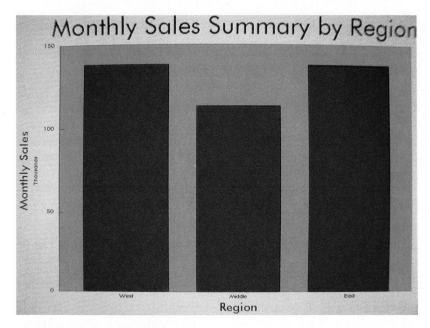

FIGURE 12–13 Bar Graph
The total sales for each region in Figure 12–12 are represented in this bar graph.

FIGURE 12–14 Stacked-Bar Graph
Regional sales for each of the three products in Figure 12–12 are represented in this stacked-bar graph.

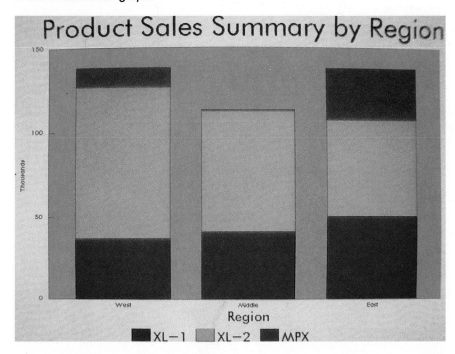

of sales. The *clustered-bar graph*, which includes a vertical bar for each product within each region, is an alternative to the stacked-bar graph in Figure 12–14. These bar graphs visually highlight the relative contribution each product has made to the total sales for each region.

Pie graphs. Pie graphs are the most basic of presentation graphics. A pie graph illustrates each "piece" of data in its proper relationship to the whole "pie." To illustrate how a pie graph is constructed and used, refer again to the monthly sales spreadsheet in Figure 12–12. Pat Kline produced the sales-by-region pie graph in Figure 12–15 by specifying that the values in the "TOTAL" column become the "pieces" of the pie. To emphasize the region with the greatest contribution to total sales, Pat decided to *explode* (or separate) the western region's piece of the pie.

Line graphs. A line graph connects similar points on a graph with one or several lines. Pat Kline used the same data in the spreadsheet of Figure 12–12 to generate the line graph in Figure 12–16. The line graph makes it easy to compare sales between regions for a particular product.

Spreadsheet Database Capabilities The database component of an integrated spreadsheet package provides the user with many of the features of a dedicated database package—all within the context of the rows and columns of a spreadsheet. When used as a database tool, spreadsheet software organizes fields, records, and files into columns, rows, and tables, respectively. For example, in the name-and-address file illustrated in Figure 12–17, each row in the spreadsheet after the first row contains the data items for each individual record (for example, Jeffrey Bates, 1401 Oak St., Framingham, MA 01710). The first row contains column head-

FIGURE 12–15 Pie Graph
The total sales for each region in Figure 12–12 are represented in this pie graph. The western region's piece of the pie is exploded for emphasis.

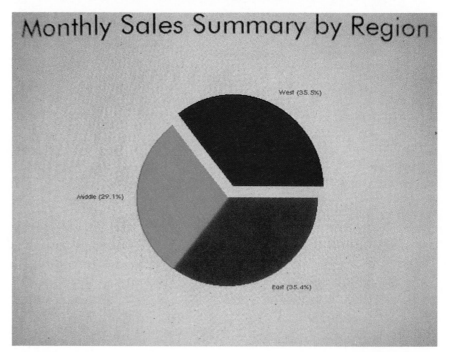

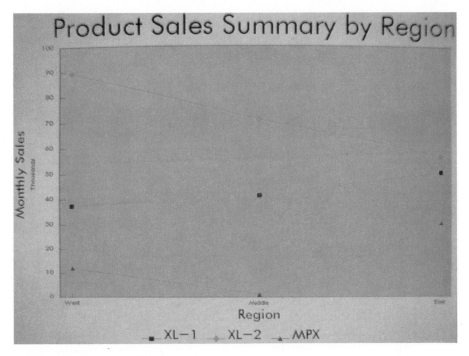

FIGURE 12–16 Line Graph

This line graph shows a plot of the data in Figure 12–12. A line connects the sales for each product by region.

FIGURE 12–17 Spreadsheet Data Base

This spreadsheet is organized as a data base (A1..E8). The name and permanent address data base contains a record for each student in a college dormitory. The labels for the fields in the record are listed in the first row (A1..E1). Each subsequent row contains one student record. This screen shows the results of an inquiry to the data base: List those students who live in Massachusetts (MA). *The criteria range (STATE="MA") is shown in A19..E20. The results of the inquiry are shown in the output range (A11..E13).*

```
A1: [W20] 'NAME

            A                B                 C           D    E
1   NAME            STREET            CITY            STATE ZIP
2   Bates, Jeffrey  1401 Oak Street   Framingham      MA    01710
3   Bell, Beverly   888 Root Road     Acoaxet         RI    02701
4   Collier, Rene   231 Fourth Street Nashua          NH    03060
5   Harper, Brian   104 Yale St.      Brockton        MA    02403
6   Hengst, Phillip Route 4D          Willimantic     CT    06226
7   Karlsen, Karla  1672 Pine Ave.    Derby Line      VT    05830
8   Mott, Leigh Anne 14 Meadowbrook Ln. Sanford       ME    04073
9
10
11  NAME            STREET            CITY            STATE ZIP
12  Bates, Jeffrey  1401 Oak Street   Framingham      MA    01710
13  Harper, Brian   104 Yale St.      Brockton        MA    02403
14
15
16
17
18
19  NAME            STREET            CITY            STATE ZIP
20                                                    MA
25-Aug-91  09:17 PM       UNDO
```

393

ings that identify the fields in a record (name, street, city, state, zip). All the records are combined in a table of rows (records) and columns (fields) to make a file. Spreadsheet rows, or records, can be sorted or extracted based on preset conditions (for example, STATE = "MA") to generate a variety of reports.

12–2 Database: Dynamic Data Tool

Function

With database software you can create and maintain a data base and extract information from it. To use database software, you first identify the format of the data, then design a display format that permits interactive entry and revision of the data base. Once the data base is created, its data can be deleted or revised and other data can be added. Notice that *database* is one word when it refers to the software that manages the data base. *Data base* is two words when the term refers to the highest level of the hierarchy of data organization (bit, character, field, record, file, and data base). The data hierarchy is discussed in detail in Chapter 6, "Data Storage and Organization."

All database software packages have these fundamental capabilities:

1. To create and maintain (add, delete, and revise records) a data base
2. To extract and list all records or only those records that meet certain conditions
3. To make an inquiry (for example, "What is the total amount owed by all customers?")
4. To sort records in ascending or descending sequence by primary, secondary, and tertiary fields
5. To generate formatted reports with subtotals and totals

The more sophisticated packages include a variety of other features, such as spreadsheet-type computations, presentation graphics, and programming.

Concepts

Creating a Data Base with Database Software   Many similarities exist between word processing packages and spreadsheet packages. With word processing, you see and manipulate lines of text. With spreadsheets, you see and manipulate data in numbered rows and lettered columns. This is not the case with database packages. What you see on the screen may be vastly different from one package to the next. However, the concepts behind these database packages are very similar. The data base example we give here is generic and can be applied to all database packages. The displays in the accompanying figures are taken from Paradox (a product of Borland International).

The organization of the data in a microcomputer data base is similar to the traditional hierarchy of data organization. Related *fields*, such as

At this television station, the nightly news anchors maintain a data base that contains background information on newsmakers in the broadcast area. The continuously updated data base helps to ensure the accuracy of stories.

company name, region, and representative name, are grouped to form *records* (for example, the customer record in the KEY_ACCT data base in Figure 12–18). A collection of related records make up a *file* or a *data base*. (In database software terminology, *file* and *data base* are often used interchangeably.)

The best way to illustrate and demonstrate the concepts of database software is by example. We have used the example of Pat Kline, the national sales manager of Zimco Enterprises, from previous examples in this chapter and Chapter 11. Pat uses a micro-based database software package to track product sales of important accounts. To do this, Pat created a KEY_ACCT data base (see Figure 12–18) that contains a record for each of the company's nine key accounts. Almost 30% of the company's worldwide sales comes from these key accounts. Each record in the KEY_ACCT data base contains the following fields:

- COMPANY (the name of a key account company)
- REGION (the sales region: west, middle, or east)
- REP_NAME (the name of field representative who services the account)
- XL1_NO (the number of XL1s installed at the account)
- XL2_NO (the number of XL2s installed at the account)
- MPX_NO (the number of MPXs installed at the account)
- LAST_ORDER (the date of the last order for one or more XL1s, XL2s, or MPXs)

To create a data base, the first thing you do is to set up a *screen format* that enables you to enter the data for a record. The data-entry screen format is analogous to a hard-copy form that contains labels and blank lines (for example, a medical questionnaire or an employment application). Data are entered and edited (deleted or revised) one record at a time with database software as they are on hard-copy forms.

The structure of the data base. To set up a data-entry screen format, first specify the *structure* of the data base by identifying the characteristics of each field in it. This is done interactively, with the system prompting

FIGURE 12–18   The KEY_ACCT Data Base
The KEY_ACCT data base contains a record for each of a company's nine key accounts. The fields for each account (customer company) are described in the text.

COMPANY	REGION	REP. NAME	PRODUCTS			
			XL1 NO.	XL2 NO.	MPX NO.	LAST ORDER
Hi-Tech	West	Rosco	22	35	5	01/11/91
Electronic	East	Allen	48	21	15	02/06/91
Compufast	Middle	Taylor	103	67	42	02/07/92
Zapp. Inc.	West	Rosco	71	85	40	01/16/92
Whizzard	East	Hill	35	45	20	10/12/91
SuperGood	Middle	Cox	24	55	4	12/24/91
Bigco	East	Hill	38	50	21	09/09/91
Actionpak	Middle	Cox	24	37	14	11/01/91
Zimco	West	Mann	77	113	40	01/13/91

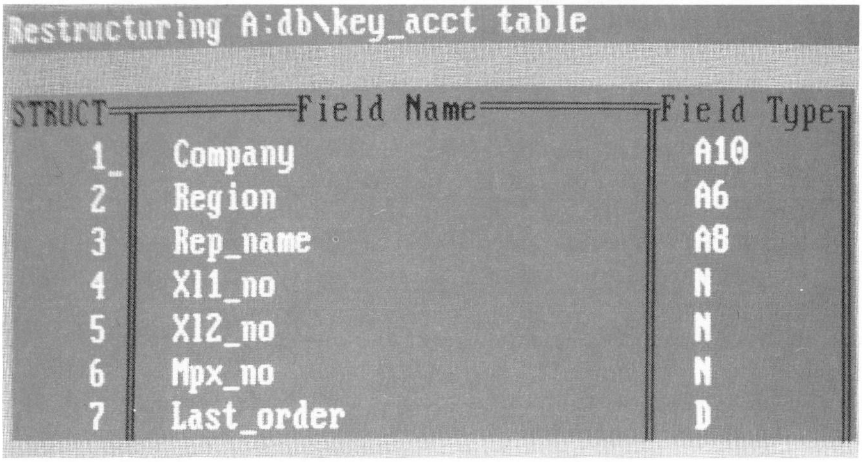

FIGURE 12–19   Structure of the KEY_ACCT Data Base
This display shows the structure of the KEY_ACCT data base for Paradox, a popular database software package. The KEY_ACCT record has three alphanumeric (A) fields, three numeric (N) fields, and a data (D) field.

you to enter the field name, field type, and so on (see Figure 12–19). The *field name* is "COMPANY," the *field length* is 10 positions, and the *field type* is alphanumeric, or character. An alphanumeric field type can be a single word or any alphanumeric (numbers, letters, and special characters) phrase up to several hundred positions in length. For numeric field types, you must specify the maximum number of digits (field length) and the number of decimal positions you wish to have displayed. Because the product sales are all defined in whole hours, the number of decimal positions for the XL1_NO, XL2_NO, and MPX_NO fields is set at zero.

Entering and editing a data base.   The screen format for entering, editing, and adding records to the KEY_ACCT data base is shown in Figure 12–20. To create the KEY_ACCT data base, the sales manager issued a command that called up the data-entry screen in Figure 12–20, entered the data for the first record, then entered the second record, and so on. On most database systems, the records are automatically assigned a number as they are entered. Records can, of course, be added to the data base and edited (deleted or revised).

Query by Example   Database software also permits you to retrieve, view, and print records based on **query by example (QBE)**. In query by example, you set conditions for the selection of records by composing one or more example *relational expressions*. A relational expression normally compares one or more field names to numbers or character strings using the **relational operators** (= [equal to], > [greater than], < [less than], and combinations of these operators). Several conditions can be combined with **logical operators** (*AND, OR,* and *NOT*). Commonly used relational and logical operators are summarized in Figure 12–21.

QBE: REGION = East.   Pat Kline wanted a listing of all key accounts in the eastern region, so the sales manager requested a list of all key

Friday the Thirteenth in Computerland We tend to expect the worst on Friday the Thirteenth. For AT&T, Friday the Thirteenth turned out to be a corporate nightmare. A minor defect in its software caused 1.8 million 800 calls to be blocked. A malfunction in its database management software caused 800 routing tables to be overwritten unintentionally by calling card routing tables. The newly developed calling card routing tables were not supposed to be used until the next year.

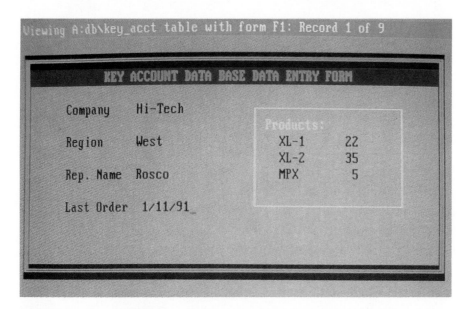

KEY ACCOUNT DATA BASE DATA ENTRY FORM

Company   Hi-Tech

Region   West

Rep. Name Rosco

Last Order 1/11/91_

Products:
XL-1   22
XL-2   35
MPX   5

FIGURE 12–20   Data-Entry Screen Format

The screen format for entering, editing, and adding records to the KEY_ACCT data base is illustrated.

Relational Operators	
COMPARISON	**OPERATOR**
Equal to	=
Less than	<
Greater than	>
Less than or equal to	< =
Greater than or equal to	> =
Not equal to	< >

Logical Operators AND and OR	
OPERATION	**OPERATOR**
For the condition to be true:	
Both subconditions must be true	AND
At least one subcondition must be true	OR

FIGURE 12–21   Relational and Logical Operators

accounts that meet the condition REGION = East in the KEY_ACCT data base (see Figure 12–18). The result is shown in Figure 12–22.

QBE: REGION = *East* AND LAST_ORDER < 7/1/91.   To produce the output in Figure 12–23, Pat Kline asks for the names of accounts in the eastern region that have not posted an order since July 1, 1991 (REGION = East AND LAST_ORDER < 7/1/91). Of course, the output can be routed to a display screen or to a printer. In addition, the sales manager can select which fields are to be displayed as a result of a query. For example, in Figure 12–23, Pat may have wanted to display only the COMPANY and LAST_ORDER fields.

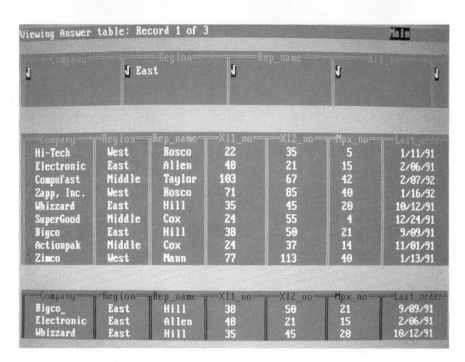

FIGURE 12–22   Query by Example, One Condition
All records in the KEY_ACCT data base (center of screen) that meet the condition REGION = East (top of screen) are displayed at the bottom of the screen.

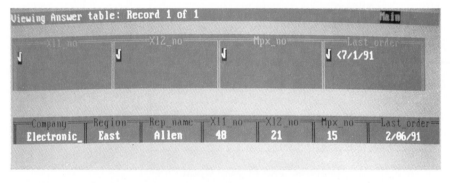

FIGURE 12–23   Query by Example, Two Conditions
All records in the KEY_ACCT data base (see Figure 12–22) that meet the condition REGION = East and LAST_ORDER < (is prior to) 7/1/91 are displayed. The LAST_ORDER condition is added to the REGION = East condition noted in Figure 12–22.

QBE: Other examples.   The following relational expressions establish conditions that will select or extract records from the KEY_ACCT data base in Figure 12–18. The records noted to the right meet the conditions set forth in the relational expressions on the left.

COMPANY = Hi-Tech	(Hi-Tech)
XL1_NO > 40 AND XL2_NO > 30	(Compufast, Zapp, Zimco)
LAST_ORDER > 10/1/91 AND LAST_ORDER < 1/1/92	(Actionpak, SuperGood, Whizzard)
REGION = West OR Middle; MPX_NO =<5	(Hi-Tech, SuperGood)
REP_NAME NOT Rosco	(All but Hi-Tech and Compufast)

The process of selecting records by setting conditions is sometimes called *filtering*; those records or fields that you don't want are "filtered" out of the display.

Memory Bits

DATABASE INQUIRIES

- Query by example (create relational expressions with)
  - Relational operators (=, >, <)
  - Logical operators (AND, OR, NOT)
- Sorts (identify)
  - Primary sort field
  - Secondary sort field (if needed)

Sorting Records Data also can be sorted for display in a variety of formats. For example, the records in Figure 12–18 can be sorted by company, representative's name, or date of last order. Figure 12–24 illustrates how the KEY_ACCT data base in Figure 12–18 has been sorted by REP_NAME within REGION. This involves the selection of a *primary* and a *secondary key field.* The sales manager selected REGION as the primary key field but wanted the account records to be listed in ascending order by REP_NAME within REGION. To achieve this record sequence, Pat selected REP_NAME as the secondary key field. In most database packages, issuing a sort command results in the creation of a temporary data base. After the sort operation, the temporary data base contains the records in the order described in the sort command.

Customized Reports Database software can create customized, or formatted, reports. This capability allows you to design the *layout* of the report. This means that you have some flexibility in spacing and can include titles, subtitles, column headings, separation lines, and other elements that make a report more readable. You describe the layout of

FIGURE 12–24 KEY_ACCT Data Base Sorted by REP_NAME Within REGION

This display is the result of a sort operation on the KEY_ACCT data base (Figure 12–18) with the REGION field as the primary key field and the REP_NAME field as the secondary key field.

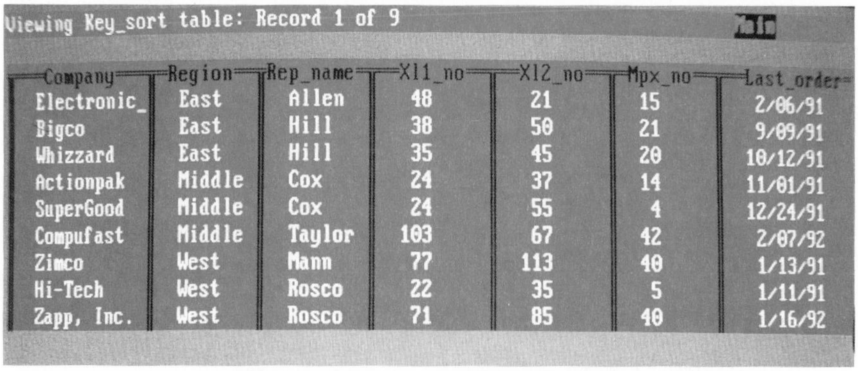

Viewing Key_sort table: Record 1 of 9

Company	Region	Rep_name	Xl1_no	Xl2_no	Mpx_no	Last_order
Electronic_	East	Allen	48	21	15	2/06/91
Bigco	East	Hill	38	50	21	9/09/91
Whizzard	East	Hill	35	45	20	10/12/91
Actionpak	Middle	Cox	24	37	14	11/01/91
SuperGood	Middle	Cox	24	55	4	12/24/91
Compufast	Middle	Taylor	103	67	42	2/07/92
Zimco	West	Mann	77	113	40	1/13/91
Hi-Tech	West	Rosco	22	35	5	1/11/91
Zapp, Inc.	West	Rosco	71	85	40	1/16/92

the *customized* report interactively, then store it for later recall. The result of the description, called a *report form*, is recalled from disk storage and merged with a data base to create the customized report. Managers often use this capability to generate periodic reports (for example, monthly sales summary reports).

Once a month, Pat Kline generates several summary reports, one of which groups the key accounts by region and provides product subtotals and an overall total for each product (see Figure 12–25). This customized report was compiled by merging a predefined report format with the KEY_ACCT data base.

Use

Database software earns the "productivity tool" label by providing users with the capability of organizing data into an electronic data base that can be maintained and queried (can permit user inquiries) easily. The examples illustrated and discussed in the "Concepts" section merely "scratch the surface" of the potential of database software. With relative ease, you can generate some rather sophisticated reports that involve subtotals, calculations, and programming. In addition, data can be presented in the form of a graph (see Figure 12–26). You can even change the structure of a data base (for example, add another field). The programming capability enables users to create their own microcomputer-based information systems.

FIGURE 12–25 Formatted Report
This formatted report was compiled by merging a predefined report format with the KEY_ACCT data base (Figure 12–18). The records are printed in alphabetical order by COMPANY within REGION.

```
                    KEY ACCOUNT SALES SUMMARY


    Company      Rep Name    XL-1     XL-2     MPX    Last Order
    ================================================================
       *** Key Acounts for Region:  East
    Bigco        Hill          38       50       21    9/09/91
    Electronic   Allen         48       21       15    2/06/91
    Whizzard     Hill          35       45       20   10/12/91
                              ------   ------   ------
          Region Totals       121      116       56

       *** Key Acounts for Region:  Middle
    Actionpak    Cox           24       37       14   11/01/91
    Compufast    Taylor       103       67       42    2/07/92
    SuperGood    Cox           24       55        4   12/24/91
                              ------   ------   ------
          Region Totals       151      159       60

       *** Key Acounts for Region:  West
    Hi-Tech      Rosco         22       35        5    1/11/91
    Zapp, Inc.   Rosco         71       85       40    1/16/92
    Zimco        Mann          77      113       40    1/13/91
                              ------   ------   ------
          Region Totals       170      233       85

                              ======   ======   ======
          Overall Totals      442      508      201
```

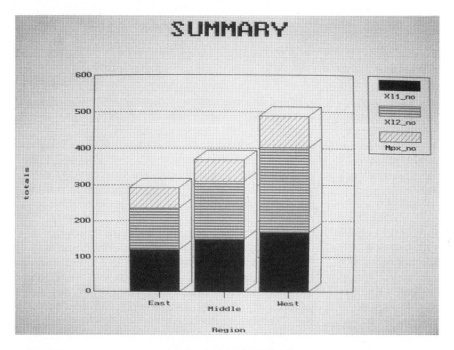

FIGURE 12–26 Database Presentation Graphics
Like spreadsheet packages, most database packages have the capability of preparing presentation graphics. This stacked-bar graph, which is derived from the data in Figure 12–18, shows the contribution of each product to regional sales.

12–3 Other Data Management Tools: Phone Books to Hypertext

One or both of the major general-purpose data management tools, spreadsheet or database, would be installed on the typical personal computer, whether in the home or office. In this section we address hypertext and a variety of application-specific data management tools. Hypertext, a general-purpose data management tool, is gaining momentum and may someday emerge as a must-have software tool for all PC users. An application-specific tool is appropriate only for those PC users who have a need for the application addressed by the tool.

Hypertext and Hypermedia

The database software discussed in this chapter manipulates data within the context of a carefully structured data base. This type of structure can be used in thousands of applications in every industry type. Another type of data management software, called **hypertext**, addresses unstructured information. Hypertext software, which is still in the infant stages of use and development, provides links between *key words* in the kinds of unstructured text-based documents that we work with every day (letters, notes, boilerplate, and so on).

"Have you seen me?" Few people have not seen this haunting question on posters and flyers from the National Center for Missing and Exploited Children (NCMEC). Over 70,000 people call its hot lines every year, challenging an organization created to coordinate the efforts of law-enforcement agencies, social service agencies, and others working to protect children.

Today the NCMEC is getting help from a network of PCs and a *geographic information system (GIS)*, database software that overlays a map with color-coded data that has a geographic component, such as a ZIP code or street address. At the NCMEC, hot-line operators log in all sightings, which are then plotted on maps with the $30,000 GIS. Beneath the map's surface, the GIS can embed data base records containing profiles of suspects and missing children, with cross-references to possibly related calls. Sometimes the plotting itself reveals a pattern in seemingly unrelated calls. Alternatively, the GIS operator can set a *filter,* a type of data base query, which highlights all calls that have certain attributes or relate to a specific area. The result: Investigators waste less time identifying and pursuing meaningful tips.

BEHIND THE GIS BOOM

GISs were first created for mainframes and minicomputers in the early 1980s, but the software has since migrated to today's powerful workstations and PCs. The trend has received a boost from the increasing afford-ability of high-capacity hard disks and CD-ROM disks and from the growing availability of demographic and cartographic data bases in digital form. Cartographic data are any facts that can be shown on a map, from physical features to political boundaries, postal ZIP code areas, Metropolitan Statistical Areas (MSAs), and television rating zones. Demographic data pertain to population characteristics such as age, income, or occupation.

A major supplier of cartographic and demographic data is the U.S. Bureau of the Census, which now sells CD-ROM disk sets containing detailed economic and population data. Although the costs may seem high (up to $11,000 for the bureau's TIGER data base), they are a bargain to many corporations and government agencies. Their need to obtain and then analyze overwhelming amounts of raw data is the most powerful factor fueling the demand for GISs.

GIS SUCCESS STORIES

Marketing executives have been especially eager to use GISs. A typical GIS assignment would be to create a "retail gravity" model—a map that combines color-coded census data, such as ethnic identity, age, and income bracket, with marketing information about hobbies and so on. Such models are used to select new store locations and to help target in-store and direct-marketing campaigns.

GISs can also help corporations comply with gov-

Hypertext is a relatively recent innovation in information technology. Prior to the creation of hypertext, the automation of applications was deemed infeasible because their data were incompatible with traditional data structures (fields, records, files). These applications generally involved long strings of unstructured text. For example, medical records provide an excellent opportunity for the use of hypertext. Once you get past basic patient data (name, social security number, insurance policy I.D., and so on), medical records are basically descriptive text (symptom descriptions, office visit summaries, and so on).

The theory behind hypertext is that it lets you work the way you think. For example, suppose you are a lawyer and one of your clients asked you to update his will. The information you need is computer-based, but in no particular format or file. Using the client's name as a

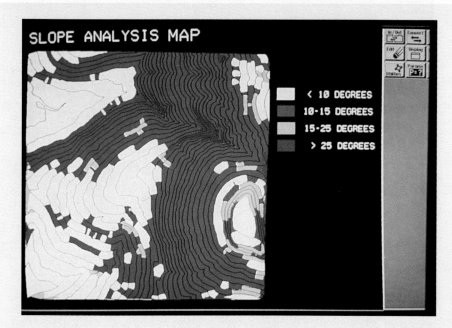

SLOPE ANALYSIS MAP

< 10 DEGREES
10-15 DEGREES
15-25 DEGREES
> 25 DEGREES

CITY PLANNING The Geographic Information and Mapping Services Department of Huntsville, Alabama, depends on GIS products for a variety of jobs. Shown here is part of a mountain slope analysis to determine soil stability in a residential area.

ernment regulations; one major bank uses a GIS to be sure its loan practices do not discriminate against poorer neighborhoods. Urban planners also use GISs, as do insurance underwriters, who use GISs to create maps showing how close a building is to a fire hydrant or fire station.

Another important application is fleet routing, the efficient planning of delivery systems, which can take in everything from devising sales territories to planning a newspaper delivery route.

Many experts predict that the number of GIS applications will keep pace with the data explosion. In fact, they say, GISs will do for demographic, cartographic, and traditional data bases what Lotus 1-2-3 did for accounting data—convert inscrutable pages of facts and numbers into easy-to-understand business graphics.

key word, you might use hypertext links to assemble needed documents: client's address from client name and address file; random notes you took at the last meeting with your client; the most recent letters you wrote to or on behalf of your client; and the client's existing will. You might use other key word links to retrieve boilerplate text that can be used as the basis for the updated will and to access your appointment calendar to schedule a meeting with your clients. In effect, the computer responds to your requests in much the same way a legal assistant would.

The potential for hypertext is enormous. For example, only a handful of companies have used hypertext to automate their sales manuals and maintenance manuals. Each says that hypertext is the only way to go. With millions of traditional hard-copy sales and maintenance manuals yet to be automated, hypertext should play a significant role in automation

World Atlas, a product of Software Toolworks, Inc., provides a geographic data base filled with thousands of facts, statistics, images, and even national anthems for over 200 countries. Information is organized in 11 major categories with over 300 subtopics of interest from animals to exchange rates. Users can create new categories or subtopics and add their own information to the permanent data base.

during the 1990s—and this is just one application. Any application that involves the storing, manipulation, and retrieval of unstructured text–based information is a candidate for hypertext.

Hypermedia is the next generation of hypertext. Hypermedia software goes one step further, enabling the integration of data, text, graphics, sounds of all kinds (including voice and music), and even full-motion video. Non-text elements of hypermedia must be associated with key words. For example, someone in aircraft maintenance can search links for "refueling 757" and opt for a word description, a drawing, or a video demonstration of the refueling procedure for Boeing 757 aircraft.

Application-Specific Data Management Tools

Some data management tools are designed to handle data for specific applications. Generally, these software tools are used by people who have ready access to a PC and use a PC routinely in their daily activities. Some of these tools are summarized in this section.

Calendar Software   For most of us, our pocket or desktop calendar is an integral part of our daily lives. On it we record appointments and notes day by day and, even, hour by hour. We refer to and/or record data in our calendars many times each day. Calendar software provides an alternative to the traditional hard-copy calendar. The electronic calendar has its advantages and disadvantages. Its primary advantage is that the calendar is in electronic format, giving you greater flexibility in what you can do. For example, you can request an overview for a month (see Figure 12–27) or an hour-by-hour accounting of the day's activities. Or, you could request the date on which you last met with a particular client. Some calendar packages automatically alert you prior to a scheduled meeting with an audible alarm or a message on the display. The primary disadvantage of calendar software is that you need a portable PC to carry it with you. This disadvantage is relatively minor in that you can print out any or all parts of your electronic calendar in minutes.

When PCs are networked (linked together) such that each worker's personal calendar is stored at a central location, calendar software takes on an added dimension. As workers schedule activities, they block out times on their electronic calendars. Let's say that a public relations manager wants to schedule a meeting to review the impact of some unexpected favorable publicity. To do this, the manager enters the names of the participants and the expected duration of the meeting. A *conference scheduling module* searches the data base containing the calendars of people affected and suggests possible meeting times. The manager then selects a meeting time, and the participants are notified by electronic mail. Of course, their calendars are automatically updated to reflect the meeting time.

FIGURE 12–27 Calendar Software
Calendar software enables you to view highlights of future events a month at a time (shown here), Details of events are displayed hour-by-hour for a given day.

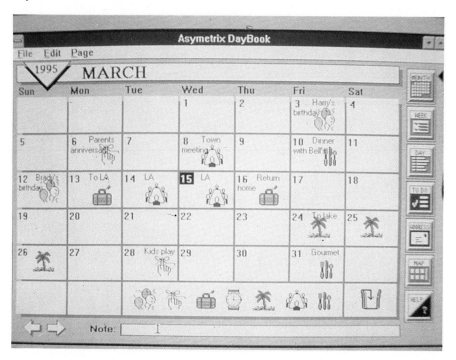

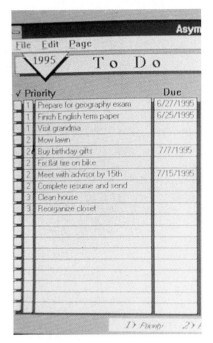

FIGURE 12–28 Things-to-Do List Software

An electronic things-to-do list can be arranged by priority with ease.

Things-to-Do List Software   PC software is available to help you manage your things-to-do (see Figure 12–28). The always changing things-to-do list is a natural for automation. Once you enter your items on the list, you can sort them by due date or group them by priority. Pop-up notes enable users to include additional explanation, if needed. Simply add or delete items to update the list.

Address Book Software   Address book software helps you organize and store pertinent information about your business contacts. Figure 12–29 illustrates a "page" from an electronic address book. The easy-access pages in the address book can be sorted in a variety of ways (by name, by city, by state, by zip, by area code, and so on). Also, you can print reports (for example, all contacts in the 617 area code) and mailing labels.

Portfolio Software   Portfolio software enables users to maintain a data base of their securities (stocks, bonds, CDs, and so on). The data base is easily updated to reflect portfolio transactions. A good portfolio program does more than data management. For example, it can suggest investment strategies based on user-defined criteria (willingness to accept risk, cash flow requirements, and so on).

Genealogy Software.   If you are interested in tracking your family lineage, then genealogy software is indispensable. Genealogy software is designed to create a data base that documents the family tree. Use it to

FIGURE 12–29 Address Book Software
The pages of an electronic address book can be sorted by user-designated fields.

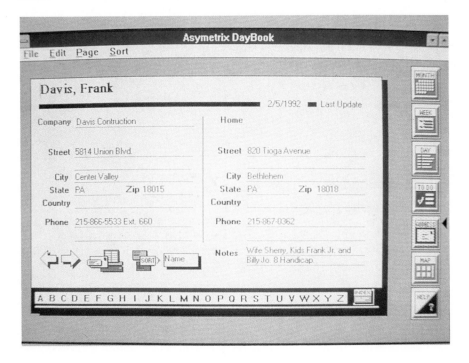

record names, dates, descendant/ancestor information, and relationships. The software enables users to print descendant charts, ancestor charts, and a variety of custom reports.

 Important Terms and Summary Outline

absolute cell
   addressing
argument
arithmetic operator
cell
cell address

function
hypermedia
hypertext
logical operator
pointer
query by example (QBE)

range
relational operator
relative cell addressing
template

12–1 THE SPREADSHEET: THE MAGIC MATRIX. Spreadsheets are simply an electronic alternative to thousands of manual tasks that involve rows and columns of data. The primary example used in this chapter illustrates spreadsheet concepts in a spreadsheet **template** of a monthly sales summary.

Spreadsheets are organized in a tabular structure of rows and columns. The intersection of a particular row and column designates a **cell**. During operations, data are referred to by their **cell addresses**. The **pointer** can be moved around the spreadsheet to any cell with the arrow keys.

To make an entry, edit, or replace an entry in a spreadsheet, move the pointer to the appropriate cell. When in edit mode, revise the entry in much the same way you would revise the text in a word processing document.

The four types of **ranges** are a single-cell, all or part of a column of adjacent cells, all or part of a row of adjacent cells, and a rectangular block of cells. A particular range is depicted by the addresses of the endpoint cells (for example, C5..E10).

An entry to a cell is classified as text (or label), numeric, or formula. A text entry is any string of alphanumeric text (spaces included) that occupies a particular cell. A numeric entry is any number. A cell may contain a formula, but it is the numeric results that are displayed in the spreadsheet. Spreadsheet formulas use standard programming notation for **arithmetic operators**.

The **relative cell address** is based on its position in relation to the cell containing the formula. When you copy, or replicate, a formula to another cell, the relative cell addresses in the formula are revised so they retain the same position in relation to the new location of the formula. When a formula is copied, the **absolute cell addresses** in the formula remain unchanged.

Predefined **functions** can be used to create formulas that perform mathematical, logical, statistical, financial, and character-string operations on spreadsheet data.

The appearance of data in a spreadsheet can be modified to enhance readability by adjusting the column width and formatting the individual numeric entries.

A spreadsheet template can be used over and over for different purposes by different people. If you change the value of a cell in a spreadsheet, all other affected cells are revised accordingly. This capability makes spreadsheet software the perfect tool for "what if" analysis.

Integrated spreadsheet packages include a presentation graphics software module. This capability enables users to create a variety of presentation graphics from data in a spreadsheet. Among the most popular presentation graphics are bar graphs (including the stacked-bar and clustered-bar graphs), pie graphs, and line graphs. Each of these graphs can be annotated with titles, labels, and legends.

12–2 DATABASE: DYNAMIC DATA TOOL. Database software permits users to create and maintain a data base and extract information from it. Once the data base is created, its data can be deleted or revised, and other data can be added to it.

In database software, the user-defined structure of a data base identifies the characteristics of each field in it. Related fields are grouped to form records. The screen format for entering, editing, and adding records to a data base is generated automatically from the specifications outlined in the structure of the data base.

Database software also permits you to retrieve, view, and print records based on **query by example (QBE)**. To do this, users set conditions for the selection of records by composing a relational expression containing **relational operators** that reflects the desired conditions. Several expressions can be combined into a single condition with **logical operators**.

Records in a data base can be sorted for display in a variety of formats. To sort the records in a data base, select a primary key field and, if needed, secondary key fields. In most database packages, issuing a sort command results in the compilation of a temporary data base.

Database software can create customized, or formatted, reports. The user describes the layout of the customized report interactively, then stores it for later recall.

12–3 OTHER DATA MANAGEMENT TOOLS: PHONE BOOKS TO HYPERTEXT. **Hypertext** is a general-purpose data management tool that addresses unstructured information by providing links between key words of related documents. **Hypermedia** enables the various forms of information (data, text, graphics, video, and sound) to be linked together so that a user can easily move from one to another.

A variety of data management tools handle data for specific applications. These applications include calendar software, things-to-do list software, address book software, portfolio software, and genealogy software.

 Review Exercises

Concepts

1. Describe the layout of a spreadsheet.
2. Give an example of a cell address. Which portion of the address indicates the row and which portion, the column?
3. Give an example of each of the four types of ranges.

4. Give examples of the three types of entries that can be made in a spreadsheet.

5. Write the equivalent formula for @AVG(A1..D1) without the use of functions.

6. If the formula B2*$B$1 is copied from C1 to E3, what is the formula in E3? If the formula in E3 is copied to D45, what is the formula in D45?

7. List three different descriptors for the range A4..P12.

8. What formula would be entered in A5 to add all numbers in the range A1..A4?

9. Name three types of graphs commonly used for presentation graphics.

10. Name two sources of data for generating pie graphs and bar graphs.

11. Name and graphically illustrate (by hand) two variations of the bar graph.

12. What is shown when a portion of a pie chart is "exploded"?

13. What is the purpose of setting conditions for a data base?

14. What is the relationship between a field, a record, and the structure of a data base?

15. Give examples and descriptions of at least two other fields that might be added to the record for the KEY_ACCT data base (Figure 12–18).

16. If the KEY_ACCT data base (Figure 12–18) were sorted so that the primary and secondary key fields were REGION and LAST_ORDER, respectively, what is the company name for the third record?

17. What records would be displayed if the selection condition for the KEY_ACCT data base (Figure 12–18) were XL1_NO > 20 AND MPX_NO <= 5?

18. What type of software provides links between *key words* in unstructured text–based documents?

Discussion

19. All commercial electronic spreadsheet packages manipulate rows and columns of data in a similar manner. What makes one spreadsheet package more desirable than another?

20. If you were asked to create a micro-based inventory management system for a privately owned retail shoe store, would you use electronic spreadsheet software, database software, or both? Why?

21. Describe two types of inquiries to a data base that involve calculations.

22. Under what circumstances is a graphic representation of data more effective than a tabular presentation of the same data?

23. Is it possible to present the same information in a stacked-bar graph and a line graph? How about stacked-bar and pie graphs?

Problem Solving

24. On a sheet of paper, draw a spreadsheet grid with 4 columns and 16 rows. On the grid create a spreadsheet template that allows you to compare this year's monthly electric bills with last year's. In Row 1, label Columns A through D as "Month," "This Year," "Last Year," and "Difference," respectively. Row 1 should contain the names of the months.

Add formulas in appropriate cells that allow you to compare this year's monthly electric bills with last year's. Also, add formulas that sum the monthly amounts for the two years.

25. *Note: This problem-solving exercise requires hands-on skills and access to a microcomputer.* Begin a spreadsheet session. Create a spreadsheet that summarizes an individual's monthly budget in two general categories: expenditures and income. Use formulas to compute the totals for the two categories, the percent of the total, and the ratio of total expenditures to total income. Use absolute cell addressing in the "Percent of Total" formulas so that you can enter each of the formulas once and copy them to the other cells. Format your spreadsheet to be similar to the following:

	A	B	C	D
	A	**B**	**C**	**D**
1	EXPENDITURES			
2	Category		Amount	Percent of Total
3	Housing		495.00	.3300
4	Utilities		125.45	.0837
5	Food		369.29	.2460
6	Clothing		85.00	.0567
7	Transportation		265.17	.1770
8	Entertainment		100.00	.0667
9	Other		59.50	.0397
10			———	
11	TOTAL		1499.41	
12				
13	INCOME			
14	Category		Amount	Percent of Total
15	Wages		2400.00	.9600
16	Tips		0.00	.0000
17	Gifts		100.00	.0400
18	Other		0.00	.0000
19	——————			
20	TOTAL		2500.00	
21				
22	Ratio of expenditures to income:			.60

Save the spreadsheet on your data disk as MONTHBUD. Print the spreadsheet.

26. The following data base was created to keep track of an individual's library of recordings: compact discs (CDs), long-playing (LP) records, and audiotapes. The data in each record is organized in five fields as shown.

FORMAT	ARTIST	TITLE	TIME	SONGS
CD	Depeche Mode	Some Great Reward	38.59	13
CD	The Cure	The Cure?	32.32	10
RECORD	London Symphony	Mozart: Requiem	61.25	1
TAPE	Pet Shop Boys	Please	32.15	10
CD	Depeche Mode	Black Celebration	41.19	12
RECORD	Depeche Mode	People Are People	32.37	11
TAPE	O.M.D.	The Pacific Age	43.00	12
CD	The Cure	Standing on the Beach	52.18	15
RECORD	The Ramones	End of the Century	36.28	16

Determine appropriate criteria and/or functions to generate and print reports that contain the records for

a. All CDs recorded by Depeche Mode

b. All tapes and LP records with playing times in excess of 40 minutes

c. The total number of songs on all CDs

d. The average playing time for all recordings in the data base

 Self-Test (by section)

12–1 **a.** The term *spreadsheet* was coined at the beginning of the personal computer boom. (T/F̂)

b. Data in a spreadsheet are referred to by their cell address .

c. The spreadsheet pointer highlights the: (a) relative cell, (b) status cell, or (c) current cell?

d. D20..Z40 and Z20..D40 define the same spreadsheet range. (T̂/F)

e. When the spreadsheet formula +H4*$Z$18 is copied from A1 to A3, the formula in A3 is +H6*$ Z$18

f. The spreadsheet formula @SUM(A1..A20) results in the computation of the sum of the values in the range A20..A1. (T̂/F)

★ **g.** A model of a spreadsheet designed for a particular application is sometimes called a template .

h. Among the most popular presentation graphics are bar graphs, pie graphs, and line graphs.

★ **i.** An alternative to the clustered-bar graph is the stacked bar graph.

12–2 **a.** If the KEY_ACCT data base in Figure 12–18 is sorted in descending order by XL1_NO, the third record would be Zapp, Inc. (T/F̂)

★ **b.** The definition of the structure of a data base would not include which of the following: (a) field names, (b̂) selection conditions for fields, (c) field lengths?

★ **c.** The relational operator for greater than or equal to is >= .

★ **d.** What record(s) would be selected from the KEY_ACCT data base in Figure 12–18 for the condition REGION = West and MPX_NO>15: (â) Zapp, Inc., Zimco; (b) Compufast; or (c) no records are selected?

★ **12–3** Hypertext enables users to assemble information from unstructured computer-based documents.

Self-test answers. **12–1 (a)** F; **(b)** addresses; **(c)** c; **(d)** T; **(e)** +H6*Z$18; **(f)** T; **(g)** template; **(h)** line; **(i)** stacked-bar. **12–2 (a)** F; **(b)** b; **(c)** >=; **(d)** a. **12–3** Hypertext.

WHERE TO BUY PCs

Each year millions of people go through the process of buying a microcomputer, micro peripheral devices, and various types of software. During the last few years the PC has emerged as the third most significant purchase—right behind homes and automobiles. The information presented here will help you spend your money wisely.

PC Retailers

Ten years ago micros were considered a highly technical specialty item and were sold almost exclusively through microcomputer retail outlets. Today micros have emerged as a popular consumer item. Microcomputers and associated hardware and software can be purchased at thousands of convenient locations.

- *Computer retailers*. About a dozen national retail chains—such as ComputerLand (over 500 locations), ENTRE (over 200 locations), and MicroAge (over 200 locations)—and many regional retail chains specialize in the sale of microcomputer hardware and software. Most market and service a variety of small computer systems. Radio Shack stores carry and sell their own line of computers. This chain has over 400 computer specialty stores and over 10,000 electronics stores, all of which sell computers. There are also over a thousand computer stores that are not affiliated with a national or regional chain.

  Most computer specialty stores offer customers the option of leasing or buying. Depending on your willingness to accept the risk of obsolescence and your tax situation, leasing may be a viable alternative to purchasing.

- *Department stores*. Micros and micro software are sold in the computer departments of most department store chains, such as Sears and Walmart.

- *Discount stores*. Discount stores, such as SAM's Club and Service Merchandise, sell a wide range of micro hardware and software.

- *Other retail stores*. Many office-supply stores, college bookstores, audio/video stores, and other specialty retailers sell computers and computer products, too.

- *Mail-order services*. The alternative to buying a computer and related products at a retail outlet is to purchase them from a mail-order service. If you know what you want, you can call any of several mail-order services, give your credit-card number, and your order will be delivered to your doorstep.

- *Direct marketers*. Some manufacturers of micro hardware and/or software are direct marketers; that is, they sell directly to the customer. For the most part, the direct marketer's "store window" is an advertisement in a PC trade magazine. The customer telephones, faxes, or mails the order and the direct marketer sends the requested product(s) by return mail. DELL Computer Corporation is a direct marketer.

- *Manufacturers*. Some manufacturers will sell directly to the customer via mail order, usually at list price. However, most will direct you to the nearest retail outlet that handles their product.

- *Used-computer retailers*. The demand for used computers has spawned a new industry during the past few years. The used-computer retailer was as inevitable as the used-car dealer. A computer that is no longer powerful enough for one user may have more than enough power for another. The used-computer dealer makes the mutually beneficial exchange possible.

- *Classified ads*. Frequently, people wishing to upgrade will opt to advertise their existing systems in the classified ad sections of their local newspapers.

The sale price of a microcomputer, a peripheral device, or a software package may vary substantially from one source to another. It pays to shop around. A word processing package may be offered at list price ($500) from the manufacturer, at $350 from one local computer retailer, at $325 from another, and at $265 from a mail-order service. Of course, the selling price does not tell the whole story. For example, the local retailers may promise to provide some technical support after the sale.

The "Perks" of Employment

You might be able to acquire a micro through your employer. Many companies offer their employees a "computer perk." In cooperation with vendors, companies make volume purchases of PCs and software at discount rates, then offer them to employees at substantial savings. Many colleges sponsor similar programs to benefit students and professors. The employee-pur-

chase program is so popular in some organizations that they set up internal computer stores.

Steps in Buying a Microcomputer

Buying a microcomputer can be a harrowing experience or it can be a thrilling and fulfilling one. If you approach the purchase of a micro haphazardly, expect the former. If you go about the acquisition methodically and with purpose, expect the latter. Follow this 10-step procedure to get the biggest bang for your buck.

Step 1: Achieve Computer Competency. You do not buy an automobile before you learn how to drive, and you should not buy a microcomputer without a good understanding of its capabilities and how you intend to use it. In effect, this book is a comprehensive buyer's guide: The informed buyer will know and understand its content. Every college and vocational college offers courses leading to computer competency. Generally speaking, the price you pay for hardware or software is for the product. Any advice or instruction is extra.

WHERE TO BUY   Retail stores are one of the PC consumer's many sources.

STEP 1: ACHIEVE COMPUTER COMPETENCY. A computer-competent colleague can be a real help during the learning process.

Step 2: Decide How Much You Are Willing to Spend. Microcomputer systems can be purchased for as little as a few hundred dollars or as much as $40,000. Assess your circumstances and decide how much you are willing to commit to the purchase of a microcomputer system.

STEP 2: DECIDE HOW MUCH YOU ARE WILLING TO SPEND. Don't forget to consider the money you can save or earn by using a computer. In pharmaceutical sales, the currency of a salesperson's information may help to foster customer loyalty.

Step 3: Determine Your Information and Computing Needs. The adage, "If you don't know where you are going, any road will get you there," certainly applies to choosing a PC. Your goal is to figure out where you want to go by answering the question "How can I use a PC to simplify my work, increase my pleasure, or both?"

For most people, this means deciding which types of software packages they want to use. The choices here range from word processing to spreadsheets, database management, data communications, personal finance, presentation graphics, and educational games. This is an important decision, since software needs frequently determine hardware needs. If you want to write your own programs, for example, you must identify the micros that support the languages you want to use. The most popular programming languages for micros are BASIC, C, COBOL, and Pascal.

STEP 3: DETERMINE YOUR INFORMATION AND COMPUTING NEEDS. Most people will be satisfied with a desktop model, but others need the flexibility and portability of a laptop or notebook computer.

Step 4: Assess the Availability and Quality of Software and Information Services. Determine what software and information services are available to meet your needs. Good sources of this type of information include general computer periodicals (*PC, Byte, Software, Computerworld,* and *MacWorld,* to name a few), application- and product-specific periodicals (*Publish, MacWorld,* and *WordPerfect: The Magazine*), salespeople at computer stores, your computer/software instructor, a local computer club, your colleagues at work, and acquaintances who have knowledge in the area.

Several hundred micro productivity software packages are available commercially, and they vary greatly in capability and price. Software with essentially the same capabilities may have price differences of several hundred dollars. Some graphics software creates displays of graphs in seconds, while others take minutes. Some software packages are easy to learn and are accompanied by good documentation while others are not. Considering the amount of time you might spend using micro software, any extra time you devote to evaluating the software will be time well spent.

STEP 4: ASSESS THE AVAILABILITY AND QUALITY OF SOFTWARE AND INFORMATION SERVICES. Different users have different computing needs. A parent may be concerned about the amount and type of educational software, while a designer may be interested in a system that assists in creating sophisticated flyers, brochures, and publications.

Step 5: Choose a Platform. At this point in the PC decision process you will need to decide on a platform. Platforms are important because software is written to run under a particular platform. The various platforms are discussed in detail in Chapter 9, "System Software and Platforms." Of course, you will need to select a platform that supports your software and information needs (Step 4). In the IBM-PC–compatible, single-user environment, the dominant platform options are MS-DOS, MS-DOS/Windows, or OS/2. In the multiuser environment, it is UNIX. High-end users will need to decide between MCA and EISA architectures. Of course, the Apple Macintosh platform is another option.

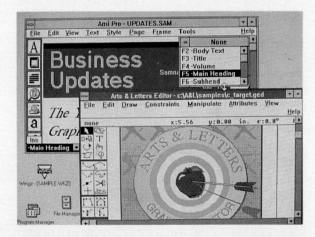

STEP 5: CHOOSE A PLATFORM. The Windows platform lets you work with several programs at the same time.

Step 6: Identify One or More Microcomputer Systems for Further Examination. If you select a specific proprietary software product (for example, desktop publishing or a general accounting system for a clinical laboratory), your selection may dictate the general microcomputer-system configuration requirements and, in some cases, a specific microcomputer system. However, if you are like most people and want to take advantage of the wide variety of microcomputer software, you will have a number of micro alternatives available to you within a given platform. Identify one or more that meet criteria established in the first five steps.

Step 7: Determine the Processor-Related Features You Want. Once you have narrowed your choice of microcomputer systems to one, two, or perhaps three, you are ready to determine which processor-related features you want. Become familiar with the options of these systems. For example, assess the availability of expansion slots, parallel ports, and serial ports. You can go with a basic processor or, if your budget allows, you can select a more powerful processor and add a few "bells and whistles." Expect to pay for each increase in convenience, quality, and speed. For example, you may wish to enhance your processor's capability by increasing the size of the random-access memory (RAM), adding a coprocessor, and including some add-on capabilities (for example, a modem for data communications or a fax board). Add-on options are discussed in Chapter 2, "Micros, Minis, Mainframes, and Supercomputers."

STEP 6: IDENTIFY ONE OR MORE MICROCOMPUTER SYSTEMS FOR FURTHER EXAMINATION. A new generation of modular computers is making it easier to upgrade both desktop and notebook computers. Upgrading this Tandon computer is as easy as pulling out one processor cartridge and sliding in another.

STEP 7: DETERMINE THE PROCESSOR-RELATED FEATURES YOU WANT. This architect uses an IBM Personal System/2 series with a tower configuration. This model is designed to rest on the floor and provides more expansion slots.

Step 8: Determine the Peripheral Devices You Want. Generally speaking, the only necessary peripheral devices are the *disk drive*, *monitor*, *keyboard*, *mouse* (or other pointing device), and *printer*. However, these and other peripheral devices come in a wide variety of speeds, capacities, and qualities. The peripherals you select depend on your specific needs, volume of usage, and the amount of money you are willing to spend. Most micros are configured with two disk drives, one for diskettes and a hard disk. You choose the type of diskette (3½-inch or 5¼-inch) and capacity of the hard disk (from 40 MB to about over 700 MB). The choice of a monitor boils down to size, resolution, and whether or not you need color. You can pay $150 for a printer or $10,000 for a desktop typesetter. This choice depends on the anticipated volume of hard-copy output; whether you need graphics output, letter-quality print, color output; and so on.

These standard peripheral devices and other devices, such as a joystick, image scanner, speech-recognition device, vision-input system, plotter, desktop film recorder, screen-image projector, speech synthesizer, and tape drive, are discussed in detail in Chapter 5, "Input/Output Devices," and Chapter 6, "Data Storage and Organization."

Step 9: "Test Drive" Several Alternatives. Once you have selected several software and hardware alternatives, spend enough time to gain some familiarity with them. Do you prefer one keyboard over another? Does a word processing system fully implement the hardware features? Is one system easier to understand than another?

STEP 8: DETERMINE THE PERIPHERAL DEVICES YOU WANT. If you are going to be doing desktop publishing, you may need an image scanner.

417

STEP 10: SELECT AND BUY YOUR SYSTEM. Once you've made your purchase, the only task left is to open up the boxes and start setting up your new system.

Many software packages have demonstration and/or tutorial disks. When you load the demo or tutorial disk on the micro, an instructional program interactively "walks you through" a simulation (demonstration) of the features and use of the software. It is a good idea to work through the demo to get a feeling for the product's features and ease of use.

Salespeople at most retail stores are happy to give you a "test drive"—just ask. Use these sessions to answer any questions you might have about the hardware or software.

Step 10: Select and Buy Your System. Apply your criteria, select, and then buy your hardware and software.

FACTORS TO CONSIDER WHEN BUYING A MICRO

- *Future computing needs*. What will your computer and information-processing needs be in the future? Make sure the system you select can grow

with your needs. For example, the difference between a 40-MB and 100-MB Winchester disk may be several hundred dollars. However, if you estimate your disk-storage needs to be in excess of 40 MB within a couple of years, you may be better off in the long run buying the 100-MB disk.

- *Who will use the system*? Plan not only for yourself but also for others in your home or office who will use the system. Get their input and consider their needs along with yours.

- *Availability of software*. Software is developed for one or several platforms, but not for all of them. As you might expect, a more extensive array of software is available for the more popular platforms (MS-DOS, Windows, and Apple Macintosh).

- *Service*. Computing hardware is very reliable. Even so, the possibility exists that one or several of the components eventually will malfunction and have to be repaired. Before purchasing a micro, identify a reliable source of hardware maintenance. Most retailers service what they sell. If a retailer says the hardware must be returned to the manufacturer for repair, choose another retailer or another system. If you plan on purchasing via mail order, identify a nearby computer-repair store or a computer retailer that does repair work on the system you intend to buy.

Most retailers or vendors will offer a variety of maintenance contracts. Maintenance-contract options range from same-day, on-site repairs that cover all parts and service to a carry-in service that does not include parts. Most domestic users elect to treat their micros like their televisions and cars: When the warranty runs out, they pay for repairs as they are needed. Under normal circumstances, this strategy will prove the least expensive. Business users are sometimes willing to pay extra for the convenience of an on-site maintenance contract.

Service extends beyond hardware maintenance. Service is also an organization's willingness to respond to your inquiries before *and* after the sale. Some retailers and vendors offer classes in programming and in the use of the hardware and software they sell.

Most hardware and software vendors offer a *technical support hot-line*. The extent of the hot-line service varies considerably. Some companies provide their licensed users with a toll-free 24-hour hot-line—free of charge for as long as they own the product. At the other end of the spectrum, companies charge their users as much as $50 an hour for using their technical support hot-lines. Typically, companies will provide hot-line service for a limited period of time (six months or a year), then charge after that.

- *Hardware obsolescence*. "I'm going to buy one as soon as the price goes down a little more." If you adopt this strategy, you may never purchase a computer. If you wait another six months, you probably will be able to get a more powerful micro

for less money. But what about the lost opportunity?

There is also a danger in purchasing a micro that is near or at the end of its life cycle. If you are planning on using a micro frequently at school, home, or work, focus your search on micros with state-of-the-art technology. Although you may get a substantial discount on a micro with dated technology, you may be better off in the long run by choosing an up-to-date one.

- *Software obsolescence*. Software can become obsolete as well. Software vendors are continually improving their software packages. Each package is assigned a *version number*. The first *release* might be identified as 1.0 (referred to as *one point zero*). Subsequent updates to Version 1.0 become Version 1.1, Version 1.2, and so on. The next major revision of the package is released as Version 2.0. Make sure you are buying the most recent release of a particular software package.

- *Product documentation (internal and external)*. PC products are consumer items and are distributed with user manuals, just like automobiles and VCRs. In most cases, the person who purchases the product installs it and uses it. To install it and use it, you will need effective product documentation. Inevitably, you will spend many hours with the product's documentation. Make sure that it is good.

When you purchase a PC or other hardware device, you will receive one or more user manuals. Examine the hardware documentation to ensure that it is visually and conceptually clear (especially the installation procedure), contains plenty of illustrations, has a good index, has a trouble-shooting guide, and lists numbers to call for help.

When you purchase a software package, you usually will receive at least one manual, the software on diskettes or CD-ROM (if requested), and often a tutorial disk. The best software documentation contains a user manual, a reference guide, and a workbook/tutorial. Depending on the complexity of the package, this documentation can be packaged in one, two, or three manuals. The user manual contains information on the features and the procedures that you would follow to use these features. (The most effective user manuals present the product at two levels—overview and in detail.) The reference guide provides a technical description of the package's capabilities (often at the menu-item level). The workbook/tutorial leads you, keystroke by keystroke, through the major features of the software.

A word of warning: Manuals and tutorials tell you everything you *can* do but say very little about what you *cannot* do. That may take a bit of experimentation to learn.

■ *Availability of training*. Proper documentation should contain everything you need to know about how to use a PC, an I/O device, or a software package. However, learning strictly from the product's documentation can be difficult unless you are a seasoned PC veteran. Most people will opt to learn about micros or a particular software package by taking a course of some kind, perhaps at a local college. Many companies offer in-house courses for their employees. Retail computer stores offer courses for their customers. Self-paced multimedia courses are available commercially for most of the more popular software packages.

Before you opt for a particular PC or software program, check the availability of training.

■ *Other costs*. The cost of the actual microcomputer system is the major expense, but there are many incidental expenses that can mount up and influence your selection of a micro. If you have a spending limit, consider these costs when purchasing the hardware (the cost ranges listed are for a first-time user): software ($100–$1500); maintenance ($0–$500 a year); diskettes and tape cassettes, including holders ($50–$200); furniture ($0–$350); cables ($0–$50); insurance ($0–$100); and printer ribbons or cartridges, paper, and other supplies ($40–$400).

PC BUYER'S WORKSHEET

After you have looked at two or three systems, their features, options, and specifications tend to blur in your mind. It is difficult to remember whether the first system had a 30-MB Winchester disk and a 40-MHz processor or a 40-MB Winchester disk and a 30-MHz processor. The best way to make an informed purchase decision is to capture pertinent information in a way that will allow an easy comparison between alternatives. The adjacent template for a PC Buyer's Worksheet is designed to help you document this information.

The two approaches to using the worksheet are:

■ *Gather information on proposed systems*. Discuss your processing and I/O needs with a sales representative, then ask the representative to propose a system to meet these needs. Complete a separate worksheet for each system configuration proposed by each sales organization.

■ *Document the ideal system for your needs*. Determine your own processing and I/O needs, then fill in the worksheet with a description of your ideal system. When you visit or talk with an organization's sales representative, discuss the worksheet description. You probably will not find exactly what you want, so be prepared to make minor modifications to your ideal system. Make copies of your ideal worksheet, then for each system discussed, note differences on a copy of your worksheet.

Once you have investigated the alternatives and are ready to make a decision, the information on the worksheet helps you in the decision-making process.

PC Buyer's Worksheet

Name of vendor_____

Contact person_____

Telephone number_(___)_____—_____ ext._____

	Cost

Processor and Memory Specifications: Make_____Model_____ $_____

      Microprocessor_____   Speed_____*MHz*

      RAM_____*KB/MB* Word *16/32 bits*

      Type system: *pocket\laptop\desktop\tower*

      Expansion slots: full___half___

      Ports: serial___parallel___

      Extra RAM ($_____ *per MB*) $_____

      Add-ons (*included in price*)_____

      Add-ons (*not included in price*)_____ $_____

      Special features (*included in price*)_____

      Special features (*not included in price*)_____ $_____

Keyboard Specifications: Make_____Model_____ $_____

      Number of keys____   Number of function keys___

      Keypad: *yes/no*   Stand-alone cursor control: *yes/no*

Monitor Specifications: Make_____Model_____ $_____

      Display: color/monochrome

      Size of display____(*inches width*)   Resolution___*X*___

      Technology (*pocket and laptop only*)_____

      Port or expansion slot requirements_____

Disk Drive Specifications:

      Interchangeable disk drive A: Make_____Model_____ $_____

      Size: *3½/5¼* Capacity: *DD/HD*

      Interchangeable disk drive B: Make_____Model_____ $_____

      Size: *3½/5¼* Capacity: *DD/HD*

      Winchester disk drive B: Make_____Model_____ $_____

      Capacity___*MB*

Tape Drive Specifications: Make_____Model_____ $_____

      Capacity___*MB*

Printer Specifications: Make_____Model_____ $_____

     Technology_____

     Speed____*(cps/ppm)*   Resolution____*(pins/dpi)*

     Port or expansion slot requirements_____

     Cable requirement (*connectors and length*)_____

     Special features (*included in price*)_____

     Special features (*not included in price*)_____ $_____

Mouse Specifications: Make_____Model_____ $_____

     Number of buttons: *2/3*

     Port or expansion slot requirements_____

Other I/O Device Specifications:

     Device_____: Make_____Model_____ $_____

     Specs:_____

     Device_____: Make_____Model_____ $_____

     Specs:_____

     Device_____: Make_____Model_____ $_____

     Specs:_____

Software (included with price of PC):

     Name_____Description_____

     Name_____Description_____

     Name_____Description_____

                   Total Hardware Cost $_____

Software Requirements:

     Name_____Description_____

     Name_____Description_____

     Name_____Description_____

                   Total Software Cost $_____

                   TOTAL SYSTEM COST $_____

General comments:_____

_____

_____

_____

_____

The MIS and Decision Support Systems

STUDENT LEARNING OBJECTIVES

▶ To describe how information needs vary at each level of organizational activity.

▶ To distinguish between programmed decisions and nonprogrammed decisions.

▶ To describe the circumstances appropriate for batch and transaction-oriented data entry.

▶ To identify the elements, scope, and capabilities of an information system.

▶ To define *data processing system, management information system, decision support system, executive support system,* and *expert system.*

▶ To identify characteristics associated with data processing systems, management information systems, decision support systems, executive support systems, and expert systems.

CHAPTER OUTLINE

When General Motors field representatives hit the road, they carry laptop computers loaded with dealer information, from market outlooks and sales forecasts to customer satisfaction indices.

 Information and Decision Making

To be successful, managers must fully understand and use four major resources: money, materials, people, and information. Managers have become adept at taking full advantage of the resources of *money*, *materials*, and *people*; but only recently have they begun to make effective use of the fourth major resource—*information*. In fact, corporate management everywhere is adopting this new concept called **information resource management (IRM)**. Information resource management treats information as a valuable resource that should be managed accordingly, just like money, materials, and people. In an all-out effort to meet the "productivity" challenge and be competitive, managers are turning to the information resource. This chapter discusses how managers can use computers to obtain more and better information.

The Decision-Making Environment

The four levels of activity within a company are *strategic*, *tactical*, *operational*, and *clerical*. Computer-based information systems process data at the clerical level and provide information for managerial decision making at the operational, tactical, and strategic levels.

- Strategic-level managers determine long-term strategies and set corporate objectives and policy consistent with these objectives. (long term) - MGMT
- Tactical-level managers are charged with the responsibility of implementing the objectives and policies set forth at the strategic level of management. To do this, managers identify specific tasks that need to be accomplished. (short term) MGMT

- Operational-level managers complete specific tasks as directed by tactical-level managers. (day-to-day) MGMT

The business system model shown in Figure 13–1 helps place the decision-making environment in its proper perspective. As you can see, it is necessary for managers to use all the resources at their disposal more effectively, meet corporate objectives, and perform the management functions of *planning, staffing, organizing, directing,* and *controlling.*

Figure 13–1 illustrates how the corporate resources of *money, materials* (including facilities and equipment), *people,* and *information* become "input" to the various functional units, such as operations, sales, and accounting. People use their talent and knowledge, together with these resources, to produce products and services.

FIGURE 13–1   A Business System Model

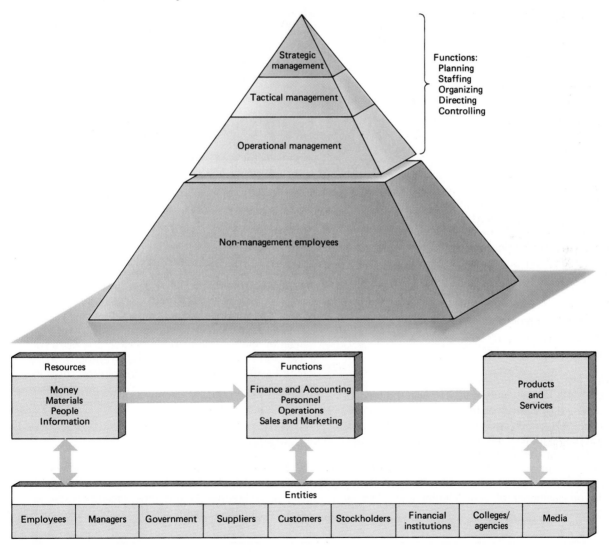

Each day your name and personal information are passed from computer to computer. Depending on your level of activity, this could happen 20 or more times a day. Thousands of public- and private-sector organizations maintain data on individuals. The data collection begins before you are born and does not end until all your affairs are settled and those maintaining records on you are informed of your parting.

TAX DATA

The Internal Revenue Service maintains the most visible stockpile of personal information. It, of course, keeps records of our whereabouts, earnings, taxes, deductions, employment, and so on. Now the IRS is supplementing basic tax information with external information to create personal profiles to tell if a person's tax return is consistent with his or her lifestyle. By law, all IRS data must be made available to about 40 different government agencies.

EDUCATION DATA

What you've accomplished during your years in school, such as grades and awards, is recorded in computer-based data bases. Included in these data bases is a variety of information such as your scores on college entrance exams, data on loan applications that include details of your family's financial status, roommate preferences, disciplinary actions, and so on. In one instance, a Chicago woman was turned down for several government jobs because of a note her third-grade teacher had entered in her file. In the note the teacher stated that in her view the girl's mother was crazy.

MEDICAL DATA

Medical files, which contain a mountain of sensitive personal data, are not always treated with the respect they deserve. In many hospitals, hundreds of employees, most of whom do not have a need-to-know, have ready access to patient information. Your medical records list all your visits to clinics and hospitals, your medical history (and often that of your family), allergies, and diseases you have or have had. They also may include assessments of your mental and physical health.

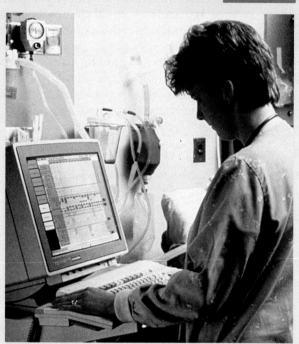

MEDICAL RECORDS   Progressive hospitals restrict staff access to patient medical histories on a need-to-know basis.

DRIVER AND CRIME DATA

State motor vehicle bureaus maintain detailed records on over 150 million licensed drivers. This information includes personal descriptive data (sex, age, height, weight, color of eyes and hair) as well as records of arrests, fines, traffic offenses, and whether your license has been revoked. Some states sell descriptive information to retailers on the open market. The FBI's National Crime Information Center (NCIC) and local police forces maintain data bases that contain rap sheet information on 20 million people. This information is readily available to thousands of law-enforcement personnel.

CENSUS DATA

With the 1990 Census still fresh in our minds, we are reminded that the U.S. Bureau of the Census maintains some very personal data: names, racial heritage, income, the number of bathrooms in our home, and persons of the opposite sex who share our living quarters. Statistics, however, are released without names.

INSURANCE DATA

Insurance companies have formed a cooperative to maintain a single data base containing medical information on millions of people. This revealing data base includes claims, doctors' reports, whether or not you have been refused insurance, how risky you would be as an insuree, and so on.

LIFESTYLE DATA

A number of cities are installing two-way cable TV that allows the accumulation of information on people's personal viewing habits. When you watch an X-rated movie, or any other movie, your choice is recorded in the family's viewing data base. As interactive cable TV matures, you will be able to use it to pay bills, respond to opinion polls, and make dinner reservations. This, of course, will add a greater variety of information to your personal file.

POLICE RECORDS Law enforcement officials routinely record and review personal information.

CREDIT DATA

Credit bureaus routinely release intimate details of our financial well-being. We, of course, hope that the information about us is up-to-date and accurate. However, this is not always the case. About one third of those who ask to review their records (you have the right to do this at any time) challenge their accuracy. Credit bureaus are bound by law to correct inaccuracies within two weeks of being notified of them.

MISCELLANEOUS DATA

Every time you make a long-distance telephone call, the number is recorded. When you make a credit-card purchase, your location at the time and the type of item you buy are recorded. Job-related information is maintained at current and past employers, including the results of performance reports and disciplinary actions. Local and state governments maintain records of property transactions that involve homes, automobiles, boats, guns, and so on. Banks not only keep track of your money, but some monitor the volume and type of transactions you make.

SUMMARY

The social security number, now assigned to all citizens, is the link that ties all our personal information together. It doubles as a military serial number, and in many states it serves as your driver's license number. It is the one item, along with your name, that appears on almost all personal forms. For example, your social security number is a permanent entry in hospital, tax, insurance, bank, employment, school, and scores of other types of records.

The few organizations discussed here represent the tip of the iceberg, so to speak. For the most part, these and thousands of other organizations are making a genuine attempt to handle personal data in a responsible manner. However, instances of abuse are widespread and give us cause for concern. Computers are now the primary vehicle for processing and storing personal information, and they will store even more information about us in the future. However, it's not computers that abuse the privacy of our personal information, it's the people who run them. We as a society must be prepared to meet the challenge with a system of laws that deals realistically with the problem.

The business system acts in concert with several *entities*, such as employees, customers, and suppliers (see Figure 13–1). An entity is the source or destination of information flow. An entity also can be the source or destination of materials or product flow. For example, suppliers are a source of both information and materials. They are also the destination of payments for materials. The customer entity is the destination of products and the source of orders.

Filtering Information

The quality of an information system is judged by its output. A system that generates the same 20-page report for personnel at both the clerical and strategic levels defeats the purpose of an information system. The information needs at these two levels of activity are substantially different. For example, a secretary might need names, date of employment, and other data to enroll employees in a pension plan. The president of the company does not need that level of detail but does need information on overall employee pension contributions.

The key to developing quality information systems is to filter information so that people at the various levels of activity receive just the information they need to accomplish their job functions—no more, no less. **Filtering** information results in the *right information* reaching the *right decision maker* at the *right time* in the *right form*.

Clerical Level   Clerical-level personnel, those involved in repetitive tasks, are concerned primarily with *transaction handling*. You might say that they process data. For example, in a sales information system, order-entry clerks key in customer orders on their terminals. In an airline reservation system, ticket agents confirm and make flight reservations.

Operational Level   Personnel at the operational level have well-defined tasks that might span a day, a week, or as long as three months, but their tasks are essentially short-term. Their information requirements often consist of *operational feedback*. In the sales information system, for example, the manager of the Eastern Regional Sales Department for Bravo International, a small high-tech firm, might want an end-of-quarter sales summary report. The report, illustrated in Figure 13–2, shows dollar-volume sales by salesperson for each of Bravo International's four products: Alphas, Betas, Gammas, and Deltas. In the report, the sales records of the top (Cook) and bottom (Ritter) performers are highlighted so that managers can use this range as a basis for comparing the performance of the other salespeople.

Managers at the operational, tactical, and strategic levels often request **exception reports** that highlight critical information. They can make such requests through the information services department, or managers can make inquiries directly to the system using a query language. For example, the eastern regional sales manager used a fourth-generation language to produce the exception report in Figure 13–2. The manager's request was:

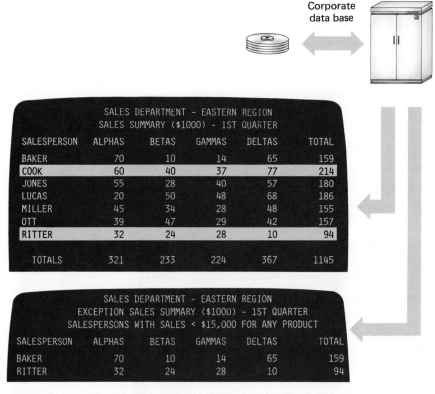

```
          SALES DEPARTMENT - EASTERN REGION
          SALES SUMMARY ($1000) - 1ST QUARTER

SALESPERSON   ALPHAS    BETAS    GAMMAS    DELTAS    TOTAL

BAKER           70        10        14        65       159
COOK            60        40        37        77       214
JONES           55        28        40        57       180
LUCAS           20        50        48        68       186
MILLER          45        34        28        48       155
OTT             39        47        29        42       157
RITTER          32        24        28        10        94

 TOTALS        321       233       224       367      1145
```

```
          SALES DEPARTMENT - EASTERN REGION
        EXCEPTION SALES SUMMARY ($1000) - 1ST QUARTER
      SALESPERSONS WITH SALES < $15,000 FOR ANY PRODUCT
SALESPERSON   ALPHAS    BETAS    GAMMAS    DELTAS    TOTAL

BAKER           70        10        14        65       159
RITTER          32        24        28        10        94
```

FIGURE 13–2   An Operational-Level Sales Summary and Exception Report
These sales reports are prepared in response to inquiries from an operational-level manager. Contrast the reports in this figure with those in Figures 13–3 and 13–4.

Display a list of all eastern region salespeople who had sales of less than $15,000 for any product in this quarter.

The report highlights the subpar performances of Baker and Ritter.

The information available for an operational-level decision is often conclusive. That is, the most acceptable alternative can be clearly identified based on information available to the decision maker. At this level, personal judgment and intuition play a reduced role in the decision-making process.

Tactical Level   At the tactical level, Bravo International managers concentrate on achieving a series of goals required to meet the objectives set at the strategic level. The information requirements are usually *periodic*, but on occasion managers require one-time and "what if" reports. *"What if" reports* are generated in response to inquiries that depict what-if scenarios ("What if sales increase by 15% next quarter?"). Tactical managers are concerned primarily with operations and budgets from year to year. In the sales information system, the national sales manager, who is at the tactical level, might want the "Corporate Sales" report of Figure 13–3. The report presents dollar-volume sales by sales region for each of

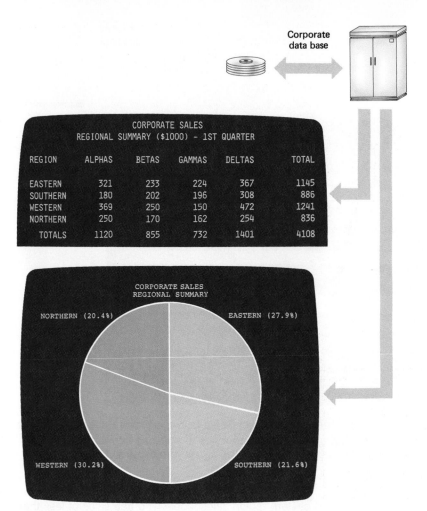

```
                    CORPORATE SALES
        REGIONAL SUMMARY ($1000) - 1ST QUARTER

REGION      ALPHAS    BETAS    GAMMAS    DELTAS      TOTAL

EASTERN       321      233       224       367       1145
SOUTHERN      180      202       196       308        886
WESTERN       369      250       150       472       1241
NORTHERN      250      170       162       254        836

  TOTALS     1120      855       732      1401       4108
```

CORPORATE SALES
REGIONAL SUMMARY

NORTHERN (20.4%)   EASTERN (27.9%)

WESTERN (30.2%)   SOUTHERN (21.6%)

Corporate
data base

FIGURE 13–3   A Tactical-Level Sales Summary Report Shown in Tabular and Graphic Formats

The sales summary report and pie graph are prepared in response to inquiries from a tactical-level manager. Contrast the reports in this figure with those in Figures 13–2 and 13–4.

the company's four products. To get a better sense of the relative sales contribution of each of the four regional offices during the first quarter, the national sales manager requested that the total sales for each region be presented graphically in a pie graph (Figure 13–3).

The information available for a tactical-level decision is seldom conclusive. That is, the most acceptable alternative cannot be identified from information alone. At this level, most decisions are made by using personal judgment and intuition in conjunction with available information.

Strategic Level   Bravo International's strategic-level managers are objective-oriented. Their information system requirements are often *one-time reports*, *"what if" reports*, and *trend analyses*. For example, the president of the company, Edward Epsilon, might ask for a report that shows the four-year sales trend for each of the company's four products and overall (Figure 13–4). Knowing that it is easier to detect trends in a graphic format than in a tabular one, Mr. Epsilon requests that the trends be summarized in a bar graph (Figure 13–4). From the bar graph, he easily can see that the sales of Alphas and Gammas are experiencing modest growth while the sales of Betas and Deltas are better.

The information available for a strategic-level decision is almost never conclusive. To be sure, information is critical to strategic-level decision making, but virtually all decision makers at this level rely heavily on personal judgment and intuition.

FIGURE 13–4   A Strategic-Level Sales-Trend-by-Product Report Shown in Tabular and Graphic Formats

The sales-trend report and bar graph are prepared in response to inquiries from a strategic-level manager. Contrast the reports in this figure with those in Figures 13–2 and 13–3.

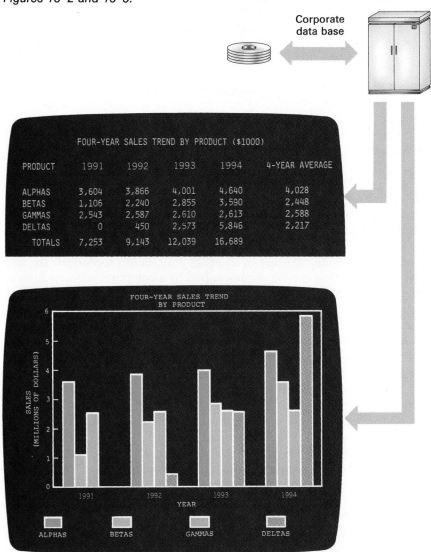

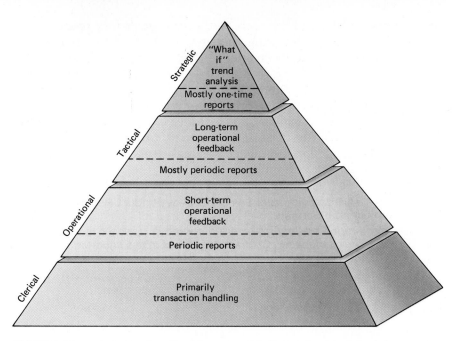

FIGURE 13–5 Information Requirement Profile by Level of Activity

The information requirements at the various levels of organizational activity are summarized in Figure 13–5.

Programmed and Nonprogrammed Decisions

The two basic types of decisions are **programmed decisions** and **nonprogrammed decisions**. Purely programmed decisions address well-defined problems. The decision maker has no judgmental flexibility because the actual decision is determined by existing policies or procedures. In fact, many such decisions can be accomplished by a computer without human intervention! For example, the decision required to restock inventory levels of raw materials is often a programmed decision that can be made by an individual or by a computer-based information system. When the inventory level of a particular item drops below the reorder point, perhaps two months' supply, a decision is made to replenish the inventory by submitting an order to the supplier.

Nonprogrammed decisions involve ill-defined and unstructured problems. Such decisions are also called **information-based decisions** because the decision maker needs information in order to make a rational decision. The information requirement implies the need for managers to use judgment and intuition in the decision-making process. Corporate policies, procedures, standards, and guidelines provide substantial direction for nonprogrammed decisions made at the operational level, less direction at the tactical level, and little or no direction at the strategic level. The greater the programmability of a decision, the greater the confidence of the decision maker that the most acceptable alternative has been selected.

These operators control the operation of a desalination plant in the Canary Islands that supplies water for drinking and irrigation. Prior to being automated, they were routinely confronted with programmed decisions. Now, the computer-based system makes such decisions, leaving the operators more time to make the more difficult information-based decisions. The trend toward relegating programmed decisions to computers is apparent in all industries.

13-2 Information System Concepts

The Information System Defined

In Chapter 1 we introduced and briefly described the concept of an information system. *Hardware, software, people, procedures,* and *data* are combined to create an *information system* (see Figure 13–6). The term *information system* is a generic reference to a computer-based system that provides the following:

- *Data processing* capabilities for a department or, perhaps, an entire company
- *Information* that people need to make better, more informed decisions

The data processing capability refers to the system's ability to handle and process data. The more sophisticated information systems provide decision makers with *on-demand reports* and *inquiry capabilities* as well as *routine periodic reports.*

Five types of information systems are discussed in this chapter: *data processing systems, management information systems, decision support systems, executive support systems,* and *expert systems.* Each is described in detail later in this chapter. The remainder of this section addresses important concepts that relate to information systems in general.

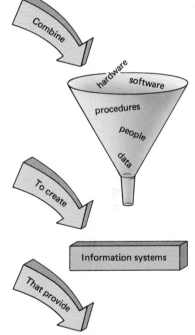

FIGURE 13–6 Creating an Information System

Information System Capabilities

Not surprisingly, an information system has the same four capabilities as a computer system: *input*, *processing*, *storage*, and *output* (Figure 13–7).

Input The information system input capability can accept

- *Source data.* Usually the recording of a transaction or an event (for example, a bank deposit or the receipt of order).

FIGURE 13–7 Information System Capabilities

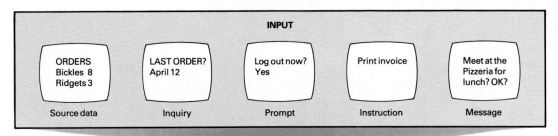

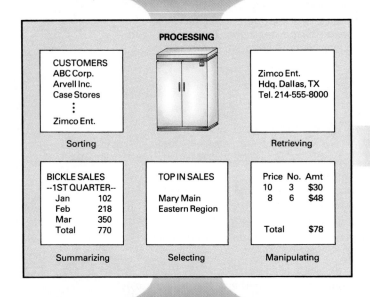

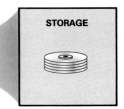

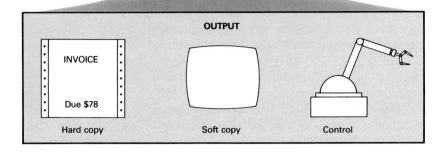

- *An inquiry.* A request for information.
- *A response to a prompt.* For example, a *Y* or an *N*.
- *An instruction.* For example, "Store file" or "Print record."
- *A message to another user on the system.*
- *A change.* For instance, editing a word processing document.

Processing   The information system processing capability encompasses

- *Sorting.* Arranging data or records in some order (for example, alphabetizing a customer file by last name).
- *Accessing, recording, and updating data in storage.* For example, retrieving a customer record from a data base for processing, entering expense data into an accounting system's data base, and changing a customer's address on a marketing data base, respectively.
- *Summarizing.* Presenting information in a condensed format, often to reflect totals and subtotals.
- *Selecting.* Selecting records by criteria (for example, "Select all employees with 25 or more years of service in the company").
- *Manipulating.* Performing arithmetic operations (addition, multiplication, and so on) and logic operations (comparing an employee's years of service to 25 to determine if they are greater than, equal to, or less than 25).

Storage   The information system storage capability permits it to store *data, text, images* (graphs, pictures), and *other digital information* (voice messages) so that they can be recalled easily for further processing.

Output   The information system output capability allows it to produce output in a variety of formats:

- *Hard copy.* For example, printed reports, documents, and messages.
- *Soft copy.* Temporary displays on terminal screens, for instance.
- *Control.* For example, instructions to industrial robots or automated processes.

Manual Systems versus Computer-Based Information Systems

When we speak of an information system today, we imply an automated system. The elements of an information system are hardware, software, people, procedures, and data. The automated elements (the hardware and software) do not play a part in manual systems. Manual systems consist of people, procedures, and data. In terms of numbers, the overwhelming majority of systems in industry, government, and education are still manual. This is true of large organizations with hundreds of computers and of two-person companies. Tens of thousands of manual systems have been targeted to be upgraded to computer-based information systems. Ten times that many are awaiting tomorrow's creative users and computer professionals to identify their potential for computerization.

Both manual systems and computer-based information systems have an established pattern for work and information flow. In a manual payroll

The paperless office is a goal that may be unreachable in the foreseeable future; however, many companies are encouraging employees to use soft copy whenever possible. These knowledge workers seldom need hard copy. When they need information, they simply request that it be displayed.

system, for example, a payroll clerk receives time sheets from supervisors; the clerk retrieves each employee's records from folders stored alphabetically in a file cabinet. The clerk uses a calculator to compute gross and net pay, then manually types the payroll check and stub. Finally, the payroll clerk compiles the payroll register, which is a listing of the amount paid and the deductions for each employee, on a tally sheet with column totals. About the only way to find and extract information in a manual payroll system is to thumb through employee folders painstakingly.

Today most payroll systems have been automated. But look in any office in almost any company and you will find rooms full of filing cabinets, tabbed three-ring binders, circular address files, or drawers filled with 3-by-5-inch inventory cards. These manual systems are opportunities to improve a company's profitability and productivity through the application of computer technologies.

Function-Based versus Integrated Information Systems

An information system can be either function-based or integrated. A **function-based information system** is designed for the exclusive support of a specific application area, such as inventory management or accounting. Its data base and procedures are, for the most part, independent of any other system. The data bases of function-based information systems invariably contain data that are maintained in other function-based systems within the same company. For example, much of the data needed for an accounting system would be duplicated in an inventory management system. It is not unusual for companies with a number of autonomous function-based systems to maintain customer data in 5 to 10 different data bases. When a customer moves, the address must be updated in several data bases (accounting, sales, distribution, and so on). This kind of data redundancy is an unnecessary financial burden to a company.

An integrated information system links people throughout the company through a common data base. When a yardmaster at this Southern Pacific switching yard in Long Beach, California, makes up a freight train, every Southern Pacific yardmaster in the system knows the content and destination of each car in the train.

During the past decade, great strides have been made in the integration of function-based systems. The resulting **integrated information systems** share a common data base. The common data base helps minimize data redundancy and allows departments to coordinate their activities more efficiently. Integrated data bases are discussed in detail in Chapter 9, "System Software and Platforms."

On-Line versus Off-Line

As we discussed earlier, the four fundamental components of a computer system are input, processing, storage, and output. In a computer system, the input, output, and data storage components receive data from and transmit data to the processor over electrical cables, or lines. These hardware components are said to be *on-line* to the processor. Hardware devices that are not accessible to nor under the control of a processor are said to be *off-line*. The concepts of on-line and off-line also apply to data. Data are said to be *on-line* if they can be accessed and manipulated by the processor. All other data are *off-line*.

On-line and off-line are important information system concepts. Consider the payroll example in Figure 13–8. In an *off-line* operation, all supervisors complete the weekly time sheets. The time sheets are then collected and *batched* for input to the computer system. When transactions are grouped together for processing, it is called **batch processing**.

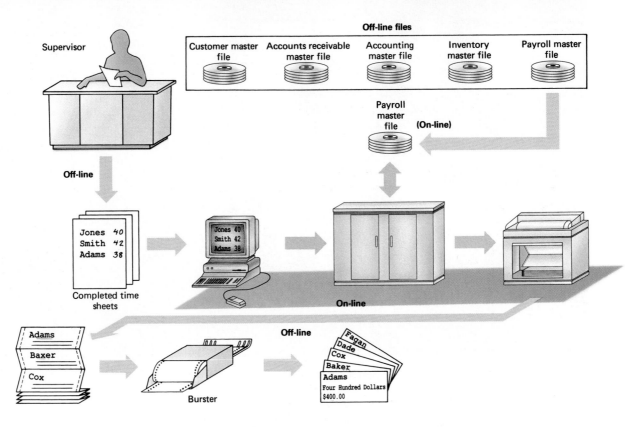

FIGURE 13–8 On-Line and Off-Line Operations

Those processing activities, hardware, and files that are not controlled by or accessible to the computer are referred to as off-line.

Before the data can be entered and the payroll checks printed, the payroll master file must be placed on-line, if it is not already. To do this, it is retrieved manually from a library of interchangeable disks and loaded to a storage component called a disk drive. Once loaded, the payroll master file is on-line. The process is analogous to selecting the compact disk you wish to play and mounting it on the turntable. (Many computer-based files and data bases are stored on permanently installed fixed disks. These files and data bases are on-line whenever the computer system is operational.)

An operator at a terminal enters the data on the time sheets directly into the computer system in an *on-line* operation. Employee data, such as name, social security number, pay rate, and deductions, are retrieved from the payroll master file and combined with the number of hours worked to produce the payroll checks. The payroll checks are produced on a printer, which is an output device.

The payroll checks are printed on continuous preprinted forms and they must be separated before distribution to the employees. In an *off-line* operation, a machine called a *burster* separates and stacks the payroll checks.

Data Entry Concepts

Source Data   Most data do not exist in a form that can be "read" by the computer. In the example of Figure 13–8, the supervisor records manually the hours worked by the staff on the time sheet. Before the payroll checks can be computed and printed, the data on these time sheets must be *transcribed* (converted) into a *machine-readable format* that can be interpreted by a computer. This is done in an *on-line* operation by someone at a terminal. The time sheet is the *source document* and, as you might expect, the data on the time sheet are the **source data**.

Not all source data have to be transcribed. For example, the numbers printed at the bottom of your bank checks are your individual account number and bank number. They are already machine-readable, so they can be read directly by an input device. Other approaches to *source data automation* are discussed in Chapter 5, "Input/Output Devices."

Approaches to Data Entry   The term **data entry** describes the process of entering data into an information system. Information systems are designed to provide users with display-screen prompts to make on-line data entry easier. The display on the operator's screen, for example, may be the image of the source document (such as a time sheet). A **prompt** is a brief message to the operator that describes what should be entered (for example, "INPUT HOURS WORKED ____").

Data can be entered on a terminal or PC in the following ways:

- *Batch processing.* In batch processing, transactions are grouped, or batched, and entered consecutively, one after the other.
- *Transaction-oriented processing.* In **transaction-oriented processing**, transactions are recorded and entered to the system as they occur.

To illustrate the difference between batch and transaction-oriented processing, consider the order-processing system for Bravo International (see Figure 13–9). The system accepts orders by both mail and phone. The

In even the most sophisticated information processing environments, much of the information is in manual systems. For example, until recently, most of the medical records at this hospital were maintained off-line in color-coded manila folders. This information was inaccessible to computer systems. Now, this and other hospitals use image processing to incorporate the images of original patient records with the existing on-line patient data base.

FIGURE 13–9   Batch and Transaction-Oriented Processing
The typical order-entry system accepts orders by mail and by phone.

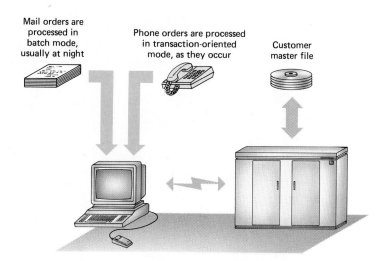

orders received by mail are accumulated, or batched, for data entry—usually at night. There are no handwritten source documents for phone orders; people taking the phone orders interact with the computer via terminals and enter the order data on-line while talking with the customer.

On-Line Data Entry   Most data entered into mainframe computer systems, both batch and transaction-oriented, is done on-line. Terminal operators enter data *directly* into the host computer system for processing as shown in Figure 13–9. The primary advantage of transaction-oriented data entry is that records on the data base are updated immediately, as the transaction occurs. With batch data entry, records are batched periodically. In a transaction-oriented environment, the data base remains continuously up-to-date and can be queried at any time. In the example of Figure 13–9, a salesperson can check the availability of an item and tell the customer when to expect delivery.

▶ 13–3   Data Processing Systems

Data processing (DP) systems are concerned with transaction handling and record-keeping, usually for a particular functional area. Data are entered and stored in a file format, and stored files are updated during routine processing. Periodic outputs include *action documents* (invoices) and *scheduled reports*, primarily for operational-level managers. The major drawback of data processing systems is that they are inflexible and cannot accommodate data processing or information needs that are not already built into the system. Most companies have moved beyond the scope of DP systems and now have systems with the flexibility of providing management with information in support of an ever-changing decision-making environment.

Household Finance Corporation and other real estate lending companies rely on management information systems for fast, accurate home mortgage information.

In the not-too-distant past, most payroll systems were data processing systems that did little more than process time sheets, print payroll checks, and keep running totals of annual wages and deductions. As managers began to demand more and better information about their personnel, payroll *data processing systems* evolved into human resource **management information systems**. A human resource management information system is capable of predicting the average number of worker sick days, monitoring salary equality between minority groups, making more effective use of available skills, and providing other information needed at all three levels of management—operational, tactical, and strategic.

The Management Information System Defined

If you were to ask any five executives or computer professionals to define a management information system, or **MIS**, the only agreement you would find in their responses is that there is no agreement on its definition. An MIS has been called a method, a function, an approach, a process, an organization, a system, and a subsystem. The following working definition of *management information system* will be used in this book:

> An MIS is an integrated structure of data bases and information flow that optimizes the collection, transfer, and presentation of information throughout a multilevel organization whose component groups perform a variety of tasks to accomplish a united objective.

Figure 13–10 depicts the concept of information flow in a multilevel organization (strategic, tactical, and so on) with component parts (finance, accounting, and so forth). The definition we provide represents

FIGURE 13–10   Information Flow in a Multilevel Organization
An MIS is the mechanism that enables information to flow throughout all levels and components of a multilevel organization.

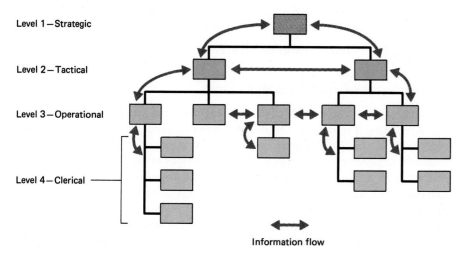

Level 1—Strategic

Level 2—Tactical

Level 3—Operational

Level 4—Clerical

Information flow

the ideal. In reality, an organization can only strive for optimization and total integration. But even if the finished product falls short of the ideal, users and computer personnel are aiming for the same target.

Characteristics of Management Information Systems

The following are *desirable* characteristics of an MIS:

- An MIS supports the data processing functions of transaction handling and record-keeping.
- An MIS uses an integrated data base and supports a variety of functional areas.
- An MIS provides operational-, tactical-, and strategic-level managers with easy access to timely but, for the most part, structured information.
- An MIS is somewhat flexible and can be adapted to meet changing information needs of the organization.
- An MIS provides an envelope of system security that limits access to authorized personnel.

The MIS versus the DP System

The basic distinctions between an MIS and a DP system are summarized as follows:

- The integrated data base of an MIS enables greater flexibility in meeting the information needs of management than the traditional file environment of DP systems.
- An MIS integrates the information flow between functional areas where DP systems tend to support a single functional area.
- An MIS caters to the information needs of all levels of management where DP systems focus on operational-level support.
- Management's information needs are supported on a more timely basis with an MIS (on-line inquiry capability) than with a DP system (usually scheduled reports).

▶ 13–5 Decision Support Systems

The Decision Support System Defined

A New Gadget for the Couch Potato Hewlett-Packard recently announced it is planning to develop an interactive peripheral device to enhance your TV viewing pleasure. With this device, you actually play along with TV game shows. Viewers can also order food or do banking while interacting with the TV. Hewlett-Packard hopes to sell about 1.5 million of this new gadget in the first year.

Managers spend much of their day obtaining and analyzing information before making a decision. Decision support systems were created to assist managers in this task. **Decision support systems (DSS)** are interactive information systems that rely on an integrated set of user-friendly hardware and software tools to produce and present information targeted to support management in the decision-making process. On many occasions, decisions makers can rely on their experience to make a quality decision, or they need look no further than the information that is readily available from the integrated corporate MIS. However, decision makers, especially at the tactical and strategic levels, are often confronted with complex decisions whose factors are beyond their human abilities to synthesize properly. These types of decisions are "made to order" for decision support systems.

A decision support system can help close the information gap and allow managers to improve the quality of their decisions. To do this, DSS hardware and software employ the latest technological innovations (for example, color graphics and database management systems), planning and forecasting models, user-oriented 4GLs, and even artificial intelligence.

In many cases, the DSS facilitates the decision-making process, helping a decision maker choose between alternatives. Some DSSs have the capability of automatically ranking alternatives based on the decision maker's predetermined criteria. Decision support systems also help remove the tedium of gathering and analyzing data. For example, managers are no longer strapped with such laborious tasks as manually entering and extending numbers (totaling rows and columns of numbers) on spreadsheet paper. Graphics software enables managers to generate illustrative bar and pie graphs in a matter of minutes. And, with the availability of a variety of user-oriented DSSs, managers can get the information they need without having to depend on direct technical assistance from an MIS professional.

In the shipping business, the accuracy of fuel estimates may mean the difference between making or losing money. These engineers rely on a decision support system that uses historical data and updated consumption data to produce reliable fuel estimates.

The DSS versus the MIS

As we have mentioned before, management information systems are oriented to supporting decisions that involve *structured* problems, such as when to replenish raw materials inventory and how much to order. This type of routine operational-level decision is based on production demands, the cost of holding the inventory, and other variables that depend on the use of the inventory item. The MIS integrates these variables into an inventory model and presents specific order information (for example, order quantity and order date) to the manager in charge of inventory management.

In contrast to the MIS, decision support systems are designed to support decision-making processes involving *semistructured* and *unstructured* problems. A semistructured problem might be the need to improve the delivery performance of suppliers. The problem is partially structured in that information comparing the on-time delivery performance of suppliers during the past two years can be obtained either from hard-copy records or directly from the integrated data base supporting the MIS. The unstructured facets of the problem, such as extenuating circumstances, rush-order policy and pricing, and so on, make this problem a candidate for a DSS.

An example of an entirely unstructured problem would be the evaluation and selection of an alternative to the raw material currently used. A decision maker might enlist the aid of a DSS to provide information on whether it would be advisable to replace a steel component with a plastic or aluminum one. The information requirements for such a decision are diverse and typically beyond the scope of an MIS.

Another distinction we can make between an MIS and a DSS is that an MIS is designed and created to support a specific application (accounting, inventory control) or set of applications (an integrated MIS). A DSS is a set of decision support tools that can be adapted to any decision environment.

Characteristics of Decision Support Systems

The following are *desirable* characteristics of a DSS:

- A DSS helps the decision maker in the decision-making process.
- A DSS is designed to address semistructured and unstructured problems.
- A DSS supports decision makers at all levels, but it is most effective at the tactical and strategic levels.
- A DSS makes general-purpose models, simulation capabilities, and other analytical tools available to the decision maker.
- A DSS is an interactive, user-friendly system that can be used by the decision maker with little or no assistance from an MIS professional.
- A DSS can be readily adapted to meet the information requirements of any decision environment.
- A DSS provides the mechanisms to enable a rapid response to a decision maker's request for information.
- A DSS has the capability of interfacing with the corporate data base.

- A DSS is not executed in accordance with a pre-established production schedule.
- A DSS is flexible enough to accommodate a variety of management styles.
- A DSS facilitates communication between levels of decision making (for example, graphic presentation of operational-level information for review by top management).

The DSS Tool Box

A decision support system is made up of a set of decision support tools that can be adapted to any decision environment (see Figure 13–11). These tools can be categorized as *software tools* and *hardware tools*. The combination of these general-purpose tools helps managers address

FIGURE 13–11   The Decision Support System
A decision support system is a set of software and hardware tools that can be adapted to any decision environment.

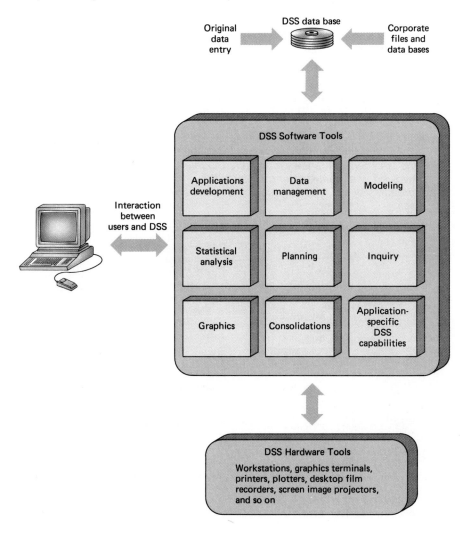

decision-making tasks in specific application areas (the evaluation and promotion of personnel, the acquisition of companies, and so on). Any input/output device that facilitates interaction with or makes use of the system would be considered a DSS hardware tool. Software DSS tools include the following:

- *Applications development.* Some decision support systems provide end users with the capability of developing computer-based systems to support the decision-making process. These applications typically involve the input, processing, and storing of data and the output of information. The ease with which DSS applications can be created has spawned a new term— **throwaway systems.** Often DSS applications are developed to support a one-time decision and are then discarded.

- *Data management.* Each DSS software package has its own unique approach to database management—that is, the software mechanisms for the storage, maintenance, and retrieval of data. This DSS tool is necessary to ensure compatibility of a DSS data base and an integrated set of DSS software tools.

- *Modeling.* Decision support systems enable managers to use mathematical modeling techniques to re-create the functional aspects of a system within the confines of a computer. Models are appropriate when decisions involve a number of factors. For example, models are often used when uncertainty and risk are introduced, when several decision makers are involved, and when multiple outcomes are anticipated. In these cases, each decision needs to be evaluated on its own merit.

Decision support systems enable managers to use network modeling techniques to model complex projects. This Gantt chart, which was created using the SAS System, shows managers the relationships between the various tasks involved in a manufacturing project. The project model helps them select the approach that optimizes the use of resources while meeting project deadlines.

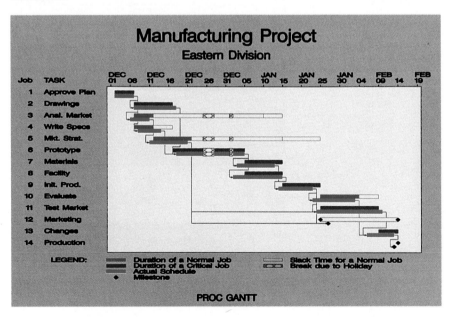

- *Statistical analysis.* The DSS statistical analysis capability includes everything from simple statistics such as average, median, and standard deviation to more analytical techniques such as regression analysis, exponential smoothing, and discriminate analysis to complex procedures such as multivariate analysis. Risk analysis and trend analysis are common applications of DSS statistical tools.

- *Planning.* End user managers are often faced with making decisions that will be implemented at some time in the future. To help them get a glimpse into the future, they rely on DSS software that permits *forecasting, "what if" analysis*, and *goal seeking* (for example, "How much do we need to increase the advertising budget to achieve a goal of $120 million sales for next year?").

- *Inquiry.* DSS software enables managers to make on-line inquiries to the DSS data base using English-like commands (for example, a natural language interface with a 4GL). End users who query corporate data bases are able to communicate with computers in much the same language that they would use to communicate with their colleagues.

- *Graphics.* With the graphics DSS software tool, managers can create a variety of presentation graphics based on data in the DSS data base, including bar graphs, pie graphs, and line graphs.

- *Consolidations.* DSS software tools are available that enable the consolidation of like data from different sources (for example, the consolidation of financial statements from subsidiary companies into a single corporate financial statement).

- *Application-specific DSS capabilities.* DSS software that supports a particular decision environment, such as financial analysis and quality control, is being introduced routinely into the marketplace.

13–6 Executive Support Systems

Just as user managers and the computer community are finally getting a handle on the scope and functionality of decision support systems, a new type of information system is conceived. Now we have the **executive support system**. Like its predecessors, the MIS and the DSS, the term *executive support system*, or **ESS**, has been introduced with fanfare and anticipation, but without a commonly accepted definition. At present ESS is viewed as a subset of decision support systems designed specifically to support decision making at the tactical and strategic levels of management. Like the MIS and DSS, the ESS may eventually gain an identity of its own, but today's commercially available executive support systems look suspiciously like what most managers and MIS professionals have come to know as decision support systems.

13–7 Expert Systems

What Is an Expert System?

The most recent addition to the circle of information systems is the *expert system.* Expert systems are associated with an area of research known as *artificial intelligence.* We introduced expert systems and artificial intelligence in Chapter 1, "The World of Computers." Artificial intelligence is the ability of a computer to reason, to learn, to strive for self-improvement, and to simulate human sensory capabilities. The scope of artificial intelligence research is discussed in Chapter 18, "Computers in Society: Today and Tomorrow." Like the DSS, expert systems are computer-based systems that help managers resolve problems or make better decisions. However, an expert system does this with a decidedly different twist. It is an interactive computer-based system that responds to questions, asks for clarification, makes recommendations, and generally helps the user in the decision-making process. In effect, working with an expert system is much like working directly with a human expert to solve a problem because the system mirrors the human thought process. It even uses information supplied by a real expert in a particular field such as medicine, taxes, or geology.

An expert system applies preset IF-THEN rules to solve a particular problem, such as determining a patient's illness. Like management information systems and decision support systems, expert systems rely on factual knowledge, but expert systems also rely on *heuristic knowledge* such as intuition, judgment, and inferences. Both the factual knowledge and the heuristic rules of thumb are acquired from a *domain expert,* an expert in a particular field. The expert system uses this human-supplied knowledge to model the human thought process within a particular area of expertise. Once completed, a knowledge-based system can approximate the logic of a well-informed human decision maker.

Technically speaking, an *expert system* is the highest form of a **knowledge-based system.** In practice, the terms *expert system* and *knowledge-based system* are used interchangeably. The less sophisticated knowledge-based systems are called **assistant systems.** An assistant system helps users make relatively straightforward decisions. Assistant systems are usually implemented to reduce the possibility that the end user will make an error in judgment rather than to resolve a particular problem.

In effect, expert systems simulate the human thought process. To varying degrees, they can *reason, draw inferences,* and *make judgments.* Here is how an expert system works. Let's use a medical diagnosis expert system as an example. Upon examining a patient, a physician might use an expert diagnosis system to get help in diagnosing the patient's illness or, perhaps, to get a second opinion. First the doctor would relate the symptoms to the expert system: male, age 10, temperature of 103°, and swollen glands about the neck. Needing more information, the expert system might ask the doctor to examine the parotid gland for swelling. Upon receiving an affirmative answer, the system might ask a few more questions and even ask for lab reports before giving a diagnosis. A final question for the physician might be whether the patient had been previously afflicted with or immunized for parotitis. Based on the information, the expert system would diagnose the illness as parotitis, otherwise known as the mumps.

In recent years expert systems have been developed to support decision makers in a broad range of disciplines, including medical diagnosis, oil exploration, financial planning, tax preparation, chemical analysis,

This output from an executive support system portrays corporate performance relative to five executive-defined critical success factors: expenses, revenues, customer service, stock prices, and net profits.

surgery, locomotive repair, weather prediction, computer repair, trouble-shooting satellites, computer systems configuration, nuclear-power plant operation, newspaper layout, interpreting government regulations, and many others.

Benefits of Expert Systems

The benefits of an expert system are somewhat different from those of other decision support systems and of management information systems.

- *An expert system enables the knowledge of experts to be "canned," so to speak.* The specialized knowledge of human experts can be captured in the form of an expert system. For example, at Campbell's Soup Company, Aldo Cimino was the only expert trouble-shooter for Campbell's giant cookers. He and his 43 years of experience were about to retire, so Campbell's executives decided to "drain his brain" into an expert system. Mr. Cimino may be retired, but Campbell's Soup Company continues to benefit from his years of experience.

- *A single expert system can expand the decision-making capabilities of many people.* In effect, an expert's knowledge can be distributed to and used by anyone associated with a specific decision environment. For example, a number of loan officers at a bank can enlist the aid of an expert system for guidance in approving and rejecting loan applications.

- *An expert system can improve the productivity and performance of decision makers.* By having ready access to an electronic partner with vast expertise in a particular area, decision makers can progress more rapidly to the most acceptable solution.

- *An expert system can provide stability and consistency to a particular area of decision making.* Unlike human beings, an expert system responds with exactly the same information when the same decision is presented. When people in similar decision-making situations have access to the advice and guidance of an expert system, the decisions they make tend to be consistent with one another.

- *An expert system reduces dependencies on critical personnel.* Human beings retire, get sick, take vacations, and only a few of them ever attain the status of expert. Computers do not take coffee breaks. Expert systems can "drain the brains" of the very limited supply of experts so that others can benefit from their expertise, immediately and after they retire.

- *An expert system is an excellent training tool.* Companies are using expert systems to train decision makers in a way similar to airlines' use of flight simulators to train pilots. During training, individuals work through a particular decision with an expert system. After making the decision, they review the documentation of the decision rationale generated by the expert system. From this documentation, they learn how decisions are made within the context of a particular environment.

Selecting an Expert System Application

Not every company has a decision-making environment appropriate for expert systems. The situation has to be just right, to justify the cost of

Memory Bits

INFORMATION SYSTEMS

- Data processing (DP) system
  Functional area support
  Transaction handling and record-keeping
- Management information system (MIS)
  Integrated data base
  DP functions plus management information
- Decision support system (DSS)
  Interactive systems
  Various tools that support decision making
- Executive support system (ESS)
  Subset of DSS
  Decision support at tactical and strategic levels
- Expert system
  Interactive knowledge-based system
  Simulates human thought process

This financial adviser sometimes requests a second opinion from an expert system before advising his clients.

developing an expert system. Typically, the development and implementation of even the most basic expert systems will involve a minimum of one work year of effort and a substantial monetary outlay for the purchase of software and hardware. Before a decision is made to create an expert system, top management should be made aware of what decision environments are appropriate for its implementation.

Those decision environments most conducive to expert systems share the following characteristics:

- A number of people will use the expert system frequently as part of their work routine.
- Decisions are complex.
- The decision logic can be translated to a hierarchy of rules.
- Applications typically focus on advice, classification, diagnosis, interpretation, explanation, selection of alternatives, evaluation of situations, or forecasting.

The number and variety of expert system applications have increased dramatically with the advent of powerful, cost-effective microcomputers. Expert systems advise financial analysts on the best mix of investments; help taxpayers interpret the tax laws; help computer repairpersons diagnose the problems of a malfunctioning computer; and help independent insurance agents select the best overall coverage for their business clients. For early versions of expert systems, the minimum hardware configuration was an expensive dedicated superminicomputer. Today expert systems can run on everything from micros to supercomputers.

The Expert System Shell

When we talk about expert systems, we usually mean systems that can help decision makers working in a particular *domain of expertise*, such as the configuration of computer systems or commercial lending. As mentioned earlier, these expert systems are the result of substantial development efforts. The software that enables the development of these expert systems has no "intelligence" and is known as the **expert system shell**.

Expert system shells are usually domain-independent proprietary software packages that have no applications "knowledge." An expert system shell contains the generic parts needed to create an expert system for a specific application. For example, the expert system shell provides companies with the capabilities needed to construct a knowledge base and the facility by which the user interacts with the knowledge base. The primary components of the expert system shell are the *knowledge acquisition facility*, the *knowledge base*, the *inference engine*, and the *user interface* (see Figure 13–12).

- *Knowledge acquisition facility.* The **knowledge acquisition facility** is that component of the expert system shell that permits the construction of the knowledge base. The knowledge base is created through the cooperative efforts of a **knowledge engineer** and one or more experts in a particular field, called **domain experts** (see Figure 13–12). The knowledge engineer

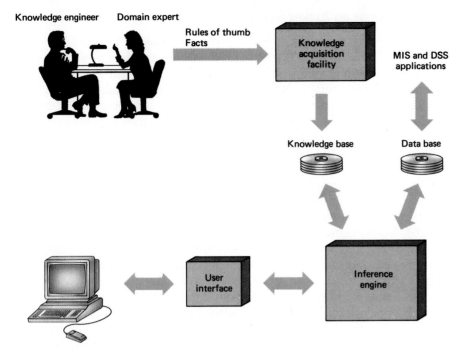

FIGURE 13–12 Components of an Expert System Shell

translates the expert's knowledge into *factual knowledge* and *rules* to create the knowledge base.

- *Knowledge base.* Appropriate facts and rules are entered into the **knowledge base** during the acquisition phase. To complete the knowledge base, the knowledge engineer, in cooperation with the domain expert, enters the following: the identification of problem(s) to be solved; possible solutions to the problem(s); and how to progress from problem to solution (primarily through facts and rules of inference). Facts (employee name and so on) needed to articulate the solution to the user are retrieved from the corporate data base (see Figure 13–12).

- *Inference engine.* The **inference engine** is the nucleus of an operational expert system (see Figure 13–12). It is the vehicle by which the facts and rules in the knowledge base are applied to a problem. The inference engine gives an expert system its ability to reason. It does this by leading the user through a logic path that results in a solution.

- *User interface.* Heuristic procedures are informal; that is, there are no formal algorithms available to solve the problem. An expert system problem is addressed by one strategy as long as it looks promising. The system always retains the option to switch to another strategy. This heuristic approach requires a flexible **user interface** (see Figure 13–12). This component of an expert system enables the type of interaction between end user and expert system needed for heuristic processing. The user interface permits the end user to describe the problem or goal. It permits both the end user and the expert system to structure questions and responses. Along with a response to a particular inquiry, an expert system usually explains and documents why a particular course of action was recommended.

An Example of an Expert System

Credit-card companies use expert system technology to provide better service to their customers, increase productivity, and save money. A case in point is the American Express Authorizer's Assistant expert system. American Express retains 300 authorizers who provide around-the-clock service to cardholders and customers. For credit-card purchases that exceed a preset amount, retailers must contact American Express to obtain authorization before completing the transaction. In cooperation with a human authorizer, the expert system ultimately recommends that a credit charge be approved or denied, or it recommends an alternative line of reasoning and the need for more information. American Express bought the system when it realized it was suffering significant losses from bad authorization decisions made by the less-experienced authorizers. To create the Authorizer's Assistant expert system, several human expert authorizers related tried-and-true rules of thumb to a knowledge engineer. From them, a knowledge engineer constructed a knowledge base that contained 520 rules. During the testing phase the number of rules grew to 850. At the end of the test period, the system demonstrated that it could reduce bad authorization decisions by 76%. Authorizer's Assistant is one of American Express' success stories. The system resulted in more consistent decision making, improved authorizer productivity, reduced credit and fraud losses, reduced operating expenses, improved service to customers and cardholders, more accurate decisions, and reduced learning time for authorizers. The system was expensive and time-consuming, but the benefits were so overwhelming that American Express recouped its entire investment during the first year of operation!

Expert System Summary

One of the myths surrounding expert systems is that they will replace human experts. While expert systems augment the capabilities of humans and make them more productive, they will never replace them. Expert systems and humans complement one another in the decision-making process. The computer-based expert system can handle routine situations with great accuracy, thereby relieving someone of the burden of a detailed manual analysis. Humans can combine the insight of an expert system with their flexible intuitive abilities to resolve complex problems.

In the short period of their existence, expert systems have operated impressively and they continue to improve. Decision makers in every environment are developing or contemplating developing an expert system. Attorneys will hold mock trials with expert systems to "pre-try" their cases. Doctors routinely will ask a second opinion. Architects will "discuss" the structural design of a building with an expert system. Military officers will "talk" with the "expert" to plan battlefield strategy. City planners will "ask" an expert system to suggest optimal locations for recreational facilities.

Some computer industry observers believe that expert systems are the wave of the future and that each of us will have "expert" help and guidance in our respective professions.

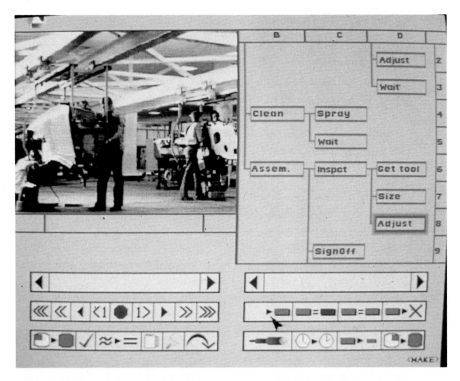

Mechanics get trouble-shooting help with this computer-based expert system. The mechanic simply keys in responses to questions asked by the "expert" about the malfunction. Through interactive questioning, the expert system eventually identifies the cause of the malfunction and demonstrates repair procedures on the video monitor.

 Important Terms and Summary Outline

assistant system	function-based	knowledge-based
batch processing	information system	system
data entry	inference engine	management information
data processing (DP)	information resource	system (MIS)
system	management (IRM)	nonprogrammed
decision support	information-based	decision
system (DSS)	decision	programmed decision
domain expert	integrated information	prompt
exception report	system	source data
executive support	knowledge acquisition	throwaway system
system (ESS)	facility	transaction-oriented
expert system shell	knowledge base	processing
filtering	knowledge engineer	user interface

13–1 INFORMATION AND DECISION MAKING. Traditionally managers have been very adept at taking full advantage of the resources of money, materials, and people, but only recently have they begun to make effective use of information, the other resource. **Information resource management (IRM)** treats information as a valuable resource that should be managed accordingly. By **filtering** information, the right information reaches the right decision maker at the right time in the right form.

Information systems help process data at the clerical level and provide information for managerial decision making at the operational, tactical, and strategic levels. Managers at the operational, tactical, and strategic levels often request **exception reports** that highlight critical information. For decisions made at the tactical and strategic levels, information is often inconclusive, and managers also must rely on their experience, intuition, and common sense to make the right decision.

The two basic types of decisions are **programmed decisions** and **nonprogrammed decisions**. Purely programmed decisions address well-defined problems. Nonprogrammed decisions, also called **information-based decisions**, involve ill-defined and unstructured problems.

13–2 INFORMATION SYSTEM CONCEPTS.   Hardware, software, people, procedures, and data are combined to create an information system. An information system provides a company with data processing capabilities and the company's people with information.

Commonly used systems terms are *information systems, data processing systems, management information systems, decision support systems, executive support systems,* and *expert systems.* The last five are types of information systems.

An information system has the same four capabilities as a computer system: input, processing, storage, and output. The processing capabilities include sorting; accessing, recording, and updating data in storage; summarizing; selecting; and manipulating.

An information system can be either function-based or integrated. A **function-based information system** is designed for the exclusive support of a specific application area. **Integrated information systems** share a common data base.

In a computer system, the input, output, and data storage components that receive data from and transmit data to the processor are said to be on-line. Hardware devices that are not accessible to nor under the control of a processor are said to be off-line. **Source data** on source documents must be transcribed into a machine-readable format before they can be interpreted by a computer. **Data entry** describes the process of entering data into an information system. Information systems are designed to provide users with display-screen **prompts** to make on-line data entry easier.

When transactions are grouped together for processing, it is called **batch processing**. In **transaction-oriented processing**, transactions are recorded and entered as they occur.

13–3 DATA PROCESSING SYSTEMS.   **Data processing (DP) systems** are file-oriented, function-based systems that focus on transaction handling and record-keeping and provide periodic output aimed primarily at operational-level management.

13–4 MANAGEMENT INFORMATION SYSTEMS.   The authors offer the following definition of a **management information system**, or **MIS**: An MIS is an integrated structure of data bases and information flow that optimizes the collection, transfer, and presentation of information throughout a multilevel organization whose component groups perform a variety of tasks to accomplish a united objective.

An MIS not only supports the traditional data processing functions, it also relies on an integrated data base to provide managers at all levels with easy access to timely but structured information. An MIS is flexible and can provide system security.

An MIS is oriented to supporting decisions that involve structured problems.

13–5 DECISION SUPPORT SYSTEMS. **Decision support systems** are interactive information systems that rely on an integrated set of user-friendly hardware and software tools to produce and present information to support management in the decision-making process.

A **DSS** supports decision making at all levels by making general-purpose models, simulation capabilities, and other analytical tools available to the decision maker. A DSS can be readily adapted to meet the information requirements for any decision environment.

In contrast to the MIS, decision support systems are designed to support decision-making processes involving semistructured and unstructured problems.

A decision support system is made up of a set of software and hardware tools. The categories of DSS software tools include applications development (frequently resulting in **throwaway systems**), data management, modeling, statistical analysis, planning, inquiry, graphics, consolidations, and application-specific DSS capabilities.

13–6 EXECUTIVE SUPPORT SYSTEMS. **The executive support system (ESS)** is a subset of decision support systems that is designed specifically to support decision making at the tactical and strategic levels of management.

13–7 EXPERT SYSTEMS. Expert systems, which are associated with an area of research known as artificial intelligence, help managers resolve problems or make better decisions. They are interactive systems that respond to questions, ask for clarification, make recommendations, and generally help in the decision-making process. An expert system is the highest form of a **knowledge-based system**, but in practice the two terms are used interchangeably. The less sophisticated knowledge-based systems are called **assistant systems**.

The following are several of the more prominent benefits of expert systems: They enable the knowledge of experts to be "canned"; they can expand the decision-making capabilities of many people; they can improve the productivity and performance of decision makers; and they can provide stability and consistency to a particular area of decision making.

The **expert system shell** is a domain-independent proprietary software package that enables the development of expert systems. The primary components of the expert system shell are the knowledge acquisition facility, the knowledge base, the inference engine, and the user interface.

The **knowledge acquisition facility** of the expert system shell permits the construction of the **knowledge base**. The knowledge base is created through the cooperative efforts of a **knowledge engineer** and one or more **domain experts**.

The knowledge base of an expert system contains facts, rules of inference, the identification of problem(s) to be solved, possible solutions to the problem(s), and how to progress from problem to solution.

An expert system's **inference engine** is the vehicle by which the facts and rules in the knowledge base are applied to a problem.

The **user interface** component of an expert system enables the interaction between end user and expert system needed for heuristic processing.

 Review Exercises

Concepts

1. MIS is an abbreviation for what term?
2. What is the purpose of an exception report?
3. What elements are combined to create an information system?
4. What are the levels of organizational activity, from specific to general?
5. Which type of information system would most closely approximate working directly with a human expert to solve a problem?
6. Which of the following information systems is designed specifically for decision support at the tactical and strategic levels of management: expert systems, management information systems, DP systems, or executive support systems?
7. Which component of the expert system shell permits the construction of the knowledge base?
8. In which type of processing are transactions grouped together for processing?
9. What are the two basic types of decisions?
10. What is meant by filtering information?
11. List seven items in the DSS software tool box.
12. Distinguish between on-line operation and off-line operation.
13. What do expert systems and assistant systems have in common?
14. What are the primary components of an expert system shell?

Discussion

15. For each of the three levels of management illustrated in the business system model in Figure 13–1, what would the horizon (time span) be for planning decisions? Explain.
16. In general, top executives have always treated money, materials, and people as valuable resources, but only recently have they recognized that information is also a valuable resource. Why do you think they waited so long?
17. It is often said that "time is money." Would you say that "information is money"? Discuss.
18. Give examples of reports that might be requested by an operational-level manager in an insurance company. By a tactical-level manager. By a strategic-level manager.

19. Contrast a DP system with an MIS. Contrast an MIS with a DSS.

20. Describe a specific decision environment that would be appropriate for the implementation of an expert system.

Problem Solving

21. Suppose the company you work for batches all sales data for data entry each night. You have been asked to present a convincing argument to top management why funds should be allocated to convert the current system to transaction-oriented data entry. What would you say?

22. The American Express Authorizer's Assistant, discussed in this chapter, paid for itself in one year. Explain briefly how you think the system was able to

   a. Provide more consistent decision making

   b. Improve authorizer productivity

   c. Reduce credit and fraud losses

   d. Reduce operating expenses

   e. Improve service to customers and cardholders

   f. Enable more accurate decision making

   g. Reduce learning time for authorizers

23. Que Realty is like most other realty companies in that at any given time, about half the sales staff is inexperienced. The owner decided to develop an expert system to help both inexperienced and veteran agents do a better job of matching buyers with available properties. The purpose of the system is to create a profile of a house that meets the buyer's needs. The owner arranged for an expert system consultant to interview David Meissner, Que's most successful agent, and create the system.

During the interview, Mr. Meissner said that he asks his clients a series of questions relating to their needs and desires. Based on the client's responses, he rates each factor's importance. He then considers these factors when searching the list of available homes to determine which ones to show the client. To help in the design of the expert system, the consultant and Mr. Meissner agreed on the following scale for client responses to questions: critical, important, advantageous, and immaterial.

Mr. Meissner always asks his clients for the following data:

   a. Number of adults and their relationship (spouse, parent, and so on)

   b. Number of children and their ages

   c. Work place location(s)

   d. Style of house preferred

Put yourself in the role of the consultant and prepare at least one rule for each of the above questions using the following format. Make any necessary assumptions (for example, style of house must be selected from a specified list consisting of ranch, bilevel, two-story colonial, and so on).

          IF: <condition>

          THEN: <action or result>

          REASON: <the rationale>

For example

IF: <There is an adult who is not a spouse>

THEN: <Ask about privacy needs>

REASON: <Client may desire separate entrance or detached living quarters for parents, in-laws, and so on>

 Self-Test (by section)

13–1 **a.** Tactical-level managers are charged with the responsibility of implementing the objectives and policies set forth at the ___strategic___ level of management.

b. It is easier for a manager to detect trends presented in a graphic format than in a tabular format. (T/F)

c. Nonprogrammed decisions are also called: (a) computer-oriented decisions, (b) information-based decisions, or (c) human decisions?

13–2 **a.** The summarizing activity would be associated with which capability of an information system: (a) input, (b) output, or (c) processing?

b. An integrated information system is designed for the exclusive support of a specific application area. (T/F)

c. A burster separates and stacks the payroll checks in an _____ (on-line or off-line) operation. ___transaction___ ___record___

13–3 The focus of data processing systems is ___handling___ and ___keeping___ .

13–4 **a.** An MIS provides an envelope of system security that limits access to authorized personnel. (T/F)

b. Which type of information system integrates the information flow between functional areas: (a) DP system, (b) MIS, or (c) DSS?

13–5 **a.** Decision support systems are designed to support decision-making processes involving semistructured and unstructured problems. (T/F)

b. A DSS is most effective at which two levels of management: (a) clerical and operational, (b) operational and tactical, or (c) tactical and strategic?

c. DSS applications that are discarded after providing information support for a one-time decision are called ___throw away systems.___

13–6 An MIS is a subset of an ESS. (T/F)

13–7 **a.** An assistant system is the highest form of a knowledge-based system. (T/F)

b. Which type of information system has the greatest potential to reduce dependencies on critical personnel: (a) MIS, (b) expert system, or (c) DP system?

c. The software that enables the development of an expert system is known as the expert system ___shell___ .

d. During the creation of an expert system's knowledge base, the ___knowledge engineer___ translates the domain expert's knowledge into facts and rules.

Self-test answers. **13–1(a)** strategic; **(b)** T; **(c)** b. **13–2(a)** c; **(b)** F; **(c)** off-line. **13–3** transaction handling, record-keeping. **13–4(a)** T; **(b)** b. **13–5(a)** T; **(b)** c; **(c)** throwaway systems. **13–6** F. **13–7(a)** F; **(b)** b; **(c)** shell; **(d)** knowledge engineer.

Applications of Information Technology

STUDENT LEARNING OBJECTIVES

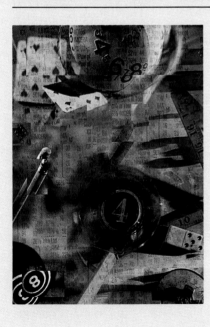

▶ To discuss computer and information system applications that have the potential of giving organizations a competitive advantage.

▶ To discuss computer and information system applications common to most organizations.

▶ To discuss a variety of computer and information system applications unique to specific types of organizations.

CHAPTER OUTLINE

14–1 The Uses of Information Technology

Life has become very competitive. Whether we like it or not, we are always engaged in some kind of competition. We compete on the tennis court and at the bridge table. We compete for favored status among friends. We compete with our fellow students for the best grades. We compete with our colleagues for promotions. The rules, the manner in which we compete, and the rewards have changed little in most of life's competitions. This, however, is not the case when we talk about how we compete with other companies. Winners in the corporate world are implementing new and innovative uses of computers and information systems to enable them to offer better products and services at a lower cost. Corporate competition is ongoing in that each company has a seemingly endless number of opportunities to use information technology to gain the *competitive advantage*.

This chapter contains an overview of the applications of computers and information systems, sometimes referred to as **information technology**, or **IT**. This overview is not intended to be an exhaustive treatment of information technology applications. However, it can acquaint you with a few of the ways information technology is contributing to and, in many instances, changing society.

Information technology applications are covered in three sections.

- *Applications that result in a competitive advantage.* The first section presents several ways in which organizations have employed information technology to achieve a competitive advantage.
- *Common systems.* The next section addresses those applications *common*

Effective use of information technology is fast becoming the ultimate strategic weapon in the business world. For example, General Motors wanted to lower the cost of producing automobiles while retaining maximum flexibility in what is made. To do this, a computer-based information system was installed to control the assembly line and enable the communication and implementation of last-minute order changes.

to just about any organization that employs people to produce goods and services (payroll processing, for example).

■ *Industry-specific applications.* The final section presents applications *unique to a particular type of industry or organization* (for example, the patient accounting system used in the health care field).

14–2 Gaining the Competitive Advantage with Information Technology

It is no longer possible for a company to achieve success and profits through good management and hard work. These organizational qualities have become prerequisites for survival, and managers must seek strategies that can give their companies the *competitive advantage*, especially those strategies that involve information technology.

In this highly competitive era, the judicious use of information technology can make the difference between profitability and failure in just about every type of organization. This section provides examples of how organizations are employing information technology to realize a competitive advantage.

Making Strategic Alliances with Customers

Electronic data interchange (EDI) (introduced in Chapter 7, "Connectivity and Data Communications") has altered the basic constructs of the wholesale drug distribution industry and it is likely to do the same with other industries as well. EDI uses computers and data communications to transmit data (for example, invoices and orders) electronically between companies. *Strategic alliances* involving EDI ultimately benefit all parties involved.

Traditionally pharmacists at over 50,000 drugstores devote many hours each week to taking inventory and creating handwritten lists of the items they need to restock. Those who have computer systems usually enter order data into their own local systems. The system prints the purchase orders, often in triplicate, and they are sent by mail to one or more wholesale distributors. It is not unusual for a single order to contain hundreds, even thousands of items. When the wholesaler receives the hard-copy order, key entry operators enter the orders into their computer system.

The trend today is toward drug wholesalers providing EDI capabilities to their customers as an incentive to do business with them. Those who provide this capability are realizing a competitive advantage and substantial increases in market share. Those who do not provide EDI capabilities are struggling or going out of business.

Pharmacists use distributor-supplied, hand-held bar-code scanners to expedite the order-entry process. The only datum keyed in by the druggist is the quantity. Order data are loaded from the portable data

A pharmaceutical company's representative is demonstrating an information-based service it offers to doctors. The system lets doctors tap directly into the company's data base to obtain information on thousands of drugs (possible side effects, interactions with other drugs, dosages, and so on). This service gives the company a strategic advantage.

entry device directly to the pharmacist's computer system, and an electronic order is transmitted from the retailer to the distributor via data communications. This approach eliminates the need for hard-copy orders and redundant key data entry.

Besides expediting the order entry process, the wholesaler provides the pharmacist with other information-based incentives as well. For example, pharmacists have only to ask for sales reports by department and product, and products are even shipped with price labels that have the customer-designated profit margin. In an ongoing effort to provide the best customer incentives and gain the competitive advantage, drug wholesalers are continuing to "up the ante." One distributor provides computer-generated suggestions for the most effective visual presentation of products. Another processes insurance forms and provides records needed for preparing income tax returns. As you can see, the EDI system provides a winning combination for the drug industry.

Taking Full Advantage of Available Technology

Perhaps the most price-sensitive market of all is the grocery business. A company can lure customers from a competitor by lowering prices by a few pennies on selected items. Supermarket managers are continually seeking ways to lower prices and reap the competitive advantage. To gain that edge thousands of supermarkets have installed automated checkout

First there was the automatic teller machine (ATM) and now there is the automated checkout machine (ACM). The move to self-checkout in supermarkets is gaining momentum. Shoppers scan their own groceries and receive visual and verbal confirmation of each purchase from the monitor. With ACMs, checkout is faster and less expensive. To pay, the customer takes a printed itemized receipt to the cashier. ACM-equipped stores can offer customers lower prices while maintaining their profit margin.

systems to take advantage of the machine-readable Universal Product Code (UPC) imprinted on each item. The automated checkout systems not only speed the checkout process but also save money that can be passed on to customers in the form of lower prices. Supermarkets experience gains in checker productivity from 20% to 50%. The system electronically tallies purchases, speeds cash flow, updates the inventory, and alerts store personnel when bad checks are presented. Even though thousands of automated checkout systems have been installed, many grocery stores still do not have them. At these supermarkets the operating costs are higher, the checkout process is slower, and management is unable to monitor inventory levels on a timely basis.

Within a few years all supermarkets will have automated checkout systems—and what then? Some supermarkets are not waiting. They are seeking new competitive strategies involving information systems. Several have installed terminals in the stores so that customers can inquire about the location of an item. Other stores give each customer a personalized shopping list and coupons based on the customer's shopping history. These strategies focus on improving customer service.

Computer-Based Training: Optimizing the Effectiveness of the People Resource

Information technology includes other aspects of business besides information systems. Computers can make significant contributions in all phases of a business endeavor, including the education of its employees. There are many sources of education: on-the-job training (OJT), college courses, seminars, professional conferences, and independent study, to mention a few. Some companies feel that the judicious use of **computer-based training (CBT)** to train employees effectively gives the company yet another competitive advantage. CBT, which has added a new dimension to education, has many benefits:

- A CBT system can give "individual attention" to a student.
- CBT is interactive and is quick to respond to a student's input.
- CBT is capable of multidimensional communication (sound, print, graphics, and color).
- CBT can demonstrate and present material, provide opportunities for drill and practice, test for understanding of the material, evaluate the test results, and provide follow-up instruction based on test results.
- CBT systems can interact with students to enhance the learning process. Through interactive computer graphics, a CBT system can demonstrate certain concepts more effectively than books, manuals, or even teachers can.
- CBT is self-paced so the student controls the speed of learning.

Educational software packages have been developed that reinforce and complement virtually every business-related topic, from word processing to project management. Companies using CBT are saving money and getting the most out of their people. This, they feel, gives them a slight competitive edge.

Sears Scores Big with New POS System Sears, Roebuck and Company recently purchased a $53-million POS (point-of-sale) system from Compuadd Corporation. Sears is installing the system in its 868 retail stores across the United States and Puerto Rico. The system will allow clerks to handle sales transactions, retrieve customer information, distribute Sears charge cards and gift certificates, and even cut down the training time of new employees from about 4 hours to just 45 minutes. It is estimated that the company will reduce expenses by $50 million a year with the installation of this system. That's a one-year payback!

A few years ago on-board computers in automobiles provided us with interesting and sometimes helpful information, such as current temperature, average trip speed, and how many miles we could go with what gas we had. On-board computers are about to take a giant leap forward.

One of the prime examples of the use of on-board computers is in long-haul truck fleet tracking. Trucking companies and their drivers want to keep those trucks rolling. A trucker, however, must stop for 30 minutes to an hour each day to call in location, estimated time of delivery, fuel consumption, and other important information. At J. B. Hunt Transport, headquartered in Lowell, Arkansas, drivers keep a fleet of 6000 eighteen wheelers rolling while on-board computers do the reporting. These sophisticated on-board computers, however, can do much more than routine reporting.

Each truck is equipped with a user-friendly (touch screen) computer in the cab and a small satellite dish on top of the cab. Transmissions from the truck's computer are picked up by a commercial communications satellite. The satellite relays the signal to a common carrier's earth station in San Diego, California. The signal is then routed via conventional ground transmission media to J. B. Hunt headquarters. The path is reversed when headquarters originates the data. Drivers, who spend only a few minutes interacting with the computer, send routine check-in data and alert dispatchers of unexpected problems. The on-board computers enable fleet managers to be in direct communication with drivers. They can alter delivery schedules, give directions, or let drivers know of family emergencies.

Trucks are equipped with instrumentation that feeds data to the on-board computers. In this way, the drivers and fleet managers can monitor speed, fuel flow and total consumption, idle time, and other information.

In the near future, trucking companies, will supplement their on-board computers with *global positioning system* (*GPS*) technology. GPS technology can be used to determine where each truck is at any time. The system is accurate to within 50 feet! Imagine, the dispatcher can pinpoint where the driver stops for lunch. GPS technology was used successfully by the U.S. Army during the Persian Gulf War with Iraq. The device, which can be hand-held or stationary, establishes a location by bouncing signals from the U.S. military's Global Positioning Satellite system, a network of 24 satellites. GPS helps fleet managers iron out routing problems when

vehicles break down, schedule deliveries, and monitor driver performance, among other things.

Within a few years, on-board computers will be considered standard equipment in long-haul trucks and in many other commercial and emergency vehicles, such as delivery trucks, police cars, and ambulances. For example, on-board computers in ambulances will continuously feed status and location data to a central computer. The central computer, which is linked to the 911 system, can automatically dispatch the closest available ambulance within seconds of the distress call. Upon receipt of the pickup order, the ambulance's on-board computer displays a map of the city with an optimal route highlighted.

Just a few years ago, Indianapolis race car drivers had to rely on intuition and feel to fine tune the operation of their race cars. Today the on-board computer is continuously monitoring and adjusting everything from the fuel mixture to the trim mechanisms that optimize aerodynamics. The pit crew can run diagnostic tests via telemetry while the driver continues to race. You can bet that many of the features being developed for Indy racers will eventually be implemented in passenger automobiles.

Today, trucks, emergency vehicles, and race cars, tomorrow your car. Sophisticated on-board computers for private cars will be economically feasible by the turn of the century. Think of the applications. Certainly the parents of a teenager would appreciate knowing where the family car is and how fast it is going!

TRUCKERS ENTER THE RANKS OF KNOWLEDGE WORKERS

The results of this pathologist's tests are entered directly to the hospital's information system, thereby making the results available as quickly as possible. Surgeons sometimes request that results be displayed on terminals in the operating room.

Cost Reduction via Source Data Automation

In recent years, the health-care industry has been faced with increased competition forcing it to seek ways to offer better service at a better price. Hospital administrators are turning to information systems to help them improve the quality of health care and increase productivity.

How can a hospital use management information systems to its advantage? A cost-reduction program involving information systems would normally encompass several facets of hospital operation. For example, a study at one hospital revealed that nurses devoted over 40% of their time to recording what they do. For example, nurses must log every prescription they deliver and every time they respond to a patient call. A computer-based data collection system was developed and installed at that hospital that enables data to be captured in machine-readable format (for example, bar codes) from bedside terminals at the *point of care*. By reducing the time nurses spend recording data about their activities from 40% to 5%, the source data automation system enabled more time to be devoted to direct patient care. In this case, the implementation of an MIS resulted in both cost reduction and improved services.

Leveraging Information to Create New Business

Another way to gain a competitive advantage is to be there first with information about a product and at timely intervals thereafter. To be successful with this strategy you must know when to arrive with the information and when to return with more information. Several manufacturers that specialize in baby products have successfully employed this strategy using management information systems.

Management at these companies knows that each birth expands the market for their products and represents a new business opportunity. One manufacturer of baby products gives an ample supply of sampler kits to hospitals to distribute to expectant mothers during the hospital's prenatal orientation sessions. The kits include samples of products and informative literature, but perhaps the most important component of the package is a return card. The mother-to-be completes a card that includes critical marketing information, such as name, address, and expected date of birth. The information on the card is all the company needs to be there first and at timely intervals thereafter.

How does the company make use of this information? The baby products company enters this information into an MIS that automatically triggers the delivery of prenatal promotional literature (coupons) and samples (shampoo) just prior to the expected delivery date. Thereafter, the company sends the consumer a monthly newsletter that focuses on the needs and expectations of mother and baby during the coming month. The newborn newsletter arrives just before the expected date of delivery. The second newsletter arrives a month later and then every month for the first year. The company provides a valuable service to potential consumers of its products while keeping its name and products in the consumer's mind.

A baby's needs are well defined during the first year. The system ensures that the mother receives samples and coupons for small, medium, or large diapers as well as baby food, toys, and other products.

After the first year, the company can use the system to anticipate the baby's needs on a quarterly basis. Competing companies must use the more costly shotgun approach to reach the consumer. The rifle approach, made possible by a sophisticated MIS, provides the company with a definite competitive advantage.

 14–3 Applications of Information Technology Common to Most Organizations

Certain computer applications and information systems are universal and equally appropriate for a manufacturing company, a university, a hospital, or even a cottage industry (where people work out of their homes). These applications normally involve *personnel* and *monetary accounting*, but they also include several other common application areas, such as inventory control. Each of these areas can be, and usually is, integrated to some extent with one or more of the other application areas.

Payroll

Having already read several payroll-related examples in earlier chapters, you should be somewhat familiar with payroll systems. The two primary outputs of a payroll system are the payroll check and stub distributed to the employees and the payroll register, which is a summary report of payroll transactions.

Thousands of software authors have created a wide variety of excellent programs, from business graphics to trivia games. However, most of these creative authors do not have the funds needed to launch their creations in the commercial software marketplace. (A million-dollar marketing campaign to launch a new software product would be considered minimal.) The alternative is to make their software available as *shareware*. Shareware is software made readily available to PC users via electronic bulletin boards and other low-cost distribution channels.

Here is how shareware works. A PC user logs on (establishes a data communications link) to an electronic bulletin board, then downloads copies of the desired software to his or her system. Or, shareware diskettes can be ordered from any of the approximately 200 companies that specialize in the distribution of shareware. Shareware distribution companies sell diskettes containing shareware. You pay the same nominal amount for a diskette (from $1.75 to $5.00), no matter whether it contains a spreadsheet program or clip art.

When you download or order shareware, it is implied that you will register the software with the developer if you like it and intend to use it. The registration fees vary from $10 for utility programs to $100 for full-featured word processing packages. Software developers use several methods to encourage registration of their software. At a minimum, developers provide technical sup-

port and update information to registered users. Some shareware is distributed with start-up documentation only: Complete documentation is sent to registered users. Some shareware developers make shareware enhancements available only to registered users.

A relatively small amount of the software available through electronic bulletin boards and software distribution companies is *public domain software*. Public domain software is not registered.

The Software Labs, one of the largest distributors of shareware, offers almost 2000 diskettes full of shareware and public domain software. Software authors submit their software creations to The Software Labs for distribution. Authors are compensated when they receive fees from users who register their software. You can get programs that print signs and banners, help you with your taxes, teach you to speak Japanese, help you manage projects, provide access to many delicious recipes, and suggest lottery numbers. You can get complete systems for church accounting, stamp collection, billing and invoicing, and investment management. You can get full-featured packages for word processing, spreadsheet, database, and graphics. And, if you're intimidated by the thought of learning a spreadsheet, why not try "Templates of Doom," a shareware program that uses an adventure game to teach spreadsheet basics. Scores of games are available from golf to martial arts. These are just the tip of the shareware iceberg.

Accounts Receivable

The accounts receivable system keeps track of money owed the company on charges for goods sold or services rendered. When a customer purchases goods or services, the customer record is updated to reflect the charge. An invoice, bill, or statement reflecting the balance due is periodically sent to active customers. Upon receipt of payment, the amount due is decreased by the amount of the payment.

Management relies on the accounts receivable system to identify overdue accounts. Reports are generated that "age" accounts to identify those customers whose accounts are overdue by more than 30, 60, or 90 days.

Accounts Payable

Organizations purchase everything from paper clips to bulldozers on credit. So the accounts payable system is the other side of the accounts receivable system. An invoice from a creditor company's accounts receivable system is input to the accounts payable system. When a company receives an invoice, the system generates a check and adjusts the balance. Most companies design their accounts payable system to take advantage of discounts for prompt payment.

General Ledger

Every monetary transaction that occurs within an organization must be properly recorded. Both payment of a bill and an interdepartmental transfer of funds are examples of monetary transactions. The general ledger system keeps track of these transactions and provides the input necessary to produce an organization's financial statement. A financial statement includes the *profit and loss statement* and the *balance sheet*.

The Securities & Exchange Commission (SEC) requires publicly held companies to file quarterly financial statements. In the past this requirement resulted in six million pages of reports being sent to the SEC every three months. Now each report is transmitted to the SEC electronically via data communications. With the current system, stockbrokers and investors can look through thousands of financial statements from their terminals, rather than wait several weeks before they could see reports.

In the not-too-distant past, accountants posted debits and credits for each account manually in a ledger book, thus the name *general ledger* for today's electronic system. Other "account" systems (accounts receivable, accounts payable, payroll, and so on) are sources of financial transactions and feed data into the general ledger system.

Inventory Management and Control

Walk into most organizations and you see desks, file cabinets, and even computers. These items are called *fixed assets*. A fixed-asset inventory record is maintained for each item and includes such data as date purchased, cost, and inventory item number. These records are maintained for asset-control and tax purposes.

Manufacturing companies must also manage *in-process* and *finished-goods inventories*. These inventory systems monitor the quantity on hand and the location of each inventory item.

Human Resource Development

Human resource development systems are essentially personnel accounting systems that maintain pertinent data on employees. Besides routine historical data (educational background, salary history, and so on), the system includes data on performance reviews, skills, and professional development.

Budgeting

Each year managers spend months preparing their departmental budgets for the coming fiscal year. To help in this task, the budget system provides

Clothiers and other retailers take an annual physical inventory of merchandise. The results are compared with the computer-based inventory data base and adjustments are made accordingly. Because items are marked with bar codes, physical inventory can be expedited with the use of hand-held wand scanners.

each manager with information on past line-item expenditures (salaries, office equipment, office supplies, and so on). Based on this information and projected budget requirements, each manager can make budget requests for the next fiscal year. The budget system matches these requests against projected revenues and generates an exception report showing those budget line items that exceed projected funding levels. The budget items are reviewed and the process is repeated until the coming year's budget is established.

Office Automation

Office automation refers collectively to those computer-based applications associated with general office work. Office automation applications include word processing (also considered a productivity tool), electronic mail, image processing, voice processing, and office information systems.

Word Processing   Word processing concerns written communication and is found wherever there is an office with a computer. Word processing, which is discussed in detail in Chapter 11, "Text and Image Processing Software," is available on virtually every micro, mini, and mainframe computer.

Electronic Mail   Computer networks enable us to route messages to each other's electronic mailbox via electronic mail. E-mail is discussed in Chapter 8, "Networks and Networking."

Image Processing   Image processing involves the creation, storage, and distribution of pictorial information. There are two levels of image processing sophistication. At the first level, facsimile (fax) equipment transfers images of hard-copy documents via telephone lines to another office. At the next level, image scanners (see Chapter 5, "Input/Output Devices") scan and digitize images (photos, traffic tickets, and so on) to be stored on disk. Once digitized, the image can be manipulated to meet applications needs.

Voice Processing   Voice processing includes **voice message switching** and **teleconferencing**. The terminal for voice message switching (a store-and-forward "voice mailbox" system) is a touch-tone telephone. Voice message switching accomplishes the same function as electronic mail, except the hard copy is not available. When you send a message, your voice is digitized and stored on a magnetic disk for later retrieval. The message is routed to the destination(s) you designate using the telephone's keyboard; then it is heard upon request by the intended receiver(s). A voice store-and-forward system permits you to send one or many messages with just one telephone call.

Teleconferencing enables people in different locations to see and talk to each other and to share charts and other visual meeting materials. The voice and video of teleconferencing are supported by the telephone network. People who are geographically scattered can meet without the need for time-consuming and expensive travel.

Companies that operate on a global scale, like Hewlett-Packard, rely on information and communications systems such as teleconferencing to enable their widely scattered employees to work together more effectively.

Harris Corporation engineers prepare for the final phase of customer checkout for this Voice Switching and Control System. The voice processing system is one of the key components of the FAA's plan to modernize air traffic control.

Office Information Systems   Several small information systems address traditional office tasks. For example, one system allows people to keep their *personal calendars* on-line. As workers schedule activities, they block out times on their electronic calendars.

There are definite advantages to having a central data base of personal calendars. Let's say that a public relations manager wants to schedule a meeting to review the impact of some unexpected favorable publicity. To do this, the manager enters the names of the participants and the expected duration of the meeting. The *conference scheduling system* searches the calendars of people affected and suggests possible meeting times. The manager then selects a meeting time, and the participants are notified by electronic mail. Of course, their calendars are automatically updated to reflect the meeting time.

Another common office application is the company *directory*. The directory contains basic personnel data: name, title, department, location, and phone number. To look up someone's telephone number, you simply enter that person's name on your terminal, and the number is displayed. The directory data base is always up-to-date, unlike hard-copy directories, which never seem to have all the current titles or phone numbers.

Other systems permit users to organize *personal notes*, keep *diaries*, document ideas in a *preformatted outline*, and keep a *tickler file*. When users log on in the morning, the tickler file automatically reminds them of things to do for that day.

At Ford's North Penn plant in Pennsylvania, an engineer monitors a computer-based manufacturing process that inserts components on the electronic engine control (EEC-IV) module. EEC-IV microprocessors perform thousands of operations per second in managing car and truck engine functions for power, fuel economy, and tailpipe emissions.

14–4 Industry-Specific Applications of Information Technology

Many applications of information technology are unique to a particular type of industry or organization. For example, fire incident reporting systems are unique to local governments. The use of automatic teller machines is unique to the banking industry. A sampling of industry-specific applications are briefly discussed in the remainder of this chapter.

Manufacturing

Traditional Manufacturing Information Systems   In a manufacturing company, the *order entry and processing system* accepts and processes customer orders. The system then feeds data to the warehouse or plant, depending on whether the order is for stock items or special order, and to the *accounts receivable system* for billing. The order entry and processing system also tracks orders and provides status information from the time the order is received until the product is delivered to the customer.

Production scheduling systems allocate manufacturing resources in an optimal manner. A well-designed system will minimize idle time for both workers and machines and ensure that materials are at the right place at the right time.

Market analysis systems rely on historical and current data to identify fast- and slow-moving products, to pinpoint areas with high sales potential, to make forecasts of production requirements, and to plan marketing strategy. For example, in Figure 14–1, the scatter plot of regional sales over the last four quarters demonstrates clearly that fourth-quarter sales in the northeast region did not keep pace with the others. Based on this finding, management might elect to focus more attention on the northeast region during the coming quarter.

Project management and control systems provide management with the information necessary to keep projects within budget and on time.

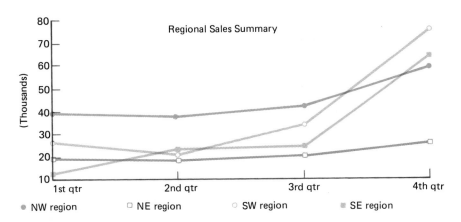

FIGURE 14–1   Scatter Plot of Regional Sales
Quarterly sales figures from four regions are plotted to help in market analysis.

Periodic reports present actual versus anticipated project costs and the number of days ahead of or behind schedule.

Other information systems commonly found in manufacturing companies include *standard costing* and *manufacturing resource planning* (MRP).

Robotics   Robotics, the integration of computers and robots, is more often than not associated with manufacturing.

Rudimentary Robotics.   The "steel-collar" work force throughout the world is made up of hundreds of thousands of industrial robots. The most common robot is a single mechanical arm controlled by a computer. The arm, called a *manipulator*, has a shoulder, forearm, and wrist and is capable of performing the motions of a human arm. The manipulator is fitted with a hand designed to accomplish a specific task, such as painting, welding, picking and placing, and so on.

An industrial robot is best at repetitive tasks and tasks that require precision movements, moving heavy loads, and working in hazardous areas. Such tasks are not unique to manufacturing; they exist in virtually every kind of industry, from hospitals to cannery row. The automotive industry is the largest user of robots (painting, welding), and the electronics industry (circuit testing, connecting chips to circuit boards) is second. Even surgeons are using robots to help in brain surgery. They can be set up to manipulate the surgical drill and biopsy needle with great accuracy, thereby making brain surgery faster, more accurate, and safer.

With the prospect of increased productivity, manufacturing companies have been rushing to install more and more applications of robotics. In the photo, an industrial robot at Deere and Company readies a windshield for installation in a tractor's cab.

Teaching Robots to Do Their Job.   A computer program is written to control the robot just as one is written to print payroll checks. It includes such commands as when to reach, in which direction to reach, how far to reach, when to grasp, and so on. Once programmed, robots do not need much attention. One plant manufactures vacuum cleaners 24 hours a day, 7 days a week, in total darkness!

Outfitting Robots with Intelligence and Human Sensory Capabilities. Most robots are programmed to reach to a particular location, find a particular item, and then place it somewhere else. This simple application of robotics is called *pick and place.* Instead of a grasping mechanism, other robots are equipped with a variety of industrial tools such as drills, paint guns, welding torches, and so on. Of course, it will be a very long time before our companions and workmates are robots. However, industrial robots are being equipped with rudimentary sensory capabilities, such as vision, that enable them to simulate human behavior. A robot with the added dimension of vision can be given some intelligence. (Robots without intelligence simply repeat preprogrammed motions.) Even though the technology for the vision systems is primitive, a robot can be "taught" to distinguish between dissimilar objects under controlled conditions. With this sensory subsystem, the robot has the capability of making crude but important decisions. For example, a robot equipped with a vision subsystem can distinguish between two boxes approaching on the conveyor. It can be programmed to place a box of particular dimensions on an adjacent conveyer and let all other boxes pass.

If vision system technology continues to improve, more and more robots will have *navigational capabilities* (the ability to move). Now most robots are stationary; those that are not can only detect the presence of an object in their path or are programmed to operate within a well-defined work area where the positions of all obstacles are known. By the turn of the century, robots will be able to move about the work area just as people do.

Computer-Integrated Manufacturing   Manufacturing companies use information technologies to streamline their operations. The integration of computers and manufacturing is called **computer-integrated manufacturing (CIM)**. The computer plays a role at every stage of the manufacturing process, from the time a part is conceived until it is shipped. In computer-integrated manufacturing, the various computer systems are linked together via data communications and feed data to one another. CIM uses an integrated network of computers to

- Design the product
- Operate and monitor production equipment
- Facilitate communication and information flow throughout the plant and the company
- Interface with the company's administrative information systems

For example, an engineer uses a *computer-aided design* (CAD) system to design the part. The design specifications are produced and stored on a

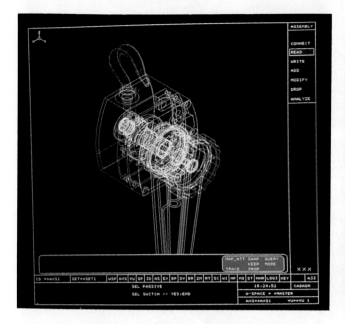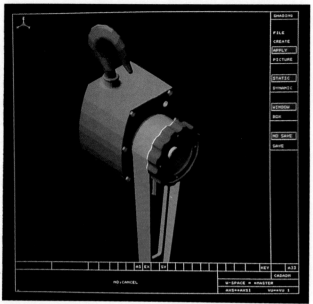

Computer-aided design (CAD) systems are used to design industrial equipment, such as this winch, consumer goods, airplanes, and just about everything else. In the design process, engineers create a wire frame image (left), then the CAD software fills in between the lines to create the three-dimensional solid model (right).

magnetic disk. The specifications, now in an electronic data base, become input to another computer system that generates programs to control the robots and machine tools that handle and make the part. These computer-driven tools are even linked to the company's MIS computers to provide data for order processing, inventory management, shop-floor scheduling, and general accounting. Some CIM systems go one step further and provide a link between the manufacturer and the customer via EDI (electronic data interchange).

Several companies in each industry are working feverishly toward the implementation of total CIM. Few, if any, have achieved it, but many have achieved at least a degree of CIM.

Financial Services

In the financial services industries, which include banking, savings and loan institutions, and brokerage firms, the computer is the impetus for some radical and progressive changes. For example, financial services organizations serve as a "money buffer" between buyer and seller. The traditional approach to money exchange has been for the seller to bill the buyer, the buyer to write a check for the amount of the bill, the seller to deposit the check, and the bank to transfer the funds from the buyer's to the seller's account. This approach is time-consuming, as well as expensive for all concerned. Throughout the remainder of the 1990s we can expect to see this traditional approach give way more and more to *electronic funds transfer (EFT)*.

On the floor of the New York Stock Exchange, securities are traded in much the same way they were during the stock market crash of 1929, but with one major difference. Today all trading data is entered into, processed by, and displayed by computers.

In electronic funds transfer, the amount owed is transferred electronically from one account to another in a bank, savings and loan, or brokerage firm. For example, rather than sending out thousands of statements, some utility companies are cooperating with customers and banks so that payments are transferred electronically at the end of each billing period. As another example, some employers are bypassing printing payroll checks. Based on data supplied to the banks, pay is electronically transferred from employer to employee accounts.

Automatic teller machines (ATMs) are the most visible symbol of EFT (see Chapter 7, "Connectivity and Data Communications"). In over 100 banks, however, EFT has been extended to the home in the form of *home banking systems*. Subscribers to a home banking service use their personal computers as terminals to pay bills, transfer funds, and inquire about account status. Some systems also provide subscribers with other services, such as "electronic shopping," electronic mail, and up-to-the-minute stock market quotations. For example, several brokerage firms permit clients to use their PCs to tap into a data base that contains their account data as well as timely information about the securities market.

All financial institutions offer *financial planning services*. Part of the service involves a computer-based analysis of a customer's investment portfolio. Input to the system includes current and anticipated income, amount and type of investments, assets and liabilities, and financial objectives (such as: minimize taxes, desired pension at age 65). The output

The computer and EFT may someday replace the armored vehicle as we move toward a cashless society. Transferring money via EFT is less expensive and not as dangerous. Moreover, branch banks such as this one become less inviting targets for robbers.

from the analysis consists of recommendations aimed at optimizing the effectiveness of a particular person's investment portfolio.

Futurists are predicting that the current system of currency exchange gradually will be replaced by EFT. More and more point-of-sale systems are being integrated with EFT systems so that what is now a *credit* transaction will be a *cash-transfer* transaction. That is, when a customer purchases an item, the amount of the sale is debited, via EFT, from the customer's checking account and credited to the account of the retail store. No further funds transfer is needed. Of course, the option of making a credit purchase will remain.

Publishing

Desktop publishing, computerized *typesetting*, computer-aided *graphics design*, and *page formatting* have revolutionized the way newspapers, books, and magazines are produced. Reporters and writers enter and edit their stories on their portable micros or on-line terminals. Once all copy is on-line, pages are automatically formatted according to type and spacing specifications. Traditionally, a manually produced document prepared with pencils, paper, and typewriters went on to the editing, retyping, composing, proofreading, cutting, pasting, and photographing of the final page format before plates could be made for the presswork.

Eventually, *customized printing on demand* will be available at bookstores. Instead of choosing from books on hand, you will make a selection from a list of virtually any current book. It will then be printed (figures and all) and bound while you wait. This approach will provide a greater selection for the customer and vastly reduce costly inventory for both bookstore and publisher.

Desktop publishing is used at Hormel Company to create the complete layout, including computer-drawn artwork, for promotional feed brochures and for insignias on wearing apparel, with considerable savings.

Brunswick Bramalea Lanes in Brampton, Ontario, is equipped with a computer-based Command Network. The management control system integrates the automatic scorers, Bowler Express systems for food and beverage ordering and in-center merchandising, cash management, and total center business operations.

Although customized printing on demand is a few years away, *magazines on a disk* are here today. These magazines are distributed in diskette format for display on microcomputers. Dictionaries, encyclopedias, and other reference materials already are being sold in the form of high-density optical laser disks.

Insurance

The information systems of an insurance company have more external interaction, or communication with people outside the company, than most other businesses. Most of this external communication is with customers. The volume of such transactions makes computer-based *policy administration* and *claims processing systems* a necessity. Insurance agents hook up to computers at headquarters so they can quote, write, and deliver insurance policies while customers wait.

An insurance company makes or loses money according to the accuracy of its *actuarial accounting system*. This system maintains countless statistics that serve as the basis for the rate structure. An actuarial system provides the following kinds of information: the probability that a 20-year-old Kansas City resident with no automobile accident history will have an accident or the life expectancy of a 68-year-old female whose parents died of natural causes.

Entertainment

The computer is now an integral part of the entertainment industry. *Pro football* coaches rely heavily on feedback from their computer systems to call plays and set defenses during a game. The system predicts what the opposing team is expected to do, based on statistics of what they have done in the past. In fact, the computer is becoming the deciding factor between evenly matched opponents in many sports.

Computers have also had an impact on the *film industry*. Many *special effects* and even the sets for some movies are generated with computer graphics. A special effect, called *morphing*, uses computer graphics to change one image to another (for example, a human being to a robot). *Animation* for cartoons and movies is no longer drawn one frame at a time. The scenes and characters are drawn, by hand or with a computer, then manipulated with computer graphics to create the illusion of motion.

Computer graphics has even made it possible to revive old black-and-white movies—in color! Imagine Laurel and Hardy in living color! Now, through an innovative use of computer technology called *colorization*, it is possible to change the old black-and-white films to color.

In the *theater*, playwrights use word processing systems especially designed for the theater environment. Besides the obvious value of word processing, there are additional benefits to having the script on-line. Actors can learn their lines by interacting with a computer that "reads" the lines of other actors; that is, only the lines of other actors are displayed on the screen unless the actor requests that all lines be displayed.

Then, of course, there are *video*—or should we say "computer"—*games*. Interest in video games has lessened as people use their computers

The Music Animals Studio in Los Angeles uses computer-controlled mixing consoles to create and record commercial jingles and albums.

for other purposes. The computer games industry, however, anticipates a resurgence of interest with the introduction of videodisk technology. With videodisk-based games (for example, "Dragon's Lair"), the images are lifelike color motion pictures instead of computer graphics.

Health Care

Hospitals   The computer is a constant companion to both patients and medical personnel. This is especially so in hospitals where, at the beginning of each day, the status of each room is updated in the *room census* data base. The *patient accounting system* updates patient records to reflect lab tests, drugs administered, and visits by a physician. This system also handles patient billing.

In the *operating room*, surgeons have on-line access to the patient's medical records. Some of these interactive systems are even voice-activated to free the surgeon's hands for more critical tasks. Computers have taken some of the risk out of complex surgical procedures by warning surgeons of life-threatening situations: During brain surgery, for example, a computer monitors the patient's blood flow to the brain. Once a patient is moved to an *intensive-care unit*, computers continue to monitor vital signs and alert attending personnel of dangerous situations. Most life-support systems (such as artificial lungs) are also computer-controlled.

Computer-controlled diagnostic equipment provides physicians and surgeons with information that simply was not available a few years ago. Because surgeons can "see" more clearly into a person's body with *CT*, or *CAT* (computer tomography), *scanners* and *MR* (magnetic resonance) *scanners*, medical procedures may be less drastic because better information is available. For example, a surgeon may not have to amputate an entire limb to stop the spread of bone cancer if an MR scan detects the cancer only in a limb's extremities. CAT scanners permit the results of several scans to be combined and forged into three-dimensional images. MR scanners, the most recent technology for viewing inside the body, combine computers and a large doughnut-shaped magnet to produce video images of a cross-section of a body. Before MR scanners, exploratory surgery was necessary to produce such internal "pictures." Physicians see and analyze the images from CAT and MR scanners on color graphics monitors.

Expert diagnosis systems (see Chapter 13, "The MIS and Decision Support Systems") help physicians identify diseases and isolate problems. The physician enters the patient's symptoms, and the system queries an expert system data base to match the symptoms with possible illnesses. If the illness cannot be diagnosed with existing information, the system requests more information.

In recent years the cost of a hospital room has soared, and some hospitals still operate in the red. To become profitable, they are implementing procedures to help control costs. Several computer systems can help hospitals optimize their resources while maximizing revenue. A *physician's accounting system* provides hospital administrators with information about how each physician is using hospital facilities. For example, such

Hearing-impaired children learn to speak more clearly with the aid of a speech-training system. Here a child, with assistance from a therapist, matches her speech to a prototype pattern displayed on the screen. This visual feedback allows the child to adjust her pitch until she makes the correct sound.

systems identify physicians who tend to admit patients who could be treated on an outpatient basis. These patients typically generate less revenue for the hospital and take up beds that could best be used by seriously ill patients.

Medical Research   The microprocessor has opened new vistas for *medical research*. Our body is an electrical system that is very compatible with these tiny computers. Researchers have made it possible for paraplegics to walk as much as two miles, pedal bicycles, and perform other motor functions under the control of external computers: Various muscle groups are electronically stimulated to cause the legs to perform a walking motion. The system has given new hope to paraplegics who thought they would never walk again. Much remains to be done, but researchers insist that someday computer implants will enable paraplegics to enjoy significantly improved mobility.

Government

Local Government   Local governments use a wide variety of information systems. Most cities supply and bill citizens for at least one of the three major utility services—water, refuse, and electricity. Besides these *utility billing systems*, a *tax collection* system periodically assesses citizens for school and real estate taxes.

Cities also have *police systems* that are used for incident reporting, inquiry, and dispatching. Many police departments even have terminals mounted in their cruisers. On these terminals, officers can see the arrest record of an individual, request a "rundown" on an auto's license number, or check on what other officers are doing. Police detectives can search data bases for suspects by matching modi operandi, nicknames, body marks, physical deformities, locations, times of day, and even footwear.

Some fire departments are electronically informed of the location of a fire by a *fire incident reporting system*. Here's how it works: Someone at the site of the fire calls a three-digit "fire reporting" number. In a split second a computer system searches its data base for the address of the phone (and the location of the fire), then automatically dispatches vehicles from the nearest fire station.

Local governments also install and support the *automated traffic-control systems* that coordinate traffic signals to minimize delays and optimize traffic flow (see Chapter 1, "The World of Computers").

State Government   At the state level of government, each major agency has its own information services department. *Welfare, employment security, highway patrol, revenue,* and *education* are only a few of the many state agencies that have such departments. In some states one of the most visible systems is the *lottery* agency. A bet is registered immediately at any of thousands of on-line terminals located in stores and restaurants throughout the state. The on-line lottery systems have made it possible for people to be "instant" winners (or losers).

Several state *crime bureaus* use computers for fingerprint identification. Once the millions of fingerprints have been converted into digital

This law enforcement officer is using a portable pen-based computer with handwriting recognition capability to record pertinent data at the scene of an accident. The 9-by-12-by-1¼-inch GRiDPad, made by GRiD Systems Corporation, can also accept and store a detailed drawing that shows how the accident happened. The violator uses the tethered electronic pen to sign the "ticket."

Prisoners Caught in the Act At Chicago's Cook County Jail, as many as 400 people are entered into the jail in a 24-hour period. Prisoners sometimes swap identities by memorizing each other's name, address, and other personal details. In 1990 the Cook County Jail adopted a biometrics system—the Criminal Eye-Dent System. Each of 24 systems is enclosed in a large gray cabinet containing an IBM PS/2 and an eye-scanning mechanism. The eye-scanners reflect a beam of light from the prisoner's retina and digitize the individual pattern of blood vessels. The digitized pattern is then transformed into an algorithm and saved in a data base. The biometrics system is said to be even more reliable than a fingerprint for identifying an individual. In its first six months, the system successfully thwarted 40 attempts at switched identities.

data and stored on magnetic disk, the system can check up to 650 prints per second. In a manual search, an investigator would take hours to do what a computer can do in a single second. This new technology doesn't give criminals much of a head start!

Federal Government   The federal government has thousands of computer systems scattered throughout the world. The Federal Bureau of Investigation (FBI) uses its *national crime information system* (*NCIS*) to help track down criminals. The Internal Revenue Service (IRS) now permits qualified accountants to *file tax returns* on-line. This service saves us and the IRS a lot of time and money. The on-line system performs all the necessary table searches and computations, and it even cross-checks the accuracy and consistency of the input data. For the IRS, no further data entry or personal assistance is required.

Computer technology has given Congress a new look. Senators and representatives have terminals in their offices that allow them to scan proposed legislation, send electronic mail, vote on legislation from their offices, do research, and correspond with constituents. The system also allows lobbyists, reporters, and other interested people to monitor voting records, session attendance, and other matters of public interest. Another benefit of the *congressional computer network* is that it lets congressional committees poll members of Congress for their feedback while legislation

Within the federal government, NASA probably exhibits the greatest variety in applications of information technology. Here, astronauts run through a simulation in the space shuttle mission simulator at Johnson Space Center in Houston, Texas. These astronauts are looking out the window of a simulated shuttle into a computer-generated scene. Astronauts practice flight control and emergency procedures while a variety of flight conditions are shown visually and simulated with the instruments.

is still in draft form, instead of waiting until the legislation is put to a vote.

The most sophisticated government computer systems are associated with *NASA* and the space program. A mind-boggling network of ground and on-board computers must work together, without malfunction, to take people to and from the moon and shuttle people between the earth and orbit around the earth.

Memory Bits

INDUSTRY-SPECIFIC INFORMATION SYSTEMS

- Manufacturing
  Order entry and processing
  Production scheduling
  Market analysis
  Project management and control
  Standard costing
  Manufacturing resource planning
  (MRP)
  Robotics
  Computer-integrated
  manufacturing (CIM)
  Computer-aided design (CAD)
- Financial services
  Electronic funds transfer (EFT)
  Automatic teller machines (ATM)
  Home banking
  Financial planning
- Publishing
  Word processing
  Typesetting
  Graphics design
  Page formatting
  Customized printing on demand
  Magazines on a disk
- Insurance
  Policy administration
  Claims processing
  Actuarial accounting
- Entertainment
  Professional sports systems
  Film industry
    Special effects
    Morphing
    Animation
    Colorization
  Theater (on-line scripts)
  Video games
- Health care
  Hospitals
    Room census

  Patient accounting
  Operating room
  Intensive-care unit
  Diagnostic equipment
  Expert diagnosis systems
  Physicians' accounting
  Source data automation
  Medical research
- Pharmaceutical
  Electronic data interchange
  Drug interaction data base
- Retail grocery
  Automated checkout system
  Personalized shopping lists
- Transportation
  Reservations
  Fleet maintenance
- Retail sales
  Point of sale (POS)
- Government
  Local
    Utility billings
    Tax collection
    Police
    Fire incident reporting
    Traffic control
  State
    Welfare
    Employment security
    Highway patrol
    Revenue
    Education
    Lottery
    Crime bureau
  Federal
    National crime information system (NCIS)
    Filing taxes
    Congressional computer network
    Space program (NASA)

Important Terms and Summary Outline

computer-based training (CBT)	information technology (IT)	voice message switching
computer-integrated manufacturing (CIM)	office automation teleconferencing	

14–1 THE USES OF INFORMATION TECHNOLOGY. New and innovative uses of computers and information systems are being implemented every day in every type of organization. The general area of computers and information systems is sometimes referred to as **information technology (IT)**.

14–2 GAINING THE COMPETITIVE ADVANTAGE WITH INFORMATION TECHNOLOGY. Corporate America is beginning to use computers and information systems to improve profitability and achieve a competitive advantage.

The strategic alliances established between the wholesale drug distribution industry and drug retailers via EDI has altered the basic constructs of the industry. The trend today is for the drug wholesalers to provide EDI capabilities to their customers as an incentive to do business with them.

Supermarkets are using automated checkout systems to speed the process and offer products at a lower price. These systems enable supermarkets to take full advantage of the automation opportunities afforded by the availability of the UPC imprinted on all packaged grocery items.

Computer-based training (CBT) has enabled some companies to be more effective in their use of people resources, the net result of which has been a competitive advantage.

At one hospital a computer-based data collection system was developed and installed that enables data to be captured in machine-readable format from bedside terminals. By emphasizing source data automation, the hospital has achieved a competitive advantage.

Some manufacturers of baby products gain a competitive advantage by leveraging information to create new business.

14–3 APPLICATIONS OF INFORMATION TECHNOLOGY COMMON TO MOST ORGANIZATIONS. Certain computer applications and information systems are universal and equally appropriate in any business environment. Computer applications found in most organizations include payroll, accounts receivable, accounts payable, general ledger, inventory management and control, human resource development, budgeting, and **office automation**.

Office automation refers collectively to computer-based applications associated with general office work. These include word processing, electronic mail, image processing (facsimile and image scanner), voice processing (**voice message switching** and **teleconferencing**), and office information systems.

14–4 INDUSTRY-SPECIFIC APPLICATIONS OF INFORMATION TECHNOLOGY. Some computer applications are unique to a particular type of business, such as production scheduling (manufacturing), electronic funds transfer (financial services), typesetting (publishing), actuarial accounting (insurance), and special effects in movies and on-line theater scripts (entertainment).

Robotics (the integration of computers and robots), **computer-integrated manufacturing (CIM)**, and computer-aided design (CAD) are three of the more prominent applications of information technology commonly found in manufacturing.

In health care, computers help hospital administrative personnel with billing and help doctors diagnose illnesses. The computer has enabled medical research to advance in leaps and bounds.

Some of the computer applications found in local government include utility billing, tax collection, and police and fire incident reporting. State governments use computers for everything from fingerprint analysis to running statewide lotteries. The federal government has thousands of computer systems throughout the world that are used in a wide variety of applications.

 ## Review Exercises

Concepts

1. Electronic funds transfer is associated with what industry?
2. Information systems common to most businesses usually involve accounting for what two corporate resources?
3. How do computers help surgeons in operating rooms?
4. Name four applications of the computer in a municipal government.
5. CAD and robotics are usually associated with what industry?
6. What computer-based applications are unique to hospitals?
7. Which common information system produces invoices? Purchase orders? Balance sheets?
8. Name three office information systems.
9. List three advantages of computer-based training.
10. Briefly describe the CIM concept.
11. What machine-readable code provides the basis for automated checkout systems in supermarkets?
12. What term is used to describe the linking of computers of different companies?

Discussion

13. Movie purists abhor the thought of great black-and-white classics, such as *Casablanca*, being changed to color with the help of computer technology. What do you think?
14. Has the application of computer technology in the theater in any way stifled artistic creativity? Has it enhanced creativity? Explain.
15. Discuss the emerging role of personal computers in electronic funds transfer.
16. Physicians' accounting systems have been implemented under a cloud of controversy. Why?
17. Would you buy a "magazine on a disk"? Why or why not?

Problem Solving

18. Suggest automation-based strategies that companies in the construction industry could employ to achieve a competitive advantage.

19. Suggest automation-based strategies that universities could employ to achieve a competitive advantage.

20. Suggest automation-based strategies that companies in the trucking industry could employ to achieve a competitive advantage.

21. The hospital data collection system that was discussed in the chapter reduced the time that nurses spend recording data about their activities from 40% to 5%. Assuming that the number of nurses on staff remained the same after system implementation, how do you think the cost of the system was justified?

Self-Test (by section)

14–1 The general area of computers and information systems is sometimes referred to as ~~information technology~~.

14–2 **a.** The trend today is for the drug wholesalers to provide ~~EDI~~ capabilities to their customers.

b. CBT is self-paced so that the student controls the speed of learning. (T/F)

14–3 **a.** The balance sheet is a by-product of a general ledger system. (T/F)

b. Accounts payable is generally associated with office automation applications. (T/F)

c. Management relies on which common information system to identify overdue customer accounts: (a) accounts receivable, (b) accounts payable, or (c) budgeting?

d. Voice message switching is an office automation application. (T/F)

14–4 **a.** The integration of the computer with manufacturing is called CIM, or ~~computer integrated manufacturing~~.

b. Automatic teller machines are an implementation of EFT. (T/F)

c. Actuarial accounting systems are associated with the ~~insurance~~ industry.

d. Computer-based traffic-control systems are implemented at the ~~local~~ level of government.

e. Among financial institutions, only brokerage firms offer computer-based financial planning services. (T/F)

f. The Internal Revenue Service is investigating the feasibility of allowing preparers to file tax returns from their personal computers, but such a service is not yet available. (T/F)

Self-test answers. **14–1** information technology. **14–2(a)** EDI; **(b)** T. **14–3(a)** T; **(b)** F; **(c)** a; **(d)** T. **14–4(a)** computer-integrated manufacturing; **(b)** T; **(c)** insurance; **(d)** local; **(e)** F; **(f)** F.

EDI - Electronic Data Interchange

THE IMAGE BANK
Computers and Movie Magic

Special effects is the discipline that sets itself a daunting but glorious challenge: to put on screen *anything* a producer or director can imagine. To meet this challenge, the special effects expert must combine the flair of a master storyteller with the skill and ingenuity of an engineer and, in recent years, a computer expert.

The discipline itself springs from the early days of cinema, when the Lumière brothers first electrified Parisians with such short films as *The Arrival of a Train* (1895). Among the dazzled observers was Georges Méliès, a successful magician and illusionist. By 1896, Méliès had discovered the first of many camera tricks that let him duplicate and even improve his magic tricks

COMPUTER GRAPHICS BRING NEW AUDIENCES TO BLACK-AND-WHITE CLASSICS This Laurel and Hardy movie is just one black-and-white film that has been *colorized* by computer technology. The colorizing process uses an electronic scanner to break each frame into 525,000 dots the computer can store and manipulate. The art director reviews the frames at the beginning, middle, and end of the scene and selects a specific color for every object. A computer operator then uses a digitizing tablet to "hand paint" these frames according to the art director's instructions. The computer software then colors the remaining frames. Movie purists would never consider watching such classics as *Casablanca* in color. However, other viewers, weaned on color television and color movies, wouldn't watch anything else.

and illusions on over 500 short films. Because so many special effects can be traced back to Méliès' work, many consider him the founder of the discipline.

Méliès is also considered the first director, for he used the camera and the images it captured to tell a story. This devotion to visual storytelling is the essence of movie making—the melding of image, character, and plot to create an engrossing emotional experience for the audience.

A devotion to visual storytelling underlies special effects to this day. In fact, the work of the special effects crew begins almost as soon as the script is in final draft. That's when the art director and his or her staff begin to develop the *story boards*, cartoon-like sketches that translate the writer's literary content into visual images. These story boards guide the special effects experts.

Today's special effects team includes experts in *visual effects*, the manipulation and capture of images on film; *physical* or *mechanical effects*, such as explosives and collapsing buildings; *sound effects*; and *makeup*. Sometimes, the special effects team can draw on a toolbox of existing techniques—many as old as the films of Méliès. Often, though, they have to improvise, adapting an existing technology to a new application. To a great extent, that's how computers got into special effects.

THE COMPUTER MAKES ITS DEBUT

For Robert Abel and Associates, it was a frustrating situation. The company was in high demand for its television commercials featuring slit-scan or streak photography, a technique first showcased in Stanley Kubrick's *2001: A Space Odyssey* (1968). This technique gets its name from the streaks and distortion produced when art is photographed through a slit while the camera, slit, or artwork—or all three—are moving. Often, this technique requires multiple passes and several exposures on the same piece of film. Because slit-scan or streak photography is an *in-camera effect* (as opposed to an effect created in the editing room), these repeated motions must be synchronized on a frame-by-frame basis.

Computers and Movie Magic

SLIT-SCAN OR STREAK PHOTOGRAPHY This logo, created for a television commercial, illustrates the use of slit-scan or streak photography to create images that seem to jump out at the audience. Movie audiences first saw this special effect in Stanley Kubrick's stunning *2001: A Space Odyssey* (1968). Near the end of the film, in a segment known as the "Stargate Corridor," the hero seems to be pulled at high speed down an endless hall of mesmerizing light streaks into a surreal world. This segment, supervised by legendary special effects wizard Douglas Trumbull, lasts only a few moments on screen but took nine months to create.

For *2001*, this motion control was automated by largely mechanical means. By the early 1970s, though, streak photography was so popular for commercials that its practitioners, like Robert Abel and Associates, needed a more reliable system of motion control. Other special effects houses, they knew, had experimented with army surplus analog computers. After checking with a local 15-year-old computer whiz, they hired him to build a computer-controlled camera out of electronic components. This innovation, combined with other just-emerging motion-control systems, helped to revolutionize visual effects.

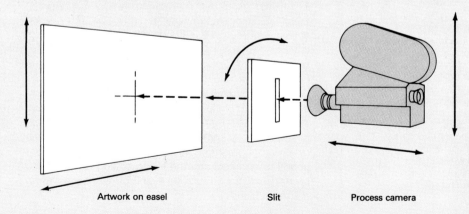

Artwork on easel   Slit   Process camera

This diagram shows the basic configuration for slit-scan work, a kind of controlled streak photography which was used to produce the light show effects near the end of *2001*. The three main components will often be capable of movement in axes other than those indicated here (the more the better).

STAR WARS SPURS THE REFINEMENT OF COMPUTERIZED MOTION-CONTROL SYSTEMS

To describe the space battles he envisioned for *Star Wars*, director George Lucas presented his visual effects team a film he had edited together from World War II footage of aerial dogfights. The black-and-white film was coarse and grainy, but it captured the cutting rhythm Lucas wanted for the climactic scenes.

These scenes presented a meaty challenge to the visual effects team headed by John Dykstra. First, they had to build convincing *miniatures*, or models of the spaceships. Then, these and other elements would be photographed separately against a blue screen. A single effects scene might involve a number of elements—two or more fighter ships, a background representing the stars of outer space, a background shot of the *Death Star,* as well as dozens of animated laser blasts. Even a simple effects shot can involve as many as 11 different strips of film, which are composited or combined in the editing room to produce the finished effect. (The same technique can be used to place live actors into effects scenes, such as the view from the *Millennium Falcon;* the main challenge here belongs to the actors, who may be emoting on an empty stage before a plain blue screen.) Sometimes the camera would swoop over and around the miniature, sometimes the miniature would move, or sometimes both would move. If either the camera or the miniature failed to duplicate the previous movements, the shot would be out of synch and wasted. In addition, Dykstra's crew had to simulate the fluid, rolling motion of the dogfights, a feat that required a camera that could move smoothly on several different axes of motion. On top of that, the crew had to shoot 365 complicated effects shots—the most in any movie since *2001*—in one-third the time (just one year).

Dykstra rose to the challenge by developing the "Dykstraflex," a track-and-boom camera rig that was controlled by a hard-wired, dedicated computer system. Its success was indicated by the Academy Award *Star Wars* received for its visual effects in 1977. Since then, computerized motion-control photography has become a standard tool of special effects.

READYING A MINIATURE FOR A MOTION-CONTROL SHOT A miniature of the *Millennium Falcon* (from the Star Wars series) is shown mounted on a self-illuminated blue neon modelmover. (Because the blue neon matches the blue background, the pylon does not show on film.) The movement of the modelmover could be duplicated, shot after shot, by the Dykstraflex's computer system.

489

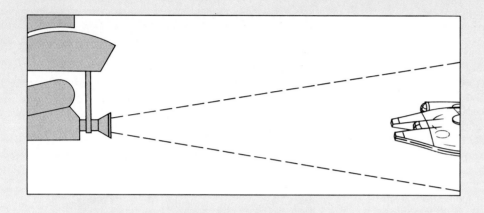

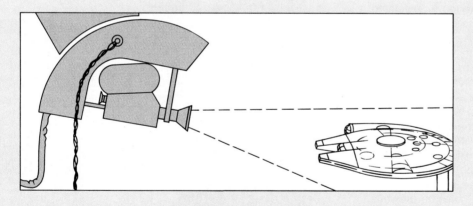

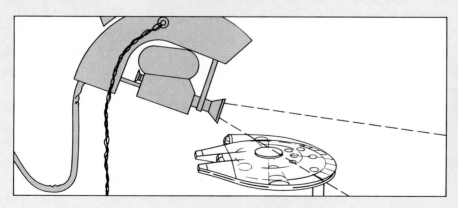

The space battles of *Star Wars* called for an electronically controlled camera rig which could repeat the same moves over and over again with great precision. A single effects shot might combine a half-dozen elements, each filmed separately against a blue screen. A rebel ship might be shot first, then a T.I.E. fighter, a star field, a portion of the *Death Star* miniature, and, lastly, a laser blast. If the camera failed to repeat its moves exactly for each component, the several elements would not fit together correctly in the final composite image.

THE ADVENT OF COMPUTER-GENERATED IMAGERY

An outgrowth of computer-aided design, computer-generated imagery (or CGI) replaces the miniature and motion-control system with graphic images that are created and animated by the computer itself.

CGI offers a number of advantages over traditional techniques. For example, CGI would make it easier to control the reflection of lights and cameras on a model's shiny surface. (The need to control reflections is one reason so many models are highly textured; this helps to break up distracting reflections.) CGI also appeals to traditional animators, who sometimes struggle for days to work out the perspective shifts involved in moving the camera through a complex scene. The computer can do the same work in just minutes—with breathtaking results. This was shown in Walt Disney Company's 1991 film, *Beauty and the Beast*, when Beast leads Beauty into his ballroom, where the camera swoops and swirls around the 3-D room. This and all the other sets were created by computer graphics; the animated actors were laid in with traditional animation techniques.

A MORPH IN PROGRESS A graphic artist uses an electronic pen on a digitizing pad to begin a morph, in this case, one that will change the model's eye, skin, and hair color. (The same technique can be used for less dramatic effects, such as retouching a photograph to eliminate a blemish.) In *Terminator 2*, the T-1000's morphs began with the filming of actor Robert Patrick walking toward and by the camera. This footage was then scanned into the computer, creating a wire-frame model that could be painted to simulate the T-1000's reflective liquid metal skin. The morph was completed by using an electronic pen on a digitizing pad to merge, frame by frame, the computer image of the T-1000 with digitized images of live-action footage of the actor in costume. The completed morph is then transferred back to film.

491

Computers and Movie Magic

Some film makers try to use CGI to simulate reality in every detail. This is a difficult and computer-intensive proposal, given the complexity of light, shadow, and reflections that play across everyday objects. (This approach, used in *Tron*, required the services of a Cray X-MP supercomputer.) Creating realistic computer-generated images of hair and clothing remains an elusive goal for these film makers.

A more pragmatic approach is epitomized by Industrial Light and Magic (ILM), the special effects house created by George Lucas. ILM's goal is to *evoke* the *illusion* of reality, using specially written graphics software and powerful but affordable workstations.

ILM's skill in evoking reality was illustrated in the Academy Award–winning special effects it created for *Terminator 2: Judgment Day* (1991), director James Cameron's sequel to his 1984 hit, *The Terminator*. An early scene, that of the nuclear destruction of Los Angeles, was rendered and animated on a Macintosh before being transferred to film. Some of the more dazzling effects, though, were created through a technique called *digital compositing,* which allows the marriage of computer-generated and filmed images inside the computer, instead of in a camera. Digital compositing is also faster and offers higher resolution. This new technique helped create the *morphs*, short for metamorphoses, that allowed the evil cyborg T-1000 to change shape and walk through bars.

T-1000 LIVES This frame shows the merging of the computer-generated image of T-1000 with live-action footage of a truck's burning wreckage. Morphs also can be seen in many commercials and in Michael Jackson's music video, *Black or White*.

Analysis and Design of Business Information Systems

STUDENT LEARNING OBJECTIVES

▶ To describe the four stages of the system life cycle.

▶ To discuss two basic approaches to satisfying an organization's information processing needs.

▶ To distinguish between the prototyping and prespecification approaches to systems development.

▶ To explain the concept of prototyping.

▶ To describe and order the major activities that take place during the systems analysis phase of systems development.

▶ To describe and order the major activities that take place during the systems design phase of systems development.

▶ To describe the scope and capabilities of CASE tools.

15–1 The System Life Cycle

An information system is analogous to the human life form. It is born, it grows, it matures, and it eventually dies. The **system life cycle** has four stages, as shown in Figure 15–1.

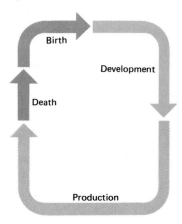

FIGURE 15–1 The System Life Cycle

Birth

Development

Death

Production

- *Birth stage.* In the *birth stage* of the system life cycle, someone has an idea about how the computer can help provide better and more timely information.
- *Development stage.* The idea becomes a reality during the *development stage* of the system life cycle. During this stage, systems analysts, programmers, and users work together to analyze a company's information processing needs and design an information system. The design specifications are then translated into programs, and the system is implemented.
- *Production stage.* Upon implementation, the information system enters the *production stage* and becomes operational, serving the information needs of the company. The production stage is the longest of the four stages and will normally last from four to seven years. During this stage, information systems are continuously modified, or maintained, to keep up with the changing needs of the company.
- *Death stage.* The accumulation of system modifications to a dynamic information system eventually takes its toll on system efficiency. The *death*

An idea often signals the birth of an information system. Eight months earlier these social workers suggested using image processing to make the information they need more readily accessible. Today, they enjoy the benefits of the system.

stage arrives when an information system becomes so cumbersome to maintain that it is no longer economically or operationally effective. At this time, it is discarded, and the system life cycle is repeated.

15–2 In-House versus Proprietary Software: Whether to Make or Buy

An organization can satisfy its information processing needs in two basic ways. The first is to use employees and/or outside consultants to create an information system that is customized to meet user specifications. The alternative is to purchase and install a **proprietary software package**. Proprietary software is developed by a software vendor to sell to a number of potential buyers. These two options offer managers the classic "make-versus-buy" decision. Each approach has its advantages and disadvantages. The best *application portfolios* contain an optimal mix of the two.

In-House Development of Information Systems

Most organizations have the capability of developing information systems using in-house personnel. Because they have limited personnel, they must weigh these decisions carefully. As a rule of thumb, companies should channel the efforts of programmers, systems analysts, and users to develop only systems whose characteristics are unique to that particular company.

There are as many ways to design an information system as there are systems analysts and end users. Invariably, each person involved has his or her ideas about how to proceed with the design.

Downsize to Save $$$$$$ Brookstone, a specialty gadget and gizmo retailer, dumped its mainframe-based custom-designed software for a minicomputer and proprietary software right out of a retail store. The use of a mainframe- and custom-designed software had become a cost burden for the growing company. This transition allowed the company to cut its information services staff in half. The conversion to a smaller computer and off-the-shelf software should save Brookstone about $1 million in the first year.

The Federal Express COSMOS system uses advanced telecommunications to monitor the status of each shipment as it moves through key handling points in the system. COSMOS was developed in-house by Federal Express personnel.

Using Proprietary Software

Virtually all installed system software (DBMS and operating system software) and general-purpose software (spreadsheet and CAD software) is proprietary. There are literally thousands of proprietary applications software packages on the market, from billing systems for veterinarians to general-ledger accounting systems for billion-dollar multinational companies. If there is a market for a software product, chances are that some entrepreneur has developed a package to meet the need.

When a company purchases a proprietary applications software package, it receives the programs (on magnetic tape, diskettes, or CD-ROM) and associated documentation. Depending on the scope and complexity of the software, on-site education, on-site consultation, and the use of a hot line may be included in the price.

▶ 15–3 The Systems Development Process

The systems development process is a cooperative effort of users and computer professionals. On one hand, computer professionals are familiar with the technology and how it can be applied to meet a business's information processing needs. On the other, users have in-depth familiarity with their respective functional areas and the information processing needs of the organization. The skills and knowledge of these two groups complement each other and can be combined to create any type of information system during the systems development process.

There are two fundamental approaches to the development of in-house information systems:

1. The prototyping approach
2. The prespecification approach

This chapter contains an overview of both approaches.

Prototyping

Prior to the early 1980s, virtually all in-house systems development was done either according to a particular systems development methodology or very informally with no guidelines for programmers and analysts. In recent years, computer technology has produced sophisticated hardware and software that enable the project team to work with users to develop a **prototype system**, a model of a full-scale system. This approach is called **prototyping**.

In effect, a prototype system permits users a "sneak" preview of the completed system. A typical prototype system

- Handles the main transaction-oriented procedures
- Produces critical reports
- Permits rudimentary inquiries

Once users gain hands-on experience with the prototype system, they are in a better position to comment on the proposed design and to fine-tune their information processing needs. Later in this chapter, we talk about the prototyping process and the tools and technologies that make it possible.

The Prespecification Approach to Systems Development

Because systems development is a team effort, most companies have adopted a standardized **systems development methodology** that provides the framework for cooperation. This *step-by-step* approach to systems development is essentially the same for an airline reservation system, an inventory management system, or another system. As members of a project team progress through the procedures outlined in a systems development methodology, the results of one step provide the input for the next step and/or subsequent steps.

The methodological approach to systems development is a tool employed by information services and user managers to coordinate the efforts of a variety of people engaged in a complex process. One of the major premises of a systems development methodology is that users must relate their information processing needs to the project team during the early stages of the project and then make a commitment to stick to these **system specifications** through system implementation. These **specs** include everything from the functionality of the system to the format of the system's output screens and reports. Because of this premise, this approach to systems development is called the **prespecification** approach.

The major advantage of the prespecification approach is that it provides a framework for all involved to coordinate their activities. The major disadvantage is that it leaves little room for flexibility in design. Figure 15–2 highlights the economics of doing it right the first time. An oversight left undetected becomes more and more difficult to correct as

FIGURE 15–2   The Cost of an Error
This chart depicts the relative personnel time required to correct a logic error when first detected in the different phases of systems development.

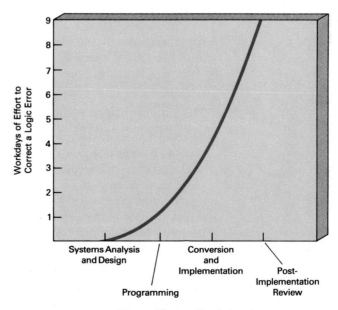

Workdays of Effort to Correct a Logic Error

Systems Analysis and Design

Programming

Conversion and Implementation

Post-Implementation Review

Phases of Systems Development

The prespecification approach to systems development requires the user to sign off on the design specifications at various stages of the process. This programmer/ analyst is demonstrating the proposed layouts of the input/ output screens for a micro-based human resources subsystem to the personnel manager. The manager is encouraged to make recommendations to improve the layouts and other aspects of the system design until he signs off, after which time the specs are frozen.

the project progresses from one phase to the next. A logic error that would take about an hour to correct in the programming phase would take nine workdays to correct after the system is implemented!

The activities of the traditional approach to systems development are typically grouped in phases, for example *Phase I—Systems Analysis, Phase II—Systems Design, Phase III—Programming, Phase IV—Conversion and Implementation*, and *Phase V—Post-Implementation*. Systems analysis and systems design are presented in this chapter, along with prototyping, the alternative approach to systems development. The other phases of the traditional approach to systems development are presented in Chapter 16, "System Implementation."

Systems Development in Practice

Over the years, MIS managers have become accustomed to the structure and success of systems development methodologies, and they are reluctant to give them up. Nevertheless, the trend is moving toward prototyping. In practice, tradition and trend are merging. Relatively few companies rely solely on prototyping for systems development. In fact those companies that have adopted the prototyping philosophy have created hybrid approaches that combine the best of the two approaches, thus realizing the advantages of the structure of a systems development methodology and the flexibility of prototyping.

15-4 Prototyping: Creating a Model of the Target System

Throughout the twentieth century, manufacturers have built prototypes of everything from toasters to airplanes. Automobile manufacturers routinely build prototypes according to design specifications. Scaled-down clay models are made to evaluate aesthetics and aerodynamics. Ultimately, a full-size, fully functional prototype is created that enables the driver and passengers to test all aspects of the car's functionality. If engineers see possibilities for improvement, the prototypes are modified and retested until they meet or exceed all specifications. Today, building prototype systems is standard procedure in software development.

The Emergence of Prototyping

Most managers have a *good idea* of what they want in an information system, but they do not know *exactly* what they want. This is a problem when it comes to developing information systems. Systems analysts and programmers must have precise specifications to create an information system. The prespecification approach forces users into committing themselves to specs long before they feel comfortable with the specs. Realistically, users cannot become comfortable with a system, nor can they recognize the potential of a system, until they have had an opportunity to work with it. In the prespecification approach, user familiarity comes after the fact and too late for quick fixes and inexpensive modifications. After implementation, even small changes to an information system can be time-consuming and expensive. This point is highlighted graphically in Figure 15–2.

Ideally, users should experiment with and familiarize themselves with the operation of the proposed system as early in the development process as possible. Systems analysts know that any action that results in the early identification of potential misdirection or errors in design will save time and money.

Prior to the early 1980s, a prototype system would probably have cost almost as much as a completed full-scale information system. But, today, project team members using *fourth-generation languages* and *application generators* can create a subset of the proposed system that, to the user at a terminal or PC, appears and acts very much like the finished product.

The Prototype System

The three objectives of prototyping are

- To analyze the current situation
- To identify information needs
- To develop a scaled-down model of the proposed system, often called the **target system**

The prototype system gives users an actual opportunity to work with the functional aspect of the proposed system long before the system is implemented. Once users gain hands-on familiarity with the prototype system, they can relate more precise information processing needs to the project team.

A prototype system can be anything from a nonfunctional demonstration of the input/output of a proposed information system to a full-scale operational system. Both the prespecification and prototype approaches can result in an information system, but, in practice, most prototype systems are merely models. These models are tested and refined until the users are confident that what they see is what they want. In some cases, the software developed to create an initial prototype system is expanded to create a fully operational information system. However, in most cases, the prototype system provides an alternate vehicle for completing the functional specifications activity of a systems development methodology. Incomplete and/or inaccurate user specifications have been the curse of the prespecification approach to systems development. Many companies have exorcised this curse by integrating prototyping into their methodologies.

As a stand-alone technique or as an augmentation to a systems development methodology, prototyping has proven to be an effective technique for creating information systems that meet users' information processing needs. Most users do not have enough experience in systems design to comprehend what a proposed system will eventually look like and how it will work. To overcome this lack of experience, project teams are building prototype systems to give users an early firsthand look at what the system will look like when it is implemented. The prototyping

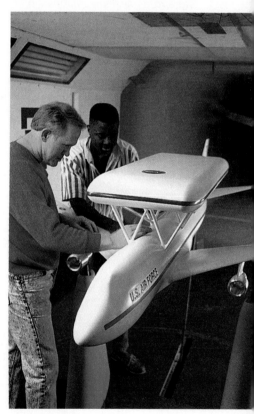

For years aircraft manufacturers have built prototype models that could be tested for aerodynamics, aesthetics, and functionality. Here a prototype of a specially equipped Boeing 747-200 is being tested in a wind tunnel at Texas A&M University. Only recently has prototyping become popular with information systems development. Now over 70% of all new information systems emerge from a prototype system, and the percentage is increasing each year.

process enables users to articulate their exact information processing needs to the project team during the early phases of the project and throughout the project. The availability of this high-quality user feedback precludes having to retrofit a less acceptable system after implementation.

Approaches to Developing Prototype Systems

Throughout the twentieth century, manufacturers have built prototypes of everything from toasters to airplanes. Automobile manufacturers routinely build prototype cars according to design specifications. However, automobile prototypes have varying degrees of sophistication. Scaled-down clay models are made to evaluate aesthetics and aerodynamics. Ultimately, a full-size fully functional prototype is created that enables the driver and passengers to test all aspects of the car's functionality. If engineers see possibilities for improvement, the prototypes at the varying levels of sophistication are modified and retested until they meet or exceed all specifications. Like prototypes of manufactured goods, software prototypes are also created in varying degrees of sophistication:

Rockwell International engineers at Cedar Rapids, Iowa, work with a prototype aircraft Electronic Library System. With the touch-sensitive flat-panel display, aircraft flight crews will be able to call up airport diagrams, approach and departure plates, weather maps, and aircraft systems information with no more than three "keystrokes."

- Nonfunctional prototype systems
- Partially functional prototype systems
- Fully functional prototype systems

In practice, a given prototype system may exhibit the characteristics of several levels of prototype sophistication.

Nonfunctional Prototypes The "quick and dirty" way to give users an opportunity to experiment with the operational aspects of a proposed information system is to create a nonworking model of the system. This approach to prototyping, sometimes called **rapid prototyping**, focuses on three aspects of the design:

- The user interface
- Data entry displays
- System outputs

Prototyping tools are available that enable project team members to design demonstration menus and screens. For example, while working with the prototype system, the user is able to select the data entry option from a menu and the desired data entry screen is displayed. Then, the user can key in data, but the data are lost when the user requests another screen; that is, the data entered are superimposed on the data entry screen, but they are not transmitted to the data base. Also, the user can select menu options that result in the display of a particular report. In a functional system, the information contained in a report is extracted from a data base, but in a nonfunctional prototype, the report is based on static test data. At this point in the system development, the content and **layout** (spacing on the screen or page) of the report are much more important than are the actual entries.

In nonfunctional prototype systems, the time-consuming technical intricacies of interfacing with an actual data base are avoided while permitting users to familiarize themselves with the proposed user interface and system input/output.

Partially Functional Prototypes   The next level of sophistication in the development of prototype systems is the partially functional prototype. The 80/20 rule is as applicable to information systems development as it is to inventory management (20 percent of the inventory items account for 80 percent of the inventory activity). When applied to information systems, the rule states that 80 percent of the features and functionality of an information system can be realized with 20 percent of the effort required to develop a fully functional system. In general, the more sophisticated but less frequently used features of an information system pose the greatest challenges and demand the lion's share of a project team's effort. The philosophy behind partially functional prototyping is that users, especially at the operational level, can work with most of the basic features of the proposed system during interactive practice sessions. They will even be able to make routine inquiries to the data base.

Many partially functional prototype systems are created under the premise that they will eventually be enhanced to the level of fully functional systems. Once all the kinks in the prototype system are worked out at one level of sophistication, the system can be enhanced to incorporate other user-requested features. After several iterations, the prototype system emerges as a fully functional information system. Those technologies that are used to develop the initial prototype system also can be employed to expand the scope of the system.

Fully Functional Prototypes   The most ambitious approach to prototyping is to create a fully functional prototype system. Typically, such systems are created for the sole purpose of enabling users to experiment with the system. The focus of fully functional prototype systems is functionality; therefore, performance characteristics are ignored. This means that prototype developers can ignore concerns that relate to system efficiency and volume of work. For example, the capacity of a fully functional prototype system may be limited to 10 transactions per minute whereas the eventual system may need to handle up to 1000 transactions per minute.

Once familiar with the operation of the proposed system, users can provide meaningful feedback on all aspects of the proposed system. Unlike the partially functional approach, the fully functional approach is not intended to result in an operational system. The results of the fully functional approach are well-defined user specifications that can be used by the project team to create an information system that uses resources more efficiently and can handle an increased volume of work.

The Prototyping Process

Forming the Project Team   The composition of the project team is essentially the same for both the prototyping and the systems development

Checking Out Imaging Banks are helping people who hate to balance their checkbooks. Customers no longer have to sort and keep their canceled checks in order—the bank does it for them. A new system captures a digitized version of the checks' images, sorts and prints them in condensed form (18 to a page), and returns the images with the statement. Besides benefiting the customer, the system also helps the bank. Sending a few sheets of paper saves a lot of money in postage. Also, microfiche of imaged checks takes up less space than paper checks. The imaging device can digitize up to 1000 check images per minute.

methodology approaches. Both have managers, users, programmers, systems analysts, and special-function personnel (user liaison, data base manager), as required. The main difference in the team makeup for the two approaches is the size of the team. The interactive nature of prototyping demands that the size of the project team be kept as small as possible. Each member of the team must be familiar with all facets of the system and be prepared to interact with any other member at any time. In the prespecification approach, project team members can work relatively independently once the specifications have been defined.

Successful Prototype Systems   There are two keys to creating successful systems:

- *Users must be willing and committed to providing ongoing and meaningful feedback.* This feedback includes recommendations and qualitative comments that enhance the functionality of the finished system. In the prespecification approach to systems development, user feedback is more of a once-and-done activity. Prototyping is an *iterative process*; therefore, users must be available to examine and comment on the system design after each addition or revision to the prototype system.
- *The prototype system must be designed and created in a manner that makes it easy to modify.* The whole idea behind prototyping is to give users an opportunity to examine a menu, a report, or the overall operation of the system so that they can render their approval or recommend changes. If it is difficult to modify the prototype system, needed changes will be ignored and the finished system will fall short of user expectations.

The Four Phases of Prototyping   The development of an information system via prototyping is done in four stages:

- Phase I—define system specifications
- Phase II—create prototype system
- Phase III—refine prototype system
- Phase IV—develop operational system

These phases are illustrated graphically in Figure 15–3.

Phase I—define system specifications.   To appreciate the benefits of prototyping fully, you need to understand what has been done in the past. Traditionally, one of the rough spots in the prespecification approach to systems development has been the definition of system specifications. In the past, users cooperated with the systems development project team to complete the functional specifications as early in the development cycle as possible. The specs had to be defined early because the technology (primarily third-generation languages and traditional flat-file processing) did not provide project team members with much flexibility to modify the design of the system or the programs. In this environment, design changes were costly and, if possible, changes were avoided (see Figure 15–2).

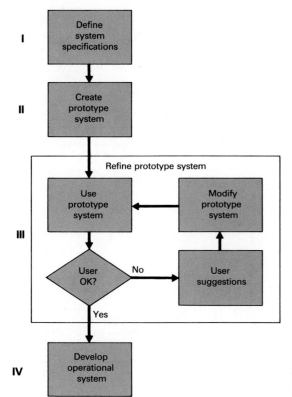

FIGURE 15–3 The Four Phases of the Prototyping Process

In the traditional prespecification approach to development, users were unable to comprehend the scope of the proposed system during the early stages of the project, and they were often unable to convey their information requirements to the project team. The resulting functional specifications were ill-defined and incomplete. Inevitably, one or more serious design oversights forced the project team to backtrack and make costly modifications. After years of backtracking, MIS professionals decided to ask users to sign-off (see Section 15–6) on the system specifications. After the sign-off, the specs were "frozen"; that is, no more changes could be made to the specs. Well, frozen specs are like ice cubes—when enough heat is applied, they melt.

Prototyping takes advantage of the capabilities of the new applications development tools. In prototyping, the specs do not need to be frozen. With these tools, the project team can develop a prototype system during interactive sessions with the user. To the user, the prototype version will look very much like the real thing. The system has menus, reports, various input/output screens, and a data base—all that a user needs to relate his or her information and information processing needs to a project team.

Phase II—create prototype system. To create a prototype system, project team members rough out the logic of the system and how the elements fit together and then work with the user to define the I/O interfaces (the system interaction with the user). During interactive ses-

We've learned that computers store data in the form of binary digits, 1s and 0s, and that these can be translated to and from the numbers and words we use our computers to work on. But images? How would a computer handle them as data —and why?

IMAGE PROCESSING APPLICATIONS

Let's look at the "why" first. Some businesses must work with literally tons of paper on a daily basis. A giant company like American Express, for example, takes in millions of credit-card slips each day from merchants, sorts the data by account, and computes invoices for customers and payments for merchants. At one time, American Express physically moved the actual charge slips from point to point during processing and returned them with the invoice to the customer. Now the slip is translated into an electronic image, processed and stored as an image, and the customer gets a copy of that image with the invoice. The result is efficiency— American Express cuts down on handling time and costs, warehouse storage space, personnel, and postage (the reconstructed images on the bills are smaller and weigh less).

In other applications, efficiency can also mean being able to do something *at all* rather than just more cheaply. In Downers Grove, Illinois, a gas station attendant was robbed and killed recently. The police were unable to recognize the assailant's face by viewing the videotape from a surveillance camera. But they saw him take and drop cigarette packs, and from one pack they got a

IMAGE PROCESSING AND HEALTH CARE   At this clinic, the image of the doctors' reports are maintained on a computer-based file with other medical information.

sions, project team members and users create whatever interactive display screens are required to meet the user's information processing needs. Project team members use prototyping tools and applications development tools (discussed later in this chapter) to create the screen images (menus, reports, inquiries, and so on) and to generate much of the programming code. In some cases, an existing data base can be modified to service the proposed system. In other cases, a new data base must be created.

Automated *prototyping tools* enable project team members to create a physical representation of a target system at one of the three levels of sophistication—a nonfunctional, partially functional, or fully functional prototype system. The basic components of prototyping tools are

- *The user interface.* This capability enables the project team to design and create the user interface. Typically the user interface consists of a hierarchy

fingerprint. The Illinois State Police entered the fingerprint into an imaging system, called the Automated Fingerprint Identification System. Comparing the fingerprint from the cigarette pack with nearly 2 million others stored by the system, a match was found—and within hours the police had the name of the killer. Searching this quantity of fingerprints the old way, by hand, would have been impossible.

The list of image processing systems is growing every day. Image processing is used by aircraft builders to store blueprints and safety documents required when designing a new plane. Hospitals use it to handle patient records. Even submarines use it to thread their way among the hazards of the ocean floor.

THE HARDWARE

In image processing, an *image scanner* "digitizes" the text, numbers, fingerprints, signatures, or whatever appears on the input paper document. A processor compresses or squeezes out any unneeded space in the digitized images to make the most efficient use of expensive secondary storage. Because digitized images take up more storage space than straightforward text and some imaging systems handle millions of images, high-capacity optical disk is often the preferred storage media. Unneeded, the input document can be shredded. To get an image out of the system, the computer decompresses it so that a copy of the original can be viewed on a screen or printed.

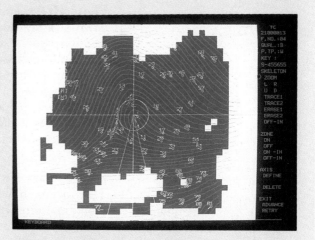

IMAGE PROCESSING AND CRIME Computers take only a few minutes to check fingerprints from the scene of a crime against a large data base of fingerprints—often with great success.

COMPUTERS LARGE AND SMALL

Major imaging systems such as that used by American Express cost millions of dollars. However, not all imaging systems cost millions. PCs configured with an image scanner, imaging software, and plenty of RAM and secondary storage can handle imaging. A PC-based imaging system works more slowly, but it costs only about $20,000. In the years to come the use of imaging may result in the paperless office.

---

of menus, which may be displayed in windows superimposed over the current display.

■ *Screen generators.* Screen generators, also called **screen formatters**, provide systems analysts with the capability of generating a mockup, or layout, of a screen while in direct consultation with the user. The layout is a detailed output and/or input specification that graphically illustrates exactly where information should be placed, or entered, on a terminal display screen or on a printer output.

■ *Report generators.* **Report generators** are similar to screen generators, with one exception. Report generators permit the calculation of summary totals by criteria and overall, and the editing of output. For example, a report generator can produce a sales report that includes summary totals for each sales region and for overall. The output could be edited so that sales amounts are displayed in currency notation ($23,462.50).

Applications development tools, discussed later in this chapter, can be used to generate much of the programming code. In some cases, an existing data base can be modified to service the proposed system. In other cases, a new data base must be created.

Phase III—refine prototype system. In this phase, users actually sit down at a terminal or PC and evaluate portions and, eventually, all of the prototype system. Invariably, users have suggestions for improving the user interfaces and/or the format of the I/O. And, without fail, their examination reveals new needs for information. In effect, the original prototype system is the beginning. From here, the system is expanded and refined to meet the users' total information needs. The use-and-modify cycle depicted in Figure 15–3 is repeated until the user is satisfied with the prototype system.

Phase IV—develop operational system. At this point in the prototyping process, users have a system that looks and feels like what they want. The system, however, is a prototype and must be enhanced (partially functional prototype system) or another system, based on the prototype system, must be developed (nonfunctional and fully functional prototype systems). In the latter case, the prototype system is discarded once the specs have been determined. From these specs, an operational information system capable of handling the required volume of work is developed.

Prototyping software tools (discussed later in this chapter) are limited in what they can do, so developing an operational information system may require a considerable amount of **custom coding**, probably written in third- and fourth-generation languages.

Prototyping Summary

Prototyping has two great advantages over the prespecification approach to systems development. First, an information system can be produced in considerably less time. And second, errors in judgment and oversights can be remedied quickly without costly redesigning or reprogramming. The greatest disadvantage of prototyping is that it assumes full cooperation on the part of users who will ultimately be affected by the information system. If the users fail to meet their obligations, the advantages of prototyping are negated.

Apparently most organizations feel that the disadvantages are offset by the advantages. Over three fourths of all new information systems emerge from a prototype system. Prototyping enables project team members to home in on exactly what the user wants early in the development cycle. This capability has endeared prototyping to the entire MIS and user communities.

 Systems Development Methodologies: The Tradition Continues

The traditional prespecification approach to systems development is based on the premise that exact information processing needs can be identified and systems specifications can be determined during the early phases of a development project. In theory, once set, the specifications are frozen (they cannot be revised) until implementation is complete. In practice, specifications are frequently revised during the development process.

A Five-Phase Systems Development Methodology System

Systems development methodologies vary in scope, complexity, sophistication, and approach. Systems development methodologies may be divided into any number of phases (3, 5, or even as many as 10), but the chronology of the activities remains essentially the same. The best methodologies involve the user throughout the development process. After all, systems development is a 50:50 proposition—users are responsible for the functional specifications and computer/MIS specialists are responsible for the implementation of those specs. A five-phase systems development methodology is discussed in this chapter to give you an overview of what is involved in developing and implementing an information system. The phases are

- *Phase I—systems analysis.* During Phase I, systems analysts and users work together to analyze the existing system and to determine input, processing, and output requirements for the target system.
- *Phase II—systems design.* During Phase II, systems analysts and users work together to design the information system. The design is submitted to programmers for coding in Phase III.
- *Phase III—programming.* During Phase III, the software needed to support the system is developed.
- *Phase IV—conversion and implementation.* During Phase IV, data files are created, and the new system is put into operation.
- *Phase V—post-implementation.* Phase V begins the *production stage* of the life cycle (see Figure 15–1). During this stage, the system is evaluated periodically to ensure that it continues to meet the information processing needs of the company.

Traditional approaches to Phases I and II are covered in this chapter as well as automated approaches to accomplishing the tasks in the first two phases. Phases III, IV, and V are covered in Chapter 16, "System Implementation: Programming, System Conversion, and Controls." These five phases are equally applicable to systems development in small, one-person businesses and in large companies with several layers of management.

The Responsibility Matrix

A systems development methodology makes it easy to identify *who* does *what*, and *when*. To help you understand better the structure of a systems development methodology, a five-phase methodology is illustrated graphically in Figure 15–4 in the form of a **responsibility matrix**.

Phases of Systems Development	Project team	MIS management	User management
Phase I Systems Analysis			
Existing system review	R		C
System objectives	R	C	C
Design constraints	R	C	C
Requirements definition	R		P
Phase II Systems Design			
General system design	R		C/A
Data base design	R		
Detailed system design	R		C/A
Phase III Programming			
System specifications review	R		
Program identification and description	R		
Program coding, testing, and documentation	R		
Phase IV Conversion and Implementation			
System and acceptance test	R		P/A
System conversion	R		P
Phase V Post-Implementation Review			
Post-Implementation review	R		C
System maintenance		R	P

Key: A = Approval   R = Primary responsibility
C = Consultation   P = Participating responsibility

FIGURE 15–4 Systems Development Responsibility Matrix
The project team has primary responsibility for most systems development activities, but MIS and user managers have participating responsibilities (P) and are called upon for consultation (C) and approval (A).

The major activities for each of the five phases are listed along the left-hand side of the responsibility matrix. Although some of the activities are accomplished at the same time, they are generally presented in the order in which they are begun.

The individuals and groups directly involved in the development of an information system are listed across the top of the matrix. Each is described as follows:

■ *Project team.* The project team normally consists of *systems analysts, programmers,* perhaps the *data base administrator,* and at least one user who will eventually use the system. The systems analysts design the system and develop the system specifications. The programmers use these "specs" as guidelines to write the programs. The data base administrator assists the team in designing and creating the data base. These and other computer specialist positions are discussed in detail in Chapter 17, "Computers in Action: Jobs and Career Opportunities."

■ *MIS management.* This group includes the director and other managers in the information services division.

■ *User management.* This group encompasses all user managers (for example, director of personnel, vice president of marketing) who affect or are affected by the proposed development project.

The entries in the matrix reflect the extent and type of involvement for each of the foregoing individuals and groups.

A   Denotes *approval* authority.

C   Denotes that the individual/group may be called in for *consultation.*

R   Denotes who has primary *responsibility* for a particular activity.

P   Denotes that although the individual or group does not have primary responsibility, it has *participating responsibility.*

Companies using systems development methodologies or the prespecification approach usually have a responsibility matrix or something similar to it. The more detailed methodologies may have literally hundreds of activities. The manual for a company's systems development methodology normally contains detailed descriptions for the numbered activities in the responsibility matrix and standardized forms (both hard-copy and on-line) to aid project team members in the development process.

15–6 Systems Analysis: Understanding the System

The systems analysis phase (Phase I of the systems development responsibility matrix of Figure 15–4) of the systems development process produces the following results:

■ Existing system review
■ System objectives
■ Design constraints
■ Requirements definition

Each of these results defines an activity that is to take place.

Existing System Review

Before designing a new or enhanced MIS, the members of the project team must have a good grasp of the existing work and information flow, whether manual or computer-based. If the existing system is computer-based, it is usually accompanied by some type of documentation. If the existing system is manual, the project team may need to compile a basic documentation package that includes a list of and examples of all reports and documents, system files (including fields), and a graphic illustration of the current work and information flow.

The work and information flow of the present system is documented by reducing the system to its basic component parts: *input*, *processing*, and *output*. A variety of design techniques can be used to depict graphically the logical relationships between these parts. The most popular technique is *flowcharting*. In certain situations, more "structured" techniques, such as *data flow diagrams* and *hierarchical plus input-processing-output* (*HIPO*) would be chosen. Data flow diagrams are introduced later in the systems design portion of this chapter. Flowcharting is covered in Chapter 10, "Programming Concepts and Languages."

System Objectives

Once the existing system is documented, the project team can begin to identify the obvious and not-so-obvious problem areas, including procedural bottlenecks, inefficiencies in information flow and storage, duplication of effort, deficiencies in information dissemination, worker discontent, problems with customer interaction, inaccuracy of operational data, and so on. Next, project team members can concentrate their

Systems analysts must consider the circumstances under which the user will be interacting with the system. The plant floor is not always conducive to the more traditional approaches to data entry, such as keyboards and wand scanners. This operator's terminal is equipped with a touch-sensitive panel with oversized buttons.

energies on identifying opportunities for the coordination of effort, the integration of systems, and the use of information.

By this time the project team should know what can be achieved with the judicious application of information. However, this knowledge needs to be formalized as system objectives. The project team arrives at general system objectives by engaging in discussions with all end user managers who will ultimately be affected by the target system. In the end, everyone should be satisfied that the system objectives are consistent with business needs. Finally, everyone concerned should have a clear picture of the direction in which the project is heading.

Design Constraints

The target system is developed with specific constraints in mind. The purpose of this activity is to detail, at the onset of the systems development process, any costs, hardware, schedule, procedural, software, data base, and operating constraints that may limit the definition and design of the target system. For example, cost constraints include any limits on developmental, operational, or maintenance costs. Constraints that may in some way limit the design of the target system are identified before the system's information processing requirements are defined. If constraints are not defined early in the project, the scope and/or direction of the project may need to be revised once the project is underway. Such revisions are unnecessary and costly.

Requirements Definition

Functional Specifications   In this activity the project team completes a *needs analysis* that results in a definition of the data processing and information requirements for the target system. To accomplish this task, the project team begins by gathering information in the following ways:

- They interview users.
- They ask users to respond to written questionnaires.
- They examine the documentation of the existing system.
- They study the decisions made within the context of the target system.

The project team uses feedback from the interviews to formulate **functional specifications** for system input, processing, and output requirements (information needs). The functional specifications describe the logic of the system (input/output, work, and information flow) from the perspective of the user.

Next, the project team turns its attention to *output requirements*. In the systems development process, the project team begins with the desired output and works backward to determine input and processing requirements. Outputs are typically printed reports, terminal displays, or some kind of transaction (for example, purchase order, payroll check). At this time, outputs are described functionally. The actual layout and detailed content of a display screen or report is specified during the systems design phase.

The User Sign-Off   In the prespecification approach to systems development, the user is asked to "sign off" at certain stages of the process. The **user sign-off** is the signature of an authorized user that in effect means

- The user has examined the work to date in detail.
- All work and specifications completed to date are consistent with user objectives.
- The user is committed to the specifications as defined by the project team.

Periodic user sign-off is important for two reasons: First, it ensures that the user is involved in and aware of project progress; second, it enables the project team to make steady progress toward project completion.

> **15-7**   Systems Design: A Science or an Art?

The following results are realized during the systems design phase (Phase II of the systems development responsibility matrix of Figure 15–4) of the systems development process:

- General system design
- Data base design
- Detailed system design

Each of these results defines an activity that is to take place.

General System Design

Systems Design—The Creative Process   The design of an MIS is more of a challenge to the human intellect than it is a procedural challenge. Just as an author begins with a blank page and an idea, the members of the project team begin with empty RAM (random-access memory) and the information requirements definitions. From here, they must create what can sometimes be a very complex information system. The number of ways in which a particular information system can be designed is limited only by the imaginations of the project team members.

Completing the General System Design   The project team analyzes the existing system, assesses information processing requirements, and then develops a **general system design** for the target system. The general system design, and later the detailed design, involves continuous communication between members of the project team and all levels of users (clerical through strategic), as appropriate. After evaluating several alternative approaches, the project team translates the system specifications (from Phase I) into a general system design.

At a minimum, the documentation of the general design of the target system includes the following:

- A graphic illustration that depicts the fundamental operation of the target system (for example, flowcharts or data flow diagrams)
- A written explanation of the graphic illustration
- General descriptions of the outputs to be produced by the system, including display screens and hard-copy reports and documents (The actual layout—for example, spacing on the page or screen—is not completed until the detailed system design.)

Data Base Design

The data base is the common denominator of any system. It contains the raw material (data) necessary to produce the output (information). In manufacturing, for example, you decide what you are going to make, then you order the raw material. In the process of developing an information system, you decide what your output requirements are, then you determine which data are needed to produce the output. In a sense, output requirements can be thought of as input to data base design.

Many companies already have integrated on-line systems and DBMS technology. As a result, at least part and perhaps all of the data base may already exist; its creation may not be necessary. However, it is likely that fields will need to be added to the data base.

The first step in data base design is to compile a **data dictionary**. A data dictionary, illustrated in Figure 15–5, is simply a listing of all fields in the data base. An existing data base will already have a data dictionary. The fields, together with certain descriptive information, are listed along the left-hand side of the data dictionary form in Figure 15–

FIGURE 15–5   Data Dictionary

Companies maintain an up-to-date data dictionary with descriptive information for all data elements. The use or occurrence of these data elements is cross-referenced to appropriate files, reports, and source documents. The entry in the Format column describes the data element's length and whether it is numeric (9) or alphanumeric (X).

						Report (R)			Data base (D)		Display screen (S)		
No.	Name	Description	Format	Coded	Responsibility	Best-seller list (R)	Overdue report (R)	On-loan report (R)	Patron data base (D)	Book data base (D)	Checkout display (S)	Acq. data entry (S)	Data base update (S)
1	TITLE	Complete title of book	X(150)	No	Acquisitions	X	X	X		X	X	X	X
2	ISBN	Int'l Std. Book No.	9(13)	No	Acquisitions				X	X	X	X	X
3	PUBYR	Year of publication	9(2)	No	Acquisitions	X				X		X	X
4	AUTHOR	Name of author	X(25)	No	Acquisitions	X				X		X	X
5	PUBL	Name of publisher	X(25)	No	Acquisitions					X		X	X
6	DUE	Due date of book	9(6)	No	Circulation		X		X		X		
7	CARDNO	Patron card number	9(4)	Yes	Circulation				X		X		
8	FNAME	First name of patron	X(10)	No	Circulation		X		X		X		

5. The data dictionary provides the basis for the creation or modification of a data base. Database management systems and structures (hierarchical, network, and relational) are discussed and illustrated in Chapter 9, "System Software and Platforms."

The remainder of the data dictionary form in Figure 15–5 is completed *after* the data base organization has been determined and *after* the reports and input screens are designed. The fields are then cross-referenced to reflect their occurrence in data base records, reports, and input screens.

Detailed System Design

The **detailed system design**—the detailed input/output, processing, and control requirements—is the result of the analysis of user feedback on the general system design. The general system design depicts the relationship between major processing activities and contains enough details for users to determine whether or not that is what they want. The detailed design includes *all* processing activities and the input/output associated with them.

The detailed design is the cornerstone of the traditional systems development process. It is here that the relationships between the various components of the system are defined. The system specifications are transformed with the project team's imagination and skill into an information system. The detailed system design is the culmination of all previous work. Moreover, it is the *blueprint* for all project team activities that follow.

A number of techniques help programmers and analysts in the design process. Each of these techniques permits the systems design to be illustrated graphically. One of these techniques, data flow diagrams, is briefly discussed here.

During detailed system design, the project team creates the detailed specifications for all input to and output from the system, including data entry screens. Typically, analysts and users experiment with several alternatives before selecting the one that enables the most effective interaction with the system.

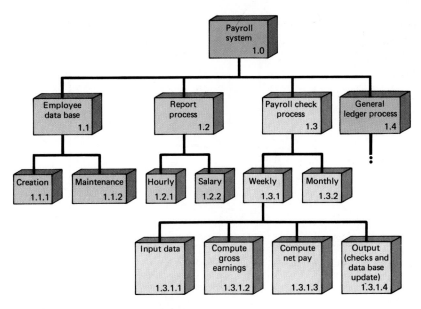

FIGURE 15–6   Structure Chart
This structure chart breaks a payroll system down into a hierarchy of modules.

Structured System Design   It is much easier to address a complex design problem in small, manageable modules than as one big task. This is done using the principles of **structured system design**. The structured approach to systems design encourages the *top-down design* technique. That is, the project team divides the system into independent modules for ease of understanding and design. The structure chart in Figure 15–6 illustrates how a payroll system can be conceptualized as a hierarchy of modules. In the hierarchy, the system is broken down into modules at finer levels of detail until a particular module can best be portrayed in terms of procedural logic. Eventually the logic for each of the lowest-level modules is represented in detail in step-by-step diagrams that illustrate the inter-actions between input, processing, output, and storage activities for a particular module.

Data Flow Diagrams   **Data flow diagrams** enable analysts to design and document systems using the structured approach to systems development. Only four symbols are needed for data flow diagrams: entity, process, flow line, and data storage. The symbols are summarized in Figure 15–7 and their use is illustrated in Figure 15–8.

FIGURE 15–7   Data Flow Diagram Symbols

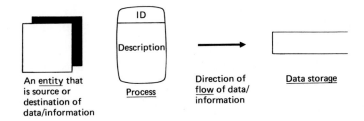

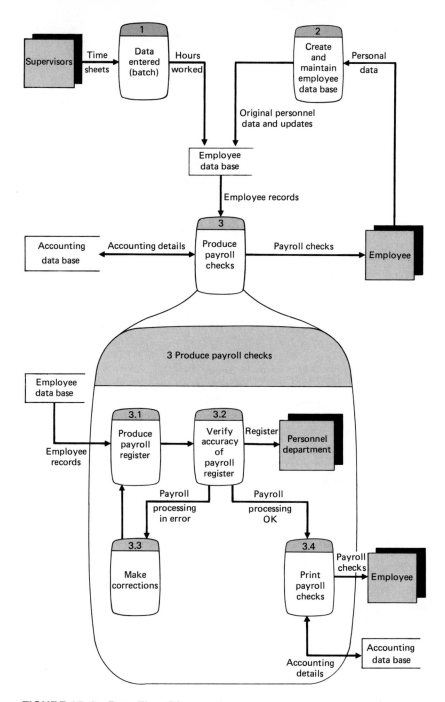

FIGURE 15–8 Data Flow Diagram

In this data flow diagram of a payroll system, Process 3 is exploded to show greater detail.

■ *Entity symbol.* The entity symbol, a square with a darkened "shadow," is the source or destination of data or information flow. An entity can be a person, a group of people (for example, customers or employees), a department, or even a place (such as a warehouse). The interactions between the various entities in a typical business system are illustrated in Appendix A, "A Management Information System Case Study."

- *Process symbol.* Each process symbol, a rectangle with rounded corners, contains a description of a function to be performed. Process symbols also can be depicted as circles. Typical processes include *enter data, calculate, store, create, produce,* and *verify.* Process-symbol identification numbers are assigned in levels (for example, Processes 1.1 and 1.2 are subordinate to Process 1).
- *Flow line.* The flow lines indicate the flow and direction of data or information.
- *Data storage.* These symbols, open-ended rectangles, identify storage locations for data which could be a file drawer, a shelf, a data base on magnetic disk, and so on.

In Figure 15–8, a data flow diagram documents that portion of a personnel system that produces payroll checks. Processes 1 and 2 deal with the employee data base, but in Process 3 the actual payroll checks are produced. In the bottom portion of Figure 15–8, Process 3 is *exploded* to show greater detail. Notice that the second-level processes within the explosion of Process 3 are numbered 3.1, 3.2, 3.3, and 3.4. Process 3.1 could be exploded to a third level of processes to show even greater detail (for example, 3.1.1, 3.1.2, and so on).

There is no one best analytical or design technique. If you elect to take a course on systems analysis and design, you will gain a deeper understanding of data flow diagrams and the other techniques. Remember, however, that design techniques are just tools. It's your skill and imagination that make an information system a reality.

The Presentation of Information Within the context of an information system, information can be presented in many ways. During the systems design process, members of the project team work in close cooperation with users to describe each output that will be generated from the target system. An output could be a hard-copy report, a display of information, or a transaction document (an invoice). Transaction documents are typically periodic (monthly invoices). Reports, or generally the presentation of information in either hard-copy or soft-copy format, can be either *periodic* or *ad hoc* (see Figure 15–9).

Both periodic and ad hoc reports can be classified with respect to *content* and *time* (see Figure 15–9). The content-based classifications are as follows:

- *Comprehensive reports.* The comprehensive report presents all pertinent information about a particular subject.
- *Summary reports.* The summary report presents a summary of information about a particular subject.
- *Exception reports.* The exception report highlights critical information (see Chapter 13).

Not surprisingly, time-based classifications deal with the past, the present, and the future.

FIGURE 15–9 Summary of Types of Reports

Periodic and ad hoc reports can be classified with respect to content and time.

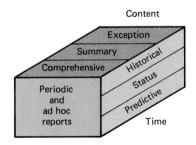

- *Historical reports.* The historical report is generated from data gathered in the past and does not reflect the current status.
- *Status reports.* The status report reflects the current status.
- *Predictive reports.* The predictive report is often the output of models based on current and historical data.

Of course, not all reports contain numbers and text. Some of the most effective ways of presenting information involve the use of graphics.

▶ 15–8 Computer-Aided Software Engineering: The CASE Tool Kit

For years most people thought the best way to improve productivity in systems development was to make it easier for programmers to create programs. *Fourth-generation languages* and *application generators* (discussed in Chapter 10, "Programming Concepts and Languages") are an outgrowth of this quest for better productivity. In essence, these languages were designed to let the computer do much of the programming. However, in the early 1980s people began asking "Why can't the power of the computer be applied to analysis and design work as well?" Now we know that it can. Many of the time-consuming manual tasks, such as creating a data dictionary and documenting information flow, can be automated. This general family of software development productivity tools falls under the umbrella of **computer-aided software engineering**, or **CASE**, tools. The term **software engineering** was coined to emphasize an approach to software development that combines automation and the rigors of the engineering discipline.

CASE tools, also called **workbench technologies**, provide automated support throughout the entire system life cycle. The CASE tool kit is made up of the following (see Figure 15–10):

- Design tools
- Prototyping tools
- Information repository tools
- Program development tools
- Methodology tools

Throughout this section, photographs illustrate the use and application of a variety of commercially available CASE tools. Each tool is discussed in more detail in the following sections. Note that there is some overlap in the functions of the various CASE tools.

CASE tools are in their infancy. To some extent, each tool is available commercially. While no comprehensive CASE tool kit to date integrates all the various tools, some companies offer packages that integrate two or three. We can reasonably expect that more sophisticated integrated CASE tool kits will be commercially available soon. **Software engineers** are developing software products to bridge the gap between design and executable program code. In a two-step process, these tool kits would enable project teams to use automated software packages to

FIGURE 15–10
The CASE Tool Kit

Design tools

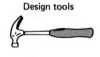

Prototyping tools

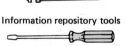

Information repository tools

Program development tools

Methodology tools

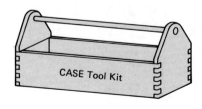

help them complete the logic design (information flow, I/O), then the CASE software would translate the logical design into the physical implementation of the system (executable program code). In fact, several existing CASE products are approaching this level of sophistication.

Design Tools

Prior to the introduction of CASE technologies, the tool kit for the systems analyst and programmer consisted of flowcharting and data flow diagram templates, lettering templates, rulers, scissors, glue, pencils, pens, and plenty of erasers and "white-out." The CASE *design tools* provide an automated alternative. They help analysts and programmers prepare schematics that graphically depict the logic of a system or program (for example, data flow diagrams, structure charts). They do this in much the same way word processing software helps a writer prepare an article for publication. They also help designers prepare screen and report layouts.

All CASE design tools use structured design techniques, such as data flow diagrams, to model the work flow, information flow, and program interactions within a system. Automated design tools enable an analyst or programmer to select and position symbols, such as the data flow diagram process and entity symbols, and to connect these symbols with flow lines (see Figure 15–8). Both symbols and flow lines can be labeled. For example,

KnowledgeWare, Inc., provides an integrated CASE environment for the planning, analysis, design, and construction of information systems. The KnowledgeWare tools function as an integrated set and independently as stand-alone products. The windows in the screen illustrate the capabilities of the Analysis Workstation, an integrated set of diagrammatic tools for requirements analysis. The techniques incorporated into the software include decomposition diagrams (top left), data flow diagrams (top right), entity relationship diagrams (middle), and action diagrams (bottom left).

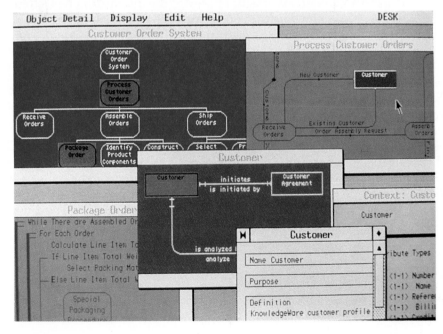

an analyst might label a process symbol "enter order data." Flow lines can be clarified with arrows to indicate the direction of flow and with descriptions of what is being transferred. Because all the design techniques supported by CASE products are structured design techniques, systems ultimately are depicted in several levels of generality. For example, at the highest level, the entire system might be represented by four process symbols of a data flow diagram. However, at the second level, each of these processes might be broken down into finer detail and presented as a more detailed data flow diagram. The processes at the second level can be broken down into finer detail, and so on.

Programmers and analysts can change the size of symbols to fit the diagram on the screen and/or change the color of a symbol or flow line to indicate special significance (a control procedure, for example). They can also help clarify the diagram by adding explanatory notations, both visible and hidden (that is, they can be called up in pop-up windows). A diagram can be exploded to the next level of generality by positioning the cursor over the appropriate symbol. The next screen would show an *explosion* (the next level of detail) of the desired process. Of course, levels of generality can be explored in both directions.

Prototyping Tools

CASE *prototyping tools* are the foundation for the creation of prototype systems. Prototyping tools include the *user interface, screen generators,* and *report generators,* all of which are discussed earlier in this chapter (Section 15–4).

Information Repository Tools

The *information repository* is analogous to the data dictionary in the traditional approach to systems design. However, the information repository contains everything the data dictionary includes and much more. It is a central computer-based storage facility for all design information. For example, in an information repository, each field is cross-referenced to all other components in the system. That is, the field *customer number* would be cross-referenced to every screen, report, graph, record/file, data base, program, or any other design element in which it occurred. Cross-references are also made to processes in data flow diagrams. Once the company has had the information repository in place for a while, cross-references can be extended between information systems. Besides the data dictionary component, the information repository permits all system documentation to be packaged electronically. That is, any part of the system—layouts, data dictionary, notes, pseudocode (nonexecutable program code), project schedules, and so on—can be recalled and displayed for review or modification. In effect, the information repository is the "data base" for the systems development project.

Program Development Tools

Program development tools focus on the back-end, or the latter phases, of the systems development effort (see Chapter 16, "System Implementation:

Programming, System Conversion, and Controls"). CASE program development tools fall into four categories:

- *Program structure charts.* The program structure chart enables programmers to create a graphic hierarchical representation of all the programs in a system. The resulting chart is similar to the one illustrated in Figure 15–6.
- *Code generators.* Code generators, which are also called application generators (see Chapter 10 for a detailed discussion) are perhaps the most valuable program development tool. Instead of actually coding programs, programmers use code generators, also called application generators, to describe the structure of a data base and to create screens and report layouts in what is essentially a fill-in-the-blank process.
- *Program preprocessors.* This tool preprocesses programmer-written programs of high-level programming languages, such as COBOL and PL/I, to point out potential problems in the program logic and syntax and to generate the documentation for the program.
- *Test data generators.* One of the more laborious tasks associated with programming is the generation of test data. Programmers using CASE tools rely on test data generators to compile test data. The programmer describes the parameters of the desired data (format, ranges, distributions, and so on), and the test data generator does the rest.

Methodology Tools

Systems development methodologies are usually presented in a hard-copy manual, but they are being automated and presented as on-line, interactive systems with increasing frequency. The *methodology tool* is a computer-based version of the traditional systems development methodology manual. Both describe phased procedures and responsibilities, and both provide forms and formats for documenting the system.

 Important Terms and Summary Outline

computer-aided
  software engineering
   (CASE)
custom coding
data dictionary
data flow diagrams
detailed system design
functional specifications
general system design
layout
prespecification

proprietary software
  package
prototype system
prototyping
rapid prototyping
report generator
responsibility matrix
screen formatter
software engineer
software engineering
  specs

structured system
  design
system life cycle
system specifications
systems development
  methodology
target system
user sign-off
workbench
  technologies

15–1 THE SYSTEM LIFE CYCLE. The four stages of a computer-based information system comprise the **system life cycle**. They are birth, development, production, and death.

15–2 IN-HOUSE VERSUS PROPRIETARY SOFTWARE: WHETHER TO MAKE OR BUY. There are two basic approaches to satisfying a company's information processing needs. The first is to use company employees and/or outside consultants to create an information system customized to meet user specifications. The alternative is to purchase and install a **proprietary software package**.

15–3 THE SYSTEMS DEVELOPMENT PROCESS. The systems development process is a cooperative undertaking by users who know the functional areas and MIS professionals who know the technology. The two fundamental approaches to the development of in-house information systems are the prototyping and prespecification approaches.

In **prototyping**, project team members create a **prototype system**, or model of a full-scale system. A prototype system normally would handle the main transaction-oriented procedures, produce the critical reports, and permit rudimentary inquiries.

The step-by-step **systems development methodology** provides the framework for the **prespecification** approach to systems development. In this approach, users commit to **system specifications**, or **specs**, early in development.

15–4 PROTOTYPING: CREATING A MODEL OF THE TARGET SYSTEM. The three objectives of prototyping are to analyze the current situation, to identify information needs (including the **layouts**), and to develop a scaled-down model, called the **target system**.

Ideally, users should experiment and familiarize themselves with the operation of a target system as early in the development process as possible. The prototyping process enables users to relate accurate information processing needs to the project team during the early phases of the project and throughout the project.

Prototype systems are also created in varying degrees of sophistication: nonfunctional (**rapid prototyping**), partially functional, and fully functional.

The four phases of prototyping are

- Phase I—define system specifications
- Phase II—create prototype system
- Phase III—refine prototype system
- Phase IV—develop operational system

Prototyping tools are used by project team members to create a physical representation of a target information system. The basic components of prototyping tools are the user interface, screen generators called **screen formatters**, and **report generators**.

Developing an operational information system may require some **custom coding**.

In practice, the MIS community is enjoying the best of both worlds by using systems development methodologies that include prototyping.

15–5 SYSTEMS DEVELOPMENT METHODOLOGIES: THE TRADITION CONTINUES. The process of developing a computer-based information system is essentially the same, regardless of the information system being developed. Some companies follow a systems development methodology that provides the framework for cooperation between the various people involved in a development project. A representative project team charged with developing an information system will normally consist of systems analysts, programmers, perhaps the data base administrator, and at least one user.

A systems development methodology is usually presented in a manual and depicts the activities to be performed, the relationship and sequence of these activities, and the key milestones. The **responsibility matrix** shows when and to what extent individuals and groups are involved in each activity of the systems development process.

A systems development methodology is organized in phases, for example:

- Phase I—systems analysis
- Phase II—systems design
- Phase III—programming
- Phase IV—conversion and implementation
- Phase V—post-implementation

15–6 SYSTEMS ANALYSIS: UNDERSTANDING THE SYSTEM. During the systems analysis phase of the systems development process, the following activities take place: existing system review, system objectives, design constraints, and requirements definition.

The work and information flow of the present system is documented by reducing the system to its basic component parts—input, processing, and output. Systems design techniques include flowcharting and other more "structured" techniques, such as data flow diagrams.

The project team arrives at general system objectives by engaging in discussions with all end user managers ultimately affected by the target system. The target information system must be developed within the boundaries of any applicable hardware, costs, schedule, procedural, software, data base, and operating constraints.

User feedback provides the basis for the **functional specifications** for system input, processing, and output requirements. These specs describe the logic of the system from the perspective of the user. The **user sign-off** indicates that the user has examined the work, that the work and specs meet the objectives, and that the user is committed to the specs.

15–7 SYSTEMS DESIGN: A SCIENCE OR AN ART? During the systems design phase of the systems development process, the following activities are completed: **general system design**, data base design, and **detailed system design**.

At a minimum, the documentation of the general system design includes a graphic illustration and explanation of the fundamental operation of the target system and general descriptions of the outputs to be produced by the system.

During systems development, designers describe the output requirements and determine which data are needed to produce the output. Fields are documented in the **data dictionary**.

The detailed design includes all processing activities and the input/output associated with them. When adhering to **structured system design**, designers divide the system into independent modules for ease of understanding and design.

Data flow diagrams enable analysts to design and document systems using the structured approach to systems development. The four symbols used in data flow diagrams are entity, process, flow line, and data storage.

Reports, or the general presentation of information, can be either periodic or ad hoc. Based on content, reports are classified as comprehensive, summary, or exception. Based on time, reports are classified as historical, status, or predictive.

15–8 COMPUTER-AIDED SOFTWARE ENGINEERING: THE CASE TOOL KIT. The general family of automated software development tools falls under the umbrella of **computer-aided software engineering**, or **CASE**, tools. The term **software engineering** was coined to emphasize an approach to software development that combines automation and the rigors of the engineering discipline.

The CASE tool kit, also called **workbench technologies**, consists of design tools, prototyping tools, information repository tools, program development tools, and methodology tools.

CASE design tools help analysts and programmers prepare schematics that graphically depict the logic of a system or program, and they help designers in the preparation of screen and report layouts. CASE prototyping tools are used by project team members to create a physical representation of a target information system. In the CASE information repository tool, each field is cross-referenced to all other components in the system. The CASE program development tools include program structure charts, code generators, program preprocessors, and test data generators. The CASE methodology tool is a computer-based version of the traditional systems development methodology manual.

 Review Exercises

Concepts

1. In which stage of the information system life cycle are systems "conceived"? "maintained"?

2. What are the two basic approaches to satisfying a company's information processing needs?

3. Name the four symbols used in data flow diagrams.

4. Classify the following outputs with respect to content and time: payroll register, third-quarter sales forecast, and delinquent accounts report.

5. The functional specifications describe the logic of a proposed system from whose perspective?

6. Describe the relationship between the data dictionary and the data base.

7. What is the design philosophy called that enables complex design problems to be addressed in small, manageable modules?

8. Name two system design techniques.

9. What is a structure chart, and how is it used?

10. Custom code written to augment a prototype system is probably written in what type of programming language?

11. What is the purpose of the CASE design tool?

12. Besides producing critical reports and permitting rudimentary inquiries, what else does a prototype system typically do?

13. Briefly describe the function of program preprocessors, one of the CASE program development tools.

14. Name three tools in the CASE tool kit.

15. What is another name for CASE tools?

16. What are two objectives of prototyping?

Discussion

17. In general, is it better to change internal procedures to fit a particular proprietary software package or to modify the software to fit existing procedures? Discuss.

18. Would it be possible for a company with 600 employees to maintain a skeleton information services division of about 5 MIS professionals and use commercially available packaged software for all their computer application needs? Explain.

19. Why is the user sign-off a controversial procedure?

20. How does adhering to a systems development methodology help a project team "do it right the first time"?

21. One of the objectives of prototyping is to develop a scaled-down model of the proposed system. However, some prototype systems are fully functional. Describe how such a prototype system is scaled down.

Problem Solving

22. Corporate management at a mail-order lingerie house is confronted with a "make-versus-buy" decision regarding software. You have been asked to argue for in-house development of a new order-entry system that will cost approximately $250,000 to develop and implement. An acceptable system can be purchased commercially for $300,000. Annual updates for the commercial system are currently $50,000. What would you say to convince management that the system should be created in-house?

23. Give examples of schedule, procedural, and hardware constraints that might limit the definition and design of a proposed marketing information system for a pharmaceutical company.

24. Design a screen layout for an on-line hospital admittance system. Design only that screen with which the hospital clerk would interact to enter basic patient data. Distinguish between input and output by underlining the input.

25. Put yourself in the role of a systems analyst. Draw a first-level data flow diagram depicting your college's student registration system. Explode one of the processes to show detail.

▶ **Self-Test (by section)**

✗**15–1** The information system becomes operational in the ~~production~~ stage of the system life cycle.

15–2 The best corporate application portfolios contain only proprietary software packages. (T/Ⓕ)

15–3 **a.** A ~~prototype~~ system is a model of a full-scale information system.

✗ **b.** A standardized (see below) provides the framework for cooperation during the systems development process.

c. The prespecification approach to systems development leaves little room for design flexibility in the latter stages of the project. (Ⓣ/F)

✗**15–4** **a.** A prototype system is essentially a complete information system, but without the data base. (T/Ⓕ)

✗ **b.** A prototype system normally would permit rudimentary inquiries. (Ⓣ/F)

✗ **c.** What prototyping tool provides systems analysts with the capability of generating a mockup of a screen: Ⓐ screen formatter, (b) report generator, or (c) user interface?

15–5 **a.** Systems development methodologies are always presented in four phases. (T/Ⓕ)

✗ **b.** Responsibility matrices typically are associated with: Ⓐ the prespecification approach to development, (b) prototyping, or (c) data flow diagrams?

15–6 **a.** Which of the following is not a design technique: (a) flowcharting, (b) data flow diagrams, or Ⓒ SAD?

✗ **b.** In the systems development process, the project team begins with the desired input and works backward to determine output and processing requirements? (T/Ⓕ)

✗ **c.** Functional specifications include system input, output, and ~~processing~~ requirements.

✗**15–7** **a.** Which results are realized during the systems design stage of the systems development process: Ⓐ data base design, (b) existing system review, or (c) design constraints?

✗ **b.** The _____ (general/Ⓓetailed) system design includes all processing activities and the input/output associated with them.

c. If data flow diagram Process 3.4 were exploded to two third-level processes, the numerical labels of the new processes would be 3.4.1 and 3.4.2. (Ⓣ/F)

15–8 **a.** Which CASE tool is analogous to the data dictionary in the traditional manual approach to systems design: (a) design tool, Ⓑ information repository tool, or (c) methodology tool?

✗ **b.** Another name for CASE tools is ~~workbench technologies~~.

Self-test answers. **15–1** production. **15–2** F. **15–3** (a) prototype; (b) systems development methodology; (c) T. **15–4** (a) F; (b) T; (c) a. **15–5** (a) F; (b) a. **15–6** (a) c; (b) F; (c) processing. **15–7** (a) a; (b) detailed; (c) T. **15–8** (a) b; (b) workbench technologies.

System Implementation

STUDENT LEARNING OBJECTIVES

▶ To describe and order the major activities that take place during the programming phase of systems development.

▶ To describe systems testing procedures and considerations.

▶ To distinguish between the different approaches to system conversion.

▶ To know what to look for during post-implementation system evaluations.

▶ To describe system controls and auditing procedures that can be employed to ensure the accuracy, reliability, and integrity of an information system.

▶ To identify points of security vulnerability for the computer center and for information systems.

CHAPTER OUTLINE

16–1 Programming: Ideas Become Reality

Chapter 15, "Analysis and Design of Business Information Services," discusses approaches and techniques used to design and create the specifications for an information system. In this chapter we are concerned with the implementation of a newly created information system and its ongoing operation. The first challenge in system implementation is to translate the system design and specifications into instructions that can be interpreted and executed by the computer. This, of course, is the *programming* phase of the systems development process.

Programming languages have improved continually during the past four decades. Early, or first-generation, programming languages required the programmer to write many complex instructions to accomplish simple tasks. Each new generation of programming languages has reduced the number of instructions required to perform tasks and made the instructions easier to comprehend and code. (Programming languages are discussed and illustrated in Chapter 10, "Programming Concepts and Languages.")

The programming phase (Phase III of the responsibility matrix of Figure 15–4) of the systems development process produces the following results:

- System specifications review
- Program identification and description
- Program coding, testing, and documentation

Each of these results defines an activity that is to be accomplished. With detailed specifications in hand, programmers are now ready to write the programs needed to make the target system operational.

System Specifications Review

During the programming phase, programmers take the system specifications completed during the systems analysis and design phases and write,

Not all programs are developed by professional programmers. These research chemists used a fourth-generation language to create the software for a minicomputer-based information system that helps them keep track of the results of experiments. Of course, users follow the same basic procedure that professional programmers follow.

or *code*, the programs to implement the information system. But before getting started, programmers should review the system specifications created during systems analysis and design. These include

- Printer output layouts of reports and transactions
- Terminal input/output screen layouts
- Data dictionary
- Files and data base design
- Controls and validation procedures
- Data entry specifications
- General system design
- Detailed system design

Once programmers have reviewed the specs and understand them, the programming task begins. A superior programming effort will be wasted if the system specifications are incomplete and/or poorly written. As the saying goes, "Garbage in, garbage out."

CASE tools, such as Teamwork/SA from Cadre Technologies, enable programmers to graphically illustrate the logic of their programs interactively at their terminals or PCs. Automated design tools have helped programmers and systems analysts make significant strides in productivity improvement.

Program Identification and Description

An information system needs an array of programs to create and update the data base, print reports, permit on-line inquiry, and so on. Depending on the scope of the system and how many programs can be generated using applications development tools, as few as three or four or as many as several hundred programs may need to be written before the system can be implemented. At this point, all programs necessary to make the system operational are identified and described. A typical program description would include

- Type of programming language (COBOL, BASIC, FOCUS, Ideal, and so on)
- A narrative of the program, describing the tasks to be performed
- Frequency of processing (for example, daily, weekly, on-line)
- Input to the program (data and their source)
- Output produced by the program
- Limitations and restrictions (for example, sequence of input data, response-time maximums, and so on)
- Detailed specifications (for example, specific computations and logical manipulations, tables)

Program Coding, Testing, and Documentation

Armed with system specifications and program descriptions, programmers can begin the actual coding of programs. The development of a program is actually a project within a project. Just as there are certain steps the project team takes to develop an information system, a programmer must take certain steps to write a program (see Figure 16–1).

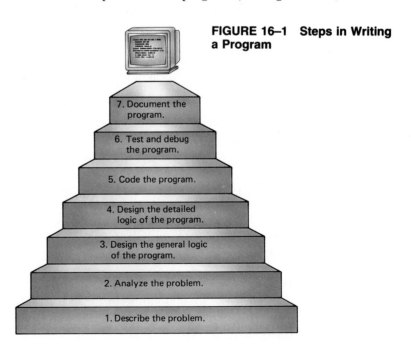

FIGURE 16–1   Steps in Writing a Program

7. Document the program.

6. Test and debug the program.

5. Code the program.

4. Design the detailed logic of the program.

3. Design the general logic of the program.

2. Analyze the problem.

1. Describe the problem.

In programming, two heads are sometimes better than one. A programmer can become so close to a program that he or she may overlook obvious errors in logic. These errors often shine as bright as a neon light when the program design is discussed with a colleague.

Step 1. Describe the problem.

Step 2. Analyze the problem.

Step 3. Design the general logic of the program.

Step 4. Design the detailed logic of the program.

Step 5. Code the program.

Step 6. Test and debug the program.

Step 7. Document the program.

These steps and programming concepts are described in detail in Chapter 10, "Programming Concepts and Languages."

A programming problem might be to write a program that accepts numeric quiz scores and assigns a letter grade. Another problem might be to write a program that identifies and prints the names of customers whose accounts are delinquent. Another might be to write a payroll check processing program.

Once the problem is described (Step 1) and its components (*output, input, processing,* and *file-interaction*) analyzed (Step 2), the programmer has to put the pieces together in the form of a logical program design (Steps 3 and 4). Any of the systems design techniques, such as flowcharting (Chapter 10) and data flow diagrams (Chapter 15), are applicable to program design as well. In the general design of a particular program, the programmer creates a logic diagram for the overall program and for each module. The detailed design encompasses *all* processing activities. Figure 16–2 contrasts the general and detailed designs for the "Compute Net Pay" module for a payroll check processing program. The level of detail portrayed in a program design is a matter of personal preference.

The best way to code (write) a program (Step 5) is to work directly from the design documentation and compose the program interactively

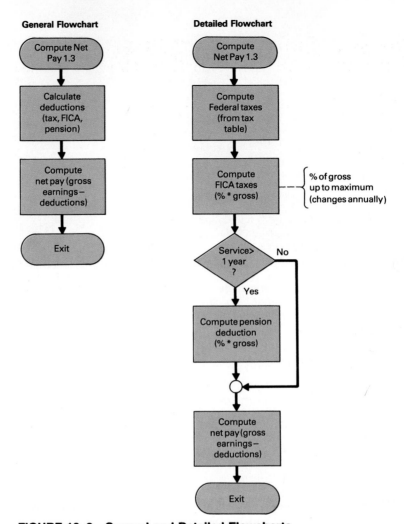

General Flowchart

Compute Net Pay 1.3

Calculate deductions (tax, FICA, pension)

Compute net pay (gross earnings — deductions)

Exit

Detailed Flowchart

Compute Net Pay 1.3

Compute Federal taxes (from tax table)

Compute FICA taxes (% * gross) — % of gross up to maximum (changes annually)

Service > 1 year ? — No / Yes

Compute pension deduction (% * gross)

Compute net pay (gross earnings — deductions)

Exit

FIGURE 16–2   General and Detailed Flowcharts

The logic of a "Compute Net Pay" module is depicted in general and detailed flowcharts.

at a terminal or PC. Not every programming task requires programmers to create code from scratch. Many organizations maintain libraries of frequently used program modules, called *reusable code*. For example, several programmers might use the same reusable code as the basis for their input modules to programs.

Testing and debugging a program (Step 6) is a repetitive process whereby each successive attempt gets the programmer one step closer to a working program. Once the syntax errors have been removed, the program can be executed. An error-free program is not necessarily a working program. The programmer now has to debug the *logic of the program* and the *input/output formats*. To do this, **test data** and, perhaps, a **test data base** must be created so that the programmer knows what to expect as output. Even though a program works, it is not finished until its documentation package is complete (source listing of instructions, detailed program design, I/O layouts, and so on).

Did you know that most money is exchanged, not from hand to hand, but between computers? Or that computers monitor the altitude and direction of aircraft flying in a dense fog around airports? We've come to trust computers—and their programs—with our money and our lives, but are they worthy of this trust?

A computer does exactly what a program tells it to do, nothing less and nothing more. Unfortunately, some programs have bugs that remain undetected, even after rigorous testing and extensive use. In fact, one popular magazine runs a "Bug Watch" column, alerting readers to bugs in PC software packages. Such bugs are relatively harmless; others can cause havoc.

- Ten million people on both the East and West coasts lost telephone service when a bug in the software used to route calls caused the telephone network to overload and crash. (Ironically, the bug represented just 3 lines in a program containing more than 2 million instructions.)
- During the Persian Gulf War, a software "glitch" in a Patriot missile's guidance system, combined with extended use, caused it to miss an incoming Iraqi Scud missile that killed 28 soldiers and wounded 97.
- The Mariner 1 spacecraft was en route to deep space when it suddenly "turned left and nosed down." An investigation into the multimillion-dollar crash revealed a little bug: Apparently a programmer had omitted *one* character from *one* equation in the guidance program. Even though the program had performed successfully in other Atlas missions, a curious set of circumstances caused it to take branches not tested or taken in previous missions. Fortunately, a similar calamity was avoided in a later manned space flight. A serious bug in the space shuttle's software lay dormant for two years, even after thousands of hours of testing. It was discovered 20 minutes before an April 1981 launch!
- Software bugs can eat up profits, too. A software error in American Airlines' Sabre reservation system gave travel and ticket agents the impression that reduced-fare tickets were not available. Thousands of potential customers were turned away while flights departed with empty seats. The company lost $50 million before the error was detected.
- Virtually all new medical diagnosis and treatment machines are controlled by computers. Machines that provide radiation therapy for cancer patients depend on exact programming to deliver the proper dosage to the malignant area. A bug in the software of one of these machines caused radiation overdoses for five patients and the death of one.
- A software bug can affect governments, too. A state government computer sent bondholders millions of dollars worth of interest checks, but the interest was not due them.
- A large bank was forced to borrow over $20 billion overnight because it was unable to complete transactions involving large amounts of government securities—all because of a bug in the software. Had the software worked properly, the loan and a $5 million interest charge would not have been needed.
- Most new automobiles are equipped with at least one microprocessor. An apparent bug in the software for the computerized fuel delivery system of a European luxury sedan caused some cars to accelerate out of control. The resulting intense negative publicity caused a sharp drop in sales. These losses pale, however, when you consider the serious injuries and deaths that have been attributed to the defective system.

These examples serve to highlight the importance of comprehensive testing. But can extremely complex systems ever be fully tested? Very large information systems, such as those for major insurance companies, may consist of millions of lines of program code and be written by hundreds of programmers. Thousands of such complex systems are currently in operation.

Star Wars, the Pentagon's Strategic Defense Initiative (SDI), is an easy choice for the most complex computer-based system ever conceived. Its objective was to seek out and destroy hostile nuclear missiles. This unbelievably complex system would have to work perfectly the first time, and it could never be fully tested. When and if Star Wars is ever needed, what are the chances of its having bugs in the system?

The following results are realized during the system conversion and implementation phase (Phase IV of the systems development responsibility matrix of Figure 15–4) of the systems development process:

- System and acceptance test
- System conversion

Each of these results defines an activity that is to take place.

System and Acceptance Test

Whether the information system is created by using the traditional prespecification approach, prototyping, or a combination of these two, the final step before system conversion and implementation is system and acceptance testing. This testing encompasses everything that makes up the information system—the hardware, the software, the end users, the procedures (for example, user manuals), and the data. If needed, the interfaces between the system and other systems are tested as well.

The importance of systems testing cannot be overemphasized. In 1988 the American Airlines reservation system, the Sabre System, lost an estimated $50 million when it stopped selling discount fares while they were still available. According to an American Airlines' spokesperson, a modification to the existing system, designed to provide an optimum mix of regular and discount seats on a given flight, "was not fully tested." This is only one of countless costly tales of inadequate testing.

Testing with Test Data   During the programming phase of systems development, programs are written according to system specifications and are individually tested. Although the programs that comprise the software for the system have undergone **unit testing** (individual testing) and have been debugged, there is no guarantee that the programs will work as a system. To ensure that the software can be combined into an operational information system, the project team performs integrated **systems testing**. An information system for inventory management and control may have a hundred programs and a comprehensive data base; all must be tested together to ensure harmony of operation. The purpose of the system test is to validate all software, input/output, procedures, and the data base. It is a safe bet that a few design errors, programming errors, procedural errors, or oversights will surface during systems testing. Minor modifications in design and programming may be required to complete the system test to the satisfaction of the users.

To conduct the system test, the project team compiles and thoroughly tests the system with test data. In this first stage of systems testing, tests are run for each subsystem (one of the functional aspects of the system) or cycle (weekly or monthly activities). The test data are judiciously compiled so that all program and system options and all error and validation routines are tested. The tests are repeated and modifications

During systems testing, systems analysts are constantly gathering feedback from users. Analysts are especially interested in hearing about errors and parts of the system where interaction is cumbersome or slow.

are made until all subsystems or cycles function properly. At this point the entire system is tested as a unit. Testing and modifications continue until the components of the system work as they should and all input/output is validated.

Testing with Live Data   The second stage of systems testing is done with *live data* by several of the people who will eventually use the system. Live data are data that have already been processed through the existing system. Testing with live data provides an extra level of assurance that the system will work properly when implemented. Testing and modifications are continued until the project team and participating users are satisfied with the results.

User-Acceptance Testing   The system is now subjected to the scrutiny of the user managers whose departments will ultimately work with the system. The purpose of this last test, called **user-acceptance testing**, is to get the user's stamp of approval. User managers examine and test the operation of the system (using live data) until they are satisfied that it meets the original system objectives. Modification and testing continue until that point is reached.

System Conversion

Once acceptance testing is complete, the project team can begin to integrate people, software, hardware, procedures, and data into an operational information system. This normally involves a conversion from the existing system to the new one.

Memory Bits

TESTING
- Unit testing
- Systems testing
  With test data
  With live data
- User-acceptance testing

Approaches to System Conversion   An organization's approach to system conversion depends on its *willingness to accept risk* and the *amount of time available* for the conversion. Four common approaches are parallel conversion, direct conversion, phased conversion, and pilot conversion. These approaches are illustrated in Figure 16–3 and discussed in the paragraphs that follow.

Parallel conversion.   In **parallel conversion**, the existing system and the new system operate simultaneously, or in parallel, until the project team is confident that the new system is working properly. Parallel conversion has two important advantages. First, the existing system serves as a backup if the new system fails to operate as expected. Second, the results of the new system can be compared to the results of the existing system.

Although this strategy provides less risk, it also doubles the workload of personnel and hardware resources during the conversion. Parallel conversion usually takes one month or a major system cycle. For a public utility company, this might be one complete monthly billing cycle.

Direct conversion.   As companies improve their systems testing procedures, they begin to gain confidence in their ability to implement a working system. Some companies forego parallel conversion in favor of a **direct conversion**. Direct conversion involves a greater risk because there is no backup in case the system fails.

Companies select this "cold turkey" approach when they have no existing system or when the existing system is substantially different. For example, all on-line hotel reservations systems are implemented cold turkey.

Phased conversion.   In **phased conversion**, an information system is implemented one module at a time by either parallel or direct conversion. For example, in a point-of-sale system, the first phase might be to convert the sales accounting module. The second phase could involve the in-

FIGURE 16–3   Common Approaches to System Conversion

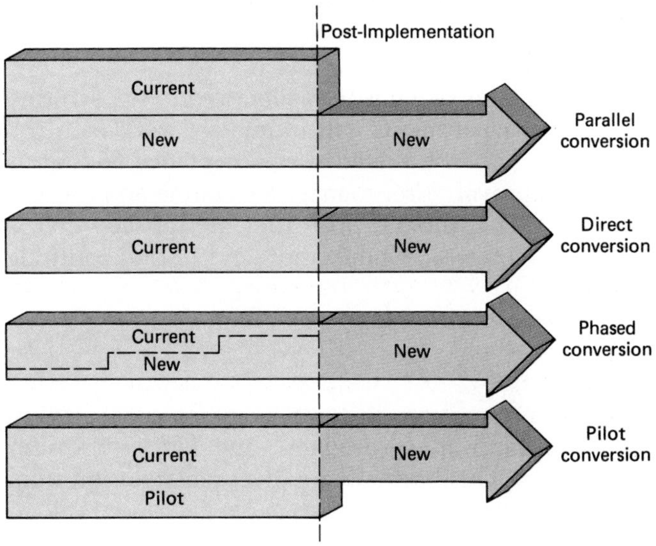

ventory management module. The third might be the credit-check module.

Phased conversion has the advantage of spreading the demand for resources to avoid an intense demand. The disadvantages are that the conversion takes longer and an interface must be developed between the existing system and the new one.

Pilot conversion.   In **pilot conversion**, the new system is implemented by parallel, direct, or phased conversion as a pilot system in only one of the several targeted areas. For example, suppose a company wants to implement a manufacturing resources planning system in its eight plants. One plant would be selected as a pilot, and the new information system would be implemented there first.

The advantage of pilot conversion is that the inevitable bugs in a system can be removed before the system is implemented at the other locations. The disadvantage is that the implementation time for the total system takes longer than if the entire system were implemented at one time.

The System Becomes Operational   Once the conversion is complete, the information system enters the production stage of the system life cycle (see Figure 15–1 in Chapter 15). During the production stage the system becomes operational and is turned over to the users. The operations function of the information services division provides operational support for the system. This function encompasses everything associated with running an information system including all interaction with the hardware that supports the system. The scope of operations support would typically include these major areas:

- Data entry and transaction processing, both batch and on-line
- Interactive inquiry, both built-in and ad hoc
- Maintenance of the data base
- Output, including reports (summary, exception, historical, graphic, and so on) and documents (for example, utility bills, mailing labels, authorizations to build, air travel tickets)
- Transition or preprocessing (massaging data to put them in the proper format for processing, a common activity for electronic data interchange applications)

16–3   Post-Implementation

Just as a new automobile will need some screws tightened after a few hundred miles, an information system will need some fine-tuning just after implementation. Thereafter, and throughout the production stage of the system life cycle, the system will be modified many times to meet the changing needs of the company.

The following results are realized during the post-implementation phase (Phase V of the systems development responsibility matrix of Figure 15–4) of the systems development process:

- Post-implementation review
- System maintenance

Each of these results defines an activity that is to take place.

Post-Implementation Review

The **post-implementation review** is a critical examination of the system three to six months after it has been put into production. This waiting period allows several factors to stabilize: the resistance to change, the anxieties associated with change, and the learning curve. It also allows time for unanticipated problems to surface.

The post-implementation review focuses on the following:

- A comparison of the system's actual performance versus the anticipated performance objectives
- An assessment of each facet of the system with respect to preset criteria
- Mistakes made during systems development
- Unexpected benefits and problems

System Maintenance

Once an information system is implemented and "goes on-line," the emphasis switches from *development* to *operations*. In a payroll system, supervisors begin to enter hours worked on their terminals, and the computer center produces and issues payroll checks. Once operational, an information system becomes a cooperative effort between the users and the information services division.

Three to six months after the hardware, software, people, procedures, and data have been integrated into an operational LAN-based information system at a real estate office, key members of the project team conduct a post-implementation evaluation to assess its overall effectiveness.

An information system is dynamic and must be responsive to the changing needs of the company and those who use it. The process of modifying an information system to meet changing needs is known as **system maintenance**.

An information system cannot live forever. The accumulation of modifications and enhancements will eventually make any information system cumbersome and inefficient. Minor modifications are known as **patches**. Depending on the number of patches and enhancements, an information system will remain operational—that is, be in the production stage—from four to seven years.

Toward the end of the useful life of an information system, it is more trouble to continue patching the system than it is to redesign the system completely. The end of the production stage signals the death stage of the information system life cycle (see Figure 15–1 in Chapter 15). A new system is then "born" of need, and the systems development process is repeated.

16–4 System Controls, Auditing, and Backup

An information system should run smoothly under normal circumstances. But as Murphy has taught us, "If anything can go wrong, it will." Users, programmers, and operators make oversights and errors in judgment. Computers sometimes fail to work as planned, and sometimes they simply cease to function. Also, there is always the threat of computer crime. Malicious hackers have vandalized thousands of systems. System controls help ensure that the system runs as planned and that errors, inappropriate procedures, or unauthorized accesses are detected before the system is affected.

System Controls

Because of the ever-present potential for human and hardware errors coupled with the threat of computer crime, it is important that an organization build in controls to ensure the accuracy, reliability, and integrity of an information system. Without controls, an enterprising computer criminal might be able to supplement his or her checking account without making a deposit. An erroneous data entry error could result in the delivery of a red car instead of a blue one. Someone expecting a monthly paycheck of $3000 might receive $300,000. A computer operator could cause chaos by forgetting to do the daily audit run. System controls are introduced to prevent these and any of a thousand other undesirable events from happening.

Information system controls minimize or eliminate errors before, during, and after processing so that the data entered and the information produced are complete and accurate. Controls also minimize the possibility of computer fraud. There are four types of controls: *input validation, processing controls, output controls,* and *procedural controls* (see Figure 16–4).

Input Validation Data are checked for accuracy when they are entered into the system. In on-line data entry, the data entry operator verifies

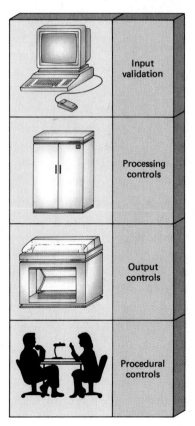

FIGURE 16–4 System Controls

Input validation

Processing controls

Output controls

Procedural controls

At USAA, an insurance company in San Antonio, Texas, much of the data is entered into the system by the customer service agents who update existing policies, write new policies, and process claims. A variety of techniques are used to validate the input. For example, written text and names are checked for spelling errors; policy numbers are validated; claim amounts are matched against those with similar circumstances; and city/ZIP code combinations are matched against a master ZIP code directory.

the data by sight checks. In addition, a variety of checking procedures are designed into the software. Two of these software-control procedures are as follows:

- *Reasonableness check.* Suppose that a customer's maximum order to date is for 250 widgets and an order is entered for 2000 widgets. Because an order for 2000 is much greater than the maximum order to date for 250, the entry is historically unreasonable, and the probable error is brought to the attention of the data entry operator.
- *Limits check.* A limits check assesses whether the value of an entry is out of line with that expected. For example, a company's policy guarantees 40 hours of work per week for each employee and limits overtime to 15 hours per week. A limits check on the "hours-worked" entry guarantees that a value between 40 and 55, inclusive, is entered.

Processing Controls   Systems analysts and programmers employ a variety of techniques to validate the fact that processing is complete and accurate. Control totals and consistency checks are two of the many techniques that can be built into the software.

- *Control total.* A control total, or hash total, is a value known to be the accumulated sum of a particular data element. Control totals are used

One class of PC programs can be loaded to RAM and left there for later recall, even during an interactive session with word processing or spreadsheet software. Once loaded, you can *terminate* the program *and* it will *stay resident* in memory. These RAM-resident programs are called, appropriately, *terminate-and-stay-resident*, or *TSR*, programs. A TSR in RAM can be activated instantly while running another program by tapping the TSR's hotkey, typically a seldom used key combination such as SHIFT + CTRL. When you are finished with the TSR, you are returned to the program you left when you tapped the hotkey—but the TSR remains in RAM.

TSRs can help you uncover a potentially devastating virus or help you access an on-line calendar, calculator, dictionary, grammar checker, scratch pad, or clock. One TSR lets you group, scan, and cross-search through thousands of pieces of "random" information. People who do a lot of desktop publishing use screen grabber TSRs to capture screen images so that they can be included in reports, newsletters, and so on.

TSR ORIGIN

TSRs grew out of an early Microsoft program that enabled a PC to communicate with a printer while con-

tinuing to respond to input from the keyboard. Other companies quickly recognized the value of having a program installed in the memory that is just a couple of keystrokes away from running, even though it's not being used.

TSRs are well-suited for functions involving network access, scanning devices, facsimile capabilities, and a host of other specialized functions. TSR creators continue to push the envelope of applications ever outward with windows designed to hold plans, lists, facts, letters, contacts, sales leads, orders, and client notes, among other things.

RAM CRAM

There are some drawbacks. If DOS provides the essential operating environment for your PC, only a limited amount of RAM is available to programs. Modern programs require more and more RAM, and giving up the memory to TSRs becomes ever harder. The quaintly named "RAM cram" has resulted from trying to squeeze more functionality into a limited RAM.

Despite these problems, the usefulness of TSRs cannot be disputed as they continue to show their value and versatility.

---

primarily to verify that processing is complete. For example, when a company's payroll checks are printed, the employee numbers are added together and compared to a known value. If the accumulated control total is not equal to the known value, the computer operator knows immediately that some checks were not processed or that some checks were processed that should not have been.

■ *Consistency check.* The consistency check compares like data items for consistency of value. For example, if a company's electric bill for March is 300% higher than its bill for March of last year, the invoice would not be processed. Management would then ask the electric company to check the accuracy of the meter reading.

Output Controls   Some people take for granted that any computer-produced output is accurate. This is not always the case. There are too many things that can go wrong. One of many methods of output control is *crossfoot checking*. This technique is used in reports, such as the one in Figure 16–5, that have column and row totals with some arithmetic relationship to one another. In Figure 16–5, the column totals for each beverage type (617) should equal the total for all delivery routes (617).

```
QUERY:  Let me see the daily delivery report.


   ROUTE NO.    COLA    FIZZ    BURP       ROUTE TOTAL

        1        41      68      32          141
        2        29      18      64          111
        3        71      65      48          184
        4        67      58      56          181

      TOTAL     208     209     200          617
```

FIGURE 16–5 Crossfoot Checking
The sum of the row totals equals the sum of the column totals.

Procedural Controls In an information system, the work is done either by the computer system or by people. Programs tell the computer what to do. Procedures guide people. Some procedures are built into the system for control purposes. For example, many companies subscribe to the *separation-of-duties* procedure. The theory behind this procedure is that if responsibilities for input, processing, and output are assigned to different people, most attempts to defraud the system will be foiled. It is unlikely that would-be computer criminals could solicit that much cooperation.

A corporation is vulnerable when one operator has sole responsibility for running a particular information system. Because of this, many companies have a mandatory vacation policy requiring programmers, operators, and others in sensitive positions to take their vacations in blocks of no less than two weeks.

Information Systems Auditing

Every corporation should have an internal information systems auditor or, perhaps, an auditing group. The information systems audit staff functions to ensure the integrity of operational information systems. There are three types of information systems audits. These are *systems development audits*, *operational audits*, and *application audits*.

Systems Development Audits In systems development audits, the information systems audit staff serve as advisers to members of the systems development project team. Their involvement in the project guarantees that appropriate audit controls are embedded in the original systems design.

Operational Audits Operational audits are periodically conducted on an MIS to ensure that proper system controls exist and are being followed. Control totals, crossfoot checking, and separation of duties (all discussed previously) are examples of such controls and procedures. Auditors use these and a number of other techniques to minimize the possibility and opportunity for abuse of a computer-based information system.

Memory Bits

SYSTEM CONTROLS
- Input validation
  Reasonableness checks
  Limits check
- Processing controls
  Control totals
  Consistency check
- Output controls
  Crossfoot checking
- Procedural controls
  Separation of duties

Application Audits The objective of periodic application audits is to validate the integrity of an information system. In an application audit, information systems auditors validate that an operational MIS is working according to design specifications. This is in contrast to a periodic systems review where present and future needs as well as system effectiveness are the key considerations. To validate an MIS, auditors may trace a summary report back to the original transactions, and vice versa. They intentionally try to block or foul the system to check internal controls. Special audit software is used to aid in the information systems audit process. For example, audit programs provide the auditor with file-sampling capabilities. The auditor uses these programs to check records for quality, completeness, accuracy, and efficiency.

System Backup

Occasionally the worst case scenario comes to pass—total system failure. To avoid catastrophe during system failure, backup and **checkpoint/restart** procedures are defined during the systems development process. These procedures describe the extra processes included in the system that cope with system failures. During the chronology of system processing, operators periodically establish a checkpoint so that any processing up to that point is saved and cannot be destroyed. When a system fails, backup files or data bases and/or backup transaction logs (see Chapter 6, "Data Storage and Organization") are used to re-create processing from the last checkpoint. The system is "restarted" at the last checkpoint and normal operation is resumed.

All the backup files and procedures in the world are worthless if there is no hardware on which to run them. Any of a number of disasters, from fire to malicious vandalism, could render a company's computer system useless. As a backup, many companies have agreements with one another to share their computing resources in case of disaster. When this happens, both companies would operate only critical systems until a new computer system could be installed. Other companies contract with a commercial disaster recovery service. These services make a fully configured computer system available to clients in case of a disaster.

16–5 Computer-Center and System Security

Security is certainly one of the most important considerations in the development and ongoing operation of an information system. As more and more systems go on-line, more people have access to the overall system. A company must be extremely careful not to compromise the integrity of its system. It must be equally careful with the "engine" of the information system—the computer.

There are too many points of vulnerability and too much is at stake to overlook the threats to the security of an information system and a computer center. These threats take many forms—white-collar crime, natural disasters (earthquakes, floods), vandalism, and carelessness.

White-collar crime exists undetected in some of the most unlikely places. It is sophisticated crime with sophisticated criminals. Most com-

Viruses on the Rise A mere 4 computer viruses existed in 1986, but over 250 viruses were reported in 1990 according to "Software Digest Ratings Report." The National Computer Security Association (NCSA) has 1200 known viruses on record, but only around 10 of these viruses are common.

puter crimes are undetected; others are unreported and, therefore, are more widespread than estimates would lead us to believe. A bank may prefer to write off a $1 million embezzlement rather than publicly announce to its depositors that its computer system is vulnerable.

In this section we discuss the measures needed to neutralize security threats to an information system or to a computer center.

Computer-Center Security

A company's computer center has a number of points of vulnerability; these are *hardware*, *software*, *files/data bases*, *data communications*, and *personnel*. Each is discussed separately in this section and illustrated in Figure 16–6.

Hardware If the hardware fails, the information system fails. The threat of failure can be minimized by implementing security precautions that prevent access by unauthorized personnel and by taking steps to keep all hardware operational.

Common approaches to securing the premises from unauthorized entry include closed-circuit TV monitors, alarm systems, and computer-

FIGURE 16–6 Security Precautions
Some or all of the security measures noted in the figure are in force in most computer centers. Each precaution helps minimize the risk of an information system or a computer system's vulnerability to crime, disasters, and failure.

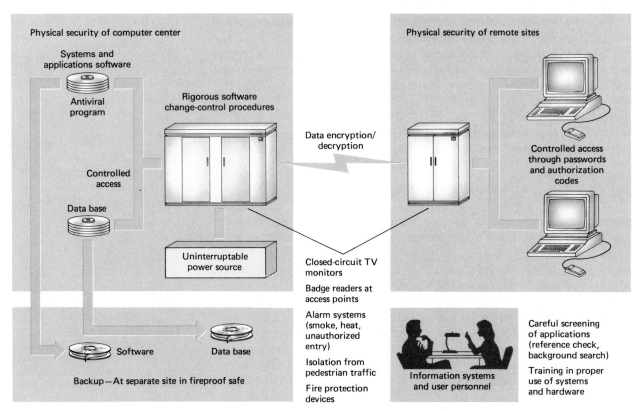

controlled devices that check employee badges, fingerprints, or voice prints before unlocking doors at access points. Computer centers also should be isolated from pedestrian traffic. Machine-room fires should be extinguished by a special chemical that douses the fire but does not destroy the files or equipment.

Computers, especially mainframe computers, must have a "clean," continuous source of power. To minimize the effects of "dirty" power or power outages, many computer centers have installed an **uninterruptible power source (UPS)**. Dirty power, with sags and surges in power output or brownouts (low power), causes data transmission errors and program execution errors. A UPS system serves as a buffer between the external power source and the computer system. In a UPS system, the computer is powered by batteries that deliver clean power, which in turn are regenerated by an external power source. If the external power source fails, the UPS system permits operation to continue for a period of time after an outage. This allows operators to either "power down" normally or switch to a backup power source, usually a diesel generator. Until recently UPS systems were associated only with mainframe computer systems. Now they are economically feasible for microcomputer systems.

Software   Unless properly controlled, the software for an information system can be modified for personal gain, or vandalized and rendered useless. Close control of software development and the documentation of an information system is needed to minimize the opportunity for computer crime and vandalism.

Unlawful modification of software.   Bank programmers certainly have opportunities to modify software for personal gain. In one case, a couple of programmers modified a savings system to make small deposits from other accounts to their own accounts. Here's how it worked: The interest for each savings account was compounded and credited daily; the calculated interest was rounded to the nearest penny before being credited to the savings account; programs were modified to round down all interest calculations and put the "extra" penny in one of the programmer's savings accounts. It may not seem like much, but a penny a day from thousands of accounts adds up to a lot of money. The "beauty" of the system was that the books balanced and depositors did not miss the 15 cents (an average of $\frac{1}{2}$ cent per day for 30 days) that judiciously was taken from each account each month. Even auditors had difficulty detecting this crime because the total interest paid on all accounts was correct. However, the culprits got greedy and were apprehended when someone noticed that they repeatedly withdrew inordinately large sums of money from their own accounts. Unfortunately, other enterprising programmers in other industries have been equally imaginative.

Operational control procedures built into the design of an information system will constantly monitor processing accuracy. We discussed these controls earlier in this section. Unfortunately, cagey programmers have been known to get around some of them. Perhaps the best way to safeguard programs from unlawful tampering is to use rigorous change-control procedures. Such procedures make it difficult to modify a program for purposes of personal gain.

Professional Intruders Companies spend large amounts of money trying to keep their computer systems from being infiltrated by competitors and nosy hackers. They hire penetration testers to try and break into their own system. It is legal and the testers get paid from $2000 to $30,000 for finding loopholes in a company's security system. Testers usually start inside the company because current and former employees are believed to be the greatest security risk. This type of testing is becoming popular, but just how popular is hard to determine. Firms are concerned they will alert real criminals of opportunities if the testing is announced.

To gain access to the computer center at this food products company, these operators must pass a security guard and open a steel door with a combination lock. Once in the machine room, they must enter a password and a personal identification number (PIN) to gain access to the system.

Viruses. The growing threat of viruses has resulted in tightening software controls. **Virus** software, which has been found at all levels of computing, "infects" other programs and data bases. The virus is so named because it can spread from one system to another like a biological virus. Viruses are written by outlaw programmers to cause harm to the computer systems of unsuspecting victims. Left undetected a virus can result in loss of data and/or programs and even physical damage to the hardware. The types of viruses and the ways in which viruses are spread are covered in an accompanying box item.

Individuals and companies routinely run antiviral programs, called *vaccines*, to search for and destroy viruses before they can do their dirty work.

Files/Data Bases The data base contains the raw material for information. Often the files/data bases are the lifeblood of a company. For example, how many companies can afford to lose their accounts receivable file, which documents who owes what? Having several *generations of backups* (backups to backups) to all files is not sufficient insurance against loss of files/data bases. The backup and master files should be stored in fireproof safes in separate rooms, preferably in separate buildings.

Data Communications Data communications applications are vulnerable because transmissions can be intercepted en route between locations. Companies address the data communications threat with encryption/decryption hardware and cryptography techniques. In effect transmissions are scrambled such that only those with the key can interpret them. Cryptography is discussed in more detail in Chapter 8, "Networks and Networking."

Personnel The biggest threat to a company's security system is the dishonesty and/or incompetence of its own employees. Managers are paying close attention to who gets hired for positions with access to computer-based information systems and sensitive data. Many companies flash a message on each terminal display such as: "All information on this system is confidential and proprietary." It's not very user-friendly, but it gets the message across to employees that they may be fired if they abuse the system. Someone who is grossly incompetent can cause just as much harm as someone who is inherently dishonest.

Information Systems Security

Information systems security is classified as physical or logical. **Physical security** refers to hardware, facilities, magnetic disks, and other items that could be illegally accessed, stolen, or destroyed.

Logical security is built into the software by permitting only authorized persons to access and use the system. Logical security for on-line systems is achieved primarily by using *passwords* and *personal identification numbers (PINs)*. Only those people with a need to know are told the password and given PINs. On occasion, however, these security codes fall into the wrong hands. When this happens, an unauthorized person can gain access to programs and sensitive files simply by dialing up the computer and entering the codes.

Keeping passwords and PINs from the computer criminal is not easy. One criminal took advantage of the fact that a bank's automatic teller machine (ATM) did not "time out" for several minutes. That is, the authorization code could be entered without reinserting the card to initiate another transaction. Using high-powered binoculars, he watched from across the street as the numeric code was being entered. He then ran over to the ATM and waited until the customer left. He quickly entered the code and made withdrawals before the machine timed out. Needless to say, this design flaw has been eliminated in existing ATM systems.

Level of Risk

No combination of security measures will completely remove the vulnerability of a computer center or an information system. Security systems are implemented in degrees. That is, an information system can be made marginally secure or very secure, but never totally secure. Each company must determine the level of risk that it is willing to accept. Unfortunately, some corporations are willing to accept an enormous risk and hope that those rare instances of crime and disaster do not occur. Some of them have found out too late that *rarely* is not the same as *never*!

 Important Terms and Summary Outline

checkpoint/restart	pilot conversion	uninterruptible power
direct conversion	post-implementation	source (UPS)
logical security	review	unit testing
parallel conversion	system maintenance	user-acceptance testing
patch	systems testing	virus
phased conversion	test data	
physical security	test data base	

16–1 PROGRAMMING: IDEAS BECOME REALITY. During the programming phase of the systems development process, programs are written to create the software necessary to make the information system operational. The following activities take place: system specifications review; program identification and description; and program coding, testing, and documentation.

For each program, the programmer describes the problem; analyzes the problem; designs the general, then the detailed logic; and codes, tests and debugs, and documents the program. When a programmer analyzes the problem, he or she breaks down the problem into its basic components (output, input, processing, and file-interaction) for analysis. The graphic display of the program logic at the detailed level of design includes all processing activities. Programmers debug programs with **test data** and a **test data base**.

16–2 SYSTEM CONVERSION AND IMPLEMENTATION. Although the programs that make up an information system have been debugged on an individual basis (**unit testing**), they must be combined and subjected to integrated **systems testing** prior to implementation.

After systems testing with live data comes **user-acceptance testing**. User managers examine and test the operation of the system until they are satisfied that it meets the original system objectives.

The four common approaches to system conversion are **parallel conversion**, **direct conversion**, **phased conversion**, and **pilot conversion**. The approach that an organization selects depends on its willingness to accept risk and the amount of time available for the conversion.

Once the conversion has been completed, the information system enters the production stage of the system life cycle and is turned over to the users.

16–3 POST-IMPLEMENTATION. The **post-implementation review**, which is a critical examination of the system after it has been put into production, is conducted three to six months after implementation.

An information system is dynamic and must be responsive to the changing needs of the company and those who use it. The process of modifying, or **patching**, an information system to meet changing needs is known as **system maintenance**.

16–4 SYSTEM CONTROLS, AUDITING, AND BACKUP. Companies build controls into their information systems to ensure system accuracy, reliability, and integrity. The four types of controls are input validation, processing controls, output controls, and procedural controls.

The information systems audit staff, which ensures the integrity of operational information systems, conducts systems development audits, operational audits, and application audits.

To avoid catastrophe during system failure, backup and **checkpoint/restart** procedures are defined during the systems development process.

16–5 COMPUTER-CENTER AND SYSTEM SECURITY. The threats to the security of computer centers and information systems call for precautionary measures. A computer center can be vulnerable in its hardware, software, files/data bases, data communications, and personnel. Organizations use a variety of approaches to secure the computer center, including the installation of an **uninterruptible power source (UPS)** and the use of cryptography to scramble messages sent over data communications channels.

Viruses are programs that infect other programs and data bases, and sometimes cause damage to hardware.

Information systems security is classified as **logical security** or **physical security**. Logical security for on-line systems is achieved primarily by using passwords and personal identification numbers (PINs). Security systems are implemented in degrees, and no computer center or system can be made totally secure.

 Review Exercises

Concepts

1. Which comes first during systems testing, testing with live data or testing with test data?

2. List three areas addressed during a post-implementation review.

3. What is the purpose of transition or preprocessing?

4. Name two types of controls for validating input. Name two types of processing controls.

5. What precautions can be taken to minimize the effects of hardware failure?

6. What advantage does direct conversion have over parallel conversion? parallel over direct?

7. Give two examples of the uses of a control total.

8. What are the first and last steps in the program development process?

9. What name is given to programs intended to damage the computer system of an unsuspecting victim?

10. List the types of information systems audits.

11. What is accomplished when we patch an information system?

12. Who evaluates the system during user-acceptance testing?

Discussion

13. Assuming that test data are designed and compiled to test all system options, why is it recommended to continue testing with live data?

14. In the past, bank officers have been reluctant to report computer crimes. If you were a customer of a bank that made such a decision, how would you react?

15. As a security precaution, some MIS managers have initiated a policy that requires two programmers to be familiar with each program. Argue for or against this procedure.

16. What is meant by the remark "Garbage in, garbage out" as applied to system specifications and programming?

Problem Solving

17. Evaluate your college's (or your company's) computer center with respect to security. Identify areas where you think it is vulnerable and discuss ways to improve its security.

18. A bank programmer developed an algorithm to determine the check digit for the bank's credit-card numbers. The programmer sold the algorithm, one of the bank's control procedures, to an underground group that specialized in counterfeit credit cards. A year later the programmer was caught and pleaded guilty. Compare this crime to common crimes (burglary, mail fraud, manslaughter, and so on) and recommend a just sentence.

19. Some programmers are accused of producing "spaghetti code," so named because their indecipherable flowcharts resemble a bowl of spaghetti. Outline steps that programming managers should take to eliminate inefficient spaghetti code and improve program quality.

20. Recommend specific input, processing, output, and procedural controls that might be built into a payroll system.

Self-Test (by section)

16–1 **a.** Programming is the only phase of systems development that can be completed out of sequence. (T/F)

⤳✗ **b.** Before coding programs, programmers must review the ~~system~~ created during systems analysis and design. *system specifications*

16–2 **a.** Individual program testing is known as: (a) unit testing, (b) module testing, or (c) hierarchical testing?

b. A newly developed information system is subjected to the scrutiny of the user managers during user-acceptance testing. (T/F)

c. Greater risk is associated with direct conversion than with phased conversion. (T/F)

d. In the *parallel* approach to system conversion, the existing system and the new system operate simultaneously until the project team is confident the new system is working properly.

16–3 **a.** The post-implementation review is normally conducted one year after system implementation. (T/F)

b. Once an information system is implemented, the emphasis is switched from development to: (a) testing, (b) operations, or (c) training?

16–4 **a.** The limits check is a procedural control. (T/F)

✗ **b.** A hash total is: (a) an input control, (b) an output control, or (c) a processing control?

c. Checkpoint/restart procedures are most closely associated with: (a) backup, (b) input controls, or (c) systems testing?

✗**16–5** **a.** Logical security for on-line systems is achieved primarily by *passwords* and PINs.

b. Virusology is the study of the assignment of security codes. (T/F)

Self-test answers.   **16–1** (a) F; (b) system specifications. **16–2** (a) a; (b) T; (c) T; (d) parallel. **16–3** (a) F; (b) b. **16–4** (a) F; (b) c; (c) a. **16–5** (a) passwords; (b) F.

Computers in Action:
Jobs and Career
Opportunities

STUDENT LEARNING OBJECTIVES

▶ To identify computer specialist positions in information services departments and in user departments.

▶ To describe the functions, responsibilities, and organization of an information services department.

▶ To identify job opportunities in organizations that provide computer-related products or services.

▶ To discuss the issue of certification of computer professionals.

▶ To appreciate the scope and charge of computer-oriented professional societies.

▶ To explore ethical questions concerning the use of computers.

▶ To become aware of the relationship between career mobility and computer knowledge.

CHAPTER OUTLINE

17–1 ## The Job Outlook

Whether you are seeking employment or perhaps a promotion as a teacher, an accountant, a writer, a fashion designer, a lawyer (or in any of hundreds of other jobs), one question is frequently asked: "What do you know about computers?" Today interacting with a computer is part of the daily routine for millions of knowledge workers and is increasingly common for blue-collar workers. No matter which career you choose, in all likelihood you will be a frequent user of computers.

Upon completion of this course, you will be part of the computer-competent minority, and you will be able to respond with confidence to any inquiry about your knowledge of computers. But what of that 90% of our society that must answer "nothing" or "very little"? These people will find themselves at a disadvantage.

Opportunities for Computer Specialists

If you are planning a career as a computer specialist, opportunity abounds. Almost every company, no matter how small or large, employs computer specialists, and most of these companies are always looking for qualified people. For the last decade people with computer/information systems education have been at or near the top of the "most wanted" list. With millions (yes, millions!) of new computers being purchased and installed each year, it is likely that this trend will continue. Of course, the number of people attracted to the booming computer field is also increasing.

(Left) These research librarians spend much of their work day interacting with computers. (Right) This computer specialist develops and maintains a variety of administrative information systems. Both need a solid foundation of computer knowledge to accomplish their jobs effectively.

According to U.S. Department of Labor employment projections, the future is bright for computer specialists. For example, during the decade of the 1990s, the number of computer programmers is expected to increase from an estimated 575,000 to over 800,000. The number of computer systems analysts is expected to increase from an estimated 400,000 to over 580,000. Other computer specialist career paths are expected to follow a similar growth pattern. New computer specialist careers are emerging each year.

This chapter should provide insight into career options and opportunities in the computer areas. Today the majority of computer specialist positions (such as operators, programmers, or systems analysts) are in a company's information services department. However, computer specialists are moving into other departments with the trend toward distributed processing (see Figure 17–1). Notice that each year a growing percentage of a company's information processing needs is met by computer specialists in user departments. Forecasters are predicting that as much as 90% of the computer specialist positions will be outside the organization's information services department by 2000. Even now, virtually every type of user group (elementary school teachers to product designers) is vigorously recruiting people with computer expertise. Job opportunities in information services departments and in the user areas are discussed later in the chapter.

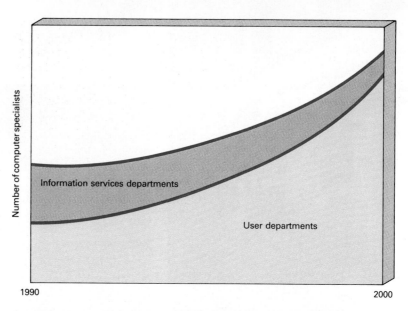

FIGURE 17–1　Computer Specialist Positions in Transition
The trend to end user computing has increased the number of computer specialists in the user areas.

Career Opportunities for the Computer-Competent Minority

This chapter presents career opportunities in the computer specialist areas and in the computer services industry in general. However, opportunities abound for computer-competent people pursuing almost any career—from actuaries to zoologists. Every facet of automation is moving closer to the people who use it. In fact, most professions put you within arm's reach of a personal computer, workstation, or terminal.

- The terminal has become standard equipment at hospital nursing stations and is often found in operating rooms.
- Draftspeople have traded drawing tables for computer-aided design (CAD) workstations.
- Teachers are integrating the power of computer-based training (CBT) into their courses.
- Economists would be lost without the predictive capabilities of their decision support systems (DSSs).
- Truck dispatchers query their information systems before scheduling deliveries.
- Advertising executives use computers to help them plan ad campaigns.
- Construction contractors keep track of on-site inventory on portable laptop computers.
- The microcomputer is the secretary's constant companion for everything from word processing to conference scheduling.
- Stockbrokers often have terminals on both sides of their desks.

In short, the capabilities of computers are being embraced by virtually all professionals. All things being equal, the person who has the knowledge

The computer revolution has had a dramatic impact on people in hundreds of professions—the way they train and, ultimately, what they do in the work place. The field of ophthalmology is one example. Here, a doctor performs eye surgery with computer-controlled precision.

of and the will to work with computers will have a tremendous career advantage over those who do not.

17–2 The Centralized Information Services Department: Organization and Personnel

In this section we will familiarize you with some of the opportunities for a computer specialist in an organization's information services department. If you are pursuing any other career, then this section will give you some insight as to who the players are in information systems development and ongoing operation and whom to contact when you have a computer-related question or request. Normally, computer users have frequent contact with people in the information services department. Besides helping to develop and maintain information systems, computer specialists in an information services department routinely respond to user inquiries about micro/mainframe links, hardware evaluation, and the use of software packages, to mention only a few.

The centralized information services department is an organization's primary source of information services. The typical department is charged with the support of the organization's information processing requirements. Information services department responsibilities are

1. Engaging in the development, the ongoing operation, and the maintenance of information systems

For most disabled workers—especially those with physical impairments—the barriers to gainful employment have been as steep as the stairs flanking many public buildings. Now this is changing, thanks to groundbreaking federal legislation and revolutionary advances in personal computer hardware and software.

The legislation, the Americans with Disabilities Act of 1990, promises to do for disabled workers what the Civil Rights Act did for racial and cultural minorities: It prohibits discrimination that might limit employment or access to public buildings and facilities. In fact, many term the law a bill of rights for the disabled—people with physical limitations, mental impairments, and chronic illnesses. The legislation promises to benefit the nation, too. Of the approximately 43 million disabled workers, only about 28% hold full- or part-time jobs at a time when experts are projecting labor shortages and a shrinking pool of *skilled* workers.

Under the law, employers cannot discriminate against any employee who can perform a job's "essential" responsibilities with "reasonable accommodations." Increasingly, these "accommodations" take the form of a personal computer with special peripherals and software. The partially sighted, for example, can benefit from software packages that create large-type screen displays, while voice synthesizers can let the blind "read" memos, books, and computer screens. For the hearing impaired, voice mail and a computer's beeps can be translated into visual cues, such as a screen display of text or flashing icons. And for people with limited use of their arms and hands, virtually any type of physical movement can be used to input commands and data to a computer. These range from relatively slow sip-and-puff devices to faster voice-recognition

THE POWER OF THE EYE   This paraplegic enters data, information, and commands by looking at keys on a monitor rather than tapping keys on a keyboard. An infrared light reflects off the back and front of the eye to determine the eye's position relative to the keyboard on the middle screen. The screen on the left monitors eye movement and the screen on the right displays the user application. In effect, the system provides a visual mouse. The user merely glances at a particular key for about a half a second to activate it.

2. Acting as an adviser to users throughout the organization on computer-related matters

3. Serving as a catalyst for improving operations through system enhancements or new systems development

4. Coordinating data and systems integration throughout the organization

5. Establishing standards, policies, and procedures relating to computers and information processing

6. Evaluating and selecting hardware and software

7. Conducting end user education programs

systems that can be trained to recognize fairly extensive vocabularies. All told, more than 18,000 technology-based products are available for the disabled.

Several studies, including ones by the U.S. Department of Labor and several private firms, concluded that 80% of all accommodations would cost less than $500 per employee. Text-to-speech software, for example, can be had for as little as $150. More sophisticated PC-based accommodations are more costly, of course. The leading speech-recognition system, for example, costs about $9000, while a PC modified for a blind word processor can cost about $8000 (versus $3000 for a standard PC). Still, the prices of these technologies, like the prices of PCs themselves, continue to drop. The cost of a "reading" device, for example, fell from $40,000 to $4000 in about a decade. Furthermore, employers who provide "assistive technologies" to their employees are eligible for tax incentives. Employers benefit, too, by gaining highly motivated and productive workers. A study at a major chemical company found that workers with and without disabilities were equal or closely matched on safety and performance.

Some of the nation's leading companies, including IBM, Apple Computer, Inc., and Electronic Data Systems Corp., initiated efforts to hire and train the disabled long before the Americans with Disabilities Act was passed. In fact, many of these disabled workers now work full-time as programmers and in other data processing jobs.

READERS NEED NOT APPLY Computer technology has made sightless people more independent. This person is "reading" several documents at a time with the aid of hand and stationary OCR scanners and a voice-response system.

Organizational Neutrality

Limited resources are available for the development and maintenance of information systems. Therefore, information services management must maintain a balance between *being responsive* to user information needs and *being responsible* (see Figure 17–2). For example, an information services manager cannot divert previously committed resources from one project in an attempt to be responsive to another user. Unless extreme circumstances dictate, information services management must strive is to keep approved projects on schedule. This is an almost daily conflict

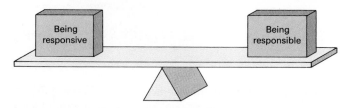

FIGURE 17–2   The Information Services Balancing Act
The information services department must maintain a balance between being responsive to user information needs and being responsible.

that information services and user managers must resolve. Because of this ever-present conflict, companies are opting for a structure that provides organizational neutrality for the information services department. Most solutions result in the director of information services reporting to the chief executive officer (CEO) in either a line or staff capacity (see Figure 17–3). This type of structural organization allows projects to be assigned priorities with the corporate good in mind.

Organization of an Information Services Department

In some information services departments, one person is the "chief cook and bottle washer"—the entire staff. Other departments employ several thousand people. Both small and large *shops* (a slang term for information services departments) must perform the same functions of systems analysis, programming, technical support, data communications, operations, and so on. Differences in staffing and organization are due primarily to the size and degree of specialization.

Figure 17–4 illustrates how an information services department in a medium-sized to large corporation might be organized. This representative organizational structure could vary considerably, depending on circumstances. The various components and specialist positions shown in Figure 17–4 are discussed in the next section.

A typical organizational structure for a small company is illustrated in Figure 17–5. Some specialty areas are not noted in the chart because personnel in small companies double up on duties. For example, a programmer might also function as the data base administrator.

FIGURE 17–3   Information Services Positioned for Organizational Neutrality
In the figure, the centralized information services department is shown as subordinate to a high-level neutral office in both a line capacity (left) and a staff capacity (right).

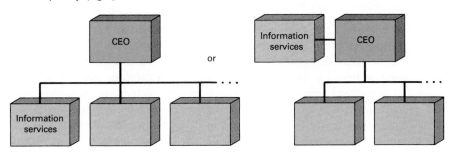

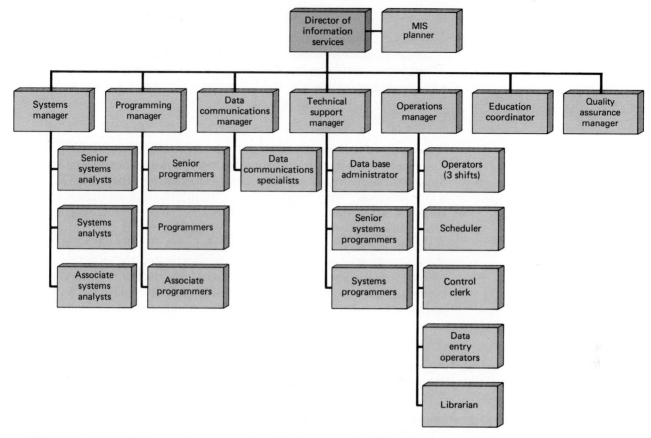

FIGURE 17–4   Organization Chart—Medium-Sized and Large Information Services Departments

No two information services departments are organized in the same way, but the example is, in general, representative.

FIGURE 17–5   Organization Chart—Small Information Services Departments

This structure is representative of a small information services department.

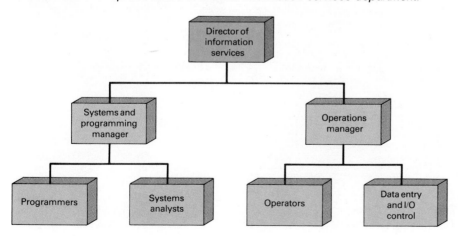

Information Services Functional Components and Specialists

This section will acquaint you with the functional components and professionals associated with the computer and information systems function. There is no "best" way to staff for the effective delivery of information services. However, each of the following components and job specialties is either implicitly or explicitly included in every company that employs computer specialists.

Information Services Management   Information services managers perform the traditional management functions: planning, organizing, staffing, directing, and controlling. The **chief information officer (CIO)**, often a vice president, has responsibility for all information services activity in the company. Often the CIO is the director of the centralized information services department. At least half the CIO's time is spent interacting with user managers and executives. In this capacity, the CIO coordinates the integration of data and information systems and serves as the catalyst for new systems development. The remainder of the CIO's time is devoted to managing the information services department. The CIO must be somewhat futuristic, predicting what information technologies will become reality so the company can position itself to use them as a strategic weapon.

Programmers, analysts, and other computer specialists in an information services department work together to meet an organization's data processing and information needs.

Systems Analysis   The systems analysis group is composed of **systems analysts**. The systems analysts, or simply *analysts*, analyze, design, and implement information systems. They work closely with people in the user areas to design information systems that meet their data processing and information needs. These "problem solvers" are assigned a variety of tasks, including feasibility studies, system reviews, security assessments, long-range planning, and hardware/software selection.

The role of systems analysts is expanding with the technology. For example, with the recent trend to prototyping (see Chapter 15, "Analysis and Design of Business Information Systems"), users and analysts can work together at a PC or terminal to design *and* implement certain information systems—without programmer involvement!

Programming   The programming component of the information services department includes **applications programmers**, or simply *programmers*, who translate analyst-prepared system and input/output specifications into programs. Programmers design the logic, then code, debug, test, and document the programs. They write programs for a certain application, such as market analysis or inventory management.

Sometimes called "implementers" or "miracle workers," programmers are charged with turning system specifications into an information system. To do this, they must exhibit logical thinking and overlook nothing. A good programmer is *perceptive, patient, persistent, picky,* and *productive*—the "five Ps" of programming.

Some companies distinguish between *development* and *maintenance* programmers. Development programmers create *new* systems. Maintenance programmers *modify* existing programs to meet changing information processing needs. At a typical company, about 50% of the applications programming tasks are related to maintenance and 50% to new development.

A person holding a **programmer/analyst** position performs the functions of both a programmer and a systems analyst. The higher-ranking people in the programming group are often programmer/analysts.

Data Communications   **Data communications specialists** design and maintain computer networks that link computers and terminals for data communications. This work involves selecting and installing appropriate hardware, such as modems, PBXs, and front-end processors, and selecting the transmission media (all discussed in Chapter 7, "Connectivity and Data Communications"). Data communications specialists also develop and implement the software that controls the flow of data between computing devices.

Technical Support   The technical support group designs, develops, maintains, and implements *system software*. System software is fundamental to the general operation of the computer; that is, it does not address a specific business or scientific problem. We discuss the various categories of system software in detail in Chapter 9, "System Software and Platforms."

The technical support group usually consists of systems programmers and the data base administrator. **Systems programmers** develop and maintain system software. The **data base administrator (DBA)** designs, creates, and maintains the integrated data base. The DBA coordinates discussions between user groups to determine the content and format of the data base so that data redundancy is kept to a minimum. The integrity and security of the data base are also responsibilities of the data base administrator.

Some companies elect to integrate data communications personnel within the system software group.

Operations   People in the operations group perform a variety of jobs, including *computer operator*, *scheduler*, *control clerk*, *data entry operator*, and *librarian*.

The **computer operator** performs those hardware-based activities needed to keep production information systems operational. An operator works in the machine room, initiating software routines and mounting the appropriate magnetic tapes, disks, and preprinted forms. The operator is in constant communication with the computer while monitoring the progress of a number of simultaneous production runs, initiating one-time jobs, and trouble-shooting. If the computer system fails, the operator initiates restart procedures to "bring the system up."

The **scheduler** strives to utilize the valuable hardware resources at optimum efficiency. Along with production information systems, the scheduler allocates and schedules computer time for program development and testing, system acceptance testing, data and file conversion, ad hoc

The nature of the work and the availability of specially equipped terminals and PCs have made computer careers particularly inviting to the physically disabled. This woman works as a data base administrator at a computer-services company. Unable to use the keyboard, she uses voice input to enter commands and data.

jobs, preventive maintenance, general maintenance, and system down-time for hardware upgrades.

The **control clerk** accounts for all input to and output from the computer center. Control clerks follow standard procedures to validate the accuracy of the output before it is distributed to the user department.

Data entry operators, sometimes called the *key operators*, use key entry devices to transcribe data into machine-readable format. At most companies, only a small data entry group is attached to information services because the majority are distributed among the user areas.

The **librarian** selects the appropriate interchangeable magnetic tapes and disks and delivers them to the operator. The operator mounts the tapes and disks on the storage devices for processing and then returns them to the librarian for off-line storage. The librarian maintains a status log on each tape and disk. Medium-sized and large companies may have hundreds, even thousands, of tapes and disks. The librarian also maintains a reference library filled with computer books, periodicals, and manuals as well as internal system and program documentation (logic diagrams, program listings, and so on).

Education The **education coordinator** manages all computer-related educational activities. Anyone who works with computers or selects a computer-related career automatically adopts a life of continuing education. Computer technology is changing rapidly, so learning is an ongoing process—new hardware, new software, new techniques, and new systems. The education coordinator schedules users and computer specialists for technical update seminars, video training programs, computer-assisted instruction, and other training. The coordinator sometimes conducts the sessions.

Administration Administration is the support function that handles the paperwork and administrative details associated with the operation of an information services department.

Planning Planning is generally considered a management function. However, the complexities of planning for the implementation of management information systems for an organization demand that medium-sized and large companies have at least one **MIS planner**.

Quality Assurance The quality assurance group encourages the "do it right the first time" approach to systems development. **Quality assurance specialists** are assigned the task of monitoring the quality of every aspect of the design and operation of information systems, including system efficiency and documentation. They also ensure that computer specialists and users adhere to standards and procedures.

Organization Summary

Figure 17–6 summarizes the relationships between computer specialty positions and users in the development and operation of an information system. A *user* request for a computer-related service, called a *service*

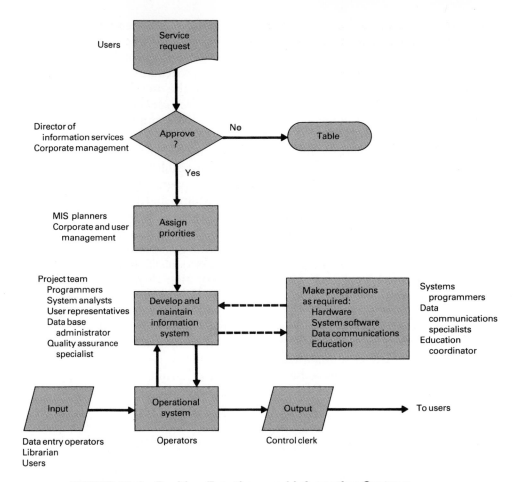

FIGURE 17–6 Position Functions and Information Systems
This chart summarizes the relationship between information services positions and user personnel in the development and operation of an information system.

request, is compiled and submitted to the information services department. Because resources are limited, not all requests are filled. The merits of service requests are evaluated by the *director of information services* and *corporate management*. Major requests are incorporated into the MIS planning process by the *MIS planner* and assigned a priority, usually in cooperation with *corporate* and *user management*.

A project team is formed to develop, implement, and maintain the information system. The project team typically is made up of *programmers*, *systems analysts*, *user representatives*, the *data base administrator*, and a *quality assurance specialist*, or some combination of the foregoing. *Systems programmers* and *data communications specialists* make changes in the hardware configuration, system software, and data communications network, as required. The *education coordinator* schedules training sessions for both computer specialists and users. Once the system is implemented, operations people handle the routine input, processing, and output activities. *Data entry operators* transcribe the raw data to machine-readable format. The *librarian* readies magnetic storage media for processing. *Operators* initiate and monitor computer runs and distribute the output to *control clerks*, who then check the output for accuracy before delivering it to the *user*.

17-3 Departmental Computing: Users Take Control

In Chapter 2, "Minis, Micros, Mainframes, and Supercomputers," we learned that *departmental computing* is a generic reference to any type of computing done at the departmental level. The trend toward departmental computing is moving hardware, software, and processing closer to the people who use them. The concept of departmental computing has emerged because users are technically more sophisticated and better prepared to assume responsibility for their own computers and information systems.

In the more sophisticated implementations of departmental computing, functional area managers find themselves managing their own miniature information services departments, often including programmers, analysts, operators, other computer specialists, and, of course, powerful computers. Departmental computing is responsible for several new computer specialist careers: user liaisons, microcomputer specialists, and office automation specialists.

Opportunities for Traditional Computer Specialists in the User Areas

Because computer specialist careers have no geographical or industry boundaries, people pursuing careers as programmers, systems analysts, and

Times are changing. (Left) Before computers, processing and information retrieval were done manually by individuals. For almost four decades after the first commercial computer was installed in 1951, the trend was to consolidate data and information processing at a centralized mainframe-based computer center. (Right) Today the trend is away from further centralization and toward departmental computing.

operators always have had a plethora of options. A decade ago, a computer specialist could choose to work in Idaho in the potato industry, in Michigan in the automobile industry, in California in the entertainment industry, or in Texas in the oil industry. But, inevitably, the search would lead to an information services department. Today the options are even greater. The emergence of departmental computing has expanded the career horizons for computer specialists. More and more are migrating to the user areas and departmental computing (see Figure 17–1). They now can seek employment in a medical research department, a consumer products marketing department, an internal auditing department, or virtually any area of business endeavor.

Emerging Computer Specialist Careers in the User Areas

User Liaisons   Computer and information processing activity is very intense in companies that seek to exploit the full potential of information technology. In this environment, someone who is attached to a particular functional area must be given the responsibility for taking full advantage of available computing resources. More often than not, this person is the **user liaison**. The user liaison can have a variety of titles, such as *internal consultant*, *functional specialist*, and *account executive*. The user liaison is a "live-in" computer specialist who coordinates all computer-related activities within a particular functional area. For example, you will often find user liaisons in finance departments and in manufacturing plants. User liaisons are intimately familiar with the functional areas to which they are assigned as well as the technical end of computers and information processing. They are often the impetus behind movements to upgrade existing information systems or to develop new systems.

Within the business community, there are many cyberphobics (people who fear computers) and people with limited computer skills. These people do not have the inclination, knowledge, or time to work effectively with a computer specialist, so they discuss what they want in general terms with the user liaison. The user liaison then does whatever is necessary to fulfill the user's request. This may involve anything from working with the computer specialist in the information services department to actually doing the programming for a department-based information system.

Microcomputer Specialists   From the growth of departmental computing and the popularity of microcomputers has emerged a new career, sometimes referred to as the **microcomputer specialist**. Micro specialists have been trained in the function and operation of microcomputers and related hardware (see Chapter 3, "Interacting with Personal Computers"). They are proficient in the use and application of all common micro software packages such as word processing, desktop publishing, communications, electronic spreadsheet, presentation graphics, and database software. (See Chapters 11 and 12 on PC software.) Often, they have expertise in the installation and maintenance of micro-based local area networks and in establishing micro/mainframe links (see Chapter 8, "Networks and Networking").

A user does not always have the time to learn the details of using a microcomputer and its software. Rather than have each person in an office learn micros and micro software packages inside out, a firm can have a micro specialist help users over the rough spots as well as implement hardware and develop new systems. In this way, users can focus their attention on applying micros to their immediate information needs rather than on system quirks.

Microcomputer specialists keep abreast of the changes in technology, both in general and as these changes relate to their application area. Because microcomputer specialists are continuously attentive to an evolving technology, the departments in which they work are in a better position to take advantage of new innovations in microcomputer hardware and software.

Office Automation Specialists   Office automation encompasses those computer-based applications generally associated with office work such as word processing, electronic mail, image processing, voice processing, and office information systems. These office automation applications are discussed in Chapter 14, "Applications of Information Technology." **Office automation specialists** know the operation of the hardware and the use of the software associated with each of the office automation applications. They help employees make effective use of office systems.

17–4   The Information Center and Information Center Specialists

The Information Center

There are managers who submit handwritten drafts for typing, secretaries who frequently refer to dictionaries, clerks who use hand calculators throughout the day, administrative personnel who assemble reports with glue and scissors, executives who would like to (but cannot) do "what if" analysis, and researchers who use pencils and graph paper to plot their results. All these people would benefit greatly from a visit to their companies' **information center**. Information centers would train these people and, therefore, allow them to use their time more productively.

An information center is a "hands-on" facility in which computing resources are made available to various user groups. Users come to an information center for the computing resources and technical support they need to help with their personal information and computing needs. The computing resources might include:

- *Video display terminals* that enable users to interact directly with the organization's central computer system, its information systems, and its integrated data base
- *Microcomputers* for personal computing
- *Plotters, color page printers, desktop film recorders, image scanners,* and other I/O devices that might not be available in the typical office

Privacy in the Work Place Are you bothered when your co-workers peek over your shoulder? Or, do you work with sensitive information in an open area? If so, you need a Privacy Filter by 3M. This filter fits over your monitor's screen, covering your work from people on either side of you. It is made of a plastic film that is inlaid with microscopic black strips, something like a Venetian blind. If you are sitting in front of the screen, you can see through the filter clearly. To others, the screen looks black.

At this information center, specialists assist users in the use and application of hardware and software until the users can become self-sufficient.

■ A wide range of *PC-based software*, including software that might not be available in the typical office, such as *desktop publishing, project management,* and *decision support system*

Information Center Specialists

Perhaps the most important component of an information center is the people who help users. These people, called **information center specialists**, conduct training sessions, answer questions, create systems that complement the information center function, and generally *help users to help themselves*. Because user computing needs run the gamut of computers and information processing, the information center specialist must be a generalist comfortable with micros, a wide variety of micro applications, and user-oriented mainframe software.

The theory behind an information center is that users have a place to go, not necessarily to request information services but to help themselves meet their own information needs. Besides providing access to user-oriented hardware and software, information centers and information center specialists provide three basic services: training, consulting, and software development.

■ *Training.* The first step toward becoming a successful user of computing and information resources is learning how to use these resources. Recognizing this, information center specialists provide ongoing training in the use and application of available hardware and software resources.

■ *Consulting.* The information center is a place where users go to get answers to their computer-related questions. The user might need help merging a spreadsheet graph into a word processing document, or debugging a query language program, or finding a cable to link a page printer with a micro.

- *Software development.* Although information centers are charged with helping users help themselves, some jobs are beyond users' capabilities. In these cases, information center specialists develop small micro-based information systems for users.

The creation of information centers has helped channel the one-time user requests away from the information services department. With users literally taking matters into their own hands (with a little help from the information center), programmers and analysts in the information services department have more time to devote to ongoing development projects.

17–5 Other Career Opportunities: Services, Hardware, Software, and Education

In the last two sections our discussion has focused on jobs typically found in an organization's information services department, in an information center, or in a user group. There are also a host of computer specialist career opportunities in organizations that provide computer-related products or services. Let's divide these organizations into four groups: services, hardware vendors, software vendors, and education. But keep in mind that a particular organization may fit into two, three, or even all four of these groups. For example, Digital Equipment Corporation markets computers and software, and it provides consulting and education services as well.

Commercial Information Services

The computer revolution is creating a tremendous demand for computer-related services. In response to this demand, a number of service organizations have emerged. These include *service bureaus*, *facilities management companies*, *turnkey companies*, *consulting firms*, *data base services*, and *computer repair stores*, to mention a few.

Service Bureaus   Service bureaus provide almost any kind of information processing services. These include but are not limited to developing and implementing information systems, providing computer time (timesharing), and transcribing source data. A service bureau is essentially a public computer center. Service bureau employees who work under contract to develop information systems for a client company are referred to as *contract programmers* and *contract systems analysts*.

Facilities Management Companies   Facilities management companies are the answer for firms that want an internal information services department but do not want the responsibility of managing it. Employees of facilities management companies physically move into a client company's computer center and take over all facets of the center's operation.

EMERGING TECHNOLOGY   Smart Houses: Houses with More than Curb Appeal

Smart houses with home automation systems have progressed from science fiction to reality. Not only do smart houses exist today, but as the twenty-first century approaches, the price should fall to where most of us can afford one.

Computers and sensors, linked by literally miles of wire and electronic adapters, enable the smart house to control security systems, entertainment centers, appliances, lights, blinds, heating and cooling systems, sprinkler systems, swimming pool systems, and other systems that can be activated by electrical apparatus. The goal of a smart house is to coordinate all domestic systems to minimize the expenditure of energy and maximize the comfort of its occupants. A central computer, called a controller, ties the threads together. We interact with the home automation system via telephone, hand-

A SMART HOUSE   This house was built by Baltimore Gas and Electric to demonstrate the savings potential and conveniences of smart houses.

Facilities management companies are often engaged for turnaround situations—where the client company wants its information services function to make a quantum leap in sophistication and capability that cannot be accomplished with existing staff.

Turnkey Companies   A **turnkey company** contracts with a client to install a complete system, both hardware and software. One of the major selling points of a turnkey company is that the hardware and/or software are installed with minimum involvement by personnel from the company purchasing them. Such companies are also called **system integrators** because they integrate various hardware and software products to provide

held remotes, keypads, touch screen televisions, and voice commands.

LIVING IN A SMART HOUSE

Do you want your home warm and cozy when you return from a trip? Just head for the nearest phone booth, call your smart house's controller, and tell it to turn up the heat. Do you want your washing machine to turn itself on at a time when electricity costs less? Just tell the controller when you want it to start.

In Japan, an experimental smart house has been built that seems warm and inviting—anything but technological. It, in fact, is filled with dozens of hidden sensors monitoring temperature, humidity, airflow, carbon dioxide, and even human presence in the house. Its sensors are part of a network linking three PCs with appliances, motor-driven windows and blinds, humidifiers, and so on.

There are lots of possibilities with a smart house. If the homeowner selects the "going out" mode on the master panel, the computer can arm the security system and adjust the lighting and ventilation systems. If it's time to celebrate at home instead of going out, the "party" setting might close the drapes, adjust the lighting, and tune in background music—all from one switch in the living room. The controller can be programmed to create whatever mood you want.

THE ENVIRONMENTALLY CONSCIOUS SMART HOUSE

Research in Holland reflects environmental concerns. On the roof of a smart house, a tunnel-like structure

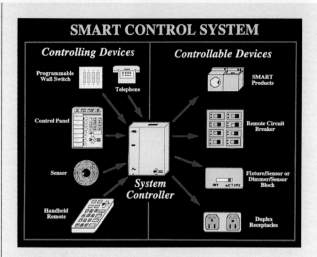

THE SMART HOUSE CONTROL SYSTEM

collects rainwater which is sent to a holding tank. The water collected is used to flush the toilets and water the garden. It reduces the need to use costly drinking-quality water when rainwater is more appropriate.

A solar boiler heats washing and bath water in the smart house, and a row of photovoltaic panels collects solar energy to charge batteries for emergency power. Gas, electricity, and water meters are integrated with the controller so that utilities and homeowners can monitor consumption.

Smart house technology isn't just a luxury for the wealthy. Those people who are energy savers and environmentally minded will probably end up using at least some smart house features in their own homes in the future.

---

a solution to a problem, such as setting up desktop publishing (for example, integrating PageMaker software, the Mac Quadra personal computer, and the Laserwriter page printer).

Consulting Firms   The peaks and valleys of MIS requirements and the lack of internal expertise in specialty areas have made the use of outside consultants and contract programmers and analysts an economic necessity. Consulting firms give advice on using computers and the information resource. Consultants usually have specialized expertise that is otherwise not available to clients. Contract programmers, analysts, and other MIS specialists, on the other hand, are retained primarily for work-force aug-

The jobs of consultants are not limited to implementation of hardware and software. Some specialize in the design of machine rooms and computer work areas. These consultants are overseeing the conversion to a larger mainframe computer system.

The rapid growth in the number of computers has resulted in the emergence of a new industry—computer repair. Fortunately, computers are very reliable. Charges for computer repair range from $50 to $250 per hour.

mentation, not because they have unique skills. For example, they may be hired to develop a high-priority information system for which internal resources are not available.

Data Base Services　A variety of applications-specific data bases are available commercially. Market researchers can obtain data bases that summarize sales by demographics for a particular type of product (such as shampoo or cough medicine). Pharmacists can purchase a data base that contains drug pairs that may result in an adverse reaction when taken together. Politicians can purchase data bases consisting of voter preferences. Entrepreneurs can purchase data bases that contain the names and addresses of the most likely buyers of their products. CEOs can tap into up-to-the-minute industry-related information.

Data bases are accessible on-line via a modem and a PC or terminal. Many on-line data bases also are distributed to subscribers on CD-ROM disk. On-line data bases are updated continuously. CD-ROM disks are current up to the most recently distributed CD-ROM disk. CD-ROM data bases are distributed as often as weekly and as infrequently as once each year, depending on the volatility of the data base.

Computer Repair Stores　One of the fastest growing service groups is computer repair stores. There weren't very many television repair shops in 1950, but look at them now. History is repeating itself with micros. Fifteen years ago, microcomputers were somewhat novel, not to mention expensive. Today they are a common consumer item, and they do "get sick" and need repair. One computer repair chain is even called the Computer Doctor.

Hardware Vendors

Computer Systems Manufacturers　The most well-known hardware vendors are the computer systems manufacturers, such as Digital Equipment Corporation, Apple, IBM, UNISYS, and Hewlett-Packard (HP). Thirty years ago fewer than a dozen companies manufactured computer systems; today there are hundreds. These companies manufacture the processor and usually some or all of the peripheral equipment (disk drives, printers, terminals, and so on).

The competition in the high-technology field of computer hardware is fierce. Manufacturers routinely purchase the competition's processors and peripheral equipment to disassemble them in search of technological innovations that can be applied to their own product line. This practice has become so widespread that the term *reverse engineering* was coined to describe it.

Leasing Companies　Most computers are available for purchase or for lease. The monthly charge for leasing a computer system is based roughly on what the monthly payments would be if the computer were purchased over a four-year period. Leasing companies purchase computers, often from manufacturers, then lease them for less than the manufacturer does. A leasing company, referred to as the *third party*, makes a profit by keeping its computers under contract for five years or more.

Plug-Compatible Manufacturers Plug-compatible manufacturers (PCMs) make peripheral devices that can be attached directly to another manufacturer's computer. A PCM might manufacture disk drives and tape drives that operate and sometimes look like those of the original computer system manufacturer. These devices are called *plug-compatible* because a PCM disk drive needs only to be plugged into the computer to become operational.

Value-Added Resellers **Value-added resellers**, or **VARs**, integrate the hardware and software of several vendors with their own software, then sell the entire package. They are called value-added resellers because they "add value" to each component of the system. For example, a VAR may integrate one vendor's microcomputer, another's electronic spreadsheet software, and yet another's voice input device to create a system on which spreadsheet applications can be run without a keyboard.

Computer Stores Until the late 1970s computer systems were sold exclusively in the customer's office. Today, computer retail outlets, such as Computerland, MicroAge Computer Stores, and Entré Computer Centers, have made it possible for customers to shop for computers in much the same way they would shop for stereo components. Because the price of a computer has been reduced so drastically, computer retail outlets and most department store chains now carry a wide variety of small computer systems, including minicomputers.

A used-computer market has also given birth to a growing number of used-computer dealers. Individuals and companies are always "trading up" to computers with greater processing capabilities. This puts a lot of "pre-owned" computers on the market.

Jobs with Hardware Vendors Hardware vendors market and service hardware. To do so they need *marketing representatives* to sell the products and *systems engineers* to support them once they have been installed. Marketing representatives hold a technical sales position that requires a broad knowledge of the company's products and their capabilities. They normally spend time with customers assessing their information processing needs, then submit proposals for their review. (Marketing reps in retail outlets spend little time with customers and seldom prepare written proposals.) A systems engineer has more technical knowledge and is schooled in the details of the company's hardware and software operation. The systems engineer is the technical expert, often called on by customers for advice on technical matters. Behind the scenes, hardware manufacturers employ programmers, analysts, and all other types of computer specialists.

Software Vendors

Software vendors that produce and market software are sometimes called **software houses**. You buy a *proprietary software package* for a particular computer-based system or application from a software house. The package contains the software on a magnetic tape, diskette, or CD-ROM, and includes its accompanying documentation. The software could be an

Jobs with hardware vendors include traditional manufacturing positions. Jobs on the line at this Compaq manufacturing facility demand computer competency because workers must use computers to test those they make.

expert system for archaeologists, an authoring system just for poets, a database management system, or any of thousands of other software options. Software prices range from about $30 to hundreds of thousands of dollars.

Software vendors copyright proprietary software by registering their creations with the Copyright Office in Washington, D.C. Copyrighted software is protected from unlawful duplication and use. When you purchase or lease a software package, you receive a *license agreement* to use it. Typically, this agreement limits the use of the software to one computer system at a time. It is a violation of copyright law to duplicate proprietary software for use on several computer systems unless permission is granted by the vendor in a *site license agreement*.

Many stories are told about successful software entrepreneurs who turned an idea into millions of dollars. These opportunities still exist today, and thousands of aspiring entrepreneurs are creating companies and placing their software on the market each year. Some struggle to marginal success and some fail, but a few make it big—very big!

Education

The computer explosion in the last decade has created an insatiable demand for computer-related education. People in the work force and those preparing to enter it need to be computer-competent to be effective in this age of information. In essence, this means that every student and virtually every person in the work force wants an opportunity to achieve computer competency. Many of those taking computer-competency courses are catching the "bug" and pursue advanced computer education in parallel with their chosen fields.

This demand for computer education is taxing the resources of our educational institutions and has given rise to a tremendous demand for *professors* and *instructors*. Over the past decade the fastest-growing curricula on most campuses are those in computer science and information systems. But the demand for computer-related education is so great that professors and instructors are being recruited to teach computer applications in a variety of curricula. Art professors teach computer graphics; physiology professors teach computer instrumentation for ergonomics experiments; sociology professors teach data base concepts as applied to the analysis of demographic trends; and music professors teach synthesized music and the use of the computer as a tool for composition.

Instructors are needed in industry as well. Programmers, analysts, and users are forever facing the announcement of a new technological innovation or the installation of a new system. In-house education is focused on the specific educational needs of the organization. Without instructors to direct this effort, a hundred new terminals may end up as bulky paperweights.

The delivery of computer education can take many forms. Several firms specialize in the development of self-paced instructional videos and computer-based training (CBT) courses. Such courses cover everything from computer competency to advanced data communications. The courses are normally accompanied by a support text and workbooks.

The manner in which we teach at every level in every subject has been affected by the computer. This speech pathologist can carry on a two-way conversation with severely disabled children with the aid of a Talking EyePoint Board. Children identify symbols by sight and a voice synthesizer speaks the word or phrase. The two-way conversation facilitates learning.

Educators that develop these self-paced courses do not have the direct student contact that instructors have, but they need similar skills plus a sensitivity to the challenge of self-paced learning.

If you wish to pursue a career in the field of computer education, you will need a solid educational foundation and several years of field experience.

17–6 Professionalism and Ethics

Licensing and Certification

If your chosen career involves the use of computers, you may be in constant contact with sensitive data and may have the power to control events. An implied responsibility to maintain the integrity of the system and its data accompanies such a job. Failure to do so could have a disastrous effect on the lives of individuals and on the stability of the organization.

At present, licensing or certification is not a requirement for programmers, operators, or any other computer professional; nor is it required for users of computers. Licensing and certification are hotly debated issues. Many professions require demonstration of performance at a certain level of competence before permission is granted to practice. Through examination, the engineer becomes a registered professional engineer, the attorney becomes a member of the bar, and the accountant becomes a certified public accountant.

Within the computer community, there are several certifications. Recruiters may view certification as favorable, but not as a prerequisite of employment. The **Certificate in Data Processing (CDP)** is a general certification in the area of computers and information systems. The **Certificate in Computer Programming (CCP)** is specifically for programmers. The CDP and CCP are administered by the Institute for Certification of Computer Professionals. The **Certified System Professional (CSP)** is a general certification administered by the Association for Systems Management. The **Certified Information Systems Auditor (CISA)** is administered by the EDP Auditor's Association, and the **Certified Data Educator (CDE)** is administered by the Data Education Certification Council. The CDP, CCP, CSP, CISA, and CDE are awarded upon successful completion of an examination.

Professional Societies

Several hundred professional societies have emerged with the information revolution. These societies promote a common bond shared by professionals with similar interests and help instill a professional attitude among the membership. A few of the more prominent professional societies organized primarily for computer specialists include:

- Association for Computing Machinery (ACM)
- Data Processing Management Association (DPMA)
- Society for Information Management (SIM)
- Data Entry Management Association (DEMA)
- Independent Computer Consultants Association (ICCA)
- Association for Systems Managers (ASM)
- Association of Information Systems Professionals (AISP)
- EDP Auditor's Association (EDPAA)

Other professional societies are organized for special-interest groups—those interested in a particular application of the computer. Whatever your chosen profession or special interest, there is probably a computer society for you to join. The following are just a few of several hundred such organizations, and the list is growing each month.

- Association of Rehabilitation Programs in Data Processing (ARPDP)
- Association of Small Computer Users in Education (ASCUE)
- Black Data Processing Associates (BDPA)
- Health and Beauty Aids Computer Users Society (HABACUS)
- Hospital Information Systems Sharing Group (HISSG)
- Library and Information Technology Association (LITA)
- Life Insurance Systems Association (LISA)
- Society for Computer Applications in Engineering, Planning, and Architecture (CEPA)
- Society for Computer Medicine (SCM)
- Steel Industry Systems Association (SISA)
- Women in Information Processing (WIP)
- Computer Law Association

The American Federation of Information Processing Societies (AFIPS) is an umbrella organization that affords societies with similar goals an opportunity to join forces on certain issues and in certain activities.

The Question of Ethics

One of the largest professional societies adopted a code of ethics over 15 years ago. The code warns members that they can be expelled or censured if they violate it. To date, not one of the society's tens of thousands of members has been expelled or censured for violating the code. Other professional societies publish a code of ethics as well, and they too rarely or never take action against delinquent members. Does this mean there are no violations? Of course not. A carefully drafted code of ethics provides some guidelines for conduct, but professional societies cannot be expected to police the misdoings of their membership. In many instances, a code violation is also a violation of the law.

A code of ethics provides direction for computer professionals and users so that they act responsibly in their application of information technology. The following code of ethics is in keeping with the spirit of those encouraged by computer societies.

1. Maintain the highest standard of professional behavior.
2. Avoid situations that create a conflict of interest.
3. Do not violate the confidentiality of your employer or those you service.

It is more the rule than the exception that people who work with computer systems will have ready access to a broad range of sensitive information. Image processing applications provide access to original documents, such as floor layouts for secured areas (shown here), medical records, wills, loan applications, and so on. Because of the potential for the abuse of this information, some professional societies have adopted a code of ethics.

4. Continue to learn so your knowledge keeps pace with the technology.
5. Use information judiciously and maintain system integrity at all times.
6. Do not violate the rights or privacy of others.
7. Accomplish each task to the best of your ability.
8. Do not break the law.

If you follow this eight-point code, it is unlikely that anyone will question your ethics. Nevertheless, well-meaning people routinely violate this simple code because they are unaware of the tremendous detrimental impact of their actions. With the speed and power of computers, a minor code infraction easily can be magnified to a costly catastrophe. For this reason, the use of computers is raising new ethical questions. The two case studies that follow illustrate the ethical overtones surrounding the application of information technology.

Case 1: Computerized Dialers Let's take as an example the case of computerized dialers, a system that automatically dials a telephone number, plays a prerecorded message, and asks the person to respond to some questions. Telephone numbers are entered into the system, then dialed one after another. If there is no answer, the number is re-dialed at a later time. Such systems are used for telemarketing a variety of products, not to mention politicians and ideologies. Is this an invasion of an individual's privacy?

Consider the company that, for a fee, will use its computerized dialing system to do telemarketing for local merchants. The system contains every telephone number in the city telephone directory. A message announcing a sale, a new service, or whatever is recorded for each client. Each day the system is activated and "the computer" makes calls from 8 A.M. to 10 P.M.

Is this application an ethical use of computers, or is it an invasion of privacy and an abuse of another person's time? During the course of a single day, the system can interrupt the lives of thousands of people. How many of us would welcome the opportunity to listen to a prerecorded commercial when we answer the phone? Is telemarketing in violation of the code of ethics just outlined? How about Item 6?

There are, of course, legitimate uses of computerized dialing systems. For example, the IRS uses them to notify delinquent taxpayers; school districts use them to notify parents of truant children; and retailers alert customers that they can pick up the items they have ordered.

Case 2: Congressional Franking Privileges Members of the U.S. Congress have franking privileges, or free mail. Before computers, most letters were sent in response to constituent inquiries. Computers, commercial mailing lists, and high-speed printers have made it possible to crank out 30,000 "individualized" letters per hour. Some members of Congress have been known to send out millions of letters a year.

Is this massive amount of correspondence an attempt to better inform the constituents, or is it politically motivated and an abuse of the power of the computer? Is this application a violation of our code of ethics? How about Items 2 and 5?

Career Mobility and Computer Knowledge

Computer competency is already a prerequisite of employment in many professions such as business and engineering. Within a few years computer literacy may well be a requirement for success in most professions. Career mobility is becoming forever intertwined with an individual's current and future knowledge of computers.

Just as advancing technology is creating new jobs, it is changing old ones. For example, people who used to work at drafting tables now work at computer-aided design (CAD) workstations. Police officers document accidents on pen-based PCs. Surgeons now rely on computer-generated three-dimensional pictures of the inside of the body instead of exploratory surgery. In time, virtually all jobs will be heavily influenced by emerging information technology.

Career advancement ultimately depends on your abilities, imagination, and performance, but understanding computers can only enhance your opportunities. If you cultivate your talents and you aspire to leave your mark on your chosen profession, the sky is the limit.

The results of major software development projects are all around us. Just lift up the hood of your car. A group of computer specialists and managers worked together closely to create the software that controls such systems as the fuel injection and brakes. Whatever your chosen career, the probability is high that you will soon be a part of a major software development project.

Important Terms and Summary Outline

applications programmer
Certificate in Computer Programming (CCP)
Certificate in Data Processing (CDP)
Certified Data Educator (CDE)
Certified Information Systems Auditor (CISA)
Certified System Professional (CSP)
chief information officer (CIO)
computer operator
control clerk

data base administrator (DBA)
data communications specialist
data entry operator
education coordinator
facilities management companies
information center
information center specialist
librarian
microcomputer specialist
MIS planner
office automation specialists

plug-compatible manufacturer (PCM)
programmer/analyst
quality assurance specialists
scheduler
service bureau
software house
system integrator
systems analyst
systems programmer
turnkey company
user liaison
value-added reseller (VAR)

17–1 THE JOB OUTLOOK. People who can include computer knowledge on their résumés will have an advantage over those who cannot. This is true in a great many professional disciplines.

Virtually every organization employs or is considering employing computer specialists. More and more of these computer specialist positions are being filled in user groups.

17–2 THE CENTRALIZED INFORMATION SERVICES DEPARTMENT: ORGANIZATION AND PERSONNEL. The information services department is the data and information "nerve center" of an organization. Its responsibilities include development, implementation, maintenance, and ongoing operation of information systems; acting as an adviser to users; serving as a catalyst; coordinating data and systems integration; establishing standards, policies, and procedures; evaluating hardware and software; and providing end user education.

An information services department must maintain a balance between being responsive to user information needs and being responsible. Because of this ever-present conflict, companies are opting for a structure that provides organizational neutrality for the information services department.

The actual organizational structure of an information services department will vary considerably from one organization to the next. Normally, individuals in smaller companies will perform several functions. Large companies have enough people to specialize.

The career fields in an information services department can be divided into eight groups: management, systems analysis, programming, data communications, technical support, operations, education, and quality assurance.

The number and type of career paths open to someone entering the computer/information systems field is expanding each year. Some of the most visible career paths are **chief information officer (CIO)**, **systems analyst**, **applications programmer**, **programmer/analyst**, **data communications specialist**, **systems programmer**, **data base administrator**

580   Part V   Opportunity, Responsibility, and Challenge

(DBA), **computer operator, scheduler, control clerk, data entry operator, librarian, education coordinator, MIS planner,** and **quality assurance specialist.**

17–3 DEPARTMENTAL COMPUTING: USERS TAKE CONTROL. Departmental computing is any type of computing done at the departmental level. The trend toward departmental computing is causing computing resources, including computer specialists, to be moved closer to the people who use them. Departmental computing is responsible for the emergence of several new computer specialist careers: **user liaisons, microcomputer specialists,** and **office automation specialists.**

The user liaison is a "live-in" computer specialist who coordinates all computer-related activities within a particular functional area served. The user liaison is familiar with computers and the functional area. The microcomputer specialist stays abreast of the latest micro hardware and software technology and helps implement this technology in user areas. The office automation specialist helps employees make effective use of office systems.

17–4 THE INFORMATION CENTER AND INFORMATION CENTER SPECIALISTS. An **information center** is a "hands-on" facility in which computing resources, including training, are made available to end users. **Information center specialists** provide three basic services: training, consulting, and software development.

17–5 OTHER CAREER OPPORTUNITIES: SERVICES, HARDWARE, SOFTWARE, AND EDUCATION. There are a host of computer-related career opportunities in addition to those in an information services department or a user group. These opportunities are found with commercial information services, hardware vendors, software vendors, and in the area of computer education.

The computer revolution is creating a tremendous demand for computer-related services. In response to this demand, a number of service organizations have emerged including **service bureaus, facilities management companies, turnkey companies** (or **system integrators**), consulting firms, data base services, and computer repair stores.

Computer system manufacturers produce the processor and usually some or all of the peripheral equipment. Leasing companies, referred to as the third party, buy computers and lease them for five or more years. **Plug-compatible manufacturers (PCMs)** make peripheral devices that can be attached directly to another manufacturer's computer. **Value-added resellers (VARs)** integrate the hardware and software of several vendors with their own software, then sell the entire package. Computer retail outlets have made it possible for customers to shop for computers as they would any other consumer product.

Hardware vendors that market and service hardware need marketing representatives to sell the products and systems engineers to support them once they have been installed.

Software houses produce and sell proprietary software packages. Such software is protected by copyright laws and is sold under a licensing agreement.

The demand for computer education has created a tremendous need for professors and instructors.

17–6 PROFESSIONALISM AND ETHICS. People whose jobs put them in contact with sensitive data can actually control events. This places even greater pressure on these people to conduct themselves as professionals. Certification programs, such as the **CDP, CCP, CSP, CISA,** and **CDE,** and professional societies help encourage professionalism.

A code of ethics provides direction for computer professionals and users so they apply computer technology responsibility.

17–7 CAREER MOBILITY AND COMPUTER KNOWLEDGE. Computer competency is a prerequisite of employment in many professions, and in a few more years it may well be a requirement in most professions.

 Review Exercises

Concepts

1. What is the difference between the job functions of development and maintenance programmers?
2. People of what job function would be involved in the selection and implementation of PBXs and front-end processors?
3. What type of programmer is usually associated with the technical support group? with the programming group?
4. What is the function of a user liaison?
5. Which job function accounts for all input to and output from a computer center?
6. Name four positions in the operations area.
7. Would every organization with an information services department have a data base administrator? Why or why not?
8. Describe the business of VARs.
9. Contrast the job of a systems engineer with that of a marketing representative. How do they complement each other?
10. What are the unabbreviated names for the following societies: SIM, DPMA, and EDPAA?
11. What are the uses of a computerized dialing system?
12. What are the three basic services provided by a typical information center?
13. What type of organization contracts with a client to install a complete system, including both hardware and software?
14. What is the function of the chief information officer?

Discussion

15. Of the jobs described in this chapter, which would you prefer? Why?
16. Some companies will have only one level of programmer or systems analyst, where other companies will have two, three, and even four levels. Discuss the advantages of having several levels for a particular position (Programmer I, Programmer II, and so on).

17. Do you feel that programmers and systems analysts should report to the same person or be organized into separate groups? Defend your answer.

18. Discuss the merit of systems analysts having programming experience.

19. Select five positions from the classified ad section of *Computerworld*. Describe what you feel would be appropriate experience and education requirements for each of the positions.

20. Relatively few computer professionals have any kind of certification. Is it really necessary?

21. Discuss the similarities shared by a company's information services function and its finance function.

22. Many, perhaps most, of the information services divisions do not have the luxury of full-time quality-control specialists. In their absence, who do you think handles the quality-control function?

Problem Solving

23. Revise the organizational chart of Figure 17–4 so only four people report to the director of information services.

24. The executive committee of Gabriel Industries, a medium-sized manufacturing company, prepared a long list of areas whose operations could be improved by the application of information technology. John Robson, manager of the computer services department, had these reactions to the list: (1) He agreed that the items on the list were valid; (2) he said that there were many other applications that could benefit from automation; and (3) he adamantly stated that the current resources of the computer services department were inadequate to implement the task force's recommendations, not to mention any other applications, within any reasonable time frame.

    John Robson's comments caused a stir among the executive committee members and they asked him for recommendations regarding the large backlog of potential computer applications. He suggested that corporate management encourage users themselves to implement smaller, locally functional applications on microcomputers. To facilitate user involvement in meeting their own information processing needs, he recommended the establishment of an information center.

    John Robson has asked you to perform the planning for the implementation of the information center for Gabriel Industries. Write a description of duties and responsibilities for the information center. List potential sources for acquiring the three people needed to staff the center. Describe the facilities (office space, hardware, software, and so on) required by the information center. In what ways do think top management can help to motivate users to develop their own applications?

 Self-Test (by section)

17–1 During the decade of the 1990s, the number of computer programmers is expected to increase. (T/F)

17–2 **a.** The librarian handles most of the training in an information services department. (T/F̲)

b. One of the responsibilities of an information services department is to act as an adviser to users regarding the interpretation of general corporate policy. (T/F̲)

c. Information services management must maintain a balance between being ~responsive~ to user information needs and being ~responsible~

d. The ~Systems Analyst~ analyzes, designs, and implements information systems.

17–3 **a.** The trend to departmental computing is causing more and more computer specialists to move to the user departments. (T̲/F)

b. Office automation specialist is a fancy name for a word processor. (T/F̲)

c. What job function is also called internal consultant or functional specialist: (a) programmer/analyst, (b̲) user liaison, or (c) CIO?

d. ~Microcomputer~ specialists are trained in the function and operation of microcomputers and related hardware.

17–4 The availability of information centers has resulted in an increase in the number of one-time user service requests received by the information services department. (T/F̲)

17–5 **a.** PCM stands for plug-compatible manufacturer. (T̲/F)

b. Turnkey companies are also called ~system integrators~.

c. What law is violated when an organization duplicates proprietary software without permission: (a) civil rights, (b) antitrust, or (c̲) copyright?

17–6 **a.** ~AFIPS~ is the umbrella organization for computer-oriented societies.

b. Professional societies are not legally obligated to expel members for code-of-ethics infractions. (T̲/F)

17–7 Computer competency is not yet a prerequisite of employment in any profession. (T/F̲)

Self-test answers.   17–1 T. 17–2 (a) F; (b) F; (c) responsive, responsible; (d) systems analyst. 17–3 (a) T; (b) F; (c) b; (d) Microcomputer. 17–4 F. 17–5 (a) T; (b) system integrators; (c) c. 17–6 (a) AFIPS; (b) T. 17–7 F.

Computers in Society:
Today and
Tomorrow

STUDENT LEARNING OBJECTIVES

▶ To put society's dependence on computers in perspective.

▶ To identify causes of illegal information processing activity.

▶ To identify and discuss controversial computer-related issues.

▶ To appreciate the scope and influence of computers in society.

▶ To identify possible computer applications of the future.

CHAPTER OUTLINE

 18–1   Information Technology: Can We Live without It?

Reaching the Point of No Return

Albert Einstein said that "concern for man himself and his fate must always form the chief interest of all technical endeavors." Some people believe that a rapidly advancing information technology exhibits little regard for "man himself and his fate." They contend that computers are overused, misused, and generally detrimental to society. This group argues that the computer is dehumanizing and is slowly forcing society into a pattern of mass conformity. To be sure, the age of information is presenting society with difficult and complex problems, but they can be overcome.

Information technology has enhanced our lifestyles to the point that most of us take it for granted. There is nothing wrong with this attitude, but we must recognize that society has made a real commitment to computers. Whether it is good or bad, society has reached the point of no return in its dependence on computers. Stiff business competition means their continued and growing use. On the more personal level, we are reluctant to forfeit the everyday conveniences made possible by computers. More and more of us find that our personal computers are an integral part of our daily activities.

Society's dependence on computers is not always apparent. For example, today's automobile assembly line is as computer-dependent as it is people-dependent: An inventory-management system makes sure that parts are delivered to the right assembly point at the right time; computer-controlled robots do the welding and painting; and a process-control computer controls the movement of the assembly line.

Turn off the computer system for a day in almost any company, and observe the consequences. Most companies would cease to function. Turn off the computer system for several days, and many companies would cease to exist. A company that helps other companies recover from disasters, Sunguard Recovery Services, estimates that a large bank would be out of business in two days if its computer systems were down. It estimated that a distribution company would last three days, a manufacturing company would last five days, and an insurance company would last six days. A University of Minnesota study examined victims of disasters that disabled computing capabilities. The study concluded that the probability of a victim company's long-term survival was low if it were unable to recover critical operations within 30 hours. Recognizing their dependence on computers, most companies have made contingency plans that provide for backup computers in case of disaster.

Give Up My Computer? Never!

Ask a secretary to trade a word processing system for a typewriter. Ask a physician for an alternative to a computer-controlled intensive-care unit. Ask an airline executive how long the organization could continue to operate without its on-line reservation system. Ask yourself if you would give up the convenience of remote banking at automatic teller machines.

Our dependence on food has evolved into the joy of eating gourmet food—and so it is or can be with information technology. Dependence is not necessarily bad as long as we keep it in perspective. However, we can't passively assume that information technology will continue to enhance the quality of our lives. It is our obligation to learn to understand computers so that we can better direct their application for society's benefit. Only through understanding can we control the misuse of information technology. We, as a society, have a responsibility to weigh the benefits, burdens, and consequences of each successive level of automation.

This electronics representative could do his job without his notebook PC. To do so, however, may impact his ability to be competitive. Realistically, he has become dependent on the processing capability and information provided by his PC.

18–2 Computers and the Law

Companies try to develop information systems and use the computer within the boundaries of any applicable law. Unfortunately, the laws are not always clear because many legal questions involving computers and information processing are being debated for the first time. To no one's surprise, computer law is the fastest growing type of law practice.

Laws governing computer and information processing are few, and those that do exist are subject to a variety of interpretations. At present, two federal laws address computer crime. They are limited, however, because they apply only to those computer systems that in some way reflect a federal interest. These laws make it a felony to gain unauthorized access to any computer system with a federal interest with the intent to obtain anything of value, to defraud the system, or to cause more than $1000 in damage. Although most states have adopted computer crime laws, they are only the skeleton of what is needed to direct an orderly and controlled growth of automation.

Existing federal and state laws concerning the privacy of personal information are being updated every year. At the same time new laws

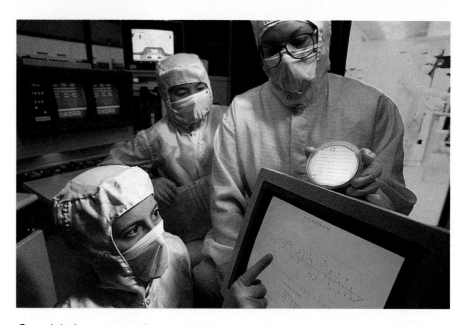

Copyright laws protect literature, music, the design of a silicon chip, and software. A sophisticated circuit design may be the result of a multimillion-dollar research effort.

are written. Current federal laws outline the handling of credit information, restrict what information the IRS can obtain, restrict government access to financial information, permit individuals to view records maintained by federal agencies, restrict the use of education-related data, and regulate the matching of computer files. States have or are considering laws to deal with the handling of social security numbers, criminal records, telephone numbers, financial information, medical records, and other sensitive personal information.

Although lawmakers recognize the impact of computers, legislation is slow in coming. Critics say that is because our lawmakers are reluctant to become computer-competent. But even with definitive legislation, prosecution of computer crimes becomes another issue. Prosecutors lack sufficient technical knowledge to prepare a case. A judge and jury understand the concept of armed robbery and have a sense of the appropriate punishment, but what about computer crimes? Sophisticated computer crimes can be extremely complex and may be well beyond the understanding of most prosecutors, judges, and jurors. Legislation must be enacted and prosecution issues resolved before the criminal justice system can begin to cope with computer crime.

Illegal Information Processing

Negligence The two main causes of illegal information processing are negligence and fraud. Negligence causes someone outside the organization to be unnecessarily inconvenienced, and it is usually a result of poor input/output control. For example, after she paid in full, a woman was

The accumulation of personal data has become a matter of concern to our information society. Whether you realize it or not, you are continuously contributing data about yourself to some computer systems. For example, when you buy or sell real estate, the transaction is recorded in a variety of data bases, including the one at this company that generates statistics and reports on real estate activity.

sent dunning notices continually and was visited by collection agencies for not making payments on her automobile. Although the records and procedures were in error, the company forcibly repossessed the automobile without thoroughly checking its procedures and the legal implications. The woman had to sue the company for the return of her automobile. The court ordered the automobile returned and the company to pay her a substantial sum as a penalty.

This is a clear case of a misinterpretation of a computer maxim—GIGO ("garbage in, garbage out"). GIGO does *not* stand for "garbage in, gospel out," as some people, who take the accuracy of computer output for granted, seem to think. The company blamed the incident on a mistake by the computer. The court stated that people enter data and interpret output and that the people affected should be treated differently from punched cards. *Trust in the infallibility of a computer does not constitute a defense in a court of law.* This incident points out the importance of careful systems design and exhaustive testing.

Fraud   The other area of illegal information processing is a premeditated or conscious effort to defraud the system. For example, a U.S. Customs official modified a program to print $160,000 worth of unauthorized federal payroll checks payable to himself and his co-conspirators. A 17-year-old high school student tapped into an AT&T computer and stole over $1 million worth of software. One person illegally transferred $10,200,000 from a U.S. bank to a Swiss bank. He probably would have gotten away with the money if he hadn't felt compelled to brag about it. These are all examples of fraud. Any illegal entry into a computer system for the purpose of personal gain is considered fraud. Over 50% of all computer frauds are internal; that is, they are committed by employees of the organization being defrauded. About 30% of those defrauding employees are computer specialists who work in information services departments.

The Privacy of Personal Information

More media and legislative attention has been focused on the issue of an individual's privacy than on computer crimes involving negligence or fraud. We as individuals have certain rights regarding the privacy of data or of information relating to us. However, these rights have yet to be uniformly defined by our lawmakers. In the absence of definitive legislative guidelines, the following principles are offered for consideration:

1. People should be made aware that data are being collected about them and made aware of how these data are to be used.
2. A person should be permitted to inspect his or her personal data and information.
3. A person should be permitted to supplement or clarify personal data and information.
4. Data and information found erroneous or irrelevant must be removed.
5. Disclosure of personal information should be limited to those with a need to know.
6. A log should be maintained of all people inspecting any individual's personal information.
7. Adequate safeguards must be in place to ensure the security of personal data and information (for example, locked doors, passwords).

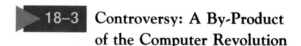

18–3 Controversy: A By-Product of the Computer Revolution

The computer revolution has generated intense controversy. Some of the more heated controversies are discussed here.

The Misuse of Personal Information

Sources of Personal Data The issue of greatest concern to the general public is the privacy of personal information. Some people fear that computer-based record-keeping offers too much of an opportunity for the invasion of an individual's privacy. There is indeed reason for concern. For example, credit-card users unknowingly leave a "trail" of activities and interests that, when examined and evaluated, can provide a rather comprehensive personal profile.

The date and location of all credit-card transactions are recorded. In effect, when you charge lunch, gasoline, or clothing, you are creating a chronological record of where you have been and your spending habits. From this information, a good analyst could compile a very accurate

These stockbrokers use computer-based systems to complete buy and sell orders. In so doing, they add name, address, and other personal information to the client data base. On average, each American is listed in about 50 government and 50 private-sector data bases. On a typical day, each person's name is passed between computers 6 times. People who are socially, economically, and politically active may be listed in hundreds of data bases.

picture of your lifestyle. For example, the analyst could predict how you dress by knowing the type of clothing stores you patronize. On a more personal level, records are kept that detail the duration, time, and numbers of all your telephone calls. With computers, these numbers easily can be matched to people. So each time you make a phone call, you also leave a record of whom you call. Enormous amounts of personal data are maintained on everyone by the IRS, your college, your employer, your creditors, your hospital, your insurance company, your broker, and on and on.

We hope that information about us is up-to-date and accurate. Unfortunately, much of it is not. Laws permit us to examine our records, but first we must find them. You cannot just write to the federal government and request to see your files. To be completely sure that you examine all your federal records for completeness and accuracy, you would have to write and probably visit each of the approximately 5800 agencies that maintain computer-based files on individuals. The same is true of computer-based personal data maintained in the private sector.

Violating the Privacy of Personal Information Most will agree that the potential exists for abuse, but are these data being misused? Some say yes. Consider the states that sell lists of the addresses of and data on their licensed drivers. At the request of a manager of several petite women's clothing stores, a state provided the manager with a list of all licensed drivers in the state who were women between the ages of 21 and 40, less than 5 feet 3 inches tall, and under 120 pounds. You be the judge. Is the sale of such a list an abuse of personal information?

Personal information has become the product of a growing industry. Companies have been formed that do nothing but sell information about people. Not only are the people involved not asked for permission to use their data, they are seldom even told that their personal information is being sold! A great deal of personal data can be extracted from public records. For example, one company sends people to county courthouses all over the United States to gather publicly accessible data about people who have recently filed papers to purchase a home. Mailing lists are then sold to insurance companies, landscape companies, members of Congress seeking new votes, lawyers seeking new clients, and so on. Those placed on the mailing list eventually become targets of commerce and special-interest groups.

The use of personal information for profit and other purposes is growing so rapidly that the government has not been able to keep up with abuses. Antiquated laws, combined with judicial unfamiliarity with computers, make policing and prosecuting abuses of the privacy of personal information difficult and, in many cases, impossible. (See the Computers and the Law section earlier in this chapter.)

Computer Matching   In computer matching, separate data bases are examined and individuals common to both are identified.

The focus of most computer-matching applications is to identify people engaged in wrongdoing. Federal employees are being matched with those having delinquent student loans. Wages are then garnisheed to repay the loans. In another computer-matching case, a $30 million fraud was uncovered when questionable financial transactions were traced to common participants. The Internal Revenue Service also uses computer matching to identify tax cheaters. The IRS gathers descriptive data, such as neighborhood and automobile type, then uses sophisticated models to create lifestyle profiles. These profiles are matched against reported income on tax returns to predict whether people seem to be underpaying taxes. When the income and projected lifestyle do not match, the return is audited.

Securing the Integrity of Personal Information   Computer experts feel that the integrity of personal data can be more secure in computer data bases than in file cabinets. They contend that we can continue to be masters and not victims if we implement proper safeguards for the maintenance and release of this information and enact effective legislation to cope with the abuse of it.

Computer Monitoring

One of the newest and most controversial applications of information technology is computer monitoring. In computer monitoring, computers continuously gather and assimilate data on job activities to measure worker performance. Today computers monitor the job performance of over 7 million American workers and millions more worldwide. Most of these workers interact with a mainframe computer system via terminals or work on a micro that is part of a local area network. Others work with electronic or mechanical equipment that is linked to a computer system.

Many clerical workers who use VDTs are evaluated by the number of documents they process per unit of time. At insurance companies, computer monitoring systems provide supervisors with information on the rate at which clerks process claims. Supervisors can request other information, such as time spent at the terminal and keying-error rate.

Computers also monitor the activities of many jobs that demand frequent use of the telephone. The number of inquiries handled by directory-assistance operators is logged by a computer. Some companies employ computers to monitor the use of telephones by all employees.

Although most computer monitoring is done at the clerical level, it is also being applied to higher-level positions such as commodities brokers, programmers, loan officers, and plant managers. For example, CIM (computer-integrated manufacturing) enables corporate executives to monitor the effectiveness of a plant manager on a real-time basis. At any given time executives can tap the system for productivity information, such as the rate of production for a particular assembly.

Workers complain that being constantly observed and analyzed by a computer adds unnecessary stress to their jobs. However, management is reluctant to give up computer monitoring because it has proved itself a tool for increasing worker productivity. In general, affected workers are opposing any further intrusion into their professional privacy. On the other hand, management is equally vigilant in its quest for better information on worker performance.

Anyone who records transactions on a computer system is a candidate for computer monitoring. A POS system has the potential to ascertain the average time required to service a customer with one item, with two items, and so on.

The "Cashless Society"

The growing number of *automatic teller machines* (ATMs) have made *electronic funds transfer* (EFT) very visible to the public. In EFT, money is transferred electronically from bank to bank, and from account to account, via computers. Each weekday, the financial institutions of the world use EFT to transfer over one trillion dollars—that's $1,000,000,000,000! Applications of EFT, such as ATMs and payroll transfer systems, are being implemented all around us. Some banks even offer *home banking* services that permit customers to pay bills and perform banking transactions via their personal computers without leaving home.

The debate rages on as we move closer to a cashless society. Is this a reasonable and prudent manner in which to handle financial transactions? In the future we may eliminate money and make the transition to a cashless society.

A first step toward a cashless society may be a universal *smart card* (smart, because of the tiny embedded microprocessor) to buy everything from candy bars to automobiles. Upon purchasing an item, a buyer would give the smart card, which serves as a *debit card*, to the seller. The seller would use the purchaser's card to log the sale on a *point-of-sale* (POS) terminal linked to a network of banking computers. The amount of the sale would then be transferred from the buyer's account to the seller's account. Smart cards are in common use throughout the world, especially in Europe. A number of American companies are using or experimenting with smart cards. (See the Emerging Technology box in Chapter 7: Smart Cards Pave the Way for a Cashless Society for more information on smart cards.)

How can expanded use of EFT be an advantage? EFT would eliminate the cumbersome administrative work associated with handling money and checks. It would also eliminate the need to carry money, eliminate rubber checks and counterfeit money, and minimize the possibility of error. It would provide a detailed record of all transactions. EFT would also eliminate the expense of making money. The cost of manufacturing a penny now exceeds the value of the coin!

The disadvantages are also worth noting. The critical issue is EFT's potential for the misuse of personal information. EFT generates a chronological record of all purchases. (See the discussion in the earlier section entitled The Misuse of Personal Information.) In effect, this type of system permits everything from a person's lifestyle to his or her location to be monitored. Opponents of EFT are also concerned about its vulnerability to crime.

Although the trend is toward more electronic funds transfer, some experts feel that EFT is about to reach its peak of acceptance. Others think that total EFT is inevitable by the turn of the century.

The Effects of Automation on Jobs

Concern over the effects of automation began two hundred years ago with the Industrial Revolution, and continues to this day. To many people, computers mean automation, and automation means loss of jobs. However, we should keep in mind that the Industrial Revolution created hundreds of new career opportunities and the computer revolution has done and will do the same.

There is no doubt that the emergence of information technology has resulted in the elimination of jobs involving routine, monotonous, and sometimes hazardous tasks. However, the elimination of these jobs has been offset by the creation of more challenging jobs. For the most part, people whose jobs have been eliminated have been displaced to jobs carrying greater responsibilities and offering more opportunities. It is common for bookkeepers to become systems analysts, for draftpersons to advance to computer-aided design, and for secretaries to become specialists in a myriad of computer applications from word processing to data management. This pattern is repeated thousands of times each month.

Automation will continue to eliminate and create jobs. Historically, advancement in technology has increased overall productivity in certain areas, thereby cutting the number of workers needed. In addition, a new wave of jobs is created in the wake of cutbacks in traditional areas. With the cost of labor increasing and the cost of computers decreasing, the trend toward the automation of routine activities will probably continue. However, to realize a smooth transition to an automated environment, industry and government must recognize that they have a social responsibility to retrain those who will be displaced to other jobs.

Presidential-Level Backing In 1992, President Bush called for a doubling of current government spending on information technology initiatives. Funding would be allocated in developing high-performance computing hardware and communications programs. A suggestion was made by the computer industry to explore and designate more funding to the development of software. D. Allan Bromley, the science and technology adviser for the President, made a statement concerning the President's request. He stated that in his opinion "there is no other single initiative that will have as widespread an impact on business, education, government, and society in general."

This laser cutting machine installed at a John Deere factory in Ottumwa, Iowa, helps the factory meet today's demands for flexible, low-volume manufacturing. The machine frees employees to focus on delivering consistent quality instead of concentrating on materials handling, machine setups, and other indirect labor. Such tasks take up time and increase costs without adding value.

The National Data Base

Many people have suggested that we use the computer technology to create a national data base, a central repository for all personal data for citizens. An individual would be assigned a unique identification number at birth. This ID number would replace the social security number, driver's license number, student identification number, and dozens of others.

A national data base would consolidate the personal data now stored on tens of thousands of manual and computer-based files. It could contain an individual's name, past and present addresses, dependent data, work history, medical history, marital history, tax data, criminal records, military history, credit rating and history, and so on. Proponents of the national data base point out that records are currently maintained but are redundant and often inaccurate or out-of-date. Therefore, they say, at least the national data base would be accurate and up-to-date.

A national data base has certain advantages. A national data base could provide the capability of monitoring the activities of criminal suspects; virtually eliminating welfare fraud; quickly identifying illegal aliens; making an individual's medical history available at any hospital in the country; taking the 10-year census almost automatically; and generating

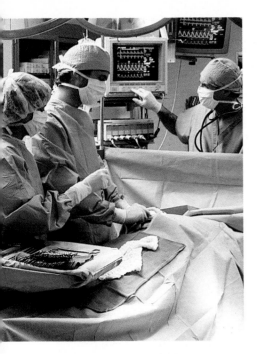

Thousands of hospitals, clinics, and doctors' offices maintain patient medical records. The medical community would like to see critical patient data made a part of national data base. In this way if you are in an auto accident 1000 miles from home, the emergency room doctor can immediately find out such information as your blood type and the drugs that might cause an allergic reaction.

valuable information. Medical researchers could isolate geographical areas with inordinately high incidences of certain illnesses. The Bureau of Labor Statistics could monitor real, as opposed to reported, employment levels on a daily basis. The information possibilities for a national data base are endless.

Those who oppose the national data base call it impersonal and an invasion of privacy. They believe that any advantages are more than offset by the potential for abuse of such a data base.

The creation of a national data base is a complex undertaking, the social implications notwithstanding. It is unlikely that we will see such a data base in this century. However, with the growing concern about welfare fraud, tax evasion, crime, and the influx of illegal aliens, the national data base may be an increasingly appealing alternative for the future.

Computer Crime

There are many types of computer crimes, ranging from the use of an unauthorized password by a student to a billion-dollar insurance fraud. It is estimated that each year the total money lost from computer crime is greater than the sum total of that taken in all robberies. In fact, no one really knows the extent of computer crime because much of it is either undetected or unreported (most often the latter). In those cases involving banks, officers may elect to write off the loss rather than announce the crime and risk losing the good will of their customers.

Computer crime requires the cooperation of an experienced computer specialist. A common street thug does not have the knowledge or the opportunity to be successful at computer crime. The sophistication of the crime, however, makes it no less criminal.

Computer crime is a relatively recent phenomenon. As a result, legislation, the criminal justice system, and industry are not yet adequately prepared to cope with it. (See the Computers and the Law section earlier in this chapter.) Only a handful of police and FBI agents in the entire country have been trained to handle cases involving computer crime. And when a case comes to court, few judges have the background necessary to understand the testimony.

Recognizing the potential severity of computer crime, the legal system and industry are trying to speed up precautionary measures. Some say a catastrophe on the same level as that of the Three Mile Island nuclear power plant failure is the only thing that will wake up industry and government.

Another problem is criminal activities of overzealous hackers. These "electronic vandals" have tapped into everything from local credit agencies to top-secret defense systems. The evidence of unlawful entry, perhaps a revised record or access during nonoperating hours, is called a **footprint**. Some malicious hackers leave much more than a footprint—they infect the computer system with a *virus*. Viruses, which were discussed in Chapter 16, "System Implementation," can wreak havoc on a computer system's data bases and software, sometimes causing millions of dollars in damage. People are concerned that these criminals are glorified by the media creating heroes for a new generation of criminals.

Everything associated with computers is growing rapidly—the number of computer professionals, robotics, EDI, expert systems, and *computer crime*. Computer crimes can be grouped into seven categories.

- *Crimes that create havoc inside a computer.* Computer viruses, Trojan horses, and logic bombs fall into this category. A *computer virus* is a program that takes control of the victim's system, with results that range from exasperating (the display of a harmless political message) to tragic (the loss of all programs and data). Furthermore, computer viruses can copy themselves from system to system when unsuspecting users exchange infected disks. A *Trojan horse* is any seemingly useful program that hides a computer virus or logic bomb. A *logic bomb*, in contrast, is a set of instructions that are executed when a certain set of conditions are met. For example, a disgruntled employee might plant a logic bomb to be "exploded" on the first Friday the thirteenth after his or her record is deleted from the personnel data base.

- *Crimes that involve the manipulation of computer systems and their data.* Embezzlement and fraud fall into this category. Embezzlement concerns the misappropriation of funds, and fraud involves obtaining illegal access to a computer system for the purpose of personal gain.

  The *salami technique* for embezzlement requires that a Trojan horse (unauthorized code hidden in a legitimate program) be planted in the program code of a financial system that processes a large number of accounts. These covert instructions cause a small amount of money, usually less than a penny, to be debited periodically from each account and credited to one or more dummy accounts. A number of less sophisticated computer-manipulation crimes are the result of *data diddling*. Data diddling is changing the data, perhaps the "ship to" address, on manually prepared source documents or during on-line entry to the system.

- *Crimes that involve telecommunications.* Illegal bulletin boards (for example, ones that distribute confidential access codes and passwords), misuse of the telephone system, and any unauthorized access to a computer system, including

eavesdropping (tapping into communications channels), fall into this category.

Unauthorized entry to a computer system is achieved in a variety of ways. The most common approach is *masquerading*. People acquire personal identification numbers (PINs) and personal information that will enable them to masquerade as an authorized user. The *tailgating* technique is used by company outsiders to gain access to sensitive information. The perpetrator simply begins using the terminal or computer of an authorized user who has left the room without terminating his or her session.

The more sophisticated user might prefer building a trap door, scanning, or superzapping. A *trap door* is a Trojan horse that permits unauthorized and undetected access to a computer system. Trap doors are usually implemented by an insider during system development, usually a programmer. *Scanning* involves the use of a computer to test different combinations of access information until access is permitted (for example, by stepping through a four-digit access code from 0000 to 9999). *Superzapping* involves using a program that enables someone to bypass the security controls.

- *Crimes that involve the abuse of personal information.* The willful release or distribution of personal information that is inaccurate would fall into this category.

- *Crimes that involve negligence.* Companies that employ computers to process data must do so in a responsible manner. Irresponsible actions that result in the deletion of a bank account or the premature discontinuation of electrical service would fall into this category. Lax controls and the availability of sensitive information invite scavenging. *Scavenging* is searching for discarded information that may be of some value on the black market, such as a printout containing creditcard numbers.

- *Crimes that support criminal enterprises.* Money laundering and data bases that support drug distribution would fall into this category.

- *Crimes that involve the theft of hardware or software.* Software piracy, theft of computers or computer components, and the theft of trade secrets belong in this category.

A few hackers and computer professionals have chosen computer crime as a profession. But the threat of computer crime may be even greater from managers and consultants because they know how the systems operate, and they know the passwords needed to gain access to the systems.

18-4 Information Technology Applications of the Future

It seems as if the computer is everywhere—yet we are only scratching the surface of possible computer applications. The outlook for innovative, exciting, and beneficial computer applications is bright, very bright indeed.

Expectations and Reality

Intense media coverage has given the computer novice the impression that bed making, dishwashing, domestic robots are just around the corner; that computer-controlled organ transplants are almost perfected; and that computers have all the answers! To be sure, we are making progress in leaps and bounds, but we have a long way to go before such applications are feasible. Nevertheless, these rising expectations are a challenge to computer professionals to deliver.

Of course, no one can see into the future, but we can extrapolate from trends and our knowledge of current research. This section paints a picture of some applications of information technology that are sociologically, economically, and technologically feasible within the next decade.

Information Networks

As the percentage of homes with micros increases, so does the potential for *information networks*. Information networks, a number of which exist today, provide certain services to an end user through a communications link to a microcomputer. Several currently available services provided by information networks are described in Chapter 8, "Networks and Networking." The two-way system provides the end user with information (for example, airline flight schedules) and permits the end user to enter data (such as reservations for airline flights).

The four components of an information network are the central computer, the data base, the network, and the microcomputers. The central computer system is accessed by end users who desire a particular service. The data base contains data and screens of information (perhaps a graphic display of a refrigerator with price and delivery information) that are presented to users. As microcomputers proliferate, a greater variety of information networks will be made available to more and more people. Even now, microcomputers that can access these networks are available in many airplanes and hotel rooms.

Hotel guests can communicate with their homes, companies, or virtually anyone else through the use of computers in their rooms. They can obtain theater or airline tickets, shop or order gifts, scan restaurant menus, and even play video games. In a few years, all major hotels will

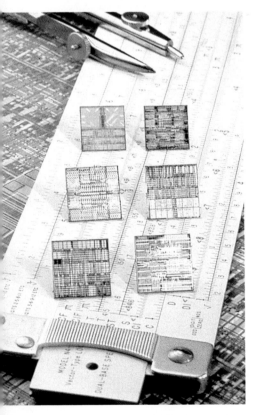

Although the state of the art of technology enables these tiny chips to hold 4 million bits, it's not enough. Our largest and fastest computers can simulate the wing, the fuselage, or the tail of an airplane in flight, but that's not enough. Aerospace engineers want the capability of simulating an entire airplane in flight. Their expectations are representative of people in other professions who already have plans for computers that are not yet developed.

Commercial information networks, such as Prodigy, offer services that range from airline reservations, to electronic mail, to games. Today over a million people subscribe to these networks. By the turn of the century, tens of millions will incorporate information networks into their everyday routine.

provide their guests with access to microcomputers and information networks.

Commercially available information networks have an endless number of yet untapped applications. Let's take real estate as an example. Suppose you live in Tucson, Arizona, and have been transferred to Salt Lake City, Utah. It is only a matter of time before you will be able to gain access to a nationwide information network that maintains an up-to-date listing of every home in the country that is for sale. Here is how it will work: You will enter your purchase criteria: Salt Lake City, Utah; $120,000 to $180,000; no more than one mile from an elementary school; double garage; and so on. The system will then present pictures and specifications of those homes that meet your criteria.

Communications

The telephone as we know it will probably disappear. In the relatively near future, the function of the telephone will be incorporated into our home computers so we can not only hear but also see the person on the other end of the line. Moreover, we will be able to pass data and information back and forth as if we were sitting at the same table.

Most of us will have ready access to microcomputers, whether at the office or on the road. From virtually anywhere, we will be able to use our microcomputers to read 50 different newspapers, turn on the heat at home, call a taxi, order groceries, buy shares of stock, or make hotel reservations.

Thousands of mobile workers could benefit from using a computer—if only the computer were lighter, freed their hands, and didn't tether them to a desk or a power outlet. Now a new generation of wearable computers promises to extend the trend begun by laptop, notebook, and pen-based computers.

Prototypes of wearable computers, long a staple of science fiction, are already being promoted by Japan's NEC Corporation. In an effort to create truly personal computers that meld a computer and its user, NEC designers have divided the PC's components into cable-connected modules that fit into headsets, drape across shoulders, hang around the neck, and fasten around the waist, forearm, or wrist. Lightweight (about two pounds or less), the components would be covered in soft plastic and strapped on with Velcro.

Many of these prototypes combine existing or emerging technologies to create customized PCs for specific types of workers. The TLC (Tender Loving Care) PC for paramedics is a good example. At an accident scene, speech-recognition software would let the paramedic dictate symptoms and vital signs into a slender microphone hanging from a headset. The computer, draped across the medic's shoulders like a shawl, would compare this data to a CD-ROM medical directory in the shoulder unit. The computer would then project possible diagnoses and suggested treatments onto the headset's goggle-type display. The TLC unit would also improve upon the two-way radio medics now use to communicate with emergency-room doctors. Instead of describing symptoms over a two-way radio, medics could use a trackball-operated video camera and body sensor strapped to their palm to *show* doctors the patients' condition. The video and additional data would be beamed to the doctors by a satellite link on the medics' back. Headphones would let the medics get feedback and additional advice from the waiting doctors.

Another of NEC's wearable PCs, geared toward clerks who take inventory, would drape their forearms with gauntlet-like terminals containing an optical scanner and bar-code reader. A shoulder unit with a small fold-down LCD display would let clerks compare inventory records to data stored in CD-ROM. Wearable PCs geared toward journalists would feature necklace-like units or electronic belts with fold-down keyboards and display screens.

Given the industry's ongoing success in miniaturizing electronics and developing more powerful but lightweight batteries, NEC projects the first commercially viable wearable PCs could appear by the late 1990s. However, Grid Systems Corporation, pioneer of the pen-based computer, isn't waiting. It recently introduced the Palmpad, a rugged 2.8-pound computer designed to be worn on a belt, slung over a shoulder, or strapped to a wrist. The MS-DOS–based Palmpad comes with 2 MB of RAM, batteries that can run up to 8 hours, a small LCD display, and a slot for high-capacity memory cards. And to increase the user's comfort, its removable battery pack can be worn around the waist, easing pressure on the user's wrist.

THE FUTURE OF PCs?   At NEC a handful of engineers and designers are creating what they believe to be the future of PCs—wearable PCs. Their objective is to blend the machine with the body. Perhaps by the twenty-first century, the PC will become as much an essential part of one's wardrobe as an indispensable business tool. The PC store of the future will be like a designer boutique, offering styles that fascinate the eye and boggle the mind.

We are only beginning to tap the potential of our PCs as tools for communication. For example, PCs, multimedia, and the telephone system can be integrated such that we can speak with and see one another while working on the same spreadsheet template. This capability surely will give telecommuting a boost.

The television of the not-too-distant future will function as a terminal and enable limited two-way communication via a keyboard. You will be able to request that the stock market reports be subtitled across the screen while you continue to watch your favorite program. Newscasters will be able to sample the thinking of tens of thousands of people in a matter of minutes. After they ask the questions, we at home will respond on our keyboards. Our responses will be sent immediately to a central computer for analysis, and the results reported almost instantaneously. In this way, television news programs will keep us abreast of public opinion on critical issues and the feeling toward political candidates on a day-to-day basis.

In the Office

The traditional letter may never become obsolete, but electronic mail will become an increasingly popular alternative, because most of us will have our own microcomputers at home and at work. To prepare and send a letter, an executive will dictate—not to a secretary, but to a computer! The executive's words will be transcribed directly into text, without key entry. The letter will then be routed to appropriate destinations via electronic mail. The recipient of the letter can request that it be displayed at a microcomputer or read using synthesized speech.

With professionals spending a greater percentage of their working day interacting with the computer, look for the telecommuting and the electronic cottage concept to gain momentum (see Chapter 8, "Networks and Networking"). At least a part of the work of most professionals will be done at home. For many professionals, their work is at their finger tips, whether at home or the office. Look for the emergence of telecommuting and cottage industries to alter the demographics of cities. Less frequent trips to the office will surely encourage urban spread. Many won't need to go to the office at all. They might prefer living in small towns hours from the nearest metropolitan area.

A Peek at the Crystal Ball

What kind of impact will information technology have on manufacturing, retail, financial services, and other industries? Let's look into the crystal ball.

Manufacturing   Manufacturing companies, especially those that are labor-intensive, face growing competition from international markets. In response to this challenge, James Baker, of General Electric, noted that American industry is confronted with three choices: ". . . automate, migrate, or evaporate." Companies can *automate*, thereby lowering costs and increasing productivity. They can *migrate* (move) to countries that offer less expensive labor. Or they can *evaporate*. Most have elected to automate, even with the blessing of organized labor. As one labor leader put it: "If we don't do it, I'm convinced we'll lose the jobs anyway."

Industries throughout the world are rebuilding to take full advantage of the potential of automation. This new Sheet Metal Center at Boeing employs automated materials handling and computer-controlled machines. When fully operational, the plant will have the capacity to fabricate up to 11 million parts per year.

With the trend toward greater use of automation, we can anticipate an increase in the number of industrial robots (see Chapter 14, "Applications of Information Technology"). As the smokestack industries become more "high-tech," the complexion of their work force will change. There will be a shift of emphasis from brawn to brains. A few unstaffed plants already exist, and this number will grow. These radical changes are a by-product of our transition from an industrial society to an information society. Traditional jobs will change or be lost forever, but new and, it is hoped, more challenging jobs will emerge to replace them.

Retail Information networks will enable us to do our shopping electronically. Instead of walking down the aisle of a grocery store or thumbing through stacks of shirts, we will be able to use our personal computer in conjunction with an information network to select and purchase almost any retail item. The items selected will be automatically picked, packaged, and possibly delivered to our doorstep. This information service will help speed the completion of routine activities, such as grocery shopping, and leave us more time for leisure, travel, and the things we enjoy.

Financial Services The overwhelming acceptance of automatic teller machines has spurred the trend toward more electronic funds transfer (EFT). Over the next decade, transaction documents, such as checks and credit-card purchase slips, will begin to disappear. Monies will be electronically transferred at the time of the purchase from the seller's account to the buyer's account. Total EFT will require an enormously complex communications network that links the computers of all financial institutions with virtually all businesses. Such a network is technologically

The manner in which we obtain information is changing rapidly. How often have you wandered through a department store looking for someone to help you? In the near future, the nearest interactive kiosk should be able to answer most of your questions. (Left) A diagram shows you where to find the sports department. (Right) When you get there, you can request specifics about a particular product (availability, price, color options, and so on).

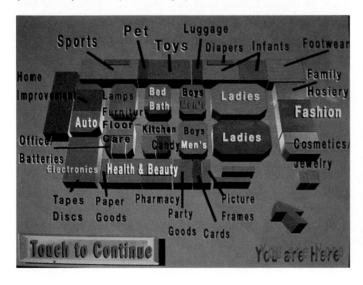

Relatively few aircraft are equipped with the Airshow Video Information System at this time, but this is changing rapidly. Airshow answers many questions frequently asked by travelers regarding the aircraft's flight path, estimated time of arrival, and related information in a real time, graphically exciting video format. In the photo, the display shows the aircraft flying over York, Pennsylvania, en route to New York City.

and economically feasible today, but sociologically we are a few years away.

Publishing   Certainly books, magazines, newspapers, and the printed word in general will prevail for casual reading and study. However, soon publishers will offer *soft-copy* publishing as an alternative to *hard-copy* publishing. We'll be able to receive books, magazines, and newspapers in electronic format, perhaps via data communications on our home computer or on a disk. A few specialized computer trade magazines are available now on disks, but in a few years a wide variety of magazines will be distributed via data communications or disks.

Can you imagine a bookstore without books? It's possible! With customized printing on demand, you will be able to browse through virtually any current book from a terminal. Then, if you wish to purchase the book, it will be printed and bound while you wait!

In the short term, CD-ROM (see Chapter 6, "Data Storage and Organization") is expected have the greatest influence on the publishing industry. Publishers can offer over 250,000 pages of text in the form of a single CD-ROM disk. Libraries, already cramped for space, are considering the possibility of providing many reference materials, such as encyclopedias and journals, in the form of CD-ROM.

Transportation   Someday soon computer-based automobile navigation systems will be standard equipment on cars. There are already enough satellites in the sky for an on-board automobile navigation system to obtain a "fix" establishing the location of the car. You will be able to call up appropriate regional or city maps from on-board optical laser disk storage. The car's location will be noted on a video display of a road map, and you will be able to plot your course and track your progress. Look for on-board computers in autos to continuously receive en route traffic density information and suggest alternate routes accordingly. The on-board computer will do much more than tell you where you are—it also will tell you how to get there.

By now you are probably saying that this Buck Rogers–type application is a bit farfetched. Well, prototypes of automobile navigation systems are now being tested—and they work!

Entertainment   How about interactive soap operas? Yes, because of the two-way communication capabilities of your television/terminal, you can be an active participant in how a story unfolds. The soaps will be shot so that they can be pieced together in a variety of ways. Imagine—you can decide whether Michelle marries Clifton or Patrick!

It won't be long before the rough drafts of television scripts are written by computers. Many weekly television shows have a formula plot. For instance, heroes are presented with a problem situation. They confront the problem, they get in trouble, they get out of trouble, stick the bad guys, and live to do it again next week. Formula plots lend themselves nicely to computer-produced rough-draft scripts. The computer systems already will have the names of the key characters on file. The systems also will have dialogues for a variety of situations. The names of non-regulars (such as the bad guys) will be generated randomly by the computer. The script writers will enter a story-line sketch, then the computer will piece together dialogues and scenes within the restrictions of the show's formula plot and the story line. The script writers will then refine the draft script.

Sculptors may someday find an interesting use for computers. For example, a sculptor will be able to create three-dimensional "sketches" on a computer, much the same way an engineer designs a part using computer-aided design (CAD). The computer will activate a robot-like sculpting tool that will rough out the general shape of the figure. The sculptor will then add the creative touches that turn a piece of clay into a work of art.

Health Care Expert systems have already benefitted physicians by helping them diagnose physical illnesses (see Chapter 13, "The MIS and Decision Support Systems"). In the near future we can anticipate expert systems that help diagnose and treat mental illnesses and emotional problems as well. Psychologists and psychiatrists will continue to work with patients in the classical manner, but with the added advantage of a "partner." This partner will be able to tap a vast storehouse of knowledge and recommend everything from lines of questioning to diagnosis and treatment.

Diagnosis will take another giant leap when scanners begin to make prognoses of illnesses directly. Today CT and MR scanners produce pictures of the inside the body. The next generation of scanners will interpret the pictures as well.

Encouraging research leads us to believe that the computer will play a vital role in tomorrow's medical "miracles." We are still a few steps away, but lifesaving computer implants are inevitable. These tiny computers will control mechanical devices that can replace organs that have ceased to function. Other medical research has given paraplegics renewed hope that they may someday walk again with the assistance of a computerized nervous system. Those who are physically challenged can look forward to improved mobility and independence. Sophisticated prostheses will be activated by voice, motion, muscle activity, breathing, and even the blinking of an eye.

Medical and technical researchers have dared to contemplate integrating computers and the brain. That is, eventually we may electronically connect tiny computer implants to the brain to enhance the brain's computational and factual-recall capabilities.

Government The emergence of computer-enhanced photography enables us to break out the finer details in photographs. With computer-enhanced photography, the headlines in a newspaper can be read from a photograph taken 150 miles above the earth (or Mars or Jupiter). Its immediate applications include law enforcement and military intelligence.

Local, state, and federal elections might not require an army of volunteers. Politicians might not have to worry about low voter turnout on a rainy Election Day. We will eventually record our votes through home or business microcomputers. Such a system will encourage greater

The automated traffic-control system in Auckland, New Zealand, is one of many examples of how municipal governments use computers to better serve their citizens.

voter participation although, of course, security and voter authenticity will be a concern. One possible solution would be to ask voters to enter their social security number and a voter registration security code known only to the voter. A few years later we won't need to carry cards or remember numbers; each voter's identity will be validated when the system reads our fingerprint and our voiceprint. All we will have to do to identify ourselves will be to enter our voiceprint by speaking a few words and our fingerprint by placing our finger near an optical scanner.

Education Computer systems are revolutionizing the education process. For example, as students learn via computer-based instruction (CBT), they can request visual reinforcement from hundreds of still and moving pictures stored on optical laser disks. There is truth to the old saying that "one picture is worth a thousand words."

Computers also are beginning to play a more active role in the education of learning-disabled children. Current human-resource limitations do not permit the luxury of constant one-on-one attention for these children. However, in between group and one-on-one sessions, a computer system capable of responding to a wide variety of inputs can be dedicated to each child. For example, computers complement the kinesthetic (touch and feel) approach to dyslexia (impaired reading ability). Children with dyslexia can engage in interactive reading that offers immediate feedback and reinforcement. At present, we are only beginning to tap the computer as an educational tool.

Computers have the potential of enabling nationwide uniform testing for elementary and secondary students. With uniform learning stan-

The computer-based alternative to the traditional book has two very inviting qualities. We can interact with it and the illustrations can be made dynamic (show movement). Such books are already proving successful in preschools and elementary schools. It's only a matter of time before college students begin to purchase disks rather than bound books.

dards for each subject at each level, students will be able to advance from one grade to the next on the basis of achievement rather than age. Computer-based uniform testing has another advantage. The system will monitor not only student progress but also the effectiveness of individual teachers and schools.

The Future of Artificial Intelligence

We have access to artificial sweeteners, artificial grass, artificial flowers—why not artificial intelligence? To some extent, we do! We introduced the field of artificial intelligence (AI) in Chapter 1, "The World of Computers." If you will remember, artificial intelligence can be divided into four categories:

- Knowledge-based and expert systems (discussed in Chapter 13, "The MIS and Decision Support Systems")
- Natural languages (discussed in Chapter 10, "Programming Concepts and Languages")
- Simulation of human sensory capabilities (discussed in Chapter 5, "Input/Output Devices")
- Robotics (discussed in Chapter 14, "Applications of Information Technology")

The concepts associated with each of these areas of AI research have been discussed in previous chapters, but where is AI headed in the future?

Expert systems already have begun to make a major impact on the way people in the business community make decisions. Today there are hundreds of expert systems, most of which were developed at great expense to service a particular company. In a few years, there will be thousands of expert systems. In the professional environment, physicians in every specialty will have at least one expert system at their disposal. During the 1990s, some doctors will accept expert systems as a critical medical instrument and bring them into the examining room. Any person who routinely does some type of screening, such as a bank loan officer or a recruiter, will do so with the help of an expert system. At home we will be able to check an expert system out of the local library to help us to decorate our homes.

Natural language software enables computer systems to accept, interpret, and execute instructions in the native language of the end user, typically English. At present, some relatively primitive natural languages enable a user-friendly interface of corporate data bases and expert systems. But as with most other software, we must use programming and the selection of menu options to tell the computer what to do. In the future, look for natural language interfaces to accompany virtually all user-oriented software, from word processing to inventory modeling packages. Instead of working through a series of menus to specify the layout of a word processing document, the user might enter, "Set the left and right margins at 1½ inches and 1 inch and double space the document."

One area of AI research involves computer simulation of human sensory capabilities. This area focuses on equipping computer systems with the capabilities of seeing, hearing, speaking, and feeling (touching). These artificial intelligence capabilities already are possible with current technology. "Intelligent" machines that can simulate human sensory

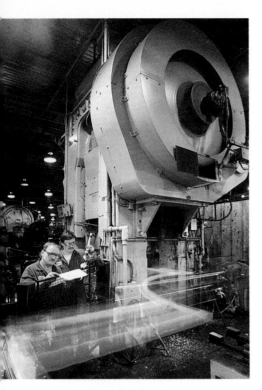

A number of expert systems are being created for the manufacturing environment. These workers frequently request assistance from an expert system when repairing this robot forge.

Robotics is one of the fastest growing areas of artificial intelligence. This robot helps assemble computers at an IBM plant.

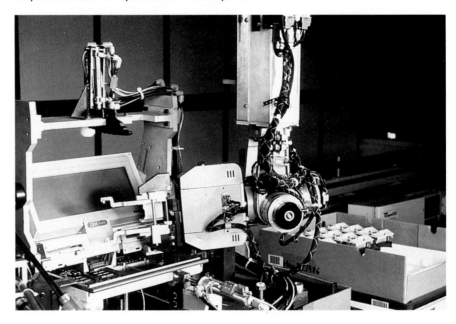

capabilities have the ability to establish a link with their environments. This link has opened the door to a number of real-world applications. Today most data are keyed in from a keyboard. Within the next decade, much of the data will be entered verbally. For example, mail-order customers will be able to verbalize order information over the telephone. The verbal information will be interpreted by a speech-recognition system and entered directly to the computer for processing. As we move into the twenty-first century, keys may be replaced by voiceprints, fingerprints, veinprints, and other unique human attributes that easily can be interpreted by computers. AI research is continually enhancing the abilities of computers to simulate human sensory capabilities. In the near future, we will have meaningful verbal conversations with computers. These computers will be able to talk, listen, and even smell the roses!

Industrial robots can be "taught" to perform almost any repetitive manipulative task, such as painting a car, screwing on a bolt, moving material, and even complex tasks, such as inspecting a manufactured part for defects. However, most existing robots are stationary—they are programmed to operate within a well-defined work area. Advances in vision systems will enable robots to move about the work area just as people do, probably within the decade of the 1990s.

On the more personal level, AI will eventually revolutionize personal computing. Within this century, the PC will become part of our portable personal paraphernalia, just like the pocket comb, compact, and billfold. Its size will enable it to be packaged as a piece of jewelry, like a wristwatch or a necklace. AI technology will be incorporated in tomorrow's PCs to give them the ultimate in the user-friendly interface. Primary input will be voice, and output will be a speech synthesizer and a miniature fold-out display. Of course, each PC will be configured with a variety of expert systems, depending on the needs of its user.

18–5 Oversights: Are We Keeping Pace with the Technology?

For whatever reasons, business, government, and education have elected not to implement computer applications that are well within the state of the art of computer technology. Many cost-effective systems are working in the laboratory but have not been implemented in practice. The implementation of these potentially beneficial systems has lagged behind the state of the art of computer technology by 5 to 10 years. Some "oversights" are presented below.

Several experimental homes feature computer-controlled lighting, temperature, and security systems. Such systems would start the coffee maker so we could awaken to the aroma of freshly brewed coffee. They would even help with paying the bills. This technology is available today and is relatively inexpensive if properly designed and installed during construction. In any case, such a system would pay for itself in a couple of years through energy savings alone.

Although some sophisticated computer-controlled medical equipment is now being used, relatively few physicians take advantage of the

Jokers Go Wild Beware! A book called *Stupid PC Tricks* has been published for the PC enthusiast who might wear water-squirting lapel flowers. The book contains programs that trick the user into thinking his or her computer is malfunctioning or contaminated by a virus. Before you jump to the conclusion that your whole system is on the blitz, check with your practical joker "friends"!

Some say that we are not tapping the full potential of computers in business—this insurance adjuster being the exception rather than the rule. By using a cellular laptop, he has eliminated the need for intermediate paperwork and the delays associated with communication by mail.

information-producing potential of the computer to improve patient care. They have expert systems that can help them diagnose diseases, drug-interaction data bases that can help them prescribe the right drug, and computer-assisted searches that can call up literature pertinent to a particular patient's illness. All the applications have the potential of saving lives.

A cashless society is technologically and economically possible. In a cashless society, the amount of a purchase would be transferred automatically from the purchaser's bank account to the vendor's bank account. Thus billing, payment, and collection problems would be eliminated, along with the need to write checks and to remember to mail them.

Why have these cost-effective and potentially beneficial computer applications not been implemented? Among the reasons are historical momentum, resistance to change, limited education, and lack of available resources. In the case of domestic-control systems, it is probably a matter of education, both of the builder and the homeowner. In the case of computer diagnosis of illness, some physicians are reluctant to admit that the computer is a valuable diagnostic aid. In the case of the cashless society, concerns about invasion of privacy are yet to be resolved.

These and thousands of other "oversights" will not be implemented until enough people have enough knowledge to appreciate their potential. This is where you come in!

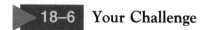 18–6 Your Challenge

Having mastered the contents of this book and this course, you are now poised to exploit the benefits of the computer in your personal and business lives. You also have an appreciation of the scope and impact of computers on society, both now and in the future. This course, however, is only the beginning. The computer learning process is ongoing. The dynamics of a rapidly advancing computer technology demands a constant updating of skills and expertise. Perhaps the excitement of technological innovation and ever-changing opportunities for application is part of the lure of computers.

By their very nature, computers bring about change. With the total amount of computing capacity in the world doubling every two years, we can expect even more dramatic change in the future. The cumulative effects of these changes are altering the basic constructs of society and the way we live, work, and play. Terminals and microcomputers have replaced calculators and ledger books; electronic mail speeds communication; word processing has virtually eliminated typewriters; computer-aided design has rendered the T-square and compass obsolete; computer-based training has become a part of the teaching process; EFT may eventually eliminate the need for money; on-line shopping is affecting consumer buying habits . . . and the list goes on.

We as a society are, in effect, trading a certain level of computer dependence for an improvement in the quality of life. This improvement in the way we live is not a foregone conclusion. It is our challenge to harness the power of the computer and direct it toward the benefit of society. To be an active participant in this age of information, we as a society and as individuals must continue to learn about and understand computers. Charles Lecht, an outspoken advocate of computers, is fond of saying, "What the lever is to the arm, the computer is to the mind."

Never before has such opportunity presented itself so vividly. This generation, *your generation*, has the technological foundation and capability of changing dreams into reality.

Francis Bacon said, "Knowledge is power." You now have a base of computer knowledge. Combine this knowledge with your innate creative abilities and you are poised to make a significant impact on whatever field you choose to pursue, be it in the business world, health care, government, education, or the arts.

 Important Term and Summary Outline

footprint

18–1 INFORMATION TECHNOLOGY: CAN WE LIVE WITHOUT IT? Society has reached a point of no return with regard to dependence on computers. Business competition demands the use of computers. We are also reluctant to give up those personal conveniences made possible by computers. Only through understanding can we control the misuse or abuse of computer technology.

18–2 COMPUTERS AND THE LAW. An information system should be developed to comply with any applicable law. At present the laws that govern the privacy of personal data and illegal computer-based activity are inadequate, but these laws are being revised and expanded. Therefore, the privacy of data and the possibility of fraud or negligence should be a consideration in the design of every information system.

18–3 CONTROVERSY: A BY-PRODUCT OF THE COMPUTER REVOLUTION. The emotions of both the general public and the computer community run high on computer-related issues. The abuse of personal information is perhaps the issue of greatest concern. Other issues include the merits of computer monitoring, the growing use of electronic funds transfer, the effects of automation on jobs, the implementation of a national data base, and coping with computer crime. The evidence of unlawful entry to a computer system is called a **footprint.**

18–4 INFORMATION TECHNOLOGY APPLICATIONS OF THE FUTURE. The number and variety of computer applications is expected to grow rapidly in the coming years. In the near future, we can anticipate an even greater variety of services available through information networks; telephones integrated into terminals; the widespread acceptance and use of electronic mail; unstaffed manufacturing facilities; electronic shopping; less use of cash; soft-copy publishing; automobile navigation systems; create-your-own-story soaps on television; robot sculptors; computer-controlled artificial limbs; voting at home via microcomputers; nationwide uniform student testing; and AI (artificial intelligence), which encompasses expert systems, natural languages, simulation of human sensory capabilities, and robotics.

18–5 OVERSIGHTS: ARE WE KEEPING PACE WITH THE TECHNOLOGY? Although society has been the beneficiary of a wide variety of computer applications, much more can be done with existing technology. Historical momentum, resistance to change, limited education, and lack of resources have slowed the implementation of technologically feasible computer applications.

18–6 YOUR CHALLENGE. The computer offers us the opportunity to improve the quality of our lives. It is our challenge to harness the power of the computer and direct it to the benefit of society.

 Review Exercises

Concepts

1. What are the four components of an information network?
2. Has society reached the point of no return with regard to its dependence on computers?
3. Most computer monitoring takes place at which level of activity: clerical, operational, tactical, or strategic?
4. Briefly describe how the business letter of the future will be composed and delivered.
5. What is the objective of computer matching?
6. What are the two main causes of illegal processing?
7. Name four human sensory capabilities that can be simulated by computers.
8. Describe two ways in which computers are contributing to the improved quality of health care.
9. What are the four categories of artificial intelligence research?

Discussion

10. Based on your knowledge of the capabilities of computers, speculate on at least three applications that we can expect within the next 10 years.

11. Why would a judge sentence one person to 10 years in jail for an unarmed robbery of $25 from a convenience store and another to 18 months for computer fraud involving millions of dollars?

12. List and discuss applications, other than those mentioned in the text, of a national data base.

13. Do you feel society's dependence on computers is good or bad? What would you suggest be done to improve the situation?

14. Describe what yesterday would have been like if you had not used the capabilities of computers. Keep in mind that businesses with which you deal rely on computers and that many of your appliances are computer-based.

15. Argue for or against a cashless society.

16. Why do you suppose our laws governing computers and information processing are inadequate?

17. Discuss the kinds of personal information that can be obtained by analyzing a person's credit-card transactions during the past year.

18. Describe problems that must be overcome to prosecute computer criminals in a court of law.

19. Compare your perspective on computers today with what it was four months ago. How have your feelings and attitudes changed?

Problem Solving

20. Explain how computers can be used to measure worker performance for any two of the following jobs: high school English teacher, fast food restaurant manager, an automobile assembly line worker, a U.S. senator, or a CPA.

21. Your company is experimenting with placing small microprocessors in charge cards as a means of thwarting theft and fraud. You have been asked to prepare a one-page report to management on how the smart card would be used during the processing of a charge transaction. Include in the report a description of the data that are input to, output from, permanently stored in, and processed by the smart card.

22. You are the spokesperson for a large metropolitan bank that was a recent victim of a successful $25-million electronic heist. You call a news conference to explain. What would you say?

23. You have just been appointed automation adviser to the President of the United States. Your first assignment is to assess the abuses of the privacy of personal information. Besides an overall assessment, the President wants specific examples of abuses.

 Self-Test (by section)

18–1 **a.** It would take at least a month to retool a typical automobile assembly line so it could function without computers. (T/**F**)

⭐ **b.** If the number of computer applications continues to grow at the present rate, our computer-independent society will be dependent on computers by the year 2000. (T/**F**)

18–2 **a.** Gaining unauthorized access to any computer system with a federal interest with the intent of defrauding the system is a: (a) violation of public ethics, (b) misdemeanor, or (c) felony?

b. Many legal questions involving computers and information processing are yet to be incorporated into the federal laws. (T/F)

c. Trust in the infallibility of a computer does not constitute a defense in a court of law. (T/F)

18–3 **a.** It is estimated that each year the total monetary loss from computer crime is greater than the sum total of all robberies. (T/F)

b. In computer monitoring computers continuously gather and assimilate data on worker activities for the purpose of measuring worker performance.

c. The number of federal government agencies that maintain computer-based files on individuals is between: (a) 50 and 100, (b) 500 and 1000, or (c) 5000 and 10,000?

d. The evidence of unlawful entry to a computer system is called a footprint.

18–4 **a.** The magazine-on-a-disk has been discussed but is beyond the state of the art. (T/F)

b. Prototypes for on-board automobile navigation systems will be ready for testing by the turn of the century. (T/F)

c. The abbreviation for artificial intelligence is: (a) artell, (b) AI, or (c) AIG?

d. Most existing industrial robots are stationary or they are programmed to operate within a well-defined work area. (T/F)

18–5 A cashless society is technologically and economically possible. (T/F)

18–6 The total computing capacity in the world is increasing at slightly less than 5% per year. (T/F)

Self-test answers.   18–1 (a) F; (b) F. 18–2 (a) c; (b) T; (c) T. 18–3 (a) T; (b) computer monitoring; (c) c; (d) footprint. 18–4 (a) F; (b) F; (c) b; (d) T. 18–5 T. 18–6 F.

An MIS Case Study

Appendix Overview

In this appendix, a variety of MIS and business concepts are discussed and illustrated in a case study. The primary objective of this case study is to demonstrate the work and information flow of an integrated MIS within the context of a business environment. The case study also sets the stage for discussion and problem solving. The case study centers on BrassCo Enterprises, a fictitious medium-sized manufacturer of free-standing, brass coat racks. BrassCo, as well as its people, are composites of real companies, real situations, and real people. Its systems, methods, and planning mirror that of other successful businesses.

A–1 BrassCo Enterprises: Background Summary

This appendix presents a case study with diagrams and supporting discussions that describe an integrated management information system (MIS) for BrassCo Enterprises, a light manufacturing company. BrassCo was founded in 1873 in Topeka, Kansas. For three decades BrassCo specialized in decorative brass candelabra. The candelabra market began a sharp decline as the electric light gained acceptance. At the turn of the century, management opted to discontinue its line of candelabra in favor of a line of high-quality brass coat racks. BrassCo coat racks are fixtures in hotels, restaurants, fine homes, and other buildings throughout the world. In 1953, the family-owned BrassCo Enterprises went public and is now owned by shareholders from every walk of life.

BrassCo management has adopted a simple entrepreneurial philosophy: Produce a limited line of high-quality consumer products for which there is relatively little competition. In keeping with its philosophy, BrassCo still makes only coat racks and only in four models: the Crown, Monarch, Curio, and Souvenir.

- *Crown.* The Crown is the flagship product. The polished-brass Crown can hold 24 coats and 12 umbrellas.
- *Monarch.* The Monarch, a smaller version of the Crown, can accommodate 12 coats and 6 umbrellas.
- *Curio.* The Curio, introduced in 1984, is BrassCo's most recent product. In contrast with the simple lines of the Crown and Monarch, the Curio is very ornate. It holds 24 coats and 12 umbrellas.
- *Souvenir.* The Souvenir is a 12 coat/6 umbrella version of the Curio.

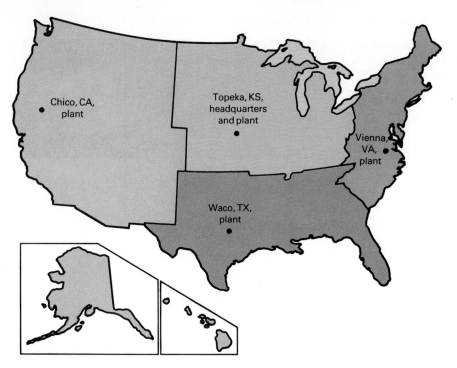

FIGURE A–1 BrassCo Headquarters and Plant Sites

BrassCo's Size and Organizational Structure

BrassCo is a $150 million (annual sales) company with about 1200 employees nationwide. Except for 40 field sales representatives, all employees work out of the Topeka, Kansas, headquarters office, the primary manufacturing facility at Topeka, or one of the three regional assembly plants: Waco (Texas), Chico (California), and Vienna (Virginia). All components for all products are manufactured in Topeka. The coat racks are assembled at each of the four plant sites. Also, each plant site serves as a *regional distribution center* and a *regional sales office* for all BrassCo products (Figure A–1).

Figure A–2 illustrates the basic structural organization of BrassCo. BrassCo is classically organized into four *line* divisions and one *staff* division. The four line divisions are the Accounting Division; the Personnel Division; the Operations Division, which includes manufacturing, distribution, research and development (R&D), and purchasing; and the Sales and Marketing Division. The Computer and Information Services Division, commonly abbreviated as CIS, provides services to all areas of corporate operation. All division heads are vice presidents and report directly to the chief executive officer (CEO) and president, *Preston Smith*. The corporate staff, which includes legal affairs, public relations, and other support groups, also reports to the CEO. The func-

tion and operation of CIS and the four functional divisions are described briefly.

- *Computer and Information Services Division (CIS)*. The vice president of the Computer and Information Services (CIS) Division, *Conrad Innis*, is charged with the support of all BrassCo Enterprises information processing requirements that are consistent with corporate objectives.
- *Finance and Accounting Division*. The head of the Finance and Accounting Division, *Monroe Green*, oversees the Finance and Accounting departments. The Accounting Department collects and manipulates monetary data to provide information that reflects BrassCo's monetary activity. The Finance Department seeks to optimize BrassCo's cash flow.
- *Personnel Division*. The vice president of the Personnel Division, *Peggy Peoples*, has the responsibility for all personnel accounting functions. Miss Peoples' division hires people to meet work force requirements and provides services to individuals and departments regarding personnel benefits, compensation, and other personnel matters. The department also maintains a skills inventory and does the background work for internal training sessions.
- *Operations Division. Otto Manning*, the vice president of the Operations Division, sees that the products are made and delivered to customers. The plant managers in Topeka, Chico, Waco, and Vienna report to the manager

of Manufacturing and Distribution, who, in turn, reports to Otto Manning. Associated with each plant is a regional distribution center for all BrassCo products. Managers of the Research and Development Department and the Purchasing Department also report to Mr. Manning.

■ *Sales and Marketing Division.* *Sally Marcio,* the vice president of the Sales and Marketing Division, is responsible for the activities of the Sales and Marketing departments. BrassCo relies exclusively on field sales representatives and telemarketing personnel to sell its products. The Sales Department field reps work out of the four regional sales offices (southern, northern, western, eastern) and call on thousands of retailers and wholesalers throughout the country. The Marketing Department is concerned primarily with making consumers aware of the products BrassCo has to offer.

Details of how these divisions interact with one another via integrated computer systems (for example, information flow) are illustrated and discussed later in this appendix.

The intensity of computer and information processing activity is very heavy in companies that seek to take full advantage of automation's potential. BrassCo, being one of these companies, has assigned a user liaison to work directly with each of the four "functional area" vice presidents. The user liaison is a "live-in" computer specialist who coordinates all computer-related activities within a particular division. The user liaison is intimately familiar with the functional area (for example, marketing, accounting, and so on) as well as the technical end of computers and information processing. The user liaison is the catalyst for new systems development and coordinates system conversions.

A–2 The Integrated Management Information System

The four functional divisions at BrassCo Enterprises (Finance and Accounting, Personnel, Operations, and Sales

FIGURE A–2 BrassCo Organizational Chart

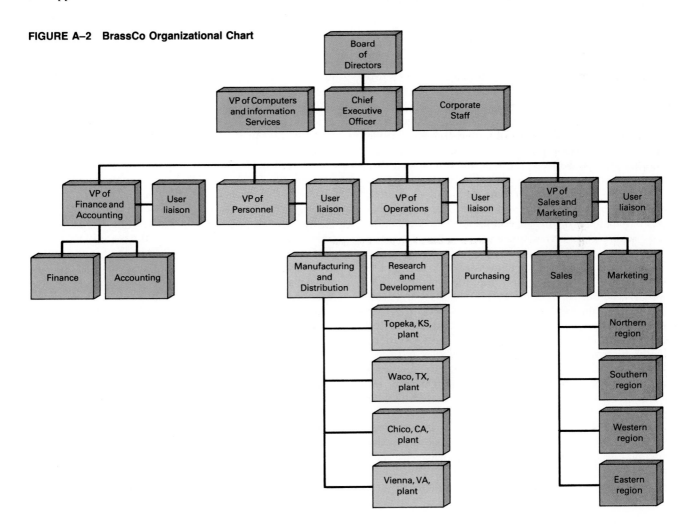

and Marketing) work together as a unit to accomplish the goals of the corporation. Each division is very much dependent on information derived from the others. In this section we'll take a *top-down view* of BrassCo's overall management information system. To do this, we'll start at the "top" (general overview) and examine a diagram that illustrates the basic information flow between the four divisions. Later in this appendix, we'll move "down" the ladder and take a closer look (greater detail) at the information flow within each of the four divisions. The design tool used to graphically illustrate the flow of information, at both the overview and detailed levels, is the data flow diagram, or DFD. The DFD technique is described in Chapter 15, "Analysis and Design of Business Information Systems."

Strategic-Level Information Flow

The CIS Division compiled the "MIS overview" of Figure A–3 to provide top management with an overview of the information flow within BrassCo Enterprises. The MIS overview diagram also provides documentation of BrassCo's information systems.

In the "business system" model presented in Figure 13–1 in Chapter 13, "The MIS and Decision Support Systems," the corporate resources (money, materials [including facilities and equipment], people, and information), the corporate functions, and the products are shown to interact with a variety of *entities* (employees, suppliers, customers, and so on), both within and outside of a company. These interactions, as well as the basic information flow between the four functional areas, are graphically portrayed in the overview data flow diagram of Figure A–3. These interactions are further expanded, or "exploded," in tactical- and operational-level DFDs in the remainder of this appendix.

The MIS overview in Figure A–3 highlights the interdependence between the four line divisions at BrassCo. For example, the Finance and Accounting Division receives purchase orders from the Operations Division, accounts receivable data from the Sales and Marketing Division, and pay and benefits data from the Personnel Division. In turn, the Finance and Accounting Division provides cost information to the Operations Division, gross sales information to the Sales and Marketing Division, and information regarding the division's work force requirements to the Personnel Division. Information flows to and from the other three divisions are illustrated in Figure A–3.

The two entities internal to BrassCo are *employees* and *managers* (see Figure A–3). The *employees* entity encompasses all employees, including managers. The *managers* entity includes managers at the operational, tactical, and strategic levels. The interaction between

BrassCo's integrated MIS and the employees entity generally falls into the areas of pay, benefits, and training. The interaction between the MIS and the managers entity is primarily in the areas of management inquiries, reports, and directives. For example, in the Sales and Marketing Division, management routinely makes inquiries regarding the progress of sales of certain products. The system also supplies forecasts of potential sales. These forecasts eventually become input to the Operations Division. There are many external entities from which the BrassCo MIS receives input and to which it must provide output.

The BrassCo Network

Through the early 1980s, the prevailing thought at BrassCo was to take advantage of the economies of scale and *centralize* all computer-based information processing in the Computer and Information Services Division. Conrad Innis convinced BrassCo's management group that information processing can be more effective and responsive if computer *hardware* (usually micros and minis), *data*, *software*, and in some cases, *personnel* are moved physically closer to the people who use these resources. To do this, he suggested a move toward distributed processing. Otto Manning concurred, saying, "With distributed processing, users control their 'information' destiny." Distributed processing is introduced in Chapter 2, "Micros, Minis, Mainframes, and Supercomputers."

At BrassCo, computer systems are arranged in a computer network, with each system connected to one or more other systems. At the headquarters location in Topeka, BrassCo has *functionally* distributed processing systems in the Finance and Accounting Division, the Sales and Marketing Division, and the home office plant. These are supported by people in CIS. *Geographically* distributed processing systems are located at each of the three plant/distribution center sites in Waco, Chico, and Vienna. Each of the remote plant sites is supported by a small staff of computer professionals. All six distributed systems are minicomputers with similar configurations.

The host computer system at Topeka serves as the hub of BrassCo's computer network, maintains the integrated data base, and services all areas of BrassCo operation. The distributed processing systems can function as part of the BrassCo computer network, or, since they are entirely self-contained, they also can operate as standalone systems. BrassCo's network encompasses over 400 terminals, about half of which are micros. Through the terminals and PCs, users can access the integrated data base supported on the host or one or more of the local data bases supported on the distributed minis.

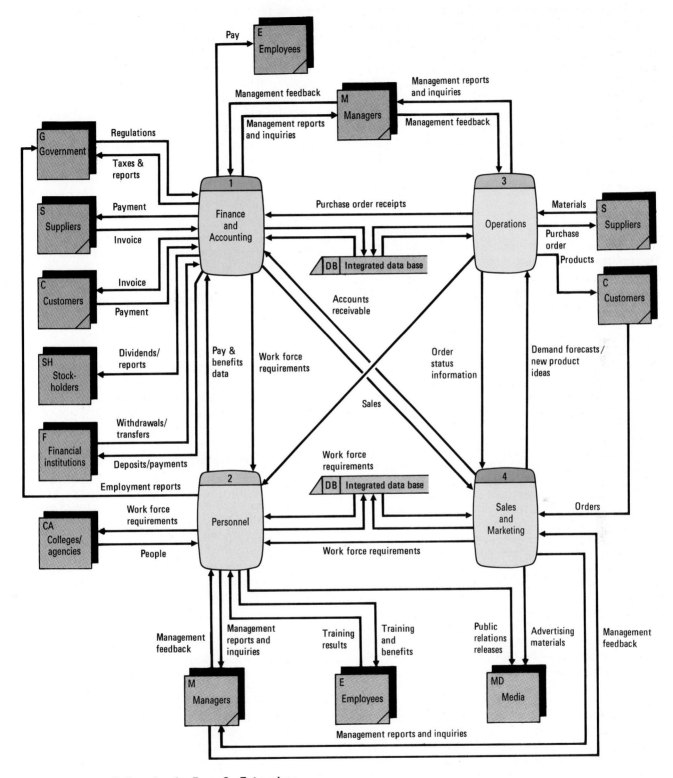

FIGURE A–3   MIS Overview for BrassCo Enterprises

The Integrated Corporate Data Base

The only data storage (the open-ended boxes in DFD diagrams) in Figure A–3 is BrassCo's integrated data base. The data base symbol is repeated to simplify the presentation of the DFD. The diagonal line on the left end of the data storage symbols indicates that the data storage is repeated elsewhere in the DFD.

To explain the concept of an integrated data base, we need to back up a few years and discuss BrassCo's data base prior to 1985. At that time, BrassCo had several dozen traditional flat files, each designed to meet a specific user group's requirements. When a file was designed and created, very little thought was given to how it would benefit BrassCo as a whole. As a result, many very similar, but different, files were created. For example, basic customer data were collected and maintained in separate files for the headquarters sales office, for the Distribution Department, for the Accounting Department, and for the Customer Service Department. Imagine, when customer data changed (for example, the name of the purchasing agent), each file would have to be updated separately!

Conrad Innis, the vice president of the CIS Division, recognized that data redundancy is costly. When he first joined BrassCo, he said, "data redundancy can be minimized by designing an integrated data base to serve BrassCo as a whole, not a single department. To do this we'll need database management system (DBMS) software." DBMS software concepts are discussed in detail in Chapter 9, "System Software and Platforms."

BrassCo first installed DBMS software in 1986 and has upgraded it several times since. The four categories of data included as part of BrassCo's integrated data base are *manufacturing/inventory*, *customer/sales*, *personnel*, and *general accounting*. The Technical Support Department of CIS is responsible for maintaining the integrated data base. BrassCo employees have access to all or part of the data base, depending on their need to know.

BrassCo's integrated data base provides its managers with enormous flexibility in the types of reports that can be generated and the types of on-line inquiries that can be made. Otto Manning, the vice president of operations, said recently that "the greater access to information provided by BrassCo's integrated data base enables me to make better decisions. As a result, we are able to produce a quality product at less cost than our competitors."

The Four Major Information Systems in BrassCo's MIS

It is no coincidence that the four major information systems in BrassCo's MIS correspond to the four functional divisions at BrassCo (see Figure A–3). BrassCo's MIS is an on-line, interactive, menu-driven system that puts data processing and information gathering at the finger tips of end users. The functional components of BrassCo's MIS are

FACS The Finance and Accounting Control System (Process 1 of MIS: Finance and Accounting)

PERES The Personnel Resource System (Process 2 of MIS: Personnel)

PICS The Production and Inventory Control System (Process 3 of MIS: Operations)

SAMIS The Sales and Marketing Information System (Process 4 of MIS: Sales and Marketing)

All the MIS component systems share a common data base, thereby eliminating much of the data redundancy that plagues other nonintegrated companies.

Review Exercises (Sections A–1 and A–2)

Discussion

1. Would you classify BrassCo's computer network as a star network or a hybrid network? Explain.

2. The trend at BrassCo is to distributed processing. Besides processing, what else is distributed?

3. The only functional division at BrassCo that does not have at least one distributed minicomputer system is the Personnel Division. Discuss possible reasons for not implementing a distributed system in the Personnel Division.

4. Conrad Innis, the VP of the CIS Division, would like to see a terminal or PC on the desktop of every white-collar worker at BrassCo. Some workers simply don't want one. Should they be excluded from Mr. Innis' plan? Explain.

5. CIS personnel use data flow diagrams to illustrate information flow within BrassCo. Why do you think they chose data flow diagrams over flowcharts?

Problem Solving

6. In Figure A–3, BrassCo's MIS is logically organized into four major processes. Suggest and justify an alternative organization that would involve five, six, or seven major processes.

7. BrassCo's full-scale support of an on-line, integrated MIS has made it possible for managers, administrative personnel, and programmers to work at home on their own PCs. BrassCo permits selected professional employees the flexibility of telecommuting up to one day a week. However, only 20% of these

people routinely take advantage of the opportunity to telecommute. Conrad Innis, the VP of CIS, feels that telecommuting is a boon to productivity and would like to see more people doing it. Suggest approaches that Mr. Innis could use to encourage greater telecommuting.

8. BrassCo established an Information Systems Policy Committee to set priorities among major information systems projects. Suggest criteria that the Information Systems Policy Committee might use to set priorities for major information systems development projects.

9. All user liaisons are in Topeka. Plant managers outside of Topeka have requested that user liaison positions be approved for the Chico, Vienna, and Waco locations. Top management refused the request and asked plant managers to use existing staff to deal with the need. What would you suggest that the plant managers do?

10. Describe the information flow between BrassCo Enterprises and all levels of government.

11. Describe the information flow between BrassCo Enterprises and its suppliers and customers.

12. Describe the information flow between BrassCo Enterprises and those financial institutions with whom it has business relations.

13. Describe the information flow between BrassCo Enterprises and those colleges/agencies with whom it has business relations.

14. Describe at least one system interaction with each of these external entities: government (state only), suppliers, customers, and stockholders.

A–3 The Finance and Accounting Information System

In 1956, BrassCo's management recognized that accounting was the obvious place to begin automating administrative activities. The tasks were repetitive, they involved numerous calculations, and they required the periodic storage and retrieval of data.

BrassCo's administrative activities have continued to evolve with the technology. Today, the Finance and Accounting Division has a sophisticated system it proudly calls the Finance and Accounting Control System, or FACS (pronounced *fax*). FACS was developed in-house by CIS in close cooperation with the Finance and Accounting Division. The systems analysts, accountants, and financial people on the team decided to divide the system into five logical subsystems (see Figure A–4). The subsystems are not necessarily aligned with particular departments because FACS is an integrated system designed to support the organization's needs as a whole.

Notice that each of the four components of the BrassCo MIS are numbered 1, 2, 3, and 4. The numbering scheme is used in data flow diagrams to identify subordinate processes. Since the Finance and Accounting process (FACS) is numbered "1," the first-level subordinate systems are identified as 1.1, 1.2, 1.3, and so on. The five subsystems are

1.1 Asset Management
1.2 Receipt Control
1.3 Disbursement Control
1.4 Financial Planning
1.5 Financial Reporting

Perhaps the best way to explain the operation of FACS is to focus on the interaction between these five subsystems and their interaction with the external (for example, financial institutions) and internal (for example, managers) entities (see Figure A–4). All subsystems interact frequently with the integrated data base, but some of these interactions are omitted in Figure A–4 so that the information flow between the subsystems is more visually apparent.

Asset Management (1.1)

Just as data are input to and output from a computer system, money is input to and output from the Asset Management Subsystem (see Figure A–4). Money is the common denominator at BrassCo and in the business world in general. The Asset Management Subsystem releases *funds* and takes in funds as needed. The funds, of course, are kept in various financial institutions. BrassCo's accounting and financial people are responsible for ensuring that enough liquid funds are on hand to meet the ongoing operational needs of the company.

Funds received from the Receipt Control Subsystem (1.2), primarily payments from customers, are deposited with financial institutions. Funds are withdrawn and distributed to the Disbursement Control Subsystem (1.3) so that these funds can be used to meet BrassCo's ongoing financial obligations. Since the Asset Management Subsystem does most of the interaction with financial institutions, the periodic payments for bonds and loans are made through the Asset Management Subsystem rather than through the Disbursement Control Subsystem.

The Asset Management Subsystem periodically generates *asset utilization reports* as input to the Financial Planning Subsystem (1.4). In turn, the Financial Planning Subsystem feeds the Asset Management Subsystem with *asset demand forecasts*. Based on the demand forecasts, the Asset Management Subsystem does the processing required to ensure that liquid funds are made available to meet short- and long-term obligations.

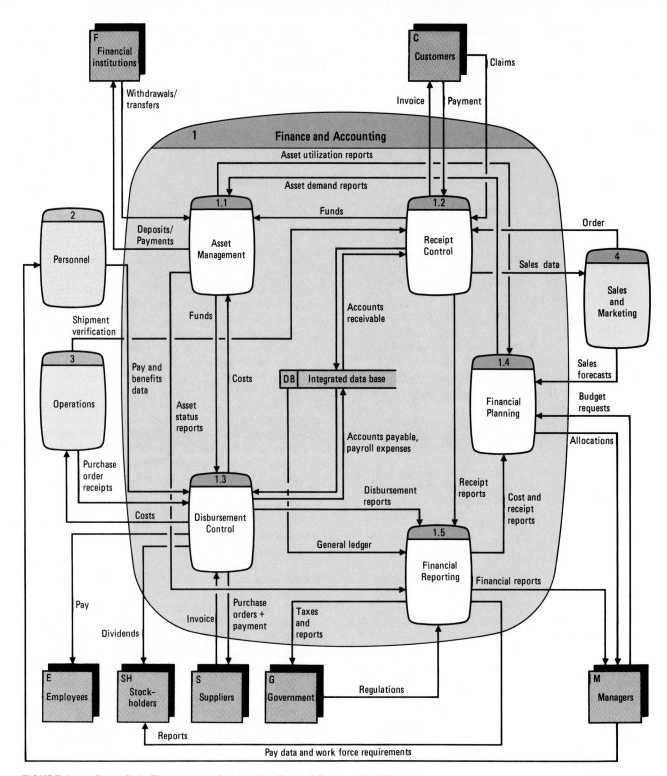

FIGURE A–4   BrassCo's Finance and Accounting Control System (FACS)
*This data flow diagram is the explosion of the finance and accounting (1) process of the
MIS overview data flow diagram of Figure A–3.*

Data generated by the Asset Management Subsystem become part of the integrated data base and are used by the Financial Reporting Subsystem (1.5) to produce BrassCo's financial statements.

Receipt Control (1.2)

The primary function of the Receipt Control Subsystem (see Figure A–4) is the *accounts receivable* application. Briefly, the Sales and Marketing Division is responsible for getting the order, the Operations Division is responsible for the manufacture and delivery of the order; and the Finance and Accounting Division is responsible for collecting for the order. The accounts receivable application keeps track of money owed the company on charges for products sold or services rendered (primarily the maintenance of products). When a BrassCo customer purchases goods or services, the customer record in the integrated data base is updated to reflect the charge.

When an *order* is verified within the Sales and Marketing Information System (SAMIS), order information is automatically recorded on the customer record and an *invoice*, which reflects the balance due, is sent to the customer. Upon receipt of *payment*, the amount due is decreased by the amount of the payment in the data base.

Management relies on the Receipt Control Subsystem (accounts receivable) to identify overdue accounts. Reports are generated that "age" accounts to identify those customers whose accounts are overdue by more than 30 days, 60 days, or 90 days. As Monroe Green, the VP of finance and accounting, puts it: "Those accounts that are 30 days overdue, we call and remind; those that are 60 days overdue, we notify that shipment of orders has been suspended; those that are 90 days overdue go on our deadbeat list and we take legal action."

BrassCo's FACS system still handles traditional data processing activities, such as aging of accounts and producing invoices, but it also provides management with tremendous flexibility to retrieve the information it needs. For example, BrassCo can provide customers with a variety of discounts to encourage their timely payment. Management and operational-level personnel have access to the information they need to do their jobs right. Customer credit histories are on-line and the data are up-to-the-minute. The FACS system can provide sales and marketing managers with *sales analysis reports* by multiple criteria. That is, they can request analysis by salesperson, territory, product, and so on. Because FACS is integrated, each *accounts receivable transaction* becomes an automatic entry in the general ledger portion of the integrated data base.

Disbursement Control (1.3)

The Disbursement Control Subsystem (see Figure A–4) ensures that all external creditor entities (except financial institutions) and employees are paid promptly. The primary applications in this subsystem are *accounts payable* and *payroll*.

Accounts payable. BrassCo purchases everything from paper clips to 18-wheelers on credit. The accounts payable application is the other side of the accounts receivable application. That is, an *invoice* from a supplier company's accounts receivable system becomes input to BrassCo's accounts payable application. When BrassCo receives an invoice, the accounts payable application generates a *check* and adjusts the balance owed. Of course, BrassCo's accounts payable application is carefully designed to take advantage of available discounts for prompt payment.

Purchase orders are generated in every department, but the Operations Division generates most of them. The purchase order is a flag to the Disbursement Control Subsystem to expect an invoice from a supplier. When the invoice is received from the supplier and receipt of the item is verified by the ordering department on the integrated data base, payment is then authorized and the supplier is sent a check.

Like accounts receivable transactions, accounts payable transactions are automatically fed to the general ledger application. The features of BrassCo's accounts payable application are numerous. It has an audit program to check entries. Invoices can be selected interactively by date or vendor. For any given invoice, the system computes the optimal discount strategy. The *invoice aging report*, the *purchase journal*, and a variety of other timely reports help managers to control purchased inventory and overhead expenses.

Payroll. The payroll application at BrassCo is a combined effort between the Personnel Division and the Finance and Accounting Division. The Personnel Division is responsible for the benefits program and for wage and salary administration. Prior to each pay period, the people in the Personnel Division verify pay and benefits data on the integrated data base. The mechanics of producing and distributing the payroll checks are handled by the Disbursement Control Subsystem in the Finance and Accounting Division. The two primary outputs of the payroll application are the *payroll check and stub*, which are distributed to the employees, and the *payroll register*, which is a summary report of payroll transactions. These transactions, of course, are logged automatically on the general ledger portion of the integrated data base.

The payroll application handles all calculations associated with gross pay, taxes, and user-defined deductions. The payroll application is capable of generating a variety of management reports, such as the *federal tax summary report* and the *retirement contribution summary report*.

Any disbursement, be it pay, dividends, or payment for goods or services, is noted in the appropriate record(s) in the integrated data base. Summary and detailed *disbursement reports* are input to the Financial Reporting Subsystem (1.5).

Financial Planning (1.4)

The Financial Planning Subsystem (see Figure A–4) operates in support of the budgeting process. Each year BrassCo's financial planners, in cooperation with management, must decide how the company's revenues can be allocated to over 400 accounts.

BrassCo's accounting is done on a calendar-year basis, so the budgeting process begins during the late summer and, if all goes well, takes effect at the beginning of the new year. During a prescribed period, managers enter their *budget requests*, with line-item detail, into the Financial Planning Subsystem from their terminals. Concurrent with the preparation of budget requests, the Sales and Marketing Division prepares a *forecast of sales* for the coming year. The Financial Planning Subsystem helps to translate these sales into *projected revenues*.

Managers often spend months preparing their departmental budgets for the coming year. To aid in this task, the *budget* application provides each manager with historical information on past line-item expenditures (for example, salaries, office equipment, office supplies, and so on). Based on this information and projected budget requirements, each manager can make budget requests for the next fiscal year.

Financial planners and top management match requests for funds against projected revenues. At BrassCo, and at other companies, managers invariably ask for more than they need, knowing full well that they will never get what they request. Eventually, a workable budget is established.

Financial Reporting (1.5)

The Financial Reporting Subsystem (see Figure A–4) includes the *general ledger* application—the glue that integrates all the other accounting applications. In the not-too-distant past, accountants manually posted debits and credits for each account in a ledger book. This is how today's electronic system got the name *general ledger*. Other "account" applications (accounts receivable, accounts payable, payroll, and so on) are sources of financial transactions and feed data to the general ledger application.

The general ledger application records every monetary transaction that occurs within BrassCo. The payment of a bill, an interdepartmental transfer of funds, the receipt of payment for an order, a contribution to an employee's retirement fund—all are examples of monetary transactions. The general ledger system keeps track of these transactions and provides the input necessary to produce BrassCo's *financial statement*.

For the purposes of accounting, BrassCo is divided into 14 general accounting categories, such as current assets, current liabilities, cost of goods sold, and so on. These, in turn, are subdivided into as many accounts as are needed to reflect monetary flow accurately within BrassCo. Monetary transactions are recorded as a debit or a credit to a particular account. The *balance sheet*, one of two major elements of BrassCo's financial statement, reflects a summary of these accounts at the end of a particular day. The other major element of the financial statement is the *profit and loss statement*. Often called the "income statement," the profit and loss statement reflects how much BrassCo makes or loses during a given period, usually a quarter or a year.

The financial planners at BrassCo routinely tap into the Financial Reporting Subsystem to ask "what if" questions. For example, they use decision support software to ask: "What if gross sales were increased by 10 percent and the cost of goods sold were decreased by 5 percent. How would net earnings be affected?" Managers also find prior-year comparisons helpful.

The Securities and Exchange Commission (SEC) requires publicly held companies such as BrassCo to file quarterly financial statements. Every three months BrassCo and thousands of other companies transmit these reports to the SEC electronically via data communications.

Maintaining FACS

All FACS subsystems are on-line 24 hours a day. Any authorized BrassCo employee can tap into the interactive, menu-driven FACS system to make inquiries or to add, delete, or revise data. The Finance and Accounting Division is responsible for maintaining that portion of the integrated data base that deals with monetary accounting, even though much of the input comes from the other divisions. On occasion, this causes some problems. Monroe Green admits that "sometimes the Personnel Division has to be prodded to get the pay and benefits data in on time. However, you can always depend on the sales reps in the field to get their expense reports in on time."

Review Exercises (Section A–3)

Discussion

15. Do acronyms, such as FACS and PERES, foster cyberphobia, or do they simplify interaction between users and computer professionals? Explain.

16. Explain the relationship between BrassCo's accounts

payable application and a supplier's accounts receivable application.

17. Getting out the payroll at BrassCo is a joint effort between the Personnel Division and the Finance and Accounting Division. Could the payroll application be made more efficient by consolidating it in one division or the other? Explain.

18. Briefly describe two transactions in each of BrassCo's four major divisions that affect the general ledger.

19. Describe the information flow to and from the Disbursement Control Subsystem (1.3) of FACS as illustrated in Figure A–4.

Problem Solving

20. Draw a data flow diagram explosion of the Receipt Control Subsystem (1.2) showing the primary information flows between appropriate processes, the customer entity, and the integrated data base. Label subordinate processes 1.2.1, 1.2.2, and so on.

21. Draw a data flow diagram explosion of the Financial Reporting Subsystem (1.5) of Figure A–4 showing the primary information flows between appropriate processes, the managers and government entities, and the integrated data base. Label subordinate processes 1.5.1, 1.5.2, and so on.

22. Describe the content of three management reports that you might expect to be generated by the Distribution Control Subsystem (1.3) of FACS. Target one report at the strategic level (CEO), one at the tactical level (vice presidents), and one at the operational level.

23. Currently, Finance and Accounting Division personnel have 37 PCs. On average the PCs are used in terminal emulation mode about 60% of the time and in stand-alone mode the rest of the time. Monroe Green, the VP of finance and accounting, is concerned about the amount of money being spent on micro productivity software and has asked you to suggest approaches that might reduce this expense. What would you suggest be done?

24. Explain how managers at BrassCo can use the Financial Planning Subsystem (1.4) to monitor expenditures in their departments. Describe an example interactive screen showing input and output.

A–4   The Human Resource Information System

PERES, which is pronounced like the French city, is an acronym for Personnel Resource System, BrassCo's human resource information system. PERES is one of the four major information systems of BrassCo's corporate-wide MIS (see Figure A–3). PERES is essentially a personnel accounting system that maintains pertinent data on employees. Peggy Peoples, the vice president of personnel, and others in the Personnel Division are the primary users of the system. Besides routine historical data, such as educational background, salary history, and so on, PERES includes data on performance reviews, skills, and professional development.

PERES is divided into three subsystems:

2.1 Recruiting
2.2 Pay and Benefits Administration
2.3 Training and Education

These subsystems are illustrated graphically in the data flow diagram of Figure A–5. Figure A–5 shows the explosion of Process 2, "Personnel," of the BrassCo MIS. Each of these subsystems is described in the following sections.

Recruiting (2.1)

It has long been a tradition at BrassCo to hire quality people and promote from within. At the beginning of each quarter, the division vice presidents enter their projected *work force requirements* into PERES. Each vice president is responsible for finding qualified candidates to fill these positions. The Recruiting Subsystem (see Figure A–5) has proven helpful in landing the best available people.

The Recruiting Subsystem (2.1) automatically distributes predefined job descriptions to selected colleges and to several personnel search agencies. About 20% of these are distributed via electronic mail; the rest are generated in hard copy and sent via the postal service. The colleges and agencies suggest possible candidates, then the Recruiting Department conducts a preliminary interview. The results of the interview, which are entered into PERES, are on-line and readily accessible to management.

Managers can make on-line inquiries directly from their terminals. The following are examples of some of the on-line reports made available by the menu-driven Recruiting Subsystem:

- Work force summary: current and authorized
- Current openings (see Figure A–6)
- Current candidate summary

Peggy Peoples, the VP of personnel, says that "the first day a new hire comes to work, he or she reports to us. We give a couple of minutes' instruction on the use of our terminals, then ask the new hire to enter his or her personal data into PERES. This is the first activity of a two-day orientation we give every new hire."

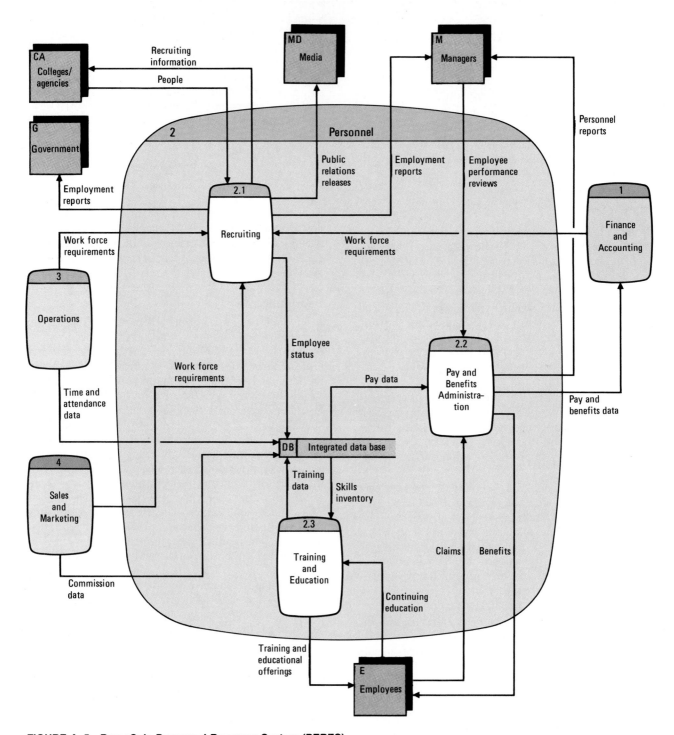

FIGURE A–5 BrassCo's Personnel Resource System (PERES)
*This data flow diagram is the explosion of the personnel (2) process of the MIS overview
data flow diagram of Figure A–3.*

		Current Openings			
Division	Position	Department	Location	Salary	Requirements
Fin./Acct.	Sr. planner	Finance	Topeka	40k-55k	MBA + exp.
	End user liason	Accounting	Topeka	28k-40k	BS, BA + 1 yr.exp.
	Adm.specialist	Accounting	Topeka	15k-22k	HS + word proc.
Sales/Mkt.	Sales rep.(2)	Sales	L.A.	18k-40k	BS, BA
Operations	Robot repair	Man./Dist.	Vienna	22k-32k	Assoc. degree
CIS	Programmer II	Programming	Topeka	27k-37k	Assoc. degree
	Sr. sys. anal.	Systems	Chico	30k-45k	BS, BA (MIS pref.)
	Librarian	Operations	Topeka	20k-28k	Assoc. degree
Total number of openings: 9					

FIGURE A–6   The Current Openings Report
This on-line current openings report is one of several that are available upon request via the Recruiting Subsystem (2.1).

Classified ads, announcing BrassCo job openings, are sent to local newspapers electronically in a format that needs no further editing by typesetters. This approach saves time and BrassCo gets a discount for delivering machine-readable ad copy. The Personnel Division receives announcements of position openings each day from several departments. It responds by preparing *releases to local newspapers*. These releases are usually, but not always, placed in the "classified ads" section.

In the past, managers complained that both internal and public announcements of position openings were being delayed too long and that they had to operate shorthanded longer than necessary. The solution was to eliminate hard-copy announcements by posting all openings on the company's *electronic bulletin board* and by transmitting the position announcements directly to newspapers via data communications. Now, minutes after a position opening is received from a department, it is posted on the BrassCo Bulletin-Board System (BBBS), affectionately known to BrassCo employees as "B-Buzz."

To post an item to B-Buzz or to scan its contents, employees simply log on to the nearest terminal. B-Buzz includes typical bulletin-board items such as softball scores, "for sale" items, messages of all kinds, and of course, position announcements. Terminals, most of which are micros, are everywhere at BrassCo, even in the halls, the cafeterias, and the executive washroom. Those employees that would like to transfer to another job or another office routinely scan the position announcements on B-Buzz.

A variety of mandatory government reports, dealing primarily with equal opportunity employment, are generated from the Recruiting Subsystem.

Pay and Benefits Administration (2.2)

Maintenance and preparation of payroll data. The *payroll application* is a joint effort between the Personnel Division and the Finance and Accounting Division. The Pay and Benefits Administration Subsystem (see Figure A–5) is the heart of the *wage and salary administration application*. Supervisors enter *hours-worked data* for hourly personnel directly into their terminals. The Personnel Division makes any adjustments to pay, such as an optional purchase of BrassCo stock, directly to an employee's record on the integrated data base. Then, prior to each pay period, the Personnel Division verifies *pay and benefits data* on the integrated data base. Once the data are prepared, the actual preparation and distribution of the checks is handled by the Disbursement Control Subsystem (1.3) of FACS.

Performance reviews. At BrassCo, every employee has a semiannual performance review—even Preston Smith, the president and CEO. Each employee is evaluated by his or her immediate manager in six areas: ability to work with others, innovativeness, contribution through achievement of goals, potential for advancement, ability to communicate, and expertise in his or her area of specialty.

Many managers record their numeric evaluations, from 1 to 10, and add a verbal support statement while interacting directly with PERES. Managers conduct performance reviews with their subordinates while both of them are seated in front of a terminal. When a subordinate comes in for an interview, the manager will have already done the rating, usually on the low side. If, by virtue of other information, a subordinate can convince the manager that he or she should be rated higher, the rating is changed on the spot. Most BrassCo managers feel that there should be some give and take between manager and subordinate. PERES gives managers the flexibility to render a mutually agreeable performance review without unnecessarily causing hard feelings.

Management reports. Managers at BrassCo use the company's fourth-generation language (4GL) to make ad hoc requests for information and reports. A manager obtains information by writing a short program that, in turn, "queries" the integrated data base. Such queries can be made to the data base for information in any functional area, not just personnel.

The 4GL used at BrassCo is called INFO-QIK. At BrassCo, 70% of the managers, including top management, know, use, and like INFO-QIK. INFO-QIK is user-friendly, and managers can get the information they need without having to wait in line for a programmer. Short user-developed INFO-QIK programs are all that are needed to respond to the following typical BrassCo management requests:

- Which employees have accumulated over 20 sick days since May 1?
- List departments that have exceeded their total budget allocation for the month of June in alphabetical order by department name.

Training and Education (2.3)

The Training and Education Subsystem (2.3) monitors and tracks the ongoing career development of BrassCo employees. Any external or internal training or education received by an employee is entered into his or her *skills inventory*. Included in an employee's skills inventory are any special skills or knowledge. As a matter of policy, managers first conduct an internal search to fill openings. They do this by listing desired skills, knowledge, and so on, then initiating an automatic search of the skills inventory section of the integrated data base. Frequently, there is a match and an opportunity for promotion is extended to an existing employee.

The Personnel Division administers ongoing in-house training programs and evaluates employee requests for external educational support. The Training and Education Subsystem automatically informs employees of *in-house offerings* by posting a notice on B-Buzz, BrassCo's electronic bulletin board.

Review Exercises (Section A–4)

Discussion

25. Many BrassCo managers conduct performance reviews with their subordinates while interacting with PERES. Discuss the pros and cons of this approach.
26. What are the advantages of having an on-line skills inventory for all employees?
27. Even though most professionals at BrassCo have ready access to the computer system, relatively few have access to sensitive data (for example, personal data on employees). Speculate on the kinds of procedures or safeguards that have been implemented to limit access to sensitive data.

28. What are the benefits of having new employees enter their own personal data into PERES?

Problem Solving

29. A proposal being seriously considered by BrassCo's top management is to change all hourly employees to salaried employees. If adopted, what impact would this proposal have on the Pay and Benefits Administration Subsystem (2.2) of PERES?
30. Describe the content and layout of three management reports that you might expect to be generated by the Training and Education Subsystem (2.3) of PERES. Target one report at the strategic level (CEO), one at the tactical level (vice presidents), and one at the operational level.
31. B-Buzz, BrassCo's electronic bulletin-board system, contains announcements of internal position openings and in-house training programs. Identify other management uses of B-Buzz that involve the enterprise-wide distribution of information.
32. Describe system controls that can be built into PERES to minimize input errors by supervisors who key in hours-worked data for hourly employees.
33. Describe the information flow to and from the Recruiting Subsystem (2.1) of PERES as illustrated in Figure A–5.
34. Describe the information flow between PERES and FACS. Be specific.
35. The current payroll system results in the distribution of checks through the mail. Suggest alternative approaches to paying employees that will result in the elimination of payroll checks.

A–5 The Production and Inventory Control Information System

PICS, BrassCo's Production and Inventory Control System, supports the Operations Division and is one of the four functional components of BrassCo's integrated management information system (see Figure A–3). Figure A–7 graphically illustrates the scope of PICS (pronounced *picks*) by showing the explosion of Process 3, "Operations," of the BrassCo MIS overview data flow diagram in Figure A–3. PICS is logically divided into five subsystems:

3.1 Production
3.2 Research and Development
3.3 Schedule and Monitor Production
3.4 Acquire and Manage Materials
3.5 Shipping

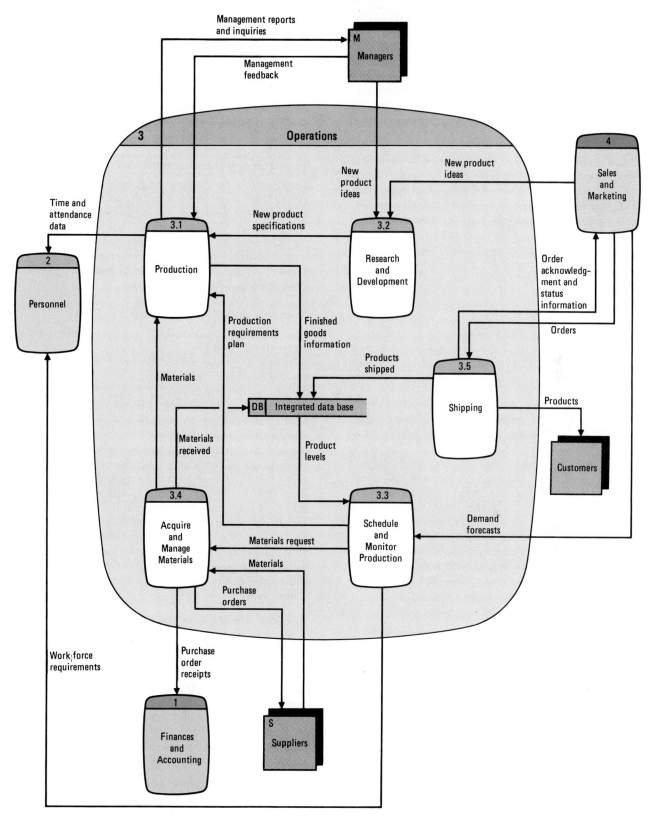

FIGURE A–7   BrassCo's Production and Inventory Control System (PICS)
This data flow diagram is the explosion of the operations (3) process of the MIS overview data flow diagram of Figure A–3.

629

The Operations Division's user liaison provides the interface between CIS people (programmers, systems analysts, and the data base administrator) and users. She made a valuable contribution to PICS during its design and implementation by facilitating and fostering verbal communication between CIS and user personnel. The user liaison explained how the project team came up with the five subsystems:

The project team analyzed the Operations Division from an information processing perspective, not from a departmental perspective. Because the information and processing requirements of the various departments overlapped substantially, it seemed only logical that we design PICS as an integrated system. Although there is some correlation between the subsystems and departmental lines, this was not a criterion during the design phase. Our primary concern was to design a system that would best meet the needs of the Operations Division, while complementing BrassCo's overall MIS.

Otto Manning, the vice president of operations, was the real force behind the development and implementation of PICS, and he was very much a proponent of designing it around an integrated data base. He said:

The Operations Division is very dynamic and hopelessly intertwined with everything we do here at BrassCo. We get input from Marketing, R&D, and Accounting. Marketing tells us what products to make, how many to make, and when to have them in stock. R&D tells us how to make them, and Accounting tells us how much we can spend. All too often Marketing wants the product before R&D is finished with the design, and Accounting doesn't allocate enough money to cover the cost of production. These and other conflicts between divisions highlight the need for people throughout the company to be better informed. To help alleviate some of our misinformation problems, we decided that the nerve center of PICS should be an integrated data base.

Production (3.1)

All activities in the Operations Division function to support the production process, and so it is with PICS. All other subsystems support the Production Subsystem (3.1). Plant managers get the *specifications* for new products and product enhancements from the Research and Development Subsystem (3.2). Each day, plant managers at the four plant/distribution center sites tap into the Schedule and Monitor Production Subsystem (3.3) to monitor *production levels*. The Acquire and Manage Materials Subsystem (3.4) ensures that raw materials needed during production are at the right place at the right time. And, of course, the Shipping Subsystem (3.5) gets the *products* out the door to the customer.

Plant managers rely heavily on the DSS (decision support system) software, such as linear programming and simulation models, that is embodied in the Production Subsystem to help them make the most effective use of available resources. These models help schedule the arrival of raw materials and components, the use of machine tools and assembly stations, the use of the work force, and maintenance shutdowns.

Research and Development (3.2)

The Research and Development Subsystem (3.2) services a small R&D department. Over the years R&D personnel have been responsible for hundreds of production and design changes. Generally, these changes improve product quality and appearance while reducing production cost. The R&D Subsystem is comprised of an array of analysis, design, and project management tools that help researchers to be more productive.

Schedule and Monitor Production (3.3)

The Schedule and Monitor Production Subsystem receives the *demand forecast* for the various BrassCo products from the Sales and Marketing Component (4) of the overall BrassCo MIS. These forecasts are what drive the production process.

Mathematical models built into the Schedule and Monitor Production Subsystem retrieve data from the integrated data base to generate a *production requirements plan*. This plan specifies week-by-week *in-stock requirements* for BrassCo products. The plan tells the plant manager what the *rate of production* for a particular product should be over a period of time, usually six months. Plant managers take immediate action if the information they get from this subsystem suggests that production levels may fall below production requirements.

The *materials request*, which is a by-product of the production requirements plan, is automatically generated and routed to the Acquire and Manage Materials Subsystem (3.4).

Acquire and Manage Materials (3.4)

Material requirements planning.   Built into the overall BrassCo MIS, and specifically the Acquire and Manage Materials Subsystem, is the philosophy of *material requirements planning*, often called *MRP*. MRP is essentially a set of mathematical models that accepts data for *production requirements* and translates these requirements into an optimal schedule for the ordering and the delivery of the *components* and *raw materials* needed to manufacture BrassCo's products.

Inventory management and control.   The Acquire and Manage Materials Subsystem gets the *materials request* from the Schedule and Monitor Production Subsystem

(3.3). The subsystem then generates *purchase orders* for the raw materials and components needed to meet production schedules. These purchase orders are sent to the suppliers, some via *electronic data interchange*, or *EDI* (see Chapter 7, "Connectivity and Data Communications," for discussions of EDI concepts and strategies). An "electronic flag" is added to the integrated data base to notify the Finance and Accounting Division of the order.

Manufacturing companies such as BrassCo must manage stock (components and raw materials) and finished goods inventories. This subsystem (3.4) monitors the quantity on hand and the location of each inventory item.

The BrassCo data base is a network data base (see Chapter 9, "System Software and Platforms"). The data base subschema in Figure A–8 illustrates that portion of the BrassCo integrated data base that relates specifically to the *inventory management and control application*. The arrows indicate the one-to-many relationships between the five data base records; that is, one record for a BrassCo product will have cross-references to the many records of the stock items that make up that product.

The data base subschema in Figure A–8 is designed to minimize data redundancy. The *product* data base record contains a list of those items (for example, components and raw materials) that are combined to produce a BrassCo product. The two inventory records, *finished goods* and *item*, maintain stock and order data. The *purchase order* record indicates what was ordered. The *supplier* record includes pertinent data about each supplier. The entire schema for BrassCo's network-based integrated data base, which is not shown, includes relationships between these and other data base records.

Shipping (3.5)

In any manufacturing company, a product is conceived, designed, manufactured, sold, and ultimately shipped to the customer. The Shipping Subsystem (3.5) of Figure A–7 supports the last major activity in the manufacturing cycle. The *orders* are entered into SAMIS (Sales and Marketing Information System) by the field sales staff or by people in the telemarketing group. Once an order is verified, a shipping notice is automatically sent to the Distribution Department via the Shipping Subsystem. Once the *product* is sent to the customer, *acknowledgment* is sent simultaneously to the Sales and Marketing Division and to the Finance and Accounting Division via the integrated data base. The sales force monitors the progress of the order, and accounting sends the customer an *invoice*.

Computer-Integrated Manufacturing

To date, automation at the factory level has grown in two separate directions at BrassCo. On one side, the MIS provides support for administrative data processing and generates information for plant-level decision makers. On the factory floors, BrassCo has done everything possible to encourage *computer-aided manufacturing (CAM)*. *Computer-aided manufacturing* is a term that was coined to highlight the use of computers in the manufacturing process. There are literally thousands of uses for special-purpose computers in the manufacturing environment. Two of the most prominent CAM applications at BrassCo are *robotics* (see Chapter 14, "Applications of Information Technology") and *computer-aided design (CAD)*. Computer-aided design has revolutionized the way BrassCo's engineers and scientists design, draft, and document a product.

At BrassCo, the movements of machine tools, such as lathes and milling machines, are also controlled by special-purpose computers. Other CAM applications for special-purpose computer systems include *automated materials handling* and *assembly-line control*.

BrassCo's strategic plans call for transitioning to a *computer-integrated manufacturing (CIM)* environment. CIM is the integration of the computer throughout the manufacturing process. In CIM, the computer is used at every stage of the manufacturing process, from the time a part is conceived until it is shipped. (CIM concepts are discussed in Chapter 14.) Eventually, all special-purpose process-control computers in the plant will be linked to the company's general-purpose MIS computers. BrassCo's plans call for the implementation of total CIM within five years.

Review Exercises (Section A–5)

Discussion

36. BrassCo Enterprises manufactures and sells four relatively low-tech products. R&D is working on high-tech versions of the traditional BrassCo coat racks. The new coat racks provide a level of security for coat rack users. The person enters a user-designated security code before placing the coat on a pressure-sensitive hook. The weight of the coat arms the system. The user must reenter the code to avoid tripping an audible alarm when removing the coat. Discuss the effects, if any, that the mixing of low- and high-tech products might have on the design of basic information systems such as an accounting system or an inventory control system.

37. Each plant maintains a local data base on its minicomputer. What data would be included in the local data base and not on the central data base at corporate headquarters?

Problem Solving

38. Describe the content and layout of three management reports that you might expect to be generated

Data Base Records

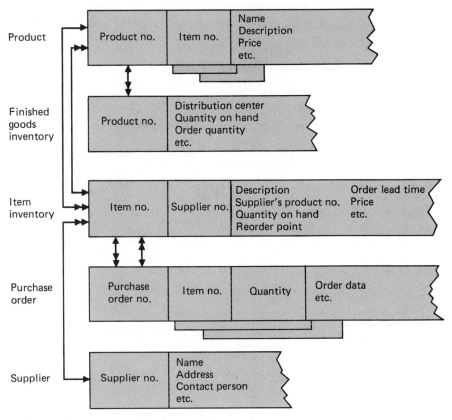

FIGURE A–8 Data Base Subschema for the Inventory Management and Control Application
This data base subschema is that portion of BrassCo's integrated data base that deals directly with inventory management and control. Links with these data base records and other data base records in accounting and finance are not shown.

by the Schedule and Monitor Production Subsystem (3.3) of PICS. Target one report at the strategic level (CEO), one at the tactical level (vice presidents), and one at the operational level.

39. Identify some of the data redundancies that might have existed in the traditional files that supported the Operations Division prior to the implementation of an integrated data base (see Figure A–8).

40. A BrassCo supplier manufactures screws and BrassCo uses every type of screw that they make. They make all screws of both brass and steel. Currently the screw lengths range from ¼ to 2 inches in ¼-inch increments, but the supplier plans to expand the product line to 3½ inches. Each length of screw is manufactured with three types of heads—round, hex, and flat. Currently, production workers have to verbally describe the screw they want. Otto Manning, the

VP of operations, would like an easier way to identify a particular screw. In that regard, he has asked you to set up a coding scheme to do this. The screw number should be coded within a minimum of positions to save disk storage. What coding scheme would you suggest?

41. Give examples of occurrences (actual data base entries) for the data base subschema in Figure A–8.

42. Describe the information flow to and from the Acquire and Manage Materials Subsystem (3.4) of PICS as illustrated in Figure A–7.

A–6 The Sales and Marketing Information System

BrassCo's original MIS strategic plan called for the inhouse development of all four components of BrassCo's

MIS (see Figure A–3): FACS (finance and accounting), PERES (human resources), PICS (operations), and SAMIS (sales and marketing). Limited resources dictated that the integrated MIS be developed and implemented in stages. The plan called for FACS to be implemented first, followed by PERES and PICS. SAMIS, the Sales and Marketing Information System, had the lowest priority, for two reasons. First, and perhaps most significant, Sally Marcio, the vice president of sales and marketing, was less vocal about the need for SAMIS than the other vice presidents were about their systems. Second, she was relatively satisfied with the information that she and her managers were receiving from an outside timesharing service.

Several years ago during the early summer, the vice president of sales and marketing remarked to the vice president of CIS that "The competition is getting the jump on us with better information. Also that timesharing service has doubled its rates! We can't wait any longer, we've got to have SAMIS by the end of the year to stay competitive!"

At that time, work was not scheduled to begin on SAMIS for another 18 months. Conrad Innis, the vice president of CIS, told Sally Marcio: "We simply don't have the resources to commit to a major new in-house development project. As an alternative, would you consider buying a commercial software package?"

BrassCo's Computer and Information Services (CIS) Division, like most centralized computer centers, suffers from a shortage of human resources. To help alleviate this problem, BrassCo managers have occasionally opted to purchase and install commercially available software packages.

Sally Marcio did not believe that the Sales and Marketing Division could wait a couple of years for CIS to develop an in-house information system. She decided to take Conrad Innis' advice and began looking for a packaged sales and marketing system. After evaluating seven such systems, a search team recommended a package developed by a firm in Cleveland. Mrs. Marcio said: "With a few minor modifications, this system will fit our needs to a tee." Since the packaged system was compatible with BrassCo's database management system, the modifications were relatively minor.

Because of the immediacy of the need and the availability of a product, BrassCo management decided to "buy" rather than "make" the fourth component of the BrassCo MIS. SAMIS went on-line in November, five months after Sally Marcio first related her sense of desperation to Conrad Innis.

SAMIS is that component of the integrated MIS that services the Sales and Marketing Division. The system interacts frequently with the other three MIS components: FACS, PERES, and PICS. The five subsystems

of SAMIS match up perfectly with the functions of the five departments in the Sales and Marketing Division. If you will remember, this is in contrast to the subsystems of FACS, PERES, and PICS, which are not aligned with the organizational structures of their respective divisions. The five subsystems of SAMIS are

4.1 Market Research
4.2 Advertising and Promotion
4.3 Customer Service
4.4 Sales and Order Processing
4.5 Sales Forecasting and Analysis

The second-level data flow diagram of Figure A–9 is the explosion of Process 4, "Sales and Marketing," of the BrassCo MIS (see Figure A–3). Each of the five subsystems is described in the following sections.

Market Research (4.1)

The Market Research Department systematically gathers all kinds of data that may in some way provide information that will help managers to make better decisions regarding the marketing and sale of BrassCo products. Unlike accounting or personnel systems, the data gathered for input to the Market Research Subsystem are very volatile (see Figure A–9); that is, data that are seemingly accurate today may be erroneous tomorrow. Because of the ever-changing nature of market research data, the data must be constantly updated so that the information derived from the data is representative of the current market. Inputs to the Market Research Subsystem are

- Data on the marketing activities of competitors
- Demographic data
- Economic indicators
- Data on consumer behavior
- Customer responses to surveys

BrassCo subscribes to several commercially available data bases that provide much of these data. The company obtains the rest of the data by periodically distributing surveys, from BrassCo's integrated data base, and from feedback from the field sales representatives.

People in the Market Research Department use SAMIS to keep an eye on demographics and customer buying trends so that they can identify untapped niches in the market. Sally Marcio says:

Without SAMIS, certain segments of the marketplace would forever remain hidden. As an example, for years we targeted our non-business marketing campaigns at homeowners. A survey conducted by market research surfaced a growing market among renters. By broadening

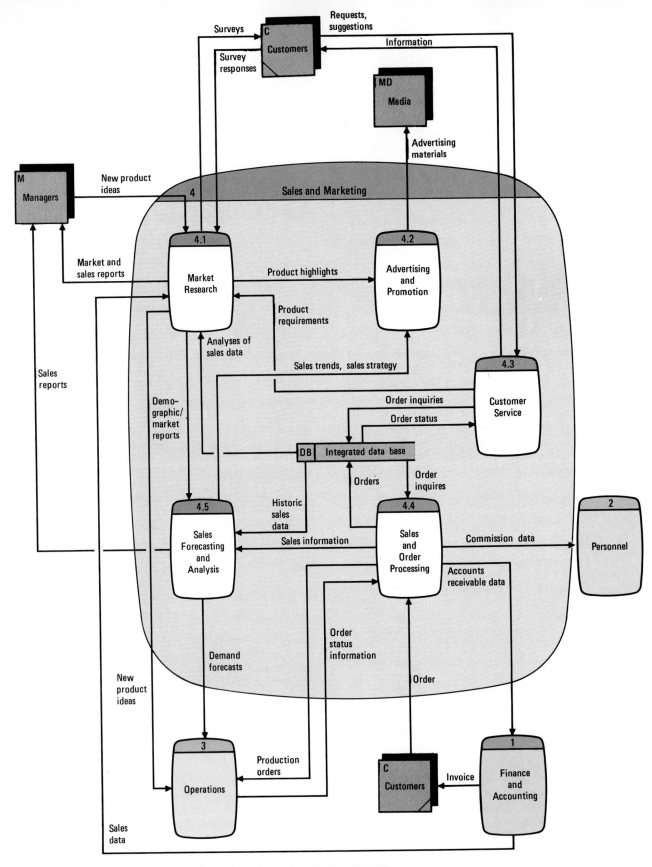

FIGURE A–9 BrassCo's Sales and Marketing Information System (SAMIS)
This data flow diagram is the explosion of the sales and marketing (4) process of the MIS overview data flow diagram of Figure A–3.

the scope of our advertising, we were able to increase sales by 11 percent during the next year.

The Market Research Subsystem automatically gathers ideas for *new products* and *enhancements to existing products* from BrassCo managers and from the Customer Service Subsystem (4.3).

The Market Research Subsystem includes a number of models that help researchers to analyze and interpret the data. For example, each week the system determines if there is any statistically significant correlation between sales trends for the various BrassCo products and other trends. For example, statistical techniques are used to correlate product sales to the consumer price index, the unemployment level, furniture sales, and numerous other factors that might in some way influence the sale of a BrassCo product. If a correlation exists, market researchers can identify trends early and give management some time to react, perhaps with an unscheduled price adjustment.

Advertising and Promotion (4.2)

BrassCo promotes its products through *personal selling* (exclusively to retailers and wholesalers), *advertising*, and *promotional campaigns*. The latter two are supported by the Advertising and Promotion Subsystem (see Figure A–9). The catalyst for the advertising and promotion activity is the information on *sales trends and strategies* provided by the Sales Forecasting and Analysis Subsystem (4.5).

About three times a year, BrassCo has promotional campaigns for each of its products. These campaigns usually involve price reductions or rebates. SAMIS has made it possible for the people at BrassCo to analyze the effectiveness of their ads and promotional campaigns on a day-to-day basis. Sally Marcio is proud of SAMIS's contribution to her division's bottom line: "By identifying the most effective advertising medium, SAMIS helps BrassCo managers to maximize the value of their advertising dollars."

The purchase price of SAMIS included the software and hardware for a computerized dialing system for *automated telemarketing*. The system, which is part of the Advertising and Promotion Subsystem, automatically dials a telephone number, then plays a prerecorded message. Sally Marcio decided to use this component of the subsystem to kick off a new promotional campaign. The telephone numbers of BrassCo customers were entered into the system, then dialed automatically, one after another. Sally Marcio said:

Telemarketing sounded like a good idea, but it wasn't. Customer feedback was all negative. They let us know immediately that they didn't appreciate these "computer"

calls, so we turned the machine off the next day and haven't turned it on since. This incident reminds us that not all applications of computer technology are worthwhile.

Customer Service (4.3)

The function of customer service representatives is to respond to any type of customer inquiry or complaint. Sally Marcio says: "Because of SAMIS, our customer service reps have on-line access to the integrated data base and just about any information that the customer would need to know."

For the more routine inquiries, many of BrassCo's customers prefer the "BrassCo Connection." BrassCo customers are given a telephone number, a password, and an authorization code that will allow them to tap directly into SAMIS from their own terminals. Customers routinely establish an *EDI link* with the Customer Service Subsystem (see Figure A–9) to track orders and shipments and to get the latest pricing information. Of course, security precautions limit what customers can access, and they can't change anything. According to Sally, "The Customer Service Subsystem has helped to build customer loyalty and has made relations with our customers much smoother. They know that if they have a question, they can ask us or they can query our data base directly."

At the end of the day, each customer service rep requests that the names and addresses of those customers with whom they have interacted be downloaded from the corporate data base to disk storage on their microcomputer terminals. Each customer service representative has a micro, with disk storage, and shares a desktop page printer. During the last hour or so of the day, the customer service terminals become stand-alone computer systems so that representatives can use word processing and mail-merge software to write "personalized" letters to the customers that they talked with during the day. The basic form letter confirms BrassCo's continuing commitment to customer service. About 50% of the time, the reps add a sentence or so that relates to the customer's particular situation. Sally Marcio says that this "immediate and personal follow-up to a customer's inquiry has provided immeasurable good will and set us apart from our competitors."

Sales and Order Processing (4.4)

The Sales and Order Processing Subsystem (see Figure A–9) provides the facility for BrassCo's field sales reps and BrassCo's customers to enter *orders* directly into SAMIS and the integrated data base. Every field sales rep has a cellular telephone and laptop PC with a built-in modem. The rep can enter an order, make an inquiry, or send a message while in a customer's office. To do this, the rep simply connects the laptop PC to the cellular telephone and dials the number of the Topeka mainframe.

Sally Marcio says that "the use of portables in the field has resulted in faster delivery to the customer, far less paperwork, and a better cash flow to BrassCo. More often than not a sales rep can guarantee the customer that his or her order will be shipped within 24 hours. The customer appreciates that."

Just having the laptop PCs gives the field reps a psychological boost. They know that they have a direct link to literally everyone in the company, even though most of them work out of their homes. All of them routinely get and receive electronic mail. Since the laptop PCs double as microcomputers, the sales reps use them in stand-alone mode to do spreadsheet analysis and word processing.

The Sales and Order Processing Subsystem (4.4) also provides support for *EDI*. Some customers prefer to enter their orders directly from their mainframe computers into BrassCo's mainframe at Topeka. Customers send the order data in a standard format, and the order is confirmed with a return message from BrassCo's main-frame computer. Sally reports: "EDI benefits our customer and us. BrassCo customers are able to cut their inventories since they get quicker delivery. It cuts our paperwork substantially, thereby reducing the overall cost of sales."

Sales Forecasting and Analysis (4.5)

The Sales Forecasting and Analysis Subsystem (see Figure A–9) uses mathematical models to combine the *historical sales data*, current sales, and a variety of predictive data to come up with a *sales forecast* for BrassCo products. The production levels at each of the plants are based on the sales forecasts. Each month, the Sales Forecasting and Analysis Subsystem generates a *6-Month Demand Schedule* for each of BrassCo's products. The bar graph in Figure A–10 illustrates the March through August 6-Month Demand Schedule for the Crown coat racks. The bar chart graphically highlights any major changes in the monthly total demand estimates. From the figure, it is obvious that there will be a far greater demand for Crowns in June than was earlier expected. The Operations Division uses these demand reports to schedule production levels at the plants and to set minimum finished goods inventory levels at each of the warehouses.

FIGURE A–10   Bar Chart for 6-Month Demand Schedule
This bar chart graphically highlights any major changes in the total product demand forecast (for example, June) by comparing the demand estimates for the current "6-Month Demand Schedule" with the estimates on the previous month's schedule.

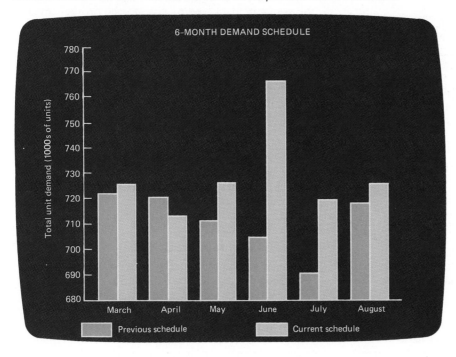

SAMIS Summary

The examples presented in this case study represent only a small fraction of the capabilities of SAMIS. Sales managers can request a sales summary or a sales history for any accounts in their regions. Orders can be received, processed, and billed without human intervention. When sales fall below the historical norm in a particular sales territory, the appropriate regional sales manager is automatically notified via electronic mail. Sally Marcio summed up her impressions of SAMIS very succinctly. "Before SAMIS, we had too much data and not enough information. Now we use information as a competitive weapon."

Review Exercises (Section A–6)

Discussion

43. The Sales and Order Processing Subsystem (4.4) permits field sales reps to make inquiries to the integrated data base from their laptop PCs while in a customer's office. Discuss the types of inquiries that a sales rep might make.

44. Of the four major systems that comprise the BrassCo MIS, only SAMIS is proprietary software. Does this make any difference to the end user? How about to BrassCo's programmers and systems analysts?

Problem Solving

45. Customers have limited access to the BrassCo data base via EDI. Discuss the types of inquiries that a customer might make. Discuss the advantages and disadvantages of this customer service.

46. Currently, BrassCo's computerized dialing system is unused. Suggest applications for this system that would benefit BrassCo.

47. Describe what had to be done to interface the SAMIS data base with existing corporate data base.

48. Describe the information flow to and from the Market Research Subsystem (4.1) of SAMIS as illustrated in Figure A–9.

Working with Numbering Systems

Appendix Overview

This appendix presents the principles of numbering systems, discusses numbering-system arithmetic, and illustrates how to convert a value in one numbering system to its equivalent in another. After studying this appendix you will be able to perform rudimentary arithmetic operations in the binary and hexadecimal numbering systems. The relationship between computers and the various numbering systems is discussed in Chapter 4, "Inside the Computer."

B–1 Principles of Numbering Systems

Binary

The binary, or base-2, numbering system is based on the same principles as the decimal, or base-10, numbering system, with which we are already familiar. The only difference between the two numbering systems is that binary uses only two digits, 0 and 1, and the decimal numbering system uses 10 digits, 0 through 9. The equivalents for binary, decimal, and hexadecimal numbers are shown in Figure B–1.

Binary (base 2)	Decimal (base 10)	Hexadecimal (base 16)
0	0	0
1	1	1
10	2	2
11	3	3
100	4	4
101	5	5
110	6	6
111	7	7
1000	8	8
1001	9	9
1010	10	A
1011	11	B
1100	12	C
1101	13	D
1110	14	E
1111	15	F
10000	16	10

FIGURE B–1   Numbering-System Equivalence Table

The value of a given digit is determined by its relative position in a sequence of digits. Consider the example in Figure B–2. If we want to write the number

639

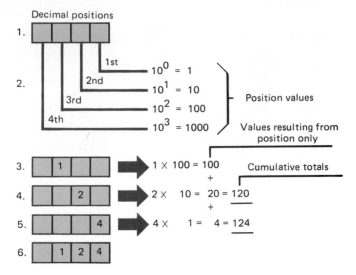

FIGURE B–2 Numbering-System Fundamentals
Ralph, our two-fingered Martian who is used to counting in binary, might go through the thought process illustrated here when counting 124 marbles in decimal. Ralph's steps are discussed in the text.

124 in decimal, the interpretation is almost automatic because of our familiarity with the decimal numbering system. To illustrate the underlying concepts, let's give Ralph, a little green two-fingered Martian, a bag of 124 (decimal) marbles and ask him to express the number of marbles in decimal. Ralph, who is more familiar with binary, would go through the following thought process (see Figure B–2).

- *Step 1*. Ralph knows that the relative position of a digit within a string of digits determines its value, whether the numbering system is binary or decimal. Therefore, the first thing to do is determine the value represented by each digit position.
- *Step 2*. Ralph knows that, as in any numbering system, the rightmost position has a value of the base to the zero power, or 1 ($10^0 = 1$). The second position is the base to the first power, or 10 ($10^1 = 10$). The third position is the base squared, or 100, and so on.
- *Step 3*. Because the largest of the decimal system's 10 digits is 9, the greatest number that can be represented in the *rightmost position* is 9 (9 X 1). The greatest number that can be represented in the *second position*, then, is 90 (9 X 10). In the *third position*, the greatest number is 900, and so on. Having placed the marbles in stacks of 10, Ralph knows immediately that there will be no need for a fourth-position digit (the thousands position). It is apparent, however, that a digit must be placed in the third position. Because placing a 2 in the third position would be too much (200 > 124), Ralph places a 1 in the third position to represent 100 marbles.
- *Step 4*. Ralph must continue to the second position to represent the remaining 24 marbles. In each successive position, Ralph wants to represent as many marbles as possible. In this case, a 2 placed in the second position would represent 20 of the remaining marbles (2 X 10^1 = 20).

- *Step 5*. There are still four marbles left to be represented. This can be done by inserting a 4 in the rightmost, or "ones," position.
- *Step 6*. The combination of the three numbers in their relative positions represents 124 (decimal).

Ralph would go through the same thought process if asked to represent the 124 (decimal) marbles using the binary numbering system (see Figure B–3). To make the binary conversion process easier to follow, the computations in Figure B–3 are done in the more familiar decimal numbering system. See if you can trace Ralph's steps as you work through Figure B–3.

Hexadecimal

Perhaps the biggest drawback to using the binary numbering system for computer operations is that programmers may have to deal with long and confusing strings of 1s and 0s. To reduce the confusion, the hexadecimal, or base-16, numbering system is used as shorthand to display the binary contents of primary and secondary storage.

Notice that the bases of the binary and hexadecimal numbering systems are multiples of 2: 2 and 2^4, respectively. Because of this, there is a convenient relationship between these numbering systems. The numbering-system equivalence table shown in Figure B–1 illustrates that a single hexadecimal digit represents four binary digits ($0111_2 = 7_{16}$, $1101_2 = D_{16}$, $1010_2 = A_{16}$ where subscripts are used to indicate the base of the numbering system). Notice that in hexadecimal, or "hex," *letters* are used to represent the six higher order digits.

Two hexadecimal digits can be used to represent the eight-bit byte of an EBCDIC equals sign (=)

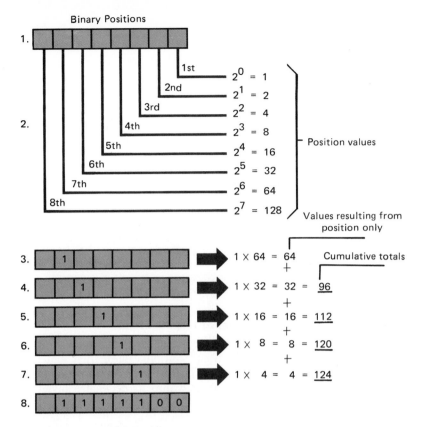

Binary Positions

1.

2.

Position	Power	Value
1st	2^0	= 1
2nd	2^1	= 2
3rd	2^2	= 4
4th	2^3	= 8
5th	2^4	= 16
6th	2^5	= 32
7th	2^6	= 64
8th	2^7	= 128

Position values

Values resulting from position only

3. $1 \times 64 = 64$ Cumulative totals
     +
4. $1 \times 32 = 32 = \underline{96}$
     +
5. $1 \times 16 = 16 = \underline{112}$
     +
6. $1 \times 8 = 8 = \underline{120}$
     +
7. $1 \times 4 = 4 = \underline{124}$

8.   1 1 1 1 1 0 0

FIGURE B–3   Representing a Binary Number
To represent 124 marbles in binary, we would follow the same thought process as we would in decimal (see Figure B–2), but this time we have only two digits (0 and 1). For ease of understanding, the arithmetic is done in decimal.

(01111110_2 is the same as $7E_{16}$). Figure B–4 illustrates how a string of EBCDIC bits can be reduced to a more recognizable form using hexadecimal.

We will now examine how to convert one number in a numbering system to an equivalent number in another numbering system. For example, there are occasions when we might wish to convert a hexadecimal number into its binary equivalent. We shall also learn the fundamentals of numbering-system arithmetic.

B–2   Converting Numbers from One Base into Another

Decimal to Binary or Hexadecimal

A decimal number can be converted easily into an equivalent number of any base by the use of the *division/remainder* technique. This two-step technique is illustrated in Figure B–5. Follow these steps to convert *decimal to binary*.

FIGURE B–4   *System* Expressed in Different Ways
The word System *is shown as it would appear in input/output, internal binary notation, and hexadecimal notation.*

Input/output (alphanumeric)	S		y		s		t		e		m	
Internal representation (binary)	1110	0010	1010	1000	1010	0010	1010	0011	1000	0101	1001	0100
Hexadecimal equivalent	E	2	A	8	A	2	A	3	8	5	9	4

The problem: 19_{10} = $?_2$

The procedure:

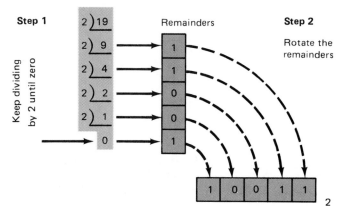

FIGURE B–5   Converting a Decimal Number into its Binary Equivalent
Use the two-step division/remainder technique to convert a decimal number into an equivalent number of any base.

- *Step 1.* Divide the number (19, in this example) repeatedly by 2, and record the remainder of each division. In the first division, 2 goes into 19 nine times with a remainder of 1. The remainder is always one of the binary digits–0 or 1. In the last division you divide 1 by the base (2) and the remainder is 1.
- *Step 2.* Rotate the remainders as shown in Figure B–5; the result (10011) is the binary equivalent of a decimal 19.

Figure B–6 illustrates how the same division/remainder technique is used to convert a decimal 453 into its hexadecimal equivalent (1C5). In a *decimal-to-hex* conversion, the remainder is always one of the 16 hex digits.

Binary to Decimal or Hexadecimal

To convert from *binary to decimal*, multiply the 1s in a binary number by their position values, then sum the products (see Figure B–7). In Figure B–7, for example, binary 11010 is converted into its decimal equivalent (26).

The easiest conversion is *binary to hex*. To convert binary to hex, simply begin with the 1s position on the right and segment the binary number into groups of four digits each (see Figure B–8). Refer to the equivalence table in Figure B–1, and assign each group of four binary digits a hex equivalent. Combine your result, and the conversion is complete.

FIGURE B–6   Converting a Decimal Number into its Hexadecimal Equivalent
The two-step division/remainder technique is used to convert a decimal number into its hex equivalent.

The problem: 453_{10} = $?_{16}$

The procedure:

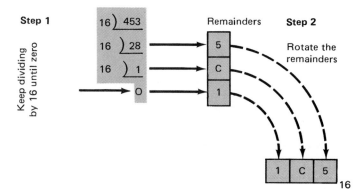

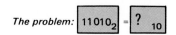

The problem: $11010_2 = ?_{10}$

The procedure:

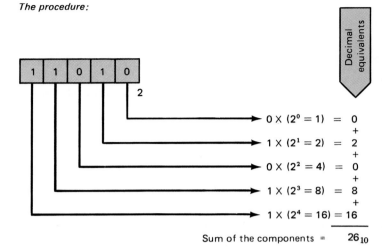

$$0 \times (2^0 = 1) = 0$$
$$+$$
$$1 \times (2^1 = 2) = 2$$
$$+$$
$$0 \times (2^2 = 4) = 0$$
$$+$$
$$1 \times (2^3 = 8) = 8$$
$$+$$
$$1 \times (2^4 = 16) = 16$$

Sum of the components = 26_{10}

FIGURE B–7   Converting a Binary Number into Its Decimal Equivalent
Multiply the 1s in a binary number by their position values.

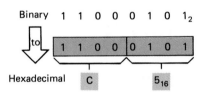

Binary   1 1 0 0 0 1 0 1_2

to

Hexadecimal   C 5_{16}

FIGURE B–8   Converting a Binary Number into Its Hexadecimal Equivalent
Place the binary digits in groups of four, then convert the binary number directly into hexadecimal.

Hexadecimal to Binary

To convert hex numbers into binary, perform the grouping procedure for converting binary to hex in reverse (see Figure B–8).

The problem: $3E7_{16} = ?_{10}$

The procedure:

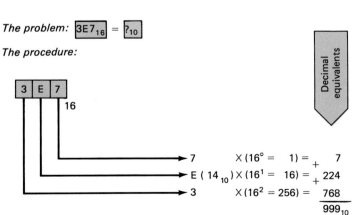

$$7 \quad \times (16^0 = 1) = 7$$
$$+$$
$$E (14_{10}) \times (16^1 = 16) = 224$$
$$+$$
$$3 \quad \times (16^2 = 256) = 768$$
$$999_{10}$$

Hexadecimal to Decimal

Use the same procedure as that used for binary-to-decimal conversions (see Figure B–7) to convert *hex to decimal*. Figure B–9 demonstrates the conversion of a hex 3E7 into its decimal equivalent of 999.

B–3   Arithmetic in Binary and Hexadecimal

The essentials of decimal arithmetic operations have been drilled into us so that we do addition and subtraction almost by instinct. We do binary arithmetic, as well as that of other numbering systems, in the same way that we do decimal arithmetic. The only difference is that we have fewer (binary) or more (hexadecimal) digits to use. Figure B–10 illustrates and compares addition and subtraction in decimal with that in binary and hex. Notice in Figure B–10 that you carry to and borrow from adjacent positions, just as you do in decimal arithmetic.

FIGURE B–9   Converting a Hexadecimal Number into Its Decimal Equivalent
Multiply the digits in a hexadecimal number by their position values.

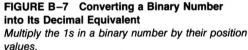

	Binary	Decimal	Hexadecimal
Addition	1111100 + 10010 10001110	124 + 18 142	7C + 12 8E
Subtraction	1111100 − 10010 1101010	124 − 18 106	7C − 12 6A

FIGURE B–10 Binary, Decimal, and Hexadecimal Arithmetic Comparison
As you can see, the only difference in doing arithmetic in the various numbering systems is the number of digits used.

Self-Test

1. The hex numbering system has a base of _____, and the binary numbering system has a base of _____.
2. The value of a particular digit in a number is determined by its relative position in a sequence of digits. T/F
3. A single hexadecimal digit can represent how many binary digits: (a) two, (b) three, or (c) four?
4. The bases of the binary and decimal numbering systems are multiples of 2. (T/F)
5. The binary equivalent of a decimal 255 is _____.
6. The binary equivalent of a hexadecimal 1C is _____.
7. The decimal equivalent of a hexadecimal 1B6 is _____.
8. The hexadecimal equivalent of a decimal 129 is _____.
9. The decimal equivalent of a binary 110101 is _____.
10. The hexadecimal equivalent of a binary 1001 is _____.
11. The binary equivalent of a decimal 28 is _____.
12. The binary equivalent of a hexadecimal 35 is _____.
13. The decimal equivalent of a hexadecimal 7 is _____.
14. The hexadecimal equivalent of a decimal 49 is _____.
15. The decimal equivalent of a binary 110110110 is _____.
16. The hexadecimal equivalent of a binary 1110 is _____.
17. The result of $101_2 + 11_2$ is _____ (in binary).
18. The result of $A1_{16} + BC_{16} + 10_{16}$ is _____ (in hexadecimal).
19. The result of $60_{10} + F1_{16} - 1001001_2$ is _____ (in decimal).
20. The result of $11_2 + 27_8 + 93_{10} - B_{16}$ is _____ (in decimal).

Self-test answers. 1. 16, 2. 2. T. 3. 4. 4. F. 5. 11111111. 6. 11100. 7. 438. 8. 81. 9. 53. 10. 9. 11. 11100. 12. 110101. 13. 7. 14. 31. 15. 438. 16. E. 17. 1000_2. 18. $16D_{16}$. 19. 228_{10}. 20. 108_{10}.

GLOSSARY

Abacus Probably the original mechanical counting device, which can be traced back at least 5000 years. Beads are moved along parallel wires to count and perform arithmetic computations.

Absolute cell address A cell address in a spreadsheet that always refers to the same cell.

Access arm The disk drive mechanism used to position the read/write heads over the appropriate track.

Access time The time interval between the instant a computer makes a request for a transfer of data from a secondary storage device and the instant this operation is completed.

Accumulator The computer register in which the result of an arithmetic or logic operation is formed. (Related to *arithmetic and logic unit.*)

Acoustical coupler A device on which a telephone handset is mounted for the purpose of transmitting data over telephone lines. Used with a modem.

Ada A multipurpose, procedure-oriented language.

Add-on boards Circuit boards that contain the electronic circuitry for a wide variety of computer-related functions (also called *add-on cards*).

Add-on cards See *add-on boards.*

Address (1) A name, numeral, or label that designates a particular location in primary or secondary storage. (2) A location identifier for terminals in a computer network.

Algorithm A procedure that can be used to solve a particular problem.

Alpha A reference to the letters of the alphabet. (Compare with *numeric* and *alphanumeric.*)

Alpha test The in-house testing of a software product by the vendor prior to its release for beta testing. (Contrast with *beta test.*)

Alphanumeric Pertaining to a character set that contains letters, digits, punctuation, and special symbols. (Related to *alpha* and *numeric.*)

Altair 8800 Considered the first personal computer (1975).

Animation The rapid repositioning of an area of a display to create movement within the display.

ANSI [American National Standards Institute] An organization that coordinates the setting of standards in the United States, including certain software standards.

APL [A Programming Language] An interactive symbolic programming language used primarily for mathematical applications.

Apple II The first commercially successful personal computer of Apple Computer, Inc. (1976).

Application A problem or task to which the computer can be applied.

Application generator A very high-level programming language in which programmers specify, through an interactive dialog with the system, which processing tasks are to be performed (also called *code generator*).

Applications portfolio The current mix of existing and proposed information systems in an organization.

Applications programmer A programmer who writes programs for specific business applications.

Applications software Software designed and written to address a specific personal, business, or processing task.

Architecture The design of a computer system.

Argument That portion of a function which identifies the data to be operated on.

Arithmetic and logic unit That portion of the computer that performs arithmetic and logic operations. (Related to *accumulator.*)

Arithmetic operators Mathematical operators (add [+], subtract [−], multiply [*], divide [/], and exponentiation [∧]) used in spreadsheet and database software for computations.

Array A programming concept that permits access to a list or table of values by the use of a single variable name.

Artificial intelligence (AI) The ability of a computer to reason, to learn, to strive for self-improvement, and to simulate human sensory capabilities.

ASCII [American Standard Code for Information Interchange] An encoding system.

ASCII file A generic text file that is stripped of program-specific control characters.

Assembler language A low-level symbolic language with an instruction set that is essentially one-to-one with machine language.

Assistant system A type of knowledge-based system that helps users make relatively straightforward decisions. (Contrast with *expert system.*)

Asynchronous transmission Data transmission at irregular intervals that is synchronized with start/stop bits. (Contrast with *synchronous transmission.*)

Attribute A field in a relational data base.

Automatic teller machine (ATM) An automated deposit/withdrawal device used in banking.

Automation The automatic control and operation of machines, processes, and procedures.

Back-end processor A host-subordinate processor that handles administrative tasks associated with retrieval and manipulation of data (same as *data base machine*).

Background (1) That part of RAM that contains the lowest priority programs. (2) In Windows, the area of the display over which the foreground is superimposed. (Contrast with *foreground*.)

Backup Pertaining to equipment, procedures, or data bases that can be used to restart the system in the event of system failure.

Backup file Duplicate of an existing file.

Badge reader An input device that reads data on badges and cards. (Related to *magnetic stripe*.)

Bar code A graphic encoding technique in which vertical bars of varying widths are used to represent data.

Bar graph A graph that contains vertical bars that represent specified numeric values.

Bar menu A menu in which the options are displayed across the screen.

BASIC A popular multipurpose programming language.

Batch file A disk file that contains a list of commands and/or programs that are to be executed immediately following the loading of the operating system to main memory.

Batch processing A technique in which transactions and/or jobs are collected into groups (batched) and processed together.

Baud (1) A measure of the maximum number of electronic signals that can be transmitted via a communications channel. (2) Bits per second (common-use definition).

Benchmark test A test for comparing the performance of several computer systems while running the same software, or comparing the performance of several programs that are run on the same computer.

Beta test Testing a software product in a live environment prior to its release to the public. (Contrast with *alpha test*.)

Binary A base-2 numbering system.

Binary notation Using the binary (base-2) numbering system (0, 1) for internal representation of alphanumeric data.

Bit A *binary digit* (0 or 1).

Bit-mapped Referring to an image that has been projected to a screen based on binary bits.

Bits per second (bps) The number of bits that can be transmitted per second over a communications channel.

Block A group of data that is either read from or written to an I/O device in one operation.

Blocking Combining two or more records into one block.

Boilerplate Existing text in a word processing file that can in some way be customized to be used in a variety of word processing applications.

Boot The procedure for loading the operating system to primary storage and readying a computer system for use.

BPI [Bytes Per Inch] A measure of data-recording density on secondary storage.

Bridge A protocol-independent hardware device that permits communication between devices on separate local area networks.

Bubble memory Nonvolatile solid-state memory.

Buffer Intermediate memory that temporarily holds data that are en route from main memory to another computer or an input/output device.

Bug A logic or syntax error in a program, a logic error in the design of a computer system, or a hardware fault. (See *debug*.)

Bulletin-board system (BBS) The electronic counterpart of a wall-mounted bulletin board that enables end users in a computer network to exchange ideas and information via a centralized data base.

Bus An electrical pathway through which the processor sends data and commands to RAM and all peripheral devices.

Bus architecture See *open architecture*.

Bus topology A computer network that permits the connection of terminals, peripheral devices, and microcomputers along an open-ended central cable.

Byte A group of adjacent bits configured to represent a character.

Bytes per inch See *bpi*.

C A transportable programming language that can be used to develop software.

C++ An object-oriented version of the C programming language.

Cache memory High-speed solid-state memory for program instructions and data.

CAD See *computer-aided design*.

CAM See *computer-aided manufacturing*.

Capacity planning The process by which MIS planners determine to what extent hardware resources are needed to meet anticipated demands.

Carrier Standard-sized pin connectors that permit chips to be attached to a circuit board.

Carrier, common [in data communications] A company that furnishes data communications services to the general public.

CASE [Computer-Aided Software Engineering] A collective reference to a family of software development productivity tools (also called *workbench technologies*).

Cathode-ray tube See *CRT*.

CBT See *computer-based training*.

CD-ROM disk [Compact-Disk–Read-Only Memory disk] A type of optical laser storage media.

Cell The intersection of a particular row and column in a spreadsheet.

Cell address The location—column and row—of a cell in a spreadsheet.

Central processing unit (CPU) See *processor*.

Centronics connector A 36-pin connector that is used for the electronic interconnection of computers, modems, and other peripheral devices.

Certificate in Computer Programming (CCP) A certification for programmers.

Certificate in Data Processing (CDP) A general certification in the area of computers and information systems.

Certified Data Educator (CDE) A certification for educators in the general area of computers and information systems.

Certified Information Systems Auditor (CISA) A certification for information systems auditors.

Certified System Professional (CSP) A general certification in the area of computers and information systems.

Channel The facility by which data are transmitted between locations in a computer network (e.g., terminal to host, host to printer).

Channel capacity The number of bits that can be transmitted over a communications channel per second.

Character A unit of alphanumeric datum.

Checkpoint/restart When a system fails, backup files/data bases and/or backup transaction logs are used to re-create processing from the last "checkpoint." The system is "restarted" at the last checkpoint, and normal operation is resumed.

Chief information officer (CIO) The individual responsible for all information services in a company.

Chip See *integrated circuit.*

CIM [Computer-Integrated Manufacturing] Using the computer at every stage of the manufacturing process, from the time a part is conceived until it is shipped.

CISC [Complex Instruction Set Computer] A computer design architecture that offers programmers a wide variety of instructions. (Contrast with *RISC.*)

Click A single tap on a mouse's button.

Clip art Prepackaged electronic images that are stored on disk to be used as needed in word processing or desktop publishing documents.

Clone A hardware device or a software package that emulates a product with an established reputation and market acceptance.

Closed architecture Refers to micros with a fixed, unalterable configuration. (Contrast with *open architecture.*)

Cluster controller See *down-line processor.*

Clustered-bar graph A modified bar graph that can be used to represent a two-dimensional set of numeric data (for example, multiple product sales by region).

Coaxial cable A shielded wire used as a medium to transmit data between computers and between computers and peripheral devices.

COBOL [COmmon Business Oriented Language] A programming language used primarily for administrative information systems.

Code (1) The rules used to translate a bit configuration into alphanumeric characters. (2) The process of compiling computer instructions in the form of a computer program. (3) The actual computer program.

Code generator See *application generator.*

Collate To combine two or more files for processing.

Column A vertical block of cells that runs the length of a spreadsheet and is labeled by a letter.

COM [Computer Output Microform] A device that produces a microform image of a computer output on microfilm or microfiche.

Command An instruction to a computer that invokes the execution of a preprogrammed sequence of instructions.

Command-driven Pertaining to software packages that respond to user directives entered as commands.

Common carrier [in data communications] See *carrier, common.*

Common User Access (CUA) The standard by which all software applications designed be to run under Microsoft's Windows must adhere.

Communications See *data communications.*

Communications channel The facility by which data are transmitted between locations in a computer network.

Communications protocols Rules established to govern the way data are transmitted in a computer network.

Communications server The LAN component that provides external communications links.

Communications software (1) Software that enables a microcomputer to emulate a terminal and to transfer files between a micro and another computer. (2) Software that enables communication between remote devices in a computer network.

Compaq Portable Considered the first portable personal computer (1982).

Compatibility (1) Pertaining to the ability of one computer to execute programs of, access the data base of, and communicate with another computer. (2) Pertaining to the ability of a particular hardware device to interface with a particular computer.

Competitive advantage A term used to describe a company's leveraging of computer and information technologies to realize an advantage over its competitors.

Compile To translate a high-level programming language, such as COBOL, into machine language in preparation for execution.

Compiler Systems software that performs the compilation process. (Compare with *interpreter.*)

Computer An electronic device capable of interpreting and executing programmed commands for input, output, computation, and logic operations.

Computer competency A fundamental understanding of the technology, operation, applications, and issues surrounding computers.

Computer console The unit of a computer system that allows operator and computer to communicate.

Computer matching The procedure whereby separate data bases are examined and individuals common to both are identified.

Computer network An integration of computer systems, terminals, and communications links.

Computer operator One who performs duties associated with the routine operation of a minicomputer, mainframe, or supercomputer system.

Computer system A collective reference to all interconnected computing hardware, including processors, storage devices, input/output devices, and communications equipment.

Computer-aided design (CAD) Use of computer graphics in design, drafting, and documentation in product and manufacturing engineering.

Computer-aided manufacturing (CAM) A term coined to highlight the use of computers in the manufacturing process.

Computer-aided software engineering See *CASE.*

Computer-based training (CBT) Using computer technologies for training and education.

Computer-integrated manufacturing See *CIM.*

Computer output microform See *COM.*

Computerese A slang term referring to the jargon associated with computers and information processing.

Concatenation The joining together of labels or fields and other character strings into a single character string in spreadsheet or database software.

Configuration The computer and its peripheral devices.

Connectivity Pertains to the degree to which hardware devices, software, and data bases can be functionally linked to one another.

Contention A line-control procedure in which each terminal "contends" with other terminals for service by sending requests for service to the host processor.

Context-sensitive Referring to an on-screen explanation that relates to a user's current software activity.

Control clerk A person who accounts for all input to and output from a computer center.

Control field See *key field.*

Control total An accumulated number that is checked against a known value for the purpose of output control.

Control unit The portion of the processor that interprets program instructions, directs internal operations, and directs the flow of input/output to or from main memory.

Conversion The transition process from one system (manual or computer-based) to a computer-based information system.

Cooperative computing An environment in which businesses cooperate internally and externally to take full advantage of available information and to obtain meaningful, accurate, and timely information. (See also *intracompany networking.*)

Coprocessor An extra processor under the control of the main processor that helps relieve it of certain tasks.

Core memory A main memory technology that was popular in the 1950s and 1960s.

Cottage industry People who do work-for-profit from their homes.

Counter One or several programming instructions used to tally processing events.

CP/M The dominant non-Apple operating system during the late 1970s.

CPU The main processor in a computer system. (See also *host processor.*)

CRT [Cathode-Ray Tube] The video monitor component of a terminal.

Cryptography A communications crime-prevention technology that uses methods of data encryption and decryption to scramble codes sent over communications channels.

Current window The window in which the user can manipulate text, data, or graphics.

Cursor, graphics Typically an arrow or crosshair which can be moved about a monitor's screen by an input device to create a graphic image or select an item from a menu. (See also *cursor, text.*)

Cursor, text A blinking character that indicates the location of the next keyed-in character on the display screen. (See also *cursor, graphics.*)

Cursor-control keys The arrow keys on the keyboard that move the text cursor vertically a line at a time and horizontally a character at a time.

Custom code Software written to handle situations unique to a particular processing environment.

Cyberphobia The irrational fear of, and aversion to, computers.

Cylinder A disk storage concept. A cylinder is that portion of the disk that can be read in any given position of the access arm. (Contrast with *sector.*)

Daisy-wheel printer A letter-quality serial printer. Its interchangeable character set is located on a spoked print wheel.

DASD [Direct Access Storage Device] A random-access secondary storage device.

Data Representations of facts. Raw material for information. (Plural of *datum.*)

Data base (1) An organization's data resource for all computer-based information processing in which the data are integrated and related to minimize data redundancy. (2) Same as a file in the context of microcomputer usage. (Contrast with *database.*)

Data base administrator (DBA) The individual responsible for the physical and logical maintenance of the data base.

Data base machine See *back-end processor.*

Data base record Related data that are read from, or written to, the data base as a unit.

Data bits A data communications parameter that refers to the number of bits in a message.

Data cartridge Magnetic tape storage in cassette format.

Data communications The collection and distribution of the electronic representation of information from and to remote facilities.

Data communications specialist A person who designs and implements computer networks.

Data dictionary A listing and description of all fields in the data base.

Data diddling The unauthorized revision of data upon being entered into a system or placed in storage.

Data entry The transcription of source data into a machine-readable format.

Data entry operator A person who uses key entry devices to transcribe data into a machine-readable format.

Data flow diagram (DFD) A design technique that permits documentation of a system or program at several levels of generality.

Data item The value of a field. (Compare with *field.*)

Data processing (DP) Using the computer to perform operations on data.

Database An alternative term for microcomputer-based data management software. (Contrast with *data base.*)

Database management system (DBMS) A systems software package for the creation, manipulation, and maintenance of the data base.

Database software Software that permits users to create and maintain a data base and to extract information from the data base.

DB2 IBM's mainframe-based relational DBMS.

DBMS See *database management system.*

Debug To eliminate bugs in a program or system. (See *bug.*)

Decimal The base-10 numbering system.

Decision support system (DSS) An interactive information system that relies on an integrated set of user-friendly hardware and software tools to produce and present information targeted to support management decision making involving semistructured and unstructured problems. (Contrast with *executive support system* and *management information system.*)

Decision table A graphic technique used to illustrate possible occurrences and appropriate actions within a system.

Decode To reverse the encoding process. (Contrast with *encode.*)

Decoder That portion of a processor's control unit that interprets instructions.

Default options   Preset software options that are assumed valid unless specified otherwise by the user.

Density   The number of bytes per linear length or unit area of a recording medium.

Departmental computing   Any type of computing done at the departmental level.

Departmental computing system   Computer systems used both as stand-alone systems in support of a particular department and as part of a network of departmental minicomputers, all linked to a large centralized computer.

Desktop computer   Any computer that can be placed conveniently on the top of a desk (same as *microcomputer, personal computer, PC*). Also called *desktop PC*.

Desktop film recorders   An output device that permits the reproduction of high-resolution computer-generated graphic images on 35-mm film.

Desktop page printer   A small printer that uses laser technology to print near-typeset-quality text and graphics one page at a time.

Desktop publishing (DTP)   Refers to the hardware and software capability of producing near-typeset-quality copy from the confines of a desktop.

Detail system design   That portion of the systems development process in which the target system is defined in detail.

Dial-up line   See *switched line*.

Dialog box   A window that is displayed when the user must choose parameters or enter further information before the chosen menu option can be executed.

Dictionary   See *information repository*.

Digitize   To translate data or an image into a discrete format that can be interpreted by computers.

Digitizing tablet   A pressure-sensitive tablet with the same x–y coordinates as a computer-generated screen. The outline of an image drawn on a tablet with a stylus or puck is reproduced on the display.

DIP [Dual Inline Package]   A toggle switch typically used to designate certain computer system configuration specifications (such as the amount of RAM).

Direct access   See *random access*.

Direct access storage device   See *DASD*.

Direct conversion   An approach to system conversion whereby operational support by the new system is begun when the existing system is terminated.

Direct-access file   See *random file*.

Direct-access processing   See *random processing*.

Director of information services   The person in an organization who has responsibility for computer and information systems.

Directory   A list of the names of the files stored on a particular diskette or in a named area on a hard disk.

Disk, magnetic   A secondary storage medium for random-access data storage available in permanently installed or interchangeable formats.

Disk address   The physical location of a particular set of data or a program on a magnetic disk.

Disk caching   A hardware/software technique in which frequently referenced disk-based data are placed in an area of RAM that simulates disk storage.

Disk cartridge   An environmentally sealed interchangeable disk module that contains one or more hard disk platters.

Disk density   The number of bits that can be stored per unit of area on the disk-face surface.

Disk drive, magnetic   A magnetic storage device that records data on flat rotating disks. (Compare with *tape drive, magnetic*.)

Disk pack   An interchangeable disk module that contains several hard disk platters mounted on a central spindle.

Diskette   A thin interchangeable disk for secondary random-access data storage (same as *floppy disk* and *flexible disk*).

Distributed data processing   Both a technological and an organizational concept based on the premise that information systems can be made more responsive to users by moving computer hardware and personnel physically closer to the people who use them.

Distributed DBMS   Software that permits the interfacing of data bases located in various places throughout a computer network.

Distributed processor   The nucleus of a small computer system linked to the host computer and physically located in the functional area departments.

Document-conversion program   Software that converts files generated on one software package into a format consistent with another.

Documentation   Permanent and continuously updated written and graphic descriptions of information systems and programs.

Domain expert   An expert in a particular field who provides the factual knowledge and the heuristic rules for input to a knowledge base.

DOS [Disk Operating System]   A generic reference to a disk-based operating system.

Dot-matrix printer   A printer that arranges printed dots to form characters and images.

Down-line processor   A computer that collects data from a number of low-speed devices, then transmits "concentrated" data over a single communications channel (also called *cluster controller*).

Download   The transmission of data from a mainframe computer to a terminal.

Downtime   The time during which a computer system is not operational.

DP   See *data processing*.

Drag   A mouse-based procedure by which an object is moved or a contiguous area on the display is marked for processing.

Draw software   Software that enables users to create electronic images. Resultant images are stored as vector graphics images.

Driver module   The program module that calls other subordinate program modules to be executed as they are needed (also called a *main program*).

DTP   See *desktop publishing*.

E-mail   See *electronic mail*.

E-time   See *execution time*.

Earth station   An earth-based communications station that can transmit and receive data from communications satellites.

EBCDIC [Extended Binary Coded Decimal Interchange Code]   An encoding system.

Echo   Referring to a host computer's retransmission of characters back to the sending device.

Education coordinator The person within an organization who coordinates all computer-related educational activities.

EFT [Electronic Funds Transfer] A computer-based system allowing electronic transfer of money from one account to another.

EGA [Enhanced Graphics Adapter] A circuit board that enables the interfacing of high-resolution monitors to microcomputers.

EISA [Extended Industry Standard Architecture] An architecture for microcomputers that use the Intel microprocessors.

Electromechanical accounting machine (EAM) A family of data processing machines that used the punched card as the basis for data storage.

Electronic bulletin board A computer-based "bulletin board" that permits external users access to the system via data communications for the purpose of reading and sending messages.

Electronic data interchange (EDI) The use of computers and data communications to transmit data electronically between companies.

Electronic data processing Same as *data processing*.

Electronic dictionary A disk-based dictionary used in conjunction with a spelling-checker program to verify the spelling of words in a word processing document.

Electronic funds transfer See *EFT*.

Electronic mail A computer application whereby messages are transmitted via data communications to "electronic mailboxes" (also called *E-mail*). (Contrast with *voice message switching*.)

Encode To apply the rules of a code. (Contrast with *decode*.)

Encoding system A system that permits alphanumeric characters to be coded in terms of bits.

Encyclopedia See *information repository*.

End user The individual providing input to the computer or using computer output (same as *user*).

End user computing A computing environment in which the end users handle both the technical and functional tasks of the information systems projects.

End-of-file (EOF) marker A marker placed at the end of a sequential file.

EPROM Erasable PROM [Programmable Read-Only Memory]. (See *PROM*.)

Exception report A report that has been filtered to highlight critical information.

Execution time The elapsed time it takes to execute a computer instruction and store the results (also called *E-time*).

Executive support system (ESS) A system designed specifically to support decision making at the strategic level. (Contrast with *decision support system* and *management information system*.)

Expansion slots Slots within the processing component of a microcomputer into which optional add-on circuit boards may be inserted.

Expert system An interactive knowledge-based system that responds to questions, asks for clarification, makes recommendations, and generally helps users make complex decisions. (Contrast with *assistant system*.)

Expert system shell The software that enables the development of expert systems.

Facilities management company For a fee, employees of facilities management companies physically move into a client company's computer center and take over all facets of the center's operation.

Facsimile Equipment that transfers images of hard-copy documents via telephone lines to another office.

Fault-tolerant system A computer system that can operate under adverse environmental conditions.

Fetch instruction That part of the instruction cycle in which the control unit retrieves a program instruction from main memory and loads it to the processor.

Fiber optic cable A data transmission medium that carries data in the form of light in very thin transparent fibers.

Field The smallest logical unit of data. Examples are employee number, first name, and price. (Compare with *data item*.)

File (1) A collection of related records. (2) A named area on a secondary storage device that contains a program, data, or textual material.

File server A micro with a high-capacity disk for storing the data and programs shared by the users on a LAN.

Filtering The process of selecting and presenting only that information appropriate to support a particular decision.

Firmware Logic for performing certain computer functions that is built into a particular computer by the manufacturer, often in the form of ROM or PROM.

Fixed disk See *hard disk*.

Flat files A traditional file structure in which records are related to no other files.

Flat-panel monitor A monitor, thin from front to back, that uses liquid crystal and gas plasma technology.

Flexible disk See *diskette*.

Floppy disk See *diskette*.

Flops Floating point operations per second.

Flowchart A diagram that illustrates data, information, and work flow via specialized symbols which, when connected by flow lines, portray the logic of a system or program.

Flowcharting The act of creating a flowchart.

Font A typeface that is described by its letter style, its height in points, and its presentation attribute.

Footprint The evidence of unlawful entry or use of a computer system.

Foreground (1) That part of RAM that contains the highest priority program. (2) In Windows, the area of the display containing the active window. (Contrast with *background*.)

Format line See *layout line*.

FORTH A programming language particularly suited for microcomputers that enables users to tailor the language's set of commands to any application.

FORTRAN [FORmula TRANslator] A high-level programming language designed primarily for scientific applications.

Fourth-generation language (4GL) A programming language that uses high-level English-like instructions to retrieve and format data for inquiries and reporting.

Frame A rectangular area in a desktop publishing–produced document that holds the text or an image of a particular file.

Front-end processor A processor used to offload certain data communications tasks from the host processor.

Frozen specifications System specifications that have been approved and are not to be changed during the systems development process.

Full-duplex line A communications channel that transmits data in both directions at the same time.

Full-screen editing This word processing feature permits the user to move the cursor to any position in the document to insert or replace text.

Function A predefined operation that performs mathematical, logical, statistical, financial, and character-string operations on data in a spreadsheet or a data base.

Function key A special-function key on the keyboard that can be used to instruct the computer to perform a specific operation (also called *soft key*).

Function-based information system An information system designed for the exclusive support of a specific application area, such as inventory management or accounting.

Functional specifications Specifications that describe the logic of an information system from the user's perspective.

Functionally adjacent systems Information systems that feed each other, have functional overlap, and/or share all or part of a data base.

Gateway Software that permits computers of different architectures to communicate with one another.

Gateway computer A subordinate computer that translates communications protocols of remote computers to a protocol compatible with the host computer, thereby enabling the transmission of data from external sources.

Gb See *gigabit*.

GB See *gigabyte*.

General system design That portion of the systems development process in which the target system is defined in general.

General-purpose computer Computer systems that are designed with the flexibility to do a variety of tasks, such as CAI, payroll processing, climate control, and so on. (Contrast with *special-purpose computer*.)

General-purpose software Software that provides the framework for a number of business and personal applications.

Geostationary orbit See *geosynchronous orbit*.

Geosynchronous orbit An orbit that permits a communications satellite to maintain a fixed position relative to the surface of the earth (also known as *geostationary orbit*).

Gigabit (Gb) One billion bits.

Gigabyte (GB) One billion bytes.

GIGO [Garbage In, Garbage Out] A euphemism implying that information is only as good as the data from which it is derived.

Graceful exit Quitting a program according to normal procedures and returning to a higher-level program.

Grammar checker An add-on program to word processing software that highlights grammatical concerns and deviations from conventions in a word processing document.

Grandfather-father-son method A secondary storage backup procedure that results in the master file having two generations of backup.

Graphical user interface (GUI) Software that permits users to select processing options simply by positioning an arrow over a graphic representation of the desired function or program.

Graphics cursor A symbol on a display screen which can be positioned anywhere on a display screen by a light pen, joystick, track ball, digitizing tablet and pen, or mouse to initiate action or to draw.

Graphics mode One of two modes of operation for PC monitors. (Contrast with *text mode*.)

Graphics software Software that enables you to create line drawings, art, and presentation graphics.

Graphics workstation See *workstation*.

Graphics-conversion program Software that enables files containing graphic images to be passed between programs.

Gray scales The number of shades of a color that can be presented on a monochrome monitor's screen or on a monochrome printer's output.

Hacker A computer enthusiast who uses the computer as a source of recreation.

Half-duplex line A communications channel that transmits data in both directions, but not at the same time.

Half-size expansion board An add-on board that fits in half an expansion slot.

Handshaking The process by which both sending and receiving devices in a computer network maintain and coordinate data communications.

Hard carriage return In word processing, a special character that is inserted in the document when the ENTER key is tapped. Typically, the character denotes the end of a paragraph.

Hard copy A readable printed copy of computer output. (Contrast with *soft copy*.)

Hard disk A permanently installed, continuously spinning magnetic storage medium made up of one or more rigid disk platters. (Same as *fixed disk*; contrast with *interchangeable magnetic disk*. See also *Winchester disk*.)

Hard-wired Logic that is designed into chips.

Hardware The physical devices that comprise a computer system. (Contrast with *software*.)

Hashing A method of random access in which the address is arithmetically calculated from the key field.

Head crash A disk drive malfunction that causes the read/write head to touch the surface of the disk, thereby resulting in the loss of the disk head, the disk, and the data stored on the disk.

Header label A file identification record found at the beginning of a sequential file.

Help command A software feature that provides an on-line explanation of or instruction on how to proceed.

Help screen The display that results from initiating the help command.

Hertz One cycle per second.

Heuristic knowledge Rules of thumb that evolve from experience.

Hexadecimal A base-16 numbering system used as a programmer convenience in information processing to condense binary output and make it more easily readable.

Hierarchical data base A data base whose organization employs the tree data structure. (Contrast with *relational data base* and *network data base*.)

High-level programming language A language with instructions that combine several machine-level instructions into one instruction. (Compare with *machine language* or *low-level programming language*.)

HIPO [Hierarchical Plus Input-Processing-Output] A design technique that encourages the top-down approach, dividing the system into easily manageable modules.

Historical reports Reports generated from data that were gathered in the past and do not reflect current status. (Contrast with *status reports*.)

Host computer See *host processor*.

Host processor The processor responsible for the overall control of a computer system. The host processor is the focal point of a communications-based system (also called *host computer*).

Hypermedia Software that enables the integration of data, text, graphics, sounds of all kinds, and full-motion video. (See also *hypertext*.)

Hypertext Data management software that provides links between key words in the unstructured text-based documents. (See also *hypermedia*.)

I/O [Input/Output] Input or output or both.

I-time See *instruction time*.

IBM Personal Computer (IBM PC) IBM's first personal computer (1981).

IBM Personal System/2 (PS/2) IBM's successor to the IBM PC (1987).

Icons Pictographs used in place of words or phrases on screen displays.

Idea processor A software productivity tool that allows the user to organize and document thoughts and ideas.

Identifier A name used in computer programs to recall a value, an array, a program, or a function from storage.

Image scanner A device which uses a camera to scan and digitize an image that can be stored on a disk and manipulated by a computer.

Index file Within the context of database software, a file that contains logical pointers to records in a data base.

Indexed-sequential organization A direct-access data storage scheme that uses an index to locate and access data stored on magnetic disk.

Industrial robot A robot used in industry. (See *robot*.)

Inference engine The logic embodied in the software of an expert system.

Information Data that have been collected and processed into a meaningful form.

Information center A facility in which computing resources are made available to various user groups.

Information center specialist Someone who works with users in an information center.

Information engineering A term coined to emphasize using the rigors of engineering discipline in the handling of the information resource.

Information management systems (IMS) IBM's mainframe-based hierarchical DBMS.

Information network Same as *information service*.

Information overload The circumstance that occurs when the volume of available information is so great that the decision maker cannot distinguish relevant from irrelevant information.

Information repository A central computer-based storage facility for all systems design information (also called *dictionary* or *encyclopedia*).

Information resource management (IRM) A concept advocating that information be treated as a corporate resource.

Information service An on-line commercial network that provides remote users with access to a variety of information services (same as *information network*).

Information services auditor Someone responsible for ensuring the integrity of operational information systems.

Information services department The organizational entity that develops and maintains computer-based information systems.

Information society A society in which the generation and dissemination of information becomes the central focus of commerce.

Information system A computer-based system that provides both data processing capability and information for managerial decision making.

Information technology A collective reference to the combined fields of computers and information systems.

Information-based decision See *nonprogrammed decision*.

Input Data to be processed by a computer system.

Input/output—bound operation The amount of work that can be performed by the computer system is limited primarily by the speeds of the I/O devices.

Inquiry An on-line request for information.

Insert mode A data entry mode in which the character entered is inserted at the cursor position.

Instruction A programming language statement that specifies a particular computer operation to be performed.

Instruction register The register that contains the instruction being executed.

Instruction time The elapsed time it takes to fetch and decode a computer instruction (also called *I-time*).

Integrated circuit (IC) Thousands of electronic components that are etched into a tiny silicon chip in the form of a special-function electronic circuit.

Integrated information system An information system that services two or more functional areas, all of which share a common data base.

Integrated services digital network (ISDN) A digital telecommunications standard.

Integrated software Two or more of the major microcomputer productivity tools integrated into a single commercial software package.

Intelligent Pertaining to computer-aided.

Intelligent terminal A terminal with a built-in microprocessor.

Interactive Pertaining to on-line and immediate communication between the end user and computer.

Interactive computer system A computer system that permits users to communicate directly with the system.

Interblock gap (IBG) A physical space between record blocks on magnetic tapes.

Interchangeable magnetic disk A magnetic disk that can be stored off-line and loaded to the magnetic disk drive as it is needed. (Contrast with *hard disk*, or *fixed disk*.)

Intercompany networking See *electronic data interchange*.

Interpreter Systems software that translates and executes each program instruction before translating and executing the next. (Compare with *compiler*.)

Interrupt   A signal that causes a program or a device to stop or pause temporarily.

Intracompany networking   The use of computers and data communications to transmit data electronically within a company. (See also *cooperative computing*.)

Invoke   Execute a command or a macro.

ISO [International Standards Organization]   An organization that coordinates the setting of international standards.

Job   A unit of work for the computer system.

Job stream   The sequence in which programs are to be executed.

Job-control language (JCL)   A language used to tell the computer the order in which programs are to be executed.

Joystick   A single vertical stick that moves the cursor on a screen in the direction in which the stick is pushed.

Kb   See *kilobit*.

KB   See *kilobyte*.

Kernel   An independent software module that is part of a larger program.

Key field   The field in a record that is used as an identifier for accessing, sorting, and collating records (same as *control field*).

Key pad   That portion of a keyboard that permits rapid numeric data entry.

Keyboard   A device used for key data entry.

Keyboard templates   Typically, a plastic keyboard overlay that indicates which commands are assigned to particular function keys.

Kilobit (Kb)   1024, or about 1000, bits.

Kilobyte (KB)   1024, or about 1000, bytes.

Knowledge acquisition facility   That component of the expert system shell that permits the construction of the knowledge base.

Knowledge base   The foundation of a knowledge-based system that contains facts, rules, inferences, and procedures.

Knowledge engineer   Someone trained in the use of expert system shells and in the interview techniques needed to extract information from a domain expert.

Knowledge worker   Someone whose job function revolves around the use, manipulation, and dissemination of information.

Knowledge-based system   A computer-based system, often associated with artificial intelligence, that helps users make decisions by enabling them to interact with a knowledge base.

LAN operating system   The operating system for a local area network.

Landscape   Referring to the orientation of the print on the page. Printed lines run parallel to the longer side of the page. (Contrast with *portrait*.)

Laptop PC   Portable PC that can operate without an external power source.

Large-scale integration (LSI)   An integrated circuit with a densely packed concentration of electronic components. (Contrast with *very large-scale integration*, or *VLSI*.)

Layout   A detailed output and/or input specification that graphically illustrates exactly where information should be placed/entered on a VDT screen or placed on printed output.

Layout line   A line on a word processing screen that graphically illustrates appropriate user settings (margins, tabs). (Also called a *format line*.)

Leased line   Same as *private line*.

Lexicon   The dictionary of words that can be interpreted by a particular natural language.

Librarian   A person who functions to catalog, monitor, and control the distribution of disks, tapes, system documentation, and computer-related literature.

Light pen   A point-and-draw input device.

Light-emitting diode (LED)   A device that responds to electrical current by emitting light.

Limits check   A system check that assesses whether the value of an entry is out of line with that expected.

Line graph   A graph in which conceptually similar points are plotted and connected so they are represented by one or several lines.

Line printer   Printers that print a line at a time.

Linkage editor   An operating system program that assigns a primary storage address to each byte of an object program.

Liquid crystal display (LCD)   An output device that displays characters and other images as composites of actuated liquid crystal.

LISP [LISt Processing]   A programming language particularly suited for the manipulation of words and phrases that is often used in applications of artificial intelligence.

Live data   Test data that have already been processed through an existing system.

Load   To transfer programs or data from secondary to primary storage.

Local area network (LAN or local net)   A system of hardware, software, and communications channels that connects devices on the local premises.

Local memory   Pertaining to the random-access memory associated with a particular processor or peripheral device.

Local net   See *local area network*.

Log on procedure   The procedure by which a user establishes a communications link with a remote computer.

Logic bomb   A Trojan horse that is executed when a certain set of conditions are met.

Logic error   A programming error that causes an erroneous result when the program is executed.

Logic operations   Computer operations that make comparisons between numbers and between words, then perform appropriate functions, based on the result of the comparison.

Logical operators   Used to combine relational expressions logically in spreadsheet and database software (such as AND, OR). (See also *relational operators*.)

Logical record   See *record*.

Logical security   That aspect of computer-center security that deals with user access to systems and data.

LOGO   A programming language often used to teach children concepts in mathematics, geometry, and computer programming.

Loop   A sequence of program instructions executed repeatedly until a particular condition is met.

Lotus 1-2-3   A popular spreadsheet package.

Low-level programming language   A language comprising the fundamental instruction set of a particular computer. (Compare with *high-level programming language*.)

Machine cycle   The cycle of operations performed by the processor to process a single program instruction: fetch, decode, execute, and place result in memory.

Machine language   The programming language that is interpreted and executed directly by the computer. (See *low-level programming language*.)

Machine-independent   Pertaining to programs that can be executed on computers of different designs.

Macintosh   Apple Computer's mainline PC.

Macro   A sequence of frequently used operations or keystrokes that can be recalled and invoked to help speed user interaction with microcomputer productivity software.

Magnetic disk   See *disk, magnetic*.

Magnetic disk drive   See *disk drive, magnetic*.

Magnetic ink character recognition (MICR)   A data entry technique used primarily in banking. Magnetic characters are imprinted on checks and deposits, then scanned to retrieve the data.

Magnetic stripe   A magnetic storage medium for low-volume storage of data on badges and cards. (Related to *badge reader*.)

Magnetic tape   See *tape, magnetic*.

Magnetic tape cartridge   Cartridge-based magnetic tape storage media.

Magnetic tape drive   See *tape drive, magnetic*.

Magnetic tape reel   Reel-based magnetic tape storage media.

Magneto-optical disk   An optical laser disk with read and write capabilities.

Mail merge   A computer application in which text generated by word processing is merged with data from a data base (e.g., a form letter with an address).

Main memory   See *primary storage*.

Main menu   The highest-level menu in a menu tree.

Main program   Same as *driver module*.

Mainframe computer   A large computer that can service many users simultaneously.

Maintenance   The ongoing process by which information systems (and software) are updated and enhanced to keep up with changing requirements.

Management information system (MIS)   An integrated structure of data bases and information flow throughout all levels and components of an organization, whereby the collection, transfer, and presentation of information is optimized to meet the needs of the organization. (Contrast with *decision support system* and *executive support system*.)

Manipulator arm   The movable part of an industrial robot to which special-function tools are attached.

Master file   The permanent source of data for a particular computer application area.

Maxicomputers   That category of computers that falls between minicomputers and supercomputers.

Mb   See *megabit*.

MB   See *megabyte*.

MCA [Micro Channel Architecture]   The architecture of the high-end IBM PS/2 line of microcomputers.

Megabit (Mb)   1,048,576, or about one million, bits.

Megabyte (MB)   Referring to one million bytes of primary or secondary storage capacity.

Memory   See *primary storage*.

Memory dump   The duplication of the contents of a storage device to another storage device or to a printer.

Memory-resident program   A program, other than the operating system, that remains operational while another applications program is running.

Menu   A display with a list of processing choices from which an end user may select.

Menu bar   A bar menu that lists menus available for the active application.

Menu driven   Pertaining to software packages which respond to user directives that are entered via a hierarchy of menus.

Menu tree   A hierarchy of menus.

Message   A series of bits sent from a terminal to a computer, or vice versa.

MHz [megahertz]   One million hertz.

MICR inscriber   An output device that enables the printing of characters for magnetic ink character recognition on bank checks and deposit slips.

MICR reader-sorter   An input device that reads the magnetic ink character recognition data on bank documents and sorts them.

Micro   See *microcomputer*.

Micro/mainframe link   Linking microcomputers and mainframes for the purpose of data communications.

Microcomputer (or micro)   A small computer (same as *desktop computer*, *personal computer*, *PC*).

Microcomputer specialist   A specialist in the use and application of microcomputer hardware and software.

Microframe   A high-end microcomputer.

Microprocessor   A computer on a single chip. The processing component of a microcomputer.

Microsecond   One millionth of a second.

Microwave radio signal   A high-frequency line-of-sight electromagnetic wave used in communications satellites.

Millisecond   One thousandth of a second.

Minicomputer (or mini)   A midsized computer.

MIPS   Millions of instructions per second.

MIS   See *management information system*.

MIS planner   The person in a company who has the responsibility for coordinating and preparing the MIS plans.

Mnemonics   Symbols that represent instructions in assembler languages.

Modem [MOdulator-DEModulator]   A device used to convert computer-compatible signals to signals suitable for data transmission facilities, and vice versa.

Modula-2   A general-purpose language that enables self-contained modules to be combined in a program.

Module   A task within a program that is independent of other tasks.

Monitor   A televisionlike display for soft-copy output in a computer system.

Motherboard   Same as *system board*.

Mouse   A small device that, when moved across a desktop a particular distance and direction, causes the same movement of the cursor on a screen.

MS-DOS [MicroSoft–Disk Operating System]   A microcomputer operating system.

Multicomputer A complex of interconnected computers that share memory while operating in concert or independently.

Multidrop The connection of more than one terminal to a single communications channel.

Multifunction add-on board An add-on circuit board that performs more than one function.

Multiplexing The simultaneous transmission of multiple transmissions of data over a single communications channel.

Multiprocessing Using two or more processors in the same computer system in the simultaneous execution of two or more programs.

Multitasking The concurrent execution of more than one program at a time.

Multiuser microcomputer A microcomputer that can serve more than one user at any given time.

Nanosecond One billionth of a second.

Natural language A programming language in which the programmer writes specifications without regard to the computer's instruction format or syntax—essentially, using everyday human language to program.

Navigation Movement within and between a software application's work areas.

Nested loop A programming situation where at least one loop is entirely within another loop.

Network, computer See *computer network.*

Network data base A data base organization that permits children in a tree data structure to have more than one parent. (Contrast with *hierarchical data base* and *relational data base.*)

Network topology The configuration of interconnection between the nodes in a communications network.

Neural network Millions of interconnected chips that are designed to enable computers to perform human-type tasks.

Node An endpoint in a computer network.

Nonprocedural language A programming language that can automatically generate the instructions needed to create a programmer-described end result.

Nonprogrammed decision A decision that involves an ill-defined and unstructured problem (also called *information-based decision*).

Notebook A notebook-size laptop PC.

NuBus The architecture of high-end Apple Macintosh computers.

Numeric A reference to any of the digits 0–9. (Compare with *alpha* and *alphanumeric.*)

Object program A machine-level program that results from the compilation of a source program. (Compare with *source program.*)

Object-oriented language A programming language structured to enable the interaction between user-defined concepts (such as a computer screen, a list of items) that contain data and operations to be performed on the data.

OCR scanner A light-sensitive input device that bounces a beam of light off an image to interpret the image.

Octal A base-8 numbering system used as a programmer convenience in information processing to condense binary output and make it easier to read.

Off-line Pertaining to data that are not accessible by, or hardware devices that are not connected to, a computer system. (Contrast with *on-line.*)

Office automation (OA) Pertaining collectively to those computer-based applications associated with general office work.

Office automation specialist A person who specializes in the use and application of office automation hardware and software. (See *office automation.*)

On-line Pertaining to data and/or hardware devices accessible to and under the control of a computer system. (Contrast with *off-line.*)

On-line thesaurus Software that enables a user to request synonyms interactively during a word processing session.

Opcode Pertaining to that portion of a computer machine-language instruction that designates the operation to be performed. Short for operation code. (Related to *operand.*)

Open architecture Refers to micros that give users the flexibility to configure the system with a variety of peripheral devices. (Contrast with *closed architecture*; also called *bus architecture.*)

Open systems interconnect (OSI) A standard for data communications within a computer network established by the International Standards Organization (ISO).

Operand Pertaining to that portion of a computer machine-language instruction that designates the address of the data to be operated on. (Related to *opcode.*)

Operating environment (1) A user-friendly DOS interface. (2) The conditions under which a computer system functions.

Operating system The software that controls the execution of all applications and systems software programs.

Operation code See *opcode.*

Operator The person who performs those hardware-based activities necessary to keep information systems operational.

Operator console The machine-room operator's terminal.

Optical character recognition (OCR) A data entry technique that permits original-source data entry. Coded symbols or characters are scanned to retrieve the data.

Optical laser disk A secondary storage medium that uses laser technology to score the surface of a disk to represent a bit.

Orphan The first line of a paragraph that is printed as the last line on a page in a word processing document.

OS/2 A multitasking PC operating system.

Output Data transferred from primary storage to an output device.

Packaged software Software that is generalized and "packaged" to be used with little or no modification in a variety of environments. (Compare with *proprietary software.*)

Packet switching A data communications process in which communications messages are divided into packets (subsets of the whole message), transmitted independent of one another in a communications network, then reassembled at the source.

Page A program segment that is loaded to primary storage only if it is needed for execution. (Related to *virtual memory.*)

Page break In word processing, an in-line command or special character that causes the text that follows to be printed on a new page.

Page offset The distance between the left edge of the paper and the left margin in a word processing document.

Page printer Printers that print a page at a time.

Page-composition software The software component of desktop publishing software that enables users to design and make up pages.

Pagination   The word processing feature that provides automatic numbering of the pages of a document.

Paint software   Software that enables users to "paint" electronic images. Resultant images are stored as raster graphics images.

Palmtop PC   See *pocket PC*.

Parallel   Pertaining to processing data in groups of bits versus one bit at a time. (Contrast with *serial*.)

Parallel conversion   An approach to system conversion whereby the existing system and the new system operate simultaneously until the project team is confident that the new system is working properly.

Parallel host processor   A redundant host processor used for backup and supplemental processing.

Parallel port   A direct link with the microcomputer's bus that facilitates the parallel transmission of data, usually one byte at a time.

Parallel processing   A processing procedure in which one main processor examines the programming problem and determines what portions, if any, of the problem can be solved in pieces by other subordinate processors.

Parallel processor   A processor in which many, even millions of, processing elements simultaneously address parts of a processing problem.

Parallel representation   The storing of bits side-by-side on a secondary storage medium.

Parameter   A descriptor that can take on different values.

Parity bit   A bit appended to a bit configuration (byte) that is used to check the accuracy of data transmission from one hardware device to another. (Related to *parity checking* and *parity error*.)

Parity checking   A built-in checking procedure in a computer system to help ensure that the transmission of data is complete and accurate. (Related to *parity bit* and *parity error*.)

Parity error   Occurs when a bit is dropped in the transmission of data from one hardware device to another. (Related to *parity bit* and *parity checking*.)

Parsing   A process whereby user-written natural language commands are analyzed and translated to commands that can be interpreted by the computer.

Pascal   A multipurpose, procedure-oriented programming language.

Password   A word or phrase known only to the end user. When entered, it permits the end user to gain access to the system.

Patch   A modification of a program or an information system.

Path   The logical route that an operating system would follow when searching through a series of directories and subdirectories to locate a specific file on disk storage.

PBX   A computer that electronically connects computers and terminals for the purpose of data communication.

PC [Personal Computer]   See *desktop computer* and *microcomputer*.

PC-DOS [PC–Disk Operating System]   A microcomputer operating system.

Pen plotter   An output device that can generate high-quality hard-copy graphic output that is perfectly proportioned.

Performance monitoring software   System software used to monitor, analyze, and report on the performance of the overall computer system and its components.

Peripheral equipment   Any hardware device other than the processor.

Personal computer (PC)   See *microcomputer*.

Personal computing   A computing environment in which individuals use microcomputers for both domestic and business applications.

Personal identification number (PIN)   A code or number that is used in conjunction with a password to permit the end user to gain access to a computer system.

Phased conversion   An approach to system conversion whereby an information system is implemented one module at a time by either parallel or direct conversion.

Physical security   That aspect of computer-center security that deals with access to computers and peripheral devices.

Pick-and-place robot   An industrial robot that physically transfers material from one place to another.

Picosecond   One trillionth of a second.

Picture element   See *pixel*.

Pie graph   A circular graph that illustrates each "piece" of data in its proper relationship to the whole "pie."

Pilferage   A special case of software piracy whereby a company purchases a software product without a site-usage license agreement, then copies and distributes it throughout the company.

Pilot conversion   An approach to system conversion whereby the new system is implemented by parallel, direct, or phased conversion as a pilot system in only one of the several areas for which it is targeted.

Pitch   Horizontal spacing (characters per inch) in printed output.

Pixel [picture element]   An addressable point on a display screen to which light can be directed under program control.

PL/I   A multipurpose, procedure-oriented programming language.

Platform   A definition of the standards followed by those who create proprietary software packages.

Plotter   A device that produces high-precision hard-copy graphic output.

Plug-Compatible Manufacturer (PCM)   A company that makes peripheral devices that can be attached directly to another manufacturer's computer.

Pocket PC   Hand-held personal computers (also called *palmtop PC*).

Point-of-sale (POS) terminal   A cash-register-like terminal designed for key and/or scanner data entry.

Point-to-point connection   A single communications channel linking a terminal or a microcomputer to a computer.

Pointer   The highlighted area in a spreadsheet display that indicates the current cell.

Polling   A line-control procedure in which each terminal is "polled" in rotation to determine whether a message is ready to be sent.

Pop-out menu   See *pop-up menu*.

Pop-up menu   A menu that is superimposed in a window over whatever is currently being displayed on the monitor (also called *pop-out menu*).

Port   An access point in a computer system that permits communication between the computer and a peripheral device.

Portable data entry Entering data on a portable device (off-line or on-line).

Portrait Referring to the orientation of the print on the page. Printed lines run parallel to the shorter side of the page. (Contrast with *landscape*.)

Post-implementation evaluation A critical examination of a computer-based system after it has been put into production.

Power down To turn off the electrical power to a computer system.

Power up To turn on the electrical power to a computer system.

Presentation graphics Business graphics, such as pie graphs and bar graphs, that are used to present information in a graphic format in meetings, reports, and oral presentations.

Prespecification An approach to information systems development whereby users determine their information processing needs during the early stages of the project, then commit to these specifications through system implementation.

Primary storage The memory area in which all programs and data must reside before programs can be executed or data manipulated. (Same as *main memory*, *memory*, and *RAM*; compare with *secondary storage*.)

Print server A LAN-based PC that handles LAN user print jobs and controls at least one printer.

Printer A device used to prepare hard-copy output.

Printer spooler A circuit board that enables data to be printed while a microcomputer user continues with other processing activities.

Private line A dedicated communications channel between any two points in a computer network. (Same as *leased line*.)

Problem-oriented language A high-level language whose instruction set is designed to address a specific problem (such as process control of machine tools, simulation).

Procedure-oriented language A high-level language whose general-purpose instruction set can be used to produce a sequence of instructions to model scientific and business procedures.

Process control Using the computer to control an ongoing process in a continuous feedback loop.

Process control system A system that uses the computer to control an ongoing process in a continuous feedback loop.

Processor The logical component of a computer system that interprets and executes program instructions.

Processor-bound operation The amount of work that can be performed by the computer system is limited primarily by the speed of the computer.

Program (1) Computer instructions structured and ordered in a manner that, when executed, causes a computer to perform a particular function. (2) The act of producing computer software. (Related to *software*.)

Program register The register that contains the address of the next instruction to be executed.

Programmable read-only memory Programmable ROM. (See *ROM*.)

Programmed decisions Decisions that address well-defined problems with easily identifiable solutions.

Programmer One who writes computer programs.

Programmer/analyst The title of one who performs both the programming and systems analysis function.

Programming The act of writing a computer program.

Programming language A language programmers use to communicate instructions to a computer.

Project leader The person in charge of organizing the efforts of a project team.

Project team A group of users and computer professionals who work together to create an information system.

Prolog A descriptive programming language often used in applications of artificial intelligence.

PROM [Programmable Read-Only Memory] ROM in which the user can load read-only programs and data. (See *EPROM*.)

Prompt A program-generated message describing what should be entered by the end user operator at a PC or terminal.

Proportional spacing A spacing option for word processing documents in which the spacing between characters remains relatively constant for any given line of output.

Proprietary software Vendor-developed software that is marketed to the public. (Compare with *packaged software*.)

Protocols Rules established to govern the way data in a computer network are transmitted.

Prototype system A model of a full-scale system.

Prototyping An approach to systems development that results in a prototype system.

Pseudocode Nonexecutable program code used as an aid to develop and document structured programs.

Puck A flat hand-held device with cross hairs used in conjunction with a digitizing tablet to translate an image into machine-readable format.

Pull-down menu A menu that is "pulled down" and superimposed in a window over whatever is currently being displayed on a monitor.

Punched cards A paper card storage medium, now obsolete, that held data in various configurations of punched holes.

Purging The act of erasing unwanted data, files, or programs from RAM or magnetic memory.

Quality assurance An area of specialty concerned with monitoring the quality of every aspect of the design and operation of information systems.

Query by example (QBE) A method of data base inquiry in which the user sets conditions for the selection of records by composing one or more example relational expressions.

RAM [Random-Access Memory] See *primary storage*.

Random access Direct access to records, regardless of their physical location on the storage medium. (Contrast with *sequential access*.)

Random file A collection of records that can be processed randomly. (Same as *direct-access file*.)

Random processing Processing data and records randomly. (Same as *direct-access processing*; contrast with *sequential processing*.)

Range A cell or a rectangular group of adjacent cells in a spreadsheet.

Rapid prototyping Creating a nonfunctional prototype system.

Raster graphics A method for maintaining a screen image as patterns of dots.

Raster scan monitor An electron beam forms the image by

scanning the screen from left to right and from top to bottom. (Contrast with *vector scan monitor.*)

Read The process by which a record or a portion of a record is accessed from the magnetic storage medium (tape or disk) of a secondary storage device and transferred to primary storage for processing. (Contrast with *write.*)

Read/write head That component of a disk drive or tape drive that reads from and writes to its respective magnetic storage medium.

Read-only memory (ROM) A memory chip with contents permanently loaded by the manufacturer for read-only applications.

Real-time computing The processing of events as they occur, usually in a continuous feedback loop.

Reasonableness check A system checking procedure that determines whether entered or generated data is reasonable when compared to historical data.

Record A collection of related fields (such as an employee record) describing an event or an item (also called *logical record*).

Register A small high-speed storage area in which data pertaining to the execution of a particular instruction are stored. Data stored in a specific register have a special meaning to the logic of the computer.

Relational data base A data base in which data are accessed by content rather than by address. (Contrast with *hierarchical data base* and *network data base.*)

Relational operators Used in spreadsheet and database formulas to show the equality relationship between two expressions (= [equal to], < [less than], > [greater than], < = [less than or equal to], > = [greater than or equal to], <> [not equal to]). (See also *logical operators*).

Relative cell address Refers to a cell's position in a spreadsheet in relation to the cell containing the formula in which the address is used.

Report generator Software that automatically produces reports based on user specifications.

Reserved word A word that has a special meaning to a software package.

Resident font A font that is accessed directly from the printer's built-in read-only memory.

Resolution Referring to the number of addressable points on a monitor's screen. The greater the number of points, the higher the resolution.

Response time The elapsed time between when a data communications message is sent and when a response is received. (Compare with *turnaround time.*)

Responsibility matrix A matrix that graphically illustrates when and to what extent individuals and groups are involved in each activity of a systems development process.

Reusable code Modules of programming code that can be called and used as needed.

Reverse video Characters on a video display terminal presented as black on a light background; used for highlighting.

RGB monitor Color monitors that mix red, green, and blue to achieve a spectrum of colors.

Ring topology A computer network that involves computer systems connected in a closed loop, with no one computer system the focal point of the network.

RISC [Reduced Instruction Set Computer] A computer-designed architecture based on a limited instruction set. (Contrast with *CISC.*)

Robot A computer-controlled manipulator capable of locomotion and/or moving items through a variety of spatial motions.

Robotics The integration of computers and industrial robots.

ROM [Read-Only Memory] RAM that can be read only, not written to.

Root directory The directory at the highest level of a hierarchy of directories.

Row A horizontal block of cells that runs the width of a spreadsheet and is labeled by a number.

RPG A programming language in which the programmer communicates instructions interactively by entering appropriate specifications in prompting formats.

RS-232C A 9-pin or 25-pin plug that is used for the electronic interconnection of computers, modems, and other peripheral devices.

Run The continuous execution of one or more logically related programs (such as printing payroll checks).

Scalable typeface An outline-based typeface from which fonts of any point size can be created.

Scheduler Someone who schedules the use of hardware resources to optimize system efficiency.

Schema A graphical representation of the logical structure of a network data base.

Screen formatter Same as *screen generator.*

Screen generator A systems design tool that enables a systems analyst to produce a mockup of a display while in direct consultation with the user (also called a *screen formatter*).

Screen image projector An output device that can project a computer-generated image onto a large screen.

Screen-capture programs Memory-resident programs that enable users to transfer all or part of the current screen image to a disk file.

Scrolling Using the cursor keys to view parts of a word processing document or a spreadsheet that extends past the bottom or top or sides of the screen.

Secondary storage Permanent data storage on magnetic disk and/or tape. (Compare with *primary storage.*)

Sector A disk storage concept of a pie-shaped portion of a disk or diskette in which records are stored and subsequently retrieved. (Contrast with *cylinder.*)

Sector organization Magnetic disk organization in which the recording surface is divided into pie-shaped sectors.

Segment A group of related fields in a hierarchical DBMS.

Self-booting diskette A diskette that contains both the operating system and an applications software package.

Semiconductor A crystalline substance whose properties of electrical conductivity permit the manufacture of integrated circuits.

Sequential access Accessing records in the order in which they are stored. (Contrast with *random access.*)

Sequential files Files containing records that are ordered according to a key field.

Sequential processing Processing of files that are ordered numerically or alphabetically by a key field. (Contrast with *direct-access processing* or *random processing.*)

Serial Pertaining to processing data one bit at a time. (Contrast with *parallel*.)

Serial port A direct link with the microcomputer's bus that facilitates the serial transmission of data, one bit at a time.

Serial printer Printers that print one character at a time.

Serial representation The storing of bits one after another on a secondary storage medium.

Serpentine A magnetic tape storage scheme in which data are recorded serially in tracks.

Server A LAN component that can be shared by users on a LAN.

Service bureau A company that provides almost any kind of information processing service for a fee.

Service request A formal request from a user for some kind of computer- or MIS-related service.

Set A network data base concept that serves to define the relationship between two records.

Shelfware Software that was purchased but never used or implemented.

Shell Software that provides a graphical user interface alternative to command-driven software.

Simplex line A communications channel that transmits data in only one direction.

Skeletal code A partially complete program produced by a code generator.

Smalltalk An object-oriented language.

Smart card A card or badge with an embedded microprocessor.

Smart modems Modems that have embedded microprocessors.

SNA See *Systems Network Architecture*.

Soft carriage return In word processing, an invisible special character that is automatically inserted after the last full word within the right margin of entered text.

Soft copy Temporary output that can be interpreted visually, as on a monitor. (Contrast with *hard copy*.)

Soft font An electronic description of a font that is retrieved from disk storage and downloaded to the printer's memory.

Soft key See *function key*.

Software The programs used to direct the functions of a computer system. (Contrast with *hardware*; related to *program*.)

Software engineering A term coined to emphasize an approach to software development that embodies the rigors of the engineering discipline. (Also called *systems engineering*.)

Software house A company that produces and markets software.

Software package One or more programs designed to perform a particular processing task.

Software piracy The unlawful duplication of proprietary software. (Related to *pilferage*.)

Sort The rearrangement of fields or records in an ordered sequence by a key field.

Source code See *source program*.

Source data Original data that usually involve the recording of a transaction or the documenting of an event or item.

Source data automation Entering data directly to a computer system at the source without the need for key entry transcription.

Source document The original hard copy from which data are entered.

Source program The code of the original program. (Also called *source code*; compare with *object program*.)

Special-purpose computer Computers designed for a specific application, such as CAD, video games, robots. (Contrast with *general-purpose computer*.)

Specialized common carrier A company that provides services over and above those offered by a communications common carrier.

Speech synthesizers Devices that convert raw data into electronically produced speech.

Speech-recognition system A device that permits voice input to a computer system.

Spelling checker An add-on program to word processing that checks the spelling of every word in a word processing document against an electronic dictionary.

Spooling The process by which output (or input) is loaded temporarily to secondary storage. It is then output (or input) as appropriate devices become available.

Spreadsheet Refers to software that permits users to work with rows and columns of data.

Stacked-bar graph A modified bar graph in which the bars are divided to highlight visually the relative contribution of the components that make up the bar.

Star topology A computer network that involves a centralized host computer connected to a number of smaller computer systems.

Statement See *instruction* (for a computer program).

Status reports Reports that reflect current status. (Contrast with *historical reports*.)

Streamer tape drive Tape drive for 1/4-inch tape cartridges that stores data in a serpentine manner.

Structure chart A chart that graphically illustrates the conceptualization of an information system as a hierarchy of modules.

Structured programming A design technique by which the logic of a program is addressed hierarchically in logical modules.

Structured Query Language (SQL) The ANSI and ISO standard data access query language for relational data bases.

Structured system design A systems design technique that encourages top-down design.

Structured walkthrough A peer evaluation procedure for programs and systems under development. It is used to minimize the possibility of something being overlooked or done incorrectly.

Style checker An add-on program to word processing software that identifies deviations from effective writing style in a word processing document (for example, long, complex sentences).

Subdirectory A directory that is subordinate to a higher-level directory.

Subroutine A sequence of program instructions that are called and executed as needed.

Summary report A report that presents a summary of information about a particular subject.

Supercomputer The category that includes the largest and most powerful computers.

Superscripts Characters that are positioned slightly above the line of type.

Supervisor The operating system program that loads programs to primary storage as they are needed.

Switched line A telephone line used as a regular data communications channel (also called *dial-up line*).

Synchronous transmission Transmission of data at timed intervals between terminals and/or computers. (Contrast with *asynchronous transmission*.)

Syntax The rules that govern the formulation of the instructions in a computer program.

Syntax error An invalid format for a program instruction.

Sysop [system operator] The sponsor who provides the hardware and software support for an electronic bulletin-board system.

System Any group of components (functions, people, activities, events, and so on) that interface with and complement one another to achieve one or more predefined goals.

System board A microcomputer circuit board that contains the microprocessor, electronic circuitry for handling such tasks as input/output signals from peripheral devices, and memory chips (same as *motherboard*).

System check An internal verification of the operational capabilities of a computer's electronic components.

System integrators See *turnkey company*.

System life cycle A reference to the four stages of a computer-based information system—birth, development, production, and death.

System maintenance The process of modifying an information system to meet changing needs.

System operator See *sysop*.

System prompt A visual prompt to the user to enter a system command.

System software Software that is independent of any specific applications area.

System specifications (specs) User-defined information processing needs for a proposed information system.

Systems analysis The analysis, design, development, and implementation of computer-based information systems.

Systems analyst A person who does systems analysis.

Systems development methodology Written standardized procedures that depict the activities in the systems development process and define individual and group responsibilities.

Systems engineering See *software engineering*.

Systems Network Architecture (SNA) IBM's overall communications strategy.

Systems programmer A programmer who develops and maintains systems software.

Systems testing A phase of testing where all programs in a system are tested together.

Tape, magnetic A secondary storage medium for sequential data storage. Available as a reel or as a cartridge.

Tape density The number of bits that can be stored per linear length of a magnetic tape.

Tape drive, magnetic The hardware device that contains the read/write mechanism for the magnetic tape storage medium. (Compare with *disk drive, magnetic*.)

Target system A proposed information system that is the object of a systems development effort.

Task The basic unit of work for a processor.

Technology transfer The application of existing technology to a current problem or situation.

Telecommunications Communication between remote devices.

Telecommuting "Commuting" via a communications link between home and office.

Teleconferencing A meeting in which people in different locations use electronic means to see and talk to each other and to share charts and other meeting materials.

Teleprocessing A term coined to represent the merging of telecommunications and data processing.

Template A model for a particular microcomputer software application.

Terminal Any device capable of sending and receiving data over a communications channel.

Terminal emulation mode The software transformation of a microcomputer so that its keyboard, monitor, and data interface emulate that of a terminal.

Test data Data that are created to test all facets of an information system's operational capabilities.

Test data base A data base made up of test data.

Text cursor A blinking character on a display screen that indicates the location of the next keyed-in character on the screen.

Text mode One of two modes of operation for PC monitors. (Contrast with *graphics mode*.)

Thermal printer A printer that uses heat elements to produce dot-matrix images.

Thesaurus, on-line See *on-line thesaurus*.

Third-party provider An intermediary who facilitates electronic data interchange between trading partners with incompatible hardware and software.

Three-tier network A computer network with three layers—a host mainframe at the top, which is linked to multiple minicomputers, which are linked to multiple microcomputers.

Throughput A measure of computer system efficiency; the rate at which work can be performed by a computer system.

Throwaway system An information system developed to support information for a one-time decision, then discarded.

Timesharing Multiple end users sharing time on a single computer system in an on-line environment.

Toggle The action of pressing a single key on a keyboard to switch between two or more modes of operation, such as insert and replace.

Top-down design An approach to systems and program design that begins at the highest level of generalization; design strategies are then developed at successive levels of decreasing generalization, until the detailed specifications are achieved.

Total connectivity The networking of all hardware, software, and data bases in an organization.

Tower PC A vertical PC that is designed to rest on the floor. A processing component of a desktop PC that has been placed on end.

Trace A procedure used to debug programs whereby all processing events are recorded and related to the steps in the program. The objective of a trace is to isolate program logic errors.

Track, disk That portion of a magnetic disk-face surface that can be accessed in any given setting of a single read/write head. Tracks are configured in concentric circles.

Track, tape That portion of a magnetic tape that can be accessed by any one of the nine read/write heads. A track runs the length of the tape.

Trackball A ball mounted in a box that, when moved, results in a similar movement of the cursor on a display screen.

Tracks per inch (TPI) A measure of the recording density, or spacing, of tracks on a magnetic disk.

Trailer label The last record in a sequential file that contains file information.

Transaction A procedural event in a system that prompts manual or computer-based activity.

Transaction file A file containing records of data activity (transactions); used to update the master file.

Transaction-oriented processing Transactions are recorded and entered as they occur.

Transcribe To convert source data into machine-readable format.

Transfer rate The number of characters per second that can be transmitted between primary storage and a peripheral device.

Transistor An electronic switching device that can be used to vary voltage or alter the flow of current.

Transmission medium The central cable along which terminals, peripheral devices, and microcomputers are connected in a bus topology.

Transparent A reference to a procedure or activity that occurs automatically. It does not have to be considered in the use or design of a program or an information system.

Trap door A Trojan horse that permits unauthorized and undetected access to a computer system.

Trojan horse A set of unauthorized instructions hidden in a legitimate program, such as an operating system. (See *logic bomb*.)

Tuple A group of related fields (a row) in a relational data base.

Turbo Pascal A microcomputer version of the Pascal programming language.

Turnaround document A computer-produced output that is ultimately returned to a computer system as a machine-readable input.

Turnaround time Elapsed time between the submission of a job and the distribution of the results. (Compare with *response time*.)

Turnkey company A company that contracts with a client to install a complete system, both hardware and software (also called *system integrators*).

Twisted-pair wire Two twisted copper wires. The foundation of telephone services through the 1970s.

Two-tier network A computer network with two layers—a host mainframe at the top that is linked directly to multiple minicomputers and/or microcomputers.

Typeface A set of characters that are of the same type style.

Typeover mode A data entry mode in which the character entered overstrikes the character at the cursor position.

Uninterruptible power source (UPS) A buffer between an external power source and a computer system that supplies clean, continuous power.

Unit testing That phase of testing in which the programs that make up an information system are tested individually.

Universal product code (UPC) A 10-digit machine-readable bar code placed on consumer products.

UNIX A multiuser operating system.

Upload The transmission of data from a PC or terminal to the mainframe computer.

Uptime That time when the computer system is in operation.

Upward compatibility A computing environment that can be upgraded without the need for redesign and reprogramming.

User See *end user*.

User acceptance testing That stage of testing where the system is presented to the scrutiny of the user managers whose departments will ultimately use the system.

User interface A reference to the software, method, or displays that enable interaction between the user and the applications or systems software being used.

User liaison A person who serves as the technical interface between the information services department and the user group.

User sign-off A procedure whereby the user manager is asked to "sign off," or commit, to the specifications defined by the systems development project team.

User-friendly Pertaining to an on-line system that permits a person with relatively little experience to interact successfully with the system.

Utility program An often-used service routine, such as a program to sort records.

Vaccine An antiviral program.

Value-added network (VAN) A specialized common carrier that "adds value" over and above the standard services of common carriers.

Value-added reseller (VAR) A company that integrates the hardware and software of several vendors with its own software, then sells the entire package.

Variable A primary storage location that can assume different numeric or alphanumeric values.

Variable name An identifier in a program that represents the actual value of a storage location.

VDT [Video Display Terminal] A terminal on which printed and graphic information are displayed on a television-like monitor and into which data are entered on a typewriterlike keyboard.

Vector graphics A method for maintaining a screen image as patterns of lines, points, and other geometric shapes.

Vector scan monitor An electron beam forms the image by scanning the screen from point to point. (Contrast with *raster scan monitor*.)

Version number A number that identifies the release version of a software package.

Very large-scale integration (VLSI) An integrated circuit with a very densely packed concentration of electronic components. (Contrast with *large-scale integration*, or *LSI*.)

VGA [Video Graphics Array] A circuit board that enables the interfacing of very high-resolution monitors to microcomputers.

Video display terminal See *VDT*.

Videodisk A secondary storage medium that permits storage and random access to video or pictorial information.

Virtual machine (VM) The processing capabilities of one computer system created through software (and sometimes hardware) in a different computer system.

Virtual memory The use of secondary storage devices and primary storage to expand effectively a computer system's primary storage. (Related to *page*.)

Virus A program written with malicious intent and loaded to the computer system of an unsuspecting victim. Ultimately, the program destroys or introduces errors in programs and data bases.

VisiCalc The first spreadsheet package.

Vision-input systems A device that enables limited visual input to a computer system.

Voice message switching Using computers, the telephone system, and other electronic means to store and forward voice messages. (Contrast with *electronic mail*.)

Voice-response unit A device that enables output from a computer system in the form of user-recorded words, phrases, music, alarms, or anything that might be recorded on tape.

Walkthrough, structured See *structured walkthrough*.

Wand scanner Hand-held OCR scanner.

Widow The last line of a paragraph that is printed as the first line on a page in a word processing document.

Wildcard (character) Usually a ? or an * that is used in microcomputer software commands as a generic reference to any character or any combination of characters, respectively.

Winchester disk Permanently installed, continuously spinning magnetic storage medium that is made up of one or more rigid disk platters. (See also *hard disk*.)

Window (1) A rectangular section of a display screen that is dedicated to a specific activity or application. (2) In integrated software, a "view" of a designated area of a worksheet, such as a spreadsheet or word processing text.

Window panes Simultaneous display of subareas of a particular window.

Windows A software product by Microsoft Corporation that provides a graphical user interface and multitasking capabilities for the MS-DOS environment.

Word For a given computer, an established number of bits that are handled as a unit.

Word processing Using the computer to enter, store, manipulate, and print text.

Word wrap A word processing feature that automatically moves, or "wraps," text to the next line when that text would otherwise exceed the right margin limit.

Workbench technologies See CASE.

Workstation A high-performance single-user computer system with sophisticated input/output devices that can be easily networked with other workstations or computers.

Worm A program that erases data and/or programs from a computer system's memory, usually with malicious intent.

WORM [Write-Once Read-Many disk] An optical laser disk that can be read many times after the data are written to it, but the data cannot be changed or erased.

Write To record data on the output medium of a particular I/O device (tape, hard copy, PC display). (Contrast with *read*.)

WYSIWYG [What You See Is What You Get] A word processing package in which what is displayed on the screen is very similar in appearance to what you get when the document is printed.

WYSIWYG–MOL WYSIWYG—more or less. (See *WYSIWYG*.)

X.12 An ANSI communications protocol that has been adopted for electronic data interchange transactions.

XENIX A spinoff of the UNIX operating system.

XMODEM A standard data communications protocol for file transfers.

XON/XOFF A standard data communications protocol.

Zoom An integrated software command that expands a window to fill the entire screen.

INDEX

PHOTO ACKNOWLEDGMENTS

CHAPTER 1   **1:** Courtesy Truevision Inc.; **3:** Rockwell International/David Perry, American Small Business Computers; **4:** Courtesy Cummins Engine Company, Inc.; **5:** Courtesy Zenith Data Systems, Courtesy of Harris Corporation; **6:** Courtesy Dr. P. Hunter Peckam, Director, Rehabilitation; **7:** Engineering Wright State University, Dayton, Ohio; **9:** Courtesy of International Business Machines Corporation; **10:** Courtesy Intermec; **16:** Courtesy of Westinghouse Electric Corporation; **18:** Courtesy TRW, Inc.; **19, 20:** Courtesy of International Business Machines Corporation; **21:** NASA; **22, 23:** Courtesy of Apple Computer, Inc.; **24:** Courtesy of Westinghouse Electric Corporation; **26:** Courtesy of International Business Machines Corporation; **28:** GE Research and Development Center; **34:** (top left) The Computer Museum, Boston, MA, (top right and bottom) Courtesy of International Business Machines Corporation; **35:** (top left and bottom) Courtesy of International Business Machines Corporation, (top right) New York Public Library Picture Collection; **36:** (top left) The Bettmann Archive/BBC Hulton, (middle and bottom) Courtesy of International Business Machines Corporation; **37:** (top left and right) Courtesy of International Business Machines Corporation; (bottom) Courtesy of Iowa State University; **38:** (top left) Courtesy of International Business Machines Corporation, (top right) United Press International Photo, (bottom) Courtesy of Unisys Corporation; **39:** (top left) Courtesy of International Business Machines Corporation, (top right) Honeywell, Inc., (bottom) Digital Equipment Corporation; **40:** Courtesy of International Business Machines Corporation.

CHAPTER 2   **41:** Courtesy of International Business Machines Corporation; **43, 45, 46:** Courtesy of International Business Machines Corporation; **48:** (Note: photos read left to right) Photo courtesy of Hewlett-Packard Company, Courtesy Toshiba, Courtesy Apple Computer, Inc., Courtesy of International Business Machines Corporation; **49:** Reprinted with permission of Compaq Computer Corporation. All Rights Reserved; **51:** Courtesy Truevision; **52:** Harcom Security Systems Corporation; **56, 58:** Courtesy of International Business Machines Corporation; **59:** Courtesy Ford Motor Company; **61** Courtesy Boeing; **62:** Genigraphics Corporation.

CHAPTER 3   **69:** Courtesy Corel Systems Corporation; **71:** Courtesy of International Business Machines Corporation; **72:** Courtesy of Apple Computer, Inc.; **73:** Courtesy of International Business Machines Corporation, Courtesy Microsoft; **75:** Courtesy Lotus Development Corporation; **76:** Reprinted with permission of Compaq Computer Corporation. All Rights Reserved; **80:** GRiD Systems Corporation; **82:** Courtesy of International Business Machines Corporation; **84:** Courtesy Microsoft; **91:** E-Systems; **93:** Reprinted with permission of Compaq Computer Corporation. All Rights Reserved; **94:** Courtesy of International Business Machines Corporation; **96:** Courtesy Central Point Software.

CHAPTER 4   **103:** Courtesy Truevision Inc.; **105:** Courtesy Sun Microsystems; Courtesy of International Business Machines Corporation; **106, 111:** Courtesy of International Business Machines Corporation; **113:** Amdahl Corporation; **116:** Reprinted with permission of Compaq Computer Corporation. All Rights Reserved; **117:** Courtesy of International Business Machines Corporation, Courtesy of Apple Computer, Inc.; **122:** Cray Research, Inc.; **123:** Courtesy of International Business Machines Corporation; **128:** 1, 2—Courtesy of International Business Machines Corporation; **129:** 3, 4—(c) M/A-COM, Inc., 5—Gould Inc., 6—AT&T Technologies, 7—National Semiconductor Corporation, 8—Courtesy of International Business Machines Corporation; **130:** 9, 11—Courtesy of International Business Machines Corporation, 10—Courtesy of Unisys Corporation, 12—Photo courtesy of Hewlett-Packard Company.

CHAPTER 5   **131:** Courtesy Truevision Inc.; **133:** Occidental Petroleum Corporation; **134:** Computer Consoles Inc.; **135:** Courtesy Microsoft, Courtesy of Apple Computer, Inc.; **136:** Courtesy Ford Motor Company; **137:** Courtesy of Hewlett-Packard, Courtesy of International Business Machines Corporation; **139:** Courtesy of International Business Machines Corporation; **141:** GRiD Systems Corporation; **142:** Courtesy Caere Corporation, Courtesy of International Business Machines Corporation; **143:** NCR Corporation; **145:** For Johnson & Johnson by Dana Duke; **146:** Reprinted with permission of Compaq Computer Corporation. All Rights Reserved; **147:** Courtesy Intermec; **148:** Courtesy Deere and Company, Courtesy Radius Inc., Courtesy Sharp Electronics Corporation, Inter-ad, Inc.; **151, 153:** Courtesy of International Business Machines Corporation; **154:** Courtesy Tektronix Computer Graphics; **156:** Houston Instrument, Photo courtesy of Hewlett-Packard Company; **157:** Reprinted with permission of Compaq Computer Corporation. All Rights Reserved; **158:** Courtesy Xerox Imaging Systems; **160:** Courtesy of International Business Machines Corporation.

CHAPTER 6   **165:** Courtesy of International Business Machines Corporation; **166:** Photo courtesy of Hewlett-Packard Company; **168:** Courtesy Ford Motor Company; **170:** Courtesy of International Business Machines Corporation; **173:** Courtesy of International Business Machines Corporation; **176:** Courtesy of International Business Machines Corporation; **177:** Microsoft Corporation, Courtesy of International Business Machines Corporation; **179:** E-Systems; **183, 184:** Seagate Technology; **185:** Courtesy of International Business Machines Corporation; **188:** Copyright © Wang Laboratories, Inc. 1989; **189:** Courtesy of Federal Express Corporation. All rights reserved; **192:** Courtesy of International Business Machines Corporation; **193:** Courtesy Disc Manufacturing, Inc.; **194:** Courtesy of International Business Machines Corporation.

CHAPTER 7   199: Courtesy Truevision Inc.; **201:** EDS photo by Steve McAlister; **203:** Reprinted with permission of Compaq Computer Corporation. All Rights Reserved; **204:** Courtesy of International Business Machines Corporation; **205:** Courtesy Ford Motor Company; **206:** GRiD Systems Corporation; **208:** Courtesy of International Business Machines Corporation; **211:** Courtesy Toshiba; **213:** Digital Equipment Corporation; **219:** Courtesy of International Business Machines Corporation; **220:** AT&T Technologies, NASA; **221:** Western Union Corporation; **223:** Courtesy of International Business Machines Corporation.

CHAPTER 8   229: Courtesy of International Business Machines Corp.; **232:** Phillips Petroleum Company; **233:** Digital Equipment Corporation; **235:** NASA; **237:** Courtesy of International Business Machines Corporation; **239:** Courtesy Home Shopping Network; **241, 242:** Courtesy of International Business Machines Corporation; **243, 245:** Reprinted with permission of Compaq Computer Corporation. All Rights Reserved; **248:** Courtesy Prodigy Services Company, (top right) Courtesy CompuServe; **250:** Courtesy Zenith Data Systems; **252:** Courtesy of Harris Corporation.

CHAPTER 9   257: Image created by Barbara Kasten at the Eastman Kodak Company Center for Creative Imaging; **259:** Courtesy Ford Motor Company; **260, 262:** Courtesy of International Business Machines Corporation; **265:** Courtesy Unisys Corporation; **269:** Official U.S. Navy photo; **271:** Courtesy Harris Corporation; **279:** E-Systems; **283:** Courtesy of International Business Machines Corporation; **290:**"The Wave of the Future" poster designed by Grafik Communications, illustrated in part by B. Pomeroy, published by Nokes Berry Graphics as a poster; **291:** Courtesy of International Business Machines Corporation, Image created by Blandon Belushin at the Eastman Kodak Company Center for Creative Imaging; **292:** Courtesy Joni Carter © USPS; (bottom left) Genigraphics Corporation, (bottom right) Courtesy Quark Inc. **293:** Courtesy SAS Institute Inc., Photograph courtesy of FTI Corporation, Annapolis, Maryland; San Francisco, California; **294:** Courtesy of International Business Machines Corporation; **295:** Courtesy Boeing Company; **296:** GE Research and Development Center, Courtesy Techmedica; **297:** M. Pique, U. Schulze-Gahmen and I. A. Wilson, The Scripps Research Institute; **298:** Courtesy National Center for Supercomputing Applications.

CHAPTER 10   299: Courtesy Truevision Inc.; **300:** Reprinted with permission of Compaq Computer Corporation. All Rights Reserved; **303:** NCR Corporation; **311:** Reprinted with permission of Compaq Computer Corporation. All Rights Reserved; **312:** Courtesy of International Business Machines Corporation; **313:** Dahlgren Museum, Naval Surface Weapons Center; **314, 318:** Courtesy of International Business Machines Corporation; **322:** Courtesy Kerr-McGee Corporation; **323:** Courtesy of International Business Machines Corporation; **324:** Courtesy Fractal Design Corporation; **325:** Courtesy Unisys Corporation; **329:** GE Research and Development Center.

CHAPTER 11   337: Image created by Hugh Dubberly at the Eastman Kodak Company Center for Creative Imaging; **339:** Used by permission, Gannet Co., Inc.; **346:** Courtesy Texas Instruments; **349, 350:** Long and Associates; **355:** Funk Software; **356:** Courtesy of Digital Equipment Corporation, Courtesy Logitech; **357:** Courtesy Sun Microsystems; **363:** Courtesy of Harris Corporation; **365:** Courtesy Aldus Corporation; **368:** Courtesy Delta Software; **369:** Courtesy Zenographics; **371:** Intergraph Corporation (Mutoh Industries).

CHAPTER 12   377: Courtesy Truevision Inc.; **378:** Used with permission of Borland International, Inc.; **388:** Long and Associates; **394:** Dynatech Corporation; **403:** Intergraph Corporation (Geographic Information and Mapping Services Department, Huntsville, Alabama); **404:** Long and Associates; **413:** Computerland; **414:** Reprinted with permission of Compaq Computer Corporation. All Rights Reserved, Courtesy Zenith Data System; **415:** Courtesy of International Business Machines Corporation, Courtesy Microsoft; **416:** Courtesy Tandon, Courtesy of International Business Machines Corporation; **417, 418:** Photo courtesy of Hewlett-Packard Company.

CHAPTER 13   423: Courtesy Truevision Inc.; **424:** Reprinted with permission of Compaq Computer Corporation. All Rights Reserved; **426:** Photo courtesy of Hewlett-Packard Company; **427:** Courtesy Zenith Data Systems; **433:** Ingersoll-Rand Co.; **436:** Courtesy of International Business Machines Corporation; **437:** Courtesy Southern Pacific Transportation; **439:** Digital Equipment Corporation; **440:** Courtesy TRW, Inc.; **443:** Photo courtesy of Hewlett-Packard Company; **446, 448:** Courtesy SAS Institute Inc.; **449:** Courtesy of International Business Machines Corporation; **453:** Courtesy Intel Corporation and Andersen Consulting.

CHAPTER 14   459: Image created by Mark Thomas at the Eastman Kodak Company Center for Creative Imaging; **461:** Courtesy General Motors; **462:** Courtesy of International Business Machines Corporation; **463:** CheckRobot Automated Checkout Machines; **464:** Reprinted with permission of Compaq Computer Corporation. All Rights Reserved; **465:** Courtesy Schneider National Trucking; **469:** Courtesy Levi Strauss and Company; **471:** Photo courtesy of Hewlett-Packard Company; **471:** Courtesy of Harris Corporation; **472:** Courtesy Ford Motor Company; **473:** Deere and Company; **475:** Courtesy of International Business Machines Corporation; **476:** Courtesy of the New York Stock Exchange; **477:** Courtesy of International Business Machines Corporation; **478:** Courtesy Hormel Co., Brunswick Corporation; **479:** Mark IV Industries, Inc.; **480:** Courtesy of International Business Machines Corporation; **481:** GRiD Systems Corporation; **482:** NASA; **487:** Mobile Image Canada Limited; **488:** Pansophic Graphics Systems, Mac Bright—artist, Illustration courtesy of Christopher Finch from his book *Special Effects: Creating Movie Magic* (New York: Abbeville Press, 1984); **489:** Courtesy 20th Century Fox Corporation; **490:** Illustration courtesy of Christopher Finch from his book *Special Effects: Creating Movie Magic* (New York: Abbeville Press, 1984); **491:** Peter Angelo Simon, Discover Magazine; **492:** Courtesy Carolco Pictures, Inc.

CHAPTER 15   493: Image created by Jay Brenner at the Eastman Kodak Company Center for Creative Imaging; **495:** Courtesy of International Business Machines Corporation; **496:** Courtesy of Federal Express Corporation. All rights reserved; **498:** Courtesy of International Business Machines Corporation; **499:** E-Systems; **500:** Rockwell International/David Perry; **504:** Courtesy of International Business Machines Corporation; **505:** Courtesy of NEC Information Systems, Inc.; **510:** Mark IV Industries, Inc.; **514:** Courtesy Honeywell; **519:** KnowledgeWare, Inc., Atlanta, GA, USA.

CHAPTER 16   527: Courtesy of International Business Machines Corporation; **529:** Digital Equipment Corporation; **530:** Cadre Technologies Inc.; **531, 535, 538:** Courtesy of International Business Machines Corporation; **540:** USAA; **546:** Courtesy of International Business Machines Corporation.

CHAPTER 17 **551:** Courtesy of International Business Machines Corporation; **553:** Photo courtesy of Hewlett-Packard Company, Courtesy Asland Oil Inc.; **555:** Courtesy of Apple Computer, Inc.; **556:** Courtesy LC Technologies; **557:** Courtesy of Xerox Corporation; **560, 562:** Courtesy of International Business Machines Corporation; **565:** Courtesy Hormel Company, Courtesy of International Business Machines Corporation; **568:** Courtesy of International Business Machines Corporation; **570, 571:** Courtesy Baltimore Gas and Electric; **572:** Digital Equipment Corporation, Microage Computer Stores, Inc.; **573:** Reprinted with permission of Compaq Computer Corporation. All Rights Reserved; **575:** Courtesy InvoTek, Inc.; **577:** Courtesy of International Business Machines Corporation; **579:** Courtesy of Harris Corporation.

CHAPTER 18 **585:** Microtime, Inc.; **587:** Courtesy Texas Instruments; **588, 589:** Courtesy TRW, Inc.; **591:** Courtesy Sun Microsystems; **593:** Courtesy of International Business Machines Corporation; **595:** Deere and Company; **596:** Photo courtesy of Hewlett-Packard Company; **598:** Courtesy of International Business Machines Corporation; **599:** Courtesy Prodigy Services Company; **600:** Courtesy NEC Corporation, Tokyo, Japan; **601:** Courtesy of International Business Machines Corporation; **602:** Courtesy Boeing; **603:** Courtesy of International Business Machines Corporation; **604:** Dynatech Corporation; **606:** Intergraph Corporation; **607:** Courtesy of International Business Machines Corporation; **608:** Courtesy TRW, Inc., Courtesy of International Business Machines Corporation; **610:** GRiD Systems Corporation; **611:** Intergraph Corporation.